New Perspectives in Criminology

New Perspectives in Criminology

John E. Conklin, Editor

Tufts University

Allyn and Bacon

Boston • London • Toronto • Sydney • Tokyo • Singapore

Vice President, Social Sciences: Susan Badger
Executive Editor: Karen Hanson
Series Editorial Assistant: Jennifer Jacobson
Manufacturing Buyer: Aloka Ratham
Marketing Manager: Joyce Nilsen
Editorial-Production Service: Electronic Publishing Services Inc.
Cover Administrator: Suzanne Harbison

Copyright © 1996 by Allyn & Bacon
A Simon & Schuster Company
Needham Heights, Massachusetts 02194

Library of Congress Cataloging-in-Publication Data

Conklin, John E.
    New Perspectives in Criminology / Edited by John E. Conklin.
      p. cm.
    Includes bibliographical references (pp. 286–316).
    ISBN 0–205–18388–3
    1. Criminology.   I. Title.
HV6025.C592 1996
364—dc20   95-24524
                                                                                                     CIP

Printed in the United States of America

10 9 8 7 6 5 4 3 2 1   99 98 97 96 95

Contents

Preface

I have designed this reader for introductory courses in criminology. In choosing the selections, I kept several criteria in mind. I wanted recent articles that would supplement rather than repeat the material typically appearing in textbooks. All of the selections here have been published in the 1990s, but because the best of contemporary criminology builds on and alludes to prior work, these selections also incorporate traditional scholarship.

I wanted readings that could be grasped by students in a first course in criminology. This meant excluding material that relied on statistical methods most of those students would not understand. In the few cases where such statistics are used, I have written footnotes to explain their meaning in simple terms.

I have written a brief introduction to each selection. To engage the reader and stimulate classroom discussion, I have also included several discussion questions at the end of each selection. These questions can be used for review and discussion, or as essay questions on examinations. I have also prepared a separate instructor's manual with multiple-choice questions. Numbered notes in the text appear after each selection. At the end of the book is a single bibliography that integrates the references used in all of the selections.

The following chart shows how instructors using different criminology textbooks might assign the readings in this book. In the few cases in which a reading did not fit with any particular chapter in a textbook, I have indicated this with a dash. Instructors may nonetheless want to assign those readings, especially because they cover material not dealt with in the assigned textbook. At the end of the chart is bibliographic information for the textbooks whose names are abbreviated in the chart with the names of the authors and the number of the most recent edition available at the time this reader went to press. Numbers at the top of columns (1–23) are for selections in the reader. Numbers in each row are for chapters in the textbook for which selections can best be assigned.

NUMBERS AT THE TOP OF COLUMNS (#1–23) ARE FOR SELECTIONS IN THE READER. NUMBERS IN EACH ROW ARE FOR CHAPTERS IN THE TEXTBOOK FOR WHICH SELECTIONS CAN BEST BE ASSIGNED.

SELECTION

TEXTBOOK	1	2	3	4	5	6	7	8	9	10	11	12	13	14	15	16	17	18	19	20	21	22	23
ADLER, MUELLER, & LAUFER 2E	9	9	4	7	10	8	2	2	17	2	6	6	6	10	10	13	13	13	12	12	17	18	18
ADLER, MUELLER, & LAUFER 2E SHORT VERSION	9	9	4	7	10	8	2	2	17	2	6	6	6	10	10	13	13	13	12	12	11	—	—
BARLOW 6E	1	1	13	17	4	14	14	3	11	11	3	6	3	3	5	9	9	9	7	7	12	12	12
BARTOL 4E	1	1	2	4	8	—	—	7	8	13	5	5	5	9	11	12	12	12	11	11	13	13	13
BIERNE & MESSERSCHMIDT 2E	1	1	14	13	4	15	3	3	15	3	13	13	13	4	5	6	6	6	7	7	5	—	—
BROWN, ESBENSEN, & GEIS 2E	1	3	6	6	11	10	4	4	2	14	8	8	8	11	11	13	13	13	12	12	5	2	2
CONKLIN 5E	1	2	5	5	7	17	4	8	13	17	8	6	6	5	8	9	9	10	10	11	14	16	16
GIBBONS 6E	1	5	7	8	8	6	5	16	16	5	11	11	11	12	9	11	11	9	13	13	20	20	20
GILSINAN 1E	2	2	6	6	9	7	7	6	4	8	7	7	7	6	—	8	8	10	10	—	13	13	13
GLICK 1E	1	2	4	4	7	5	5	6	11	11	5	5	5	7	7	10	10	10	9	9	12	12	12
HAGAN 3E	1	2	4	5	6	14	3	3	3	14	7	7	7	6	6	13	13	13	10	10	8	14	14
HOLMAN & QUINN 1E	1	1	4	6	6	11	11	7	14	14	11	11	11	6	7	7	7	12	13	13	7	6	6

NUMBERS AT THE TOP OF COLUMNS (#1–23) ARE FOR SELECTIONS IN THE READER. NUMBERS IN EACH ROW ARE FOR CHAPTERS IN THE TEXTBOOK FOR WHICH SELECTIONS CAN BEST BE ASSIGNED.

SELECTION #

TEXTBOOK	1	2	3	4	5	6	7	8	9	10	11	12	13	14	15	16	17	18	19	20	21	22	23
JEFFERY 1E	15	15	10	16	16	16	16	18	15	15	—	—	16	13	13	18	18	18	17	17	9	12	12
LIVINGSTON 1E	2	2	10	10	6	11	4	4	16	2	11	11	11	5	5	7	5	8	9	9	16	15	15
MASTERS & ROBERSON 1E	1	1	12	19	21	20	7	19	1	1	10	10	10	21	21	20	20	20	21	21	21	1	1
REID 7E	1	2	4	4	7	5	5	2	5	2	5	5	5	7	7	8	7	8	9	9	3	14	14
SACCO & KENNEDY 1E	6	6	3	4	8	11	2	3	8	11	3	3	3	3	3	—	—	4	10	10	4	11	11
SCHMALLEGER IE	12	12	5	6	6	7	7	7	8	8	7	7	7	6	6	10	10	10	9	9	6	13	13
SIEGEL 5E	1	3	6	10	4	7	3	3	15	15	7	7	7	11	11	14	14	14	13	13	12	18	18
SIEGEL 5E SHORT VERSION	1	3	6	10	4	7	3	3	15	15	7	7	7	11	11	14	14	14	13	13	12	—	—
SUTHERLAND, CRESSEY, & LUCKENBILL 11E	1	1	7	10	10	26	11	8	13	13	9	9	9	7	12	7	7	12	11	11	14	22	22
SYKES & CULLEN 2E	2	2	9	9	6	15	4	4	12	12	9	9	9	6	5	7	7	7	8	8	12	12	12
VITO & HOLMES 1E	1	2	5	6	13	18	8	12	10	18	8	8	8	13	12	16	16	16	17	17	14	18	18
YABLONSKY 4E	1	1	14	14	4	15	3	3	17	3	15	15	15	5	6	9	9	6	11	11	17	16	16

Criminology Textbooks

Adler, Freda, Gerhard O. W. Mueller, and William S. Laufer. *Criminology,* 2nd ed. New York: McGraw-Hill, 1995.

Adler, Freda, Gerhard O. W. Mueller, and William S. Laufer. *Criminology: The Shorter Version,* 2nd ed. New York: McGraw-Hill, 1995.

Barlow, Hugh D. *Introduction to Criminology*, 6th ed. New York: HarperCollins, 1993.

Bartol, Curt R. *Criminal Behavior: A Psychosocial Approach*, 4th ed. Englewood Cliffs, NJ: Prentice Hall, 1995.

Bierne, Piers, and James Messerschmidt. *Criminology*, 2nd ed. Fort Worth, TX: Harcourt Brace, 1995.

Brown, Stephen E., Finn-Aage Esbensen, and Gilbert Geis. *Criminology: Explaining Crime and Its Context*, 2nd ed. Cincinnati, OH: Anderson, 1996.

Conklin, John E. *Criminology*, 5th ed. Boston: Allyn & Bacon, 1995.

Gibbons, Don C. *Society, Crime, and Criminal Behavior*, 6th ed. Englewood Cliffs, NJ: Prentice Hall, 1992.

Gilsinan, James F. *Criminology and Public Policy: An Introduction*. Englewood Cliffs, NJ: Prentice Hall, 1990.

Glick, Leonard. *Criminology*. Boston: Allyn & Bacon, 1995.

Hagan, Frank E. *Introduction to Criminology*, 3rd ed. Chicago: Nelson-Hall, 1994.

Holman, John E., and James F. Quinn. *Criminology: Applying Theory*. St. Paul, MN: West, 1992.

Jeffery, C. Ray. *Criminology: An Interdisciplinary Approach*. Englewood Cliffs, NJ: Prentice Hall, 1990.

Livingston, Jay. *Crime & Criminology*. Englewood Cliffs, NJ: Prentice Hall, 1992.

Masters, Ruth, and Cliff Roberson. *Inside Criminology*. Englewood Cliffs, NJ: Prentice Hall, 1990.

Reid, Sue Titus. *Crime and Criminology*, 7th ed. Dubuque, IA: Brown and Benchmark, 1994.

Sacco, Vincent F., and Leslie W. Kennedy. *The Criminal Event: An Introduction to Criminology*. Belmont, CA: Wadsworth, 1996.

Schmalleger, Frank. *Criminology Today: An Introductory Text for the 21st Century*. Englewood Cliffs, NJ: Prentice Hall, 1995.

Siegel, Larry J. *Criminology,* 5th ed. St. Paul, MN: West, 1995.

Siegel, Larry J. *Criminology: The Shorter Version*, 5th ed. St. Paul, MN: West, 1995.

Sutherland, Edwin H., Donald R. Cressey, and David F. Luckenbill. *Principles of Criminology*, 11th ed. Dix Hills, NY: General Hall, 1992.

Sykes, Gresham M., and Frances T. Cullen. *Criminology,* 2nd ed. Fort Worth, TX: Harcourt Brace Jovanovich, 1992.

Vito, Gennaro F., and Ronald M. Holmes. *Criminology: Theory, Research, and Policy*. Belmont, CA: Wadsworth, 1994.

Yablonsky, Lewis. Criminology: *Crime and Criminality*, 4th ed. New York: HarperCollins, 1990.

Acknowledgments

I want to thank Karen L. Hanson, Executive Editor at Allyn & Bacon, for her support and for the opportunity to do this book. Her assistants, Jennifer Jacobson and Sarah Dunbar, provided me with prompt and useful advice when I needed it. I am grateful for Jennifer McGlashan's production assistance, Carol Anne Peschke's copyediting, and Regina Shelley's proofreading. I also wish to thank Jim Ennis for his advice and Peg Bruno for her help in preparing the chart on pages x and xi.

John E. Conklin

New Perspectives in Criminology

P a r t *I*

Conceptualizing Crime

The Social Construction of Serial Homicide

Philip Jenkins

Only some of the many crimes that occur receive intense attention from the news media, law-enforcement agencies, and the public. White-collar crime gets less attention than its enormous costs warrant, and arson is rarely the basis of news stories, official investigation, and public fear. In recent years, two relatively uncommon forms of crime—serial homicide and the murder of children abducted by strangers—have dominated press reports on crime, television documentaries, police investigations, and popular attention.

In this selection, Philip Jenkins shows how serial murder—a pattern of several homicides by an offender over a period of time—is a socially constructed problem whose cultural meaning has been influenced by the efforts of the FBI. Claims-makers such as the FBI stake out ownership of an issue, present statistics and interpretations of the problem, and shape the way the problem is interpreted by the mass media and the public. The media and the public, in turn, place limits on the kind of official interpretation of the issue that will be accepted, and so the cultural image of serial murder is shaped through an ongoing social process.

During the 1980s, the issue of serial murder was established as a major social problem, and the stereotypical serial killer became one of the best-known and most widely feared social enemies. For research in problem construction, the process raises three fundamental questions: Why did the problem arise at the time it did? Why did it take the particular form that

Source: Reprinted with permission from: Jenkins, Philip. *Using Murder: The Social Construction of Serial Homicide,* pp. 211–225. (New York: Aldine de Gruyter) Copyright © 1994 Walter de Gruyter, Inc., New York.

it acquired in these years? And why did the diverse claims enjoy such outstanding and quite rapid success?

In each case, particular attention should be directed toward the identification of claims-makers, those individuals and groups who attempt to present an issue in a particular way. The study of such claims-makers is central to the constructionist approach to social problems, in which "the theoretical task is to study how members define, lodge and press claims; how they publicize their concerns, redefine the issue in question in the face of political obstacles, indifference or opposition; how they enter into alliances with other claims-makers" (Kitsuse and Schneider, 1989:xii–xiii). This chapter will describe the development of the claims that shaped public perceptions of the serial murder problem, and the means by which claims came to be established as authoritative. It will be suggested that such an exploration has important implications both for the framing of social problems, and for the study of the mass media.

Our first question is one of chronology: Why did the problem arise when it did? The answer may seem obvious, in that from the mid-1970s onwards, there appeared to be a significant increase in both the number of sensational cases and the scale of victimization in the separate incidents. This marked a genuine departure from conditions in the 1950s and 1960s. Every few years brought a case that broke previous records for the total number of known victims, while several of the major instances lasted for months or years before arrests were made, permitting far-reaching speculation by pressure groups and the media. It was therefore likely that concern would peak by about 1980–1981 and that some endeavor would be made to provide a context that incorporated the diverse cases in a general social problem.

On the other hand, there have been many other years in American history when there was a similar concatenation of nationally publicized multiple-murder cases. To take only the most spectacular periods, this was true of the mid-1870s, the years between 1910 and 1915, the mid-1920s, and the late 1930s. Yet neither in 1915, 1928, nor 1939 was there a national murder panic on anything like the model observed in 1983.

Equally, it is by no means inevitable that a multiple homicide problem would be constructed in the particular way that has recently occurred in the United States. In midcentury, it was the psychiatric and therapeutic experts who had exercised ownership of an earlier manifestation of the problem, when it had been understood as part of the general issue of sex crime and mental illness. It was not then typified as a criminal justice issue, and the political context determining the appropriate responses was generally liberal. The experience of offenders like Charles Whitman, Richard Speck, or Lee Harvey Oswald could be cited to support more enlightened policies of child rearing and community mental health, or extending the scope of psychiatric detection and intervention (see, for example, Menninger, 1968). Moreover, such individual-oriented and psychodynamic theories might have led to multiple murder continuing to be viewed through the medium of discrete case studies, rather than in terms of a general problem.

By 1980–1981, moreover, there were several other competing groups of claims-makers, each with its distinctive interpretation of the murder issue: black groups who viewed it as part of systematic racial exploitation; feminists who saw the offense as serial femicide, a component of the larger problem of violence against women; children's rights activists concerned with missing and exploited children; as well as religious and other advocates of a ritual murder threat. That such activism could promote an alternative construction is suggested by the experience of contemporary England, in which the Yorkshire Ripper case of the late 1970s secured the dominance of an essentially feminist analysis of serial murder. This gave the femicide theory an authoritative position, which profoundly influenced the mass media and academic criminology and also shaped law enforcement practice (Jenkins, 1992). Moreover, this occurred in a conservative political environment quite reminiscent of Reagan's America.

The Role of Federal Law Enforcement

In any event, the interpretation that prevailed in the 1980s defined the new problem in terms of interjurisdictional cooperation, intelligence gathering, and overcoming linkage blindness [the failure to see connections among crimes committed in different jurisdictions]—in short, as a problem of law enforcement and federal power rather than one of mental health or social dysfunction. This construction does much to illuminate the composition of the groups most active in developing or pressing claims, as well as their motives and interests. The serial murder problem was defined according to the specifications of the U.S. Justice Department, and above all the FBI's behavioral science experts at Quantico. This recognition goes far toward explaining why the problem was defined in the manner it was, while the timing should be seen as at least in part a response to the bureaucratic needs of an expanding agency.

The dominance of the FBI's experts can be observed throughout the process of construction. They successfully presented themselves as the best (or only) authorities on the topic, and they assisted journalists and writers who reciprocated with favorable depictions of the agency. It was the FBI that originated and popularized the high statistics about the scale of the crime, and once disseminated, these figures shaped the public perception that serial murder represented a grave social threat. The same group at Quantico also guided the debate in other ways, above all in drawing attention to the "roaming" killers who operated in several states.

In terms of their underlying interests in making these claims, the federal officials stood to gain substantially in terms of their bureaucratic position because establishing the reality of a problem provided added justification for the BSU [Behavioral Sciences Unit], a new and rather unorthodox agency seeking to validate its skills in areas such as profiling and crime scene analysis. In terms of the agency as a whole, focusing on a social menace of this sort was likely to erode public opposition to the enhancement of FBI powers and resources, at a time when such a development was politically opportune. The successful creation of the serial murder problem marked a critical expansion of what both public and legislators felt to be the appropriate scope of federal police powers.

Moreover, this could easily be seen as the thin end of the wedge: Once it was established that the FBI could and should have jurisdiction over this type of crime, it was not difficult to seek similar involvement in other offenses that could plausibly be mapped together with serial homicide. In 1986, it was proposed that the NCAVC [National Center for the Analysis of Violent Crime] might soon expand its powers over other serial crimes, including "rape, child molestation, arson and bombing" (Jenkins, 1988). This represents an ingenious form of verbal sleight-of-hand, by which the simple adjective *serial* has come to mean much more than merely *repeated,* and implies sinister characteristics such as irrationality, compulsiveness, extreme violence, highly transient offenders, and so on. Serial offenses of any kind are thus framed as ipso facto both federal in nature, and the peculiar responsibility of the mind-hunters.

In terms of the FBI's broad interests in defining the problem, it is necessary to see this incident as part of a long bureaucratic tradition. Historically, federal law enforcement was virtually non-existent in the United States before the present century, and agencies only established themselves gradually during the Progressive era and afterwards. In the case of the FBI, the agency was founded in 1908, but made virtually no impact before the early 1930s, when it was regarded as the essential antidote to a perceived wave of kidnapping (Powers, 1983). The *New York Times* described this as "a rising menace to the nation" (quoted in Schechter, 1990:101). The media presented the offense as the work of ruthless and itinerant predators assaulting American children in their homes, and the official response was to declare the action a federal crime (Alix, 1978). The law was to be enforced by an enhanced FBI under its director J. Edgar Hoover, who presented himself as the head of a national super-police agency leading a "war on crime" (Powers, 1983, 1987; Summers, 1993).

This was only the first of several successive panics through which the unit developed immense prestige and widespread jurisdiction (Kessler, 1993). Respectively, these supposed public enemies included gangsters and bank robbers like John Dillinger, Nazi fifth columnists, and Communist spies. The bureau suggested that each problem in turn was a severe public threat and was moreover interjurisdictional in nature, so that on both counts federal action was required. The FBI was presented as the appropriate agency because of its superior professionalism and forensic skills, exactly the sort of technocratic arguments that were employed in the 1980s demands for federal war against serial killers (Ungar, 1976). These ideas were often portrayed in the mass media, for example, in the 1959 James Stewart film *The FBI Story,* which was made under the close supervision of the bureau. Federal law enforcement thus had a long record of benefiting from public panics about itinerant predatory criminals, especially where children were said to be involved.

The FBI also had vast resources in making its claims, and were par excellence insider claims-makers with an unchallenged right to present their views before legislative and policymaking bodies. They had much to offer journalists or investigators that might encourage them to accept their view of an emerging problem. J. Edgar Hoover had cultivated the closest possible links with the media, and there was thus a long tradition of regarding the FBI as an authoritative source on law enforcement matters. In the specific instance of serial murder, the agency benefited from being literally the only group offering a systematic overview of the phenomenon, an unchallenged position suggested by the absence of skepticism about its early quantitative claims, either from law enforcement agencies or academics.

On a personal basis, BSU agents could also claim immense authority due to their extensive personal contacts with the imprisoned killers, who were an unparalleled resource. Agents like Robert Ressler and John Douglas were articulate speakers who could be relied on to provide interesting and lively accounts of the crimes they had investigated, and their views were substantiated by their wide and somewhat perilous experiences in border crossing—attempting to enter the minds of heinous offenders. This offered the potential for vicarious excitement for a news audience, while the empirical nature of their research confirmed the prima facie likelihood that these officials were, in fact, the best qualified experts in the field. Since they could draw freely on the language of both practical investigation and personal observation on the one hand, and theoretical psychology and criminology on the other, they could be viewed neither as "just cops" nor as ivory-tower intellectuals. The image presented was both attractive and convincing.

The opinions of the BSU experts thus appeared to be of great value, even when they were addressing quantitative or political issues in which their expertise was far more dubious. Once this perception of authority was established, the FBI had much discretion in the access it provided to these valuable resources. It could permit or deny the interviews that would be essential for any writer seeking to investigate serial murder, either with federal experts like Ressler, Heck, Hazelwood, or Douglas or (to some extent) with the killers themselves. Obviously, these favors were more likely to be granted to those journalists or academics likely to show themselves sympathetic to the interests of the organization. Meanwhile, anyone with access to the information and opinion controlled by the BSU had the potential for frequent stories and features that were almost guaranteed to be newsworthy. Certainly in 1983 and 1984, the FBI made shrewd use of the information it was acquiring in the area of serial murder, developing a reciprocal relationship with the journalists, academics, and filmmakers who obtained access to the agency.

Ressler has written with refreshing candor about the development of the serial murder problem:

> There was somewhat of a media feeding frenzy, if not a panic, over this issue in the mid-1980s and we at the FBI and other people involved in urging the formation of VICAP [Violent Criminal Apprehension Program] did add to the general impression that there was a big problem and that something needed to be done about it. We didn't exactly go out seeking publicity, but when a reporter called, and we had a choice whether or not to cooperate on a story about violent crime, we gave the reporter good copy. In feeding the frenzy, we were using an old tactic in Washington, playing up the problem as a way of getting Congress and the higher-ups in the executive branch to pay attention to it. The difficulty was that some people in the bureaucracy went too far in their quest for attention. (Ressler and Schachtman, 1992:203)

Ressler describes how his hospitable treatment of a reporter resulted in a flattering 1980 article in the *Chicago Tribune,* which in turn "led to a flood of other articles, including important ones in *The New York Times, People* and *Psychology Today,* just to name a few, as well as invitations for me to appear on various radio and television programs" (p. 232). He also stresses the importance of the unit's outreach to academic psychology and criminology, and, of course, to the popular media. He advised authors like Thomas Harris and Mary Higgins Clark, and in 1987 he addressed the annual meeting of the Mystery Writers of America. And he obviously knew the sort of pithy phrases that the news media would delight in quoting ("Serial killing—I think it's at epidemic proportions"; "America is going to turn into *A Clockwork Orange*" . . .). The BSU experts were from an early stage quite familiar with the necessity to cultivate the media and the means of so doing.

This assistance might pay very rich dividends indeed, though it is difficult to imagine anyone in the agency foreseeing that the aid accorded to Thomas Harris would reap quite such splendid rewards. . . . At the end of the decade, the decision to permit location shooting at Quantico for *The Silence of the Lambs* was brilliantly effective in reinforcing the linkage between the real-life behavioral sciences experts and Harris's fictional heroes, while the ensuing publicity more than negated the disastrous consequences of the recent *Iowa* investigation.

Also valuable as a resource was the FBI's ability to present plausible statistical evidence, which was of special value in the early 1980s. As has been noted, there then existed several interest groups seeking to present their interpretation of a serial murder problem, but both the media and the diverse activist groups all had a common vested interest in emphasizing certain aspects of the murder problem, above all its very large scale. Whether pressure groups wished to stigmatize child abductions, sexual violence, or satanist conspiracies, they all shared a desire to see very high statistics presented for the numbers of serial killings. The FBI helped to secure its ownership of the issue by being the first and indeed only group to offer such a quantitative foundation, one that seemed sufficiently high to satisfy the various claims-makers. It established the critical frame around which other groups could embellish; so that the simple four or five thousand serial murder victims swiftly became five thousand women and children, or five thousand victims of ritual murder.

In addition, there were many points of underlying agreement between FBI experts like Hazelwood and the feminist theorists, both of whom emphasized the sexual content of the violence and the role of pornography in the etiology of serial homicide. It is remarkable to note the respectful attention often paid to Justice Department claims by feminists like Jane Caputi, who rarely makes positive remarks about law enforcement agencies (Downs, 1989). This tactical alliance assured that federal claims were less likely to be assailed from liberal critics in Congress, the news media, or the academic world. Intentionally or otherwise, the FBI's sympathy for the sexual violence construction did much to create a consensus for its interpretations.

Since the early 1980s, it has been unthinkable to present either a news story or a fictional account of serial murder without due acknowledgment of the assistance granted by BSU experts, who in more or less fictionalized form often appear as the heroes of the novels and films. This has had a cyclical effect in that these media depictions reinforce the stereotype of the experts as well-informed and heroic, and ensures that future accounts will continue to rely on these unquestioned authorities. In consequence, the media have still returned to the FBI personnel for comments and quotes even after they have been shown to be fallible or even wrong about key issues. And in the cases where the FBI authorities were not quoted directly, their views and theories still permeate the literature through the use of terminology like *organized* and *disorganized* offenders, *unsubs,* and *blitz* attacks, and the emphasis on the offender's acting out of violent fantasies. The language and theory of serial murder study were created at Quantico.

In terms of social problem construction, there are few examples where a federal agency has so decisively acquired ownership of a topic: the all-but-unchallenged right to interpret the issue according to its assumptions and interests. The media came to rely for information and opinion on a very small body of accredited experts, in this case the FBI investigators and some of their associates in the academic or law enforcement worlds. This reliance meant that the views of each individual claims-maker acquired disproportionate significance, while such a highly focused approach created a high likelihood that errors or misstatements would remain uncorrected, or that views hostile to these initial claims-makers were unlikely to be expressed. The point is illustrated by what we might call the *negative* claims-making activity of another BSU agent, Kenneth Lanning, who resisted considerable pressure to grant the FBI's imprimatur to satanic murder and ritual abuse claims. This individual decision was of critical importance in ensuring that these ideas remained firmly on the intellectual fringe and never developed into the full-fledged panic that often seemed imminent in the late 1980s.

Nor was this influence confined to the United States, as the new construction of serial murder had by the late 1980s caused a general reevaluation of multiple homicide in several industrialized countries. In Great Britain, serial murder has been a recognized phenomenon at least since the time of Jack the Ripper in 1888, but the media of the 1980s affected to discover it as something new, startling, and specifically American. During a wave of such cases during 1986, it was the prestigious *Sunday Times* that claimed, "With thousands of police in the hunt for the Stockwell Strangler and the Railway Killer in London, the specter of the serial murderer, now common in America, has been established in Britain" (Deer, 1986). There was "growing alarm . . . that Britain could be seeing the growth of what their American counterparts are calling recreational murder, where there is no apparent motive" (*Sunday Times,* July 27, 1986).

The responses were predictable, with the emergence of a centralized HOLMES data bank to collect information on serious crimes (Jenkins, 1991, 1992). Quantico profilers were also invited to assist in several investigations from 1981 onwards. In 1986, it was announced that "Scotland Yard and the American FBI have launched an unparalleled joint campaign to give Britain the benefit of the FBI's experience of serial murders, where the same killers strike again and again" (*Sunday Times,* July 27, 1986). Serial murder and the mind-hunter image were the subject of two major television programs in the early 1990s, both of which made great use of American experts like Robert Ressler (Clark and Morley, 1993). Britain now has a specialized True Crime publishing imprint specializing in serial murder stories, with a heavy emphasis on Quantico-style profiling (see, for example, Berry-Dee and Odell, 1992, 1993; Wilson and Seaman, 1992).

In Australia and Canada, similarly, a serial murder problem was noted during the 1980s, and the exemplars cited were almost entirely American cases, supplemented by one or two domestic offenders (Mann, 1989; Rule, 1988). The new problem provided a media tag for coverage of local incidents, as in 1989 when the Australian press reported a Sydney serial murder case. Many articles contextualized the case with reference to the United States, where "up to five thousand people a year" were victims of such crimes, and "up to 350 [sic] serial killers are thought to be on the loose" (Robinson, 1989). In response, Australian criminal justice experts called for a national homicide register, to provide some of the information available to the American NCAVC.

American true-crime case studies were widely available in translation throughout Western Europe, and France even published accounts of American cases that were not available in the country of origin. Florida serial killer Gerard Schaefer has become a well-known figure in France through a memoir and a television documentary, though he remains little known in the United States (Bézard, 1992:44, 90–94). Even the phrase *serial killer* has entered French parlance, untranslated. It seems that American criminals and investigators have come to define the expected international norms for this problem.

Federal law enforcement agencies such as the FBI have a long history of employing the mass media to promote their own interests, while suppressing or discouraging rival views; and it must be asked how far a deliberate policy of manipulation explains the successful imposition of the Justice Department view of serial murder. Ressler (see above) portrays the BSU as opportunistic rather than manipulative, but it would be disingenuous to ignore the immense weight carried by statements from such a specialized FBI unit. It is—to say the least—surprising that the authorities who issued the terrifyingly high statistics about the prevalence of the offense were unaware of the serious methodological flaws in these data or that they did not foresee the enormous public impact that these figures would have.

Constraints and Opportunities

On the other hand, it would be simply unacceptable to attribute the emergence of the serial murder problem to any sort of conscious or conspiratorial abuse of evidence. The facts and figures offered by the BSU became significant only when they were accepted as a fair and accurate analysis of circumstances, a process that implies the agency was in a sense telling the public what they wished and expected to hear. The statistics were important because they achieved instant credibility with the politicians and interest groups involved in the successive congressional hearings, suggesting that such a threatening picture must have responded to political or rhetorical needs. The prominence of the many news stories on this subject can only be understood if in fact the FBI's interpretations of the problem were closely attuned to media perceptions of popular needs and fears, and if the images presented matched substantially with underlying expectations. Furthermore, it is more difficult to trace a Justice Department role in the second panic during the early 1990s, which achieved an intensity little inferior to that of 1983–1985.

In other words, the success of the Justice Department model was shaped by a number of constraints and opportunities in the general social and political environment. Especially significant were prevailing ideological conditions, above all the New Right perspective then at its zenith. While not absolutely determining the interpretations that were be likely to be successful for the new problem, the political environment did impose constraints, by discouraging any view that partook of the "failed liberalism" of the previous two decades. This effectively made it impossible to resuscitate the therapeutic model of earlier years, while implicitly favoring a justice-oriented scheme that emphasized the extreme predatory violence of the offenders.

It is equally important to consider the lateral dimension to any given problem: that is, to take account of other problems and panics that were under way more or less simultaneously and that helped form popular thinking on criminal violence and related menaces. Problem construction is a cumulative or incremental process, in which each issue is to some extent built upon its predecessors, in the context of a steadily developing fund of socially available knowledge. The nature of these other issues provides the intellectual environment for the formulation of the new problem, and again provides both constraints and opportunities.

It is difficult to understand the serial murder panic of 1983–1985 without tracing its relationship to other originally separate scares of earlier years, especially the concern over missing and exploited children, and organized pedophilia, as well as ill-defined concerns about the prevalence of homosexuality. These issues acted as essential precursors, though they originally had little obvious or necessary relevance to multiple homicide. None of these incidents should be seen in isolation from the others: The later panics would not have had the force they did if they had not built upon earlier memories and preconceptions, especially about threats to children.

The Making of News

Perhaps the most important opportunities were those provided by the news media themselves, and for both print and electronic media, the claims presented by the FBI from the early 1980s were both timely and valuable. For several years, there had been numerous stories about multiple homicide, and these met obvious public interest. Now, however, claims about an emerging murder problem gave the theme several new elements that made it appear all the more frightening or exciting.

Multiple homicide has long occupied a high position in media perceptions of what constitutes a newsworthy story, as suggested by numerous incidents from the Ripper murders of 1888 through the New York child murders of 1915, the Son of Sam case of the 1970s, and the more recent affairs of Jeffrey Dahmer and Joel Rifkin. This attraction is not difficult to comprehend. Different newspapers and television programs have different values about what constitutes worthwhile news, but there are some common criteria, and serial murder fulfills most of them. Like great drama, a newsworthy story should evoke an emotional response such as fear, outrage, or pity, which is why innocent victims like children or animals feature so regularly. The story should also suggest a phenomenon that appears to be a real threat, that affects or could affect a large number of the readers or viewers of that particular item. It might offer excitement or shock value in the form of unusual sexual activity or violence, and often concerns well-known people in whom there is a good deal of established public interest. Ideally, the story should also offer a platform for social action ("something must be done"), perhaps indicated by the demands of politicians, police, or bureaucrats.

All these criteria are illustrated by a typical serial murder story. It offers drama in the confrontation of good and evil; excitement in the pursuit of the villain; and fear in the likelihood of potential violence befalling members of the news audience. The themes of the coverage are epitomized by the formulaic devices that occur in the television news programs on such cases, which almost invariably include interviews with the family of a victim or victims. Such encounters serve to emphasize the ordinariness and decency of the bereaved parents as individuals and clearly invite identification. This is intended to attract sympathy and to heighten the contrast with the wanton brutality of the offender. Parental interviews also stress the very common nature of the danger, which may exist in apparently safe environments, and thus the universality of the murder threat is reinforced. This is confirmed by the interviews with the perpetrator's neighbors or colleagues, who generally declare that he appeared harmless and innocent, thus indicating once more the random danger from a "stranger next door."

In a sense, serial murder represents for the media the perfect social problem, in that there is no need to resort to any of the rhetorical devices that are normally required to package an issue to make it palatable or interesting for the audience. In the case of an issue like AIDS, child abuse, or homelessness, a story will normally need an opening "grabber," some dramatic story or incident to secure the reader's attention, and some effort has to be expended ensuring that the reader will realize that this issue causes genuine harm or damage. In addition, a story has to be personalized in such a way as to provide reader or viewer identification, as illustrated by the effect on AIDS coverage of sensational cases like those of Rock Hudson and Kimberly Bergalis.

In contrast, serial murder stories usually have such elements built in. The crime may well be discovered in a particularly gruesome way, with the finding of a mass graveyard or a body in a car, and the press has an automatic grabber in its accounts of this extremely aberrant behavior. There may also be a powerful visual image, which can encapsulate public fears and concerns: John Wayne Gacy's crawl space, Jeffrey Dahmer's apartment, Joel Rifkin's pickup truck. Furthermore, any arrested offender immediately acquires celebrity status, so that coverage is inevitably personalized. Nor is there any doubt that such behavior involves authentic harm, especially when the crimes so often involve archetypally evil activities such as cannibalism, necrophilia, or human butchery.

It is not difficult to understand why the cases of the late 1970s were all so attractive to newspapers and television, and all were treated as headline-making stories. However, the FBI's presentation of a wave of serial murder presented the chance to contextualize individual cases as part of a highly newsworthy national phenomenon. This greatly amplified the potential threat of the behavior by bringing the danger home to every community and household across the nation, and moreover the new construction emphasized the danger to children and the young. It was an ideal news story at several distinct levels, offering as it did the opportunity to indulge in political advocacy, demands for the reform of legislation and policing, as well as wide-ranging social analysis. The value was all the greater when it offered such rich rhetorical opportunities to many different interest groups. The FBI earned the credit for bringing the issue to public attention, and also appeared to be the only group with a serious practical agenda to combat the new menace.

The potency of the new problem is illustrated by its longevity. As Best has noted,

> Claims-makers must compete for attention. Social problems drop from view when they no longer seem fresh or interesting. New waves of claims-making may depend on the claims-makers' ability to redefine an issue, to focus on a new form of an old threat (e.g., crack or heavy metal music) or to find other wrinkles. (Best, 1989:140)

In the case of serial murder, the panic of 1983–1985 was followed by several years of simmering interest, and then a dramatic growth of renewed concern from 1990 onwards, while there is no reason to doubt that there will be an indefinite number of future revivals.

The resilience of the topic owes much to its pervasive presence in popular fiction, especially from the end of the 1980s, and the novels, films, and true-crime books vastly increased the fund of socially available knowledge. This reinforced public expectations about the severity of the threat and provided numerous tags that could be employed for further media coverage of the story. Apart from its inherent qualities, the serial murder theme also fit well with the changing news priorities of the 1980s and the growth of sensationalistic "trash television" epitomized by successive Geraldo Rivera specials (and Rivera made this type of homicide one of his favorite topics).

Nor is it difficult to speculate about the next manifestations of the issue, as there are already potentially newsworthy developments merely awaiting a sensational case or discovery to provide a focus for concern. For instance, we know that the VICAP system is already indicating apparent links between murders that would not hitherto have been connected. The resulting upsurge in alleged murder series will almost certainly be taken as proof of a rise in the behavior itself, rather than a simple change in investigative technology. In addition, demographic changes make it likely that future fears will be directed toward multiple killers who prey on the elderly, sick, and institutionalized. There always have been such offenders, who are the subjects of several books and other studies, but they are likely to be the subject of much sharper concern in a rapidly aging population. It is also possible that a quite unforeseen circumstance might reawaken dormant fears about cult or racial conspiracies underlying serial homicide.

Shaping the Image

The serial murder problem illustrates the complex relationship between three apparently independent forces: the law enforcement bureaucracy, the news media, and popular culture. Once the original theme was established, innovative interpretations of the problem ("other wrinkles") could originate in any of the three areas, before spreading rapidly to gain acceptance in both the other components of the triangle. This process serves not only to keep alive an interest in serial murder, but also to define ever more sharply the image of the killer in the monster stereotype formulated during the 1980s, to the exclusion of other possible interpretations.

During 1991, this interaction was well illustrated by the complex relationship between reality and fiction in the construction of both villains (Hannibal Lecter and Jeffrey Dahmer) and heroes (Jack Crawford, his BSU prototypes, and his countless fictional imitators). The Justice Department formulates the image, which is transformed and publicized in fiction, which in turn shapes public attitudes and expectations; while the news media present stories that respond to these images and stereotypes. In turn, the investigative priorities of bureaucratic agencies are formed by public and legislative expectations, which are derived from popular culture and the news media. Media images can also frame the expectations and behavior of individual agents and administrators: "New applicants to the BSU are taking Jodie Foster's character as a role model: they too want to be supersleuths" (Ressler and Schachtman, 1992:242).

In this process, the killers themselves often play a claims-making role that is important, if sparsely explored. In any discussion of serial homicide, particular weight is attached to the remarks of incarcerated offenders, which are felt to provide the best validation for particular theories about the etiology of violence or the development of the homicidal personality. In documentaries of the 1980s, there were frequent appearances by killers like Ted Bundy, Henry Lee Lucas, and Edmund Kemper, while more recently interviews with Westley Alan Dodd have often been aired and cited. Published confessions by notorious killers are the most popular of true-crime books, as is illustrated by the great popularity of Ted Bundy's published interviews (Michaud and Aynesworth, 1983, 1989). There has even appeared a *Diary* controversially ascribed to the original Jack the Ripper (Harrison, 1993).

It is widely assumed that these statements enjoy a peculiar authority as firsthand autobiography and self-analysis, but this view is open to question. There is a well-known sociological process by which offenders come to be labeled, to accept not only the deviant status that is imputed to them by agents of control, but also to accept the interpretations of this evil that are proffered to them. Serial killers are influenced by the media as well as by academic psychology, and many make a specific study of earlier offenders. Peter Kürten was one of many to have found a role model in the original Jack the Ripper, while recent killers like Joel Rifkin possess substantial libraries about true-life murder cases.

This influence may go far to explaining why killers in different eras tend to reproduce explanations of their offense that closely mimic the prevailing ideological perspective of the day or even of the particular investigator to whom they are confessing. Thus the psychodynamic confessions of an earlier day have given way to common assertions that the criminal in question had been the victim of extreme sexual abuse during childhood. Others aggressively affect the monster image, as when Westley Dodd declared, "At that point, I became a hunter and a killer, and that's all that I was" (interview on CBS's "48 Hours," May 8, 1991).

There are also legal considerations, in that a killer may wish to present himself or herself in such a way as to promote a particular judicial outcome, above all an insanity defense. In contrast, Westley Dodd apparently tried to present himself as a ruthless monster with the explicit goal of preventing obstacles being placed in the path of his much desired execution. Other individuals have certainly confessed to crimes far beyond those they actually committed. By definition, this is neither a rational nor a conventional population, so much caution should be exercised in accepting its statements at face value.

In addition, the psychopathic personality type so frequently represented among serial killers often manifests itself in a desire to please and manipulate, to tell whatever story will win the sympathy of the listener, and this may explain why the final confessions of Ted Bundy to an evangelical writer laid so much emphasis on the sinister influence of pornography. Moreover, the successive confessions of a given killer over the years are likely to contain numerous contradictions, so that a particular claims-maker can choose whatever quotation may seem opportune for his or her cause. Medical murderer Donald Harvey has asserted the influence on his conduct of early childhood sex abuse with quite the confidence with which he had earlier denied the same interpretation.

Whatever the explanation, the serial killers add an important element to the complex feedback relationship between investigators, media, and popular culture. Though they often do little more than reflect the commonplaces of the culture and the academic environment, the offenders do this with such apparent authority that their remarks are likely to be taken as the ultimate warrant for any desired view or explanation.

Discussion Questions

1. Why did the FBI, particularly its Behavioral Sciences Unit, select serial murder rather than some other crime problem as an issue to focus on during the mid-1980s? How did the FBI's position in American society and in the federal government influence its use of the serial homicide issue?

2. Does the "social construction of social problems" approach imply that some of the issues highlighted by claims-makers are unimportant, or that they are given more attention than they warrant? Does this approach suggest that other aspects of social reality should receive more attention, or that with more attention other issues would be just as likely to be seen as important problems?

3. In 1992, an apparent epidemic of carjackings received much attention in the press. The FBI was quick to point out that the forcible theft of cars from drivers was not a new crime and was really a form of robbery. The FBI did add carjackings to the list of violent crimes investigated by its Operation Safe Streets task force, and a federal law was passed to punish "robbery auto theft" more severely. Less than two years later, this crime was rarely getting much attention in the press, even though there was no evidence that the offense was no longer being committed. Why didn't the FBI make more effort to define carjacking as an important crime problem, as it did with serial murder? Was it because the press didn't cooperate in redefining carjacking as a serious issue, or did the public resist making more out of this offense?

$C\ h\ a\ p\ t\ e\ r$ 2

The Myth and Fear of Child Abduction

Victor E. Kappeler, Mark Blumberg, and Gary W. Potter

This selection looks at the consequences of distorting the magnitude of one aspect of the crime problem: the abduction of children by strangers. The authors show how the media, politicians, and law enforcement agencies have exaggerated this problem by mixing together a relatively small number of stranger kidnappings with a much larger number of runaways and children taken by noncustodial parents in violation of court orders. They then explore the negative effects of these exaggerated claims for children, their parents, and society as a whole.

To be unaware of the issue of missing children in America is to be totally isolated from newspapers, television, mail, or other forms of communication. Beginning in the early 1980s, barely a week went by when the public was not exposed to photographs, stories, and debates on the issue of missing and abducted children. Virtually every form of media was used to circulate the faces and stories of missing children. From milk cartons to flyers in utility bills to television documentaries, Americans were made aware of the child abduction "epidemic" (Kappeler and Vaughn, 1988:56). "Toy stores and fast-food restaurants distributed abduction-prevention tips for both parents and children. Parents could have their children finger-printed or videotaped to make identification easier; some dentists even proposed attaching identification disks to children's teeth" (Best, 1987:102).

The image of missing and exploited children commands public attention and causes emotional response in even the most callous individuals. One cannot be exposed to the

Source: Reprinted by permission of Waveland Press, Inc., from Victor E. Kappeler, Mark Blumberg, and Gary W. Potter, *The Mythology of Crime and Criminal Justice,* 2nd ed. (Prospect Heights, IL: Waveland Press, Inc., 1996). All rights reserved.

stories and images of these victims and not feel some emotion. Shedding the issue of emotionalism, however, produces serious questions concerning the true magnitude of the missing children problem and the necessity of drastic social changes aimed at its prevention. Several factors have culminated in the creation of an unprecedented level of fear and concern about the possibility of child abduction in America. Combining the concepts of missing children and exploited children precipitates increased emotionalism and concern. The thought of a child being abducted conjures images of strangers hiding under cover of darkness, waiting to whisk away someone's child, intent on committing some unspeakable crime.

Indisputably, there are hideous acts committed against children. These incidents often receive great media attention and remain embedded in the public's mind for extended periods of time. The media has and continues to focus extensively on sensational cases like the abduction and murder of Adam Walsh and the serial murders of children in both Atlanta and Texas. More recently the media focused on the abduction and abuse of ten-year-old Katie Beers from her home in Bay Shore, New York. Katie was abducted and held for seventeen days by John Esposito, a friend of Katie's family, in an underground room. Newspapers across the country reported the incident, focusing almost exclusively on the attempted sexual abuse and the "hidden dungeon," "secret room," and "coffin of confinement" where the child was held. The horror of such examples becomes the key ingredient in the public's perception of the child abduction problem. As one group of researchers remarked, the popular stereotype of kidnapping "draws its imagery from nationally notorious and tragic cases of abduction . . ." (Finkelhor, Hotaling, and Sedlak, 1992:226).

Besides drawing on the imagery of notorious cases, the media and politicians alike have linked child abduction with sexual exploitation. In 1981 when the issue of missing children was first taking shape, Senator Hawkins remarked that "once they [missing children] are on the street they are fair game for child molestation, prostitution, and other exploitation" (Hawkins, 1991:2; as quoted in Best, 1987:105). Little has changed in the 1990s. In November of 1992 and again in May of 1993, the television show *America's Most Wanted* aired specials devoted to child abduction. To promote the first show, the producers ran advertisements in *TV Guide* stating that "over one million children are reported missing every year" (*TV Guide,* 1992:123). The 1992 special spent considerable time forging the imagery of child abduction with talk of "serial child molesters" and "child predators," vowing to get "the people who hunt our children" (*America's Most Wanted,* 11/20/92).

Media imagery aside, children can be missing without being the victims of sexual exploitation or abuse. Conversely, exploitation and abuse can occur in the child's own home; unfortunately, these acts are not limited to strangers. The media did attract enormous public attention in 1994 when Susan Smith's two young sons were allegedly kidnapped in a carjacking. The nation watched in horror as it was later revealed that Susan Smith had released the parking brake on her van and let it roll with her sons strapped in their car seats into a lake. Countless other cases do not receive national attention. Consider a few incidents of "missing" and abused children that were given only passing mention by the media:

- Alice Brown of Leavenworth, Kansas pleaded guilty to involuntary manslaughter in the death of her 4-year-old son, Steven. His body was found encased in concrete on the family's back porch (*USA Today,* 5/18/93:3A).

- Tanisha Nobles of Dayton, Ohio who reported her son, Erick, age 2, missing from a shopping mall was charged with murder after she admitted to police that she had drowned her child because he "got on her nerves" (*USA Today,* 1/14/93:6A).
- Reenee Lyoyd and Bertha Toombs, the aunt and grandmother of five-year-old Marquisha Candler, were charged with murder after police uncovered the child's remains in a California desert. The two women had made public pleas for help in locating the missing child (*USA Today,* 9/30/92).

The issue of child abduction is further complicated by the lack of a clear criterion for defining the term "missing children." While this may seem to be a trivial point, an analysis of the issue illustrates that the ambiguity of the definition "missing" distorts the public's perception of the "reality" and "extent" of the missing children problem. Joel Best (1987) perhaps best captured the context in which the definition of missing children was constructed when he contended that reforms advocating new laws to address the missing children problem "preferred an inclusive definition of missing children" (Best, 1987:105). Under their definition a child would have included people as old as twenty, people missing for a few hours, and the events surrounding the child's disappearance would include most "misadventures which might befall children" (Best, 1987:105).

Eventually because of the political pressure generated by individuals, reform groups, and the media, Congress took action to address the problem of missing children in America. The Missing Children's Assistance Act (MCAA) of 1983 defined "missing child" as:

1. any missing person thirteen years of age or younger, or;
2. any missing person under the age of eighteen if the circumstances surrounding such person's disappearance indicate that such person is likely to have been abducted (Sec. 272).

The Missing Children's Assistance Act, passed in 1984, created the National Center for Missing and Exploited Children (NCMEC) and defined "missing" in the following language:

1. . . . "missing child" means any individual less than eighteen years of age whose whereabouts are unknown to such individual's legal custodian if—

   a. the circumstances surrounding such individual's disappearance indicate that such individual may possibly have been removed by another from the control of such individual's legal custodian without such custodian's consent; or
   b. the circumstances of the case strongly indicate that such individual is likely to be abused or sexually exploited. . . . (Sec. 5772).

The text of the new law clearly forged a linkage between sexual exploitation and child abduction. Persons encompassed by these definitions may be missing for a variety of reasons unrelated to stranger abductions. Children can be abducted by a parent who does not have legal custody, an act commonly termed "child stealing" (McCoy, 1978). They may be missing because they ran away from home, or they may be suffering from some form of illness such as amnesia, or in some cases they may have committed suicide. Clearly, not all children counted as missing are lost as a result of some stranger's criminality. It is with these broad definitions of missing children that the reality of the problem becomes distorted.

The failure to formulate clear typologies of missing children combined with law enforcement's merging the two categories—exploited and missing—contribute to the public's perception of the extent and context of the problem. Taken together, these factors produce a situation conducive to imprecise reporting of statistics to the public, often in such a fashion as to exaggerate the potential danger of a child being abducted by strangers.

For the purposes of clarity, the terms child stealing, child snatching and parental abduction (often used interchangeably) are defined as the taking of a child by a parent in violation of a court's custody order. Child kidnapping is defined as a stranger's abduction of a child in violation of criminal law. With these distinctions in mind, let's begin considering how the "reality" of missing children is created and how the problem has become defined in American society.

Creating Reality and Defining the Problem

The public is exposed to statistics on missing children published by sources varying from newspaper articles and private organizations to governmental reports. These reports generally indicate that anywhere between 1.5 and 2.5 million children are missing from their homes each year (Treanor, 1986; Regnery, 1986; *Congressional Record-Senate*, 1983; Dee Scofield Awareness Program, 1983b). Of those reported missing, it is predicted that as many as 50,000 children will never be heard from again (Thornton, 1983; Schoenberger and Thomas, 1985). It is also estimated that as many as 5,000 of these missing children will be found dead (*Congressional Record-Senate*, 1983).

These are the statistics distributed by various sources for public consumption. A more critical examination of these statistics finds that within some jurisdictions between 66 and 98 percent of those children listed as missing are in reality runaways and were not abducted at all (Treanor, 1986; Schoenberger and Thomas, 1985). Police departments receive many more reports of missing runaways than other types of missing cases. Regnery (1986) estimates that nearly 1 million of the reportedly 1.5 million missing children are runaways. As many as 15 percent of the missing children may be parental abductions (Schoenberger and Thomas, 1985). In fact one author has maintained that about one out of twenty-two divorces ends in child theft (Agopian, 1981). Others estimate that between 25,000 and 100,000 incidents of missing children are parental abductions (Foreman, 1980; *Congressional Record-Senate*, 1983).

In a Michigan study (Schoenberger and Thomas, 1985), the researchers found that 76 percent of the 428 entries examined in Michigan's lost children files should have been removed because the persons entered as missing had been located. These 325 children had been found but were not removed from the active files. The vast majority of children listed as missing in law enforcement records are found within 24 hours. Similarly, the Massachusetts State Police Missing Persons Unit estimates that 40 percent of their computer listings on missing persons are in reality solved cases that have not been removed from the data base (*Crime Control Digest*, 1985). These files along with data from other states are used to support contentions about the scope of the missing children problem. The presence of inaccurate data in many law enforcement record systems has contributed to dramatically overestimating the number of children missing.

Bill Treanor, Director of the American Youth Center, presents even more conservative figures:

> Up to 98 percent of so-called missing children are in fact runaway teenagers. . . . Of the remaining 2 percent to 3 percent, virtually all are wrongfully abducted by a parent. That leaves fewer than 200 to 300 children abducted by strangers annually. The merchants of fear would have you believe that 5,000 unidentifiable bodies of children are buried each year. In truth, it's less than 200 dead from all causes, such as drowning, fire and exposure, not just murder. (1986:B1)

To compound the problem, statistics are presented regarding the number of children murdered each year. It is maintained that approximately 2,500 children are murdered yearly including homicides committed by ". . . psychopathic serial murderers, pedophiles, child prostitution exploiters and child abusers" (Regnery, 1986:42). However, of these 2,500 children murdered, the number reported missing prior to their victimization was not determined. Additionally, it is not reported how many of these victims were killed by their parents or other family members.

By 1992 researchers had determined that each year only 200 to 300 cases of missing children met the imagery of the stereotypic kidnapping (Finkelhor, Hotaling, and Sedlak, 1992:233). These distinctions are easily blurred in the public's eyes. Statistics, often without qualification, are distributed to the public from official governmental sources. Such findings raise serious doubts as to the accuracy of the statistics presented to the public concerning the number, nature and ultimate fate of missing children in America. Growing public awareness and concern over the missing children issue has been promoted through the use of inconsistent and inaccurate statistics. Such statistics and the effect they have on the public and its perception of the extent of the missing children problem have both obvious and unintended consequences.

Latent Functions of Prevention

The primary obvious function of increased awareness of the problem of child abduction is prevention. Public preoccupation with child safety has become evident in the proliferation of children's literature addressing safety and the prevention of abduction. With increasing frequency, books and other forms of literature are becoming available to children illustrating the dangers of social contact with persons who are not considered a member of the family or extended family unit. These texts often inform children of the danger of speaking or having contact with strangers.

Children's books of this nature can have at least three negative latent functions. First, through children's literature the feelings of danger are equated with social contacts outside the family unit. This perception can result in increased social isolation and alienation of children from the community. As both parents and children begin to equate social contact outside the family with danger and impending harm, community interaction may decrease.

The fear of child abduction, while limiting social interaction, may reduce the family's dependence on third parties for child care. Parents may begin to rely less and less on day care facilities, in-house sitters, and other third party child care sources. As parents take greater responsibility for the care of their children, the contact within the family unit may increase and greater dependence may be placed on the interactions of family members. The family unit may gain greater solidarity as social interaction with community decreases, but the cost may be increased fear and stunted social development.

Second, these texts often give questionable information to children. A specific case in point is a children's book entitled *Never Talk to Strangers* (Joyce, 1967), which advises children through the use of animal characters that they should never talk to strangers, but that it is acceptable to become friendly with acquaintances of the family. This notion is reinforced by a government program sponsored by the National Child Safety Council (NCSC). According to H. R. Wilkins of the Michigan-based NCSC, millions of milk cartons were printed utilizing animal characters to instruct children of the dangers of contact with strangers (*Juvenile Justice Digest,* 1985b). Yet, the literature and research on both sexual abuse of children and child abduction indicates that children are more often victimized by acquaintances rather than strangers. Consider these statistics:

- A study of three states found that 96 percent of female rape victims under the age of 12 knew their attackers (Bureau of Justice Statistics, 1994a:2).
- A study of murder in families found that 63 percent of the children murdered under the age of 12 were killed by family members. In 57 percent of these cases children were murdered by a parent (Bureau of Justice Statistics, 1994b:5).

As children are taught to run from unfamiliar persons, they are also being taught to run into the arms of those most often engaged in child abuse. These media also promote the notion that if properly educated, children can distinguish between those individuals who are "safe" and those persons to avoid, a distinction even criminologists are reluctant to make. The fear invoked by the spread of prevention literature and the indoctrination of children with safety tips like avoiding strangers may be a zero sum game. Such prevention measures only replace the unfounded fear of child abduction with a new and equally unfounded fear of strangers. These approaches to prevention may confuse children and promote paranoia and insecurity. Where would a child abused by a family member turn given such mixed messages—to a stranger?

Third, the proliferation of literature on child safety stresses that it is the duty of the parents to educate their children. This responsibility in itself is not damaging and may very well contribute to prevention. However, placing blame on parents for failing to educate their children allows the responsibility for child safety to be shifted from social control agencies such as the police and society as a whole to individual family members. In effect, what these texts suggest is that if parents fail to educate their children and if children fail to heed their warnings, they will be abused or abducted and the responsibility rests on them alone—rather than on the offender or society as a whole. We in effect begin to "blame the victim" and shift focus from the offender and crime control agencies to the child and the nonvigilant parent.

The link between literature and the behavior of adolescents has been well illustrated by the works of David McClelland (1961). He found that the economic performance of a culture varied with the degrees of achievement portrayed in literature. Parallels were drawn between the declines and increases in achievement, and the decline and increase of literature depicting economic success. This research shows that literature has an effect on behavior. Whether it is motivation to excel economically or motivation to withdraw socially, the effect is profound. By depicting strangers as the persons to fear and avoid due to the possibility of abduction and exploitation, we circumvent serious consideration of the extent to which relatives, friends, and family members are involved in child abuse and abduction. We also divert attention away from the fact that most missing children are runaways.

Concern for child safety and fear of child abduction have not been limited to children's literature. The fear of child abduction is beginning to motivate legal reform designed to criminalize a vast scope of behavior involving children. Society is turning to solutions to a problem which has been defined based on fear and inaccurate information.

Legal Reform: Creating Crime and Criminals

The emotional furor and fear of child abduction has created an atmosphere conducive to the creation of a new crime and class of criminals. In California, prior to 1976, if a parent took his or her child in violation of a custody order, it was not considered a criminal offense. Since October 1, 1977, legislation in California has been enacted making it a criminal offense for parents to take custody of their own children in violation of a court custody order (Agopian, 1980, 1981).

The state of New York has enacted similar legislation, making parental child abduction a felony offense. In February of 1985, the National Governors' Association called for all states to adopt legislation making child snatching a felony offense, regardless of whether the violator was a parent or stranger to the child. As of 1983, forty-eight states had adopted the Uniform Child Custody Jurisdiction Act and forty-two states had classified child snatching as a felony (Silverman, 1983). The legal response to this behavior has also been addressed at the federal level.

Prior to 1983, the United States Department of Justice restricted the issuance of warrants for the arrest of parents who took illegal custody of their children and subsequently crossed state lines. Since December 23, 1982, federal and local law enforcement officials can seek federal arrest warrants for child snatching even if there is no evidence to suggest the child is in physical danger (*United States Attorneys Bulletin,* 1983). In the Sixth Report to Congress on the implementation of the Parental Kidnapping Prevention Act of 1980, the Department of Justice indicated that during 1982, thirty-two "fugitive parents" were arrested by the Federal Bureau of Investigation (FBI). These arrests took place prior to removal of the warrant restrictions imposed by the Department of Justice. During the first nine months of 1983, after the removal of restrictions, the number of parents arrested by the FBI doubled to sixty-four (U.S. Department of Justice, 1983). With these reforms at both the state and federal levels, we have created the crime of child stealing and the criminal classifications of "fugitive parents" and "custody criminals."

While in some circles this easing of restrictions on the FBI and the criminalization of custody violations may be viewed as a positive step in solving the problem of child abduction by parents, there are certainly negative effects associated with the increased arrests of fugitive parents. An undetermined number of these children are physically and emotionally better off with the parent who committed the illegal act. This point was illustrated in the case of a Long Island girl who was abducted by her mother after the father was awarded custody. After lengthy consideration of the case, New York Justice Alexander Vitale ordered that the mother should retain custody of the child, having decided that this was in the best interest of the child's welfare. The best interests of the child are not always paramount in the court's decision-making process; jurisdictional concerns are often given equal importance in deciding custody cases after an abduction has occurred (*In re Nehra* v. *Uhlar,* 1977).

The second problem arises out of labeling as criminal the parent who removes his or her child from an abusive atmosphere. While not all parents who abduct their children do so with such noble intentions, these parents often have little recourse. They must decide either to comply with the law and allow their children to endure further abuse or to violate the law in the best interest of the child. Legal avenues are often closed to parents. Fees associated with custody battles often restrict a parent's ability to obtain legal redress in these matters. Regardless of the individual's ability to access the courts, child abduction is often seen as the last alternative to maintaining a full-time parental relationship (Agopian, 1980). While some degree of formal social control may be required to prevent parental abductions, better screening and investigation by the courts before awarding custody could reduce the incidence of well meaning child abduction. We can only speculate as to the motivations of a parent who would abduct a child or children from an apparently stable family, but the abducting party must (at a minimum) feel that an inadequate custody arrangement was made in the judicial process. More equitable custody arrangements may be one way of reducing child abduction by parents.

A more pragmatic consideration is the utility of fugitive warrants. A fugitive warrant does not allow the FBI to take a child into custody or even to return the child to the parent with legal custody. These children are often kept in foster homes or other community shelters while courts review the custody arrangements. In some cases these environments may be more damaging than staying with the abducting parent. Arrests on fugitive warrants do not reflect the number of children who are actually returned to their legal guardians as a result of arrest. Furthermore, the warrant does not allow agents to effect arrests of persons other than those named on the warrant, who may have materially participated in the abduction or currently have physical custody of the child.

The emotional atmosphere created by increased publicity of the dangers of child abduction has been used as a political tool to advocate stiffer punishments for offenders. In the cases of true stranger abductions, this may be a desirable prevention measure. It is, however, questionable whether stiffer sanctions would prevent hideous crimes against children. The desire to control and sanction stranger abduction often becomes politicized with calls for stiffer penalties for all offenders who commit crimes against children. Calling for legislative "reform," Congressman Henry J. Hyde advocated mandatory life sentences for persons who kidnap a child and the death penalty for child abduction that results in death. The Congressman stated, "I do not feel it is too harsh to say that one who kidnaps or murders a child has forfeited his right to freedom forever" (*Juvenile Justice Digest,* 1985a:4). A call for the death penalty for child snatchers has not been limited to the political arena. Private organizations devoted to the location of missing children have also called for legislative "reform." Dee Scofield Awareness Program (1983a), a private organization located in Tampa, Florida, recommends that child abduction should be elevated to a federal offense punishable by either death or life imprisonment. The most disturbing point here is that the proposed reform fails to make a clear distinction between parental custody violations and stranger abductions.

Conclusion

McClintock and Haden (1970) have pointed out that the manner in which a problem is defined is related to the type of social control systems available to address that problem. The problem of missing children in America is no exception to their contention. It becomes clear from the analysis of the missing children problem that the issue has been defined as epidemic in proportion and criminal in nature. Given this definition and perception of the issue, the current course of action—the criminalization of this behavior—is clearly a logical consequence. As a society, we have defined the problem as an abnormal behavior on the part of a select group of individuals we have chosen to call criminal. We have chosen social control agencies and criminal sanctions as the solutions for this epidemic. In an attempt to prevent this behavior, we have subsequently created a new classification of crime and criminals without distinguishing the motives and reasoning behind this behavior. In short, we have defined missing children in America as a legal problem with legal solutions.

As long as this definition and solution dominate the missing children problem, a solution is not forthcoming. The legal "solution" is merely a reaction to an undesirable behavior. However, if we define the scope of the problem more accurately and develop a clear understanding of the various types of incidents that collectively compose the problem, an alternative solution may yet emerge.

As previously mentioned, the missing children problem includes runaways, parental abductions, and stranger abductions. Incorporating runaways into missing children statistics produces the perception of an epidemic. The inclusion of stranger abduction in the composite figures permits the problem to be defined as criminal. Linking sexual abuse and exploitation provokes emotionalism. Incorporating parental abductions and then criminalizing all abductions promotes conceptualization of the issue as both epidemic and criminal.

In order to begin to address the problem of missing children in America, we must first understand the problem in a social rather than a legal context. Only then can we begin to take preventive rather than reactive measures. The nature of family relationships must be explored in order to begin to understand why 1.5 million children flee their homes each year. We must also begin to realize that our legal system, both criminal and civil, is not a panacea for all social problems. We must begin to separate the missing children problem into its parts—social and legal. The fact that thousands of children each year are abducted by their parents raises serious questions about our legal system's ability to define family relations equitably through divorce and child custody orders.

Our adversarial trial system, so often alluded to in the criminal process, is omnipresent in civil courts as well. The adversarial process creates what amounts to custody battles. These events can only be seen as creating conflict, setting the stage for continued discord between the winners (those awarded custody) and the losers (those denied custody). Unless a more equitable process is developed—one void of the conflicts resulting from the current system—child stealing will remain a result of custody battles. If we cannot adequately understand the behavior of runaway children and the reaction of parents who are denied the custody of their children, or develop workable solutions to custody arrangements, how can we hope to understand or prevent child abductions by strangers?

While this chapter has attempted to address some of the latent and manifest functions of the fear of child abduction, the true effects of increased awareness, fear, and use of prevention programs may not become evident for some time. It is too early to speculate on the possible effects the promotion of these fears will have on future generations of parents, children, and legal reforms.

The preliminary indications are that we will continue to attempt to handle the issue through increased legislation and stiffer penalties for offenders. However, it is evident that the campaign against missing children, while well intended, will have negative effects socially. It would appear prudent to consider the social effects of prescribing criminalization and prevention in mass dosages. It is readily apparent that critical research designed to reflect accurately the scope of the problem of missing children in America is desperately needed. Furthermore, we can no longer afford to implement prevention programs without first giving critical thought to both the manifest and latent social functions of these policies.

Discussion Questions

1. What organizations and individuals do you think are responsible for exaggerating the number of child abductions by strangers? How do they create a distorted picture of the problem of missing children? What do they have to gain from defining the problem in the way they do?

2. What might be the short-term and long-term consequences for children exposed at an early age to the message "Never talk to strangers"? Were you exposed to such advice when young and, if so, how did you react to it then and how do you regard it today?

3. Will efforts at prevention and legal reform to deal with the problem of missing and abducted children strengthen the American family or weaken it? What will be the likely effects of these changes for society as a whole? Consider the possible impact of the specific measures discussed by Kappeler, Blumberg, and Potter.

Part *II*

Sources of Criminal Behavior

$$Chapter \quad 3$$

The Biology of
Antisocial Behavior

Diana H. Fishbein

Criminologists have explored many sources of criminal behavior, from genetic inheritance to personality type, from child abuse to unemployment. In this selection, Diana Fishbein proposes that criminology will benefit from integrating the perspectives of various disciplines and that criminologists should pay close attention to recent advances in behavioral sciences that indicate that biological factors are important influences on antisocial behavior. She cites evidence that individuals with certain biological traits are especially vulnerable to social environmental influences, helping to explain why only some people who are abused as children or who grow up in poverty turn to crime.

Consistent observations that a small percentage of offenders are responsible for a preponderance of serious violent crime (Hamparian et al., 1978; Moffitt et al., 1989; Wolfgang, Figlio, and Sellin, 1972) suggest that this particular population is unusually vulnerable to repetitive antisocial behavior. Numerous studies report that chronically violent criminals have an early history of crime and aggression (Loeber and Dishion, 1983; Moffitt et al., 1989); in fact, the best predictor of present and future behavior is past behavior. Findings that conduct disorders and delinquent acts precede drug abuse and related criminal behaviors (see Fishbein, 1991) provide further fuel for the suggestion that a subgroup of offenders is at high risk for many forms of antisociality. The possibility that biological conditions may play a role in the development of antisocial and criminal behavior is accentuated by

Source: This paper was written for this book and is an updated and revised version of Diana H. Fishbein, "Biological Perspectives in Criminology," *Criminology* 28 (February 1990), pp. 41–72. Used with permission of the author.

these reports and has spurred a search for biological markers in "vulnerable" subgroups (Fishbein, 1990; Mednick et al., 1987).

The primary purpose of this chapter is to present a more balanced view of antisocial behavior, a view which integrates findings from various behavioral sciences relevant to the study of crime. The central question addressed is "Given similar environmental and socio-cultural experiences, why does only a subgroup engage in antisocial and sometimes violent behavior?" Sociological research has well established the link between particular adverse environmental and social conditions, but has been unable to explain individual differences in vulnerability to these conditions. Using this "integrationist" approach, reliable biological aspects of criminal behavior may be incorporated into sociological paradigms to provide a comprehensive understanding of antisociality. This chapter provides only a condensed introduction to the vast amount of work accomplished in the behavioral sciences.

The theoretical parameters for integrating biological, psychological and sociological findings are consistent with the diathesis–stress model (see Tarter and Edwards, 1987) constructed to explain many forms of antisocial behavior. According to this model, individuals vary considerably with respect to their biological strengths and weaknesses. Biological weaknesses, referred to as "vulnerabilities," are influential in an individual's risk for antisocial behavior. Rather than acting alone, however, these biological features operate by setting the stage for how adaptively an individual will respond to personal stressors. In other words, a stressful environment is more likely to contribute to some form of psychopathology when it is received by a biological system that is somehow compromised. Learning disability, brain damage or functional irregularity, drug exposure, genetic predisposition to temperamental disturbances, and other biological disadvantages lay the groundwork for a pathological response to a stressful environment. Prior learning experiences and situational factors contribute further by either increasing or decreasing the risk.

Although the probability of a pathological response is a function of the number of these risk factors present, the probability is even greater in the presence of an adverse environment with severe stressors (e.g., poverty, unemployment, crime and drug infestation, poor parenting, lack of education, abuse/neglect, and social immobility). For example, hyperactive children may function well if given appropriate intervention. In the presence of family instability, alcoholism, absence of educational programs, and a delinquent peer group, however, the child may be more prone to antisocial behavior, possibly resulting in criminal acts. Thus, environmental factors play a facilitating role in determining an antisocial outcome in vulnerable persons. Environmental factors may be even more potent determinants of antisociality than strictly biological vulnerabilities when the environment is unusually harsh or conducive to such behavior, as we may readily observe in our inner cities. Once again, however, not all inner city residents engage in antisocial behavior; that outcome remains somewhat dependent on individual vulnerability. The reverse may also apply—even in the presence of a protective environment, a biological disadvantage may be so severe as to overwhelm a positive environmental influence. An example of that particular outcome may be seen in fetal alcohol syndrome, when the biological odds frequently outweigh prosocial influences.

The following discussion concentrates on biological aspects of this multifaceted relationship. A variety of disciplines have examined antisocial behaviors, and at least one example from each topical area will be discussed. Note that the majority of so-called multidisciplinary studies have examined only a few variables in isolation, without accounting for interactive effects between biological and socio-environmental conditions. A truly collaborative research project promises to yield more informative results regarding bio-socio-environmental influences on antisocial behavior. (See Fishbein, 1990; Mednick et al., 1987; and Raine, 1993, for detailed critiques of biological approaches.)

Evolutionary Dictates

Sociobiology is a field devoted to the study of evolutionary bases for human behavior. According to this theory, human instinctual drives (e.g., eating, reproduction, and defensive behavior) ensure our survival and are essentially stable over time. The mechanisms for acting on these drives, however, especially within the brain, continuously evolve to enhance our survival capabilities. With the advent of human consciousness, psychological forces and cultural values interact and sometimes compete with biological drives dictated by evolutionary trends (Thiessen, 1976). Thus, human behavior is a product of the profound and complex interaction of biological and social conditions. Due to the intricacy of this interaction and the elusiveness of evolutionary directions, the nature and outcome of this process are difficult to identify and to study.

Most behaviors have some adaptive significance (i.e., they reflect an attempt to adapt to environmental conditions) and, thus, can be studied in an evolutionary context. Aggression is one form of behavior that facilitates adaptations to the environment and is, under normal conditions, functional. On the other hand, aggressive behavior can become dysfunctional under "abnormal" environmental conditions, particularly conditions that have been associated with a display of extreme, overt aggression because they are perceived as threats to survival. For example, the administration of an electrical shock, loud noises, extreme heat, starvation, crowding, and other conditions elicit or exacerbate fighting behaviors in many primate species, including humans (Carlson, 1977; Thiessen, 1976; Valzelli, 1981). Similar responses are elicited by stimulating areas in the brain responsible for the perception and assimilation of painful stimuli, enabling the identification of neural mechanisms involved. Abnormal environmental conditions characterize prisons and may contribute to the incidence of overt aggressive behavior among inmates; they may also partially explain the relationship between contacts with the criminal justice system (e.g., amount of time incarcerated) and recidivism rates. Also, the prevalence of abnormal conditions has increased with the ever-increasing breakdown of the family structure, community disorganization, disparity between public policy and biological needs, crowding, learned helplessness, and other frequently cited characteristics of U.S. urbanization (Archer and Gartner, 1984:98–117; Larson, 1984:116–141).

A recent article presenting an evolutionary perspective on antisocial behavior (Mealey, forthcoming) suggests that "sociopathy" in particular is an expression of a life history strategy which is selected for naturally in response to certain environmental circumstances. In other words, "sociopaths are designed for the successful execution of social deception and ... are the product of evolutionary pressures which, through a complex interaction of environmental and genetic factors, lead some individuals to pursue a life history strategy of manipulative and predatory social interactions." Because antisocial behavior, including sociopathic behavior which may be selected for in an evolutionary context, is most likely to be expressed under conducive environmental circumstances, manipulations of these circumstances can help to curb its expression. Investigation of how these deleterious conditions exacerbate antisocial behavioral mechanisms may eventually lead to socioenvironmental programs to enhance, rather than detract from, adaptive capabilities.

Genetic Contributions

As a rule, what is inherited is not a behavior; rather, it is the way in which an individual responds to the environment—it provides an orientation, predisposition, or tendency to behave in a certain fashion. Also, genetic influences on human behavior are polygenic—no single gene effect can be identified for most behaviors. The bulk of genetic research on various aspects of antisocial behavior indicates that traits predisposing to antisociality which may be inherited are behavioral, temperamental, and personality dispositions, and include irritability, proneness to anger, high activity levels, low arousal levels, dominance, mania, impulsivity, sensation-seeking, hyperemotionality, extraversion, depressed mood, and negative affect (Biederman et al., 1986; Cadoret et al., 1985; DeFries and Plomin, 1978; Ghodsian-Carpey and Baker, 1987; Plomin et al., 1990; Rowe et al., 1987; Rushton et al., 1986). In the presence of a negative mood state, antisocial behavior more likely results under conditions of stress and when social learning supports such responses. Intellectual deficits (Bouchard and McGue, 1981; Cattell, 1982), having a large degree of heritability, have also been shown to increase the risk for antisocial behavior. Individuals with several of these traits report an increased familial incidence of similar behavioral problems and show differences, along with their family members, in certain biochemical, neuropsychological, and physiological parameters (Biederman et al., 1986; Cadoret et al., 1975; DeFries and Plomin, 1978; Hare and Schalling, 1978; Plomin et al., 1990; Rushton et al., 1986; Tarter et al., 1985; Zuckerman, 1983).

Numerous studies have attempted to estimate genetic contributions to the development of criminality, delinquency, aggression, and antisocial behavior, using one of four methods: family, twin, adoption, and molecular genetics studies. Because it is difficult to isolate genetic factors from developmental events, cultural influences, early experiences, and housing conditions, findings of genetic studies on criminal behavior are not always straightforward, depending on the design and measures used (Mednick et al., 1987; Plomin et al., 1990; Rowe and Osgood, 1984; Walters and White, 1989; Wilson and Herrnstein, 1985). Genetic research designs and selected studies are briefly described and evaluated below.

Family Studies

The family study seeks to identify genetic influences on behavioral traits by evaluating similarities among family members. Cross-generational linkages have been reported for personality and behavioral attributes related to criminal behavior, including temper outbursts (Mattes and Fink, 1987), sociopathy (Cloninger et al., 1975, 1978; Guze et al., 1967), delinquency (Robins et al., 1975; Rowe, 1986), hyperactivity and attention deficit disorder (Cantwell, 1979), conduct disorder, aggression, violence, and psychopathy (Bachy-Rita et al., 1971; Stewart et al., 1980; Stewart and DeBlois, 1983; Stewart and Leone, 1978; Twito and Stewart, 1982).

Despite conclusions from these studies that genetic effects are largely responsible for criminal behavior, this method does not directly assess genetic contributions. Environmental influences on measures of behavior may be common to parents and offspring, and thus, large environmental correlations among relatives cannot be accounted for. Diet, environmental toxins, neighborhood conditions, and television-viewing habits are only a few examples of environmental factors that similarly influence family members. We may conclude only that the incidence of criminal and related behaviors appears to have a familial basis.

Twin Studies

The classic twin design involves the testing of identical (monozygotic or MZ) and fraternal (dizygotic or DZ) twins. MZ twins share genetic material from the biologic parents and are, thus, considered genetically identical. DZ twins are approximately 50 percent genetically alike, as are regular siblings. The extent to which MZ twins share a characteristic as compared to DZ twins provides evidence for a genetic influence on the variable. To the extent that there is still some degree of DZ resemblance after genetic influences have been accounted for, there is evidence for the influence of common family environment on the trait. For example, if a sample of MZ twins is 60 percent similar for IQ and a matched sample of DZ twins is 25 percent similar for IQ, we can conclude that IQ is largely a function of heredity.

Overall, twin studies provide strong evidence for a genetics–environment interaction, showing that MZ twins were more alike in their antisocial activity than DZ twins (see reviews by Christiansen, 1977, and Raine, 1993). Significant genetic effects have been found for both self-report and official rates of delinquent or criminal behavior (Rowe, 1983; Rowe and Osgood, 1984) and for personality or temperamental traits related to criminal behavior, for example, aggression (Coccaro et al., 1993; Ghodsian-Carpey and Baker, 1987; Rowe, 1986; Rushton et al., 1986; Tellegen et al., 1988), although discrepant studies exist (Owen and Sines, 1970; Plomin et al., 1981). Plomin et al. (1988) examined numerous twin studies of criminal/delinquent behavior and aggression and noted that the results were highly inconsistent, possibly because no uniform measure of self-reported aggression and its constructs has been applied.

Twin studies commonly suffer from a number of unique methodological weaknesses (see Plomin et al., 1980). First, sampling techniques may favor the selection of MZ pairs that are similar in relevant behavioral traits, which may bias results. Second, MZ twins tend to share more similar environments than do DZ twins because of their similar appearance. Because environmental assessments are not commonly conducted, such similarities cannot be estimated to determine their relative influence. In favor of the validity of the twin method, however, is evidence that physical and environmental similarities among MZ twins do not bias studies of personality in general (see DeFries and Plomin, 1978: 480; Plomin and Daniels, 1986). Third, only recently have researchers employed biochemical tests to verify the zygosity of the twins; prior studies may have underestimated genetic influence. Fourth, measurement errors may further increase underestimations. On the other hand, the twin method can only examine the level of genetic contribution over and above environmental influence. Thus, there may be contamination from an unknown amount of environmental contribution. Nevertheless, twin studies in general provide fairly consistent findings providing intriguing evidence for a genetic effect.

Adoption Studies

This method examines individuals who were raised from infancy by nonrelated adoptive parents rather than biological relatives. To the extent that subjects resemble biological relatives and not nonbiologic relatives, heredity is thought to play a contributory role. The adoption study method provides richer information about the relative contribution of heredity to behavioral traits and for genetics–environment interactions. Nevertheless, the method also has some weaknesses (see Mednick et al., 1984; Plomin et al., 1990; Walters and White, 1989).

Fourteen adoption studies indicate noteworthy genetic effects on criminal or delinquent behavior and related psychopathology, i.e., psychopathy (see Raine, 1993). For the most part, these studies suggest that biological relatives of criminal or antisocial probands have a greater history of criminal convictions or antisocial behavior than the biological relatives of noncriminal control adoptees. In general, family environment, including such indices as social class, rearing styles, and parental attitudes, played a smaller role than did purported genetic effects. Three of these studies indicate that property offending is more heritable than violent crime (Bohman et al., 1982; Mednick et al., 1984; Sigvardsson et al., 1982). This is likely due to the failure of researchers to examine repetitively violent offenders; frequently offenders categorized as violent do not show a chronic pattern of aggressiveness and their crimes may be more situational.

Genetic influences on criminality may differ for those who are also alcoholic (Bohman et al., 1982). Specifically, when the biological parents are both criminal and alcoholic, crimes of adoptees tend to be more violent. Cadoret et al. (1995) further demonstrated a strong effect of a biologic parent with both alcohol problems and antisocial personality on the eventual substance abuse and antisocial behavior in the adopted-away offspring. Antisocial personality in individuals with biologic antisocial parents is first manifested in childhood and adolescence as a conduct disorder, followed by the early onset of substance use. The factor most predictive of drug abuse was aggressivity and was correlated with biological parent antisocial personality.

Adoption studies highlight the importance of gene–environment interaction models (Rowe and Osgood, 1984). Having a criminal adoptive parent most profoundly affects those with a genetic propensity for criminality (Mednick et al., 1984). In other words, those who inherited certain antisocial personality and temperamental traits are more likely to manifest criminal behaviors in the presence of deleterious environmental conditions, e.g., criminal parents.

Molecular Genetic Studies

While family, twin, and adoption studies have predominated efforts to assess genetic contributions to antisocial behavior, they do not directly identify the actual biological features transmitted. Molecular genetic techniques are increasing our understanding of causal links between genetics, brain function, temperament, and the behavioral outcome. Investigators have isolated DNA from blood to identify specific genetic features that may be involved (Comings et al., 1994; Noble et al., 1993). Genetic defects in two neurotransmitters, dopamine and serotonin, have been identified in certain drug abusers and appear to play a role in forms of excessive and compulsive behaviors, including aggressivity, conduct disorder, obsessive–compulsive disorder, and post-traumatic stress disorder, all of which are associated with violence. The sensitivity of brain regions to both abusable drugs and aggressive behavior is a function of these neurotransmitters. Thus, the use of drugs and/or aggressivity may provide relief from or stimulation to systems that are chronically imbalanced. Theoretically, vulnerable individuals may attain a "neurological high" from both drug use and antisocial or violent behavior (Gove and Wilmoth, 1990).

As previously mentioned, genetic studies of criminal behavior have been criticized (Mednick et al., 1987; Plomin et al., 1990; Rowe and Osgood, 1984; Walters and White, 1989; Wilson and Herrnstein, 1985). This research, like other studies in criminology, suffers from a high level of abstraction because "criminal behavior" is a legalistic label, not descriptive of actual behavior. Criminal behavior, as a single phenomenon, is far too variable and subject to individual and cultural judgments to be defined for reliable and valid investigation. Instead, research should be predicated on disaggregated behaviors that are reflective of actual acts that can be consistently and accurately measured. Accordingly, genetic studies that focus on criminal behavior per se may be inherently flawed; as criminal behavior is heterogeneous, genetic effects may be more directly associated with particular traits that place individuals at risk for criminal labeling. Mednick et al. (1984) took a first step toward this goal by differentiating violent from property offenders. Nevertheless, categories are still based on criminal offenses rather than behavioral constructs such as impulsive-aggression, depression, alcoholism, and psychopathy to which specific identifying criteria can be applied (Plomin et al., 1990). Also critical particularly in genetic research is the need to examine subjects who exhibit a history of repetitive violent behavior relative to those who do not. Most current studies include subjects who committed only one or two violent offenses, without a history of violence. It is likely that those who become excessively aggressive may do so only as a result of present circumstances rather than an inherent predisposition.

Biological Contributions

Genetic foundations for behavior are manifested in the resulting, visible expression of a genetic trait, called a phenotype. Although we can rarely trace a behavioral disorder to a specific gene, we can measure the manifestation of a genetic blueprint in nervous system features. Other biological traits associated with behavioral problems are not directly genetic in origin; they may be due to genetic mutations, biochemical exposures, or a deleterious social environment. All of these conditions, from the genetic to the environmental, exert their influence on the nervous system and, thus, can be directly measured and manipulated. The following correlates of behavioral disorders illustrate selected ways in which genetic and environmental factors impact on the nervous system to alter behavior.

Biochemical Correlates

A number of biochemical differences have been found between controls and individuals with psychopathy, antisocial personality, violent behavior, conduct disorder, and other behaviors associated with criminal behavior. These groups have been discriminated on the basis of levels of certain hormones, neurotransmitters, peptides, toxins, and metabolic processes (Brown et al., 1979; Comings et al., 1994; Davis et al., 1983; Eichelman and Thoa, 1972; Fishbein et al., 1989a; Mednick et al., 1987; Rogeness et al., 1987; Roy et al., 1986; Valzelli, 1981; Virkkunen and Narvanen, 1987).

Current investigations of biochemical mechanisms of aggressiveness focus on the same neurotransmitter systems examined in molecular genetics studies. Animal and human studies, for example, consistently indicate that serotonin globally inhibits behavioral responses to emotional stimuli and modulates aggression (Muhlbauer, 1985; Soubrie, 1986; van Praag et al., 1987). Several indicators of lower levels of serotonin activity in individuals characterized as violent or impulsive, in comparison with those who are not, have been reported (Brown et al., 1979; Coccaro, 1989; Coccaro and Astill, 1990; Fishbein et al., 1989a; Linnoila et al., 1983; Virkkunen et al., 1987, 1989). These studies indicate that serotonin functioning is altered in some types of human aggressiveness and violent suicidal behavior. Thus, a decrease in serotonin activity produces disinhibition in both brain mechanisms and behavior, resulting in increased aggressiveness and impulsivity.

Examination of neurotransmitters that interact with serotonin is necessary to provide a more complete understanding of the neural mechanisms involved. Dopamine (DA) and norepinephrine (NE) are excitatory transmitters that counterbalance the inhibiting influence of serotonin. In a sense, DA and NE operate as the "fuel" while serotonin provides the "brakes" for behavioral responses. An imbalance between the activity of these chemicals may lead to a psychiatric disorder, mood disturbance, or behavioral dysfunction. For example, low levels of norepinephrine are associated with clinical depression; many antidepressants work by raising norepinephrine activity. High levels of DA, on the other hand, are associated with certain mood disorders and behavioral agitation. The location of the imbalance within the brain determines the behavioral outcome. Alcohol can substantially contribute to antisocial behaviors by its influence on these systems; alcohol lowers serotonin activity while raising dopamine, a virtual "double-whammy."

Biological factors contributing to individual differences in temperament, arousal, or vulnerability to stress may be important in the etiology of female criminal behavior (Widom, 1978). Socioenvironmental influences may differentially interact with biological sex differences to produce variations in male and female criminality (see, for example, Ellis and Ames, 1987). For example, in males, high levels of the sex hormone testosterone may increase aggressive behavior (Archer, 1995; Kreuz and Rose, 1971; Olweus et al., 1988; Rada et al., 1983; Schiavi et al., 1984), although discrepant studies exist (Coe and Levine, 1983). Because in utero exposure to various levels of sex hormones plays a role in determining later sensitivity to sex hormone release, unusually high levels of exposure may increase sensitivity in adolescence. For example, exposure to abnormally high levels of testosterone in utero may precipitate a heightened response to the release of testosterone in puberty among males affected. As a result, testosterone levels in puberty may be normal, but the response may be exaggerated. A similar situation may theoretically be true for affected females, particularly those who are constitutionally masculinized, possibly resulting in increased risk for antisocial behavior. Masculine features such as abnormal hair growth, large musculature, low voice, irregular menses, fertility disorders, hyperaggressiveness, and other features reflecting sensitivity to male hormones (androgenization) can only develop as a result of prenatal exposure to sex hormone imbalances, steroid use (a testosterone derivative), or certain medical disorders (see Archer, 1995; Fishbein, 1992).

Premenstrual and postpartum periods have also been associated with elevated levels of aggressivity and irritability in some women. These phases of the cycle are marked by a hormonal upset which may trigger both physical and psychological impairments in a subgroup of women, e.g., sharp changes in mood, depression, irritability, aggression, difficulty in concentration, and substance abuse (Haskett, 1987; Trunnell and Turner, 1988). A significant number of females imprisoned for aggressive criminal acts were found to have committed their crimes during the premenstrual phase, and female offenders were found to be more irritable and aggressive during this period (see Ginsburg and Carter, 1987). Despite methodological shortcomings (see Harry and Balcer, 1987), there remains a general impression that a small percentage of women appear to be vulnerable to cyclical hormonal changes which cause them to be more prone to anxiety and hostility (Carroll and Steiner, 1987; Clare, 1985; Ginsburg and Carter, 1987).

Exposure to toxic trace elements is yet another factor that has been shown to interfere with brain function and behavior. Exposure to lead, for example, has a deleterious effect on brain function by damaging organ systems, impairing intellectual development, and subsequently interfering with the regulation of behavior. Sources of lead include our diet and environment, and contamination among children may be grossly underestimated (Bryce-Smith and Waldron, 1974; Moore and Fleischman, 1975). Resulting impairments may be manifested as learning disabilities and cognitive deficits (hyperactivity and attention deficit disorder), particularly in measures of school achievement, verbal and performance IQ, and mental dullness (see Benignus et al., 1981; Lester and Fishbein, 1987; Needleman et al., 1979; Pihl and Parkes, 1977), all of which are risk factors for delinquency (Denno, 1988). Research has also demonstrated that lead intoxication is significantly associated with violence (Pihl et al., 1982). Accumulating evidence strongly suggests that lead exposure substantially increases the risk for antisocial behavior (see Rimland and Larson, 1983).

Psychophysiological Correlates

Psychophysiological variables are quantifiable indices of nervous system function, e.g., heart rate, blood pressure, attention and arousal levels, skin conductance, and brain waves. These measurable responses directly reflect emotional state. Studies have repeatedly found psychophysiological evidence for mental abnormality and central nervous system disturbances as putative markers for antisocial behavior. Psychopaths, who are relatively unemotional, impulsive, immature, thrill-seeking, and "unconditionable" (Cleckley, 1964; Moffitt, 1983; Quay, 1965; Zuckerman, 1983), have been characterized as having low levels of perceptible anxiety and physiological responses during stressful events (Hare and Schalling, 1978; House and Milligan, 1976; Syndulko et al., 1975; Venables, 1987; Yeudall et al., 1985). Psychopaths differ from nonpsychopathic controls in several physiological parameters, including: (a) electroencephalogram (EEG) differences, (b) cognitive and neuropsychological impairment, and (c) electrodermal, cardiovascular, and other nervous system measures (see Raine, 1993). In particular, psychopathic individuals tend to show relatively more slow wave activity in their EEG compared with controls, which may be related to differences in cognitive abilities (Fishbein et al., 1989b; Hare, 1970; Howard, 1984; Pincus and Tucker, 1974; Syndulko, 1978). Relatively high levels of EEG slowing found in psychopathic subjects may reflect a maturational lag in brain function (Kiloh et al., 1972; Pontius and Ruttiger, 1976). Thus, individuals with EEG slowing who also demonstrate immature behavior and an inability to learn from experience may be developmentally delayed.

EEG slowing among some psychopaths is consistent with findings of hypoaroused autonomic nervous system function (ANS: a portion of the nervous system that regulates emotional state via certain bodily functions, e.g., heart rate, blood pressure, hormone release, and skin conductance) and other differences in psychophysiologic parameters mentioned above. When the ANS is underactive, the need for external stimulation is higher and more difficult to satisfy due to a lower level of internal stimulation. Consequently, psychopaths with low ANS activity tend to be more sensation-seeking (Blackburn, 1978; Quay, 1965; Wilson and Herrnstein, 1985) and more prone to risky, dangerous, and perhaps criminal activity. This condition appears to exist in many children with hyperactivity, who require Ritalin, an amphetamine, to provide the internal stimulation required to physically relax in order to concentrate and respond to the environment appropriately. Thus, it is not surprising that significantly more psychopaths than nonpsychopaths were hyperactive as children (see Wilson and Herrnstein, 1985).

On the other hand, when the ANS is stimulated, subjective feelings of anxiety result. Individuals experience anxiety when the threat of a negative repercussion exists due to the learned association between the behavior and its likely consequence. Thus, the brain initiates a release of hormones that stimulates feelings of stress whenever we contemplate a behavior that we have been conditioned to avoid. Individuals with a properly functioning nervous system become conditioned to avoid stressful situations given the learned contingencies discussed above. Most of us, for example, would experience psychological and physical discomfort at the thought of picking a pocket or burglarizing a convenience store. Thus, we make a rational choice based on a calculation of costs and benefits and deterrence is most likely achieved.

The learning and conditioning of behavior occur differentially among individuals with different neurological statuses. Theoretically, psychopaths do not sufficiently experience the discomfort of anxiety associated with a proscribed behavior due to an underactive ANS, and thus are not easily conditioned or deterred (Hare and Schalling, 1978). They make a rational choice based on the calculation that the benefits of the act (e.g., monetary gain) outweigh the costs (e.g., anxiety of detection). Accordingly, psychopaths encountered by the criminal justice system tend to be resistant to most deterrence programs.

Psychopharmacological Inducements

Psychopharmacology is the study of drug effects on the brain and their psychological and behavioral consequences. Certain psychoactive drugs are reported to increase aggressive responses (see Fishbein and Pease, in press), for example, amphetamines, cocaine, alcohol, and phencyclidine (PCP). The actual expression of aggressive behavior depends on the dose, route of administration, genetic factors, and type of aggression.

Several biological mechanisms have been proposed as explanations for alcohol-induced aggression: (1) pathological intoxication, sometimes involving psychomotor epilepsy or temporal lobe disturbance (Bach-y-Rita et al., 1970; Maletsky, 1976; Marinacci, 1963); (2) hypoglycemic (low blood sugar) reactions (Cohen, 1980; Coid, 1979; Wallgren and Barry, 1970); and (3) alterations in neurotransmitter activity (Weingartner et al., 1983). Because most drinkers do not become aggressive, indications are that alcohol either changes the psychological state or the psychological state has an effect on the behavioral outcome of alcohol consumption. In the second scenario, alcohol would stimulate an existing psychiatric condition or psychological predisposition to aggress or misbehave (Pihl and Ross, 1987). For most individuals, behaviors under the influence of a psychoactive drug are not completely uncharacteristic or bizarre; drugs simply act as a trigger for underlying tendencies to be expressed. Because serotonin plays a modulating role in drinking behavior, individuals with low serotonin are more likely to drink to excess and also to exhibit aggressive behavior under the influence. Administration of drugs that elevate serotonin activity reduce craving for alcohol and its consumption. Hence, alcohol does not appear to "cause" aggression, but rather permits its expression under specific circumstances and biological conditions.

Chronic use of PCP (phencyclidine) has been repeatedly associated with extreme violence to self and others (Aronow et al., 1980; Fauman and Fauman, 1980; Linder et al., 1981; Schuckit and Morrissey, 1978; Seigal, 1978; Smith and Wesson, 1980). Violent reactions appear to be an extension of PCP toxic psychosis, which affects some users (Fauman and Fauman, 1980). Because only a subpopulation of users manifests violent behavior, additional research is needed to determine the nature of the vulnerability that causes certain individuals to be particularly susceptible to that behavioral effect. PCP-related aggression may be due to influences on hormonal and neurotransmitter activity (Domino, 1978, 1980; Marrs-Simon et al., 1988). Also, neuropsychological impairments have been observed that minimally reflect a temporary organic brain syndrome (Cohen, 1977; Smith and Wesson, 1980) sometimes associated with aggressiveness. Studies of PCP users indicate that factors in the user's background, personality, and drug history are also important determinants of the drug-related experience (Fauman and Fauman, 1980; McCardle and Fishbein, 1989). These observations suggest that the consequences of PCP use, independent of the drug's purity and varying strengths, are determined by a number of individual factors, including pharmacological, psychological, and situational ones.

"Vulnerability" studies suggest that certain personality types may be more at risk for drug abuse than others (Brook et al., 1985; Deykin et al., 1986; Kellam et al., 1980; McCardle and Fishbein, 1989). This does not mean, however, that these individuals will inevitably become drug abusers due to an inherited predisposition. There is evidence for the substantial contribution of family support systems in the final determination of whether an individual with a vulnerable personality type will, in fact, abuse drugs (Tarter et al., 1985:346–47). Natural and acquired traits interact dynamically in a given environment and are inseparable in the evaluation of such a complex phenomenon as human behavior.

Closing Remarks

Exactly how biological variables interact with social and psychological forces to produce human behavior generally and antisocial behavior specifically is not well understood. Over the past twenty years, the bulk of "multidisciplinary" studies have examined only a few isolated variables and have generally failed to evaluate dynamic interrelationships among biological and socioenvironmental conditions (Denno, 1988; Wilson and Herrnstein, 1985). Only in recent years has there been a concerted effort to assess relative and interactive relationships, and advances in statistical and methodological techniques have facilitated that development.

While caution against the premature application of biological findings is clearly advised, insights from these behavioral sciences strongly indicate that a number of social programs will reduce biological vulnerabilities to antisocial behavior. Rather than some vague recognition that certain social conditions are deleterious to human functioning, we now have a better understanding of how such conditions influence biological systems to alter risk status. Child abuse, for example, heightens later risk for an antisocial outcome in the victim. Not all victims, however, become victimizers. What differentiates those more vulnerable from those seemingly "protected" from such adversity? While the answer to that question would enable society to identify vulnerable children and provide individualized interventions, even without an answer, global social changes need to be undertaken to protect children's rights. Such a tack is necessary, not just for humanitarian reasons, but also to protect society from the victimizers we are creating. Also illustrative is the consistent finding that adverse and stressful environmental conditions lower serotonin levels, increasing impulsivity and impairing coping skills. Perhaps this observation partially explains the level of violence and drug abuse presently occurring in our inner cities in general, but it more directly speaks to the issue of why only a subgroup manifests these behaviors. Specifically, individuals with lower initial levels of serotonin activity may be more vulnerable to adversity than others who do not become antisocial under the same social circumstances. These findings support sociologists' century-old appeal to initiate and properly fund programs that provide social insulation from both the psychological and biological results of environmental stress.

Evidence to suggest that biological conditions have a profound impact on the adaptive, cognitive, and emotional state of the individual is compelling. Investigation of the discriminants for behavioral dysfunctions indicates that the impact of these factors is substantial. When a biological disadvantage is present due to genetic influences or when a physical trauma occurs during developmental stages of childhood, the resultant deficit may be compounded over time and drastically interfere with behavioral functions throughout life. Such conditions appear to place an individual at high risk for persistent problematic behavior. Disturbances associated with poor environmental and social conditions coupled with impaired brain function may eventually be amenable to intervention. As it stands, the tendency in society is to ignore the developmental and emotional needs of children at risk until they are old enough to incarcerate. The unfortunate reality for those who come into contact with the courts by virtue of their dysfunction, however, is that the underlying causes of their disorder are inaccurately evaluated or simply left unattended. The capability to identify and predict the factors responsible for antisocial behavior may eventually enable society to employ innovative methods of early detection, prevention, remediation, and evaluation.

Criminal justice policies must be based on well-founded theories and findings that survive scientific scrutiny. The application to criminal justice programs of scientific findings that are well recognized and accepted by the discipline has more value than trial and error approaches in preventing or minimizing antisocial behavior. Although biological techniques in the assessment of human behavior are still under the microscope and definitive answers have yet to surface, the foregoing description of biological foundations for behavior provides evidence of their applicability and value. By undertaking a collaborative strategy, we can implement more effective prevention and therapeutic programs and develop a legal system that reflects public consensus, meets human needs, and maintains an ethical and organized social structure.

Discussion Questions

1. What questions about crime might biological criminologists answer that sociological ones cannot? How can biological and sociological perspectives on crime be better integrated?

2. Genetic influences on antisocial behavior have been explored through the study of families, twins, adoptees, and molecular genetics. How does each of these four research methods try to determine the influence of genetic factors on antisocial behavior and try to separate that influence from the influence of social environmental factors? What are the advantages and disadvantages of each of the four methods?

3. What are some of the biochemical correlates of antisocial behavior? What roles do serotonin, dopamine, and norepinephrine play in antisocial behavior? How might biochemical factors explain male–female differences in criminal activity? What role do toxic trace elements play in antisocial behavior?

$$C \ h \ a \ p \ t \ e \ r \quad 4$$

Criminality and Low Self-Control

Michael R. Gottfredson and Travis Hirschi

In their influential book *A General Theory of Crime,* Gottfredson and Hirschi (1990:15) define crime as "acts of force or fraud undertaken in pursuit of self-interest." They explain such acts as the outcome of the individual characteristic of low self-control in combination with situational conditions conducive to such behavior. This selection first looks at several elements of self-control and the way that these traits can be inferred from the nature of crime itself. The authors cite research that indicates that people with low self-control are especially likely to engage in a wide variety of criminal acts. They conclude by looking at the way that socialization and discipline within the family can lead to the development of low self-control in children.

We are now in position to describe the nature of self-control, the individual characteristic relevant to the commission of criminal acts. We assume that the nature of this characteristic can be derived directly from the nature of criminal acts. We thus infer from the nature of crime what people who refrain from criminal acts are like before they reach the age at which crime becomes a logical possibility. We then work back further to the factors producing their restraint, back to the causes of self-control. In our view, lack of self-control does not require crime and can be counteracted by situational conditions or other properties of the

Source: Excerpted from "The Nature of Criminality: Low Self-Control," pp. 88–94, 97–105 in *A General Theory of Crime*, by Michael R. Gottfredson and Travis Hirschi, with the permission of the publishers, Stanford University Press. © 1990 by the Board of Trustees of the Leland Stanford Junior University.

individual. At the same time, we suggest that high self-control effectively reduces the possibility of crime—that is, those possessing it will be substantially less likely at all periods of life to engage in criminal acts.

The Elements of Self-Control

Criminal acts provide *immediate* gratification of desires. A major characteristic of people with low self-control is therefore a tendency to respond to tangible stimuli in the immediate environment, to have a concrete "here and now" orientation. People with high self-control, in contrast, tend to defer gratification.

Criminal acts provide *easy or simple* gratification of desires. They provide money without work, sex without courtship, revenge without court delays. People lacking self-control also tend to lack diligence, tenacity, or persistence in a course of action.

Criminal acts are *exciting, risky, or thrilling.* They involve stealth, danger, speed, agility, deception, or power. People lacking self-control therefore tend to be adventuresome, active, and physical. Those with high levels of self-control tend to be cautious, cognitive, and verbal.

Crimes provide *few or meager long-term benefits.* They are not equivalent to a job or a career. On the contrary, crimes interfere with long-term commitments to jobs, marriages, family, or friends. People with low self-control thus tend to have unstable marriages, friendships, and job profiles. They tend to be little interested in and unprepared for long-term occupational pursuits.

Crimes require *little skill or planning.* The cognitive requirements for most crimes are minimal. It follows that people lacking self-control need not possess or value cognitive or academic skills. The manual skills required for most crimes are minimal. It follows that people lacking self-control need not possess manual skills that require training or apprenticeship.

Crimes often result in *pain or discomfort for the victim.* Property is lost, bodies are injured, privacy is violated, trust is broken. It follows that people with low self-control tend to be self-centered, indifferent, or insensitive to the suffering and needs of others. It does not follow, however, that people with low self-control are routinely unkind or antisocial. On the contrary, they may discover the immediate and easy rewards of charm and generosity.

Recall that crime involves the pursuit of immediate pleasure. It follows that people lacking self-control will also tend to pursue immediate pleasures that are *not* criminal: they will tend to smoke, drink, use drugs, gamble, have children out of wedlock, and engage in illicit sex.

Crimes require the interaction of an offender with people or their property. It does not follow that people lacking self-control will tend to be gregarious or social. However, it does follow that, other things being equal, gregarious or social people are more likely to be involved in criminal acts.

The major benefit of many crimes is not pleasure but relief from momentary irritation. The irritation caused by a crying child is often the stimulus for physical abuse. That caused by a taunting stranger in a bar is often the stimulus for aggravated assault. It follows that people with low self-control tend to have minimal tolerance for frustration and little ability to respond to conflict through verbal rather than physical means.

Crimes involve the risk of violence and physical injury, of pain and suffering on the part of the offender. It does not follow that people with low self-control will tend to be tolerant of physical pain or to be indifferent to physical discomfort. It does follow that people tolerant of physical pain or indifferent to physical discomfort will be more likely to engage in criminal acts whatever their level of self-control.

The risk of criminal penalty for any given criminal act is small, but this depends in part on the circumstances of the offense. Thus, for example, not all joyrides by teenagers are equally likely to result in arrest. A car stolen from a neighbor and returned unharmed before he notices its absence is less likely to result in official notice than is a car stolen from a shopping center parking lot and abandoned at the convenience of the offender. Drinking alcohol stolen from parents and consumed in the family garage is less likely to receive official notice than drinking in the parking lot outside a concert hall. It follows that offenses differ in their validity as measures of self-control: those offenses with large risk of public awareness are better measures than those with little risk.

In sum, people who lack self-control will tend to be impulsive, insensitive, physical (as opposed to mental), risk-taking, short-sighted, and nonverbal, and they will tend therefore to engage in criminal and analogous acts. Since these traits can be identified prior to the age of responsibility for crime, since there is considerable tendency for these traits to come together in the same people, and since the traits tend to persist through life, it seems reasonable to consider them as comprising a stable construct useful in the explanation of crime.

The Many Manifestations of Low Self-Control

Our image of the "offender" suggests that crime is not an automatic or necessary consequence of low self-control. It suggests that many noncriminal acts analogous to crime (such as accidents, smoking, and alcohol use) are also manifestations of low self-control. Our image therefore implies that no specific act, type of crime, or form of deviance is uniquely required by the absence of self-control.

Because both crime and analogous behaviors stem from low self-control (that is, both are manifestations of low self-control), they will all be engaged in at a relatively high rate by people with low self-control. Within the domain of crime, then, there will be much versatility among offenders in the criminal acts in which they engage.

Research on the versatility of deviant acts supports these predictions in the strongest possible way. The variety of manifestations of low self-control is immense. In spite of years of tireless research motivated by a belief in specialization, no credible evidence of specialization has been reported. In fact, the evidence of offender versatility is overwhelming (Hirschi, 1969; Hindelang, 1971; Wolfgang, Figlio, and Sellin, 1972; Petersilia, 1980; Hindelang, Hirschi, and Weis, 1981; Rojek and Erickson, 1982; Klein, 1984).

By versatility we mean that offenders commit a wide variety of criminal acts, with no strong inclination to pursue a specific criminal act or a pattern of criminal acts to the exclusion of others. Most theories suggest that offenders tend to specialize, whereby such terms as robber, burglar, drug dealer, rapist, and murderer have predictive or descriptive import. In fact, some theories create offender specialization as part of their explanation of crime. For example, Cloward and Ohlin (1960) create distinctive subcultures of delinquency around particular forms of criminal behavior, identifying subcultures specializing in theft, violence, or drugs. In a related way, books are written about white-collar crime as though it were a clearly distinct specialty requiring a unique explanation. Research projects are undertaken for the study of drug use, or vandalism, or teen pregnancy (as though every study of delinquency were not a study of drug use and vandalism and teenage sexual behavior). Entire schools of criminology emerge to pursue patterning, sequencing, progression, escalation, onset, persistence, and desistance in the career of offenses or offenders. These efforts survive largely because their proponents fail to consider or acknowledge the clear evidence to the contrary. Other reasons for survival of such ideas may be found in the interest of politicians and members of the law enforcement community who see policy potential in criminal careers or "career criminals" (see, e.g., Blumstein et al., 1986).

Occasional reports of specialization seem to contradict this point, as do everyday observations of repetitive misbehavior by particular offenders. Some offenders rob the same store repeatedly over a period of years, or an offender commits several rapes over a (brief) period of time. Such offenders may be called "robbers" or "rapists." However, it should be noted that such labels are retrospective rather than predictive and that they typically ignore a large amount of delinquent or criminal behavior by the same offenders that is inconsistent with their alleged specialty. Thus, for example, the "rapist" will tend also to use drugs, to commit robberies and burglaries (often in concert with the rape), and to have a record for violent offenses other than rape. There is a perhaps natural tendency on the part of observers (and in official accounts) to focus on the most serious crimes in a series of events, but this tendency should not be confused with a tendency on the part of the offender to specialize in one kind of crime.

Recall that one of the defining features of crime is that it is simple and easy. Some apparent specialization will therefore occur because obvious opportunities for an easy score will tend to repeat themselves. An offender who lives next to a shopping area that is approached by pedestrians will have repeat opportunities for purse snatching, and this may show in his arrest record. But even here the specific "criminal career" will tend to quickly run its course and to be followed by offenses whose content and character is likewise determined by convenience and opportunity (which is the reason why some form of theft is always the best bet about what a person is likely to do next).

The evidence that offenders are likely to engage in noncriminal acts psychologically or theoretically equivalent to crime is, because of the relatively high rates of these "noncriminal" acts, even easier to document. Thieves tend to smoke, drink, and skip school at considerably higher rates than nonthieves. Offenders are considerably more likely than nonoffenders to be involved in most types of accidents, including household fires, auto crashes, and unwanted pregnancies. They are also considerably more likely to die at an early age (see, e.g., Robins, 1966; Eysenck, 1977; Gottfredson, 1984).

Good research on drug use and abuse routinely reveals that the correlates of delinquency and drug use are the same. As Akers (1984) has noted, "compared to the abstaining teenager, the drinking, smoking, and drug-taking teen is much more likely to be getting into fights, stealing, hurting other people, and committing other delinquencies." Akers goes on to say, "but the variation in the order in which they take up these things leaves little basis for proposing the causation of one by the other." In our view, the relation between drug use and delinquency is not a causal question. The correlates are the same because drug use and delinquency are both manifestations of an underlying tendency to pursue short-term, immediate pleasure. This underlying tendency (i.e., lack of self-control) has many manifestations, as listed by Harrison Gough (1948):

> unconcern over the rights and privileges of others when recognizing them would interfere with personal satisfaction in any way; impulsive behavior, or apparent incongruity between the strength of the stimulus and the magnitude of the behavioral response; inability to form deep or persistent attachments to other persons or to identify in interpersonal relationships; poor judgment and planning in attaining defined goals; apparent lack of anxiety and distress over social maladjustment and unwillingness or inability to consider maladjustment qua maladjustment; a tendency to project blame onto others and to take no responsibility for failures; meaningless prevarication, often about trivial matters in situations where detection is inevitable; almost complete lack of dependability . . . and willingness to assume responsibility; and, finally, emotional poverty. [p. 362]

This combination of characteristics has been revealed in the life histories of the subjects in the famous studies by Lee Robins. Robins is one of the few researchers to focus on the varieties of deviance and the way they tend to go together in the lives of those she designates as having "antisocial personalities." In her words: "We refer to someone who fails to maintain close personal relationships with anyone else, [who] performs poorly on the job, who is involved in illegal behaviors (whether or not apprehended), who fails to support himself and his dependents without outside aid, and who is given to sudden changes of plan and loss of temper in response to what appear to others as minor frustrations" (1978:255).

For 30 years Robins traced 524 children referred to a guidance clinic in St. Louis, Missouri, and she compared them to a control group matched on IQ, age, sex, and area of the city. She discovered that, in comparison to the control group, those people referred at an early age were more likely to be arrested as adults (for a wide variety of offenses), were less likely to get married, were more likely to be divorced, were more likely to marry a spouse with a behavior problem, were less likely to have children (but if they had children were likely to have more children), were more likely to have children with behavior problems, were more likely to be unemployed, had considerably more frequent job changes, were more likely to be on welfare, had fewer contacts with relatives, had fewer friends, were substantially less likely to attend church, were less likely to serve in the armed forces and more likely to be dishonorably discharged if they did serve, were more likely to exhibit physical evidence of excessive alcohol use, and were more likely to be hospitalized for psychiatric problems (1966:42–73).

Note that these outcomes are consistent with four general elements of our notion of low self-control: basic stability of individual differences over a long period of time; great variability in the kinds of criminal acts engaged in; conceptual or causal equivalence of criminal and noncriminal acts; and inability to predict the specific forms of deviance engaged in, whether criminal or noncriminal. In our view, the idea of an antisocial personality defined by certain behavioral consequences is too positivistic or deterministic, suggesting that the offender must do certain things given his antisocial personality. Thus we would say only that the subjects in question are *more likely* to commit criminal acts (as the data indicate they are). We do not make commission of criminal acts part of the definition of the individual with low self-control.

Be this as it may, Robins's retrospective research shows that predictions derived from a concept of antisocial personality are highly consistent with the results of prospective longitudinal and cross-sectional research: offenders do not specialize; they tend to be involved in accidents, illness, and death at higher rates than the general population; they tend to have difficulty persisting in a job regardless of the particular characteristics of the job (no job will turn out to be a good job); they have difficulty acquiring and retaining friends; and they have difficulty meeting the demands of long-term financial commitments (such as mortgages or car payments) and the demands of parenting.

Seen in this light, the "costs" of low self-control for the individual may far exceed the costs of his criminal acts. In fact, it appears that crime is often among the least serious consequences of a lack of self-control in terms of the quality of life of those lacking it. . . .

Child-Rearing and Self-Control: The Family

The major "cause" of low self-control appears to be ineffective child-rearing. Put in positive terms, several conditions appear necessary to produce a socialized child. Perhaps the place to begin looking for these conditions is the research literature on the relation between family conditions and delinquency. This research (e.g., Glueck and Glueck, 1950; McCord and McCord, 1959) has examined the connection between many family factors and delinquency. It reports that discipline, supervision, and affection tend to be missing in the homes of delinquents, that the behavior of the parents is often "poor" (e.g., excessive drinking and poor supervision [Glueck and Glueck, 1950:110–11]); and that the parents of delinquents are unusually likely to have criminal records themselves. Indeed, according to Michael Rutter and Henri Giller, "of the parental characteristics associated with delinquency, criminality is the most striking and most consistent" (1984:182).

Such information undermines the many explanations of crime that ignore the family, but in this form it does not represent much of an advance over the belief of the general public (and those who deal with offenders in the criminal justice system) that "defective upbringing" or "neglect" in the home is the primary cause of crime.

To put these standard research findings in perspective, we think it necessary to define the conditions necessary for adequate child-rearing to occur. The minimum conditions seem to be these: in order to teach the child self-control, someone must (1) monitor the child's behavior; (2) recognize deviant behavior when it occurs; and (3) punish such behavior. This seems simple and obvious enough. All that is required to activate the system is affection for *or* investment in the child. The person who cares for the child will watch his behavior, see him doing things he should not do, and correct him. The result may be a child more capable of delaying gratification, more sensitive to the interests and desires of others, more independent, more willing to accept restraints on his activity, and more unlikely to use force or violence to attain his ends.

When we seek the causes of low self-control, we ask where this system can go wrong. Obviously, parents do not prefer their children to be unsocialized in the terms described. We can therefore rule out in advance the possibility of positive socialization to unsocialized behavior (as cultural or subcultural deviance theories suggest). Still, the system can go wrong at any one of four places. First, the parents may not care for the child (in which case none of the other conditions would be met); second, the parents, even if they care, may not have the time or energy to monitor the child's behavior; third, the parents, even if they care *and* monitor, may not see anything wrong with the child's behavior; finally, even if everything else is in place, the parents may not have the inclination or the means to punish the child. So, what may appear at first glance to be nonproblematic turns out to be problematic indeed. Many things can go wrong. According to much research in crime and delinquency, in the homes of problem children many things have gone wrong: "Parents of stealers do not track ([they] do not interpret stealing . . . as 'deviant'); they do not punish; and they do not care" (Patterson, 1980:88–89; see also Glueck and Glueck, 1950; McCord and McCord, 1959; West and Farrington, 1977).

Let us apply this scheme to some of the facts about the connection between child socialization and crime, beginning with the elements of the child-rearing model.

The Attachment of the Parent to the Child

Our model states that parental concern for the welfare or behavior of the child is a necessary condition for successful child-rearing. Because it is too often assumed that all parents are alike in their love for their children, the evidence directly on this point is not as good or extensive as it could be. However, what exists is clearly consistent with the model. Glueck and Glueck (1950:125–28) report that, compared to the fathers of delinquents, fathers of nondelinquents were twice as likely to be warmly disposed toward their sons and one-fifth as likely to be hostile toward them. In the same sample, 28 percent of the mothers of delinquents were characterized as "indifferent or hostile" toward the child as compared to 4 percent of the mothers of nondelinquents. The evidence suggests that stepparents are especially unlikely to have feelings of affection toward their stepchildren (Burgess, 1980), adding in contemporary society to the likelihood that children will be "reared" by people who do not especially care for them.

Parental Supervision

The connection between social control and self-control could not be more direct than in the case of parental supervision of the child. Such supervision presumably prevents criminal or analogous acts and at the same time trains the child to avoid them on his own. Consistent with this assumption, supervision tends to be a major predictor of delinquency, however supervision or delinquency is measured (Glueck and Glueck, 1950; Hirschi, 1969; West and Farrington, 1977; Riley and Shaw, 1985).

Our general theory in principle provides a method of separating supervision as external control from supervision as internal control. For one thing, offenses differ in the degree to which they can be prevented through monitoring; children at one age are monitored much more closely than children at other ages; girls are supervised more closely than boys. In some situations, monitoring is universal or nearly constant; in other situations monitoring for some offenses is virtually absent. In the present context, however, the concern is with the connection between supervision and self-control, a connection established by the stronger tendency of those poorly supervised when young to commit crimes as adults (McCord, 1979).

Recognition of Deviant Behavior

In order for supervision to have an impact on self-control, the supervisor must perceive deviant behavior when it occurs. Remarkably, not all parents are adept at recognizing lack of self-control. Some parents allow their children to do pretty much as they please without interference. Extensive television-viewing is one modern example, as is the failure to require completion of homework, to prohibit smoking, to curtail the use of physical force, or to see to it that the child actually attends school. (As noted, truancy among second-graders presumably reflects on the adequacy of parental awareness of the child's misbehavior.) Again, the research is not as good as it should be, but evidence of "poor conduct standards" in the homes of delinquents is common.

Punishment of Deviant Acts

Control theories explicitly acknowledge the necessity of sanctions in preventing criminal behavior, but do not suggest that the major sanctions are either legal or corporal. On the contrary, they suggest that disapproval by people one cares about is the most powerful of sanctions. Effective punishment by the parent or major caretaker therefore usually entails nothing more than explicit disapproval of unwanted behavior. The criticism of control theories that dwells on their alleged cruelty is therefore simply misguided or ill-informed (see, e.g., Currie, 1985).

Not all caretakers punish effectively. In fact, some are too harsh and some are too lenient (Glueck and Glueck, 1950; McCord and McCord, 1959; West and Farrington, 1977; see generally Loeber and Stouthamer-Loeber, 1986). Given our model, however, rewarding good behavior cannot compensate for failure to correct deviant behavior. . . .

Given the consistency of the child-rearing model with our general theory and the research literature, it should be possible to use it to explain other family correlates of criminal and otherwise deviant behavior.

Parental Criminality

Our theory focuses on the connection between the self-control of the parent and the subsequent self-control of the child. There is good reason to expect, and the data confirm, that people lacking self-control do not socialize their children well. According to Donald West and David Farrington, "the fact that delinquency is transmitted from one generation to the next is indisputable" (1977:109; see also Robins, 1966). Of course our theory does not allow transmission of criminality, genetic or otherwise. However, it does allow us to predict that some people are more likely than others to fail to socialize their children and that this will be a consequence of their own inadequate socialization. The extent of this connection between parent and child socialization is illustrated by the West and Farrington study, which revealed that fewer than 5 percent of the families accounted for almost half of the criminal convictions in the entire sample. (In our view, this finding is more important for the theory of crime, and for public policy, than the much better-known finding of Wolfgang and his colleagues [1972] that something like 6 percent of *individual* offenders account for about half of all criminal acts.) In order to achieve such concentration of crime in a small number of families, it is necessary that the parents and the brothers and sisters of offenders also be unusually likely to commit criminal acts.[1]

Why should the children of offenders be unusually vulnerable to crime? Recall that our theory assumes that criminality is not something the parents have to work to produce; on the contrary, it assumes that criminality is something they have to work to avoid. Consistent with this view, parents with criminal records do *not* encourage crime in their children and are in fact as disapproving of it as parents with no record on criminal involvement (West and Farrington 1977). Of course, not wanting criminal behavior in one's children and being upset when it occurs does not necessarily imply that great effort has been expended to prevent it. If criminal behavior is oriented toward short-term rewards, and if child-rearing is proented toward long-term rewards, there is little reason to expect parents themselves lacking self-control to be particularly adept at instilling self-control in their children.

Consistent with this expectation, research consistently indicates that the supervision of delinquents in families where parents have criminal records tends to be "lax," "inadequate," or "poor." Punishment in these families also tends to be easy, short-term, and insensitive—that is, yelling and screaming, slapping and hitting, with threats that are not carried out.

Such facts do not, however, completely account for the concentration of criminality among some families. A major reason for this failure is probably that the most subtle element of child-rearing is not included in the analysis—the *recognition* of deviant behavior. According to Gerald Patterson (1980), many parents do not even recognize *criminal* behavior in their children, let alone the minor forms of deviance whose punishment is necessary for effective child-rearing. For example, when children steal outside the home, some parents discount reports that they have done so on the grounds that the charges are unproved and cannot therefore be used to justify punishment. By the same token, when children are suspended for misbehavior at school, some parents side with the child and blame the episode on prejudicial treatment by teachers. Obviously, parents who cannot see the misbehavior of their children are in no position to correct it, even if they are inclined to do so.

Given that recognition of deviant acts is a necessary component of the child-rearing model, research is needed on the question of what parents should and should not recognize as deviant behavior if they are to prevent criminality. To the extent that our theory is correct, parents need to know behaviors that reflect low self-control. That many parents are not attentive to such behaviors should come as no surprise. The idea that criminal behavior is the product of deprivation or positive learning dominates modern theory. As a consequence, most influential social scientific theories of crime and delinquency ignore or deny the connection between crime and talking back, yelling, pushing and shoving, insisting on getting one's way, trouble in school, and poor school performance. Little wonder, then, that some parents do not see the significance of such acts. Research now makes it clear that parents differ in their reaction to these behaviors, with some parents attempting to correct behaviors that others ignore or even defend (Patterson, 1980). Because social science in general sees little connection between these acts and crime, there has been little systematic integration of the child development and criminological literatures. Furthermore, because the conventional wisdom disputes the connection between child training and crime, public policy has not focused on it. We do not argue that crime is caused by these early misbehaviors. Instead, we argue that such behaviors indicate the presence of the major individual-level cause of crime, a cause that in principle may be attacked by punishing these early manifestations. Nor do we argue that criminal acts automatically follow early evidence of low self-control. Because crime requires more than low self-control, some parents are lucky and have children with low self-control who still manage to avoid acts that would bring them to the attention of the criminal justice system. It is less likely (in fact unlikely), however, that such children will avoid altogether behavior indicative of low self-control. Put another way, low self-control predicts low self-control better than it predicts any of its specific manifestations, such as crime.

Family Size

One of the most consistent findings of delinquency research is that the larger the number of children in the family, the greater the likelihood that each of them will be delinquent. This finding, too, is perfectly explicable from a child-rearing model. Affection for the individual child may be unaffected by numbers, and parents with large families may be as able as anyone else to recognize deviant behavior, but monitoring and punishment are probably more difficult the greater the number of children in the family. Greater numbers strain parental resources of time and energy. For this reason, the child in the large family is likely to spend more time with other children and less time with adults. Children are not as likely as adults to be effective trainers. They have less investment in the outcome, are more likely to be tolerant of deviant behavior, and do not have the power to enforce their edicts.

If the analysis of criminality of parents and size of family is sufficient to establish the plausibility of our child-rearing explanation, we can now attempt to apply it to some of the more problematic issues in the connection between the family and crime.

The Single-Parent Family

Such family measures as the percentage of the population divorced, the percentage of households headed by women, and the percentage of unattached individuals in the community are among the most powerful predictors of crime rates (Sampson, 1987). Consistent with these findings, in most (but not all) studies that directly compare children living with both biological parents with children living in "broken" or reconstituted homes, the children from intact homes have lower rates of crime.

If the fact of a difference between single- and two-parent families is reasonably well established, the mechanisms by which it is produced are not adequately understood. It was once common in the delinquency literature to distinguish between homes broken by divorce and those broken by death. This distinction recognized the difficulty of separating the effects of the people involved in divorce from the effects of divorce itself. Indeed, it is common to find that involuntarily broken homes are less conducive to delinquency than homes in which the parent was a party to the decision to separate.

With the continued popularity of marriage, a possible complication enters the picture. The missing biological parent (in the overwhelming majority of cases, the father) is often replaced at some point by a stepparent. Is the child better or worse off as a result of the presence of an "unrelated" adult in the house?

The model we are using suggests that, *all else being equal,* one parent is sufficient. We could substitute "mother" or "father" for "parents" without any obvious loss in child-rearing ability. Husbands and wives tend to be sufficiently alike on such things as values, attitudes, and skills that for many purposes they may be treated as a unit. For that matter, our scheme does not even require that the adult involved in training the child be his or her guardian, let alone a biological parent. Proper training can be accomplished outside the confines of the two-parent home.

But all else is rarely equal. The single parent (usually the mother) must devote a good deal to support and maintenance activities that are at least to some extent shared in the two-parent family. Further, she must often do so in the absence of psychological or social support. As a result, she is less able to devote time to monitoring and punishment and is more likely to be involved in negative, abusive contacts with her children.

Remarriage is by no means a complete solution to these problems. As compared to natural parents, stepparents are likely to report that they have no "parental feelings" toward their stepchildren, and they are unusually likely to be involved in cases of child abuse (Burgess, 1980). The other side of the coin is the affection of the child for the parent. Such affection is conducive to nondelinquency in its own right and clearly eases the task of child-rearing. Affection is, for obvious reasons, less likely to be felt toward the new parent in a reconstituted family than toward a biological parent in a continuously intact family.

The Mother Who Works Outside the Home

The increase in the number of women in the labor force has several implications for the crime rate. To the extent this increase contributes to the instability of marriage, it will have the consequences for crime just discussed. Traditionally, however, the major concern was that the mother working outside the home would be unable to supervise or effectively rear her children. Sheldon and Eleanor Glueck (1950) found that the children of women who work, especially the children of those who work "occasionally" or "sporadically," were more likely to be delinquent. They also showed that the effect on delinquency of the mother's working was *completely* accounted for by the quality of supervision provided by the mother. (Such complete explanations of one factor by another are extremely rare in social science.) When the mother was able to arrange supervision for the child, her employment had no effect on the likelihood of delinquency. In fact, in this particular study, the children of regularly employed women were least likely to be delinquent when supervision was taken into account. This does not mean, however, that the employment of the mother had no effect. It did have an effect, at least among those in relatively deprived circumstances: the children of employed women were more likely to be delinquent.

More commonly, research reports a small effect of the mother's employment that it is unable to explain. The advantage of the nonemployed mother over the employed mother in child-rearing remains when supervision and other characteristics of the mother, the family, and the child are taken into account. One possible implication of this explanatory failure is that the effects of employment influence children in ways not measurable except through their delinquency. One way of addressing this question would be to examine the effect of mother's employment on measures of inadequate self-control other than the commission of criminal acts—such as on accidents or school failure. If we are dealing with a social-control effect rather than a socialization effect, it should be possible to find a subset of deviant behaviors that are more affected than others by mother's employment. Although our scheme does not allow us *a priori* to separate the enduring effects of child "rearing" from the temporary effects of child "control," it alerts us to the fact that self-control and supervision can be the result of a single parental act.

Another consequence of female labor-force participation is that it leaves the house unguarded for large portions of the day. The unoccupied house is less attractive to adolescent members of the family and more attractive to other adolescents interested only in its contents. As we indicated earlier, research shows that the absence of guardians in the home is a good predictor of residential burglary.

Author's Notes

1. It is commonly observed (in an unsystematic way) than in an otherwise law-abiding family, individual children can be seriously delinquent. This observation is taken as evidence against family or child-rearing explanations for crime. Such observations do not dispute the strong tendencies toward consistency within families mentioned in the text. They do suggest that family child-rearing practices are not the only cause of crime.

Discussion Questions

1. What are the elements of self-control identified by Gottfredson and Hirschi? What is the relationship between self-control as a personality trait and crime as a form of behavior?

2. Gottfredson and Hirschi propose that their theory of crime is a *general* one, i.e., that it applies to all forms of crime. They argue elsewhere in their book that white-collar crime does not differ from more conventional forms of crime and delinquency. This suggests that white-collar workers who turn to crime are lower in self-control than workers who do not break the law. How would you carry out a research project to test this hypothesis?

3. What is meant by the "versatility" of criminal offenders? According to Gottfredson and Hirschi, do most offenders specialize in one kind of crime, or are they versatile in their choice of crimes? What is the significance of versatility or specialization for the authors' theory of crime?

4. What is ineffective child-rearing and how does it produce low self-control in children? What is the significance of parental criminality, family size, single-parent families, and mothers working outside the home for the rearing of children and the development of self-control? What national policies might reduce crime by improving the likelihood that parents will teach their children self-control?

Chapter 5

The Cycle of Violence*

Cathy Spatz Widom

This selection looks at another aspect of family life that is conducive to crime and delinquency: child abuse. Widom's comparison of a sample of children who had official records of abuse or neglect with a sample of children who had no such records demonstrates that maltreated children are more likely to be arrested for delinquent and criminal acts, as well as more likely to engage in other undesirable forms of behavior. The author concludes with several implications of her findings for policymakers.

Does childhood abuse lead to adult criminal behavior? How likely is it that today's abused and neglected children will become tomorrow's violent offenders?

In one of the most detailed studies of the issue to date, research sponsored by the National Institute of Justice (NIJ) found that childhood abuse increased the odds of future delinquency and adult criminality overall by 40 percent. The study followed 1,575 cases from childhood through young adulthood, comparing the arrest records of two groups:

- A study group of 908 substantiated cases of childhood abuse or neglect processed by the courts between 1967 and 1971 and tracked through official records over the next 15 to 20 years.
- A comparison group of 667 children, not officially recorded as abused or neglected, matched to the study group according to sex, age, race, and approximate family socioeconomic status.

---

* Findings and conclusions of the research reported here are those of the researcher and do not necessarily reflect the official position or policies of the U.S. Department of Justice.

Source: Cathy Spatz Widom, *The Cycle of Violence,* pp. 1–6, a Research in Brief of the National Institute of Justice. Washington, D.C.: U.S. Department of Justice, October 1992.

While most members of both groups had no juvenile or adult criminal record, *being abused or neglected as a child increased the likelihood of arrest as a juvenile by 53 percent, as an adult by 38 percent, and for a violent crime by 38 percent.*

The "cycle of violence" hypothesis suggests that a childhood history of physical abuse predisposes the survivor to violence in later years. This study reveals that victims of neglect are also more likely to develop later criminal violent behavior as well. This finding gives powerful support to the need for expanding common conceptions of physical abuse. If it is not only violence that begets violence, but also neglect, far more attention needs to be devoted to the families of children whose "beatings" are forms of abandonment and severe malnutrition. An example of intervention for the prevention of neglect is described later.

The first phase of this study relied on arrest records to measure delinquency and criminality. A second phase calls for locating and interviewing a large sample of the previously abused and neglected children to draw a more complete picture of the consequences of childhood victimization. The remainder of this report presents Phase I results in greater detail and introduces preliminary findings from Phase II.

Study Design

Several important design features distinguish this research from prior efforts to study the intergenerational transmission of violence (for further information on the design and sampling procedures, see Widom, 1989). First, by following a large number (1,575) of cases from childhood through adolescence into young adulthood, this "prospective" study was able to examine the long-term consequences of abuse and neglect. The sample, drawn from a metropolitan area in the Midwest, was restricted to children who were 11 years or younger at the time of the incident of abuse or neglect. At the time that juvenile and criminal records were checked, subjects ranged in age from 16 to 33; most were between ages 20 and 30, with a mean age of 25.

Matching members of the study group to others whose official records showed no childhood abuse or neglect was an equally important feature of the research. This design allowed the study to separate the effects of known correlates of delinquency and criminality (age, sex, race, and socioeconomic status) from the experience of abuse and neglect. Both groups were approximately two-thirds white and one-third black and were about evenly divided between males and females. Most were between 6 and 11 years old at the time the abuse was documented.

The study design also featured clear operational definitions of abuse and neglect. Combined with large sample sizes, this permitted the separate examination of physical abuse, sexual abuse, and neglect, defined as follows:

- Physical abuse cases included injuries such as bruises, welts, burns, abrasions, lacerations, wounds, cuts, bone and skull fractures, and other evidence of physical injury.
- Sexual abuse involved such charges as "assault and battery with intent to gratify sexual desires," "fondling or touching in an obscene manner," rape, sodomy, and incest.

- Neglect cases represented extreme failure to provide adequate food, clothing, shelter, and medical attention to children.

Family members (often parents) were the primary perpetrators of the abuse and neglect. The most frequent type of perpetrator varied, however, by type of maltreatment.

Juvenile court and probation records were the source of information on the abuse and neglect, as well as the characteristics of the family. Arrest data were obtained from Federal, State, and local law enforcement records. Recognizing that much child abuse (as well as later delinquent and criminal behavior) never comes to the attention of any official authority, Phase II will supplement these official records with interview results.

Study Findings

Of primary interest was the question, "Would the behavior of those who had been abused or neglected be worse than those with no reported abuse?" The answer, shown in Table 5-1, was evident: those who had been abused or neglected as children were more likely to be arrested as juveniles (26 percent versus 17 percent), as adults (29 percent versus 21 percent), and for a violent crime (11 percent versus 8 percent). The abused and neglected cases were also more likely to average nearly 1 year younger at first arrest (16.5 years versus 17.3 years), to commit nearly twice as many offenses (2.4 percent versus 1.4 percent), and to be arrested more frequently (17 percent of abused and neglected cases versus 9 percent of comparison cases had more than five arrests).

Sex

Experiencing early child abuse or neglect had a substantial impact, even on individuals with little likelihood of engaging in officially recorded adult criminal behavior. Thus, although males generally have higher rates of criminal behavior than females, being abused or neglected in childhood increased the likelihood of arrest for females—by 77 percent over comparison group females. As adults, abused and neglected females were

TABLE 5-1   Extent of Involvement in Delinquency, Adult Criminality, and Violent Criminal Behavior

Type of Arrest	Abused and Neglected (n=908) Percent	Comparison Group (n=667) Percent
Juvenile	26.0	16.8
Adult	28.6	21.1
Violent crime	11.2	7.9

Note: All differences significant.

more likely to be arrested for property, drug, and misdemeanor offenses such as disorderly conduct, curfew violations, or loitering, but not for violent offenses. Females in general are less likely to be arrested for street violence and more likely to appear in statistics on violence in the home. Through interviews, Phase II will examine the incidence of unreported violence to learn more about the possible existence of hidden cycles of family violence.

Race

Both black and white abused and neglected children were more likely to be arrested than comparison children. However, as shown in Table 5-2, the difference between whites was not as great as that between blacks. In fact, white abused and neglected children do *not* show increased likelihood of arrest for violent crimes over comparison children. This contrasts dramatically with the findings for black children in this sample who show significantly increased rates of violent arrests, compared with black children who were not abused or neglected. This is a surprising finding and one that may reflect differences in an array of environmental factors. Phase II will investigate a number of explanations for these results, including differences in poverty levels, family factors, characteristics of the abuse or neglect incident, access to counseling or support services, and treatment by juvenile authorities.

Juvenile Record

Previously abused or neglected persons were at higher risk of beginning a life of crime, at a younger age, with more significant and repeated criminal involvement. Notably, how-

TABLE 5-2   Involvement in Criminality by Race

	Abused and Neglected (n=908)	Comparison Group (n=667)	Significance*
Any arrest	Percent	Percent	
Juvenile			
Black	37.9	19.3	<.001
White	21.1	15.4	<.05
Adult			
Black	39.0	26.2	<.01
White	24.4	18.4	<.05
Violent			
Black	22.0	12.9	<.01
White	6.5	5.3	NS

*[If the level of significance is <.001, the probability that the two percentages in the row are different because of chance factors in the selection of the two samples is less than one in a thousand. In other words, the difference between the percentages is very likely to be a "real" one. If the level of significance is less than .05, the difference is considered to be a meaningful one. "NS" means "not significant."]

ever, among those arrested as juveniles, abused or neglected persons were no more likely to continue a life of crime than other children:

- In both groups, roughly the same proportion of children with juvenile arrests also had arrests as adults (53 percent versus 50 percent).
- Similarly, in both groups, about the same proportion of those with violent juvenile arrests also had violent arrests as adults (34.2 percent versus 36.8 percent).

In short, childhood abuse and neglect had no apparent effect on the movement of juvenile offenders toward adult criminal activity. Distinguishing the factors that promote the onset of criminal behavior from those that affect persistence in a criminal career is clearly an important topic for future research.

Does Only Violence Beget Violence?

To test the notion that childhood victims of violence resort to violence themselves in later years, violent criminal behavior was examined as a function of the type of maltreatment experienced as a child. The results are presented in simplified form below.

Abuse Group	Number	Percent Arrested for Violent Offense
Physical abuse only	76	15.8%
Neglect only	609	12.5
Physical abuse and neglect	70	7.1
Sexual abuse and other abuse or neglect	28	7.1
Sexual abuse only	125	5.6
Comparison group	667	7.9

The physically abused children (as opposed to those neglected or sexually abused) were the most likely to be arrested later for a violent crime. Notably, however, the physically abused group was followed closely by the neglected group.

Because different types of abuse and neglect are not distributed evenly by age, race, and sex, these frequencies present an oversimplified picture. Even after controlling for age, race, and sex, however, a relationship between childhood neglect and subsequent violence remained evident.

This finding offers persuasive evidence for the need to take concerted preventive action. Nationwide, the incidence of neglect is almost three times that of physical abuse (15.9 per 1,000 children in 1986, compared to 5.7 per 1,000 for physical abuse, and 2.5 per 1,000 for sexual abuse) (Westat, Inc., 1988). Neglect also is potentially more damaging to the development of a child than abuse (provided the abuse involves no neurological impairment). In one study of the influence of early malnutrition on subsequent behavior, previously malnourished children had attention deficits, reduced social skills, and poorer emotional stability than a comparison group (Galler et al., 1983). Other researchers have found an array of developmental differences associated with childhood neglect (see, for instance, Allen and Oliver, 1982; Egeland, Stroufe, and Erickson, 1983; Frodi and Smetana, 1984). This study now suggests that those differences include a greater risk of later criminal violence.

Research findings show how imperative are improved procedures for the identification of child abuse and neglect. Referring to the connection between child maltreatment and adult criminality, New York City instituted new procedures for police response and followup in cases involving suspected child abuse and neglect (Ward, 1989).

Out-of-Home Placement and Criminal Consequences

Not all abused and neglected children grow up to become delinquents, adult criminals, or violent criminal offenders. What are some of the possible mediating variables that act to buffer or protect abused and neglected children? Placement outside the home is one possible buffer that was investigated with Phase I data. Scholars and practitioners have often criticized out-of-home placements (foster care, in particular). Children placed outside the home are considered a particularly vulnerable group, since they have experienced both a disturbed family situation and separation from their natural parents. Accordingly, child welfare policies today often seek to avoid removing the child from home and instead to mitigate negative family situations through counseling and related support.

In contrast to today's practices, the vast majority of a sample of the children abused and neglected roughly 20 years ago were placed outside the home during some portion of their childhood or early adolescence. Year-by-year information was available from juvenile court and probation records on 772 cases. For these children, out-of-home placements included foster care, guardian's home, and schools for the retarded or physically handicapped. Only 14 percent of these abuse and neglect cases had no record of having been placed up through age 18. The average amount of time in placement was about 5 years, and sometimes lasted through childhood and adolescence.

As Table 5-3 shows, there was remarkably little difference between the arrest records of those who remained at home and those who were placed outside the home due to abuse and neglect. (Predictably, both of these groups were strikingly different from those placed outside the home due to delinquency as well as abuse and neglect.) At least for this sample, then, an out-of-home placement did not lead to negative effects on the arrest measure for those who were removed from their homes due only to abuse and neglect.

The study also showed that stability may be an important factor in out-of-home placements. Children who moved three or more times had significantly higher arrest rates (almost twice as high) for all types of criminal behaviors—juvenile, adult, and violent—than children who moved less than three times. In turn, children with multiple placements typically had behavior problems noted in their files. These notations covered a wide spectrum of problem behavior, including chronic fighting, fire setting, destructiveness, uncontrollable anger, sadistic tendencies (for example, aggressiveness toward weaker children),

TABLE 5-3 Juvenile and Adult Arrests as a Function of Placement Experiences for Juvenile Court Cases Only (n=772)

Type of Placement	N	Any Juvenile (n=209)	Any Adult (n=217)	Both Juv. & Adult (n=115)	Any Violent (n=93)
No placement	106	15.1	29.2	6.6	10.4
Abuse/neglect placement only	489	17.8	23.3	8.6	8.4
Delinquency placement plus abuse/neglect	96	92.7***	60.4***	55.2***	34.4***

Note: Adult arrest rates restricted to subjects age 21 and older in March 1988.
p<.001 [The probability that the percentages marked "" differ from the above percentages only because of chance factors in the selection of samples is less than one in a thousand. In other words, there seems to be a "real" difference in the probability of arrest between the cases in the third row and those in the first two rows.]

and extreme defiance of authority. Whether the behavior problems caused the moves, or the moves contributed to the behavior problems, is unclear. In either case, children with numerous placements obviously need special services.

These findings challenge the assumption that it is necessarily unwise to remove children from negative family situations. While stability of placement appears to be important, the potential damage of removing an abused and neglected child from the home did not include a higher likelihood of arrest or violent criminal behavior.

Phase II: Followup and In-Person Interviews

While the findings from Phase I demonstrate convincingly that early child abuse and neglect place one at increased risk for officially recorded delinquency, adult criminality, and violent criminal behavior, a large portion of abused and neglected children did not have official arrest records. Indeed, the linkage is far from inevitable, since the majority of abused and neglected children did not become delinquents, adult criminals, or violent offenders. However, because the findings from Phase I were based on official arrest records, these rates may be underestimates of the true extent of delinquency and criminality. Phase I findings also do not tell us about general violent behavior, especially unrecorded or unreported family violence.

Phase II was designed to address many of the unanswered questions from the first phase by finding and interviewing a large number of these people 20 years after the childhood victimization. Most are now young adults in their early 20's and 30's; some are beginning to have their own children. The followup study aims to examine the full consequences of maltreatment as a child and to determine why some victims of childhood abuse and neglect fare well, while others have negative outcomes. The interviews will explore recollections of early childhood experiences, schooling, adolescence, undetected alcohol and drug problems, undetected delinquency and criminality, and important life experiences.

Preliminary Phase II findings, based on 2-hour followup interviews with 500 study and comparison group subjects, indicate that other negative outcomes may be as common as delinquency and violent criminal behavior. These interviews suggest that the long-term consequences of childhood victimization also may include:

- Mental health concerns (depression and suicide attempts).
- Educational problems (inadequate cognitive functioning, extremely low IQ, and poor reading ability).
- Health and safety issues (alcohol and drug problems).
- Occupational difficulties (lack of work, employment in low-level service jobs).

In addition to documenting the broader consequences of childhood victimization, Phase II is geared to identify "protective" factors that may act to buffer the negative results of abuse and neglect. The ultimate goal is to provide a base of knowledge on which to build appropriate prevention and treatment programs.

Conclusion and Implications

Childhood victimization represents a widespread, serious social problem that increases the likelihood of delinquency, adult criminality, and violent criminal behavior. Poor educational performance, health problems, and generally low levels of achievement also characterize the victims of early childhood abuse and neglect.

This study offers at least three messages to juvenile authorities and child welfare professionals:

- *Intervene early.* The findings of Phase I issue a call to police, teachers, and health workers for increased recognition of the signs of abuse and neglect, and serious efforts to intervene as early as possible. The later the intervention, the more difficult the change process becomes. Specialized attention needs to be paid to abused and neglected children with early behavior problems. These children show the highest risk of later juvenile and adult arrest, as well as violent criminal behavior.
- *Develop policies that recognize the high risks of neglect as well as abuse.* Also important in its implications for juvenile court and child welfare action is the fact that neglect alone (not necessarily physical abuse) was significantly related to violent criminal behavior. A picture emerges where physical abuse is only one point on a continuum of family situations that contribute to violence. Whether those situations result in active physical abuse, or more passive neglect, it is now quite clear that both forms of child maltreatment are serious threats. Neglect cases represent the majority of cases taxing the child protection system. Research shows that today's victim of neglect may well be a defendant in tomorrow's violent criminal case.

- *Reexamine out-of-home placement policies.* This NIJ study focused on cases during the period 1967–1971, when out-of-home placements were a common intervention. Detailed information available for 772 cases revealed that the vast majority (86 percent) were placed outside their homes for an average of 5 years. This contrasts sharply with today's efforts to avoid out-of-home placement on the assumption that separation may aggravate, rather than ameliorate, a child's problems. Yet, there was no evidence that those who were separated from their families fared any worse on the arrest measures than those who remained at home. Though these results are far from definitive, they do suggest that child protective policies in this area deserve close scrutiny. The assumption that removal from the home offers additional risk could not be confirmed by this study. Any policy founded on this assumption ought to be tested through careful local studies of the full consequences of out-of-home placement.

Discussion Questions

1. How do abused and nonabused children differ in terms of the likelihood that they will engage in delinquency and crime? What is it about physical and sexual abuse or neglect that increases the chance of breaking the law? How does this research fit with Gottfredson and Hirschi's theory (selection #4) about child-rearing and low self-control?

2. Why is neglect nearly as strongly associated with crime and delinquency as is physical abuse?

3. What are the policy implications of this research? Why do you think policymakers in the past moved away from a policy of taking children out of their parents' homes and placing them in foster homes or institutions, even though there was no research supporting that change? Is there now a national inclination against taking abused or neglected children from their parents and, if so, why?

Chapter 6

Crime and
Social Reproduction

Mark Colvin

Unlike the previous three selections, this one focuses on broad social-structural and economic sources of crime. Colvin outlines eight proposals for reducing crime through programs that would enhance human productivity, strengthen social bonds, create career opportunities, and increase democratic participation in such institutions as school and the workplace. Implicit in Colvin's proposals is the notion that crime is the product of factors that cannot simply be influenced by better child-rearing techniques, increased numbers of police officers, or more effective correctional programs.

Don C. Gibbons (1990) recently called for some "outrageous" proposals to address the crime problem in the 1990s. Gibbons made it clear that he was interested in seeing proposals that contrast with the general right-wing trends in criminal justice policies offered by the Reagan and Bush administrations. In response to Gibbons's call, this article outlines an eight-point comprehensive plan to reduce crime through enhancement of human development and human capital. It proposes to shift national priorities by increasing public investments in our institutions of social reproduction.

The problem of crime in the United States is connected to the processes of social reproduction (Colvin and Pauly, 1983). Social reproduction involves the institutions of socialization that prepare people for productive roles in society. Rising crime rates since the 1960s are a by-product of a fractured process of social reproduction that does not articulate with our society's productive needs in an increasingly global economy. The institu-

Source: Mark Colvin, *Crime & Delinquency* (Vol. 37, No. 4), pp. 436–48, copyright © 1991 by Sage Publications, Inc. Reprinted by permission of Sage Publications, Inc.

tions of social reproduction (primarily families and schools) have, except in the rhetoric of politicians, been largely neglected by policymakers. As a result, growing numbers of young people fail to create social bonds with legitimate avenues to adulthood; and many become marginal to our nation's economic institutions.

Our society's failure to invest in human development and human capital costs us dearly in productive capacity and international competition, and ultimately results in both high rates of crime and soaring social expenses for welfare and prisons. Both the problems of crime and economic decline spring from a lack of social investments in our future. Both of these problems can be addressed by a national comprehensive program aimed at spurring economic growth, human development, and grass-roots, democratic participation in the major institutions affecting our lives and those of our children.

A telling moment that highlights a central problem with our national priorities occurred on January 16, 1991. A special report on public television dealing with the crisis in education and child welfare, which was scheduled to be broadcast that night, was pre-empted by the U.S.-led offensive on Iraq. No matter the arguments in favor or against this particular military action, it points to a major contradiction in both U.S. priorities and the meaning of national security. Expenditures for the military have skyrocketed, and the government has retreated over the last decade from its constitutional obligation to promote the general welfare. In the process, our true national security, based on our productive capacity and competitiveness in the world economy, has been undermined. Crime in our society is a by-product of this failure of public policy.

And crime policies themselves have largely failed. Most crime-reduction proposals are reactive; they attempt to respond to crime by focusing on offenders after involvement in criminal activities. These include both conservative approaches of deterrence and incapacitation and liberal approaches aimed at rehabilitation. Neither has demonstrated much success for overall crime reduction.

Other proposals that focus on preventive measures aimed at potential offenders before they break the law offer a proactive approach that usually falls short because these programs are not adequately funded or sufficiently comprehensive. Many proactive programs focus exclusively on the individual's immediate situation without addressing the larger context that shapes that person's socialization. These programs often lack public commitment and financing because they are seen as helping specific groups (i.e., the poor) at the expense of middle class taxpayers who receive no direct benefits from these programs.

For a crime-reduction program to work, it must deal with the underlying sources of crime through comprehensive, proactive measures aimed at prevention. To receive wide public support, the program must be aimed not directly at crime or the poor, but rather at broader economic and human development problems (related to crime and poverty) that directly affect large segments of the population. (Indeed, the difference in the level of public support for Social Security as opposed to welfare programs for the poor is due to the more widespread, cross-class benefits of Social Security.) Crime-reduction would thus be a by-product of a comprehensive program dealing with economic growth and human development that affects the mass of the population. A comprehensive program that reduces crime by addressing the underlying processes of social reproduction must offer benefits to a wide constituency and must simultaneously address the broader problems of our economic production and international competitiveness.

That a comprehensive proposal that seeks to affect the social reproduction process in the United States must be viewed as "outrageous" is more a reflection of the truly outrageous state of our political-economy than of the proposal itself. In most industrialized democracies the development of human capital is taken as a serious public obligation and is seen as an investment in these societies' continued well-being. The more "privatized" nature of social reproduction and economic production in the United States creates enormous dislocations. Future social needs are neglected as the bases for public investments are undermined by private investment decisions that move capital into wild speculation, into nonproductive ventures, and generally out of the United States. Most industrialized societies in Western Europe and the Far East intervene in investment decisions in ways that protect their larger economic well-being. It is recognized in these nations that unbridled private investment has enormous negative social consequences. These societies also direct a much larger share of their economic surplus from private hands to public investments in human capital. That is, they consciously attempt to shape the social reproduction process in ways that ensure the young will move into productive roles as adults.

These nations' investments in human capital and infrastructure allow them to compete effectively in a global economy. They become beneficiaries of a "virtuous cycle" set in motion by their public investments:

> A work force possessing a good basic education, which can efficiently bring the fruits of its labors to the global economy, can attract global capital for its performance of moderately complex tasks. The experience gained by performing these tasks generates additional on-the-job training and experience, which serve to lure global capital for more complex activities. As skills build and experience accumulates, the nation's citizens receive more and more from the rest of the world in exchange for their services—which permits them to invest in better schools, transportation, research, and communications systems. . . . [T]heir links with the world steadily improve, their income rises. (Reich, 1991:43)

However, nations that fail to make these public investments fall into a "vicious cycle in which global money and technology are lured only by low wages and low taxes" (Reich, 1991:43). With these enticements to global capital, the financing of education and infrastructure becomes more problematic as the tax base erodes, and training and experience in more complex, higher-paying jobs are not provided. This vicious cycle "can continue to push wages downward until citizens of the nation (or region, or city) have a standard of living like that typical of the Third World" (Reich, 1991:43). Since the late 1970s, the United States has been moving toward such a vicious cycle; rising crime rates and blighted inner cities are visible symptoms.

Yet other nations' experiences show that this is not an inevitable process. A country need not attract global capital through low wages; it can thrive through an abundance of skilled workers and "world-class" infrastructure:

> The average worker in the former West Germany earns a higher hourly wage than the average American, but global capital is nonetheless attracted to Germany by the nation's pool of skilled workers and its first-class transportation and communications facilities. (Reich, 1991:43–44)

The same is true of France and Japan. "All three of these nations are spending significant sums of money on education, training, research and development" (Reich, 1991:44). But as Reich (1991) reports, "even as other nations have been increasing their public investments in people and infrastructure, the United States as a nation has been cutting back" (p. 46).

Neither Japan nor Germany can be held up as models for the United States. Although there may be much to learn from their experiences, the United States has its own traditions of democratic participation. Any comprehensive program affecting the social reproduction process must also aim to expand the democratic process in new and imaginative ways. The enhancement of social bonding, the key to any crime-reduction program, entails the maximization of democratic participation at the grass-roots level in schools, communities, and workplaces.

A comprehensive crime reduction policy simultaneously must be a plan that reshapes the social reproduction process and radically enhances our nation's investment in human capital. The focus is less on "what to do about crime" and more on "what to do about our declining infrastructure and competitiveness in the world economy." The latter question entails the first. Crime reduction is bound up with the question of resources for human capital and human development.

The following proposals draw freely from and expand on ideas developed by Elliott Currie (1985), Samuel Walker (1989), Lynn Curtis (1989), and the Eisenhower Foundation (1990), all of which present a similar focus on crime prevention through addressing economic and human needs. A major problem with their approaches, in my view, is that most of their proposed programs focus exclusively on poor communities. Although such programs are a necessary part of a comprehensive approach, they risk public rejection, as many of the 1960s' war on poverty programs did, because they are targeted at a minority of the population. To be successful and to avoid class and racial polarization, programs must receive broad-based public support by directly benefiting more than just the poor.

In the section that follows, I present a specific outline of a comprehensive public policy. Some aspects are more "outrageous" than others. The proposal is offered in the spirit of eliciting discussion. I strongly feel that in the next few years, as it appears that we are running out of answers to the difficult problems we face, opportunities for fresh starts and new ideas will multiply. The aim is to develop an outline for a comprehensive strategy that increases productive capacity and aggregate demand in the economy, and, as an important by-product, draws young people away from the social processes that induce criminal involvement and toward those that encourage participation in legitimate activities.

"Outrageous" Proposals

A comprehensive plan, such as the one proposed here, will require a major change in our priorities. National investments must be moved away from military toward education and human development (Eisenhower Foundation, 1990). We need to establish an "educational–industrial complex" to replace the military–industrial complex that has driven economic and public policies since World War II. Such a major shift is now possible with the lessening of the Soviet military threat; and it is imperative because our national security is now threatened to a much greater extent by domestic decline.

An educational–industrial complex would be the web of social institutions that develop human beings for useful and productive roles in our society. Education is understood as a broader project than the formal education now offered in public schools. It must include families, schools, workplaces, and communities. And, of greatest importance for crime prevention, it must reduce the marginalization of young people. Eight specific proposals make up this comprehensive approach.

1. Short-Term Emergency Measures

In the short term, to deal with the immediate situation of joblessness and human suffering, CETA [Comprehensive Employment and Training Act] and other "war on poverty" job-training and placement programs need to be reinstituted. Income subsidies for poor families can provide a stop-gap measure while more comprehensive job-training and job development programs are established. But a reliance on entitlement programs that do not enhance human capital but only keep poor people in place is inadequate. The goal should be public investments that move individuals off welfare and into jobs that produce growth in public revenues; but this may not be possible until other aspects of this plan have time to emerge. These job programs, in fact, will have little impact on joblessness unless they are incorporated into a much more comprehensive approach that affects economic growth. One danger in these short-term measures is the possible political backlash from those not directly benefiting from these programs. To mitigate this opposition, implementation of these short-term measures should accompany the initial start of other proposals in this plan that affect broader constituencies.

2. Nationwide Parent-Effectiveness Programs

A nationwide program of parent-effectiveness training needs to be instituted. Disciplining children in a noncoercive, consistent, and nonhumiliating fashion is perhaps the most important measure for establishing affective social bonds between them and their parents, who are the first authority figures in the children's lives (Gottfredson and Hirschi, 1990; Patterson, Chamberlain, and Reid, 1982; Larzelere and Patterson, 1990). These initial social bonds set the stage for a child's future encounters with other authority figures in the school and community. Success in school is greatly determined by early childhood experiences in families (Jencks et al., 1972).

Parent-effectiveness training should be required in the senior year in all high schools and offered as an adult education class in all high schools to new parents. These classes should be supplemented by parent-effectiveness counseling programs attached to local schools. Parents can be induced to participate in parent-effectiveness classes through enhanced tax exemptions for participation. Gerald Patterson's experimental programs in training impoverished parents in effective disciplining techniques show that this approach has promise (Patterson, Chamberlain, and Reid, 1982). Of course, as with each of the specific proposals included in this comprehensive plan, by itself parent-effectiveness training will have a very limited impact if basic economic and other social issues are left untouched.

3. Universal "Head Start" Preschool Programs

All children should be prepared early for participation in school. This can be done either through parents themselves who have the time, talent, and inclination to provide preschool development or through an enhanced program modeled after the current Head Start program. For parents who can provide such preschool development themselves, a program for certification and training by local schools would be a necessary prerequisite for this approach. For most working parents, however, time is too limited to adequately provide an effective preschool experience. Certified private and public preschool centers can be coupled with free day-care programs for children of working parents. Combined with effective parenting, these preschool programs can provide the cognitive and emotional basis for early success in school.

4. Expanded and Enhanced Public Education

Public education in the United States has fallen far behind systems of education in other industrial nations (Barrett, 1990). Radical improvement of public education is the next necessary component of a comprehensive approach.

An essential reform is greatly increased teachers' salaries and changes in teacher education and certification, aimed at opening this profession up to noneducation majors. We need to attract specialists, especially in science and math, who can also teach. The current teacher education and certification process in many states precludes such specialists from entering public school classrooms until they complete often superfluous education courses (which may take more than a year at their own expense) before they can receive certification. Such obstacles combined with relatively low pay makes it unlikely that many of these professionals who have the desire and talent to teach will enter the field. We need to attract teachers who have had not only graduate education but also practical experiences in which they have developed problem-solving and problem-identifying skills that they can pass on to their students. In short, our brightest and best citizens need to be recruited into the teaching profession.

The school year should be lengthened to 230 days to accelerate learning in mathematics, the sciences, and humanities. Such an expansion from our current national average 180-day school year would make us competitive with the Japanese and Germans, who have about 240 days of school each year (Barrett, 1990). A special focus on problem-solving and problem-identification needs to be incorporated into the curriculum in all disciplines. Such skills are a premium in the global economy (Reich, 1991). An expanded school year would allow such skills to be learned in many traditional courses and in many nontraditional educational activities, such as "outward bound" experiences in wilderness areas for all children 10 years and older; paid apprenticeship programs that give young people specific role models and experiences in professions and occupations (Hamilton, 1990); tutoring and summer reading programs; and the parent-effectiveness training discussed above.

Education can also be enhanced through the use of peer counseling programs, student-tutoring programs in which more gifted students are involved in teaching other students, and the elimination of "tracking" (Oakes, 1985). Such programs and reforms are aimed at creating a cooperative educational experience in which individual success is seen to depend on group success. These educational approaches move away from the hyper-competitiveness characteristic of so many of our current educational programs and thus reduce the invidious distinctions among students which lower self-esteem for many and contribute to student alienation and marginalization.

The problem of student dropout should be ameliorated by this more cooperative approach to education. But to further enhance the attractiveness of school, an incentive-based learning system can be instituted whereby students are paid stipends to attend school and are given "bonuses" for good grades. These payments for attending and doing well in school would greatly reduce the need for students to work. This not only would create more time for students to concentrate on educational activities (which include education-ally appropriate paid apprenticeships) but would free up a number of nonskilled jobs for unemployed adults.

Schools also can become arenas in which responsible democratic participation and skills in conflict resolution are instilled. Students should be actively involved in develop-ing school policies. The obvious conflicts between interested parties over school policies is not something that school administrators should avoid. Rather, such conflict should be seen as an important resource for educating students as active participants in a democratic society. Such experiences will get students used to democratic involvement and the identi-fication and solving of problems between people. Effective, nonviolent methods of conflict resolution can be instilled through actual practice. An enhanced sense of empowerment among students will increase bonding to the school and decrease the sense of alienation and isolation that spurs marginalization. In fact, schools can become an arena for commu-nity-wide involvement. Local community groups, students, parents, teachers, and school administrators should all be involved in developing educational programs. The responsi-bility for teaching should be transferred from educational bureaucracies to classroom teachers with important input from students and parents. The current stultifying bureau-cracy in many schools can be opened up through democratic participation; parent, student, and teacher alienation from the current educational process can be overcome through enhanced participation by those who are immediately affected. Schools then become a true training ground for citizenship, not just in the abstract but through concrete, everyday activities. Students emerging from such an educational experience should be much better prepared to accept the challenges and deal with the conflicts inherent in a complex indus-trial society. They will be better prepared to become the problem solvers and problem iden-tifiers who can attract global capital to the United States.

5. National Service Program

On completion of secondary education, young people should have the opportunity to com-plete a 2-year national service program, after which educational and vocational training stipends would be awarded to those participating. Each young volunteer would be involved in developing his or her own specific service commitment, although community needs will obviously influence the choice of assignments. Military service could be another option, but one that should be assigned *only* with the participant's consent. Payment during the national service commitment should be at a subsistence level.

National service can include all types of service related to environmental improvements, poverty programs, literacy programs, health care, nursing homes, construction, day care, and so on. National service volunteers could provide needed labor for public works projects aimed at improving both our environment and infrastructure; for community development programs aimed at improving social services for the poor, children, and the elderly; and for educational programs as teachers' assistants, tutors, day care workers, and counselors' assistants. (Many of the enhanced school year activities called for in Proposal 4 can be implemented with these national service volunteers.) National service volunteers should be intimately involved in the problem-identification and problem-solving processes in all these areas, thus honing their skills through practical application.

The program should not be mandatory, but it is hoped the incentive for participation will be quite high. For completion of 2 years of national service, complete tuition, room and board should be paid for 4 years of college or for completion of vocational training. Additionally, national service volunteers should be eligible for scholarships for postgraduate work if they excel as undergraduates. Those not participating in national service would receive none of these benefits.

Such a program provides at least two important benefits. First, young people between ages of 18 and 20 would be actively participating in the community in adult roles that lead to a promising future. During these 2 years they would gain experiences in life that will help them decide on their futures and give them insights that will enhance their later education. Second, for a very low price, the community would be able to use the enormous energy of young people in activities that improve the life of the community, rebuild the infrastructure, and contribute to the educational development of their younger brothers and sisters.

6. Enhancement of Workplace Environments

Another important aspect of a comprehensive plan is the general improvement of the workplace environment for adults. Young people must know that they are eventually heading into a good quality job; otherwise, the sense of hope that the education process is trying to instill will be undermined. In addition, adults' workplace experiences have profound effects on family relations (Kohn, 1977). Coercive workplace environments create alienated workers who often duplicate these coercive relations in the home (Colvin and Pauly, 1983), thus recreating the cycle that creates marginalization (and crime) in our society.

Enhanced labor laws that emphasize workplace democracy and expanded collective bargaining are needed to create the types of noncoercive work environments for which we will be educating our young people to enter. Their experiences with democratic participation in schools should prepare them for democratically controlled workplaces. Such workplaces are necessary for the type of self-directed and creative employees that attract capital in the new global economy (Reich, 1991). In the process, democracy in the United States will become a profound everyday affair, not just an election-day exercise. The noncoercive practices of conflict resolution that take place in the schools and in workplaces on an everyday basis will become the model for conflict resolution in other daily interactions, which can only have a positive effect in reducing crime in the wider community.

7. Programs for Economic Growth and Expanded Production

Enhancement of human capital (the desired outcome of the educational process) is meaningless if production and the economy are not concurrently enhanced. Financial investments need to be publicly guided, not placed solely in the hands of a few wealthy people who may seek short-term profits at the expense of national growth and security, as they did during the 1980s (Phillips, 1990). Economic investments need to focus on sustained growth in industries that meet basic human needs and services. Investment decisions of major corporations need to be made by boards composed of owners, managers, workers, and consumers. Public funds can be used to direct production, research and development. (This has been routinely done in the military–industrial complex since World War II. Why not apply the same process in a more democratic fashion to nonmilitary production?) There are huge investments in our basic infrastructure that need to be made. Our cities are declining largely because of the lack of private investment. We have fallen behind the Germans and Japanese in basic research and industrial techniques, because we have not invested in such areas. During the 1980s, the lure of short-term profits guided investments in the United States. The types of long-term investments that do not create an immediate profit, but do create a stronger economic base that attracts global capital, have not occurred. Much can be done with a democratically planned investment strategy that creates jobs and rebuilds the basis for a vibrant economy (Harrison and Bluestone, 1988).

8. A Progressive Income Tax System

The tax system in the United States needs to be made truly progressive. The wealthy in the United States are paying far lower taxes than they did 30 years ago; and middle-class citizens, if payroll deductions for Social Security are included, are paying much more (Phillips, 1990). "Americans are not overtaxed. In 1989, we paid less in taxes as a percentage of GNP . . . than the citizens of any other industrialized country. Wealthy Americans, in particular, are not overtaxed. Their marginal income-tax rate is the lowest top tax rate in any industrialized nation" (Reich, 1991:51). Higher income taxes especially on the wealthy and on corporations, coupled with the jobs and education programs proposed earlier, would pump more money into the civilian economy for purchase of basic needs and services, and thus would increase aggregate demand. "Were the personal income tax as progressive as it was even as late as 1977, in 1989 the top tenth would have paid $93 billion more in taxes than they did. At that rate, from 1991 to 2000 they would contribute close to a trillion dollars more, even if their incomes failed to rise" (Reich, 1991:51). Revenues from such tax increases, if invested in infrastructure and human capital development, would help spur the flagging economy, attract global capital, and thus increase overall tax revenues that could then be pumped back into economic and human development. Thus we would begin to move our economy toward the "virtuous cycle" currently enjoyed in Germany and Japan. This spurring of the civilian economy through tax reform and government spending could be accelerated even further through diversion of money from military toward educational programs. The approximately $500 million a day that it cost us to project military strength to the Persian Gulf could have gone a long way toward educational programs and civilian job development, not to mention development of alternative energy sources. As evidenced by our experience in the booming 1950s and 1960s when the wealthy were paying a much greater share of taxes, a growing economy ultimately benefits both the wealthy and working classes. Such economic growth, coupled with the human development and education programs outlined above, should have an ameliorating effect on crime, because more young people would be drawn into our more viable social institutions, and far fewer of them would be left to drift in marginal, nonproductive positions.

Conclusion

The above steps are, of course, controversial. But each component of the plan is necessary if it is going to have a chance to be effective. Political leadership is the key ingredient for implementation. Public concerns about education and the future of our children have not been adequately addressed by political leaders. Growing concern about the economy coupled with these issues can provide the basis for a popular political movement that our governmental leaders cannot ignore if they expect to be elected. The issues of our children's future and the U.S. economy can provide the basis for a consensus for a new approach. What has been lacking in recent decades is any clear vision of a hopeful future that might inspire progressive political action. Generally, people are dissatisfied with present circumstances, but do not see any alternative except continued deterioration. The above proposals are an outline of a hopeful alternative that through discussion and debate can be fine tuned into a plan of action. Political leadership is required to articulate this new approach, build a consensus for it, and transform it into national policy. Whether this will occur is as yet unknown and unpredictable, but one fact is clear: the solutions to our economic and crime problems are not just technical but, more fundamentally, are also political ones.

The comprehensive program outlined above at each step prepares children for a dynamic future which they will be involved in actively planning and building. As hope for the future rises (both nationally and personally) a sense of enhanced social bonding should be created. Throughout, the focus of these "outrageous" proposals is on inducing voluntary participation through positive incentives and reinforcements, not through coercion and punishments that only increase the sense of humiliation and sever social bonds. Through these positive incentives, we can produce children who are imaginative, productive, and willing to actively participate in their community. In this environment created by the renewed socialization process, crime can be reduced as individual bonding increases and national and community ties improve. Our investment in human capital can enhance our nation's ability for economic competition and can unleash the human productive potential that has been deadened by the economic and spiritual malaise of the last 20 years (Chafe, 1991).

Discussion Questions

1. What does Colvin mean by "social reproduction"? What are "human capital" and "human development"? What does Colvin mean by the "marginalization" of youth?
2. Colvin focuses on broad measures that might reduce the crime problem, but he says little about crime itself. What theory of crime causation is implied by Colvin's

proposals to reduce crime? Would he agree or disagree with Gottfredson and Hirschi's theory (selection #4) that crime is a product of low self-control? Can the two approaches be reconciled in a single explanation of criminal behavior?

3. Do you think that Colvin's proposals for change would be accepted by the American people, given their current political mood? If so, do you think the changes would reduce crime? Look at each proposal separately and examine how it might reduce crime.

Part ***III***

Class, Gender, and Race

Chapter *7*

The Poverty of a
Classless Criminology

*John Hagan**

The concept of social class is central to several important theories of crime causation, but research has yielded such mixed results about the relationship between class and crime that some criminologists have suggested that the two are not strongly connected. This view contrasts sharply with the position of many sociologists and historians, as well as much of the general public, that class is inextricably interwoven with crime. In this article, his 1991 presidential address to the American Society of Criminology, John Hagan acknowledges the complexity of the class–crime relationship while arguing strongly that criminologists should continue to give class a central place in their theories and research.

When criminologists write of the "Myth of Social Class and Criminality" (Tittle et al., 1978) or ask "What's Class Got to Do With It?" (Jensen and Thompson, 1990), they express a skepticism about the connection of class with crime that distinguishes them from other scholars as well as laypersons. Popular discourse of earlier eras included frequent references to the "dangerous" and "criminal classes," and scholarly discourse

* The writing of this address was supported by a Killam Research Fellowship. Gwynn Nettler stimulated many of my thoughts about the topic of this address in ways that go beyond what I can formally reference. I am grateful to Fiona Kay for research and editorial assistance, and to my colleagues, A.R. Gillis and David Brownfield, for helpful comments. I alone assume responsibility for views expressed.

Source: John Hagan, "1991 Presidential Address: The Poverty of a Classless Criminology," *Criminology* 30 (February 1992), pp. 1–19. Reprinted by permission of the American Society of Criminology.

today features discussions of an "underclass," which is assumed to prominently include criminals.

The dangerous and criminal class concepts probably are heard infrequently today because they were used in such an invidious and pejorative fashion. The underclass conceptualization has the potential to be used in the same way, even though it was invented to call attention to processes of disadvantagement and subordination. Thus, new as well as old depictions of class and crime can prove problematic, and their uses demand careful scrutiny. However, the simple omission of class from the study of crime would impoverish criminology.

Conversations About Class and Crime

Riesman (1964) describes sociology as a "conversation between the classes." Although "conversations" linking class and crime predate both modern sociology and criminology, this metaphor usefully highlights the layers of meaning that are often communicated in discussions of class and crime.

Discussions of criminal or dangerous classes are traced by Silver (1967) to eighteenth- and nineteenth-century Paris and London (see also Gillis, 1989; Ignatieff, 1978; Tombs, 1980), and they were common as well in nineteenth- and twentieth-century Canada and the United States (Boritch and Hagan, 1987; Monkkonen, 1981). Daniel Defoe (1730:10–11) wrote of eighteenth-century London that "the streets of the City are now the Places of Danger," and Charles Brace (1872:29) warned nearly a century and a half later, in *The Dangerous Classes of New York,* that

> let but law lift its hand from them for a season, or let the civilizing influences of American life fail to reach them, and, if the opportunity afforded, we should see an explosion from this class which might leave the city in ashes and blood.

As Silver (1967:4) makes clear, the dangerous or criminal classes referred primarily to the unattached and unemployed, and to their associations with crime.

Historians continue to write about conceptions of the dangerous and criminal classes of earlier periods and places, while popular and scholarly discussions of contemporary affairs refer to the "underclass." Myrdal (1963) introduced discussion of the underclass to draw attention to persons driven to the economic margins of modern society. Marks (1991) has detailed the development of the concept of the urban underclass, calling particular attention to the place of crime within it.

Marks (1991) notes that Auletta (1982:49) distinguishes four distinct elements of the underclass: "hostile street and career criminals, skilled entrepreneurs of the underground economy, passive victims of government support and the severely traumatized," while Lemann (1986:41) characterizes this class in terms of "poverty, crime, poor education, dependency, and teenage out-of-wedlock childbearing." Often race also is embedded in these characterizations, leading to debate about the extent to which the U.S. underclass is a black underclass. But what is most striking in these discussions is the extent to which the modern underclass, like its historical predecessors described by Silver (1967), is defined by the association of the unattached and unemployed with crime. Marks (1991:454) asks, "Is . . . criminality the major ingredient of . . . underclass status?" Her concern is that, "the underclass has been transformed from surplus and discarded labor into an exclusive group of black urban terrorists."

Declassifying Crime

There are scientific as well as ideological reasons to be skeptical of the modern linkage between class and crime in the concept of the underclass. Gans (1990:272) argues that this new concept is itself "dangerous" because by focusing on crime and other nonnormative behaviors in discussing the underclass, "researchers tend to assume that the behavior patterns they report are caused by norm violations on the part of area residents and not by the conditions under which they are living, or the behavioral choices open to them as a result of these conditions." Gans concludes that the effect is to identify and further stigmatize a group as "the undeserving poor."

However, this criticism surely is unfounded in its association with William Julius Wilson's (1987) discussion of the underclass in *The Truly Disadvantaged*. This book focuses on concentrations of joblessness among the ghetto poor as explicit causes of crime and violence in these communities. Wilson (1991:12) is also careful to make clear that his thesis is not confined to black American ghettoes, noting that, "the concept 'underclass' or 'ghetto poor' can be theoretically applied to all racial and ethnic groups, and to different societies if the conditions specified in the theory are met." Wilson's work has stimulated important new research on urban crime and poverty (e.g., Matsueda and Heimer, 1987; Sampson, 1987), and he (1991:6) worries that "any crusade to abandon the concept of underclass, however defined, could result in premature closure of ideas just as important new studies on the inner-city ghetto, including policy-oriented studies, are being generated." Wilson (1991) interchanges the term "ghetto poor" for "underclass" in his recent writing.

Meanwhile, the scientific utility of some uses of the underclass concept is also open to question, at least for the purposes of theorizing about crime. Insofar as the conceptualization of the underclass includes within it the cultural (e.g., attitudes and values) and structural (e.g., joblessness) factors assumed to cause crime, as well as crime itself, it may be little more than a diffuse tautology. And it may indeed be this feature of some discussions of the underclass, like the dangerous and criminal class conceptualizations before it, that has engendered skepticism in criminology and limited our understanding of connections between class and crime.

From Class and Crime to Status and Delinquency

Prominent theories of criminogenesis also emphasize the harsh class circumstances experienced by the most desperate and disreputable segments of the population (see Hirschi, 1972; Matza, 1966), and they causally connect these adverse class conditions with serious crime (e.g., Cloward and Ohlin, 1960; Cohen, 1955; Colvin and Pauly, 1983; Merton, 1938; Miller, 1958; Shaw and MacKay, 1942). However, in so doing these theories separately identify class conditions and criminal behavior as distinct and independent phenomena. The correlation proposed in these theories is largely taken for granted in ethnographic research (Anderson, 1978; Hagedorn, 1988; Howell, 1973; Liebow, 1967; Monroe and Goldman, 1988; Rose, 1987; Sullivan, 1989), and it also is observed in most if not all areal studies (e.g., from Chilton [1964] to Sampson and Groves [1989]).

But the correlation of class and crime is only weakly if at all reflected in self-report analyses based on surveys of individual adolescents attending school (e.g., Tittle et al., 1978; Weis, 1987), which has led to calls for the abandonment of class analyses of crime. Since the latter self-report studies are at variance not only with lay and scholarly theories of criminogenesis, but also with ethnographic and areal research, there might seem grounds to simply reject the former method and its results as artifactual. However, doing so risks underestimating the valuable role that self-report studies have played in the advancement of criminological theory. Self-report methodology (e.g., from Nye and Short [1957] through Hindelang et al. [1981]) has facilitated systematic and extensive measurement of explanatory variables, while freeing researchers from reliance on official records of criminality; and this methodology has underwritten classic contributions to theory testing in criminology (e.g., Hirschi, 1969; Matsueda, 1982).

In such efforts, self-report survey researchers have usefully disentangled the concepts of class and crime. In doing so they implicitly have questioned the taken-for-granted nature of associations of crime and poverty in the densely descriptive ethnographic studies, as well as the mixtures of measures of poverty and crime that sometimes tautologically and ecologically have confounded areal studies. Self-report survey researchers rightly insist on independent measures of class and crime that can provide the building blocks for testing explanations of crime. Literary or statistical descriptions of crime-prone areas, the modern sociological analogues to Dickens's and Mayhew's early depictions of the dangerous and criminal classes of London, are not enough for the purposes of theory testing. In their place, self-report researchers moved into the schools of America (and later other countries) to collect extensive information on family, educational, community, and other experiences of adolescents. Three substitutions characterized this process: (1) schools replaced the streets as sites for data collection; (2) delinquency replaced crime as the behavior to be explained; and (3) parental-status origins replaced criminal actors' more immediate class conditions as presumed exogenous causes of delinquency.

In some ways, these substitutions enhanced the scientific standing of criminological research, but they also distanced self-report studies from the conditions and activities that stimulated attention to the criminal or underclass in the first place. For example, while sampling frames could more accurately be established from schools than from the streets, it was street youths who were more likely than school youths to be involved in delinquency and crime. Further, while adolescent self-reports of delinquency might be free from some kinds of mistakes and biases involved in official recordkeeping about adolescents and adults, the more common self-reported adolescent indiscretions were also less likely to be the crimes of more general concern to citizens. Parental status could be indexed (with attractive measurement properties for persons regularly employed in conventional occupations) independently of the adolescent behaviors that researchers were seeking to explain. However, the status continua underlying these measures assumed that the parents had occupations, and the measures were not actually measures of the positions of those whose behaviors were being explained. These substitutions made self-report survey research more systematic, but they also produced the unintended result that less theoretically relevant characteristics (i.e., status in place of class) were used to explain the less serious behaviors (i.e., common delinquency in place of serious crime) of less criminally involved persons (i.e., school youths rather than street youths and adults).

Reclassifying Crime

Serious attempts have been made to improve on these features of the self-report paradigm. These efforts most significantly have involved the use of parental and youth unemployment measures, which better represent class positions and conditions, instead of or in addition to the occupational statuses of parents.

Wright (1985:137) explains why this kind of reconceptualization is important when he notes that definitions of specific classes can be understood as a particular form of proposition. He writes that, "all things being equal, all units within a given class should be more like each other than like units in other classes *with respect to whatever it is that class is meant to explain*" (emphasis in original). The key to defining a class in this way is to identify relevant linking conceptual mechanisms. For example, in economics or sociology, when income is the theoretical object of explanation, educational attainment, whether as an indicator of certification or skill transmission, is an obvious linking mechanism that must be incorporated in the measurement of class.

In criminology, our theoretical objects of explanation—delinquency and crime—demand their own distinct conceptual consideration. So we need to more directly conceptualize and measure our own linking causal mechanisms. These mechanisms may involve situations of deprivation, desperation, destitution, degradation, disrepute, and related conditions. Tittle and Meier (1990:294) speak to the importance of such factors when they suggest that, "it would make more sense to measure deprivation directly than to measure SES [socioeconomic status], which is a step removed from the real variable at issue."

That is, when serious street crime is the focus of our attention, the relevant concern is with class more than status—especially as the former operates through such linking mechanisms as deprivation, destitution, and disrepute. These linking mechanisms are more directly experienced when actors themselves are, for example, hungry, unhoused, ill-educated, and unemployed, but they may also operate indirectly through parental unemployment and housing problems, for example, involving associated family disruption, neglect and abuse of children, and resulting difficulties at school. Youth and parental unemployment experiences are important exogenous sources of these kinds of direct and indirect class effects, and some survey researchers therefore have focused on these measures in self-report studies.

However, Brownfield (1986:429) reports that efforts in school surveys to identify class circumstances in terms of parental joblessness (perhaps the most promising of parental class measures) reveal that "researchers have considerable difficulty finding and studying the disreputable poor." Consider briefly the few studies that are available. By counting any spell of unemployment over three preceding years, 16% of the family heads in Hirschi's (1969) Richmond study were designated unemployed. By oversampling multiple dwelling units and depressed neighborhoods, Hagan et al. (1985) produced a Toronto sample in which 9% of the family heads were unemployed. Johnson (1980:88) also focused on parental joblessness and selected three Seattle high schools, "in order to obtain a sufficient number of underclass students," who constitute 8% of this sample. The Research Triangle Institute (see Rachal et al., 1975) oversampled ethnic communities and produced a sample in which about 7% of the youth lived in a household with an unemployed head. Finally, the Arizona Community Tolerance Study (see Brownfield, 1986:428) overrepresented rural families, 3% of which had unemployed heads, including many "miners who were temporarily laid off." These are the only self-report studies I can find that report parental joblessness as a measure of underclass position. All use samples stratified on exogenous variables intended to overrepresent jobless parents, and all still find relatively few underclass families.

The limited study of, and variance in, parental unemployment diminishes the likelihood of finding stable or substantial parental class-of-origin effects on adolescent delinquency. And there is the further and possibly more important factor that the influence of class of origin on delinquency is from a distance. For example, the class-of-origin effect is assumed to operate over as long as a three-year lag in the case of the Richmond study described above. Furthermore, the parental class effect is presumably also indirect, operating through the variety of family, school, and other mediating variables noted above. This combination of factors suggests that the impact of parental class of origin on delinquency *should* be weak. And it is therefore not surprising that this indirect class effect is elusive and uncertain in self-report research (see McCarthy and Hagan, 1991).

This shifts our attention to the potentially more immediate and direct class effects of youth unemployment on crime and delinquency. Although there are many aggregate-level studies of crime and unemployment (Chiricos, 1987), and even some attempts to disaggregate neighborhood-level effects on individuals (see Jencks and Mayer, 1990:155–62), there are again surprisingly few studies that focus on individuals. However, these individual-level studies reveal higher levels of youth unemployment than is present in the studies focused on parents; and, perhaps most important, these studies report the expected correlation between youth unemployment and involvement in delinquency and crime, even if the full nature of this correlation is only beginning to be understood.

For example, Farrington et al. (1986) report that nearly half of the sample of 411 London males followed in their panel research from ages 8 to 18 experienced some unemployment, and the youths self-reported more involvement in delinquency during the periods of their unemployment. This study (and further research reported below) allows some consideration of the timing of crime and unemployment, and as well attempts to remove concerns about spuriousness arising from joint causes. However, this study (like others) does not definitively determine the *direction* in which the causal influence between unemployment and crime flows. A problem is that the relationship between unemployment and crime may be instantaneous or simultaneous, as well as lagged. Farrington et al. consider the simultaneous occurrence of crime and unemployment during coterminous periods, making it uncertain whether crime or unemployment can be identified as coming first.

This issue is salient because there are several classic studies which show that juvenile delinquency is nonspuriously correlated with later *adult* unemployment. Perhaps the best-known study is Robins's (1966) *Deviant Children Grown Up*. This study followed a clinic-based sample of predominately low-status, "severely antisocial children" into adulthood and compared them with a "control group," who were without adolescent behavior problems and matched with the clinic sample on race, age, sex, IQ, and socioeconomic status

(SES). As adults the clinic sample experienced more frequent and longer spells of unemployment.

The Gluecks (1950, 1968) used a similar matched-group design to study white males from Boston who, because of their persistent delinquency, were committed to one of two correctional schools in Massachusetts. In their reanalysis of these data, Sampson and Laub (1990) find greater adult unemployment among the delinquent sample.

Two of the most systematic efforts to establish the direction of influence between youth unemployment and delinquency and crime are by Bachman et al. and Thornberry and Christenson. Bachman et al. (1978) analyze self-report panel data gathered through a nationally representative sampling of 87 public high schools in the United States. They ask, "Does unemployment really heighten aggression and drug use?" They conclude, "Our findings in this area are suggestive, but not definitive. In each case an alternative path of causation is possible" (p. 218). Similarly, Thornberry and Christenson (1984) use a linear-panel model to analyze unemployment and crime among 567 subjects from a 1945 Philadelphia birth cohort; they conclude that unemployment and crime mutually influence one another over the individual's life span, with no indication of which problem occurs first.

The importance of these studies is that they are unified in indicating that there is a nonspurious correlation between unemployment and crime that endures over the life course. Much important work remains to be done in establishing the direction and dynamic of this relationship, as I discuss further below. However, insofar as unemployment is a core component of class, and insofar as unemployment and crime form important causal components in the formation of life course trajectories, there can be little doubt that the relationship between class and crime is a key element in criminological research.

High Class Crimes and Misdemeanors

Thus far I have focused exclusively on delinquency and crime at the lower end of the class hierarchy. However, too much criminological theorizing and research have operated from the simplistic assumption that the relationship between class and crime is linear and monotonic, as if with each step down a class or status hierarchy, the likelihood of crime could be expected to increase along a fixed gradient. This is unlikely. Individual-level class locations are connected to crime in different ways in different settings. For example, we do not expect to find complicated securities schemes undertaken by unemployed street youths, or street muggings and robberies performed by corporate executives. However, this does not mean that the relationship between class and crime is nonexistent or unimportant, but again that our conceptualization and operationalization of class and crime must be linked to the context in which they are applied.

It is in this sense that Sutherland's rejection of the relationship between poverty and crime has often been misunderstood. Gaylord and Galliher (1988:68) note of Sutherland that

> he accepted the official criminal justice statistics as being more or less accurate in gauging the extent of criminality in the lower classes. His complaint was that the official statistics gave an appearance of the concentration of crime in the lower class only because middle- and upper-class crime systematically escaped official notice.

The challenge is to conceptualize and operationalize class and crime to capture the distinctiveness of these different class connections.

One way of doing this is to more generally focus on socially organized resource relationships in the conceptualization of class. Access to resources can determine the power relationships that are central to modern conceptions of class (e.g., Hagan, 1989; Wright, 1985). Lack of food, shelter, and employment define one extreme of class-structured power relationships, while ownership, authority, and access to money define another. Depending on the setting and purpose involved, one or another of these conditions and relationships may be most relevant. I have already discussed research on the relationship between youth unemployment and crime. There is increasingly important research at the other end of the class hierarchy as well.

For example, Stanton Wheeler and his colleagues have undertaken a series of studies that isolate and identify the ways in which corporate resources are used to perpetrate white-collar crimes. They demonstrate that individuals operating through formally organized associations and businesses perpetrate larger-scale crimes than individuals acting alone (see Wheeler and Rothman, 1982); and these crimes are further linked into the ownership and authority structures of corporate settings (Hagan and Parker, 1985). The class-specific nature of these high-class crimes is nicely captured by Wheeler and Rothman (1982:1406) when they note that the corporation and its resources are "for white-collar criminals what the gun or knife is for the common criminal—a tool to obtain money from victims." The point of such an observation, of course, is that the relationship between class and crime is class and crime specific.

Research is also emerging on the importance of access to resources among adolescents. For example, Cullen et al. (1985) have demonstrated that having access to money is correlated with delinquency. Tanner and Krahn (1991) find that part-time employment among adolescents still in school is associated with delinquency. Hagan and Kay (1990) show that male children of employer-class parents are more likely to engage in the copyright violations that involve, for example, copying audio cassettes. And Agnew (1985) shows that under specified conditions the weekly pay of employed adolescents is positively related to delinquency. These studies indicate that access to, as well as denial of, class-structured sources of power can be causally related to delinquency and crime, so that delinquency and crime are causally linked to high as well as low positions in the class structure (Hagan et al., 1985).

Class Conditions and Crime

Finally, it is important to note that class is relevant to the study of crime not only for its main effects, but also through its interaction and conditioning effects. From this perspective, class contexts set conditions and parameters within which other factors influence and are influenced by delinquency and crime (e.g., Colvin and Pauly, 1983; Hagan et al., 1985; see especially Tittle and Meier, 1990:294).

One of the most interesting examples of potential conditioning effects of class involves the linkage between juvenile delinquency and adult employment outcomes noted above. Two of the studies I mentioned, Robins (1966) and Sampson and Laub (1990), find lasting negative effects of delinquency. However, both of these studies are based on samples of subjects drawn from predominantly lower-class backgrounds. Jessor et al.'s (1991) recent panel analysis based on more representative samples of middle- and upper-class subjects involved in less serious activities finds fewer long-term effects, and no effects on occupational outcomes. This research suggests that class origins in part condition the effects of delinquency on life course trajectories.

This conditioning process could occur in several ways. On the one hand, in the middle and upper classes, the openness of the opportunity structure, processes of community absorption, and access to second chances may mitigate the effects of early involvements in delinquency (Jessor et al., 1991). On the other hand, restricted legitimate opportunities and alternative illegitimate opportunities, as well as labeling effects, may increase the salience of early involvements in delinquency in underclass settings (Hagan, 1991).

Freeman (1987, 1991) points out that contexts of low legitimate earnings can give rise to criminal activity in several ways. He cites micro-level data on inner-city youths analyzed by Viscusi (1986), which reveal a clear relationship between illegal activity and expectations of relative earnings in legal and illegal work. The rational choice implication, of course, is that those who expected higher earnings "on the street" were more likely to participate in crime than those who did not. Similarly, Freeman (1991; see also Freeman, 1987) reports that despite a booming labor market in the greater Boston area in the 1980s, the fraction of black males in the inner city who perceived higher earnings potential in crime relative to legitimate earnings rose substantially. Freeman and Holzer (1991:18) observe that this perception is consistent with the declining earnings of the less educated, and perhaps with the growing market for illicit drugs as well, leading to the conclusion that "criminal activity among young and less-educated blacks should hardly be surprising in this light."

Meanwhile, at least from the pioneering work of Schwartz and Skolnick (1964), there is evidence that contacts with the criminal justice system have especially negative effects for underclass males. Even if most underclass males who are arrested do not go to jail, the experience of arrest can have long-term, even intergenerational repercussions (Hagan and Palloni, 1990). Both Freeman (1991) and Grogger (1991) report that a criminal arrest record has detrimental consequences for labor market outcomes, with negative effects on employment as much as eight years later. Presumably, some of this is due to the reluctance of employers who check for criminal records to employ ex-offenders. However, there are other possibilities as well. Incarceration, or even prolonged processing through the criminal justice system (Feeley, 1979), can date job skills and networks of contacts for employment. As well, the attitudes and interests that signal employability to prospective employers may be chronically undermined (Hagan, 1991). Freeman (1991:18) writes that, "either way, declining labor market opportunities for the less-educated and participation in crime seem to reinforce each other for growing fractions of less-educated young males." These less-educated males are the core of the underclass.

The latter discussion acknowledges the further relevance of class to juvenile and criminal justice processing decisions. One of the classic findings of research on the policing of adolescents indicates the influence of class- and race-related demeanor on arrest decisions (Clark and Sykes, 1974; Piliavin and Briar, 1964; Smith and Visher, 1981). More direct effects of class are a part of juvenile and criminal court processing decisions when, for example, unemployment is incorporated into the legal criteria used to make bail and probation decisions (see Bernstein et al., 1977; Hagan and Bumiller, 1983). The embedment of demeanor and employment considerations in statutory guidelines makes the meaning of these effects moot for some legal purposes, but not for the theoretical purposes of understanding and explaining criminal justice operations.

Meanwhile, perhaps equally important are the ways in which these police and court experiences are perceived by citizens. Such experiences recently have been brought to public attention by graphic videotapes and audio recordings of police–citizen encounters replayed by the media. Yet, we know relatively little about the ways in which these messages about our justice system are received by the public.

However, two possibilities seem likely. One possibility is that personal as well as vicarious experiences with the justice system are a part of the process by which ghetto youths develop hostile attitudes and perhaps also behaviors that impair transitions to adult employment. Another possibility is that minorities who have escaped poverty and moved into more advantaged class locations remain uniquely sensitive to these early experiences and continuing intrusions into their lives. A quarter century ago, the star center of the Boston Celtics basketball team, Bill Russell (1966), wrote in his autobiography of the continuing harassment he had experienced in encounters with the police. A year ago, the Boston Celtics first-round draft pick, Dee Brown, received an apology from suburban Boston police for "racial implications" in his search by officers looking for a black bank robber (*New York Times,* November 4, 1990, VII, 8:1). Research confirms (Hagan and Albonetti, 1982) that black professionals more generally have an acute sensitivity to criminal injustice that is reflective of Russell's and Brown's experiences. This interaction of class with race in the perception of criminal justice is likely an important and continuing base of support for criminal justice reform in America.

Advancing Theories of Class and Crime

Some of the greatest advances of criminology over the past several decades have involved its evolution into a more systematic and precise science. These advances have demanded greater clarity and testability of our theories, and these advances have occurred through the dedicated efforts of some of our field's most practiced contributors. However, some of these efforts risk being regarded as irrelevant by other scholars, policymakers, and the general public when they are interpreted as moving from the identification of flaws in conceptualizations and operationalizations of class and crime, to the dismissal of this relationship and its significance for the study of crime.

A better starting point is to acknowledge the variety and complexity of the relationship between class and crime. We need to know more about the ways in which our ideology as well as our science influence our conceptualizations and operationalizations of class and crime. Once they are conceptualized and operationalized, we need to learn more about the ways in which class and crime relationships vary across time and place, within the life course, between historical periods, as well as across societies. But perhaps most important, we need to better understand the ways in which cultural and structural forces operate to change as well as conserve relationships between class and crime. An example may help to clarify the kinds of cultural and structural processes I have in mind.

Earlier in this essay I discussed results from Sampson and Laub's fascinating reanalysis (1990) of the Glueck's data that follow adolescents of predominately lower-class backgrounds into adulthood. Further results from this research reveal evidence of change as well as persistence in behavioral trajectories across the life course. The evidence of change is especially exciting: Former delinquents who obtained stable employment and established strong marriages were less likely to persist in adult crime. Since the Gluecks' Massachusetts sample is predominately lower class, and since several studies suggest that it is in the lower class that negative effects of delinquency on adult employment are most likely to be found (see Hagan, 1991, and above), Sampson and Laub's results are especially noteworthy. One of the most valuable features of this research is that it stimulates further questions, contributing to a new agenda of criminological research.

For example, we need to learn more about how and why many formerly delinquent youths are able to find stable adult employment and form strong marriages, often despite disadvantaged backgrounds. How are many of these youths able to develop the kinds of social and cultural capital that are necessary to establish successful adult lives? Disadvantaged class origins imply little access to the forms of social and cultural capital that seem so essential in the life course. Yet when those youths who reform, as well as those who are never involved in serious delinquency, are traced into adulthood, it becomes obvious that most youths, even from significantly disadvantaged circumstances, do succeed in adulthood. We need a theory of social and cultural capital that is sensitive to issues of class disadvantage and that can account for successful life trajectories, as well as careers in crime.

Meanwhile, we also know that contacts with the juvenile justice system are associated with the kinds of impaired employment prospects, and probably impaired marriage prospects as well, that are also associated with the persistence in crime observed in the Gluecks' Massachusetts data, as well as in Farrington's panel data from working-class London (see Hagan and Palloni, 1990). The juvenile justice system must occupy a central place in *a theory of class reproduction* that accounts for persistence in these career trajectories. Again, we need to learn more about how this process operates and accounts for persistence in crime: For example, whether it is the stigma of a police or court record, interruptions in employment and job seeking caused by police, court, and/or detention experiences, or attitudes and behaviors associated with system contacts that are most salient in determining adult outcomes.

Of course, theories of cultural capital and class reproduction will often, if not usually, be complementary. For example, police and court contacts are one way in which the cultural capital of ghetto youths is diminished, reproducing intergenerational problems of unemployment as well as crime, with attitudinal as well as behavioral ramifications. But we have much to learn about how these processes work, especially in the underclass. The advancement of our knowledge about such processes will not be enhanced by dismissing or simplifying connections between class and crime for ideological or other purposes.

Discussion Questions

1.   What is social class? How have criminologists measured class? Do some definitions of class (e.g., the underclass) actually incorporate crime? Why is it important to define class and crime independently of one another?
2.   Hagan says that researchers who have done self-report studies have collected data in schools rather than on the streets, for delinquency rather than crime, and on parental

status rather than the class conditions of the youths who are reporting their delinquent and criminal activity. What is the significance of these three substitutions for understanding the relationship between class and crime? How might researchers still use self-report questionnaires but avoid the problems that result from these substitutions?

3. What are the short-term and long-term consequences of unemployment for young people? What implications do these consequences have for national employment policies? How might the proposals made by Mark Colvin in selection #6 minimize these negative consequences?

4. What does Hagan mean when he writes about studying the impact of specific "class contexts" on crime and delinquency? Have some criminologists dismissed the influence of class on crime prematurely because of a failure to acknowledge what Hagan calls "the variety and complexity of the relationship between class and crime"?

Men and the Meaning of Violence

Anne Campbell and Steven Muncer

The relationship between gender and crime is clearer than the relationship between class and crime: For all societies for which we have data, men are more likely than women to engage in most crimes, especially violent crimes. It is less clear why this is the case. Campbell and Muncer argue that men and women differ in their interpretations of aggression. Men are more likely to regard the use of aggression, even violence, in instrumental terms, as a means to control others to get their way. Women, on the other hand, more often see aggression in expressive terms, as a breakdown of self-control. Robbery and domestic violence are used to illustrate the authors' argument.

It is men who commit 90 percent of violent crime. Violence and the male sex are virtually synonymous—the two are interwoven seamlessly in our minds as part of the natural order of things. Yet women are not devoid of the capacity for anger and aggression. As infants they cry and display temper tantrums as often as boys (Goodenough, 1931) and in adulthood they experience anger as frequently and as intensely as do men (Frost and Averill, 1982; Tavris, 1989). In this chapter we want to examine the differences between men's and women's understanding of aggression in order to focus on how men's interpretation makes them much more likely to engage in violent behaviour. The behavioural differences between the sexes, we believe, can be traced to the distinctive social representations or implicit theories that they hold about the meaning of aggression.

Source: Anne Campbell and Steven Muncer, "Men and the Meaning of Violence," in John Archer, ed., *Male Violence.* London: Routledge, 1995, pp. 332–46. Reprinted by permission of Routledge and the authors.

Male violence is marvellously heterogeneous in form. It manifests itself in acts as disparate as robbery, assault, football hooliganism, school bullying, date rape and pub brawls. Yet as diverse as these behaviours may appear to be, they share certain common features. They all serve a clear instrumental purpose—they achieve interpersonal ends. Robbery is about monetary gain but it is also about the effective use of threat as a means of interpersonal control (Katz, 1988; Lejeune, 1977). Assaults are character contests in which neither participant will back down for fear of losing face (Luckenbill, 1977). Bullying is about the achievement of social status through the humiliation of peers (Besag, 1980). Saturday afternoons provide football hooligans with a forum in which they can demonstrate courage and loyalty between the mundane weeks of stultifying work and anonymity (Marsh et al., 1978). Date rape is about the use of force to coerce compliance for purposes of sexual gratification or the exercise of power (Felson, 1993). Drunken brawls as often as not result from power struggles between customers and bar staff about who has the right to regulate behaviour in the pub (Felson et al., 1986; Marsh and Campbell, 1979). No matter how much the media plays up the idea of "senseless" or "mindless" violence, it is clear to the actors involved and to the researchers who study them that the behaviour is in fact goal-directed and functional despite its prohibited criminal status. Violence, amongst some men, serves to demonstrate their control over others and in that control resides power and so self-esteem.

Sex and the Understanding of Aggression

Violence and aggression differ principally in their outcomes. Violence results in actual bodily injury which is subject to criminal prosecution. Aggression encompasses a variety of verbal, emotional as well as physical attacks that share in common the actor's intent to hurt or control and the victim's desire to avoid these outcomes. But in terms of the motives espoused by the male actors, violence and aggression share much in common. Listen to John Allen (1978:181, 183), a convicted violent criminal explaining his position on the crime of robbery and on the intimately related issue of self-esteem:

> You know when people are going to rip you off. You know when somebody up to something. They give theirself away, the way they look or the way they act or the way they talk. The amount of money really don't make no difference: *you just can't let them get out on you.* It don't matter who you are or what you are; they'll try, and you gotta stop them. At all times you gotta stop them. . . . *You got to maintain who you are at all times. You do it for the people watching.* I remember one time in Lorton the psychiatrist asked me, 'Do you sometimes grow weary of portraying the image of a tough guy?' And I say 'Yeah, I really do.' Because you can't let your guard down. Once you start one way, people expect this of you at all times. This thing where you just had to show you had the heart, you could do it.

Now listen to the words of a Wall Street broker and a New York journalist (from Campbell, 1993), men with no history of criminal violence but with normal exposure to male conflicts, discussing what aggression means to them:

Mike: I want that guy to know I'm going to beat him and I want him to back down. I don't want to hit him. I want that guy to be the guy to say "OK we're not going to fight." *I want to maintain my self-respect.* That's the kind of person I am. . . . *I just want to get one up on him* and walk away and go "Haha."

Robert: But do you do it for the other guys? I think sometimes I'm like that. There comes a point where I don't know if I do it for me or for the acceptance. I think maybe you first start doing it for yourself and you really get pissed off and you get in there and start something. And then you realize that people are listening. And it's kind of uplifting because *you're on-stage,* you know? Everyone is going "Ooh, look at that over there." You enjoy the fact that people are watching and all. You feel good. You feel like "I have some power here. I have something over them."

These texts come from speakers with very different backgrounds. They differ in race, social class, family backgrounds and life opportunities, but as men they share a great deal when it comes to the subject of aggression. They inhabit a world beset with threat from other men. The perception of threat sets in motion a zero-sum game in which self-esteem is either won or lost. To back down from challenge means that the game is lost before it has begun, so, for these men, there is no alternative but to enter the fray. Once committed to the contest, public honour in the form of audience expectation raises the stakes above mere private self-esteem. Violence is not relished for its own sake—Mike hopes that the other guy will back down and John Allen gets tired of living up to his fearless image—but when challenged it is the only conceivable response.

Analysis of men talking about aggression suggests that they view it as an instrumental act concerned with issues of interpersonal control (Campbell and Muncer, 1987). This view is also taken by many academic accounts of aggression which can be united under the general rubric of instrumental theories. They focus upon the consequences of aggression in terms of social or material rewards accruing to the actor. The proposed rewards include coercive power (Tedeschi et al., 1974), social control (Black, 1983), normative approval (Wolfgang and Ferracuti, 1967), self-esteem (Toch, 1969), the management of identity (Felson, 1982, 1984; Athens, 1977) and a variety of other social and material reinforcers such as the acquisition of territory, money and peer approval (Bandura, 1973). Though differing in their specifics, these theories share a common concern with aggression as a personally functional and learned behaviour with a clear focus upon the interpersonal context and rewards for aggression.

In recent years instrumental theories have become so widely accepted that their assertions about the motivations for aggression seem self-evident. But by contrasting them with a very different theoretical position—expressive theories—we can see more clearly the unique properties of such a view. Expressive theories focus upon the build-up of drive, stress or arousal which is discharged through aggressive action. Theorists such as Freud (1946), Lorenz (1966), Storr (1968) and the Yale group (Dollard et al., 1939) are particularly concerned with the motivational component that energizes or potentiates the behaviour. Others have devoted more attention to the discharge mechanisms by which this drive is expressed in aggressive action. Candidates include catharsis (Freud, 1946), genetically linked deficiency in learning (Eysenck, 1964), inadequate imposition of external social control (Gottfredson and Hirschi, 1990), environmental cues (Berkowitz, 1965), failure of cognitive guidance at high levels of arousal (Zillmann, 1979) and deficient ego functions (Perls, 1969; Redl and Toch, 1986). Expressive theories share a belief in aggression as socially and personally dysfunctional and a concern with the intrapsychic rather than interpersonal dynamics of the act.

If we listen to women speaking about violence, expressive concerns feature very prominently in their talk. The following extract is from a New York woman in her mid-twenties:

Karen: We had a really terrible fight. It probably was about nothing important. *I can't remember what it was about.* But it did terminate with him going in and taking a shower and I was so furious. I just sort of whirled around and tried to pick up the phone. *I don't know if I wanted to throw it* but I knew it wasn't going to go far enough. So I picked up this frying pan that was right there and I tossed it right through the curtain. I didn't even think about it and then he came out dripping, holding the frying pan. And he said "You could have killed me. You could have killed me, do you know that?" I still didn't realize I could have killed him because I didn't feel like I wanted to kill him. I mean it wasn't even in my head at the time I was throwing it. *I could have flung it against the wall.* I did fling it at him but it wasn't that I was thinking "I am going to aim for his head or someplace else." I just threw it. I can do that. I really have a very blind kind of rage sometimes when *I seem to get really crazy.*

In this text, there is little to suggest that her aggression is about maintaining self-esteem or demonstrating control. Control features in the role of *self-control* and specifically in the consequences of its breakdown. So powerful is the impact of the erupting anger that she remembers little of what preceded the fight or of the aims of her actions. She clearly recalls the terrifying potential of her aggression—the possibility that she could have killed someone—but insists that this was not her motivation. She needed to discharge her anger and frustration and realizes that she could have achieved the same effect by throwing something at the wall. She was in the throes of a blind rage which took possession of her, making her temporarily "crazy." Whereas in instrumental accounts of aggression acts are directed at physically incapacitating the challenger, in expressive accounts they are about the discharge of anger. In the former the actor must maintain a level of control in order effectively to subdue his challenger, but in the latter the actor's behaviour is seen as out of control as if she were possessed by some demonic force.

Social Representations of Aggression

Before elaborating upon the consequences of the social representations of aggression held by men and women, we shall digress briefly to clarify the concept of "social representation." The term was coined by Moscovici (1976) in his seminal work tracing the diffusion of psychoanalytic theory into modern lay consciousness. Derived from Durkheim's (1953) "collective" and "individual" representations, the term was designed to capture the middle ground between sociology and psychology by focusing upon social representations which "are shared by many individuals and as such constitute a *social* reality which can influence *individual* behavior" (Jaspars and Fraser, 1984:104). Moscovici has been deliberately evasive in defining the term (Farr, 1987), but has perhaps come closest in this quotation:

> cognitive systems with a logic and language of their own. . . . They do not represent simply "opinions about," "images of" or "attitudes towards" but "theories" or "branches of knowledge" in their own right, for the discovery and organization of reality. . . . Systems of values, ideas and practices with a two-fold function; first, to establish an order which will enable individuals to orientate themselves in their material and social world and to master it; secondly, to enable communication to take place among members of a community by providing them with a code for social exchange and a code for naming and classifying unambiguously the various aspects of their world and their individual and group history. (Moscovici, p. xiii, in his foreword to Herzlich, 1973)

Because social representations are explanatory and interpretative devices, they appear to share some common ground with attribution theory and problem-solving. Yet they differ fundamentally; the latter are constructivist in approach whereas the former focus upon social transmission. Constructivist approaches maintain that consensus amongst persons with regard to, for example, moral judgement or causal attribution results from similar methods of problem-solving. They further assume that there are optimal solutions to such problems, that the development of problem-solving is internally generated and that the outcome of development is perfect intellectual autonomy. Development is social only to the extent that the problems to be solved may be social in nature. Such theories "assume that each individual has arrived independently at an objective understanding of the same reality" (Emler, 1987:376). Emler goes on to argue that life is simply too short for the individual discovery of many non-obvious causal connections and that the consensus that people achieve arises from the cultural dissemination of social representations. Children acquire "currently employed and acknowledged ways of thinking and talking within the social system to which (they) belong." Recent research (Campbell et al., 1992; Campbell et al., 1993; Campbell and Muncer, forthcoming) has confirmed quantitatively, using more than 450 subjects, the significant correlation between being male and showing a preference for an instrumental interpretation of aggression. The prevalence of two distinct representations of aggression associated with sex precludes the notion of 'optimal solutions' to attributional dilemmas. Each model does a good job of accounting for the facts of social life since the act of holding a given model tends to encourage selective attention to variables which confirm it (Moscovici, 1981). In addition, the relationship between sex and preference for instrumental or expressive representations suggests that either (1) the sexes have distinct problem-solving styles which independently lead men in one attributional direction and women in another, or (2) that part of gender socialization entails the acquisition of appropriate social representations of specific phenomena, including aggression. We favour this latter interpretation.

It is likely that gendered differences in social representations of aggression may be traced to contemporary structural factors and to the socialization experiences of boys and girls. Men and women differ in the mundane occupational and social roles that they hold. Men's work legitimates the controlled use of aggression (Eagly and Steffen, 1986; Eagly, 1987). In the world of business it is used as a means of encouraging competition and maintaining hierarchies of power while in the military it is actively trained and encouraged. Women occupy subordinate work positions often in professions which encourage caring and support (teaching, nursing, social work). These same qualities are also called upon in their domestic work as homemakers and mothers. In both cases the expression of aggression is strongly discouraged. For women both the nature of their work roles and their lesser power are consonant with an expressive view of aggression as a dysfunctional force to be controlled, while for men an instrumental interpretation of aggression gels with its function as a source of social influence and personal power (Bakan, 1966; Gilligan, 1982; Parsons and Bales, 1955).

Developmentally, the aggression of boys and girls is not differentially sanctioned by mothers (Maccoby, 1980; Newson and Newson, 1968). The critical differences between the sexes seem to lie in their peer-group experiences (Maccoby, 1988). Boys' peer groups are larger, more public and organized hierarchically (Archer, 1992). Language is used as a means of achieving status within the group, as is physical aggression in the early years (Maltz and Borker, 1982). Aggression is a particularly potent means of evoking a response from male peers (Fagot and Hagan, 1985; Fagot et al., 1985). In the peer group boys learn that aggression is critical in asserting interpersonal control and achieving respect, and this message is clearly reinforced on television where popular male "superheroes" employ violence as a legitimate and socially applauded means of controlling the villains. Girls, on the other hand, typically have one or two best friends, construct their friendships more privately and avoid direct confrontation as a means of settling disputes (Archer, 1992). Language is a means of establishing bonds and cementing friendship through self-disclosure rather than a combative device. Outright aggression tends to produce not censure but a lack of response (Fagot and Hagan, 1985; Lloyd and Smith, 1986). Girls learn that aggression is both ineffective as a means of interpersonal influence and a threat to the harmony of relationships.

We turn now to a consideration of the implications of gendered social representations for male and female involvement in criminal violence. There are significant variations in the sex ratio in violent crime as a function of specific offence (Kruttschnitt, 1990). Self-reported and official data indicate that robbery is the most predominantly male form of violent crime (with the exception of rape). In contrast, national surveys of spousal violence show that men and women admit to similar numbers of aggressive acts toward their spouses. How can a theory of differential social representations of aggression interpret data in each of these two areas?

Robbery

Robbery is the most frequent stranger-to-stranger crime in the United States and it is a largely male enterprise. There are between ten and fifteen male robberies for every one committed by a female (Hindelang et al., 1979; Laub and McDermott, 1985). Robbery—defined as theft employing force or the threat of force—is perhaps the prototype of instrumental violence. It is an act characterized by the absence of anger (indeed the absence of any relationship between the parties involved), where the principal goal is monetary and the secondary benefits include the symbolic humiliation of the victim and consequently a sense of power and mastery on the part of the criminal (Gabor et al., 1987; Lejeune, 1977; Luckenbill, 1981; Walsh, 1986). Such an act by its nature appeals to a masculine and instrumental understanding of aggression and is foreign to women's expressive representation of aggression. But before considering the merits of such an argument, let us first look at four alternative explanations of the sex imbalance in this crime.

Robbery requires the use or potential use of *physical strength*. Studies suggest that in adolescence ghetto youth perfect the art of yoking (grabbing an unsuspecting peer round the neck with a bent arm) as part of routine street games (Allen, 1978; Katz, 1988) and that in adulthood many robbers display a marked concern with their physical fitness and physique (Walsh, 1986). Perhaps it is merely women's lesser strength that deters them from engaging in robbery? Such a straightforward proposal, however, presupposes that the only potential victims of robbery are males. If a female robber were to restrict her 'marks' to other females she would be at no more of a physical disadvantage than would a male in a same-sex confrontation. In fact, 53 percent of victims of female robbers are male, suggesting that such women do not fear the physical disparity between them (Fortune et al., 1980; Girouard, 1988). In addition, the physical strength argument should also apply to all forms of violent crime. Yet the sex imbalance for robbery is considerably higher than for assault or domestic violence (Laub and McDermott, 1985; Straus and Gelles, 1990). Furthermore, the disparity in physical strength can easily be equalized by the use of a gun or other lethal weapon. Clearly, women are able to gain access to firearms since in domestic homicides guns are used equally by men and women (Cook, 1982).

Perhaps women lack the *motives* for robbery. Interviews with robbers unambiguously endorse the speedy acquisition of money as the chief motive for the crime. Yet in the United States it is women, not men, who form the bulk of those living below the poverty line; the sex ratio for poverty is 1.51:1. Amongst blacks, who are disproportionately represented in poverty statistics, half of all children under 18 live with their mothers only, and half of these families are below the poverty line. With child-support payments erratic or non-existent, scant day-care facilities for those who want to work and the lower average wage earned by women, surely it is women who have the greater financial motive for robbery. Yet an analysis of sex differentials in crime trends from 1930 to 1980 indicates that there has been no change for robbery in spite of the fact that the differential for other property crimes rose steadily from 7 to 32 percent over the same period (Steffensmeier and Cobb, 1981). Women, especially those in poverty, are not adverse to crime. Forty percent of female arrests are for shoplifting, forgery and fraud. But though women engage in property crime and in violent assaults, they rarely combine both in the act of robbery.

The thrill of robbery is often cited as a secondary motive for the crime (Gabor et al., 1987; Katz, 1988; Lejeune, 1977; Walsh, 1986). But we should be cautious in uncritically accepting such verbal reports by offenders. The term tends to imply a risky confrontation between equal adversaries, whereas this is rarely the case (Harlow, 1987). Fifty percent of robberies are by multiple offenders, 50 percent use weapons, one-third are committed against women and a further one-third against children under 15 or older people over 50 years of age. In addition, the offender has the clear advantage of surprise. The rhetorical presentation of robbery as "risky business" serves to perpetuate a romantic myth about the equality of the parties involved and so to offer grounds for self-congratulation on the part of the successful robber. Thrill seems to be an inadequate basis for explaining the gender imbalance in robbery.

A vital element in crime commission is *opportunity*. The majority of robberies—about 70 percent—are situational or opportunistic acts occurring without prior planning (Gabor et al., 1987; Nugent et al., 1989). The typical robbery occurs on the street after dark in the inner city. Ethnographic studies portray inner-city streets as the territory of men—there are few 'street corner' women (Anderson, 1978; Campbell, 1986; Hannerz, 1969; Liebow, 1967). Unemployed and irregularly employed men gather on the stoops to while away the long hours with beer and conversation. Playful and not-so-playful masculine banter centres on the demonstration of essential qualities such as "coolness" (autonomy and grace under pressure), "smartness" (the ability to dupe or con others) and "heart" (courage). These qualities are seen to coalesce in the crime of robbery. Robberies often occur as a result of peer pressure and a determination not to chicken out—what Fagot and Hagan (1985), in a quite different context, have eloquently termed "the tyranny of the male group." If women are simply absent from such settings, perhaps this explains their desistance from robbery. The problem with such an explanation is that women are not absent. At least one-third of victims are women, and if they are present as victims (Harlow, 1987), they must be also present as potential criminals. Even if they are excluded from the male groups in which robberies are spawned there is nothing to prevent them from conspiring in their apartments to engage in planned robberies. Yet the ratio of planned to spontaneous robberies amongst women who do rob is the same as that of men (Fortune et al., 1980; Girouard, 1988). Opportunities for crime can be created where there is a desire, but we believe women do not see robbery as an option because of their different orientation to the meaning of aggression.

A robbery has been described by Luckenbill (1981) as a four-stage process: the offender establishes co-presence with the victim, he announces the robbery and is taken seriously, he takes the goods and then makes his escape. Perhaps women's difficulty lies in their *lack of credibility* at the second stage of the process—they are unable to convince the victim that they are in earnest and that they will use force if required. Some data suggest that this may be the case. Women are more likely than men to use incapacitating force on the victim probably in an attempt to convince the victim of the seriousness of the encounter (Harlow, 1987). (There is an inverse relation between weapon use and injury in robbery for the obvious reason that the presence of a knife or gun is usually successful in subduing the victim; see Cook, 1986. Because women are less likely to carry guns, they must find other means of instilling fear.) Apparently this tactic is effective, because women and men are identical in the rate of 'success' in robbery. Though credibility may present a problem to the female robber, it is clearly not an insurmountable one.

Katz (1988:247) came close to summarizing our position when he noted, "Unless it is given sense as a way of elaborating, perhaps celebrating, distinctively male forms of action and ways of being . . . stickup has almost no appeal at all." We want to be more specific about these "male forms of action," identifying them as the embodiment of the far end of the continuum of an instrumental representation of aggression. Robbers are men who use aggression to material and social ends with such frequency that it becomes a way of life. Robbers have a higher rate of recidivism than other serious criminals; a three-year follow-up study of arrestees indicated that 44 percent of robbers were re-arrested for robbery (Cook and Nagin, 1979). Nor do they confine themselves to robbery; violent predators identified in one study had high rates of involvement in robbery, assault and drug offences (Chaiken and Chaiken, 1982). All three form part of a lifestyle characterized by exploitation and material hedonism. With respect to the former, ethnographic studies and biographies indicate a highly antagonistic and competitive view of other men. Because of this marked distrust and their aversion to being the underdog, the prevailing attitude seems to be "Get them before they get you." Because of this acute awareness of the ignominy of being conned or duped, such men take pride in their ability to humiliate others (Toch, 1969). Cutting or diluting drugs, pimping, conning and robbing are all ways of "getting over on someone." Robbery holds a particular attraction since in the critical moment of the transaction, the victim is humiliated not only into submission but also into giving up his money. The rewards are both monetary and social. By insisting at a rhetorical level that it is an even contest (despite the obvious advantages which the robber possesses, including the element of surprise and weaponry), the robber can augment his self-esteem by demonstrating his capacity to terrorize and subdue.

At the same time the financial rewards not only reinforce the act itself but also support a hedonistic lifestyle which in addition confers a particular social identity. One study found that 76 percent of robbers spend the proceeds on clothes, cars, holidays and travel (Gabor et al., 1987). Ethnographic work endorses this finding, noting the cycle of "earning and burning" in which parties, drug-taking, womanizing and shopping sprees follow robberies and necessitate further stick-ups (Allen, 1978; Williamson, 1965; Willwerth, 1974). For young men from areas of urban blight, such a lifestyle sets them apart from those around them and confirms their relative "smartness."

Such cold-blooded use of aggression is foreign to most women. For them, anger is a necessary (though far from sufficient) condition for aggression, and violence is only comprehensible in the context of at least a minimal relationship between the parties. Women may be driven to violence by frustration, jealousy or abuse, but not by poverty or a need to demonstrate material or physical superiority. The equation of money, control and social status is a masculine one, as is the use of violence as a means to these ends.

Domestic Violence

In 1975 and in 1985 two national probability samples of intact couples were interviewed about their involvement in domestic violence (Straus et al., 1980; Straus and Gelles, 1990). Approximately 16 percent of all married couples had experienced physical aggression in the year prior to the survey; 28 percent had experienced physical aggression at some point in their relationship. More controversially, 3.8 percent of women and 4.6 percent of men were the victims of severe violence. It appears that wives are as aggressive as husbands in the private domain of the home and in dating relationships (Archer and Ray, 1989; Cate et al., 1982; Marshall and Rose, 1987), although this parity does not extend to injuries sustained (Stark et al., 1979; Straus, 1989).

There has been no shortage of empirical data and theorizing about wife-beaters. The predominant explanation of their behaviour is in terms of their need to maintain power and control (Dobash and Dobash, 1979; Dutton and Strachen, 1987; Kantor and Straus, 1987; McClelland, 1975). This is consonant with an instrumental framework for male aggression generally, and indeed Fagan et al. (1983) found that males with arrests for stranger violence were the most frequent and severe wife-abusers.

Those who support a power motivation theory of wife assault offer data from a variety of measures. Structurally, wife-beating is more common where status differentials in education or occupational status place the husband in an inferior position to the wife (Coleman and Straus, 1986; Gelles, 1974). Attempts to assert or maintain control over decision-making, social relations, family finances and spouse's freedom of movement have all been identified as salient factors in wife-beating (Frieze and Browne, 1989; Frieze and McHugh, 1981; Pagelow, 1984; Walker, 1984), as well as attempts to compensate for deficits in power outside the home (Frieze and Browne, 1989). Bowker (1983) concluded that male subcultures play a role in supporting wife-beating; men who are most integrated into peer subcultures which support patriarchal dominance of the family are more severe in their domestic violence. Personality measures have endorsed a connection between wife-beating and low self-esteem (Ganley and Harris, 1978; Pagelow, 1984), jealousy (Bowker, 1983; Davidson, 1978), depression (Shields et al., 1988), need for control (Elbow, 1977) and poor verbal skills (Novaco, 1976; Rosenbaum and O'Leary, 1981), all of which offer either tangential or direct support for a power motivation theory.

Developmentally, exposure to violence as a child is a powerful precursor of adult domestic violence in men (Caesar, 1988; Fagan et al., 1983; Gelles, 1974; Hotaling and Sugarman, 1986; Pagelow, 1984; Rosenbaum and O'Leary, 1981). Boys in violent families acquire an instrumental theory of violence through modelling, vicarious and, ultimately, direct reinforcement (Bandura, 1973; Pagelow, 1984). Sonkin and Durphy (1985) note that men use violence in the home because it is effective in allowing them to win arguments and control situations. The "gratifications" described by criminologists (Bowker, 1983; Herzberger, 1983) translate simply into psychologists' reinforcers. These include the power to control the spouse's behaviour, increases in feelings of power and self-esteem, denial of dependence, and physical rewards such as access to economic resources and sexual gratification (Bowker, 1983; Browne, 1987; Frieze, 1983; Shields et al., 1988). The literature, then, is very largely in agreement that male violence in the home is an instrumental act aimed at asserting or maintaining control and that men who beat their wives are most likely to be those who in terms of marital power structure, personality, sex-role adherence or peer-group affiliation have a particular sensitivity to issues of masculine control.

Very little has been written on the causes of aggression by wives. Indeed, the primary responses to the well-replicated finding that similar percentages of women and men admit to at least one act of serious violence in the preceding year have been to question the validity of the measures (Pleck et al., 1977–78), to minimize the importance of this area of inquiry (Berk et al., 1981) or to assert that violence by wives is a defensive response to male-initiated violence (Saunders, 1986). Straus (1980) used the national survey data to estimate that at most 50 percent of acts of female domestic violence could be considered to be acts of self-defence.

If women view aggression as an expressive act involving loss of self-control (rather than attempts at control over others), then aggression is most likely when stress or frustration is high and/or when self-control is low. We believe that both these elements of the female "violence equation" are affected in marriage. "Push" forces are heightened in the domestic arena. Despite women's increased involvement in the workforce, they are frequently employed in part-time or short-term jobs as a means of augmenting the family income and work is an adjunct to rather than a replacement of their major arena of responsibility—the home. This is particularly true of mothers, who, despite increases in husbands' "helping out," remain the primary caretakers of children. Although the major focus for many women is their family and home, male dominance in domestic decision-making remains high. Added to this is the day-to-day responsibility of child-rearing, a 24-hour-a-day job usually without vacations. Self-report data and community studies indicate higher levels of stress and neurotic symptoms amongst women compared to men (Fujita et al., 1991; Gove and Tudor, 1973; Dohrenwend and Dohrenwend, 1976). Sex differences in the relation between stress and domestic aggression also lend support to an expressive aggression position (Straus and Gelles, 1990). Men's violence increases regularly as a function of stress. Women's violence remains considerably lower than men's until a high level of stress is present, when their violence shows a dramatic increase. This is in line with the assertion that women suppress their stress more effectively until some critical level is reached. Another very significant factor in stress is the behaviour of husbands. In discussing marital homicide we shall raise more fully the traumatic long-term effects of physical abuse and alcoholism by husbands.

What factors might contribute to a failure of self-control by women in the domestic arena? We believe that the critical variable may be privacy. Although we argue that women internalize behavioral restraint in the form of self-control, there is no denying the powerful additional force of public surveillance. Public aggression by women involves the potential for negative evaluation by the audience as well as the woman herself. In private this source of censure is lacking. She is still subject to her husband's evaluation of her behavior, but we believe that two factors are relevant here. First, the private nature of marriage may erode public standards of gender-appropriate behaviour. Secondly, if the message which women attempt to convey by aggression is a plea for help, then it is the husband to whom it is usually directed. If women are announcing that their daily life is intolerable, then it is the husband who has the principal power to alter it for the better. In support of this expressive interpretation of female aggression we again note that women, more than men, engage in a range of acts not all of which involve injury. Indeed, women are more likely to cry rather than hit in domestic disputes (Averill, 1982; Campbell and Muncer, 1987; Straus et al., 1980). The aim is to issue a plea for help rather than, as with men, to coerce by the use of force.

Approximately 40 percent of family homicides are committed by women. Yet a comparison of male and female spouse-killers indicates that "the motivations of women who commit marital homicide differ significantly from male homicide perpetrators" (Fagan and Browne, 1990). Wolfgang (1967) and Wilbanks (1983) both found that men who were killed by their wives were more likely to have beaten their spouses (60 percent) than were women who were killed by their husbands (5 percent). Browne (1987) compared women who killed in marital relationships with other women in abusive relationships who did not kill. The factors which differentiated the groups were those associated with the extremity of the *husbands'* behaviour. Women who killed lived with men who drank daily, used street drugs, had threatened them with murder, physically attacked them more frequently, more severely and caused more serious injuries. From an expressive aggression perspective, the salient dimension of the women's experience is the traumatic build-up of stress. The husband's ability to restrain her movement and to isolate her from social and legal assistance, combined with the constant threat and use of violence, leads to the build-up of an intolerable level of stress in which self-control snaps and lethal violence ensues.

Contrast this scenario with accounts of men who kill their wives. Several studies (Browne, 1987; Gelles, 1974; Luckenbill, 1977) suggest that male spousal homicide is the result of an escalating series of events in which the wife fails to obey orders or challenges his self-esteem or power. Katz (1988) and Zahn (1989) suggest that homicide is the culmination of a series of attempts to regain control over the wife's behaviour or affections. Men who kill can be characterized as demanding that the wife "Do what I tell you to do." Women who kill seem to be saying, "I can't take this any more." Though the result in both cases is equally tragic, these two messages are quite distinct and a predictable result of men and women's differing understanding of aggression.

Diversity in Men's Representations

In this chapter we have focused heavily on gendered, socially transmitted ways of thinking as the basis of behavioural differences between men and women in aggression and violence. But there is variation within sex in representations of aggression—not all men subscribe to an instrumental view of aggression. Social representations are cultural phenomena, not biological requirements; there is no necessary link between masculinity and instrumentality. What, then, are the social factors that might explain variation between men in their understanding of aggression?

Social representations of aggression (and indeed a variety of other social phenomena) provide the cognitive glue that holds together social structural variables on the one hand and individual action on the other. Relative *power* is perhaps the most politically visible and contentious aspect of the differences between the sexes. And power differentials are also relevant to the use of instrumental aggression amongst men. As Hannah Arendt (1970:56) notes: "Power and violence are opposites; where one rules absolutely the other is absent. Violence appears when power is in jeopardy." So instrumental approaches to aggression may be the hallmark of those men whose positions are under threat—the office bully, the dispensable middle manager, the estranged husband—rather than amongst those whose power is institutionalized and confirmed. For those who are confident of their power, the use or threat of force is a line of last resort against resistant subordinates in the workplace or the home.

Outright violence between equals as a route to interpersonal power is more likely where the means for achieving legitimate respect and recognition are absent, where the subculture itself encourages violence as a route to community esteem and where formal social control is weak (see Archer, 1994). These conditions, tied to both *social class and age,* are most likely to be met amongst teenagers, economically disadvantaged groups and criminal subcultures and in societies where the rule of law has broken down (Brownfield, 1986). Reciprocally middle-class lifestyles are likely to engender a more expressive orientation to aggression and violence. Emphasis is placed upon the demonstration of superiority through organized competition in education and professional life (David and Brannon, 1976). This socially sanctioned means of demonstrating worth and gaining respect actively debars direct aggression and violence except within the rule-governed arena of the Rugby pitch or the boxing ring. Boys who reject middle-class values of academic success and upward social mobility as "sissy" may be more likely to seek status through direct physical confrontation (Cohen, 1955; Willis, 1977, 1978).

Differences in orientation to aggression may also be tied to *social roles.* Men and women differ in their typical daily occupations, with women overrepresented in caring roles whereas men are more likely to be engaged in competitive and even confrontational daily activities like policing, the armed forces and business. Those whose daily life involves the support and nurturing of others are more likely to view aggression as destructive and self-indulgent, whereas mundane involvement in coercion and competition meshes with a more instrumental attitude. We found in a recent study (Campbell and Muncer, forthcoming) that male and female nurses held a more expressive view of aggression than did army personnel of both sexes. Men engaged in a traditionally "female" caring occupation viewed aggression very much like their women co-workers, whereas men in the army were by far the most instrumental in their view of aggression. From the viewpoint of social change, opening up new avenues of work to both sexes is likely to result in alterations in the typical gender patterns of social representations of aggression. To the extent that men assume increasing responsibility for child care, for example, we might expect a corresponding shift in their attitude towards violence compared to men who remain in the traditionally competitive and individualistic world of business.

Though power, class, age and role can be identified as potential mediators of individuals' orientation towards aggression, they are in the real world often interdependent both between and within sexes. Middle-class, middle-aged men are more likely to hold jobs in business with in-built power. Working-class boys are more likely to be unemployed and to reside in areas where the demonstration of physical prowess is accepted as a source of status. To tease out the factors that influence the way in which men view aggression is a formidable task, but, if it is true that social representations are not merely interpretive but generative, it will be a worthwhile one. If men were to relinquish the idea that aggression is a legitimate means of social coercion and a source of status, a range of social problems from schoolyard bullying and domestic violence to terrorism and international conflicts might be brought under control.

Discussion Questions

1. What is a "social representation?" What is the difference between instrumental and expressive interpretations of aggression? How do men and women differ in the social representations of aggression they hold? Why do these differences exist? Do all men share the male social representation of aggression presented here? If not, why not?

2. Why are criminals who commit robbery overwhelmingly male? What explanations of the underrepresentation of women among robbers do Campbell and Muncer consider but dismiss? Why do some women commit robbery, and why do most men not commit robbery?

3. Why was there controversy over survey results that showed that aggression by wives against their husbands was as common, or more common, than aggression by husbands against their wives? Why were efforts made to dismiss or explain away those findings? How do Campbell and Muncer explain the beating of wives by their husbands? How do they explain the beating of husbands by their wives?

4. How might Campbell and Muncer fit Gottfredson and Hirschi's theory (selection #4) of low self-control as a cause of crime into their theory of gender differences in social representations of aggression?

C h a p t e r   *9*

The Death Penalty and Gender Discrimination

Elizabeth Rapaport*

The two preceding selections look at class and gender as factors linked to the commission of crime; the next two articles focus on the ways that gender and race influence criminal justice system responses to those who break the law. Rapaport considers the idea that women are especially unlikely to be sentenced to death because of "chivalry," but rejects that notion in favor of the idea that male murderers are more likely than female ones to have committed the kinds of murder that our society finds most reprehensible. She then shows how the law supports a patriarchal tradition by treating only some types of murder as deserving of capital punishment.

It would seem, superficially at least, that if there is gender discrimination in the U.S. capital punishment regime, it favors female offenders. At most 2 percent of those executed from colonial times to the present have been female (Bedau, 1982:3). In the modern death penalty era, which begins with the Supreme Court's constitutional invalidation of then existing capital statutory schemes in 1972 and the imposition of novel constitutional requirements on the fashioning of such statutes in 1976, approximately 2 percent of those condemned have been female.[1] Only one woman has been among the 143 persons

* I would like to thank David Baldus, Philip Cook, and Alex Keyssar for helpful conversations about gender and the death penalty, and Shari Diamond for invaluable assistance in the preparation of this article. I would also like to thank Charles Dainoff and Anna Tefft for research assistance.

Source: Elizabeth Rapaport, "The Death Penalty and Gender Discrimination," *Law & Society Review* 25:2 (1991), pp. 367–82. Reprinted by permission of the Law and Society Association.

executed since executions resumed in 1977, after a decade-long moratorium during which the future of capital punishment in the United States had been in doubt (NAACP Legal Defense and Educational Fund, 1991:1). A gross comparison of the death-sentencing rates for men and women suggests that women convicted of murder are underrepresented on death row. Two percent of men but only one tenth of 1 percent of women convicted of murder are condemned to die.[2]

For a feminist to raise the issue of gender discrimination and capital punishment is not an altogether comfortable undertaking. At worst, it suggests a campaign to exterminate a few more wretched sisters. In my view, however, the issue is worth confronting. The reputed leniency that women receive with respect to death sentencing supports the view widely held in our society that women are incapable of achieving, nor are they in fact held to, the same standards of personal responsibility as are men. Although there may well be fields of endeavor in which the most profound forms of equality call for recognition of difference, equal democratic citizenship can proceed from no other premise than that of equal personal responsibility for decisions and actions.[3] The chivalry from which women supposedly benefit is too costly: In ideological coin it is supposed to be repaid with tacit recognition of the moral inferiority of females and our lack of aptitude for full citizenship. As a matter of both logic and political necessity, then, feminists must embrace either gender-neutral evenhandedness or abolitionism.

There has been very little research on the death penalty and gender discrimination, either before or after the Supreme Court mandated a new constitutional regime for the administration of capital punishment in 1976; yet the charge that women receive favorable treatment has been aired, notably by Justice Marshall in his concurring opinion in *Furman v. Georgia* (1972), in which he asks, rhetorically, how the disparity between the number of murders women commit and the number of women executed can be explained other than by discrimination in favor of women (ibid., p. 365).[4]

Does the sparseness of women on death row result from a chivalrous disinclination to mete out death to women under circumstances in which men would be consigned to this fate? Or does the apparent underrepresentation of women have an explanation other than gender discrimination in our favor? Two hypotheses, singly or in combination, would account for the gender profile of America's death rows: (1) women offenders are benefiting from gender discrimination in their favor; (2) women are represented on death row in numbers commensurate with the infrequency of female commission of those crimes our society labels sufficiently reprehensible to merit capital punishment.

In the first part of this article, I explore what the currently available information can tell us about the extent of gender discrimination in selection for death. I then offer a profile of condemned men and women in order to compare the crimes and the characteristics of male and female capital offenders. The question explored there is whether men and women are selected for the most severe sanction our society can impose for the same or different sorts of reasons. In the final part, I discuss a form of gender discrimination built into U.S. death penalty law that expresses and reinforces the subordination of women: Under modern era law, the death penalty is a possible punishment only for crimes and criminals that evoke our society's most extreme condemnation. The crimes whose prohibition we solemnize by treating as death eligible are those which, overwhelmingly, are predatory crimes committed by men against other men or against women and children not their own. The death penalty, therefore, is a dramatic symbol of the lesser dignity attached to the security and peace of the domestic sphere as compared with the realms of commerce and intercourse among nonintimates.

I. *Characteristics of Male and Female Murderers and of Offenders Selected for Death*

According to FBI Supplementary Homicide Reports (SHR) data, in the twelve years 1976–87, women made up 14.3 percent of murder and nonnegligent manslaughter suspects known to the police.[5] If women commit 14 percent of all such killings, they commit substantially fewer of those murders that are subjected to capital adjudication. The great majority of capital sentences are meted out to those who have committed felony murder, murder committed during the course of another serious felony, and other predatory murders. More than 80 percent of the death sentences in some jurisdictions that have been studied are pronounced on felony murderers; nationally the percentage exceeds 75 percent.[6] Women seldom commit felony murders. Of 20,905 persons suspected by the police of the felony murders of rape, burglary, robbery, auto theft, arson, and the catch-all category of other felony for 1976–87, only 6.2 percent were women.[7] Table 9-1 reveals the suspected involvement of women in the categories of murder most likely to yield a death sentence.[8] Of particular interest is robbery murder: 67.4 percent of the 20,905 felony murders for 1976–87 were robbery murders.

Most murders, whether committed by men or women, are not sufficiently aggravated to tempt prosecutors to pursue a death penalty.[9] An important reason why so few women are eligible for capital sentences is that women who kill are more likely than men to kill family and other intimates in anger rather than to kill for a predatory purpose. Predatory murder is committed to gain some material or other advantage, in contrast with killing that appears to be stimulated by powerful emotion. Felony and other predatory murders are committed most often against strangers and least often committed against family and other

TABLE 9-1   Categories of Murder Most Likely to Receive the Death Sentence, Male and Female Suspects, 1976-1987

		Percent Committed by	
	Number	Males	Females
Felony murder	20,905	93.8	6.2
Robbery murder	14,093	96.0	4.0
Rape murder	1,505	96.1	3.9
Stranger murder	31,506	96.1	3.9
Multiple victim murder	5,218	92.8	7.2
All murders	172,961	85.7	14.3

Source: FBI SHR data. See Author Note 5.
Note: In 25.8 percent of the cases the gender of the suspect was unknown.

TABLE 9-2   Distribution of Murder Victims by Relationship to Female and Male Murder Suspects, 1976–1987

Relationship of Victim to Suspect	Female Suspect	Male Suspect
Intimate:	65.5%	22.1%
Spouse, lover, and ex	48.9	11.8
Child	10.4	2.7
Other family	6.2	7.6
Acquaintance, friend, and other known	26.9	47.1
Stranger	5.0	20.4
Unknown	3.3	10.2
	100.0%	99.8%
Number of victims	24,786	146,175

Source: FBI SHR data. See Author Note 5.
Note: Rows are defined as follows: *Spouse, lover, and ex*-husband/wife, common-law — husband/wife, ex-husband/wife, boyfriend/girlfriend, homosexual relationship; *child*— both adult and minor children, includes stepchild; *other family*—parent, sibling, in-law, other family; *acquaintance, friend, and other known*—friend, acquaintance, neighbor, employer, employee, and other known to victim; *stranger*—not known to victim.

intimates. The victims of women killers are substantially more likely than those of men to be family members and less likely to be strangers (Table 9-2).

If men and women received evenhanded treatment, and no factor other than the broad category of the offense was causally related to sentencing outcomes, we would expect the percentage of women on death row to be about 4 percent—reflecting female participation in the most heavily sanctioned felony murders, robbery, and rape murders—or perhaps as high as 6 percent—reflecting female participation in felony murder of all kinds (see Table 9-1). We would certainly not expect the proportion of death-sentenced women to be 14 percent, to reflect the extent of female participation in murders of any and every kind. That other factors in addition to broad offense categories affect sentencing outcomes further decreases the proportion of women one would expect to find among the condemned.

The great majority of felony murderers and other categories of prime death-eligible murderers are not death sentenced. At least three additional factors legitimately influence which felony murderers and other potential capital defendants are subject to capital trials and death sentences. The "legitimacy" I speak of here is that conferred by legislative enactment and the sentencing policies embodied therein. Some aspects of these policies will be treated critically in part III. My concern here is limited to assessing the impact of current statutory sentencing schemes on the gender composition of U.S. death rows. Three factors that legitimately influence selection for death, then, are prior criminal record, offense seriousness, and degree of culpability.[10] There are indications that at least two of these factors, prior record and offense seriousness, legitimately expose more male than female murderers to capital sentencing.

A majority of death penalty states treat prior history of violence as a factor in aggravation of murder which, if not outweighed by mitigating factors, permits a jury to impose the death penalty. Such factors as a prior felony conviction, prior history of violence, and prior conviction for murder express the condemnation of a history of violence common in the capital statutes. Male murderers with prior convictions for a violent felony are substantially more likely to face trial than are female murderers with a comparable record. Twenty percent of male murderers but only 5 percent of female murderers convicted in state courts in 1986 had a prior conviction for a violent felony.[11] Thus male murderers were four times more likely to possess a disadvantageous prior history that would induce a prosecutor to seek a capital trial and a jury to impose a death sentence.

An important measure of offense seriousness as interpreted by modern death penalty statutes is the amount of violence or brutality employed by the offender. The statutes stigmatize excessive violence and attempt to measure it by asking juries to consider such factors as whether the murder was brutal, whether torture was employed, whether persons other than the victims were placed at grave risk, and whether more than one victim perished. Men are demonstrably more prone than women to commit violent crime:[12] If men are also likely to employ more violence during the commission of murder than are women, then the gap between the expected representation of men and women on death row would again narrow. Notoriously, many of the measures of excessive violence employed by the statutes lend themselves to subjective variation in the responses of juries who are asked to determine whether a murder is markedly vile, heinous, or brutal. However, the only completely objective measure of brutality, the number of victims, is also especially salient in influencing sentencing outcomes. Although multiple homicides are quite rare, they are substantially more likely to lead to death sentences than are single victim killings.[13] In the twelve-year period 1976–87, only 7.2 percent of multiple murder suspects were female,[14] again suggesting that one should not expect female death sentences to approach the 14 percent mark reflecting female involvement in murder of every category.

Finally, there is the question of the relative culpability of male and female murderers. If female perpetrators of felony murders and other predatory murders are legitimately perceived as being less culpable than similar males, women would legitimately receive fewer death sentences than male murderers. For example, if women who figure in multiple perpetrator felony murders (most robbery murders are multiple perpetrator crimes; see Block, 1985:18) are commonly mere accomplices of men, one would expect a lower rate of death sentences for female robbery murderers. Relative culpability is much in need of further study, since it is an area in which at present we have little to guide us except unexamined stereotypical thinking. Common sense would incline many observers to suppose that women are often both perceived by prosecutors and juries to be, and objectively are, mere accomplices of dominant males. Others may be drawn to the equally stereotypical if perhaps more misogynist conjecture of Otto Pollak (1950), who speculated that women criminals control unsuspecting male colleagues through surreptitious manipulation, exposing the men to the brunt of the blame in the event of legal consequences. Not even tentative conclusions can be drawn about relative culpability without further study.

In sum, although there is ample scope for further study before fully satisfactory conclusions can be reached, the explanation for much, if not all, of the apparent disparity between the proportion of murderers who are women and the proportion of women on death row is not chivalrous regard for the female sex. It is to be found in the differences between the kinds of murders men and women commit and the kinds of personal history they present to prosecutors and sentencers: Female murderers are dramatically less likely than male murderers to have committed predatory murder and to appear in the dock as habitual and exceptionally violent felons. The sparseness of women on death row reflects our society's judgments about the nature of the most reprehensible and hence most severely sanctioned crimes rather than our protectiveness of women.

The soundness of our society's grading of homicide offenses is the subject of part III. In part II, I compare men and women who are selected for death row: Are the admissions criteria for death row the same for the men and women? How like or unlike are these men and women and the crimes they have committed?

II. Profiles of Death Sentenced Women and Men

Death sentences are rare for both sexes. Only 2 percent of those convicted of murder or nonnegligent manslaughter are capitally sentenced (U.S. Bureau of Justice Statistics, 1990:9), and thus far only 3 percent of those condemned in the modern era have actually been executed.[15] Whether or not there is greater reluctance to death sentence women, a small stream of women have been death sentenced; each year has brought new female inmates to death row. The relative rareness of the capital sentencing of women creates both opportunities and impediments for the researcher. On the one hand, the small number of cases invites in-depth study of female death row. On the other hand, the inquirer must canvass a relatively long span of years and large number of states in order to gather cases for study. The small number of cases also limits the confidence one can have that the data reflect meaningful shifts or stable levels.

To learn whether women and men come to death row by similar or different routes, I compared a set of male and a set of female death row inmates—thirty-nine women sentenced between 1978 and 1987, and eighty-four men sentenced in North Carolina between June 1977 and January 1989.[16] Because the postconviction review process is so lengthy and uncertain, and because so few death-sentenced persons have actually been executed in the modern era (and only one woman, North Carolina's Velma Barfield, has been among them), I have focused on death sentences rather than executions.[17] The central question pursued is, "what leads a modern era jury to sentence a man or woman to die?"

Table 9-3 presents a comparison of the contemporary male and female death row cases with respect to three factors identified in the first part of this article as likely to lead to the capital sentencing of convicted murderers—that the murder was committed in the course of another felony, that there was more than one victim, and that the killer had a prior conviction for a felony of violence. Although the men exceed the women in each of these indications, it is only with respect to prior felony convictions that the gap between the sexes is statistically significant.

These figures do not allow us to test directly whether the women defendants sentenced to death are selected from among women murder defendants according to the same criteria as are the males who are sentenced to death. It is possible, for example, that fewer of the women sentenced to death have a history of a prior violent felony because fewer women who murder have such a history.

On one important variable, however, we can compare the characteristics of men and women sentenced to death with the pattern among murder suspects. While the SHR figures (see Table 9-2) show that 22.1 percent of the murders committed by male suspects are against intimates, only 12 percent of the males sentenced to death in North Carolina had

TABLE 9-3   Women Sentenced to Death 1978–1987 and North Carolina Men Sentenced to Death 1977–1989 Whose Cases Included the Aggravating Factors of Felony Murder, Multiple Victims, or Prior Convictions for Violent Felonies

	Women	Men	Chi-Square (1df, Corr. Cont.)[†]
Felony murder	38%	55%	2.21
Prior conviction for violent felony	3	32	6.46, $p < .05$
Multiple victims*	18	24	.19
At least 1 of the 3 factors	49	81	6.28, $< .05$
Number of offenders	39	84	

* Seven women were tried for more than one count of murder: juries heard evidence implicating women in multiple killing in an additional four cases, which in this table are treated as single-victim cases.
† Chi-Square is a statistical measure of the association between two variables, here between gender and each of the four measures of aggravating factors at the left of the table. For two measures, "prior conviction for violent felony" and "at least 1 of the 3 factors," the relationship with gender is statistically significant beyond the .05 level, meaning that the chance that there was actually no "real" relationship between gender and the factor was less than five in one hundred. In other words, the data strongly suggest that such relationships do exist and are not just due to chance factors in the selection of samples.

killed intimates; these figures suggest that murders of nonintimates by men are twice as likely to lead to the death penalty as are murders of intimates. In contrast, the percentage of intimacy murders among women on death row more equally represents the percentage of intimacy murders women committed; 65.5 percent of the female murder suspects killed intimates, and 49 percent of the women sentenced to death did so. The high percentage of intimacy murders among death-sentenced women may reflect differential treatment of male and female murders of intimates or differences in other attributes of the male and female offenders who commit murders. It may also reflect societal reaction to a particular kind of intimacy murder. Eleven of the nineteen women death sentenced for murder of an intimate in 1976–87 killed for pecuniary profit, a crime resembling paradigmatic stranger murder in motive. A full exploration of the relationship between gender, intimacy murder, and the death penalty must await further study when we have data on offender attributes and the prevalence of intimacy murder among nondeath-sentenced killers of both sexes.

III.   A Gendered Interpretation of the Conception of Offense Seriousness Embedded in Capital Punishment Law

In a series of cases beginning in 1976, the Supreme Court has placed jurisdictions wishing to impose the death penalty under constitutional obligation (1) to guide and limit the discretion of sentencers in order to avoid the arbitrariness in death sentencing that infected the system in the past and (2) to abjure the death sentence altogether for crimes that our society no longer regards as sufficiently reprehensible to merit capital punishment. The Court has interpreted both mandatory death sentencing for a particular crime and death as a penalty for a crime that does not involve a fatality as violating contemporary U.S. perceptions of the limits of retributive justice. Most states that retain the death penalty, thirty-four out of thirty-seven, have responded to the requirement that discretion be guided by enacting statutes that enumerate the aggravating factors, which, if found to be present, and if not outweighed by mitigating factors, would permit the sentencing authority to impose the death penalty (see, e.g., Fla. Stat. Ann. § 921.141(5) (1989)). Analysis reveals that three broad categories of murders are stigmatized as death eligible in the death penalty statutes of this type: (1) predatory murder, (2) murder that hinders or threatens the enforcement of law or other governmental functions, and (3) murder that evinces excessive violence or brutality.

1. A predatory murder is one that is carried out for gain or advantage. The gain sought is usually, although not always, economic;[18] it may be sexual, or it may involve some other form of domination of others; it may be revenge or the elimination of a rival. Under the felony murder rule, the full weight of the risk of a victim's death during certain predatory crimes, such as robbery and rape, is placed on the offender (see, e.g., Fla. Stat. Ann. § 921.141(5)(d) (1989)). The offender may be death sentenced even if he or she did not intend to kill the victim or if the victim is killed by a confederate. The apparent harshness of the felony murder rule reveals the depth of our distaste for predatory crime. Murdering for hire or hiring another to commit murder are also common predatory murder factors found in the statutes (see, e.g., Ariz. Rev. Stat. Ann. § 13-703(F)(4) (1989)).

2. Stigmatizing the murders of police officers, fire fighters, or correction officials are the most common of the ways in which the statutes protect the state's authority.[19] Most death penalty statutes also make killing to prevent arrest or to escape custody and killing while incarcerated aggravating factors. Killing a judge, prosecuting attorney, or witness is a common aggravating factor while a few states make killing any governmental official a potentially capital matter (see, e.g., Cal. Penal Code § 190.2(a)(11)-(13) (1990)).

3. Excessive violence is condemned in the great majority of statutes: to kill cruelly (see, e.g., La. Code Crim. Proc. Ann. art. 905.4(A)(7) (1989)), to kill more than one victim (see, e.g., Ky. Rev. Stat. Ann. § 532.025(2)(a)(6) (1989)), to endanger others in addition to taking the life of a victim (see, e.g., Ga. Code § 17-10-30(b)(3) (1982)), to have killed before (Colo. Rev. Stat. § 16-11-103(6)(a) (1986)) or resorted to violence before are all forms of excess condemned by the statutes. A number of statutes mark the use of torture, explosives, or poison as rendering a murder susceptible to a capital sentence in addition to the blanket factor of cruelty or brutality. A prior history of violence or a prior felony conviction (see, e.g., Fla. Stat. Ann. § 921.141(5)(b) (1989)) or a prior murder conviction (see, e.g., Ga. Code § 17-10-30(b)(1) (1982)) are commonly among the enumerated factors, as is creating a grave risk to more than one person (see, e.g., Fla. Stat. Ann. § 921.141(5)(c) (1989)).

If we examine the results of this analysis of the statutes with the eye of a feminist critic, we will note that special protection is not given to domestic life or relationships. The worst cases of domestic violence, unlike the worst cases of robbery violence, are not, as such, eligible for capital adjudication. Domestic crimes may nonetheless become capital cases if they are regarded as especially brutal crimes or if they are also pecuniary crimes. But the paradigmatic domestic killing, arising out of hot anger at someone who is capable, as it were by definition, of calling out painful and sudden emotion in his or her killer, is virtually the antithesis of a capital murder. Yet there are features of domestic homicides that could plausibly be regarded as among the most reprehensible crimes: They involve the betrayal of familial trust and responsibility on which not only domestic peace but presumably our civilization depends, as much it depends on honoring the law of mine and thine and respecting the authority of the state. They also have characteristics that could be read as inherent extreme brutality. The victims of family murders are typically especially vulnerable to their killers because of physical weakness and psychological dependency. Often the victims have been the objects of prior and habitual violence by their killers.

Whether or not one endorses or opposes capital punishment on moral or other grounds, and whether or not one would wish to see its domain enlarged for any purpose, there is, from a feminist point of view, an invidious subordination of the interests of women involved in the failure of the statutes to attach our society's most profound condemnation to crimes that destroy the domestic peace. These murders are also far more likely to have women and children as victims than are economic crimes. Our law reveals a disposition to regard killing a stranger for gain as more heinous than killing a spouse or child in anger. This hierarchy of opprobrium both privileges the interests of men over those of women and children and supports patriarchal values. In what follows I first elaborate a feminist critique of the hierarchy of opprobrium in the statutes. I then argue that including the worst domestic murders among the most severely stigmatized crimes, despite the apparent counterintuitiveness of such a proposal, is consistent with the doctrinal structure of our law of homicide and the policies that may be inferred to underlie it.

The kinds of crimes that are most likely to result in death sentences—felony murders and other predatory murders—are most likely to be committed by men against other men and against women and children in other men's families. Of stranger murders, 96 percent are committed by males; 80 percent of the victims in stranger murders are also male (see FBI SHR data). Women are much more likely to be victimized by family—especially current and former spouses and lovers—than are men. In 1988, 31 percent of female victims but only 5 percent of male victims were accounted for in this fashion (Federal Bureau of Investigation, 1989:13). Children, especially young children, are even more likely to be murdered at home. Child abuse fatalities have been estimated to exceed 1,000 per year (for estimates for 1986, 1987, and 1988, see Daro and Mitchel, 1989).

Although women are more likely to be victimized by intimates than men, they are also more likely to have intimates for victims. Indeed it is only in the domain of family murder that women kill nearly as many victims as do men. Nonetheless, it is in the interests of women that society treat domestic murder in its most aggravated forms as among the most heinous crimes.

Creating parity of opprobrium for the worst cases of domestic homicide—let us say by elevating serious and habitual abuse of a spouse or child to the status of a felony and including this felony among the enumerated felonies rendering a homicide eligible for capital sentencing—challenges directly the proposition that violence in the home, from which women and children suffer disproportionately, is less reprehensible than violence directed at a luckless clerk on night duty at a convenience store.[20] The supposition that predatory violence is more reprehensible than domestic violence is a symptom or effect of the ancient family privacy doctrine that has supported male domestic authority, and the parental authority of both sexes, at the price of tolerating if not encouraging a culture of domestic violence.

Despite women's high rates of domestic murder, male efforts to maintain their domination in the domestic sphere may be the most fundamental cause of the majority of spousal homicides, regardless of the sex of the perpetrator. In the majority of cases when wives kill husbands, they have been provoked by the violence of husbands (see Wolfgang's classic 1958 analysis). Husbands, on the other hand, are most likely to kill wives not because they themselves are under physical attack but out of retaliation for what they perceive to be desertion or infidelity (Barnard et al., 1982). Recent studies have also uncovered a facet of fatal child abuse murder that also underscores the breadth and causative nature of the male role in domestic violence. The presence of a man in the home has been identified as a major risk factor for a fatal outcome to child abuse. Men, often boyfriends of the mother rather than men with a legal or biological relationship to the child victim, are involved in the majority of fatality cases (Alfaro, 1988).

One piece of evidence that on the surface suggests social valuing of female victims is the finding that murderers of women are more likely to be death sentenced than murderers of men (Gross and Mauro, 1989:50). We cannot, however, infer from this finding that the higher likelihood of a death sentence reflects a societal judgment that murders of female victims are in all circumstances more serious than murders of male victims. The greater likelihood that a female victim's killer will be death sentenced reflects, at least, the opprobrium with which we regard rape murder. Even if it proves to be the case that felony murderers of other types who kill female victims are at greater risk of a death sentence than those who kill males, we can conclude nothing from such a finding about the propensity of domestic killers of females to be death sentenced. The claim I am making here is that the capital statutes do not single out domestic killing as especially reprehensible; indeed, they single out crimes generally thought of as virtually opposite or complementary in type for that designation. If, however, it should prove to be the case that all predatory stranger killing of females, not merely rape murder, puts murderers at greater risk of a death sentence, the result would be compatible with the feminist analysis advanced here: It is congruent with patriarchal values, and offensive to feminist values, that violence against women belonging to others be more heavily sanctioned than violence against your own women.

At least three counterarguments are likely to be leveled at the feminist critique of the exclusion of the worst domestic homicides from among the most severely punished crimes. A consideration of their merits reveals the essentially ideological origin of the current moral grading of homicide offenses.

1. The most plausible defense for the relative leniency of our response to domestic murder takes the following form: It is a generalization of Wolfgang's (1958) theory of victim-precipitated homicide. If acquaintances, friends, and most especially family members quarrel and a homicide ensues, we are disposed to view the victim as sharing some responsibility with his or her killer for the killing—whether or not the provocation would be considered legally sufficient to reduce the charge from murder to manslaughter. The victim is regarded as having assumed a measure of the risk of victimization simply by remaining in an intimate relationship with the killer whom he or she may have known to be disposed to violence. We assume that the victim possessed some degree of control over the circumstances of his or her victimization, which puts the homicide in a less frightening light and diminishes the degree of punishment that appears appropriate.

There is a fatal objection to this theory: It is unable to account for the lesser opprobrium ascribed to the killing of a young child. Nor can it account for the relative leniency of response to the murder of an adult who is psychologically or otherwise dependent on his or her killer, as may be the case with a battered spouse.

2. The feminist critique of capital statutes offered here could also be accused of failing to respect the theory of relative culpability inherent in our law of homicide. Our law of homicide regards the unprovoked and calculated killer, the cold-blooded killer, as more reprehensible than the hot-blooded killer. Therefore, it may be said, because family murders are paradigms of hot-blooded crime, they ought not to be dealt with as harshly as cold-blooded, predatory murder. However, it must be noted that ever since the introduction of degrees of murder, first-degree murder has included, in addition to deliberate and premeditated murder, felony murder. Conviction for felony murder does not require that the offender killed intentionally, much less with deliberation and premeditation. Felony murderers are not held capitally responsible for their actions because their crimes were cold-blooded in the sense that they were deliberate or premeditated. Our society places the full measure of the risk of a victim's death on the one who would use violence for a predatory end. Similarly, if we chose to do so, our traditional law of homicide offers no conceptual barrier to treating child abuse or spouse abuse as a felony capable of sustaining a capital sentence if a fatality results from it. To do so would be to make the moral and ideological choice to place the risk of a victim's death on someone using violence in the interests of domestic tyranny.

3. The feminist critic could also be taxed for failing to appreciate that cold-blooded killings are more apt to be subjected to the death penalty because cold-blooded killing is more susceptible to deterrence through severity of sanction than hot-blooded crime. I will not comment here on the vexing and contested question of whether the death penalty does in fact possess deterrent value. Suffice it to say that other kinds of murder now deemed capital are not obviously more or less susceptible to deterrence through severity of sanction than murder in the course of felonious domestic violence. Killing in the course of an armed robbery or killing a peace officer to avoid arrest are capital crimes that may not be either planned or coolly executed; they may be the product of panic, confusion, or lack of self-control. If such potential offenders are deterrable, deterrence presumably often takes the form of dissuading them from predatory crime rather than self-mastery in the midst of commission of felonies. By parity of reasoning, if we choose to, we could similarly attempt to deter severe family abuse by putting potential abusers on notice that society regards killing in the course of aggravated and habitual domestic abuse as among the most reprehensible forms of killing.

My purpose in offering a feminist critique of our capital punishment system is not in fact to advocate capital punishment for domestic murder. Nor would I wish to endorse the view that criminal law is the best, or the only, or an adequate, tool for dealing with all facets of the problem of domestic violence. My purpose rather is to expose the ideological biases of the status quo in which domestic homicide is treated, invidiously, as almost always less reprehensible than predatory murder. The logic of the argument suggests that egregious cases of domestic murder should be among the most severely condemned crimes and therefore eligible for the heaviest sanctions, whatever these may be. Such an allocation of penalties would use the law of homicide in the inculcation of new social values and the concomitant guiding of conduct.

It may well be that the underevaluation of the heinousness of domestic murder is the most serious form of gender discrimination to be discovered in our capital punishment system. In the present state of our knowledge, I have tried to show, we have no credible evidence that women are spared the death penalty in circumstances where it would be pronounced on men. The gender composition of death row rather appears to reflect differences between the kinds of homicides men and women commit. Additionally, there is some evidence that the admissions standards for death row may be somewhat different for the two sexes. Although women are indeed sent to death row for crimes that lead men to the same fate, a strikingly high percentage of the women on death row, unlike the men, killed family or intimates. The question of the death penalty and gender discrimination, then, appears to be fundamentally a question of social ideology. Women are doubly disserved by the current climate of belief and policy. First, women are disserved by the misleading or false belief that we are spared the most extreme criminal sanction because of our sex. Second, the criminal law is not being mobilized to sufficiently discredit, discourage, and sanction crimes of domestic oppression from which women and children suffer disproportionately.

Author's Notes

1. See Strieb (1991:2), who makes an informed estimate based on review and collation of the sources of information available. See also Strieb, 1990.
2. U.S. Bureau of Justice Statistics (1990:9), reporting findings of a survey of state prison inmates in 1986.
3. There has been considerable debate among feminist legal theorists as to whether women ought to seek formal equality with men or to urge what is often called special treatment, i.e., legal rights recognizing pertinent gender differences, such as employee leave for pregnant women. The position I take on gender and the death penalty resembles the position taken by Williams (1982) in that I maintain that acceptance of special treatment would be purchased at the price of leaving damaging stereotyping practices intact. I agree with Williams on issues that implicate women's status as full-fledged citizens, with the moral and political capacities thereof, e.g., laws protecting minor females but not minor males under statutory rape laws, or the blanket female exemption from the military draft; but the recognition of biological and social-functional realities supports, I think, a different treatment stand on some issues. See Littleton (1987) and Minow (1987). If gender-neutral equality is the goal of criminal law reform, this ought not to be misconstrued to mean endorsing legal regimes that promote a spurious equality at the expense of genuine gender neutrality. E.g., the law of self-defense, which typically imposes on female defendants some requirements that can only reasonably be expected of males, is not gender neutral (see Gillespie, 1989). Nor, as I argue in part III below, is the law of capital punishment gender neutral as it currently exists.

4. Sellin (1980:66–68) concluded that women received favorable treatment in his study of the pre-*Furman* death penalty system. However, two researchers who to determine whether racial bias was present studied the post-*Furman* system found no evidence of gender bias in the cases they examined. In a study of 604 defendants arrested for homicide in North Carolina 1977–78, 18.7 percent of whom were women, Nakell and Hardy (1987:93, 139–40) found no significant differences between the sexes in the likelihood of being tried or sentenced for first-degree murder or of receiving a life or death sentence. Baldus, Woodworth, and Pulaski (1985:1385; 1990:494) found that gender did not have a statistically significant impact on sentencing outcomes in their study of the operation of the death penalty in Georgia 1979–81, although they do report a weak correlation between being a female defendant and a non-death penalty sentencing outcome. They studied 607 cases of persons convicted of murder, 10 percent of whom were women. These results must be received with caution because the number of women in each study was small.

5. Supplementary Homicide Reports (SHR) are compiled by the FBI's Uniform Crime Reporting

(URC) section from information filed by local law enforcement agencies. I would like to thank James Alan Fox of the National Crime Analysis Program at Northeastern University for supplying me with the FBI SHR data on which the murder statistics in this article are based. SHR statistics reflect both murder and nonnegligent manslaughter, defined by the FBI URC as "willful nonnegligent killing." In my discussion of the import of SHR data, I use the term "murder" expansively to include all willful nonnegligent killing, including nonnegligent manslaughter.

6. Gross and Mauro (1989:45) found that in 1976–80 over 80 percent of the death penalties in Florida and Georgia were in felony murder cases, as were 75 percent in Illinois. Ekland-Olson (1988:859) reports that in 1974–83 in Texas, 72 percent of death sentences involved cases of robbery, burglary, or sexual assault. According to the NAACP Legal Defense and Educational Fund, which monitors America's death rows, in 1986 more than 75 percent of death row cases involved felony murder. See Baldus, Pulaski, and Woodworth, 1986:139.

7. These SHR data, it must be said, are relevant to the inquiry only if police suspicions reflect the underlying distribution of murders by men and women.

8. Gross and Mauro (1989:45–50) found that commission of murder during the course of another felony, stranger victim, and multiple victims were the three factors most likely to lead to a death sentence.

9. Nakell and Hardy (1987:136), e.g., report that in a year period in 1977–78 in the middle-sized death penalty state of North Carolina, in most judicial districts between 5 and 15 percent of all homicide cases went to trial as first-degree murder cases, thus having the potential for capital sentencing.

10. Thirty-four of the thirty-seven death penalty states have enacted statutes that stipulate the factors in aggravation, which, in the absence of overbalancing factors in mitigation, permit sentencers to impose the death penalty. See *Cornell Law Review* 1984, which tallies the number of instances of each type of aggravating factor in the statutes of states that have the aggravating factor format. Since the publication of this catalog, Massachusetts has abandoned the death penalty and Ver-

mont has adopted a statute of the same type; there have also been a number of statutory emendations. See Rapaport (1990) for a detailed analysis of the statutory categories and survey of developments since the *Cornell Law Review* article appeared. Texas, Utah, and Virginia have distinctive statutory schemes that narrow the class of murders eligible for death sentencing through other statutory devices. See Blumstein et al. (1983:69–125) for a review of the literature on determinants of sentences.

11. These results were arrived at by analyzing data collected by the U.S. Department of Justice, which surveyed felons convicted in state courts in 1986. Unlike in the discussion of FBI SHR data above, "murderer" is used here more strictly and hence excludes persons convicted of nonnegligent manslaughter. The data were obtained through the Inter-University Consortium for Political and Social Research. I would like to thank Dr. Bruce Burchett of the Duke University Center for the Study of Aging and Human Development for assistance in analyzing the survey tapes. For the published results of the Bureau of Justice Statistics survey of felons convicted in state courts in 1986, see U.S. Bureau of Justice Statistics (1990).

12. According to FBI Uniform Crime Report (URC) data, e.g., in 1983 males accounted for 89 percent of arrestees for the violent crimes of homicide, rape, robbery, and assault. See U.S. Bureau of Justice Statistics (1988:41).

13. See Gross and Mauro (1989:48–50), who found that killing more than one victim was one of the factors mostly likely to lead to a death sentence in their study of Florida, Georgia, and Illinois in 1976–80.

14. FBI SHR data. See note 5 *supra.*

15. U.S. Bureau of Justice Statistics (1989:8). Almost 40 percent of those death sentenced in 1977–88 have left death row without suffering execution, a few because of death by other causes or commutation, the great majority as the result of appellate court action.

16. Note that North Carolina gave more than two times the number of death sentences to men during June 1977–January 1989 than the entire country gave to women in the ten years of 1978–89. In the typical study of sentencing discrimination, the researcher examines the probability of a particular

outcome, e.g., death sentences for black versus white defendants. The difficulty confronting research on gender discrimination and the death penalty is that the number of death-sentenced women is minuscule for any jurisdiction and in fact tiny for the nation as a whole. As a result, I have focused here on offenders selected for death in order to determine what characterizes the few women who are sent to death row.

17. Thus far, 53.9 percent of these women and 47.6 percent of the men have had sentencing relief for numerous reasons spanning appellate rulings that their sentences were excessive to procedural grounds that did not address the appropriateness of a death sentence in their cases.

18. Thirty-three of the thirty-four state statutes that enumerate aggravating factors include murder for pecuniary gain among the factors.

19. The majority of statutes of this type have this provision. See, e.g., Ga. Code § 17–10–30(b)(8) (1982).

20. Although no statute offers its protection to victims of spousal murder, two states (Mississippi and Utah) have recently amended their statutes to include felony child abuse among the felony circumstances that render a homicide eligible for capital sentencing. Five states (Arizona, Illinois, Louisiana, South Carolina, and Tennessee) treat the murder of a child as an aggravating factor. Delaware treats murder of any defenseless person as a factor in aggravation. Seven states, including both capital punishment and noncapital punishment states, have elevated child abuse homicide to first-degree murder. See Repella (1989:2).

Discussion Questions

1. What is meant by the "chivalrous" treatment of women accused of murder? What evidence is there that this accounts for the relatively low proportion of women on death row? What factors does Rapaport find best explain the disproportionately low percentage of women sentenced to death for murder?

2. How do men and women sentenced to death differ in terms of the kinds of murder they have committed, prior convictions for violent felonies, and the killing of multiple victims? Do these differences account for the disproportionately low percentage of female murderers who are sentenced to death?

3. How do the kinds of murders that are and are not subject to capital punishment reflect a patriarchal tradition of male dominance in both domestic and nondomestic contexts? Why are predatory murders more likely than domestic murders to lead to capital punishment?

4. If the law were changed to treat as a capital crime the murder of a spouse or a child by an adult with a prior conviction for a domestic violence felony, what would be the effect on the number of people sentenced to death? What impact would such a change have on the proportion of men and women sentenced to death?

C h a p t e r **10**

Racial Politics, Racial Disparities, and the War on Crime*

Michael Tonry

In this selection, Tonry demonstrates that measures enacted since 1980 to "get tough on crime," especially drug offenses, have fallen much more harshly on blacks than on whites. He presents evidence that scholars agreed, even before these more severe penalties were implemented, that such measures would not reduce crime. As did Rapaport with gender in selection #9, Tonry here shows how race influences the response of the criminal justice system to crime.

Racial disparities in arrests, jailing, and imprisonment steadily worsened after 1980 for reasons that have little to do with changes in crime patterns and almost everything to do with two political developments. First, conservative Republicans in national elections "played the race card" by using anticrime slogans (remember Willie Horton?) as a way to appeal to anti-Black sentiments of White voters. Second, conservative politicians of both parties promoted and voted for harsh crime control and drug policies that exacerbated existing racial disparities.

The worsened disparities might have been ethically defensible if they had been based on good faith beliefs that some greater policy good would thereby have been achieved. Sometimes unwanted side effects of social policy are inevitable. Traffic accidents and

---

* This article draws on Tonry's *Malign Neglect: Race, Crime, and Punishment in America* (1994).

Source: Michael Tonry, *Crime & Delinquency* (Vol. 40, No. 4), pp. 475–92, copyright © 1994 by Sage Publications, Inc. Reprinted by permission of Sage Publications, Inc.

fatalities are a price we pay for the convenience of automobiles. Occupational injuries are a price we pay for engaging in the industries in which they occur.

The principal causes of worse racial disparities have been the War on Drugs launched by the Bush and Reagan administrations, characterized by vast increases in arrests and imprisonment of street-level drug dealers, and the continuing movement toward harsher penalties. Policies toward drug offenders are a primary cause of recent increases in jail and prison admissions and populations. Racial disparities among drug offenders are worse than among other offenders.

It should go without saying in the late 20th century that governments detest racial injustice and desire racial justice, and that racial disparities are tolerable only if they are unavoidable or are outweighed by even more important social gains. There are no offsetting gains that can justify the harms done to Black Americans by recent drug and crime control policies.

This article presents data on racial trends in arrests, jailing, and imprisonment; examines the rationales for the policies that have produced those trends; and considers whether the adoption of policies known to have disparate adverse effects on Blacks can be ethically justified. First, the evidence concerning the effectiveness of recent drug and crime control policies that have exacerbated racial disparities is examined. Next, data on arrests, jail, and imprisonment trends are presented and demonstrate that racial disparities have worsened, but not because Blacks are committing larger proportions of the serious offenses (homicide, rape, robbery, aggravated assault) for which offenders were traditionally sent to prison. Finally, the reasons why recent policies were adopted and whether they can be ethically justified are considered.

Crime Reduction Effects of Crime Control Policy

There is no basis for a claim that recent harsh crime control policies or the enforcement strategies of the War on Drugs were based on good faith beliefs that they would achieve their ostensible purposes. In this and other countries, practitioners and scholars have long known that manipulation of penalties has few, if any, effects on crime rates.

Commissions and expert advisory bodies have been commissioned by the federal government repeatedly over the last 30 years to survey knowledge of the effects of crime control policies, and consistently they have concluded that there is little reason to believe that harsher penalties significantly enhance public safety. In 1967, the President's Commission on Law Enforcement and Administration of Justice observed that crime control efforts can have little effect on crime rates without much larger efforts being directed at crime's underlying social and economic causes. "The Commission . . . has no doubt whatever that the most significant action that can be taken against crime is action designed to eliminate slums and ghettos, to improve education, to provide jobs. . . . We shall not have dealt effectively with crime until we have alleviated the conditions that stimulate it."

In 1978, the National Academy of Sciences Panel on Research on Deterrent and Incapacitative Effects, funded by President Ford's department of justice and asked to examine the available evidence on the crime-reductive effects of sanctions, concluded: "In summary, we cannot assert that the evidence warrants an affirmative conclusion regarding deterrence" (Blumstein, Cohen, and Nagin, 1978). Fifteen years later, the National Academy of Sciences Panel on the Understanding and Control of Violent Behavior, created and paid for with funds from the Reagan and Bush administration departments of justice, surveyed knowledge of the effects of harsher penalties on violent crime (Reiss and Roth, 1993). A rhetorical question and answer in the panel's final report says it all: "What effect has increasing the prison population had on violent crime? Apparently very little. . . . If tripling the average length of sentence of incarceration per crime [between 1976 and 1989] had a strong preventive effect," reasoned the panel, "then violent crime rates should have declined" (p. 7). They had not.

I mention that the two National Academy of Sciences panels were created and supported by national Republican administrations to demonstrate that skepticism about the crime-preventive effects of harsher punishments is not a fantasy of liberal Democrats. Anyone who has spent much time talking with judges or corrections officials knows that most, whatever their political affiliations, do not believe that harsher penalties significantly enhance public safety.

Likewise, outside the United States, conservative governments in other English-speaking countries have repudiated claims that harsher penalties significantly improve public safety. In Margaret Thatcher's England, for example, a 1990 White Paper (an official policy statement of the government), based on a 3-year study, expressed its skepticism about the preventive effects of sanctions:

> Deterrence is a principle with much immediate appeal. . . . But much crime is committed on impulse, given the opportunity presented by an open window or an unlocked door, and it is committed by offenders who live from moment to moment; their crimes are as impulsive as the rest of their feckless, sad, or pathetic lives. It is unrealistic to construct sentencing arrangements on the assumption that most offenders will weigh up the possibilities in advance and base their conduct on rational calculation. (Home Office, 1990)

Canada is the other English-speaking country that has recently had a conservative government. In Brian Mulroney's Canada, the Committee on Justice and the Solicitor General (in American terms, the judiciary committee) proposed in 1993 that Canada shift from an American-style crime control system to a European-style preventive approach. In arguing for the shift in emphasis, the committee observed that "the United States affords a glaring example of the limited effect that criminal justice responses may have on crime. . . . If locking up those who violate the law contributed to safer societies then the United States should be the safest country in the world" (Standing Committee on Justice and the Solicitor General, 1993). Six years earlier, the Canadian Sentencing Commission (1987) had reached similar conclusions: "Deterrence cannot be used, with empirical justification, to guide the imposition of sanctions."

There is no better evidentiary base to justify recent drug control policies. Because no other western country has adopted drug policies as harsh as those of the United States, a bit of background may be useful before I show why there was no reasonable basis for believing recent policies would achieve their ostensible goals. In drug policy jargon, the United States has adopted a prohibitionistic rather than a harm-reduction strategy and has emphasized supply-side over demand-side tactics (Wilson, 1990). This strategic choice implies a preference for legal threats and moral denunciation of drug use and users instead of a preference for minimizing net costs and social harms to the general public, the law enforcement system, and drug users. The tactical choice is between a law enforcement emphasis on arrest and punishment of dealers, distributors, and importers, interdiction, and source-country programs or a prevention emphasis on drug treatment, drug-abuse education in schools, and mass media programs aimed at public education. The supply-side bias in recent American policies was exemplified throughout the Bush administration by its insistence that 70% of federal antidrug funds be devoted to law enforcement and only 30% to treatment and education (Office of National Drug Control Policy, 1990).

It has been a long time since most researchers and practitioners believed that current knowledge justifies recent American drug control policies. Because the potential income from drug dealing means that willing aspirants are nearly always available to replace arrested street-level dealers, large-scale arrests have repeatedly been shown to have little or no effect on the volume of drug trafficking or on the retail prices of drugs (e.g., Chaiken, 1988; Sviridoff, Sadd, Curtis, and Grinc, 1992). Because the United States has long and porous borders, and because an unachievably large proportion of attempted smuggling would have to be stopped to affect drug prices significantly, interdiction has repeatedly been shown to have little or no effect on volume or prices (Reuter, 1988). Because cocaine, heroin, and marijuana can be grown in many parts of the world in which government controls are weak and peasant farmers' incentives are strong, source-country programs have seldom been shown to have significant influence on drug availability or price in the United States (Moore, 1990).

The evidence in support of demand-side strategies is far stronger. In December 1993, the President's Commission on Model State Drug Laws, appointed by President Bush, categorically concluded, "Treatment works." That conclusion is echoed by more authoritative surveys of drug treatment evaluations by the U.S. General Accounting Office (1990), the National Institute of Medicine (Gerstein and Jarwood, 1990), and in *Crime and Justice* by Anglin and Hser (1990). Because drug use and offending tend to coincide in the lives of drug-using offenders, the most effective and cost-effective way to deal with such offenders is to get and keep them in well-run treatment programs.

A sizable literature now also documents the effectiveness of school-based drug education in reducing drug experimentation and use among young people (e.g., Botvin, 1990; Ellickson and Bell, 1990). Although there is no credible literature that documents the effects of mass media campaigns on drug use, a judge could take judicial notice of their ubiquity. It is not unreasonable to believe that such campaigns have influenced across-the-board declines in drug use in the United States since 1980 (a date, incidentally, that precedes the launch of the War on Drugs by nearly 8 years).

That the preceding summary of our knowledge of the effectiveness of drug control methods is balanced and accurate is shown by the support it receives from leading conservative scholars. Senator–scholar Daniel Patrick Moynihan (1993) has written, "Interdiction and 'drug busts' are probably necessary symbolic acts, but nothing more." James Q. Wilson (1990), for two decades America's leading conservative crime control scholar, observed that "significant reductions in drug abuse will come only from reducing demand for those drugs. . . . The marginal product of further investment in supply reduction is likely to be small" (p. 534). He reports that "I know of no serious law-enforcement official who disagrees with this conclusion. Typically, police officials tell interviewers that they are fighting either a losing war or, at best, a holding action" (p. 534).

Thus a fair-minded survey of existing knowledge provides no grounds for believing that the War on Drugs or the harsh policies exemplified by "three strikes and you're out" laws and evidenced by a tripling in America's prison population since 1980 could achieve their ostensible purposes. If such policies cannot be explained in instrumental terms, how can they be explained? The last section answers that question, but first a summary of recent data on racial trends in arrests, jailing, and incarceration.

Racial Disparities in Arrests, Jail, and Prison

Racial disparities, especially affecting Blacks, have long bedeviled the criminal justice system. Many hundreds of studies of disparities have been conducted and there is now widespread agreement among researchers about causes. Racial bias and stereotyping no doubt play some role, but they are not the major cause. In the longer term, disparities in jail and prison are mainly the result of racial differences in offending patterns. In the shorter term, the worsening disparities since 1980 are not primarily the result of racial differences in offending but were foreseeable effects of the War on Drugs and the movement toward increased use of incarceration. These patterns can best be seen by approaching the recent increases in racial disparities in imprisonment as a mystery to be solved. (Because of space limitations, jail data are not discussed here at length, but the trends parallel those for prisons. Between 1980 and 1991, e.g., the percentage of jail inmates who were Black increased from 40% to 48%.)

Figure 10-1, showing the percentages of prison inmates who were Black or White from 1960 to 1991, reveals two trends. First, for as long as prison population data have been compiled, the percentage of inmates who are Black has by several times exceeded the percentage of Americans who are Black (10% to 13% during the relevant period). Second, since 1980 the Black percentage among prisoners has increased sharply.

Racial disproportions among prison inmates are inherently undesirable, and considerable energy has been expended on efforts to understand them. In 1982, Blumstein showed that around 80% of the disproportion could be explained on the basis of racial differences in arrest patterns. Of the unexplained 20%, Blumstein argued, some might represent bias and some might reflect racial differences in criminal history or arguably valid case-processing differences. Some years earlier, Hindelang (1976, 1978) had demonstrated that racial patterns in victims' identifications of their assailants closely resembled racial differences in arrests. Some years later, Langan (1985) skipped over the arrest stage altogether and showed that racial patterns in victims' identifications of their assailants explained about 80% of disparities in prison admissions. In 1990, Klein, Petersilia, and Turner showed that, after criminal history and other legitimate differences between cases were taken into account, the offender's race had no independent predictive effect in California on whether he was sent to prison or for how long. There the matter rests. Blumstein (1993b) updated his analysis and reached similar conclusions (with one important exception that is discussed below).

Although racial crime patterns explain a large part of racial imprisonment patterns, they do not explain why the Black percentage rose so rapidly after 1980. Table 10-1 shows Black and White percentages among people arrested for the eight serious FBI Index

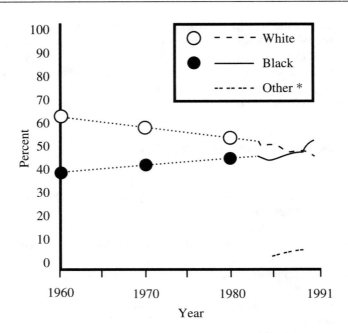

FIGURE 10-1.   Prisoners in State and Federal Prisons on Census Date by Race, 1960–1991

Sources: For 1960, 1970, 1980: Cahalan, 1986, table 3.31; for 1985–1991: Bureau of Justice Statistics, 1993, 1991a, 1991b, 1989a, 1989b, 1987.
* = Hispanics in many states, Asians, Native Americans.

Crimes at 3-year intervals from 1976 to 1991 and for 1992. Within narrow bands of fluctuation, racial arrest percentages have been stable since 1976. Comparing 1976 with 1992, for example, Black percentages among people arrested for murder, robbery, and burglary were slightly up and Black percentages among those arrested for rape, aggravated assault, and theft were slightly down. Overall, the percentage among those arrested for violent crimes who were Black fell from 47.5% to 44.8%. Because prison sentences have traditionally been imposed on people convicted of violent crimes, Blumstein's and the other analyses suggest that the Black percentage among inmates should be flat or declining. That, however, is not what Figure 10-1 shows. Why not?

Part of the answer can be found in prison admissions. Figure 10-2 shows racial percentages among prison admissions from 1960 to 1992. Arrests of Blacks for violent crimes may not have increased since 1980, but the percentage of Blacks among those sent to prison has increased starkly, reaching 54% in 1991 and 1992. Why? The main explanation concerns the War on Drugs.

Table 10-2 shows racial percentages among persons arrested for drug crimes between 1976 and 1992. Blacks today make up about 13% of the U.S. population and, according to National Institute on Drug Abuse (1991) surveys of Americans' drug use, are no more likely than Whites ever to have used most drugs of abuse. Nonetheless, the percentages of

TABLE 10-1 Percentage Black and White Arrests for Index I Offenses 1976-1991 (3-year Intervals)*

	1976		1979		1982		1985		1988		1991		1992	
	White	Black	White	Black	White	Black	White	Black	White	Black	White	Black	White	Black
Murder and nonnegligent manslaughter	45.0	53.5	49.4	47.7	48.8	49.7	50.1	48.4	45.0	53.5	43.4	54.8	43.5	55.1
Forcible rape	51.2	46.6	50.2	47.7	48.7	49.7	52.2	46.5	52.7	45.8	54.8	43.5	55.5	42.8
Robbery	38.9	59.2	41.0	56.9	38.2	60.7	37.4	61.7	36.3	62.6	37.6	61.1	37.7	60.9
Aggravated Assault	56.8	41.0	60.9	37.0	59.8	38.8	58.0	40.4	57.6	40.7	60.0	38.3	59.5	38.8
Burglary	69.0	29.2	69.5	28.7	67.0	31.7	69.7	28.9	67.0	31.3	68.8	29.3	67.8	30.4
Larceny-theft	65.7	32.1	67.2	30.2	64.7	33.4	67.2	30.6	65.6	32.2	66.6	30.9	66.2	31.4
Motor vehicle theft	71.1	26.2	70.0	27.2	66.9	31.4	65.8	32.4	58.7	39.5	58.5	39.3	58.4	39.4
Arson	—	—	78.9	19.2	74.0	24.7	75.7	22.8	73.5	25.0	76.7	21.5	76.4	21.9
Violent crime†	50.4	47.5	53.7	44.1	51.9	46.7	51.5	47.1	51.7	46.8	53.6	44.8	53.6	44.8
Property crime§	67.0	30.9	68.2	29.4	65.5	32.7	67.7	30.3	65.3	32.6	66.4	31.3	65.8	31.8
Total crime index	64.1	33.8	65.3	32.4	62.7	35.6	64.5	33.7	62.4	35.7	63.2	34.6	62.7	35.2

Sources: Sourcebook of Criminal Justice Statistics. Various years. Washington DC: Department of Justice, Bureau of Justice Statistics; FBI 1993, Table 43.
* Because of rounding, the percentages may not add to total.
† Violent crimes are offenses of murder, forcible rape, robbery, and aggravated assault.
§ Property crimes are offenses of burglary, larceny-theft, motor vehicle theft, and arson.

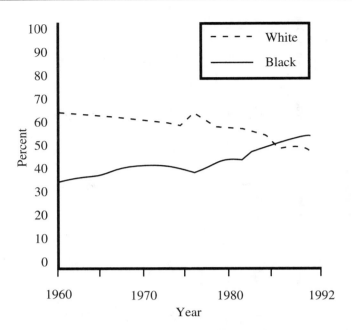

FIGURE 10-2.   Admissions to Federal and State Prisons by Race, 1960–1992

Sources: Langan, 1991; Gilliard, 1992; Perkins, 1992, 1993; Perkins and Gilliard, 1992.
Note: Hispanics are included in Black and White populations.

Blacks among drug arrestees were in the low 20% range in the late 1970s, climbing to around 30% in the early 1980s and peaking at 42% in 1989. The number of drug arrests of Blacks more than doubled between 1985 and 1989, whereas White drug arrests increased only by 27%. Figure 10-3 shows the stark differences in drug arrest trends by race from 1976 to 1991.

Drug control policies are a major cause of worsening racial disparities in prison. In the federal prisons, for example, 22% of new admissions and 25% of the resident population were drug offenders in 1980. By 1990, 42% of new admissions were drug offenders as in 1992 were 58% of the resident population. In state prisons, 5.7% of inmates in 1979 were drug offenders, a figure that by 1991 had climbed to 21.3% to become the single largest category of prisoners (robbers, burglars, and murderers were next at 14.8%, 12.4%, and 10.6%, respectively) (Beck et al., 1993).

The effect of drug policies can be seen in prison data from a number of states. Figure 10-4 [omitted here] shows Black and White prison admissions in North Carolina from 1970 to 1990. White rates held steady; Black rates doubled between 1980 and 1990, rising most rapidly after 1987. Figure 10-5 [omitted here] shows prison admissions for drug crimes in Virginia from 1983 to 1989; the racial balance flipped from two-thirds White, one-third non-White in 1983 to the reverse in 1989. Similarly, in Pennsylvania, Clark (1992) reports, Black male prison admissions for drug crimes grew four times faster (up

TABLE 10-2   U.S. Drug Arrests by Race, 1976-1992

Year	Total Violations	White	White Percentage	Black	Black Percentage
1976	475,209	366,081	77	103,615	22
1977	565,371	434,471	77	122,594	22
1978	592,168	462,728	78	127,277	21
1979	516,142	396,065	77	112,748	22
1980	531,953	401,979	76	125,607	24
1981	584,776	432,556	74	146,858	25
1982	562,390	400,683	71	156,369	28
1983	615,081	423,151	69	185,601	30
1984	560,729	392,904	70	162,979	29
1985	700,009	482,486	69	210,298	30
1986	688,815	463,457	67	219,159	32
1987	809,157	511,278	63	291,177	36
1988	844,300	503,125	60	334,015	40
1989	1,074,345	613,800	57	452,574	42
1990	860,016	503,315	59	349,965	41
1991	763,340	443,596	58	312,997	41
1992	919,561	546,430	59	364,546	40

Sources: FBI 1993, Table 43; *Sourcebook of Criminal Justice Statistics—1978–1992.*
Various Tables. Washington, DC: U.S. Department of Justice, Bureau of Justice Statistics.

1,613%) between 1980 and 1990 than did White male admissions (up 477%). In California, according to Zimring and Hawkins (1994), the number of males in prison for drug crimes grew 15 fold between 1980 and 1990 and "there were more people in prison in California for drug offences in 1991 than there were for *all* offences in California at the end of 1979" (p. 89; emphasis in original).

Why, if Blacks in their lives are no more likely than Whites to use illicit drugs, are Blacks so much more likely to be arrested and imprisoned? One possible answer, which is almost certainly wrong, is that Blacks are proportionately more likely to sell drugs. We have no representative surveys of drug dealers and so cannot with confidence paint demographic pictures. However, there is little reason to suspect that drug crimes are more interracial than are most other crimes. In addition, the considerations that make arrests of Black dealers relatively easy make arrests of White dealers relatively hard.

Drug arrests are easier to make in socially disorganized inner-city minority areas than in working- or middle-class urban or suburban areas for a number of reasons. First, although drug sales in working- or middle-class areas are likely to take place indoors and in private spaces where they are difficult to observe, drug sales in poor minority areas are likely to take place outdoors in streets, alleys, or abandoned buildings, or indoors in public places like bars. Second, although working- or middle-class drug dealers in stable areas are unlikely to sell drugs to undercover strangers, dealers in disorganized areas have little choice but to sell to strangers and new acquaintances. These differences mean that it is easier for police to make arrests and undercover purchases in urban minority areas than elsewhere. Because arrests are fungible for purposes of both the individual officer's personnel file and the department's year-to-year statistical comparisons, more easy arrests look

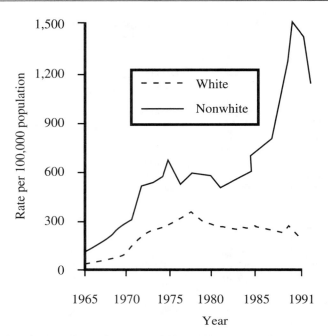

FIGURE 10-3.   Arrest Rates for Drug Offenses by Race, 1965–1991

Source: Blumstein, 1993a.

better than fewer hard ones. And because, as ethnographic studies of drug trafficking make clear (Fagan, 1993; Padilla, 1992), arrested drug dealers in disadvantaged urban minority communities are generally replaced within days, there is a nearly inexhaustible potential supply of young minority Americans to be arrested.

There is another reason why the War on Drugs worsened racial disparities in the justice system. Penalties for drug crimes were steadily made harsher since the mid-1980s. In particular, purveyors of crack cocaine, a drug used primarily by poor urban Blacks and Hispanics, are punished far more severely than are purveyors of powder cocaine, a pharmacologically indistinguishable drug used primarily by middle-class Whites. The most notorious disparity occurs under federal law which equates 1 gram of crack with 100 grams of powder. As a result, the average prison sentence served by Black federal prisoners is 40% longer than the average sentence for Whites (McDonald and Carlson, 1993). Although the Minnesota Supreme Court and two federal district courts have struck down the 100-to-1 rule as a denial of constitutional equal protection to Blacks, at the time of writing, every federal court of appeals that had considered the question had upheld the provision.

The people who launched the drug wars knew all these things—that the enemy troops would mostly be young minority males, that an emphasis on supply-side antidrug strategies, particularly use of mass arrests, would disproportionately ensnare young minority males, that the 100-to-1 rule would disproportionately affect Blacks, and that there was no valid basis for believing that any of these things would reduce drug availability or prices.

Likewise, as the first section showed, there was no basis for a good faith belief that the harsher crime control policies of recent years—more and longer mandatory minimum sentences, tougher and more rigid sentencing guidelines, and three-strikes-and-you're-out laws—would reduce crime rates, and there was a good basis for predicting that they would disproportionately damage Blacks. If Blacks are more likely than Whites to be arrested, especially for drug crimes, the greater harshness of toughened penalties will disproportionately be borne by Blacks. Because much crime is intraracial, concern for Black victims might justify harsher treatment of Black offenders if there were any reason to believe that harsher penalties would reduce crime rates. Unfortunately, as the conservative national governments of Margaret Thatcher and Brian Mulroney and reports of National Academy of Sciences Panels funded by the administrations of Republican Presidents Ford, Reagan, and Bush all agree, there is no reason to believe that harsher penalties significantly reduce crime rates.

Justifying the Unjustifiable

There is no valid policy justification for the harsh drug and crime control policies of the Reagan and Bush administrations, and for their adverse differential effect on Blacks. The justification, such as it is, is entirely political. Crime is an emotional subject and visceral appeals by politicians to people's fears and resentments are difficult to counter.

It is easy to seize the low ground in political debates about crime policy. When one candidate campaigns with pictures of clanging prison gates and grief-stricken relatives of a rape or murder victim, and with disingenuous promises that newer, tougher policies will work, it is difficult for an opponent to explain that crime is a complicated problem, that real solutions must be long term, and that simplistic toughness does not reduce crime rates. This is why, as a result, candidates often compete to establish which is tougher in his views about crime. It is also why less conservative candidates often try to preempt their more conservative opponents by adopting a tough stance early in the campaign. Finally, it is why political pundits congratulate President Clinton on his acumen in proposing federal crime legislation as or more harsh than his opponents'. He has, it is commonly said, "taken the crime issue away from the Republicans."

Conservative Republican politicians have, since the late 1960s, used welfare, especially Aid to Families with Dependent Children, and crime as symbolic issues to appeal to anti-Black sentiments and resentments of White voters, as Thomas and Mary Edsall's *Chain Reaction: The Impact of Race, Rights, and Taxes on American Politics* (1991) makes clear. The Edsalls provide a history, since the mid-1960s, of "a conservative politics that had the effect of polarizing the electorate along racial lines." Anyone who observed Ronald Reagan's portrayal in several campaigns of Linda Evans, a Black Chicago woman, as the "welfare queen" or George Bush's use of Black murderer Willie Horton to caricature Michael Dukakis's criminal justice policies knows of what the Edsalls write.

The story of Willie Horton is the better known and makes the Edsalls' point. Horton, who in 1975 had been convicted of the murder of a 17-year-old boy, failed to return from a June 12, 1986, furlough. The following April, he broke into a home in Oxon Hill, Maryland, where he raped a woman and stabbed her companion.

Lee Atwater, Bush's campaign strategist, after testing the visceral effects of Willie Horton's picture and story on participants in focus groups, decided a year later to make Horton a wedge issue for Republicans. Atwater reportedly told a group of Republican activists that Bush would win the presidency "if I can make Willie Horton a household name." He later told a Republican gathering in Atlanta, "there's a story about a fellow named Willie Horton who, for all I know, may end up being Dukakis's running mate." Atwater for a time denied making both remarks but in 1991, dying of cancer, recanted: "In 1988, fighting Dukakis, I said that I would . . . make Willie Horton his running mate. I am sorry."

The sad reality is that tragedies like the crimes of Willie Horton are inevitable. So are airplane crashes, 40,000 to 50,000 traffic fatalities per year, and defense department cost overruns. Every person convicted of a violent crime cannot be held forever. Furloughs are used in most corrections systems as a way to ease offenders back into the community and to test their suitability for eventual release on parole or commutation. Horton had successfully completed nine previous furloughs, from each of which he had returned without incident, under a program established in 1972 not by Michael Dukakis but by Governor Francis Sargent, a Republican.

Public discourse about criminal justice issues has been debased by the cynicism that made Willie Horton a major participant in the 1988 presidential election. That cynicism has made it difficult to discuss or develop sensible public policies, and that cynicism explains why conservative politicians have been able year after year successfully to propose ever harsher penalties and crime control and drug policies that no informed person believes can achieve their ostensible goals.

Three final points, arguments that apologists for current policies sometimes make, warrant mention. First, it is sometimes said to be unfair to blame national Republican administrations for the failures and disparate impacts of recent crime control policies. This ignores the efforts of the Reagan and Bush administrations to encourage and, through federal mandates and funding restrictions, to coerce states to follow the federal lead. Attorney General William Barr (e.g., 1992) made the most aggressive efforts to compel state adoption of tougher criminal justice policies, and the Bush administration's final proposed crime bills restricted eligibility for federal funds to states that, like the federal government, abolished parole release and adopted sentencing standards no less severe than those in the federal sentencing guidelines. In any case, as the Edsalls' book makes clear, the use of crime control issues (among others including welfare reform and affirmative action) to elicit anti-Black sentiments from White voters has long been a stratagem of both state and federal Republican politicians.

Second, sometimes it is argued that political leaders have merely followed the public will; voters are outraged by crime and want tougher policies (DiIulio, 1991). This is a half-truth that gets the causal order backwards. Various measures of public sentiment, including both representative surveys like Gallup and Harris polls and work with focus groups, have for many years consistently shown that the public is of two minds about crime (Roberts, 1992). First, people are frustrated and want offenders to be punished. Second, people believe that social adversity, poverty, and a troubled home life are the principal causes of crime, and they believe government should work to rehabilitate offenders. A number of surveys have found that respondents who would oppose a tax increase to pay for more prisons would support a tax increase to pay for rehabilitative programs. These findings of voter ambivalence about crime should not be surprising. Most people have complicated views about complicated problems. For example, most judges and corrections officials have the same ambivalent feelings about offenders that the general public has. Conservative politicians have seized upon public support of punishment and ignored public support of rehabilitation and public recognition that crime presents complex, not easy, challenges. By presenting crime control issues only in emotional, stereotyped ways, conservative politicians have raised its salience as a political issue but made it impossible for their opponents to respond other than in the same stereotyped ways.

Third, sometimes it is argued that disparate impacts on Black offenders are no problem and that, because much crime is intraracial, failure to adopt tough policies would disserve the interests of Black victims. As former Attorney General Barr (1992) put it, perhaps in ill-chosen words, "the benefits of increased incarceration would be enjoyed disproportionately by Black Americans" (p. 17). This argument also is based on a half-truth. No one wants to live in unsafe neighborhoods or to be victimized by crime, and in a crisis, people who need help will seek it from the police, the public agency of last resort. Requesting help in a crisis and supporting harsh policies with racially disparate effects are not the same thing. The relevant distinction is between acute and chronic problems. A substantial body of public opinion research (e.g., National Opinion Research Center surveys conducted throughout the 1980s summarized in Wood, 1990) shows that Blacks far more than Whites support establishment of more generous social welfare policies, full employment programs, and increased social spending. The congressional Black and Hispanic caucuses have consistently opposed bills calling for tougher sanctions and supported bills calling for increased spending on social programs aimed at improving conditions that cause crime. Thus, in claiming to be concerned about Black victims, conservative politicians are responding to natural human calls for help in a crisis while ignoring evidence that Black citizens would rather have government support efforts to ameliorate the chronic social conditions that cause crime and thereby make calls for help in a crisis less necessary.

The evidence on the effectiveness of recent crime control and drug abuse policies, as the first section demonstrated, cannot justify their racially disparate effects on Blacks, nor, as this section demonstrates, can the claims that such policies merely manifest the people's will or respect the interests of Black victims. All that is left is politics of the ugliest kind. The War on Drugs and the set of harsh crime control policies in which it was enmeshed were adopted to achieve political, not policy, objectives, and it is the adoption for political purposes of policies with foreseeable disparate impacts, the use of disadvantaged Black Americans as means to the achievement of White politicians' electoral ends, that must in the end be justified. It cannot.

Discussion Questions

1. What evidence does Tonry cite to support his argument that scholars agree that harsher penalties do not deter crime? Do you know of any evidence to support the contention that more punishment will reduce crime? If research shows no deterrent effect of punishment, why has there been so much support among politicians for harsher penalties?

2. What rationale do you think was used for making the penalty for crack cocaine so much more severe than the penalty for cocaine in the form of powder? How did this change affect blacks and whites convicted of drug offenses? How have state and federal courts responded to the racial disparity in sentences that resulted from this change in penalties?

3. What evidence does Tonry cite to support his argument that a significant racial disparity in prison admissions has occurred since 1980? Why does he think this has occurred?

4. How has the race issue been used by politicians as a symbolic appeal to voters fearful of crime? How has the public responded to the definition of crime as a race issue?

Part IV

Juvenile Gangs

Chapter *11*

Gang Involvement: The Individual and the Decision to Become a Member

Martín Sánchez Jankowski

From his study of thirty-seven street gangs in New York, Los Angeles, and Boston, Martín Sánchez Jankowski concludes that the concern of those organizations with their own survival determines the methods they use to recruit new members. Gangs have to let their members pursue their own goals while still tying them to the group through self-interest, moral incentives, and a code of behavior. This selection focuses on the reasons that individuals choose to become gang members.

Before proceeding, it is important to dismiss a number of the propositions that have often been advanced. The first is that young boys join gangs because they are from broken homes where the father is not present and they seek gang membership in order to identify with other males—that is, they have had no male authority figures with whom to identify. In the ten years of this study, I found that there were as many gang members from homes where the nuclear family was intact as there were from families where the father was absent.[1]

The second proposition given for why individuals join gangs is related to the first: it suggests that broken homes and/or bad home environments force them to look to the gang

Source: Martín Sánchez Jankowski, *Islands in the Street: Gangs and American Urban Society.* Berkeley: University of California Press, 1991, pp. 39–47. Copyright © 1991 The Regents of the University of California. Reprinted by permission of the University of California Press and the author.

as a substitute family. Those who offer this explanation often quote gang members' statements such as "We are like a family" or "We are just like brothers" as indications of this motive. However, I found as many members who claimed close relationships with their families as those who denied them.

The third reason offered is that individuals who drop out of school have fewer skills for getting jobs, leaving them with nothing to do but join a gang. While I did find a larger number of members who had dropped out of school, the number was only slightly higher than those who had finished school.

The fourth reason suggested, disconfirmed by my data, is a modern version of the "Pied Piper" effect: the claim that young kids join gangs because they are socialized by older kids to aspire to gang membership and, being young and impressionable, are easily persuaded. I found on the contrary that individuals were as likely to join when they were older (mid to late teens) as when they were younger (nine to fifteen). I also found significantly more who joined when they were young who did so for reasons other than being socialized to think it was "cool" to belong to a gang. In brief, I found no evidence for this proposition.

What I did find was that individuals who live in low-income neighborhoods join gangs for a variety of reasons, basing their decisions on a rational calculation of what is best for them at that particular time. Furthermore, I found that they use the same calculus (not necessarily the same reasons) in deciding whether to stay in the gang, or, if they happen to leave it, whether to rejoin.

Reasons for Deciding to Join a Gang

Most people in the low-income inner cities of America face a situation in which a gang already exists in their area. Therefore the most salient question facing them is not whether to start a gang or not, but rather whether to join an existing one. Many of the reasons for starting a new gang are related to issues having to do with organizational development and decline—that is, with the existing gang's ability to provide the expected services, which include those that individuals considered in deciding to join. This section deals primarily, although not exclusively, with the question of what influences individuals to join an existing gang. However, many of these are the same influences that encourage individuals to start a new gang.

Material Incentives

Those who had joined a gang most often gave as their reason the belief that it would provide them with an environment that would increase their chances of securing money. Defiant individualists* constantly calculate the costs and benefits associated with their efforts to improve their financial well-being (which is usually not good). Therefore, on

---

* [Jankowski (1991:24–26) defines defiant individualists in terms of seven character traits: an intense sense of competitiveness, a sense of mistrust or wariness, self-reliance, social isolation, survival instinct, a Social Darwinist worldview, and a defiant air.]

the one hand, they believe that if they engage in economic ventures on their own, they will, if successful, earn more per venture than if they acted as part of a gang. However, there is also the belief that if one participates in economic ventures with a gang, it is likely that the amount earned will be more regular, although perhaps less per venture. The comments of Slump, a sixteen-year-old member of a gang in the Los Angeles area, represent this belief:

> Well, I really didn't want to join the gang when I was a little younger because I had this idea that I could make more money if I would do some gigs [various illegal economic ventures] on my own. Now I don't know, I mean, I wasn't wrong. I could make more money on my own, but there are more things happening with the gang, so it's a little more even in terms of when the money comes in. . . . Let's just say there is more possibilities for a more steady amount of income if you need it.

It was also believed that less individual effort would be required in the various economic ventures in a gang because more people would be involved. In addition, some thought that being in a gang would reduce the risk (of personal injury) associated with their business ventures. They were aware that if larger numbers of people had knowledge of a crime, this would increase the risk that if someone were caught, others, including themselves, would be implicated. However, they countered this consideration with the belief that they faced less risk of being physically harmed when they were part of a group action. The comments of Corner, a seventeen-year-old resident of a poor Manhattan neighborhood, represent this consideration. During the interview, he was twice approached about joining the local gang. He said:

> I think I am going to join the club [gang] this time. I don't know, man, I got some things to decide, but I think I will. . . . Before I didn't want to join because when I did a job, I didn't want to share it with the whole group—hell, I was never able to make that much to share. . . . I would never have got enough money, and with all those dudes [other members of the gang] knowing who did the job, you can bet the police would find out. . . . Well, now my thinking is changed a bit 'cause I almost got hurt real bad trying something the other day and so I'm pretty sure I'll join the gang 'cause there's more people involved and that'll keep me safer. [He joined the gang two weeks later.]

Others decided to join the gang for financial security. They viewed the gang as an organization that could provide them or their families with money in times of emergency. It represented the combination of a bank and a social security system, the equivalent of what the political machine had been to many new immigrant groups in American cities.[2] To these individuals, it provided both psychological and financial security in an economic environment of scarcity and intense competition. This was particularly true of those who were fifteen and younger. Many in this age group often find themselves in a precarious position. They are in need of money, and although social services are available to help during times of economic hardship, they often lack legal means of access to these resources. For these individuals, the gang can provide an alternative source of aid. The comments of Street Dog and Tomahawk represent these views. Street Dog was a fifteen-year-old Puerto Rican who had been in a New York gang for two years:

Hey, the club [the gang] has been there when I needed help. There were times when there just wasn't enough food for me to get filled up with. My family was hard up and they couldn't manage all of their bills and such, so there was some lean meals! Well, I just needed some money to help for awhile, till I got some money or my family was better off. They [the gang] was there to help. I could see that [they would help] before I joined, that's why I joined. They are there when you need them and they'll continue to be.

Tomahawk was a fifteen-year-old Irishman who had been in a gang for one year:

Before I joined the gang, I could see that you could count on your boys to help in times of need and that meant a lot to me. And when I needed money, sure enough they gave it to me. Nobody else would have given it to me; my parents didn't have it, and there was no other place to go. The gang was just like they said they would be, and they'll continue to be there when I need them.

Finally, many view the gang as providing an opportunity for future gratification. They expect that through belonging to a gang, they will be able to make contact with individuals who may eventually help them financially. Some look to meet people who have contacts in organized crime in the hope of entering that field in the future. Some hope to meet businessmen involved in the illegal market who will provide them with money to start their own illegal businesses. Still others think that gang membership will enable them to meet individuals who will later do them favors (with financial implications) of the kind fraternity brothers or Masons sometimes do for each other. Irish gang members in New York and Boston especially tend to believe this.

Recreation

The gang provides individuals with entertainment, much as a fraternity does for college students or the Moose and Elk clubs do for their members. Many individuals said they joined the gang because it was the primary social institution of their neighborhood—that is, it was where most (not necessarily the biggest) social events occurred. Gangs usually, though not always, have some type of clubhouse. The exact nature of the clubhouse varies according to how much money the gang has to support it, but every clubhouse offers some form of entertainment. In the case of some gangs with a good deal of money, the clubhouse includes a bar, which sells its members drinks at cost. In addition, some clubhouses have pinball machines, soccer-game machines, pool tables, ping pong tables, card tables, and in some cases a few slot machines. The clubhouse acts as an incentive, much like the lodge houses of other social clubs.[3]

The gang can also be a promoter of social events in the community, such as a big party or dance. Often the gang, like a fraternity, is thought of as the organization to join to maximize opportunities to have fun. Many who joined said they did so because the gang provided them with a good opportunity to meet women. Young women frequently form an auxiliary unit to the gang, which usually adopts a version of the male gang's name (e.g., "Lady Jets"). The women who join this auxiliary do so for similar reasons—that is, opportunities to meet men and participate in social events.[4]

The gang is also a source of drugs and alcohol. Here, most gangs walk a fine line. They provide some drugs for purposes of recreation, but because they also ban addicts from the organization, they also attempt to monitor members' use of some drugs.[5]

The comments of Fox and Happy highlight these views of the gang as a source of recreation.[6] Fox was a twenty-three-year-old from New York and had been in a gang for seven years:

> Like I been telling you, I joined originally because all the action was happening with the Bats [gang's name]. I mean, all the foxy ladies were going to their parties and hanging with them. Plus their parties were great. They had good music and the herb [marijuana] was so smooth. . . . Man, it was a great source of dope and women. Hell, they were the kings of the community so I wanted to get in on some of the action.

Happy was a twenty-eight-year-old from Los Angeles, who had been a gang member for eight years:

> I joined because at the time, Jones Park [gang's name] had the best clubhouse. They had pool tables and pinball machines that you could use for free. Now they added a video game which you only have to pay like five cents for to play. You could do a lot in the club, so I thought it was a good thing to try it for awhile [join the gang], and it was a good thing.

A Place of Refuge and Camouflage

Some individuals join a gang because it provides them with a protective group identity. They see the gang as offering them anonymity, which may relieve the stresses associated with having to be personally accountable for all their actions in an intensely competitive environment. The statements of Junior J. and Black Top are representative of this belief. Junior J. was a seventeen-year-old who had been approached about becoming a gang member in one of New York's neighborhoods:

> I been thinking about joining the gang because the gang gives you a cover, you know what I mean? Like when me or anybody does a business deal and we're members of the gang, it's difficult to track us down 'cause people will say, oh, it was just one of those guys in the gang. You get my point? The gang is going to provide me with some cover.

Black Top was a seventeen-year-old member of a Jamaican gang in New York:

> Man, I been dealing me something awful. I been doing well, but I also attracted me some adversaries. And these adversaries have been getting close to me. So joining the brothers [the gang] lets me blend into the group. It lets me hide for awhile, it gives me refuge until the heat goes away.

Physical Protection

Individuals also join gangs because they believe the gang can provide them with personal protection from the predatory elements active in low-income neighborhoods. Nearly all the young men who join for this reason know what dangers exist for them in their low-income neighborhoods. These individuals are not the weakest of those who join the gang, for all have developed the savvy and skills to handle most threats. However, all are either tired of being on the alert or want to reduce the probability of danger to a level that allows them to devote more time to their effort to secure more money. Here are two representative comments of individuals who joined for this reason. Chico was a seventeen-year-old member of an Irish gang in New York:

> When I first started up with the Steel Flowers, I really didn't know much about them. But, to be honest, in the beginning I just joined because there were some people who were taking my school [lunch] money, and after I joined the gang, these guys laid off.

Cory was a sixteen-year-old member of a Los Angeles gang:

> Man I joined the Fultons because there are a lot of people out there who are trying to get you and if you don't got protection you in trouble sometimes. My homeboys gave me protection, so hey, they were the thing to do. . . . Now that I got some business things going I can concentrate on them and not worry so much. I don't always have to be looking over my shoulder.

A Time to Resist

Many older individuals (in their late teens or older) join gangs in an effort to resist living lives like their parents'. As Joan Moore, Ruth Horowitz, and others have pointed out, most gang members come from families whose parents are underemployed and/or employed in the secondary labor market in jobs that have little to recommend them.[7] These jobs are low-paying, have long hours, poor working conditions, and few opportunities for advancement; in brief, they are dead ends.[8] Most prospective gang members have lived through the pains of economic deprivation and the stresses that such an existence puts on a family. They desperately want to avoid following in their parents' path, which they believe is exactly what awaits them. For these individuals, the gang is a way to resist the jobs their parents held and, by extension, the life their parents led. Deciding to become a gang member is both a statement to society ("I will not take these jobs passively") and an attempt to do whatever can be done to avoid such an outcome. At the very least, some of these individuals view being in a gang as a temporary reprieve from having to take such jobs, a postponement of the inevitable. The comments of Joey and D.D. are representative of this group. Joey was a nineteen-year-old member of an Irish gang in Boston:

> Hell, I joined because I really didn't see anything in the near future I wanted to do. I sure the hell didn't want to take that job my father got me. It was a shit job just like his. I said to myself, "Fuck this!" I'm only nineteen, I'm too young to start this shit. . . . I figured that the Black Rose [the gang] was into a lot of things and that maybe I could hit it big at something we're doing and get the hell out of this place.

D.D. was a twenty-year-old member of a Chicano gang in Los Angeles:

> I just joined the T-Men to kick back [relax, be carefree] for awhile. My parents work real hard and they got little for it. I don't really want that kind of job, but that's what it looked

like I would have to take. So I said, hey, I'll just kick back for a while and let that job wait for me. Hey, I just might make some money from our dealings and really be able to forget these jobs. . . . If I don't [make it, at least] I told the fuckers in Beverly Hills what I think of the jobs they left for us.

People who join as an act of resistance are often wrongly understood to have joined because they were having difficulty with their identity and the gang provided them with a new one. However, these individuals actually want a new identity less than they want better living conditions.

Commitment to Community

Some individuals join the gang because they see participation as a form of commitment to their community. These usually come from neighborhoods where gangs have existed for generations. Although the character of such gangs may have changed over the years, the fact remains that they have continued to exist. Many of these individuals have known people who have been in gangs, including family members—often a brother, but even, in considerable number of cases, a father and grandfather. The fact that their relatives have a history of gang involvement usually influences these individuals to see the gang as a part of the tradition of the community. They feel that their families and their community expect them to join, because community members see the gang as an aid to them and the individual who joins as meeting his neighborhood obligation. These attitudes are similar to attitudes in the larger society about one's obligation to serve in the armed forces. In a sense, this type of involvement represents a unique form of local patriotism. While this rationale for joining was present in a number of the gangs studied, it was most prevalent among Chicano and Irish gangs. The comments of Dolan and Pepe are representative of this line of thinking. Dolan was a sixteen-year-old member of an Irish gang in New York:

I joined because the gang has been here for a long time and even though the name is different a lot of the fellas from the community have been involved in it over the years, including my dad. The gang has helped the community by protecting it against outsiders so people here have kind of depended on it. . . . I feel it's my obligation to the community to put in some time helping them out. This will help me to get help in the community if I need it some time.

Pepe was a seventeen-year-old member of a Chicano gang in the Los Angeles area:

The Royal Dons [gang's name] have been here for a real long time. A lot of people from the community have been in it. I had lots of family in it so I guess I'll just have to carry on the tradition. A lot of people from outside this community wouldn't understand, but we have helped the community whenever they've asked us. We've been around to help. I felt it's kind of my duty to join 'cause everybody expects it. . . . No, the community doesn't mind that we do things to make some money and raise a little hell because they don't expect you to put in your time for nothing. Just like nobody expects guys in the military to put in their time for nothing.

In closing this section on why individuals join gangs, it is important to reemphasize that people choose to join for a variety of reasons, that these reasons are not exclusive of one another (some members have more than one), that gangs are composed of individuals whose reasons for joining include all those mentioned, that the decision to join is thought out, and that the individual believes this was best for his or her interests at the moment.

Author's Notes

1. Although the present study is not a quantitative study, the finding reported here and the ones to follow are based on observations of, and conversations and formal interviews with, hundreds of gang members.
2. For a discussion of the political machine's role in providing psychological and financial support for poor immigrant groups, see Merton (1968:126–36). Also see Riordan (1963).
3. There are numerous examples throughout the society of social clubs using the lodge or clubhouse as one of the incentives for gaining members. There are athletic clubs for the wealthy (like the University Club and the Downtown Athletic Club in New York), social clubs in ethnic neighborhoods, the Elks and Moose clubs, the clubs of various veterans' associations, and tennis, yacht, and racket ball clubs.
4. See Campbell (1987).
5. For the use of drugs as recreational, see Virgil (1988) and Fagan (1989), who reports varying degrees of drug use among various types of gangs. For studies that report the monitoring and/or prohibition of certain drugs by gangs, see Virgil (1988), on the prohibition of heroin use in Chicano gangs; and Mieczkowski (1986).
6. See Thrasher (1927:84–96). He also discusses the gang as a source of recreation.
7. See Moore (1978: Chapter 2); Horowitz (1983: Chapter 8); and Virgil (1988); Hagedorn (1988).
8. For a discussion of these types of jobs, see Piore (1972).

Discussion Questions

1. What reasons have others given for boys' joining gangs? What evidence does Jankowski cite in rejecting those explanations?
2. According to Jankowski, why do boys join gangs? Which of the reasons that he gives do you think are most important, and which are incidental or less important? How do gangs make themselves attractive to potential recruits?

Stealing and the Juvenile Gang

Felix M. Padilla

In his participant-observation study of the Diamonds, a Puerto Rican gang living in a Chicago neighborhood called "Suburbia," Padilla describes the group as a business establishment supported primarily by street-level drug dealing and based on the ideology that its members' well-being can best be improved through collective rather than individual effort. Here, Padilla describes a secondary source of income for the gang, theft by its youngest members. Stealing serves functions for the group in addition to profit; it is an important step in joining the gang, demonstrating commitment, and moving up the ranks.

Stealing is one way members of the Diamonds raise money for themselves and the gang. Though the gains from this activity are relatively limited, stealing represents an important step one takes to move up the ranks of the gang.

The job of stealing is usually assigned to the Pee Wees, or Littles, the younger gang members, who are typically thirteen to fifteen years in age. There are several reasons for charging the Pee Wees with the responsibility of carrying out stealing and other similarly hazardous job assignments. First, as newcomers, the Pee Wees are expected to demonstrate their commitment and loyalty to the gang. Stealing is regarded as one task designed specifically for this purpose. Second, gang leaders recognize that the legal justice system is less than efficient when dealing with minors, when these youngsters are apprehended for committing acts that are in direct violation of the law. Third, Pee Wees are perceived by older gang members as "crazies"—youngsters who think and care very little about their actions. Some Pee Wees willingly adopt this identity and, indeed, carry out their activities much in line with the typecast. They believe it is to their advantage to perform in accordance with the gang's expectations, hoping that this form of behavior will be generously rewarded. It is not uncommon to hear, for example, such arguments as: "We can count on Jimmy—he's crazy. He's down for the gang; he will do it. We should take care of Jimmy because he is never scared to do anything for the gang." This is the kind of positive evaluation Pee Wees aspire to. Fourth, there are some individuals within the ranks of the Pee Wees who come to the gang already possessing a background or reputation in stealing. These youngsters do not hesitate to display their talent, believing that it will gain them prestige over others with less experience.

Stealing represents work that is very risky because the potential for discovery is extremely high. Therefore, almost by necessity, stealing becomes a group undertaking. Most stealing activities described to me by members of the Diamonds are said to have been carried out by a group, or crew, of two to five gang members. More dangerous jobs require additional manpower at which time the size of the crew increases. It is rare for an individual to "pull a job" or "score" on his own. In cases when this does occur the gang will not sanction the behavior. In fact, there have been cases when individuals were severely penalized for carrying out thefts on their own. Overall, as shown before, the Diamonds live and die by the fundamental principle of collectivism, which discourages individual action.

The significance of the group approach to stealing can be seen in the following remarks, which also tell a great deal about the repercussions for individuals who decide to work on their own.

Felix: When we were talking earlier about stealing you phrased it in terms of "we were stealing this and that." What did you mean by *we?*

Carmelo: Actually, that's what starts it—the gang. Back then we were called the "Littles," so they would say, "Let's get the Littles to do it." And we would go out as a team and do a job.

Felix: What's a team?

Carmelo: Just a number of guys. Sometimes there were three guys; other times we would go out with eight.

Felix: Why would you need eight guys?

Carmelo: They were our watchdogs. Sometimes people who saw what we were doing would come out and try to intimidate us, but when they see all these other guys they become scared. Besides, the gang would get real upset if they ordered us to do a job and we did it alone. Sometimes we would get a *V.* A *V* stands for violation, and, if you get one, you get rolled on by a bunch of guys.

Felix: But why were you given a *V* for stealing? After all, if you got into trouble, you would have to pay for it yourself.

Carmelo: Well, maybe you're right, but it doesn't work like that in the gang. Because, you see, if guys go on their own and do jobs on their own and make money, then the gang doesn't get no money. Besides, the gang doesn't want people to get greedy.

In addition, the partnership offers a greater probability of accuracy in defining situations and solving problems since groups have a greater number of resources for coming up with ideas and for dealing with circumstances of error than individuals. Hence, as a group, youngsters can better plan and execute a job. Even when an individual member presents a robbery plan to his associates, there is always deliberation about it by crew members before executing the plan. Similarly, the partnership allows for task specialization, necessary for carrying out different robberies and planning strategies. Task specialization is usually determined on the basis of personal work preferences and a related repertoire of skills, which can be adopted to fit various stealing activities should reasons of practicality, economics, and unique opportunities so dictate. It is not uncommon to find a stealing group that includes an individual whose mechanical prowess is great. Some youngsters, for example, are especially good at breaking into cars. Most members of the Diamonds who have been involved in stealing have developed skills in car burglary.

Rafael's memories of his burglary crew provide us with a clear picture of the dynamics of this type of work association:

> I used to work with two of the boys all the time. We came into the gang together, so we knew each other real good. For a while we worked separately, but then we came together, and that was really "bad." I think we had the baddest crew in the Diamonds. The thing about our group is that we went after the things we liked and were good for selling. We knew what we wanted to go after. We were car thieves, and my boy Pete—Pete is serving time for something that some other shithead did, but Pete was good. Not once were we ever busted.
>
> I just remember this one time we were chased, but we knew where to hide. There was this gangway that he [Pete] knew about. So, we ran a few blocks then, and, real quickly, we were gone. We ran through this gangway, then we crossed the alley and then another gangway, and we were at this schoolyard, and there was a park next to the school. There were other fellas playing ball there, so we pretended to be with them. We hung out for a while and then headed to the hood.
>
> This is why we were good. We always informed one another. We were always on the alert. We knew where to go when things got dangerous and messy. And because of that we were always clean. The law just couldn't catch up with us.

It may be argued that, in terms of the explicit goals of the partnership, this type of arrangement, into a cooperative crew, is functional. Forcing an unwilling or dissident member to join a robbery would only endanger the stealing crew. To diverge from one's line of expertise, however, encourages the hazards implicit in lack of practice and unfamiliarity. Only in unusual circumstances does someone from a crew engage in robberies he dislikes and for which his skills are ill-suited.

Pee Wees learn to steal by working together with another gang member who has experience, whose role is that of mentor and leader. In an informal conversation Coco provides insight into this process:

Felix: What do you mean by "turning you on"?

Coco: He [Coco's mentor] was the one who was teaching me the ropes.

Felix: And who was that person?

Coco: My main man.

Felix: What about stealing? How did you learn this?

Coco: From my main man. He would teach me everything. I was under his wing. So, what he knew he was going to teach me.

Felix: Why did he do this?

Coco: He was supposed to. Part of his job was to train the new ones like me. What did we know when we came? Not much. I didn't know too much at this time. There are some people that come in bragging. They want to make everybody believe that they are bad and that they have done jobs before. But everybody knows that they ain't shit. We know who's doing what out in the streets. That's our business—to stay in tune with what's happening. So, these guys . . . all they be is a lot of talk, you know, *mucha mierda* [lots of shit].

Felix: So, what are some of the things you learned from the guy you call your main man?

Coco: Like in stealing autos, he taught me to put the screwdriver on the corner of the window; it pops the window without shattering it—no noise. He taught me how to peel the column. You peel the bottom piece, and the rod is right there. You pull up the shoehorn, and it is straight; you turn on the car; you steer the steering wheel, put the car in drive, and you're gone. That's how he taught me. He would stand by the window of the car telling me "Hurry up—do this and do that."

Felix: He wasn't helping you?

Coco: No, he was watching to see that nobody was coming. He was watching me, too. He had to make sure that I was doing it right.

Felix: And how long did he work with you?

Coco: Well, because I learned fast and good, he kept me. My main man liked me a lot, so that too. We were good friends. I think you have to be to do this kind of work.

Gang members define specific items or goods as attractive for stealing and fencing (passing stolen goods along from one person to another to blur the identity of the actual thief)—for example, cars and their parts and household goods, such as VCRs, stereos, TVs, and jewelry. Preference is given to those items with the highest consumer demand. Youngsters steal merchandise they know can be easily sold to permanent customers. Some youngsters usually sell their goods to neighborhood residents who the youngsters know cannot afford to purchase from regular retailers. As indicated by Elf:

> We knew that some of the older guys in the neighborhood were in need of a car or parts for a car. So, we would tell them that we could get the parts and all they had to do was to leave their garage door unlocked. We would come, steal the car, and stick it inside the garage. If they only needed a certain part, we would put the car inside the garage, strip it, leave him the parts he needed, and take the rest with us. Sometimes they used to come to us to order whatever they needed.

There were other instances when goods were stolen precisely for use by individuals running "chop shops," legal business operations described by members of the Diamonds as being heavily dependent on stolen goods. I was told many stories about the business of the chop shop; many youngsters indicated knowing of at least one, and most claimed to be aware of many. In the dialogue that follows Coco provides a penetrating account of the nature of the chop shop operation.

Felix: You mentioned the idea of a chop shop. What is that exactly?

Coco: These are legal corporations or businesses that buy stolen merchandise cheap and sell it at a higher price.

Felix: Give me an example.

Coco: We would steal a car and leave it at a certain spot, and they pick it up. They would pay us in advance, and they would come with tow trucks and drive it away.

Felix: A certain spot, like what?

Coco: Well, like a street. We would drive the car to the street they tell us and leave it there, go to them, they give you the money, and you tell them where it is, and they come and pick it up. They take all the parts themselves. All the parts' serial numbers are changed, and the parts become ready for sale.

Felix: So, a chop shop is a legal business?

Coco: Yes, it could be an auto body shop, auto parts, a mechanic's garage—they might need certain things to sell to their customers. So, they come to us and tell us to get them this or that part. We get them the part, and they put their own serial number on it, and that makes it legal. Like stolen radios, you can take them to an electronics shop, and they include them with their stock, and it can't never be proven that it's stolen because it is part of their stock, and it has a legal serial number. We call this a tag job.

Felix: Are the chop shops local, like in this neighborhood?

Coco: They are all over the place, not only in this neighborhood but in others. There could be one right here in this community, and nobody knows.

Felix: How do you find them? How do they find you guys?

Coco: They go out and look into what they consider bad neighborhoods, like our neighborhood. This is not a bad neighborhood, but they know that we are here. They got connections. These guys think that because we are gang-bangers that we can do these things for them.

Felix: What do you mean by that?

Coco: Well, that just because we are bangers we are supposed to know how to do this kind of work—that we are good at this because they think that that's what we do. Besides, if we get caught, who are we? We're just bangers. If we squeal on them, they know they're safe because the law is not going to take our word.

Felix: So these guys are keeping you guys employed?

Coco: Yes, but it's not legal. This is not the kind of job you want to tell people about. Like, if you go to McDonald's or wherever to look for a job, you just don't tell them that you had this kind of job. They're going to want to know what kind of experience you have, but this is not a legal gig. So, we don't tell what we do in this line of work. Anyway, these guys are slick. They make the operation seem legal. They come in with their own tow trucks, so the police would think that it's legal; they come in with their own equipment, and nobody knows that they are illegal. Then they stick a number on the stuff and make it legal.

Felix: And what do you think of these guys?

Coco: Hey, man, like, they have to survive. This is survival out here. They are beating the law. That's what everybody learns.

Felix: Would you do something like that if you were in the same position as these guys?

Coco: I don't know. That's dangerous. If I had my own business, I would try to stay clean.

Another major skill young members of the Diamonds must learn during this stage of burglary work is locating and selecting potential "scores." That is, they need to learn of places in which they can secure the merchandise they are involved in peddling. According to members of the Diamonds, they do not burglarize in their own neighborhood. There is, in fact, a gang policy that serves to discourage youngsters from including neighborhood residents and their property as part of their stealing pool. As stated by several members of the Diamonds, the view shared by most youngsters is that they need to keep the neighborhood fairly stable and peaceful to ensure that their drug operations run smoothly and to prevent their parents from discovering that they are affiliated with the gang.

For these reasons thefts and burglaries committed in Suburbia are often blamed on local neighborhood youth not associated with gangs. Tony explains:

> I know the two guys who are terrorizing the hood. These two guys are stoned thieves. But, since they look like everybody, you know, like other teenagers or like regular bangers, people think it's us. But these guys don't belong to a gang. They are not Diamonds. They are some of these neutrons that sometimes try to make trouble for us. But you know what? Anything that happens here is blamed on us. When things are stolen around here, when things are missing, do you know who is fingered? Us! What some people don't understand is that we have respect for where we live. Our guys don't steal around here. We want our neighborhood clean and without trouble. We got enough trouble as it is. But you know what is interesting about these two guys? Well, I'll tell you. They could go loose. The

police could come after us and forget about the people who are really going around giving people a hard time and taking their things.

Carmelo adds:

You really have to be stupid to steal in your own neighborhood. Come on, now—we are not that damn stupid. If you want people coming after you, then go and take their shit. Once you steal in your neighborhood, forget it—people will find you, and they try getting on your case. Who wants that? And, you know, where can we go if we mess with the people here? Besides, if you take their stuff, where are you going to sell it? I just think that people should know that we are a little smarter than what they think. That's just too stupid to do. Maybe other gangs do it that way. But around here we have respect.

It is also believed that members from rival gangs deliberately burglarize local neighborhood residents for the purpose of upsetting relations between the Diamonds and their neighbors. Coco elaborated on this perception:

There are guys from enemy gangs who are sent out to our hood to give people a hard time and even to steal from them. What they want to do is to put us in a bad situation with the people around here so the people can turn against us. When we find out that this is happening we play the same game, too. We call this a risk game.

There was this one time that one of the neighbors that we know, and they know us too, told us that they had seen a guy breaking into the house next door. They told us what the dude looked like, and we knew that he was not with us. So, the chief got really pissed off and told us to go and do a number in the hood of [the opposition gang]. So, I went with my main man and this other guy and ransacked this apartment. We went and took some shit from there. It was nothing important, but we turned the apartment inside out. And you know why we did this shit? Because they did it to us.

Because of their commitment to maintaining Suburbia in a state of serenity, members of the Diamonds who steal must develop appropriate methods for locating potential scores outside of their neighborhood. One of the most regularly employed approaches involves traveling by car in search of areas in the city which seem to contain desired goods, principally car models youngsters believe will "bring the most amount of cash." On these "scouting trips" youngsters are accompanied by an older and experienced member who has knowledge of these neighborhoods. During these early trips youngsters are shown a neighborhood with potential, its apparent dangerous spots (that is, places to avoid), and the different car models desired. Carmelo recalls going out on his first "expedition" and the knowledge he gained from it:

We didn't steal anything the first time we went. This guy wanted to show me the neighborhood and the things he thought I needed to learn. We drove around, and then he took me over to a street. We got out of the car and walked half a block. He took me behind one car and said, "Look, if we are going to steal this car, you can see from here how dangerous it is. This street is not protected. Anywhere in this street people can see us." So, I learned not to mess in places like that. I'm sure that, if I was by myself that day, I would have gotten caught because there were some Saabs and Toyotas, and, you know, the cars we are after— but [places] that are usually patrolled.

Another major source of information that youngsters use for locating potential scores are the customers themselves. Chop shop operators and regular customers provide youngsters with tips about merchandise they want and its location. Coco describes an ongoing relationship he has established with one chop shop operator, who frequently visits him to request certain merchandise and provides him with information about where to obtain it:

> This guy started trusting me. He knew I needed the cash and I wasn't going to rat, and, besides, nobody believes a gang member. Anyway, he would tell me of specific places where I could find this or that. He was as much a thief as I was. My biggest score with this guy was a Mazda car. He described the kind of car he wanted and told me of several places to go. One was by the ballpark—you know, where the Cubs play. I drove by there with my main man. This was very dangerous because this was the hood of an opposition gang. So, we had to be really on the alert. We found a car on Wayne Street. It was blue, and we brought it back to where he was going to pick it up.

Elf recounts a similar experience: "Without the tips from this guy who owned [the electronics] shop I never would had learned of [that area]. He knew the different places there real good. He knew houses and apartments where I could go for VCRs and stereos. I only did it several times because the other guys thought that he was a narc and was setting us up. So, we stopped. And I wasn't sure about this guy. Everybody was suspicious."

While the act of stealing is dangerous, risky, and requires much preparation and planning, sales of stolen goods usually produce small earnings for these youngsters. In the following account Tito provides a brief description of the monetary payoff of stealing: "We stole this one car because it had some little seats a guy in the neighborhood needed. And, so, we went and took the car, and this car had a nice radio, and I took the radio and sold it, and that's how we used to keep money in our pockets so we could get new gym shoes and things like that. What was I making? Sometimes I pocketed fifty [dollars]. Sometimes my take was twenty. You know, enough to get me by." In a similar way Lobo describes making only enough money to take his girlfriend to the movies and, at times, out for dinner: "I never made a lot of money through stealing. Most of the money I got I used it for being with my girlfriend. We would go to get a bite and then to the show. Sometimes we did it the opposite way, but always I spent the money quick and on her."

From the descriptions provided above by Lobo and Tito as well as those by other youngsters it is not difficult to discern the "profit-sharing" dimension of group theft. Simply put, youngsters are expected to share equally with their partners whatever they make from stolen goods. According to Coco, "We were making spending money—only enough to buy little things. So, why not split the money three ways or four ways? I always liked working with my partner, and sometimes we brought one other guy with us, so it was a three-way split. We knew that we were not going to get rich from one job, so what we made was split between the three of us. And it didn't matter what I did or the other guy did; I never took more than what we gave him. That was our policy—even sharing."

When the job of stealing produces negative results it is expected that the entire working crew absorbs the blame. That is, as partners, members of the Diamonds not only share the profits but also any losses from stealing. Elf provides a vivid description of this element of sharing while recounting one incident that led to the apprehension of his entire crew:

We went to get this car for a chop shop deal, and after we got it we decided to drive around for a while. It was a new Toyota—you know, one of those Camrys that . . . they have everything. So, we were cruising through the north side, trying it out. Hell, we decided to have some fun with the car before giving it up. But then the law spotted us, and they started chasing us. And I was with my boys; there were three of us. I was driving, so I took the car through alleys and shit, but they got us because I got into one alley that was blocked by a garbage truck. So, we closed the windows of the car, and the police came, and we refused to open the windows or the doors. Then I said to the guys that it was cool, that I was going to open up but that nobody say nothing. So, we walked out, and the cops proceeded to search us and the car, and then they started punching us and beating all three of us. But we didn't talk. We all said that someone else gave us the car to take someplace. We stuck to that story. We all got busted together. That's how it is with us; we do it together, and we pay together.

In effect, the major outcome of stealing is seldom measured by economic benefit but, rather, by the sense of achievement experienced by youngsters who manage the operation successfully and use their mechanical expertise. A "beautiful job" does not necessarily indicate that a large amount of money was taken or made; it also suggests an appreciation of a crew's craftsmanship. In this way, the youngster working in stealing operations resembles the craftsman whose reward is more psychological than economic.

Additionally, it is more appropriate to speak of gang members involved in stealing—in particular, the Pee Wees or Littles—as "career thieves" rather than "professional thieves": They view stealing strictly as a stage in their participation in the life of the gang and not as a permanent business. Through acts of stealing these newer gang members demonstrate "how much heart they have" and the skills they have learned and can offer to the gang—all of which are essential ingredients for measuring the kind of recognition and acceptance bestowed upon an individual member. (Pee Wees make a distinction between the "skilled" and "inept" thief. In most cases this contrast has to do with one's orientation toward law enforcement. To be a skilled thief is to have developed skills that minimize one's chances of being apprehended. The gang responds quite favorably to those youngsters possessing this special competence.) Thus, the major significance of stealing stems from its symbolism as an expression of fidelity and an act of commitment to the virtues of the gang. Consider the following explanation taken from an interview with Rafael, who reached the level of cocaine dealer: "In gangs there are members that are different in their own way. You might have the quiet type of guy; you might have the real wild one that likes to steal; you might have another that likes to do drugs; you might have all different types of characters. But there is one thing if you want to advance and show that you're bad and that you're real cool and that the gang could trust you selling drugs—if that's what you want, then you must prove yourself by stealing, by writing on the walls of another gang and showing that you're not a snitch."

Discussion Questions

1. If the Diamonds make most of their money from drug dealing, why do they engage in the relatively high-risk crime of theft? What functions does stealing serve for the group besides profit?

2. Why is the job of stealing assigned to the younger gang members? Why don't gang members progress from relatively petty theft when young to more organized and lucrative forms of theft as they get older?

3. How do members of the Diamonds who steal minimize the risks of stealing? What functions does working in a crew serve for the thieves? Why do they usually select targets outside their own community?

4. What sorts of property do the gang members steal? Where do they get information about what to steal? How do they convert stolen property into cash? How do they divide their profits?

*Homeboys, Dope Fiends, Legits, and New Jacks**

John M. Hagedorn

Does the money to be made from the drug trade keep members of groups such as the Diamonds active in gangs into their adult years, or do gang members eventually adopt more legitimate lifestyles? In this paper, John Hagedorn documents the great variation among members of Milwaukee gangs in their commitment to conventional or criminal ways of life, and he looks at changes in that commitment over time for the same individual. He also explores the policy implications of his findings.

This paper addresses issues that are controversial in both social science and public policy. First, what happens to gang members as they age? Do most gang members graduate from gangbanging to drug sales, as popular stereotypes might suggest? Is drug dealing so lucrative that adult gang members eschew work and become committed to the drug economy? Have changes in economic conditions produced underclass gangs so deviant and so detached from the labor market that the only effective policies are more police and more prisons?

Second, and related to these questions, are male adult gang members basically similar kinds of people, or are gangs made up of different types? Might some gang members be

* This paper was based on a paper presented at the 44th annual meetings of the American Society of Criminology. Helpful comments on earlier drafts were made by Manuel Chavez, Lavelle Cox, Mary Devitt, Jeff Fagan, Ansley Hamid, Clint Holloway, Joan Moore, Steve Percy, Jorge Silva, Edward Smith, Claire Sterk-Elifson, Angelo Vega, and Jerome Wonders. Send correspondence to Hagedorn, UWM Urban Research Center, PO Box 413, Milwaukee, WI 53201.

Source: John M. Hagedorn, "Homeboys, Dope Fiends, Legits, and New Jacks," *Criminology* 32 (May 1994), pp. 197–216. Reprinted by permission of the American Society of Criminology.

more conventional, and others less so? What are the implications of this "continuum of conventionality" within drug-dealing gangs for public policy? Data from a Milwaukee study on gangs and drug dealing shed some light on these issues.

Gang Members, Drugs, and Work

An underlying question is whether the drug economy provides sufficient incentives to keep gang members away from legal work. If drug sales offer highly profitable opportunities for all who are willing to take the risks, we might expect many adult gang members to be committed firmly to the drug economy. On the other hand, if drug dealing entails many risks and produces few success stories, gang members might be expected to have a more variable relationship to illicit drug sales. In that case we could look at variation within the gang to explain different behaviors.

The research literature contains few empirical studies on the pull of the drug economy away from licit work. On the more general level, Carl Taylor (1990:120) asserts that "when drug distribution becomes the employer, $3.65 or $8.65 can't compare with drug business income." Martín Sánchez Jankowski (1991:101), in his study of gangs in three cities, found an "entrepreneurial spirit" to be the "driving force in the world view and behavior of gang members." This "entrepreneurial spirit" pushes gang members to make rational decisions to engage in drug sales. Jerome Skolnick (1990) and his students argue that gangs are centrally involved with profitable mid-level drug distribution, although these findings have been challenged by researchers (Klein and Maxson, 1993; Waldorf, 1993).

Others have found that gang involvement in drug sales varies substantially (see Cummings and Monte, 1993; Huff, 1990). Klein et al. (1991) remind us that not all gangs are involved with drug sales, a point that is often overlooked in the discussion of an invariant gang/drug nexus. Among those who sell drugs, actual income varies. Fagan (1991) points out that earnings from drug dealing in two Manhattan neighborhoods ranged from about $1,000 to nearly $5,000 per month. Although most drug sellers had little involvement with the formal economy, 25% of Fagan's dealers also worked in conventional jobs, and most reported both illegal *and* legal income for each month. This finding suggests that incentives from drug sales were not always sufficient to make dealing a full-time job.

Similarly, a Rand Corporation study (MacCoun and Reuter, 1992:485) found that the typical Washington, D.C. small dealer made about $300 per month and the typical big dealer $3,700, with an average of about $1,300. Sullivan (1989) found illicit economic activities in Brooklyn to be a youthful enterprise, quickly outgrown when "real" jobs offered themselves. The seriousness of criminal activity varied with the intactness of networks providing access to legitimate work. Most of Williams's (1989) New York "cocaine kids" matured out of the drug business as they became young adults and their drug-dealing clique broke up. Padilla's (1992:162) "Diamonds" became "disillusioned" with the empty promises of street-level dealing and aspired to legitimate jobs.

These few studies suggest substantial variation in the degree and duration of gang involvement in drug dealing. The drug economy is not an unquestionably profitable opportunity for gang members; rather, its promise appears to be more ambiguous. If that conclusion is valid, research must examine both the actual amounts of money earned by adult gang drug dealers *and* variation within the gang to understand gang involvement in drug dealing. We have a few studies on how much money gang members make from selling drugs, but hardly any contemporary data on different types of gang members.

Variation Within the Gang

Some research has portrayed gang members as relatively invariant. Walter Miller (1958) viewed gang delinquents as representative of a lower-class cultural milieu; his six "focal concerns" are persistent and distinctive features of the entire American "lower class." Similarly, Jankowski (1991:26–28) said that male gang members were one-dimensional "tough nuts," defiant individuals with a rational "social Darwinist worldview" who displayed defiant individualism "more generally" than other people in low-income communities.

Other research, however, has suggested that gang members vary, particularly on their orientation toward conventionality. Whyte (1943) classified his Cornerville street corner men as either "college boys" or "corner boys," depending on their aspirations. Cloward and Ohlin (1960:95), applying Merton's (1957) earlier typology, categorized lower-class youths in four cells of a matrix, depending on their aspirations and "criteria for success." Many of their delinquents repudiated the legitimacy of conventional society and resorted to innovative solutions to attain success goals. Cloward and Ohlin took issue with Cohen (1955) and Matza (1964), whose delinquents were internally conflicted but, as a group, imputed legitimacy to the norms of the larger society.

Some more recent researchers also have found variation in conventionality within gangs. Klein (1971), echoing Thrasher (1927), differentiated between "core" and "fringe" members, a distinction that policy makers often use today as meaning more or less deviant. In the same view, Taylor (1990:8–9) saw gang members as "corporates," "scavengers," "emulators," "auxiliaries," or "adjuncts," mainly on the basis of their distance from gang membership. Fagan (1990:206), like Matza and Cohen, found that "conventional values may coexist with deviant behaviors for gang delinquents and other inner city youth." MacLeod (1987:124) observed surprising variation between ethnic groups. The white "hallway hangers" believed "stagnation at the bottom of the occupational structure to be almost inevitable" and were rebellious delinquents, whereas the African American "brothers" reacted to similar conditions by aspiring to middle-class status.

Joan Moore is one of the few researchers who have looked carefully at differentiation within gangs. In her early work (1978), she discovered both square and deviant career models among East Los Angeles gang members. In an impressive restudy (1991) she found that most adult gang members were working conventional jobs, but those who had been active in the gang in recent years had more difficulty finding employment as job networks collapsed. Many veteran gang members had been addicted to heroin for years, but by the 1990s few were dealing drugs to support themselves. Moore found that both male and female Chicano gang members could be categorized as "tecatos," "cholos," or "squares," a typology similar to those suggested for the nongang poor by Anderson (1978, 1990) and Hannerz (1969).

If gang members in fact vary on orientation to conventionality, and if the drug economy itself offers only an ambiguous lure, jobs and other programs that strengthen "social capital" (Coleman, 1988) might be effective means of integrating many adult gang members into the community (see Sampson and Laub, 1993). On the other hand, if adult gang members are look-alike criminals who are dazzled by the prospect of vast profits in the drug trade, jobs and social programs would have little effect, and our present incarceration strategy may be appropriate.

This paper provides quantitative and qualitative data on the conventional orientations of young adult gang members in Milwaukee. First we report on the licit work and illicit drug-dealing patterns of adult gang members. Then we offer a typology, drawn from Milwaukee data, that demonstrates a "continuum of conventionality" between core members of drug-dealing gangs. In conclusion, we discuss research and public policy consequences of the study.

Research Methods and Sources of Data

The interpretations presented here draw on observation and extensive fieldwork conducted over a number of years, specifically from two funded interview studies, in 1987 and in 1992. During the early 1980s I directed the first gang diversion program in the city and became acquainted with many leaders and other founders of Milwaukee's gangs. I have maintained a privileged relationship with many of these individuals.

In the 1987 study, we interviewed 47 members of 19 Milwaukee male and female gangs (Hagedorn, 1988). These "founders" were the core gang members who were present when their gangs took names. Founders are likely to be representative of hard-core gang members, not of peripheral members or "wannabes." As time has passed, the gang founders' exploits have been passed down, and younger Milwaukee gang members have looked up to them as street "role models." Our research design does not enable us to conclude how fully our sample represents subsequent groups of adult gang members.

As part of our current study, we conducted lengthy audiotaped interviews with 101 founding members of 18 gangs in the city; 90 were male and 11 female. Sixty percent were African American, 37% Latino, and 3% white. Their median age was 26 years, with 75% between 23 and 30. Twenty-three respondents also had been interviewed in the 1987 study; 78 were interviewed here for the first time. Members from two gangs interviewed in the earlier study could not be located. Each respondent was paid $50.

The interview picks up the lives of the founding members since 1987, when we conducted our original study, and asks them to recount their careers in the drug business, to discuss their pursuit of conventional employment, and to reflect on their personal lives. The respondents also were asked to describe the current status of their fellow gang members. In the 1987 study, we collected rosters of all members of each gang whose founders we interviewed. In the current study, we asked each respondent to double check the roster of his or her gang to make sure it was accurate. In both studies, we asked respondents to tell us whether the other members were still alive, had graduated from high school, were currently locked up, or were working. In the 1992 study, we also asked whether each of the founding members was selling or using dope (in our data "dope" means cocaine), had some other hustle, or was on the run, among other questions.

To understand more clearly the variation between and within the gangs, we interviewed nearly the entire rosters of three gangs and about half (64 of 152) of the original founding members from eight male gangs in three different types of neighborhoods. In each of these gangs, we interviewed some who still were involved with both the gang and the dope game and some who no longer were involved. This paper reports on data on all of the 90 males we interviewed and on their accounts of the present circumstances of 236 founders of 14 male gangs.

The interviews in this most recent study were conducted in late 1992 and early 1993.[1] As in the original study, the research follows an inductive and collaborative model (see Moore, 1978), in which gang members cooperate with the academic staff to focus the research design, construct interview schedules, conduct interviews, and interpret the findings.

Findings: Drug Dealing and Work

As expected, gang members appear to be working more today than five years ago, but participation in the formal labor market remains quite low (see Table 13-1).[2]

These low levels of labor market participation apply to more than gang members. A recent Milwaukee study revealed that in 1990, 51% of jobs held by *all* African American males age 20 to 24, slightly younger than our study population, lasted less than six weeks. The average *annual* income in retail trade, where most subjects held jobs, was $2,023; for jobs in service, $1,697; in education, $3,084 (Rose et al., 1992). African American young adults as a whole (and probably nongang Latinos) clearly were not working regularly and were not earning a living wage.

Selling cocaine seems to have filled the employment void. In 1987 only a few gang members dealt drugs, mainly marijuana. Within African American gangs, at least, cocaine dealing was not prevalent. By 1992, however, cocaine had become a major factor in Milwaukee's informal economy, evolving into widespread curbside sales and numerous drug

TABLE 13-1   1992 Status of Male Gang Founders, 236 Founding Members of 14 Male Groups

Predominant Activity/Status	African American	White	Latino	Total
Working: Part-Time or Full-Time	22.2%	68.8%	27.6%	30.5%
Hustling: Nearly All Selling Cocaine	50.4	15.4	56.3	47.9
Deceased	7.7	6.3	5.7	6.8
Whereabouts Unknown	19.7	9.4	10.3	14.8
Total N =100%	N =117	N =32	N =87	N =236

Note: Column percentages may not equal 100% because of rounding.

houses (see Hamid, 1992). Of the 236 fellow gang founders, 72% reportedly had sold cocaine at some time in the last five years.[3]

That involvement has not been steady, however. We collected detailed data on the length of involvement in the drug economy and the amount of money made by those we interviewed. We asked our respondents to indicate how they had supported themselves in each month of the past three years, and then asked how much money they made in both legal and illegal employment. For most respondents, selling cocaine was an on-again, off-again proposition. About half (35) of those who had sold cocaine sold in no more than 12 months out of the past 36; only 12% (9) sold in more than 24 of the past 36 months. Latinos sold for slightly longer periods than African Americans, 17.7 months to 13.1 months ($p = .07^*$).

When gang members did sell dope, they made widely varying amounts of money. About one-third of those who sold reported that they made no more than they would have earned if they worked for minimum wage. Another one-third made the equivalent of $13 to $25 an hour. Only three of the 73 sellers ever made "crazy money," or more than $10,000 per month, at any time during their drug-selling careers. Mean monthly income from drug sales was approximately $2,400, or about $15 per hour for full-time work. By contrast, mean monthly income for legal work was only $677; Latinos made more than African Americans ($797 per month to $604 per month, $p = .08^*$; table not shown). The *maximum* amount of money earned monthly by any gang member from legal income was $2,400, the *mean* for gang drug sales (see Table 13-2).[4]

Qualitative data from our interviews support the view that for some respondents, the dope game indeed lives up to its stereotype. One dealer credibly reported income from his three drug houses at about $50,000 per month for several months in 1989. Another told how he felt about making so much money:

Q: Did you ever make crazy money?

R#220: Yeah . . . one time my hands had turned green from all that money, I couldn't wash it off, man, I loved it. Oh man, look at this . . . just holding all that money in my hand turned my hands green from just counting all that money. Sometimes I'd sit back and just count it maybe three, four times, for the hell of it.

Even for big dealers, however, that money didn't last. Some "players" were "rolling" for several years, but most took a fall within a year or so. As with Padilla's Diamonds, disappointments with the drug trade seemed to exceed its promise for most gang members. Prison and jail time frequently interrupted their lives. More than three-quarters of all gang founders on our rosters had spent some time in jail in the past five years, as had two-thirds of our respondents. Even so, our respondents had worked a mean of 14.5 months out of the last 36 in legitimate jobs, had worked 14.5 months selling dope, and had spent the

---

* [The values of p mean that the differences between the two figures in each set (17.7 and 13.1, and $797 and $604) are statistically significant at the .07 and .08 levels, respectively. This means that the likelihood that the differences are due to chance factors in the selection of samples and are not "real" differences are seven in 100 and eight in 100, respectively. In neither case do the values of p suggest great differences between the figures; a value of less than .05 is usually regarded as indicative of a meaningful difference.]

TABLE 13-2   Mean Monthly Income from Drug Dealing: 1989–1991, 87 African American and Latino Respondents

Average Monthly Income from Drug Sales	African American	Latino*	Total
Never sold	15.8%	23.3%	18.4%
Less than $1,000 monthly (equivalent to less than $6/hour)	28.1	30.0	28.7
Between $1,000 and $2,000 monthly (equivalent to $7-$12/hour)	28.1	6.7	20.7
Between $2,00 and $4,000 monthly (equivalent to $13-$25/hour)	25.3	33.3	28.7
More than $10,000 monthly	1.8	6.7	3.4
Total N =100%	N =57	N =30	N =87

* Three whites were excluded from the analysis. One white founder never sold, and the other two made less than $2,000 monthly.
Note: Column percentages may not equal 100% because of rounding.

remaining seven months in jail. Twenty-five percent of our respondents had worked legitimate jobs at least 24 of the past 36 months.

Yet an anomaly confronted us as we analyzed our data on work. As might be expected, nine out of 10 of those who were not working at the time of our interview had sold dope in the past three years. We also found, however, that three-quarters of those who *were* working in 1992 had sold dope as well within the previous five years (see Table 13-3).

These findings lend themselves to alternative explanations. It may be that three-quarters of those who were working had sold cocaine in the past, but had stopped and were getting their lives together. A second interpretation is that full-time employment is nothing more than an income supplement or "front" for continuation in the drug game. Some gang founders indeed fit into one or the other of these categories.

A third interpretation evolved as we received reports from our staff and respondents about the current status of their fellow gang members. A few days after an interview with "Roger," one of our staff members would report that "Roger" was no longer working for a temporary agency, as he had reported, but was "back in the dope game." The next week "Roger" might call us from jail. A week or so later, we would learn that he was out on bail, his "lady" had put pressure on him, and he was now working full-time in construction with his brother-in-law. Our offices were flooded with similar reports about dozens of people on our rosters. Working and selling drugs were both part of the difficult, topsy-turvy lives led by our respondents. Elliot Liebow's (1967:219) colorful description of the confused lives on Tally's Corner also fits our data: "Traffic is heavy in all directions."

TABLE 13-3   1992 Work Status by Involvement in Cocaine Sales, 220 Surviving Members of 14 Male Gangs

Sold Dope in Last Five Years?	Working Now	Not Working Now*	Work Status Unknown	Totals
Have sold dope	75.0%	91.2%	40.0%	77.7%
Have not sold dope	16.7	5.3	2.9	8.6
Unknown	8.3	3.5	57.1	13.6
Total N =100%	N =72	N =113	N =35	N =220

* Includes selling cocaine, being "on the run," being locked up, and being involved in other street hustles.

These vicissitudes became too complicated for us to track, so we "froze" the status of founders on our rosters at the time of the last and most reliable interview. Some of our founders seemed to be committed to the dope business and a few had "gone legit," but most of those we were trying to track appeared to be on an economic merry-go-round, with continual movement in and out of the secondary labor market. Although their average income from drug sales far surpassed their income from legal employment, most Milwaukee male gang members apparently kept trying to find licit work.

To help explain this movement in and out of the formal labor market, we created a typology of adult gang members, using constant comparisons (Strauss, 1987). This categorization has some similarities to earlier typologies, but it differs in that it intends to account for the different orientations of gang members in an era of decreased legitimate economic opportunities and increased drug-related, illicit opportunities.

A Typology of Male Adult Gang Members

We developed four ideal types on a continuum of conventional behaviors and values: (1) those few who had gone *legit,* or had matured out of the gang; (2) *homeboys,* a majority of both African American and Latino adult gang members, who alternately worked conventional jobs and took various roles in drug sales; (3) *dope fiends,* who were addicted to cocaine and participated in the dope business as a way to maintain access to the drug; and (4) *new jacks,* who regarded the dope game as a career.

Some gang members, we found, moved over time between categories, some had characteristics of more than one category, and others straddled the boundaries (see Hannerz, 1969:57). Thus a few homeboys were in the process of becoming legit, many moved into and out of cocaine addiction, and others gave up and adopted a new jack orientation. Some new jacks returned to conventional life; others received long prison terms or became addicted to dope. Our categories are not discrete, but our typology seemed to fit the population of gang members we were researching. Our "member checks" (Lincoln and Guba, 1985:314–16) of the constructs with gang members validated these categories for male gang members.

Legits

Legits were those young men who had walked away from the gang. They were working or may have gone on to school. Legits had not been involved in the dope game at all, or not for at least five years. They did not use cocaine heavily, though some may have done so in the past. Some had moved out of the old neighborhood; others, like our project staff, stayed to help out or "give back" to the community. These are prime examples of Whyte's "college boys" or Cloward and Ohlin's Type I, oriented to economic gain and class mobility. The following quote is an example of a young African American man who "went legit" and is now working and going to college.

Q: Looking back over the past five years, what major changes took place in your life—things that happened that really made things different for you?

R#105: I had got into a relationship with my girl, that's one thing. I just knew I couldn't be out on the streets trying to hustle all the time. That's what changed me, I just got a sense of responsibility.

Today's underclass gangs appear to be fundamentally different from those in Thrasher's or Cloward and Ohlin's time, when most gang members "matured out" of the gang. Of the 236 Milwaukee male founders, only 12 (5.1%) could be categorized as having matured out: that is, they were working full time *and* had not sold cocaine in the past five years. When these data are disaggregated by race, the reality of the situation becomes even clearer. We could verify only two of 117 African Americans and one of 87 Latino male gang founders who were currently working and had not sold dope in the past five years. One-third of the white members fell into this category.[5]

Few African American and Latino gang founders, however, were resigned to a life of crime, jail, and violence. After a period of rebellion and living the fast life, the majority of gang founders, or "homeboys," wanted to settle down and go legit, but the path proved to be very difficult.

Homeboys

"Homeboys" were the majority of all adult gang members. They were not firmly committed to the drug economy, especially after the early thrill of fast money and "easy women" wore off. They had reached an age, the mid-twenties, when criminal offenses normally decline (Gottfredson and Hirschi, 1990). Most of these men were unskilled, lacked education, and had had largely negative experiences in the secondary labor market. Some homeboys were committed more strongly to the streets, others to a more conventional life. Most had used cocaine, some heavily at times, but their use was largely in conjunction with selling from a house or corner with their gang "homies." Most homeboys either were married or had a "steady" lady. They also had strong feelings of loyalty to their fellow gang members.

Here, two different homeboys explain how they had changed, and how hard that change was:

Q: Looking back over the past five years, what major changes took place in your life—things that happened that really made things different for you?

R#211: The things that we went through wasn't worth it, and I had a family, you know, and kids, and I had to think about them first, and the thing with the drug game was, that money was quick, easy, and fast, and it went like that, the more money you make the more popular you was. You know, as I see it now it wasn't worth it because the time that I done in penitentiaries I lost my sanity. To me it feels like I lost a part of my kids, because, you know, I know they still care, and they know I'm daddy, but I just lost out. Somebody else won and I lost.

Q: Is she with somebody else now?

R#211: Yeah. She hung in there about four or five months after I went to jail.

Q: It must have been tough for her to be alone with all those kids.

R#211: Yeah.

Q: What kind of person are you?

R#217: Mad. I'm a mad young man. I'm a poor young man. I'm a good person to my kids and stuff, and given the opportunity to have something nice and stop working for this petty-ass money I would try to change a lot of things. . . .

I feel I'm the type of person that given the opportunity to try to have something legit, I will take it, but I'm not going to go by the slow way, taking no four, five years working at no chicken job and trying to get up to a manager just to start making six, seven dollars. And then get fired when I come in high or drunk or something. Or miss a day or something because I got high smoking weed, drinking beer, and the next day come in and get fired; then I'm back in where I started from. So I'm just a cool person, and if I'm given the opportunity and if I can get a job making nine, ten dollars an hour, I'd let everything go; I'd just sit back and work my job and go home. That kind of money I can live with. But I'm not going to settle for no three, four dollars an hour, know what I'm saying?

Homeboys present a more confused theoretical picture than legits. Cloward and Ohlin's Type III delinquents were rebels, who had a "sense of injustice" or felt "unjust deprivation" at a failed system (1960:117). Their gang delinquency is a collective solution to the failure of institutional arrangements. They reject traditional societal norms; other, success-oriented illegitimate norms replace conventionality.

Others have questioned whether gang members' basic outlook actually rejects conventionality. Matza (1964) viewed delinquents' rationalizations of their conduct as evidence of techniques meant to "neutralize" deeply held conventional beliefs. Cohen (1955:129–37) regarded delinquency as a nonutilitarian "reaction formation" to middle-class standards, though middle-class morality lingers, repressed and unacknowledged. What appears to be gang "pathological" behavior, Cohen points out, is the result of the delinquent's striving to attain core values of "the American way of life." Short and Strodtbeck (1965), testing various gang theories, found that white and African American gang members, and lower- and middle-class youths, had similar conventional values.

Our homeboys are older versions of Cohen's and Matza's delinquents, and are even more similar to Short and Strodtbeck's study subjects. Milwaukee homeboys shared three basic characteristics: (1) They worked regularly at legitimate jobs, although they ventured into the drug economy when they believed it was necessary for survival. (2) They had very conventional aspirations; their core values centered on finding a secure place in the American way of life. (3) They had some surprisingly conventional ethical beliefs about the immorality of drug dealing. To a man, they justified their own involvement in drug sales by very Matza-like techniques of "neutralization."

Homeboys are defined by their in-and-out involvement in the legal and illegal economies. Recall that about half of our male respondents had sold drugs no more than 12 of the past 36 months. More than one-third never served any time in jail. Nearly 60% had worked legitimate jobs at least 12 months of the last 36, with a mean of 14.5 months. Homeboys' work patterns thus differed both from those of legits, who worked solely legal jobs, and new jacks who considered dope dealing a career.

To which goal did homeboys aspire, being big-time dope dealers or holding a legitimate job? Rather than having any expectations of staying in the dope game, homeboys aspired to settling down, getting married, and living at least a watered-down version of the American dream. Like Padilla's (1992:157) Diamonds, they strongly desired to "go legit." Although they may have enjoyed the fast life for a while, it soon went stale. Listen to this homeboy, the one who lost his lady when he went to jail:

Q: Five years from now, what would you want to be doing?

R#211: Five years from now? I want to have a steady job, I want to have been working that job for about five years, and just with a family somewhere.

Q: Do you think that's gonna come true?

R#211: Yeah, that's basically what I'm working on. I mean, this bullshit is over now, I'm twenty-five, I've played games long enough, it don't benefit nobody. If you fuck yourself away, all you gonna be is fucked, I see it now.

Others had more hopeful or wilder dreams, but a more sobering outlook on the future. The other homeboy, who said he wouldn't settle for three or four dollars an hour speaks as follows:

Q: Five years from now, what would you want to be doing?

R#217: Owning my own business. And rich. A billionaire.

Q: What do you realistically expect you'll be doing in five years?

R#217: Probably working at McDonald's. That's the truth.

Homeboys' aspirations were divided between finding a steady full-time job and setting up their own business. Their strivings pertained less to being for or against "middle-class status" than to finding a practical, legitimate occupation that could support them (see Short and Strodtbeck, 1965). Many homeboys believed that using skills learned in selling drugs to set up a small business would give them a better chance at a decent life than trying to succeed as an employee.

Most important, homeboys "grew up" and were taking a realistic look at their life chances. This homeboy spoke for most:

Q: Looking back over the past five years, what major changes have taken place in your life—things that made a difference about where you are now?

R#220: I don't know, maybe maturity. . . . Just seeing life in a different perspective . . . realizing that from sixteen to twenty-three, man, just shot past. And just realizing that it did, shucks, you just realizing how quick it zoomed past me. And it really just passed me up without really having any enjoyment of a teenager. And hell, before I know it I'm going to hit thirty or forty, and I ain't going to have nothing to stand on. I don't want that shit. Because I see a lot of brothers out here now, that's forty-three, forty-four and ain't got shit. They's still standing out on the corner trying to make a hustle. Doing this, no family, no stable home and nothing. I don't want that shit. . . . I don't give a fuck about getting rich or nothing, but I want a comfortable life, a decent woman, a family to come home to. I mean, everybody needs somebody to care for. This ain't where it's at.

Finally, homeboys were characterized by their ethical views about selling dope. As a group, they believed dope selling was "unmoral"—wrong, but necessary for survival. Homeboys' values were conventional, but in keeping with Matza's findings, they justified their conduct by neutralizing their violation of norms. Homeboys believed that economic necessity was the overriding reason why they could not live up to their values (see Liebow, 1967:214). They were the epitome of ambivalence, ardently believing that dope selling was both wrong and absolutely necessary. One longtime dealer expressed this contradiction:

Q: Do you consider it wrong or immoral to sell dope?

R#129: Um-hum, very wrong.

Q: Why?

R#129: Why, because it's killing people.

Q: Well how come you do it?

R#129: It's also a money maker.

Q: Well how do you balance those things out? I mean, here you're doing something that you think is wrong, making money. How does that make you feel when you're doing it, or don't you think about it when you're doing it?

R#129: Once you get a (dollar) bill, once you look at, I say this a lot, once you look at those dead white men [*presidents' pictures on currency*], you care about nothing else, you don't care about nothing else. Once you see those famous dead white men. That's it.

Q: Do you ever feel bad about selling drugs, doing something that was wrong?

R#129: How do I feel? Well a lady will come in and sell all the food stamps, all of them. When they're sold, what are the kids gonna eat? They can't eat the dope cause she's gonna go smoke that up, or do whatever with it. And then you feel like "wrong." But then, in the back of your mind, man, you just got a hundred dollars worth of food stamps for thirty dollars worth of dope, and you can sell them at the store for seven dollars on ten, so you got seventy coming. So you get seventy dollars for thirty dollars. It is not wrong to do this. It is not wrong to do this!

Homeboys also refused to sell to pregnant women or to juveniles. Contrary to Jankowski's (1991:102) assertion that in gangs "there is no ethical code that regulates business ventures," Milwaukee homeboys had some strong moral feelings about how they carried out their business:

R#109: I won't sell to no little kids. And, ah, if he gonna get it, he gonna get it from someone else besides me. I won't sell to no pregnant woman. If she gonna kill her baby, I want to sleep not knowing that I had anything to do with it. Ah, for anybody else, hey, it's their life, you choose your life how you want.

Q: But how come—I want to challenge you. You know if kids are coming or a pregnant woman's coming, you know they're going to get it somewhere else, right? Someone else will make their money on it; why not you?

R#109: 'Cause the difference is I'll be able to sleep without a guilty conscience.

Homeboys were young adults living on the edge. On the one hand, like most Americans, they had relatively conservative views on social issues and wanted to settle down with a job, a wife, and children. On the other hand, they were afraid they would never succeed, and that long stays in prison would close doors and lock them out of a conventional life. They did not want to continue to live on the streets, but they feared that hustling might be the only way to survive.[6]

Dope Fiends

Dope fiends are gang members who are addicted to cocaine. Thirty-eight percent of all African American founders were using cocaine at the time of our interview, as were 55% of Latinos and 53% of whites. African Americans used cocaine at lower rates than white gang members, but went to jail twice as often. The main focus in a dope fiend's life is getting the drug. Asked what they regretted most about their life, dope fiends invariably said "drug use," whereas most homeboys said "dropping out of school."

Most Milwaukee gang dope fiends, or daily users of cocaine, smoked it as "rocks." More casual users, or reformed dope fiends, if they used cocaine at all, snorted it or sprinkled it on marijuana (called a "primo") to enhance the high. Injection was rare among African Americans but more common among Latinos. About one-quarter of those we interviewed, however, abstained totally from use of cocaine. A majority of the gang members on our rosters had used cocaine since its use escalated in Milwaukee in the late 1980s.

Of 110 gang founders who were reported to be currently using cocaine, 37% were reported to be using "heavily" (every day, in our data), 44% "moderately" (several times per week), and 19% "lightly" (sporadically). More than 70% of all founders on our rosters who were not locked up were currently using cocaine to some extent. More than one-third of our male respondents considered themselves, at some time in their lives, to be "heavy" cocaine users.

More than one-quarter of our respondents had used cocaine for seven years or more, roughly the total amount of time cocaine has dominated the illegal drug market in Milwaukee. Latinos had used cocaine slightly longer than African Americans, for a mean of 75 months compared with 65. Cocaine use followed a steady pattern in our respondents' lives; most homeboys had used cocaine as part of their day-to-day life, especially while in the dope business.

Dope fiends were quite unlike Cloward and Ohlin's "double failures," gang members who used drugs as part of a "retreatist subculture." Milwaukee dope fiends participated regularly in conventional labor markets. Of the 110 founders who were reported as currently using cocaine, slightly more were working legitimate jobs than were not working. Most dope fiends worked at some time in their homies' dope houses or were fronted an ounce or an "eightball" (3.5 grams) of cocaine to sell. Unlike Anderson's "wineheads," gang dope fiends were not predominantly "has-beens" and did not "lack the ability and motivation to hustle" (Anderson, 1978:96–97). Milwaukee cocaine users, like heroin users (Johnson et al., 1985; Moore, 1978; Preble and Casey, 1969), played an active role in the drug-selling business.

Rather than spending their income from drug dealing on family, clothes, or women, dope fiends smoked up their profits. Eventually many stole dope belonging to the boss or "dopeman" and got into trouble. At times their dope use made them so erratic that they were no longer trusted and were forced to leave the neighborhood. Often, however, the gang members who were selling took them back and fronted them cocaine to sell to put them back on their feet. Many had experienced problems in violating the cardinal rule, "Don't get high on your own supply," as in this typical story:

R#131: . . . if you ain't the type that's a user, yeah, you'll make fabulous money but if you was the type that sells it and uses it and do it at the same time, you know, you get restless. Sometimes you get used to taking your own drugs. . . . I'll just use the profits and just do it . . . and then the next day if I get something again, I'd just take the money to pay up and keep the profits. . . . You sell a couple of hundred and you do a hundred. That's how I was doing it.

Cocaine use was a regular part of the lives of most Milwaukee gang members engaged in the drug economy. More than half of our respondents had never attended a treatment program; more than half of those who had been in treatment went through court-ordered programs. Few of our respondents stopped use by going to a treatment program. Even heavy cocaine use was an "on-again, off-again" situation in which most gang members alternately quit by themselves and started use again (Waldorf et al., 1991).

Alcohol use among dope fiends and homeboys (particularly 40-ounce bottles of Olde English 800 ale) appears to be even more of a problem than cocaine use. Like homeboys, however, most dope fiends aspired to have a family, to hold a steady job, and to find some peace. The wild life of the dope game had played itself out; the main problem was how to quit using.[7]

New Jacks

Whereas homeboys had a tentative relationship with conventional labor markets and held some strong moral beliefs, new jacks had chosen the dope game as a career. They were often loners, strong individualists like Jankowski's (1991) gang members, who cared little about group norms. Frequently they posed as the embodiment of media stereotypes. About one-quarter of our interview respondents could be described as new jacks: they had done nothing in the last 36 months except hustle or spend time in jail.

In some ways, new jacks mirror the criminal subculture described by Cloward and Ohlin. If a criminal subculture is to develop, Cloward and Ohlin argued, opportunities to learn a criminal career must be present, and close ties to conventional markets or customers must exist. This situation distinguishes the criminal from the violent and the retreatist subcultures. The emergence of the cocaine economy and a large market for illegal drugs provided precisely such an opportunity structure for this generation of gang members. New jacks are those who took advantage of the opportunities, and who, at least for the present, have committed themselves to a career in the dope game.

Q: Do you consider it wrong or immoral to sell dope?

R#203: I think it's right because can't no motherfucker live your life but you.

Q: Why?

R#203: Why? I'll put it this way . . . I love selling dope. I know there's other niggers out here love the money just like I do. And ain't no motherfucker gonna stop a nigger from selling dope . . . I'd sell to my own mother if she had the money.

New jacks, like other gang cocaine dealers, lived up to media stereotypes of the "drug dealer" role and often were emulated by impressionable youths. Some new jacks were homeboys from Milwaukee's original neighborhood gangs, who had given up their conventional dreams; others were members of gangs that were formed solely for drug dealing (see Klein and Maxson, 1993). A founder of one new jack gang described the scene as his gang set up shop in Milwaukee. Note the strong mimicking of media stereotypes:

R#126: . . . . it was crime and drug problems before we even came into the scene. It was just controlled by somebody else. We just came on with a whole new attitude, outlook, at the whole situation. It's like, have you ever seen the movie *New Jack City,* about the kid in New York? You see, they was already there. We just came out with a better idea, you know what I'm saying?

New jacks rejected the homeboys' moral outlook. Many were raised by families with long traditions of hustling or a generation of gang affiliations, and had few hopes of a conventional future. They are the voice of the desperate ghetto dweller, those who live in Carl Taylor's (1990:36) "third culture" made up of "underclass and urban gang members who exhibit signs of moral erosion and anarchy" or propagators of Bourgois's (1990:631) "culture of terror." New jacks fit the media stereotype of all gang members, even though they represent fewer than 25% of Milwaukee's adult gang members.

Discussion: Gangs, the Underclass, and Public Policy

Our study was conducted in one aging postindustrial city, with a population of 600,000. How much can be generalized from our findings can be determined only by researchers in other cities, looking at our categories and determining whether they are useful. Cloward and Ohlin's opportunity theory is a workable general theoretical framework, but more case studies are needed in order to recast their theory to reflect three decades of economic and social changes. We present our typology to encourage others to observe variation within and between gangs, and to assist in the creation of new taxonomies and new theory.

Our paper raises several empirical questions for researchers: Are the behavior patterns of the founding gang members in our sample representative of adult gang members in other cities? In larger cities, are most gang members now new jacks who have long given up the hope of a conventional life, or are most still homeboys? Are there "homeboy" gangs and "new jack" gangs, following the "street gang/drug gang" notion of Klein and Maxson (1993)? If so, what distinguishes one from the other? Does gang members' orientation to conventionality vary by ethnicity or by region? How does it change over time? Can this typology help account for variation in rates of violence between gang members? Can female gang members be typed in the same way as males?

Our data also support the life course perspective of Sampson and Laub (1993:255), who ask whether present criminal justice policies "are producing unintended criminogenic effects." Milwaukee gang members are like the persistent, serious offenders in the Gluecks' data (Glueck and Glueck, 1950). The key to their future lies in building social capital that comes from steady employment and a supportive relationship, without the constant threat of incarceration (Sampson and Laub, 1993:162–68). Homeboys largely had a wife or a steady lady, were unhappily enduring "the silent, subtle humiliations" of the secondary labor market (Bourgois, 1990:629), and lived in dread of prison. Incarceration for drug charges undercut their efforts to find steady work and led them almost inevitably back to the drug economy.

Long and mandatory prison terms for use and intent to sell cocaine lump those who are committed to the drug economy with those who are using or are selling in order to survive. Our prisons are filled disproportionately with minority drug offenders (Blumstein, 1993a) like our homeboys, who in essence are being punished for the "crime" of not accepting poverty or of being addicted to cocaine. Our data suggest that jobs, more accessible drug treatment, alternative sentences, or even decriminalization of nonviolent drug offenses would be better approaches than the iron fist of the war on drugs (see Hagedorn, 1991; Reinarman and Levine, 1990; Spergel and Curry, 1990).

Finally, our typology raises ethical questions for researchers. Wilson (1987:8) called the underclass "collectively different" from the poor of the past, and many studies focus on underclass deviance. Our study found that some underclass gang members had embraced the drug economy and had forsaken conventionality, but we also found that the *majority* of adult gang members are still struggling to hold onto a conventional orientation to life.

Hannerz (1969:36) commented more than two decades ago that dichotomizing community residents into "respectables" and "disrespectables" "seems often to emerge from social science writing about poor black people or the lower classes in general." Social science that emphasizes differences within poor communities, without noting commonalities, is one-sided and often distorts and demonizes underclass life.

Our data emphasize that there is no Great Wall separating the underclass from the rest of the central-city poor and working class. Social research should not build one either. Researchers who describe violent and criminal gang actions without also addressing gang members' orientation to conventionality do a disservice to the public, to policymakers, and to social science.

Author's Notes

1. This study was funded by NIDA Grant RO1 DA 07218. The funding agency bears no responsibility for data or interpretations presented here.

2. Rosters of gangs in 1992 were refined and new gangs were added; thus it was difficult to make comparisons with 1987 rosters. In 1987, with $N = 225$, 20% of white male gang members, 10% of Latinos, and 27% of African Americans were working.

3. Selling cocaine is not only a gang-related phenomenon. Half of those who were reported as no longer involved with the gang also had sold cocaine within the last five years.

4. We asked respondents to report on the number of months they worked legitimate jobs, worked selling dope, and were in prison. We then asked them to tell us the average amount of money they made in those months working or selling dope. Hourly estimates are based on the monthly average divided by 160 hours. Most respondents reported that they worked selling dope "24/7," meaning full time.

5. About 15% of the founders' whereabouts were not known by our informants, but "unknown" status was no guarantee that the missing member had gone legit. One founder of an African American gang was reported to us in a pretest as having "dropped from sight," but later we learned that he had been a victim of one of serial killer Jeffrey Dahmer's grisly murders. Others, with whom our respondents no longer have contact, may be heavy cocaine users who left the gang and the neighborhood because they were no longer trustworthy.

6. Homeboys varied as well. Some were entrepreneurs or "players"; typically they were the "dope-men" who started a "dopehouse" where other gang members could work. Others worked only sporadically in dopehouses as a supplement to legitimate work or during unemployment. Finally, some, often cocaine users, worked most of the time at the dopehouse and only sporadically at legitimate jobs. Although homeboys also varied over time in their aspirations to conventionality, as a group they believed that the lack of jobs and the prison time were testing their commitment to conventional values. We found no significant differences between Latino and African American homeboys.

7. It is too early to tell how many persons will succeed at freeing themselves from cocaine use. Ansley Hamid (1992) found that by the 1990s, most New York crack users were in their thirties and poor; their heavy drug involvement had ruined their chances for conventional careers.

Discussion Questions

1. What have other researchers found about the long-term commitment of gang members to drug selling? Does Hagedorn's study confirm or contradict their results?

2. What are the four types of adult gang members described in Hagedorn's typology? In what ways do the four types differ from one another? Do they have anything in common? What factors do you think might predict which of the four types a teenage gang member will become when he or she becomes an adult?

3. What are the policy implications of Hagedorn's findings? Do they support a crime-control model with harsher penalties for drug offenders like that criticized by Tonry (selection #10), or do they support an approach more like that favored by Colvin (selection #6)

Violent Crime

Chapter *14*

Trauma-Control Model of the Serial Killer

Eric W. Hickey

Explanations of serial killing often cross disciplinary boundaries, drawing from research in such fields as sociology, psychology, and biology. Here, sociologist Eric Hickey, who studied more than two hundred serial killers, develops a psychological explanation of serial murder, focusing on early childhood traumatizations and the role of such "facilitators" as pornography. In his book, he also examines sociological factors such as the social background of the murder victims and differences in the behavior of male, female, and team serial killers.

We are beginning to learn that serial offenders are influenced by a multitude of factors that inevitably lead them to kill. It is unlikely that any one factor is directly responsible for homicidal behavior. People are no more likely to be born to kill than offenders are to acquire homicidal inclination from watching violence on television. However, this does not preclude the existence of a predisposition for violent behavior or the fact that we may be influenced by what we see.

In addition, no one factor has been useful thus far in predicting who may be prone to serial murder. Social scientists have long engaged in creating models for predicting criminal behavior. Unfortunately, in serial murder research, everyone wants to be the first to predict causation. Whether the explanation is excessive television viewing, head traumas, biogenics, childhood victimization, or a host of other "causes," it has been offered too quickly, without having a basis of sufficient and valid data.

Source: Eric W. Hickey, *Serial Murderers and Their Victims*, pp. 65–73. Pacific Grove, Calif.: Belmont/Cole, 1991.

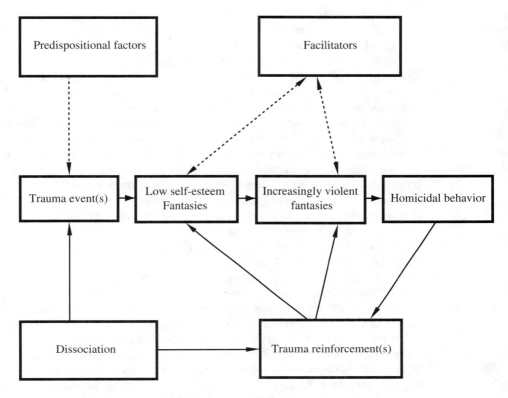

FIGURE 14–1.   Trauma-Control Model for Serial Murder

Predispositional factors and facilitators may or may not influence the serial killing process.

Among serial killers there may exist one or more predispositional factors that may influence their behavior. Some violent offenders have been known to possess an extra Y chromosome, but some men who possess an extra chromosome never become violent offenders. Similarly, there are many who drink heavily and indulge in pornography—even violent pornography—and never become serial killers. Thus even for those influenced by predispositional factors, whether they be biological, sociological, psychological or a combination thereof, an event or series of events, or traumas, seem to be required that gradually influence a person to kill. Figure 14–1 shows a proposed trauma-control model for understanding the process by which individuals may become involved in serial murder.

In discussing the trauma-control model, the destabilizing event(s) that occur in the lives of serial offenders will be referred to as *traumatizations*. These include unstable home life, death of parents, divorce, corporal punishments, sexual abuse, and other negative events that occur during the formative years of the offender's life. There are literally millions of U.S. citizens who experience one or more of these traumatizations in their lives and never become offenders of any sort. Also, it is possible that individuals who have some predilection for criminal behavior and who experience some form of traumatization do not become violent offenders.

In the case of serial murderers, the triggering mechanism within the trauma may well be the individual's inability to cope with the stress of the events. For serial murderers the most common childhood traumatization reported was rejection, including rejection by relatives and parent(s). It must be emphasized that an unstable home was reported as one of the major forms of rejection. The child or teen feels a deep sense of anxiety, mistrust, and confusion when psychologically or physically abused by an adult. Eth and Pynoos (1985) noted some of the effects of traumatization when children witnessed murder, rape, or suicidal behavior. These effects included images of violence involving mutilations, destabilization of impulse control, and revenge fantasies. However, instability in the home environment may not be sufficient to trigger homicidal behavior. Other factors may be involved that in combination create a synergistic response, or enhanced reaction.

The combined effect of various traumatizations is greater than any single trauma. In other words, the combined effects should be viewed exponentially rather than arithmetically. As Nettler (1982) observed, "In synergistic situations, a particular effect may be 'more than caused.' It is not merely a metaphor to speak of 'causal overkill'" (p. 77). Other possible contributing forms of rejection include failure, ostracism in school, and exclusion from a group. Most individuals appear to constructively cope with rejection or at least to deal with the stress of rejection from a "self-centered" perspective. In other words, the individual deals with his or her feelings without the involvement of others. This may include physical exercise, hobbies, travel, and so on. Others may become self-destructive through, for example, excessive eating, anorexia nervosa, bulimia, and other types of eating disorders. In more severe cases, rejection may prompt individuals to take their own lives rather than live with such uncomfortable feelings. Rejection as a stressor may contribute to a number of psychosomatic illnesses. For some people, confronting rejection may necessitate seeking out others who are able to provide emotional support to again restore their psychological equilibrium.

Some individuals deal with rejection within a more destructive framework—perhaps by beating the family dog, breaking objects, or assaulting a spouse, a friend, or a relative. Each person deals with rejection differently depending on its perceived degree, frequency, and intensity. Similarly, children cope with various childhood traumatizations in numerous ways. In the case of children who later become serial killers, many have experienced some form of childhood trauma that was not or could not be effectively countered by therapeutic strategies. In some cases there appeared to be series of traumatizations that psychologically affected these offenders. At this juncture in our research we can only speculate as to the number or strength of predispositions or predilections offenders may have had toward violent behavior. However, we do know that most of them have a history of childhood traumatizations. Hazelwood and Warren (1989) reported in their study of 41 serial rapists that 76% had been sexually abused as children. Considering that some serial killers in this study were rapists before they graduated to murder, we must not ignore the implication that sexual victimization during childhood may readily manifest itself in a negative manner during adulthood.

Traumatization experienced by the offender as a child may nurture within him or her feelings of low self-esteem. A common characteristic of most, if not all, serial offenders is feelings of inadequacy, self-doubt, and worthlessness. They do not cope constructively with the early trauma(s) and subsequently perceive themselves and their surroundings in a distorted perspective. It is during this time of childhood development that a process of dissociation occurs. In an effort to regain the psychological equilibrium taken from them by people in authority, serial offenders appear to construct masks, facades, or a veneer of self-confidence and self-control. The label of *psychopath,* given to most serial killers, may actually describe a process of maintaining control of oneself, of others, and of one's surroundings.

The offender may suppress the traumatic event(s) to the point where he or she cannot consciously recall the experience(s). This can be referred to as splitting off, or blocking out, the experience. Tanay (1976), in describing this state of dissociation, noted that the murderer appears to carry out the act in an altered state of consciousness. Such an ego-dystonic homicide, whereby the individual is faced with a psychologically unresolvable conflict, results in part of the psychic structure splitting off from the rest of the personality. Danto (1982) noted that dissociative reactions are types of anxiety states in which the mind is "overwhelmed or flooded by anxiety" (p. 6). For some children, certain traumatizations can generate extremely high anxieties. To defend oneself against a psychologically painful experience a person may block the experience from recall or, instead, not consciously suppress the fact the trauma occurred but suppress the hurt, fear, anger, and other feelings caused by the event(s). However, the pain of a traumatic event will eventually surface in some way. For the offender, a cycle of trauma and quest for regaining control can be generated at a very early age.

Facilitators

At some point in the trauma-control process the offender may begin to immerse him- or herself in facilitators. Facilitators may include alcohol and other drugs, pornography, and books on the occult. Alcohol appears to decrease inhibitions and inhibit moral conscience and propriety, whereas pornography fuels growing fantasies of violence. During the Reagan Administration, the Meese Commission found that violent pornography was linked to violent sexual behavior. However, the connection made between pornography and violence can be misleading, because saying the two are "linked" can be interpreted in several ways. In any case, the serial murderers who insisted that pornography was a major factor in their killing young women and children should not be ignored. In February, 1989, Richard Daniel Starrett was arrested and charged in the murder of a 15-year-old girl in South Carolina. He was also believed to have participated in the abduction and sexual assault and murders of several other young women and girls. Starrett observed that the proliferation of pornography influenced his violent behavior. As police searched a miniwarehouse rented by Starrett, they seized 935 books and magazines depicting nudity and sexual violence, as well as 116 posters depicting bondage, violence, or sex, 18 calendars depicting sex or violence, a number of books on sex crimes, and dozens of hardcore videos—all belonging to him.

Murray Straus and Larry Baron (1983) found that states with the highest readership of pornographic magazines, such as *Playboy* and *Hustler,* also had the highest rape rates. Dr. Victor Cline (1990), of the University of Utah, outlined a four-factor syndrome that appears similar to the process experienced by serial killers who are reported to have used pornography extensively. The offender first experiences "addiction" similar to the physiological/psychological addiction to drugs, which then generates stress in his or her everyday activities. The person then enters a stage of "escalation," in which the appetite for more deviant, bizarre, and explicit sexual material is fostered. Third, the person gradually becomes "desensitized" to that which was once revolting and taboo-breaking. Finally the person begins to "act out" the things that he or she has seen.

We must remember, however, that some serial murderers do not use pornography to any extent. Given the current state of limited research in serial homicide, it is dangerously premature to suggest facilitators as *causal* factors. What we can say is that a tendency to use pornography, alcohol, and texts on the occult has been noted frequently in serial offenders. But, we must recognize that pornography is produced in many different forms, both qualitatively and quantitatively. There exists not only difficulty in defining the parameters of pornography but also in discerning the effects it may or may not have on any particular person. In a recent study conducted by the Federal Bureau of Investigation, it was found that 36% of serial rapists collected pornography (Hazelwood and Warren, 1989). Does this mean they all read *Playboy, Penthouse,* and *Hustler* or perhaps the many publications that include hardcore acts of sadomasochism, bestiality, and other forms of sexual degradation? Can we give the same weight to all forms of pornography, including acts of violent sexual conduct?

Also, can we exclude the possibility that pornography, like alcohol, may affect those people who harbor a predisposition for such stimulation more than others? In addition, pornography may actually serve as a retardant to serial offenders. If we are to believe, regardless of the presence or absence of pornography, that serial killers will commit acts of murder, then it is possible that some people may find sufficient gratification in and catharsis through various forms of pornography to avoid violence. As a release valve, the pornography lessens the demand for victims. We might argue that some serial offenders might have been motivated to kill earlier if pornography had not been available through which they could exercise their fantasies of control.

Proper scientific verification of these and other implications of pornography are needed in the construction of serial murder etiology. We must be cautious in suggesting there exists anything more than a tendency for pornography to affect those offenders involved in serial killing, regardless of how we may feel about it. If an argument is to be made that pornography (hardcore) is a primary causal agent for serial murder, then how are we to explain the behavior of serial killers who lived before the media explosion of the twentieth century? Serial murderers have existed for several hundreds of years, if not longer. Before technology permitted society to produce violent and sexually graphic material, serial killers were at work in America.

However, one could also argue that the emergence of large numbers of serial killers beginning in the 1960s was a direct result of the media explosion of recent years. Alcohol and pornography are not mandatory elements in the construction of a serial killer, but they tend to provide vehicles the offender uses to express the growing rages from within. In most instances these facilitators tend to be present to some degree in the profile of a serial killer. It is my contention, however, that without alcohol or pornography the offender in all likelihood would kill anyway. The circumstances of the acts may be altered, but the murders would inevitably occur. The offender still must gain control of inner feelings, anxieties, anger, rage, and pain. Using alcohol, pornography or other such types of graphic literature may be useful in expediting the offender's urge to kill.

Fantasy

The most critical factor common to serial killers is violent fantasy. Prentky and colleagues (1986), who studied repetitive sexual homicides, found that daydreams of causing bodily harm through sadism and other methods of sexual violence were common among offenders. The researchers concluded that the offender attempts to replicate his fantasies. Since the offender can actually never be in total control of his or her victim's responses, the outcome of the fantasy will never measure up to his or her expectations. In any case, each new murder provides new fantasies that can fuel future homicides. Ressler and his colleagues (1988) concluded that "sexual murder is based on fantasy" (p. 33). Fantasy becomes a critical component in the psychological development of a serial killer. Although fantasies are generally associated with sexual homicides, they are likely to be found in the minds of most, if not all, serial killers.

The following case illustrates how consuming and powerful fantasies can become: Carl had been arrested for attempted rape and murder. Visiting a young woman in whom he was interested, Carl suddenly attacked and tried to rape her. During the course of the attack the girl's mother returned home. Enraged, Carl killed the mother and fled the home. Carl was adjudicated to be insane at the time of the attack and was confined to a mental institution until he could be considered safe to return to the community. After seven years and extensive therapy in a sex offender program, Carl was permitted to begin a community reintegration program. Working as an electrician's helper, Carl worked during the day and stayed at the hospital at night. He was also allowed certain weekend privileges provided he followed the specific rules of his therapy program. One of Carl's problems had been his propensity for fantasy. When he was younger, he loved to set fires so he could view the flashing lights of the police and fire trucks. Over time he had graduated into some extremely violent fantasies that were believed by psychiatrists to have contributed to his homicidal behavior. During his years in the sex offender program Carl appeared to learn how to control his fantasies. On weekends he attended dances, movies, and other recreational activities. He was not permitted, however, to attend movies that contained any explicit sexual violence for fear he could still become caught up in his own fantasies of violence. One evening he violated his weekend pass by attending the movie *Dressed To Kill* featuring Angie Dickinson. Later, he would report how he had attempted to "pick up a girl" during the movie but was rejected. Even before the violence in the movie had ended, Carl was also ready to kill. Going to his car engulfed in raging fantasies of violence, Carl located his electrician's knife and waited in the shadows while four unsuspecting female college students exited from the theater. His fantasy was to enter their car and cut each girl's throat. Walking quickly to the rear door of the vehicle, Carl reached for the handle. Just as he was about to open the door, the driver, unaware of his presence, stepped on the accelerator and drove off.

Frustrated and in the grips of his violence fantasies, Carl later explained how he had then gone to the local park, hunting for a lone female jogger. He had decided to cut her into pieces. Waiting in some bushes for several minutes, Carl saw a woman jogging toward him. It was 11:30 P.M., and the park was deserted. Fortunately for his intended victim, a male jogger emerged from another direction at about the same time. Thwarted in his bid to kill and in fear of detection, Carl returned to his car. After driving around for a while and unable to locate any more suitable victims, Carl calmed down and returned to the hospital where he explained to hospital staff his evening's experiences. It was decided that Carl was still in need of closer supervision, and his passes were revoked (author's files).

Most people's fantasies generally are perceived as harmless and often therapeutic. Fantasies can involve a continuum of benign to aggressive thoughts that usually generate little or no action on the part of the fantasizer. For serial offenders, however, fantasies appear to involve violence, often sexual in nature, whereby the victim is controlled totally by the offender. The purpose of the fantasy is not the immediate destruction of another human being but the total control over that person. The element of control is so intense in the serial killer that in some cases the actual death of the victim is anticlimactic to the fantasized total control over the victim. In one case, an offender who is believed to have killed 14 young women used to place his revolver on the forehead of his victim and order her to perform fellatio. Those victims who cried and begged for mercy would invariably receive a bullet in their heads during the sexual assault. Those victims who cooperated with the killer but remained calm and did not show fear were spared. During an interview with one of the victims who survived the assault I was told how she, a store owner, was ordered to kneel on the floor. In this instance the offender had placed tape over his victim's mouth. After he had taped her mouth the killer proceeded to rub his penis against her face and insisted she look him in the eyes while he performed his sexual assault. The victim later recalled how she managed to remain calm and did exactly as he ordered her to do even though her attacker held a gun to her head. After a few moments the killer realized his victim was not responding the way he expected (and according to his fantasies), and so he abruptly fled the store (author's files).

The control fantasy becomes the highlight of the attack. The sexual assault is one vehicle by which the offender can attempt to gain the total control of a victim. Sexual torture becomes a tool to degrade, humiliate, and subjugate the victim. It is a method to take away all that is perceived to be personal, private, or sacred from the victim. The offender physically and mentally dominates his or her victims to a point where he or she has fantasized the ultimate control over another human being. Once that sense of control has been reached, the victim loses his or her purpose to the offender and is then killed. One serial killer noted in a personal interview that he developed a ritual for torturing his victims and that he seldom varied from those methods.

It is during the sexual assault, torture, and degradation that fantasies of the original childhood trauma may manifest themselves in acts of violence. In some cases, ten or twenty years may have lapsed since the traumatic event(s) occurred; in others, only a short period of time may have passed. During the time elapsed between the traumatic events(s) and the homicides, the offender may have completely split off from the traumatic experience and have protected him- or herself further by assuming a life of control and confidence. Psychologically the offender has been drawing farther and farther away from self-control but desperately seeks to retain control of his inner self. Often the victims selected by the killers stand as proxies for the traumatic event(s) experienced by the offenders. In one instance an offender had received electroshock treatments as corrective therapy for his involvement in a gang rape while he was a teenager. In 1984, 22 years after his electroshocks, the offender tortured some of his victims by wiring their toes to electrical outlets and then turning the power on and off. In yet another case, an offender had been sexually abused, beaten, bound with heavy cords, and left in terrifyingly dark closets. Several years later he began torturing boys by beating them, tying them with heavy cords, and holding them captive in dark places. His attempts to replicate his childhood traumas were nearly successful except he lacked the elusive sense of control. Each victim experienced more extensive tortures and depravities than the previous victim until he died, at which time the killer butchered the corpse. His last victim was slowly dismembered and disemboweled while still alive (author's files).

Fantasies may be fueled by pornography and facilitated by alcohol. The anger that has continued to grow over the years is allowed to be expressed in images of violence and death. Once the total domination and destruction of the victim has occurred, the killer momentarily regains the sense of equilibrium lost years before. One offender described this as the "restoration stage," which allows the killer to "feel good" again. He explained that for many serial killers, the frequency of victimization is a direct function of the degree of completion of the restoration. In other words, if the offender is stymied or frustrated in some way as he ritualistically kills the victim, he or she may be prompted to quickly seek out another victim. Once the killer is able to complete the ritual of killing and feeling that sense of control restored, he or she may not need to kill again for some time.

But fantasies can never be completely fulfilled or the anger removed or the lack of self-esteem reversed. For some, the experience of killing may generate new fantasies of violence. Exactly what does occur in the killer's mind between murders? It is possible for some offenders to become so consumed by their attempts at fantasy fulfillment that killing becomes a frequent experience. Yet, there are many serial killers who wait long periods of time, months or even years, before they seek out their next victim. According to one offender, he felt good about himself and more in control of his life directly following a murder. Eventually he would experience another failure in his life, such as criticism of job performance or rejection by a girlfriend. He believed that such events should not have bothered him, but they seemed to act as catalysts for depression and low self-esteem. The sense of failure or rejection never failed to put him into a spiral of self-pity, anger, loss of confidence, and increased fantasies. Sometimes it would be months, but inevitably he would go hunting for young women to torture and kill (author's files).

The trauma-control model of violent behavior then becomes a cyclical experience for serial offenders. Fantasies, possibly fueled by pornography or alcohol, reinforced by "routine" traumatizations of day-to-day living, keep the serial killer caught up in a self-perpetuating cycle of violence. Contrary to some claims, serial killers do not all wish to be caught, although some do and even allow themselves to be apprehended. Ed Kemper, after murdering several women in California, drove to Colorado, called the police and told them he was the killer, and was even accommodating enough to wait by the pay phone until police arrived and arrested him. Some serial killers can go on for many years and never allow their fantasies to become so consuming that they lose control of their surroundings and their abilities to remain obscure. For the killer, the cycle becomes a never-ending pursuit of control over one's own life through the total domination and destruction of others' lives.

Discussion Questions

1. What does Hickey mean by "traumatizations"? How does he account for the fact that many children who suffer such traumatizations never go on to commit serial murder or other serious crimes? How would he account for the fact that some people who do commit serial murder apparently have not suffered such traumatizations, or have not suffered more serious traumatizations than people who do not commit serial murder?
2. How might Hickey's trauma-control model incorporate Gottfredson and Hirschi's theory of low self-control (selection #4)? In Hickey's model, what is the difference between internal control and control over other people, and how are the two related to one another?
3. What does Hickey mean by a "facilitator" of serial murder? What are the facilitators he discusses, and how are they related to serial murder?
4. What role does fantasy play for the serial killer? Do people who do not commit serial murder have similar violent fantasies, but not act on them? If so, what keeps them from acting out their fantasies?

C h a p t e r *15*

The Motivation of the Persistent Robber

Jack Katz

In *Seductions of Crime: Moral and Sensual Attractions in Doing Evil* (1988), Jack Katz considers the subjective appeal of shoplifting, murder, robbery, and street gangs. In this paper, he looks at the motivations of the small number of people who remain persistently involved in robbery. He explores why the use or threat of violence against their victims is appealing to them, arguing that their actions go beyond rationality in order to establish dominance over those from whom they steal and transcend the "chaotic circumstances" they create and confront.

The motivations that animate robbery vary so greatly that they seem to defy generalization. Keeping in mind a loose definition of robbery as the taking of something valuable by force or threat of force, then the offense is found quite commonly in childhood. Much of the "bully's" behavior might be seen as robbery, as might much of the unkindness that gives sibling rivalry its bad reputation.

The personal consequences and social dimensions of robbery are so disturbing that an allusion to the nasty and rough play of early childhood may seem frivolous. Yet biographies of hard-core robbers describe early offenses that occur close to home, if not against kin, and then within local social circles and on local streets.[1] These mean and predatory actions do not seem to warrant the archetype of "robbery," perhaps because they are more clearly expressive than economic projects: intimidating a classmate to "give" pocket change; using a tough posture to deflect requests by a friend that he be repaid money that

Source: Jack Katz, "The Motivation of the Persistent Robber," in Michael Tonry, ed., *Crime and Justice: A Review of Research,* Vol. 14., pp. 277–289, 298–300. Chicago: The University of Chicago Press, 1991. Reprinted by permission of The University of Chicago Press. © 1991 by The University of Chicago. All rights reserved.

was, some time before, handed over as a "loan;" seizing an item of clothing from another youth because it represents membership in an enemy group; approaching strangers in public spaces with a humble monetary "request" that subtly but quickly becomes recognized as an arrogant and inexorable demand.

Robbery is often a group activity for young, officially apprehended offenders (Zimring, 1981). In recent surveys, crime victims report they were attacked by multiple offenders in about 25 percent of the robberies in which the offenders appeared to be between the ages of twelve and twenty, compared to about 8 percent of robberies in which the offenders seemed to be thirty or over (Bureau of Justice Statistics, 1989c, table 47, p. 52). The group character of youth robberies suggests that, qualitatively, the details of individual offenses will display numerous moments of interactional fireworks. The following case, drawn from Chicago police information, illustrates what youths might well deem to be a "cool" strategy for drawing a victim, as well as a pattern of spontaneously and interactively escalating violence.

> Four teenagers planned to rob a pizza delivery man. They called in an order, and when the delivery man reached their area, the youngest of the group, a 14-year-old, approached him on foot and declared, "This is a stickup, don't make it a murder." The victim, 55 years old, threw up his hands and dropped the money he was holding. The 14-year-old then asked, "Where is the rest of the money, man?" The victim ran to his car, got inside, and started it, but the two of them jumped in and began to struggle with him. Then one pulled a shotgun from his overcoat and shot the victim in the throat and chest. The four split with $27 to divide. (Katz, 1988:186)

Materialistic interests, playful maneuvers, and intensely hostile emotions all swirl around the motivations governing youthful robbery. Indeed, a series of colloquialisms ("stickup," "wilding," "mugging," "yoking," "purse snatching") has emerged to grasp street distinctions among behaviors that statutory law may treat equally as "robbery."

But if robbery has a widely experienced and highly varied appeal to children and male adolescents, the appeal is usually not very deep, at least not for officially recognized instances of the offense. Robbery arrests have often been found to peak in late adolescence or the early twenties (Miller, Dinitz, and Conrad, 1982); in recent arrest data, robberies peak at ages seventeen and eighteen (Federal Bureau of Investigation, 1987, table 33, p. 174; Federal Bureau of Investigation, 1988, table 33, p. 178). Historical research on arrest data indicates that robbery has become increasingly concentrated among the young. The peak age of robbery has declined from nineteen in 1940 to seventeen in 1980; in age distributions of robbery arrests, the age at which the number of arrests is at half the number produced by the peak age was twenty-nine in 1940, dropped to twenty-seven in 1960, and dropped to twenty-four in 1980 (Steffensmeier et al., 1989, table 2, p. 815). In national U.S. data on arrests for robbery, within the five-year age set of males forty to forty-four, there is an average of about 500 robbery arrests for each year, compared to almost 7,000 arrests of eighteen-year-old males (Federal Bureau of Investigation, 1988, table 34, pp. 180–81). Various studies indicate that many young people who are intensely active in thieving cultures during their adolescence are vividly aware that penalties will increase when they reach the age of majority; their desistance appears to be a response (West, 1978;

Sullivan, 1983). These age-related data suggest that those who persist with robbery late in their twenties or into their thirties are likely to be a rather special set of criminal actors.

Over the last decade, several studies have documented the existence of a relatively small number of unusually persistent offenders who commit a disproportionate number of robberies. Variously labeled "violent predators," "heavies," "habitual," "chronic," and "career" robbers, these persistent offenders are not crime specialists. Typically they also commit nonviolent property crimes, undertake assaults independent of acquisitive objectives, and, at one or another phase of their criminal careers, participate intensively in vice (drug, prostitution, illegal gambling) markets. A famous self-report study of 2,200 U.S. jail and prison inmates identified a set of "violent predators" who reported that they commit robbery, deal drugs, and assault persons. Ten percent of "violent predators" reported committing an average of 135 robberies per year of release time, compared to 90 percent of robbers who reported that they did not deal drugs or commit assaults and who committed an average of ten robberies per year (Chaiken and Chaiken, 1982:55). A team of researchers in French Canada classified a sample of thirty-five armed robbers into "chronic" and "occasional" offenders and found that the former had committed an average of twenty to fifty robberies, compared to an average of one to six for the latter group. The occasionals were specialists in crime, while the chronics were generalists, although with a special aversion for fraud crimes (Gabor et al., 1987:55). And in a national U.S. sample of over 1,800 felons in state prisons, Wright and Rossi (1986:76) identified through self-reports a set of handgun "predators" who constituted 17 percent of the sample but were responsible for over 50 percent of the total crimes committed by the sample, leading in nonviolent as well as the violent types of crime.[2]

These studies might be read to suggest that a commitment to the use of violence, in robbery and personal relations, is an inevitable response to the chaos that characterizes the lives of street criminals, except that the same studies have also documented the lack of significant involvement in robbery on the part of many who persist in nonviolent theft and vice activities. If robbery is not sufficiently rewarding to maintain the involvement of most young offenders who try it, and if robbery is not necessary to persist through young adulthood in a life of street crime, what motivates the small set of persistent robbers?

Utilitarian or materialistic explanations that point to the offender's lack of legitimate economic opportunities or suggest that he is immune from punishment are not very helpful. As to employment opportunities, offenders may not have economically attractive legitimate alternatives, but the rewards of street robbery are often minimal. Gas station robberies averaged a loss of $303 in 1986 (Federal Bureau of Investigation, 1986); convenience store robberies averaged a loss of $344 in 1988 (Federal Bureau of Investigation, 1988:19); only 15 percent of noncommercial victims reported losses of $500 or more in 1987, and in 40 percent of the robberies the victims reported theft losses of less than $100 (Bureau of Justice Statistics, 1989c, tables 82 and 83, pp. 74, 76). And given the familiarity of persistent robbers with nonviolent theft and rich vice markets, materialistic factors cannot explain their specialization in a violent form of criminal career. As to punishment, the career criminal data, combined with the biographical accounts, indicate that persistent robbers continue despite lengthy periods of incarceration during youthful years. When offenders desist in their late twenties or in their thirties, it is usually after a number of stretches in confinement had failed to provoke desistance, and it cannot be that, after years of imprisonment, their legitimate economic opportunities exceed what they were before they compiled a lengthy criminal record.

Gender differences in robbery offense rates also indicate the inadequacies of utilitarian or materialistic explanations. The pressures of poverty are equal, if not greater, on females than they are on males, yet males recurrently make up about 90 percent of those counted in arrest data (Federal Bureau of Investigation, 1988, table 37) and in conviction records of bank robbers (Haran, 1982); in the national victims survey for 1987, victims identified only 7 percent of single offender robbers as female (Bureau of Justice Statistics, 1989c, table 39, p. 46; see also Hindelang, 1981).

A difference by sex in anxiety about physical danger cannot fully explain the gender difference in robbery. Criminal practices that are more attractive than robbery to poor women, such as prostitution and drug dealing, are not obviously safer. Nor can a psychobiological male tendency toward violence account for the enormous gender disproportion in robbery. The male-to-female ratio in assaults is much smaller than it is in robbery. In victim survey data organized to permit comparisons within race, Laub and McDermott (1985, table 2, p. 90) found a male-to-female ratio of between 3:1 and 4:1 for "assaultive violence without theft"; within arrest data they found a male-to-female ratio of about 3:1 for "simple assaults." And in domestic criminal homicides, in several American cities it is almost as likely, in some times and locations more likely, that the female will be the one who survives and is arrested (Riedel and Zahn, 1985:41).

Differences in the representation of ethnic groups in robbery statistics also militate against materialistic explanations. In Canada, predominantly French Quebec has had armed robbery rates that are two to three times the rates in the English provinces, even while the rates of nonrobbery violent crimes and nonviolent property crimes have been lower in French than in English Canada (Gabor et al., 1987:13, 23).

Ethnic group comparisons are more meaningful when they attempt to control for economic status. Although neither arrest nor victim-based data provide information on the offenders' economic status, if we assume that robbery offenders come from poverty populations, we can easily generate useful ethnic comparisons. Because the historical mixture of Hispanic and black populations in the Caribbean is significantly represented in eastern and midwestern U.S. cities, ethnic comparisons among poverty populations in the U.S. Southwest, where Hispanics are primarily of Mexican and Central American origin, give a more clear-cut picture. In Southern California, the rate of robbery arrests of poor blacks is four to five times that of poor Hispanics; for homicides (violence usually without theft) as well as for burglaries (theft without violence), the black rates are only about twice the Hispanic rates (Katz, 1988, p. 240, table 7.1).

In sum, a variety of patterns indicates that persistent robbers have motivations that distinguish them from other persistent offenders, that are sufficiently powerful to transcend heavy costs of punishment, and that are apparently not grounded in sex or race dispositions either toward violence in particular or toward crime in general. One way to explore the motivations of persistent robbers is to try to identify uniquely correlated background factors—some bizarre form of abuse in early childhood, an odd feature in contemporaneous socioeconomic ecology, or a deep predisposition measurable on psychological inventories. No such factors have as yet been identified, and several considerations point to the futility of a research strategy focused on background factors. Involvement in robbery changes over the life course and from moment to moment within an offender's day on the streets, while the offender's socioeconomic context and psychologically formative experiences remain constant. More important, the attractions of persisting in robbery are so peculiar that to pursue a significant, discrete background cause, even presuming it exists, would be to search for a needle in a haystack. To justify such a search, one must have faith that some form of evil genius in biology or social organization cunningly guides offenders to a peculiar form of criminality that is quite rare even among persistent or "career" criminals.

We might better appreciate the contributions of demographic research, not by looking for age, race, sex, social ecological or other background causes, but by acknowledging an implication of the gross character of demographic correlations: the motivation to rob is relatively rare and obviously not easy to sustain. We are then led to wonder *how* persistent robbers overcome the many discouragements to their "careers." The inquiry into criminal motives becomes a question of understanding what makes robbery attractive for those few who persist in it or, more precisely, how offenders construct and sustain the attractions of robbery. If a search for background explanations for such a rare form of criminality implies theories of evil genius in nature or social organization, it must be admitted that an inquiry into the methods by which offenders themselves make robbery attractive indulges a humanistic prejudice. . . .

When asked, robbers often define themselves as rational actors, doing crime "to make money the best way I know how" and using violence prudently by attacking victims only when they resist. But a close examination of interaction within robberies indicates that this is not the sort of "job" that, through weighing costs and benefits, one can sensibly elect to make one's career. And the suggestion that offenders typically monitor their use of violence according to a utilitarian calculus about the means of intimidation that they possess (bare arms, knives, guns) and the minimal use of force necessary to control victims ignores the nonrational commitment that is essential for persistently committing the offense (e.g., Skogan, 1978; Luckenbill, 1980; Feeney, 1986).

Data describing high correlations between victim resistance and violence by robbery offenders have frequently been reported. In perhaps the first significant study that bore on the question, Conklin (1972:115) found, in two Boston samples totaling 1,242 robberies, that offenders used force in less than half the cases where victims did not resist and in almost two-thirds of the cases where victims did resist.[3] Luckenbill (1981) reconstructed 257 robbery events from police records in a Texas city and found that, although gun-armed offenders always began with a threat alone, in those cases in which the victim resisted, half the time the offender would abandon the scene and half the time he would shoot. Block (1977) examined over 1,000 robberies as described in Chicago police reports and found that, in robberies by gun in which the victim did not resist, only 7 percent of victims were injured, while 78 percent of resisting victims were injured.

As Philip Cook (1986) has stressed, any inference that victim conduct can control offender violence depends on a questionable reading of causal direction. Does victim resistance provoke violence by offenders? Or does incipient violence by offenders provoke resistance by victims? In his study, Block (1977:81) addressed this issue and found that two-thirds of resisting victims resisted *before* the robber used force. But in close examinations of police files, offenders sometimes appear so wild or so bent on "vicious" conduct (Cook, 1980a:31) that a reasonable victim might well "resist" just before or just as the offender begins to launch his attack. It is not clear that routine police records, created for law enforcement purposes and examined after the fact for evidence on a question of causal direction that a researcher brings to and imposes on them, can provide data of sufficiently high quality to resolve the matter.

More significant, the subtly interactive nature of each party's conduct creates substantial difficulties for interpreting causal direction in any given case. Not only are victims intensely concerned to read offenders' posture and gestures to anticipate being attacked, offenders enter the scene geared to read their victims for signs of likely resistance. Just as with victims who see the offender provide a cue for a preemptory strike, offenders who strike victims who had not resisted may simply be trying to strike first. More complex still, we cannot be sure of the accuracy of these readings: offenders and victims alike may strike first on a mistaken belief that the other is about to act.

The subtlety and complexity of social interaction in robbery, and the risk of a fateful misreading, is a problem not only for the researcher but, initially, for the robber. Offenders who discover the intrinsic difficulties of rationally managing violence within robbery have reason to abandon the offense. Those who persist must either be especially skilled in dramatizing violent behavior or unusually indifferent to the dictates of reason.

Biographical evidence indicates that ironically both are true. "Career" robbers recall adolescent years dedicated to the perfection of "badass" identities, the key to which is the portrayal of a personal character that is committed to violence beyond calculations of legal, material, or even physical costs to oneself. They learn that what wins in a showdown with another "badass" is not so much superiority in fighting skill or firepower but escaping the ghost of reason and continuing to attack when an opponent, haunted by anticipations of injury or imprisonment, will back off (see Keiser, 1979; Dietz, 1983).

That the criminal predator's career is originally shaped through adolescent peer testing creates fundamental problems for analyzing the common forms of statistical data in order to understand the relationship between offender violence and victim resistance. Such data, whether compiled from police records or victim reports, are seriously biased against including robberies committed against victims who are similar to offenders in social identity. If robbery offenders are engaged in vice and other, nonviolent activities, they have special reasons for not reporting their own victimization in robberies to the police, and they are likely to be living in ways that make them especially inaccessible to phone surveys that attempt to identify victims. And if conventional citizens, when faced with an offender, may sometimes detect cues that seem to them to justify anticipatory resistance, the offender's mirror-image peers must quite often provide heavy-handed cues that they will try preemptive strikes.

Violent predators typically reside near other violent predators, on ghetto streets and in state confinement. It is revealing that the research literature on victim–offender interaction in robbery makes virtually no mention of the absence from its statistical data base of offenses conducted within confinement settings. If one's interest is in advising conventional citizens how to behave within robberies, this neglect is understandable. But for an understanding of offenders' motivations, it is essential to appreciate the contexts for robbery that are familiar to them. Research on gun possession indicates that, in order to seize emergent opportunities but also in order to defend against surprise attacks, violent predators maintain a constant readiness for violence, often literally sleeping with a weapon under the pillow and driving with a gun in the glove compartment (Wright and Rossi, 1986:14). In the context of this lifestyle, there are so many good reasons for anticipating situationally unprovoked attacks that a complementary, nonrational commitment to violence would itself be rational.

The rational basis for the persistent robber to become committed beyond reason to violence appears even stronger if we appreciate the many prudent, practical considerations that recommend unprovoked violence to robbers. Although it is common to consider "victim resistance" as a "reason" for offender violence, and "unprovoked violence" as an indicator of nonrational behavior, the "resistance" concept is much more open than is usually appreciated, with the result that "unprovoked violence" often has a readily located, reasonable, practical, and utilitarian basis for the offender.

Thus, whether a victim is resisting or not depends on how ambitious and elastic are the offender's expectations and desires. In the research literature, "resistance" is variously applied to cover physically expressed protests, attempts to flee and calls for help, and failures to comply quickly with offenders' demands. But, however facile the researcher's coding of the phenomena, the judgment of victim resistance from the offender's perspective is often quite ambiguous. The offender, after all, will usually not know what the victim has to offer in exchange for the offender's withholding of violence; "unprovoked" violence may serve to reveal valuables that an initial request did not uncover. Faced by an offender who seems violently impatient, victims may discover valuables to offer that they otherwise would not consider to be part of the criminal exchange. A phrase currently popular among armed robbers, "Give it up!" contains a denotative ambiguity that neatly serves the exploratory aspects of the robber's crime.

Because contemporary robberies are commonly "spur-of-the-moment" affairs with little advance planning of methodology or "casing" of targets (Dietz, 1983; on bank robberies, see Johnston, 1978), the robber will often be determining the limits of what he is willing to demand within the robbery interaction itself. Victims initially targeted for their cash or drugs may, on closer inspection, wear jewelry, clothing, or even gold fillings that might as well be demanded (Katz, 1988:190). Unprovoked violence is also useful for the offender to gauge just how compliant the victim is willing to be. Although such events are rare, offenders may discover other, nonmonetary desires that victims might serve, and offenders may perceive in victim compliance an invitation to extend the robbery relationship beyond its initial setting, for example, through kidnapping the victim and using him or her as a guide to treasures stored at home.

First, then, the rationality of unprovoked offender violence is an open matter because, for the offender, what the victim has to offer and what the offender himself desires are both phenomena that emerge within the robbery situation. For both reasons, a robber is well-advised to appear to be at least somewhat outside the limitations of reason. A robber who appears too civil might not effectively convey his commitment to back demands with force; a robber who articulates his desires too precisely might miss valuables that a victim might supply in an effort to identify and satisfy the desires of a brusque, crude assailant.

Second, the rational basis of offender violence is unclear even when the victim *does* resist first. If offenders often have empirically justifiable reasons to employ violence when they are not provoked, the inverse also holds: offenders often lack firmly based reasons to use violence when victims do resist. When victims resist, they rarely threaten to disable the offender physically or to block his escape (an indication of just how rare is given in Katz, 1988:186). Given the minimal amount of investment robbers usually make in setting up a particular offense, when victims resist, the rational course of action for offenders would not be to respond with violence but to abandon the immediate crime scene for another they could easily find and enter. Were robbers truly rational or solely instrumental in their use of violence, they would commonly use some violence *before but rarely after* victims resist.[4]

Cool, retrospective statements by offenders that they limit violence to practical necessity (Allen, 1978; Feeney, 1986) misrepresent their motivation by obscuring the wild possibilities of the interaction. Offenders know that they do not know what victims will do; some report a self-conscious paranoia that victims will counterattack with guns. When they act with confederates, they often have good reasons to believe that the confederates may not be reliable partners because of their potential for unreliable conduct within the robbery, vulnerability to law enforcement pressure related to other offenses, or inclination toward predatory attacks on colleagues.

Building on all the other uncertainties and most difficult to control is the offender's uncertainty as to how he, himself, will respond within the robbery scene. Those who act under the influence of intoxicating substances are not unaware that their strategic ability may be affected. And while persistent offenders often decry the "stupid" or "hotheaded" practices of novice robbers, their posture of professionalism is belied by detailed accounts of their own mature offenses. They relate crimes in which they attacked what they regard as low-status targets, such as gas stations, out of loyalty to overly spontaneous colleagues (Allen, 1978:192); their pride in knowingly taking on unusual risks by acting with colleagues they regard as weak willed, just for the ironic purpose of demonstrating their superior self-control (Taylor, 1985:72); and a retrospective awareness of their own tendencies toward explosive violence.

Novice offenders may be unaware of all these uncertainties and fantasize robbery as an occasion for enacting an efficient, cold-blooded control. They may be lured in by street comments that recommend robbery as "easy," a way to get money within a matter of moments, virtually whenever one needs it, without requiring any special skills; a rhetoric that celebrates the crime as a neatly bounded task, something one can "get in, get out, and get away with" quickly; a deviant culture that portrays the crime as a routine matter analogous to going shopping. But persistent robbers know intimately that the crime is shot through with uncertainties and uncontrollable risk. Thus, although they may enjoy distinguishing themselves as more sophisticated and business-like about the crime than amateurs and those who start robbing and then soon desist, they know that neither the payoffs from the crime nor the offender's conduct within it can be systematically managed to make sense on a utilitarian calculation.

Against this background knowledge, seemingly gratuitous violence becomes sensible to the persistent offender for a reason that specifically overrides situational risk calculations. In order to persist as a robber, it is necessary to steel oneself against utilitarian thinking, becoming, in one contemporary street phrase, a "hardhead" who is impervious to attacks of reason. For some careers, the commitment to persist depends on accepting the gambler's maxim that one should not throw good money after bad. Professional card players, for example, protect their career commitments by sacrificing their earlier stakes when an unexpected turn of the cards shows that the risk of loss has suddenly increased. But "professional" robbers cannot afford routinely to abandon offenses when victims resist and simply move on to the next crime scene. The adoption of such a finely calculating perspective on crime would block them from doing robberies in the first place. Much of the "gratuitous violence" in robberies makes sense within the uniquely demanding needs of "career" robbery offenders. By leaping over a retail counter, putting a gun to the side of a clerk's head and slamming him to the floor, an offender sends a strong message to the victim, and to himself as well, that material profit may not be all that the event is about. And by taking victim resistance as a "reason" for a violent response, offenders ritualize their criminal commitments in ceremonies that sometimes portray intentions in blood.

In sum, the study of interaction within robbery events indicates that, in order to conduct robbery persistently, one must commit oneself spiritually and emotionally beyond what material and mundane calculation can recommend. "Nonrational" violence makes sense as a way of committing oneself to persist in robbery in the face of the risks and chaos inherent in the criminal event. . . .

A similar social fabric of illicit action can be found in the careers of nonviolent and violent, persistent property offenders. While it is essential to appreciate how violent predators may use drugs, sexual relationships, gambling, and robbery offenses to embody their desires in a social world that will then promote their persistent criminality, their motivations contain a more distinctive theme. In juxtaposition to the self-consciously sensual dynamics they work into their lives is their generalized commitment to violence, a commitment that serves the emphatically disembodied purpose of being mean.

Violent predators appear to become distinguished from nonviolent "career" criminals at an early age. Their biographies reveal their experience of an early, critical test. However strong they may be—and they do not describe themselves uniformly as particularly capable of physical aggression—they come to realize, through battles with peers, that fighting skills or weapons possession will never be sufficient to guarantee dominance. Battles, they learn, are decided ultimately by a fierceness of will that has no substantive objective other than dominance itself: the victor is the one who manages best not to be concerned about his own legal liability or physical survival; conversely, so long as there is a possibility of continuing to attack, or returning another day to attack again, the loser is ultimately defined as the one who begins to worry and then backs off. In a phrase, they learn that they must be mean, to insist that their meaning or definition of the situation prevail regardless of its utility for any further purpose. Much of the culture of the "badass" that is popular in high-crime areas celebrates the substantively purposeless yet highly expressive styles and symbols of being mean (Katz, 1988:99–112).

The challenges of humiliating dominance that are represented in early adolescence primarily by insults from neighboring peers become constant and more diffuse for the persistent offender in his young adult years. The life histories of violent and nonviolent "career" thieves alike show them recurrently struggling against powerful chaotic forces that threaten to make fools of them, to abuse them physically, to lock them up, or to kill them. Habitual participation as a customer and as a seller in drug markets has its well-known risks. Jealous and vengeful, abandoned mistresses appear to be valuable resources for law enforcement investigators. If confederates in property crimes are pressured by the police, the contemporary offender has little basis to anticipate that traditions of honor will protect him. In addition to the chaos stimulated by boom-and-bust financial cycles, by the complexities of managing multiple and shifting intimate relationships, and by episodic abandonment to the powers of intoxicating substances, the persistent offender keeps in mind that, because of the variety of his previous criminal involvements, he may currently be sought by the police and seized in connection with any of a number of offenses he no longer keeps in mind.

Against this background of chaos, persistent violent property offenders are known in a variety of cultural contexts as "hard-legged," "hard-headed," and "hardmen." What distinguishes robbery from sneak, con, and other surreptitious forms of theft is the offender's demand that everyone on a scene in effect "shut up" and comply to his will. The relatively broad appeal of robbery to young offenders suggests the attractiveness of this posture; and the relatively narrow appeal of persisting in robbery indicates that, as costs and benefits begin to weigh in, career motivation comes to depend increasingly on the personal importance of overtly demanding compliance without giving reasons.

That a posture of readiness to use violence is significant to violent predators not only as a discretely applied criminal skill but as a generalized personal stance toward chaotic circumstances is indicated by data describing their common, extensive assault histories and their virtually continuous maintenance of weapons close at hand (Wright and Rossi, 1986). Scenes from life histories vividly convey a readiness to settle disagreements over personal debts with a show of force that brooks no protest; to silence discordant mates with sudden, overwhelming acts of violence; and to abuse small children verbally and physically with a quick and cold indifference (Willwerth, 1974; Carr, 1975; Allen, 1978; Dietz, 1983).

In several respects, the robber exploits in his crime the specifically transcendent potential of criminal violence. He creates and transcends chaos by first establishing fearful victims, overcoming any resistance they may mount, and either freezing the scene or transforming victims into compliant accomplices who locate valuables and clear paths for escape. As a stunning physical act, an offender's violence goes one significant step beyond the career criminal's effort to embody his acts with a sensual self-awareness: the offender's violence dramatizes the dominance of his purpose unforgettably in another's body. And in light of the multitude of uncertainties that block a calculated election of robbery as a rational offense, the offender's violence becomes invaluable as a ritual to sustain a will always threatened by the temptations of reason. While robbery may not fare well in materialistic cost–benefit comparisons with other lines of criminal involvement, the robber's generalized embrace of violence has the special virtue of helping steel oneself continually to "get over" the omnipresent threat of chaos in contemporary, urban, street criminal life.

Author's Notes

1. Farrington (1986:233) suggests "that more attention should be given to 'offending' before the age of criminal responsibility."

2. See also Petersilia, Greenwood, and Lavin (1977) and Haran (1982).

3. For evidence from victim survey data, see Hindelang, Gottfredson, and Garofalo (1978).

4. Compare Zimring and Zuehl (1986:30–31), who advise victims not to resist armed robbers, implying that robbers restrain their violence unless given practical reasons to unleash it, but who also offer the observation that "'recreational violence' seems to us not only evocative but descriptive of a large number of . . . [robberies]."

Discussion Questions

1. Are persistent robbers motivated primarily by the money they steal from their victims? Is money secondary to other motives, and if so, what are they? Why do some robbers persist in that crime despite its risks?

2. In what sense do persistent robbers go "beyond rationality" in their actions? What are the reasons for their seemingly irrational or nonrational behavior? What functions does violence or the threat of violence serve for these robbers? Would changes such as Colvin suggests in selection #6 (such as job training programs) reduce crime by persistent robbers?

3. How would Katz deal with such explanations of crime as Gottfredson and Hirschi's theory of low self-control (selection #4) or Widom's focus on the long-term consequences of child abuse (selection #5)? Does Katz think that such background factors cause crime? Why does he think this way?

Part VI

Drugs and Crime

C h a p t e r 16

Drugs and Predatory Crime

Jan M. Chaiken and Marcia R. Chaiken

A widely held perception is that property crime is common in the United States because of the country's high rate of illegal drug use; drug users are thought to turn to predatory or income-producing crime to support their expensive habits. In this selection, Chaiken and Chaiken review the research on the association between predatory crime and drug use and selling. They find that the relationship is a complex one, with predatory crime often occurring before rather than after drug use begins. They use the criminal careers perspective to examine changes in predatory crime and drug use over the life course.

A strong association has long been surmised between illicit drug use and predatory crime. Almost twenty years ago, Sutherland and Cressey (1970:164) pointed out that in the United States "felons are overrepresented in the addict population, [and] crime rates are increased considerably by drug addiction." But, although they proposed several hypotheses to explain the relationship, they summarized the state of knowledge at the time by saying that "a precise definition of the process by which narcotic drugs are related to criminal behavior has not been made" (p. 167).

Ten years later, numerous studies of incarcerated or addicted populations had increased knowledge of the drug/crime nexus; but the information was still complex and incomplete. Only in regard to heroin addiction did a coherent viewpoint prevail, but it was not universally accepted. The prevailing view, summarized by Gandossy et al. (1980), was that drug use propelled income-producing crime primarily because addicts required money to buy drugs. This view was supported by the following findings: many serious offenders

Source: Jan M. Chaiken and Marcia R. Chaiken, "Drugs and Predatory Crime," in Michael Tonry and James Q. Wilson, eds., *Drugs and Crime,* Vol. 13, of *Crime and Justice: A Review of Research,* pp. 203–207, 210–216, 218–221, 234–235. Chicago: The University of Chicago Press, 1990. Reprinted by permission of The University of Chicago Press. © 1990 by The University of Chicago. All rights reserved.

were drug users and had started using drugs as juveniles; not all drug users became addicts, but continued drug use frequently led to heroin addiction; minority group members were proportionately more likely than nonminority group members to be drug users and to be arrested for crimes; many (although not all) drug users became addicted before they were involved in criminal pursuits or arrest; among arrestees and prisoners, drug users were more likely than nondrug users to have been arrested for income-generating crimes rather than crimes of violence; drug users in treatment were more likely to have been arrested for property crimes than for violent crimes; and the drug users who were most likely to commit numerous crimes were heroin addicts.

At the time, some researchers and many policymakers were convinced from this evidence that a fairly simple causal relation existed between drug use and criminality, especially for minority group members who were disproportionately likely to become involved in drug use: first came some form of drug use as juveniles, then drug use progressed to heroin addiction, and, as heroin addicts, these users committed many nonviolent income-producing crimes to support their habits. But many countervailing facts were already known, such as that a substantial number of casual users of heroin (nonaddicts) existed and were not heavily involved in crime (e.g., Robins, Davis, and Wish, 1980).

The picture available from today's research indicates that, while the progression to heroin addiction and income-producing crimes may apply to some drug users, other behavioral sequences also occur often (even *more* often), for example, patterns involving drugs other than heroin, or predatory crime before drug addiction, or violent rather than nonviolent criminality. Some patterns are applicable only in particular subgroups of the population.

In short, no single sequential or causal relationship is now believed to relate drug use to predatory crime. When the behaviors of large groups of people are studied in the aggregate, no coherent general patterns emerge associating drug use per se with participation in predatory crime, age at onset of participation in crime, or persistence in committing crime. Rather, different patterns appear to apply to different types of drug users (Chaiken and Johnson, 1988). But research does show that certain types of drug abuse are strongly related to offenders' committing crimes at high *frequencies*—violent crimes as well as other, income-producing crimes. The observed relationship applies to various population subgroups, including groups defined by age, race, or sex.

This essay summarizes the known research information—with emphasis on quantitative research—about the association between drug use and *predatory crime*. The association between drug dealing and predatory crime is also discussed, because it is often more pertinent or stronger than the association between drug use and crime.

In discussing predatory crime, we have in mind instrumental offenses committed for material gain. We do not include aggressive crimes such as marital violence, homicide, or assault unrelated to robbery or burglary; public disorder crimes; driving under the influence of alcohol or drugs; or consensual crimes such as prostitution. However, in reviewing the results of published works, some nonpredatory crimes may be included with predatory crimes if they were studied together or summarized together by the original authors.

In summarizing and commenting on the literature on drug use and predatory crime, we use a specialized vocabulary that has been developed in the study of criminal careers (Blumstein et al., 1986). The terms *onset, participation, frequency, desistance,* and *persistence* are drawn from the concept of a criminal career as a sequence of crimes committed by an individual offender (Blumstein et al., 1986). A person's criminal career has its *onset* when he or she commits a crime for the first time, at which time the offender is said to be *participating* in crime. A *participation rate* is the proportion of a group of people who engage in crimes during a specified period. The *frequency* or *rate* of crime commission is the number of crimes committed per year when the offender is free to commit crime (that is, unincarcerated). *Desistance* is the end of the criminal career, and *persistence* refers to a career that lasts a long time between onset and desistance.

Since this essay focuses on predatory crime and not on assaultive or other destructive behavior resulting from physiological effects of drugs, we do not distinguish among pharmacological classes of drugs such as amphetamines, barbiturates, or hallucinogens. However, as shown in the sections that follow, the types of drugs used by offenders and the frequency with which they use them are important in understanding the connections between drug abuse and predatory crime. Most drug users abuse at least two types of substances; therefore many research studies summarized in this essay categorize types of *drug abuse* rather than types of *drugs* abused. Commonly employed categories of drug abuse, in order of increasing seriousness, are: marijuana and alcohol abuse; use of other nonopiate illicit drugs (possibly in addition to marijuana and alcohol); and opiate or cocaine use, including various derivative forms of those substances.

People are generally considered to be involved in a specific category of drug abuse if they have a sustained pattern of involvement. For example, most researchers would not classify as a drug abuser a person who has used marijuana two or three times. Similarly, a person who frequently drinks and also smokes marijuana would be classified by most researchers as involved in marijuana use; this would be the case even if he or she is also known to have used cocaine on one occasion. However, people who have a sustained pattern of relatively serious drug abuse would be classified as involved in that form of drug abuse even though they were more likely to indulge in less serious forms of abuse. For example, people who use heroin every week would be classified as heroin users even if they drank alcohol and smoked marijuana every day.

Almost all the studies discussed in this essay were based on self-reports of drug use and crime. Self-reports are less likely than criminal justice system records or other forms of agency records to underestimate study subjects' involvement in crime, delinquency, or drug use. However, the validity of self-report information about drug abuse and criminality is questionable because respondents may have had difficulty recalling past behavior, may not have understood the questions they were asked, or may either have concealed or exaggerated their illegal activities. Researchers who conduct these studies are aware of these validity issues and use methods that minimize the possible distorting effects on their findings.

The studies most likely to avoid problems of recall are those in which subjects are interviewed at set intervals over a period of time. These studies provide valuable information on the relationships between predatory crime and drug use over the life course. However, many other studies learn about respondents' past behavior retrospectively. When findings from prospective and retrospective studies are similar, they reinforce each other.

The methods used for collecting data about drug use and criminality range from relatively large national surveys to in-depth interviews and observations of small groups. The study subjects include random samples of the nation's youth, groups of school children, addicts in treatment centers, inmates in prisons and jails, defendants whose cases had been just concluded, samples of inner-city youth, probationers, and adult street populations. Aside from studies of addicts in treatment, important data sources drawn on in this essay are the National Youth Survey, a Rand Corporation inmate survey, and interview data from street addicts in New York City. . . .

I. Summary of Findings from Recent Research

People who commit predatory crimes over long periods tend also to commit other crimes and to have begun their criminal careers at young ages. Similarly, people who use illicit drugs often or in large quantities tend to use a variety of drugs and to have begun using drugs during adolescence. These seemingly similar groups of persistent offenders and persistent drug users are not necessarily the same people. There appears to be no simple general relation between high rates of drug use and high rates of crime.

A. Patterns of Criminal Behavior and Drug Use

Research on criminal behavior over the past decade has demonstrated strong interrelationships among age at onset of a criminal career, persistence of criminal activity, rates of committing offenses, and types of offenses committed. In any population of offenders, most commit nonviolent offenses and at low rates. Even adult offenders who were incarcerated for violent crimes such as robbery or assault typically committed only one or two of these offenses in the year preceding their incarceration (Chaiken and Chaiken, 1982; Visher, 1986; Mande and English, 1988; Chaiken and Chaiken, 1989). However, a relatively small group of offenders commits crimes at very high rates—hundreds of crimes per year when they are free to do so (Chaiken and Chaiken, 1982; Ball, Shaffer, and Nurco, 1983; Johnson et al., 1985; Ball, 1986; Mande and English, 1988; Chaiken and Chaiken, 1989). Those who frequently commit violent crimes also are very likely to commit other crimes, such as burglary and theft, and to commit one or more of these types of crimes at high rates (Chaiken and Chaiken, 1982; Chaiken and Chaiken, 1985; Johnson et al., 1985). Moreover, this small group of adult offenders is likely to have started committing crimes as young adolescents (Chaiken and Chaiken, 1982; Hanson et al., 1985; Johnson et al., 1985).

Studies of patterns of drug use have produced parallel findings. Most people who use illicit drugs confine their use to sporadic use of marijuana, while relatively few use other illicit drugs such as barbiturates, amphetamines, cocaine, or heroin (Miller et al., 1983; Johnston, O'Malley, and Bachman, 1985, 1986). An even smaller number of people use these drugs frequently (e.g., daily or more often); and those who use any drug in high quantities or at high frequencies are likely to be using also several other types of illicit drugs frequently, often in combination with alcohol (Elliott and Huizinga, 1985; Wish and Johnson, 1986; Elliott, Huizinga, and Menard, 1989). The high-frequency users are also more likely than other users to have started using drugs as adolescents (Newcomb and Bentler, 1988).

While these parallel patterns of criminal behavior and drug abuse are strongly interrelated, research does not support the view that they are basically overlapping descriptions of the same people. There are a few severely addicted people who commit no crimes aside from illegal possession of drugs (Collins et al., 1982); and there are criminals who commit numerous serious crimes but are not involved in drug use (Chaiken and Chaiken, 1985; Innes, 1988). Moreover, for most people, changes over time in individuals' use or nonuse of drugs are not systematically related to changes in their participation or nonparticipation in criminal activity (Kandel, Simcha-Fagan, and Davies, 1986; Newcomb and Bentler, 1988). One exception is a repeated finding that, among heroin-using high-rate offenders, intensity of offending appears to vary directly with intensity of drug use (e.g., Anglin and Speckart, 1986; Nurco et al., 1988).

Research does not support the view that drug abuse necessarily precedes onset of criminal activity, nor does it demonstrate a causal ordering between drug use and criminality. A more coherent interpretation is that drug abuse and participation in crime coexist in some social groups. Rather than having a cause-and-effect relationship, the onset of drug use, the onset of predatory crime, or both, can occur in early puberty as products of similar external factors. Fagan and others have found that both or either of these behaviors can be explained by intervening variables such as destructive factors in the environment (e.g., physical abuse or criminal siblings) or the absence of traditional social controls (e.g., lack of parental attention or participation in rewarding school activities) (White, Pandina, and LaGrange, 1987; Fagan and Weis, 1990). The more deviant the environment, the more likely an adolescent is to perform poorly in school, to use multiple forms of illicit drugs frequently, and to participate frequently in predatory crime (Williams and Kornblum, 1985; Simcha-Fagan and Schwartz, 1986).

From analysis of self-report surveys of male prison and jail inmates in three states in the late 1970s, we concluded that predatory criminals may be involved in drug use as a part of their nontraditional lifestyle, which in most instances is also evidenced by other factors such as irregular employment and absence of marital ties (Chaiken and Chaiken, 1982). However, many long-term offenders in these inmate surveys had never used drugs; in fact, nearly half (47 percent) of inmates who had never used drugs were persistent offenders (they had committed crimes for more than five years prior to their arrest). Generally, older criminals are less likely than younger offenders to use illicit drugs (Wish and Johnson, 1986); but even among young delinquents who committed crimes such as robbery, burglary, or serious assaults in inner-city areas, most have been found not to use drugs (Fagan and Weis, 1990).

Where, then, lies the strong relationship between drug use and criminality? A large body of research, discussed in the remainder of this essay, shows that, among predatory offenders, the ones who are *high-frequency* drug users are also very likely to be *high-rate* predators and to commit many different types of crimes, including violent crimes, and to use many different types of drugs. This finding has been confirmed for adolescents and adults, across states, independent of race, and in many countries. It also is the same for both males and females with one notable exception: females who use drugs frequently are less likely than males to commit violent crimes (but women drug users are more likely to resort to prostitution, shoplifting, and similar covert, nonviolent crimes at high rates [Sanchez and Johnson, 1987]).

The relationship between high-frequency drug use and high-frequency criminality is intensified by long durations of involvement in drug use and predatory crime (Nurco et al., 1988). Adult offenders who commit robbery and burglary at the highest rates typically have been persistent offenders and drug users since they were juveniles, for example, using heroin as juveniles and starting to commit predatory crimes before they were sixteen years old (Chaiken and Chaiken, 1982). The earlier the age of onset of cocaine or heroin use, the more likely persistent offenders are to be serious predatory offenders as adults (Chaiken and Chaiken, 1985; Collins and Bailey, 1987).

B. Drug Sellers

In all studies that have examined the issue, the relationship between drug use and criminality has been found to be substantially weaker than the relationship between drug *sales* and other forms of criminality (Chaiken and Chaiken, 1982; Johnson et al., 1985; Chaiken, 1986). Most people who sell drugs do so occasionally and privately and are not likely to be involved in predatory crimes. But those who sell drugs publicly, for example in parks, streets, or back alleys, are likely to commit predatory crimes and to commit them at higher rates than people who commit the same type of offenses but do not sell drugs (Johnson et al., 1985; Williams and Kornblum, 1985).

Based on surveys of inmates and interviews with other offenders, adult robbers who sell drugs on average report committing many more robberies than robbers who do not sell drugs; these *robbers* also report committing more *burglaries* than many other burglars, especially burglars who do not distribute drugs (Johnson et al., 1985; Chaiken, 1986). Among urban youth, drug sales were also found to have a strong association with committing numerous serious crimes, including armed robbery (Fagan and Weis, 1990).

While many public drug dealers are themselves frequent users of various types of drugs, others are careful not to mix business with pleasure; they only sporadically use their own illicit merchandise. Yet these nonuser drug dealers still commit predatory crimes, including numerous robberies and burglaries (Chaiken and Chaiken, 1982; Williams and Kornblum, 1985; Mieczkowski, 1986).

Some of the robberies and other assaultive crimes committed by offenders who also sell drugs are systemic aspects of the drug trade (Johnson et al., 1985). Given the highly competitive nature of drug distribution (Kleiman and Smith, 1990; Moore, 1990) and the obvious lack of official regulation, violence and robbery are sometimes used to drive competitors out of business or to protect a dealer's money, supplies, and connections (Adler, 1985; Johnson et al., 1985). Other assaults and predatory crimes committed by drug dealers arise from their need for money for drugs and are opportunistically focused on the first available target (Williams and Kornblum, 1985)—although many addicts are able to sustain their use by committing less serious crimes (Goldstein, 1985; Hunt, 1990). However, many predatory crimes are committed by dealers who find vulnerable victims with cash, follow them to a secluded area, threaten or actually injure them, and take their money (Chaiken and Chaiken, 1985; Hanson et al., 1985). . . .

II. Chronology of Participation in Use of Illegal Drugs and Predatory Crime

The criminal careers model provides a useful framework for organizing the discussion of research on the relationship between drug use and predatory crime. Similarities and differences between the onset and persistence of these two types of behaviors are discussed in this section. Particular emphasis is given to research on the interrelatedness of the onset and persistence of drug use and predatory crime.

A.   *Onset of Criminal Behavior*

Research does not support the hypothesis that use of illicit drugs ultimately results in the user's involvement in predatory crime, or even that this is a predominant pattern. Studies of youths' drug use and crime that refute this hypothesis have included repeated interviews with over 1,500 youngsters selected as a representative sample for a National Youth Survey (Elliott and Huizinga, 1985); in-depth interviews with 100 youngsters in a medium-size upstate city in New York (Carpenter et al., 1988); surveys of over 800 inner-city youth including almost 200 school dropouts (Fagan and Weis, 1990); repeated surveys from age fifteen to age twenty-five with a sample of over 1,000 youths selected to be representative of students enrolled in New York State secondary schools (Kandel, Simcha-Fagan, and Davies, 1986); and repeated interviews over a period of eight years with a sample of 1,000 youths who originally attended Los Angeles County schools (Newcomb and Bentler, 1988).

Virtually all these studies have found that many more youngsters use illicit drugs than are involved in predatory crime. As youthful users of illicit substances approach adulthood, they are likely to continue to use drugs, but they are less likely—not more likely—to commit predatory crimes (Kandel, Simcha-Fagan, and Davies, 1986). Moreover, youths who commit serious predatory crimes are more likely to use illicit drugs frequently than are youthful users of illicit drugs to engage in predatory crime (Fagan and Weis, 1990).

Research evidence provides little support for the popular conception that most drug-involved offenders begin committing predatory crimes because they want money to buy drugs. In fact, many of them were involved in juvenile delinquency, including minor forms of predatory crime, before they were involved in illicit drug use. The data are more consistent with the commonsensical notion that minor predatory crime is a precursor to serious predatory crime. Prospective longitudinal self-report data from the National Youth Survey (Elliott and Huizinga, 1985) and studies based on a sample of New York youngsters (Kandel, Simcha-Fagan, and Davies, 1986) demonstrate that, among youngsters who both use drugs and commit nondrug offenses, delinquency is about as likely to begin before as after initial use of illicit drugs. . . .

In sum, use of illicit drugs may be a primary cause for initial participation in predatory crime for some offenders; however, for the vast majority of offenders who commit predatory crimes, use of illicit substances appears to be neither a necessary nor a sufficient cause of onset of predatory criminal behavior. Even onset of *narcotic addiction* often does not appear to be causally related to onset of involvement in property crime. Rather, the onset of heroin addiction is often a key point in accelerating an existing criminal career.

B.   *Persistence of Drug Use and Predatory Crime*

Studies that have followed the behavior of youngsters over the span of early adolescence to young adulthood indicate that drug use is more likely to persist over this life span than is involvement in predatory crime (Kandel, Simcha-Fagan, and Davies, 1986; Newcomb and Bentler, 1988). Further, continued criminality is more predictive of future drug use than is drug use predictive of criminality. Although over two-thirds of youthful users of drugs are likely to continue use as adults, as they approach their late teens and early twenties, half of the juveniles who commit crimes stop (Elliott and Huizinga, 1985; Kandel,

Simcha-Fagan, and Davies, 1986). As they grow older, delinquents are likely to use more addictive drugs—starting with marijuana, progressing to hallucinogens, sedatives and analgesics, and then to cocaine and heroin (Inciardi, 1987). Delinquents most likely to engage in drug use are those who have been sexually abused as children (Dembo et al., 1987). Moreover, almost all persistent serious delinquents are likely eventually to use drugs. Only 18 percent of chronic, serious offenders in the National Youth Survey remained drug free as they aged (Elliott and Huizinga, 1985).

A review of cohort studies covering nearly 12,000 boys in Philadelphia, London, Racine (Wisconsin), and Marion County (Oregon) suggests that youngsters are most likely to continue committing serious crimes as adults if they behave badly in school, come from poor families, have other criminals in their immediate family, have a low IQ, and receive inadequate parental attention (Blumstein, Farrington, and Moitra, 1985). Retrospective studies of the careers of predatory adult offenders suggest that essentially the same factors are characteristic of persistent offenders who commit the most serious predatory crimes (robbery and burglary) at high rates (Chaiken and Chaiken, 1985). While drug abuse may often be concomitant with these predictive factors, it generally has not been shown to have independent value as a predictor of persistent offending.

Although sustained drug use cannot, in general, be considered a cause of predation, involvement in predatory crime increases the probability of serious forms of drug use which in turn enhance continuation and seriousness of a "predatory career." This self-reinforcing relationship has been demonstrated by interviews conducted with patients in methadone treatment about their "addiction careers"; in these studies, Anglin and Speckart (1986) found that theft precedes addiction more frequently than it follows addiction; however, burglary and robbery are more likely to follow than precede addiction; and there is positive covariation between the levels of narcotics use and the numbers and seriousness of crimes committed.

Ethnographic studies of street addicts suggest that these relationships may be explained by involvement in a lifestyle of "taking care of business" in which "the hustle" is any legitimate or illegal activity that can generate income (Hanson et al., 1985). Theft and other minor predatory crimes become a "normal" activity for relatively many elementary school–aged boys raised on inner-city streets. As they approach adolescence, boys in many major cities have the opportunity to participate in the drug trade (Mieczkowski, 1986; Hunt, 1990). Part of the street drug trade often involves keeping a small amount of drugs for personal use and robbing street drug distributors or other community residents of drugs or cash (Johnson et al., 1985). As adults, heroin use may continue as part of this lifestyle, but even regular users of heroin may abstain for relatively long periods in the absence of a safe and lucrative hustle (Hanson et al., 1985). Among hustlers, robbery is not generally considered a safe means of obtaining money; however, a relatively small proportion of adult hustlers like to do "stick-ups" (robberies) because they consider the activity adventuresome and exciting (Hanson et al., 1985).

Little is known about the end of hustling lifestyles or the termination of predatory careers among drug-involved persistent offenders. Recent research suggests that addicted adult offenders often continue to use drugs and commit crimes for twelve or more years in the absence of effective treatment and supervision (Anglin, Piper, and Speckart, 1987). There is some evidence that mortality rates are relatively high for this population and that almost half of the deaths are due to drug use (Joe and Simpson, 1987). There is also evidence, based on in-depth interviews with over 100 ex-addicts, that the end of a hustling lifestyle can be self-initiated because of a personally negative incident endemic to hustling, such as a threat of bodily harm from another dealer, and can take place in the absence of formal treatment (Biernacki, 1986).

Future research is urgently needed on the causes and reasons for desisting from a life of drug use, crime, or both. Most pertinent for policy purposes will be improved information on the manner and extent to which drug addiction extends an addict's criminal career. . . .

III.   *Conclusions and Implications for the Justice System*

Use of illicit drugs does not appear to be strongly related to onset and participation in predatory crime; rather, drug use and crime participation are weakly related as contemporaneous products of factors generally antithetical to traditional United States lifestyles. Most of the underlying causative factors, such as irregular employment or weak attachment to school or parents, are not amenable to intervention by the justice system. Moreover, general prevalence figures for drug use do not give much hope that even major reductions in the numbers of people who use illicit drugs could significantly reduce the numbers of incidents of predatory crime.

More specifically, among adolescents and adults who use illicit drugs, most do not commit predatory crimes. Reducing the number of adolescents who are sporadic users of illicit drugs, especially marijuana, may possibly affect the incidence and prevalence of some types of crime, such as disorderly conduct and driving under the influence of controlled substances, but not predatory crime. In addition, most adults who sporadically use drugs such as hallucinogens, tranquilizers, or cocaine do not commit predatory crimes. Therefore, reducing the number of *adults* who are sporadic users of these types of drugs may also affect the incidence and prevalence of some types of crime, but is unlikely to affect the incidence of predatory crime.

About 50 percent of delinquent youngsters are delinquent before they start using drugs; about 50 percent start concurrently or after. Reducing the number of adolescents who sporadically use illicit drugs may potentially reduce the incidence and prevalence of minor predatory crime; but these types of crime are more likely to be reduced through comprehensive delinquency prevention measures which do not focus exclusively or particularly on drug abuse.

Persistent use of drugs other than heroin (and perhaps also excluding cocaine) appears to be unrelated to persistence in committing predatory crimes. Among youngsters who use drugs and commit theft or other predatory crimes, most continue to use drugs as adults but stop committing crimes at the end of adolescence. Moreover, almost half of convicted offenders who are persistent offenders never used drugs. Therefore preventing persistent use of drugs other than heroin and cocaine is not likely to reduce the numbers of persistent predatory offenders.

However, there is strong evidence that predatory offenders who persistently and frequently use large amounts of multiple types of drugs commit crimes at significantly higher rates over longer periods than do less drug-involved offenders, and predatory offenders commit fewer crimes during periods in which they use no heroin.

These findings suggest that criminal justice programs that focus resources on high-rate predatory offenders should include among their selection criteria evidence of persistent, frequent use of multiple types of illicit drugs. In addition, criminal justice system programs that effectively prevent addicted predatory offenders from using heroin appear promising when measured against the goal of reducing the incidence of predatory crime.

Discussion Questions

1. What is the criminal careers perspective? What do the terms *onset, participation, frequency, desistance,* and *persistence* mean? How do Chaiken and Chaiken use these concepts to look at careers in predatory crime and careers in drug use and selling?

2. Does drug use inevitably lead to predatory crime to pay for drugs? Does research show that drug use typically precedes predatory crime, that predatory crime typically precedes drug use, or that the two usually occur at about the same time?

3. Is the association between drug use and predatory crime stronger or weaker than the association between drug selling and predatory crime? Why do you think this is the case?

4. How much of an impact on predatory crime would there be if governmental policies significantly reduced the number of people using illegal drugs? What policies does this paper suggest for reducing predatory crime and illegal drug use?

Chapter 17

Street Kids and Crack Cocaine: The Drugs/Violence Connection

James A. Inciardi, Ruth Horowitz, and Anne E. Pottieger

This selection is part of a study of 611 serious delinquents studied on the streets of Miami. Twenty percent of them were twelve or thirteen years old, 38 percent were fourteen or fifteen, and the rest were sixteen or seventeen. Males were 84 percent of the sample. Whites were 41 percent of the total, blacks 42 percent, and Hispanics 16 percent. This selection looks at the involvement of these delinquents in the crack trade and at the link between crack use and dealing and involvement in violent crime. A delinquent's involvement in the crack business was categorized as "none," "minor," "dealer," or "dealer+" (a person who sells crack and also manufactures, smuggles, or wholesales it.)

The general relationship between drugs and violence within this population can be examined within the context of Goldstein's (1985) "tripartite" conceptual framework. The serious delinquents interviewed for this study, like most drug/crime samples, demonstrate the impact of three simultaneous connections between drug use and violent behavior. Goldstein labels these the *psychopharmacological, economically compulsive,* and *systemic* models of violence.

Source: James A. Inciardi, Ruth Horowitz, and Anne E. Pottieger, *Street Kids, Street Drugs, Street Crime: An Examination of Drug Use and Serious Delinquency in Miami.* Belmont, Calif.: Wadsworth, 1993, pp. 104–106, 108–112.

The *psychopharmacological model of violence* suggests that some individuals, as the result of short-term or long-term use of certain drugs, may become excitable, irrational, and violent. Some 5.4% of the sample reported committing this form of violence at least once during the 12-month period prior to interview, and 4.6% reported being the *victims* of it during this same period. In both cases, the impatience and irritability associated with drug withdrawal or the paranoia and edginess associated with stimulant abuse were the typical causes of this behavior. During mid-1989 a 17-year-old daily crack user summed up both situations:

> It doesn't seem to matter whether you're on or off crack . . . you're crazy both times. If you're high, you think someone's goin' ta do something to you, or try an' take your stuff. If you're comin' down or are waiting to make a buy or just get off, you seem to get pissed off easy. . . . A lot of people been cut just because somebody looked at them funny or said somethin' stupid.

Similarly, a 16-year-old female crack user reported in 1990:

> I was in this *graveyard* [a room in an abandoned building used for selling and smoking crack or for exchanging sex for crack] off 103rd [Street], givin' this man a blow job [oral sex] for a *taste* [a share of drugs; in this case, a *hit* from a crack pipe] of his crack. But he was so strung out, so wasted, so fucked up from doin' crack that he couldn't *get it up* [get an erection]. Like it was my fault, the mother fucker. . . . The touchy asshole. He keeps slappin' me, sayin' that I couldn't give good *head* [oral sex]. . . . Another time I saw this same man, with some other lady, and the same thing was happenin' and he got fuck-all kick-ass mad and beat her up bad.

A second view, the *economically compulsive model of violence,* holds that some drug users engage in economically oriented violent crimes to support their costly drug use. The majority of respondents in this study participated in robberies during the 12-month period prior to interview. That most robberies were committed to purchase drugs is suggested by answers to the question "Of the money you make illegally, how much goes to buying drugs?" Some 61.9% of all 611 respondents said 90% or more, and 91.0% said over half their crimes went toward purchasing drugs. In this regard, a 17-year-old male reported in 1988:

> To get enough money for whatever we wanted to do [whatever drugs], sometimes me an' a friend would go downtown, maybe down the street from some nice restaurants, and wait for them [potential victims] to go to their cars. We'd know what cars they'd be goin' to. It was the rental cars—Hertz, Alamo, you know, those cars—for the tourists. When the guy would bend down to unlock the door, we'd run from across the street real fast, knock him with a club an' kick him a few times, take his wallet, jewelry. And the guy would always have a lady with him, and she would stand there in shock, so I'd run around the car an' take her bag, a chain from the neck if she had it.

In addition, 24.1% of the 611 respondents had taken drugs away from another drug user in the prior 12 months by means of force or threat of force, and 21.1% had themselves been the *victim* of a drug robbery during that time. An additional 39.9% were not robbed of drugs in the past year but had been victimized this way at some previous time. For example, a 15-year-old female explained in 1989 that, because of her size and her sex, she had been continually victimized by the drug users and sellers that she dealt with:

> Maybe it was because I'm a girl, maybe because I'm little, but everybody was rippin' me off. I'd get my stuff and somebody would knock me down and take it. I would lie to my mother about the bruises. Once I was beat so I had two black eyes, and I told my mother somebody tried to rape me, and she went crazy, wanted to call the police.

Third, the *systemic model of violence* maintains that violent crime is intrinsic to involvement with any illicit substance, due to the traditionally aggressive patterns of interaction within illegal drug-trafficking and -distribution systems. Many of the youths interviewed in this study reported involvement in systemic violence as both perpetrators (8.3%) and victims (9.0% in the last 12 months; another 7.2% earlier). The violence typically emerged in this population as fights resulting from territorial disputes, the sale of poor-quality drugs, and instances of "messing up the money." One incident involved the execution in 1987 of two crack user/dealers in Miami's Liberty City community who were suspected of being police informants. As the reported perpetrator of these homicides indicated:

> I'm not sayin' *when* I did it, *how* I did it, or *where* I did it. But I will say why. Because they were cheatin', lyin' mother fuckers, takin' money from cops and sellin' out. . . . So I was told to teach 'em a good lesson, and make a good example of 'em. (Inciardi, 1990:100)[1]

Our data suggest a clear relationship between a youth's proximity to the crack market and his or her overall involvement in crime, *including violent crime.* Specifically, the more involved a youth is in crack distribution, the earlier he or she first committed a crime and was first arrested, convicted, and incarcerated. Moreover, the greater the crack-business involvement, the higher the likelihood of an arrest resulting in incarceration. This suggests that the youths most likely to become deeply involved in the crack trade were those with the earliest and most serious general crime history.

Current crime—i.e., crime in the year prior to interview—shows the same pattern: the greater the crack-business participation, the greater the level of other crime commission. As indicated in Table 17-1, this held for both major felonies and property offenses. This pattern was not seen for the vice offenses, due primarily to the small number of females in the sample.[2]

Of particular interest in Table 17-1 are the figures regarding violence—robberies and assaults. Specifically, the greater the crack-business participation, the greater the involvement in violent crime. Moreover, those in the "dealer" and "dealer+" groups committed more violent crimes on a per capita basis than those in the "none" and "minor" groups. Of youths who committed *any* robberies, those with no or only minor crack-market ties averaged 6.1 robberies each, compared to 13.9 for dealers and 18.2 for the dealer+ group.

In terms of absolute numbers, these 254 youths were responsible for a total of 223,439 criminal offenses during the 12 months prior to interview. Some 61.1% of these offenses were drug sales, 11.4% were vice offenses, 23.3% were property offenses, and 4.2% were major felonies, including robberies, assaults, burglaries, and motor vehicle thefts. As

TABLE 17-1   Specific Crimes in the 12 Months Prior to Interview

	Crack-Business Involvement				Total Crack Sample (N =254)
	None (N =50)	Minor (N =20)	Dealer (N =138)	Dealer+ (N =46)	
Major felonies	44.0%	65.0%	87.7%	95.7%	78.7%
Robbery	12.0	40.0	66.7	73.9	55.1
Assaults	4.0	0.0	8.0	17.4	8.3
Burglary	24.0	25.0	70.3	91.3	61.4
Motor vehicle theft	30.0	35.0	57.2	73.9	53.1
Property offenses	94.0%	95.0%	100.0%	100.0%	98.4%
Shoplifting	90.0	95.0	100.0	100.0	97.6
Theft from vehicle	34.0	30.0	75.4	84.8	65.4
Pickpocketing	2.0	5.0	13.0	10.9	9.8
Prostitute's theft	8.0	5.0	20.3	4.3	13.8
Other larcenies	4.0	0.0	0.7	0.0	1.2
Con games	6.0	5.0	53.6	63.0	42.1
Bad paper	10.0	5.0	60.1	73.9	48.4
Stolen goods	76.0	85.0	94.9	97.8	90.9
Property destruction	16.0	0.0	35.5	34.8	28.7
Other crimes	0.0	0.0	0.7	0.0	0.4
Vice offenses	18.0%	5.0%	33.3%	17.4%	25.2%
Prostitution	18.0	5.0	22.5	6.5	17.3
Procuring	4.0	5.0	30.4	15.2	20.5
Drug business (any)	86.0%	100.0%	100.0%	100.0%	97.2%

indicated in Table 17-2, the relationship between crack-trade participation and level of other criminal involvement is quite clear. The mean number of crimes per subject during the 12-month period ranges from 375.9 for those with no involvement in the crack business to 1419.1 offenses for those in the dealer+ category. Furthermore, this pattern was apparent not only for total crimes but also for three of the four primary crime categories: major felonies, property crimes, and total drug-business offenses (it did not hold for vice offenses).

Table 17-2 also indicates that, although less than 1% of the 223,439 offenses resulted in arrest, some 87.4% of the respondents were arrested during the 12 months prior to interview. The fact that the subjects were youths, that 358 (88.4%) of the 405 crimes resulting in arrest were either drug, vice, or petty property offenses (i.e., not major felonies), and that Miami-Dade has a seriously overburdened criminal justice system, explains why these youths were still in the free community at the time of interview.

Street Kids, Street Crime

Recent media reports appear to be correct in assessing youthful involvement in the crack business as a significant crime trend in some locales. If anything, media reports may underestimate its importance, for three reasons: (1) the crack trade is related to not only heavier

TABLE 17-2   Crimes and Arrests in the 12 Months Prior to Interview

	Crack-Business Involvement				Total Crack Sample (N =254)
	None (N =50)	Minor (N =20)	Dealer (N =138)	Dealer+ (N =46)	
Number done					
Major felonies	444	164	5,857	2,938	9,403
Property offenses	5,479	3,937	32,360	10,203	51,979
Drug business	9,785	6,630	70,365	49,766	136,546
Vice offenses	3,115	2,020	18,006	2,370	25,511
Total offenses	18,823	12,751	126,588	65,277	223,439
Mean number per respondent					
Major felonies	8.9	8.2	42.4	63.9	37.0
Property offenses	109.6	196.9	234.5	221.8	204.6
Drug business	195.7	331.5	509.9	1081.9	537.6
Vice offenses	62.3	101.0	130.5	51.5	100.4
Total offenses	375.9	637.6	917.3	1419.1	879.6
Percent arrested for					
Major felonies	6.0	10.0	17.4	26.1	16.1
Property offenses	30.0	25.0	46.4	32.6	39.0
Drug business	46.0	90.0	76.1	58.7	68.1
Vice offenses	4.0	5.0	6.5	2.2	5.1
Any offense	64.0	100.0	94.9	84.8	87.4

crack use but also more use of other drugs, (2) young crack dealers commonly violate not just drug laws but also those protecting persons and property, and (3) the crack business appears criminogenic in ways that go beyond any potential it may have as a *lure* into crime.

This last point is particularly well illustrated by the data in this study. For these youths, money to be made in the crack business was *not* the motive for initial criminal activities. Future research may show such cases, but, as it happened, crack was not widely available until most of these subjects had been engaged in some sort of regular crime for at least a year or two. Due to this timing, most had actually *sold* marijuana before ever *using* crack. But this means that, crime initiation aside, the crack business is criminogenic in that it leads serious delinquents to become even more seriously involved in crime.

In particular, these data suggest that it is not drug sales in general but specifically the crack business that is so highly problematic. Tables 17-1 and 17-2 show that 86% of the no-crack-business group were selling *some* drug, averaging around 200 sales per year. But the involvement of this group in major felonies and petty property crime was distinctly lower than that of youths with even minor involvement in the crack business, let alone compared to that of crack dealers. At the other end of the scale, one might expect that more crack-trade participation would lead to less time for, or less interest in, other crime. But there is only a slight dropoff in petty property crime for the dealer+ group compared to other dealers, and for the most serious offenses—major felonies—the dealer+ group averaged nearly 50%

more crimes per offender than other crack dealers, who in turn committed nearly five times as many crimes as subjects with minor or no crack-trade participation.

So what explains the criminogenic effects of the crack trade? The general drugs/crime literature suggests that one factor is the interactive pattern typical of crime/drug relationships for addictive, expensive drugs: crime finances use; use encourages more use; more use encourages more crime. Crack certainly appears eligible for this general pattern, since it is highly addictive and, although cheaper than other forms of cocaine, is expensive for unemployed users with anything more than a sporadic use pattern. At retail prices, a big crack habit—dozens or even scores of hits per day—can be at least as expensive as a big heroin habit, since the latter entails considerably fewer daily doses.

Thus, one major problem with the crack trade is that it facilitates crack addiction. Every single youth in the subsample who was involved in the crack business to even a minor degree was a crack user; of the crack dealers, over 70% used crack every day whereas under 15% used it less than regularly. Furthermore, even though greater crack-trade participation meant more crack earned directly, as payment for drug sales, it also meant heavier use patterns, so that crack dealers were paying an average of over $8,000 a year to purchase crack for personal use. The fit to the classic crime/drug interactive cycle seems clear: crack dealing finances crack use, crack use encourages more crack use, and more crack use requires more profit-making crimes of all sorts to support an ever-growing addictive use pattern.

This cycle was readily apparent in the lives of many of the youths interviewed. As one stated:

> It's like the vicious circle—the more cracks you use, the more cracks you want, and the more you have to do to get the cracks.

Another remarked:

> Ya get to a step in the business that everyone is out t' get ya. They know'd ya have stuff an' they want it, but they'd just as soon take it first. So ya have t' start protectin' yourself, 'cause they're carryin' [weapons] too. And when yer carryin' yer gonna use it. An' so ya use it to protect yerself, an' also t' *take off* [rob], because yer so far into it [using so much drugs] that yer money's burnin' up fast.

And a third:

> Dan Rather says that we street kids are into this for the gold chains, the leather coats, the sunglasses, the designer jeans. I believed that shit too, once. Ol' Dan never been out on the street. He don't know what the fuck he's talking about. I work hard, but there's not that much money in dealin' crack. The more you use, the more you have to sell, and hustle. You get caught up in it, like a big snowball going down a hill. You end up doing all kinds of things.

To the degree that one driving force for this cycle is indeed crack use, one possibility for breaking the cycle is forced intervention into the addiction pattern. This step requires that these youths be located, but the criminal justice system is in fact finding them: 92% of the crack-data subsample had been arrested at some time (true for almost 98%—

199/204—of those with any crack-business involvement at all). Further, over 87% had been arrested just within the 12 months prior to interview. This is a much higher percentage than that typical of young adult heroin users in street studies 10 or 20 years ago. But although these youths have been located, intervention has not occurred. Fewer than 4% of this extremely drug-involved sample had *ever* been in drug treatment. This reflects not only an overburdened juvenile court system but also inadequate treatment resources for adolescents. Both problems are commonplace across the nation.

But an additional criminogenic aspect of the crack business—and another reason why compulsory intervention is required—is the crack trade's strong attractiveness as a lifestyle to the youths involved in it. This fascination is reminiscent of descriptions applied some years ago to the heroin-user subculture: the joys of hustling and "taking care of business," the thrills of a "cops and robbers" street life (see Preble and Casey, 1969; Sutter, 1969). Interviews with some young crack dealers give the impression that the crack trade is, for them, not only all this but much more. Demand for crack makes dealing it remarkably easy and sometimes profitable—more so than selling heroin used to be. Further, crack-business networks give the appearance of upward mobility and therefore a feeling of achievement; movement up the ranks is rare for heroin dealers. A likely additional factor is that the rewards for crack dealing include a drug that makes its users feel not merely unworried but omnipotent. Finally, the sheer youth of these young crack dealers means that dangers—street violence, arrest, overdose, and potential death—are perceived with particularly giddy enthusiasm as challenges to be outwitted and overcome. Participation in the crack trade, in short, provides its own kind of intoxication for many youths entangled in it.

In conclusion, the crack/crime dynamic, at least for adolescent crack dealers, represents an intensified version of the classic drug/crime relationship originally described for (adult) heroin users. Both patterns rest on addiction; however, for crack, addiction onset appears to be more rapid, and maximum physiological intake—and thus financial requirements—seems more limitless. For both, sales of the drug of choice are the most common criminal offense, but the rewards of the crack trade go well beyond those of "getting by" through heroin dealing. Finally, whereas both patterns ensnare youth in their formative years, young crack dealers are astonishingly more involved in a drugs/crime lifestyle at an alarmingly younger age.

Authors' Notes

1. The perpetrator of these executions, sampled for the study in 1987, was interviewed by the senior author two years later, in early 1989. A black male and high school dropout, he was 17 years of age at the time of the homicides. In his neighborhood he had the reputation of being an aggressive youth who had been arrested on several occasions for serious assaults. Local crack-using informants never doubted his assertions about the 1987 killings. In fact, they claimed that from 1986 through early 1989 he was responsible for at least four killings in the Miami-Dade drug community.

2. Only 15% of the sample were females ($N = 38$), who were distributed in the crack-business categories as follows: "None" ($N = 13$), "Minor" ($N = 1$), "Dealer" ($N = 22$), and "Dealer+" ($N = 2$).

Discussion Questions

1. What are the three models of the drugs/violence relationship discussed by Inciardi, Horowitz, and Pottieger? What do they conclude about the relationship between involvement in the crack trade and the commission of serious delinquent acts? Which of the three models is best supported by their data?

2. Are the conclusions of this study of crack use and violent crime consistent with those reached by Chaiken and Chaiken in their review of the relationship between drug use and predatory crime (selection #16)?

3. How does the crack/crime relationship differ from the heroin/crime relationship? What explains the crime-generating effects of the crack trade?

Chapter 18

Deviant Careers
and Reintegration

Patricia A. Adler

In the 1970s, Patricia Adler carried out an observational study of sixty-five upper-level marijuana and cocaine dealers and smugglers in the southwestern United States. She looked at the way they organized their deviant activities, at the rewards and risks of their lifestyle, and at the criteria they used to measure success and failure. In the early 1990s, she returned to the scene of her original study and located thirteen members of her original sample. In this selection, she spells out the factors or "career contingencies" that permitted her subjects to disengage from their former lives in the drug world.

Direct or indirect follow-ups on thirteen of my major subjects showed them all to be out of the drug business and involved in other ventures. When I originally described the scene, all of my subjects had been between 25 and 40. The people I returned to find were now well into their forties or fifties and retired. Although their level of involvement in the business (carrying with it a greater potential for insulation and profit), coupled with the exit barriers they encountered (the treadmill of the dealing lifestyle and the removal of their credentials for legitimate professional work), might have hypothetically enabled or induced them to remain with the activity longer, they burned out, bottomed out, busted out, grew out, and quit.[1] Some quit with the help of Narcotics Anonymous, some with the help of other detoxification programs. Some quit because they got arrested. Some quit because they had

Source: Patricia Adler, *Wheeling and Dealing* 2nd edition, pp. 169–182. Copyright © 1993 by Columbia University Press. Reprinted with permission of the publisher.

near-arrest escapes. Some got killed while involved in dangerous work. Many of the people I knew, however, just quit on their own.

They quit for many reasons that were intrinsic to the character and experience of their dealing careers. People's participation in every deviant activity follows a career trajectory, such that their later years of involvement differ significantly from their earlier years. Some aspects of the experience fade while others arise. Those that faded were most commonly associated with the novelty of the experience. My subjects quit, first, because the rewards of dealing, from the thrills, to the power, to the money, to the unending drugs, became less gratifying. These were no longer new or exciting; they became commonplace and taken for granted. The aspects of the deviant career that arose were most commonly those associated with aging, health, and increased vulnerability to law enforcement. These dealers also quit because, like Waldorf, Reinarman, and Murphy's (1991) cocaine users, their troubles, from the physical burnout, to the diminished excitement, to the paranoia and real risks associated with their activities, mounted. As they saw people around them getting killed, arrested, divorced, and becoming haggard, they finally decided, either at some major turning point, or over a gradual period of time, that they were tired of or unable to traffic in large quantities any longer. They had aged through the career and reached a point where they were ready to move out of it.

Their attempts at getting out were not all successful. Many factors continued to hold them to the drug world and undermined their success in the legitimate world. Their exits, then, tended to be fragile and temporary, followed by periods of relapse into dealing. Reintegration formed the mirror image to the shifts and oscillations they made out of dealing: a series of forays into the legitimate world, many of them unsuccessful and temporary, that were often followed by subsequent re-endeavors. Each attempt at reintegration, however, brought them further back into society and away from the insulated world of the fast life. Yet even once made, their reattachment to conventional society was problematic due to their many years out of the mainstream economy.

Factors Affecting Reintegration

What factors affected these people's lives and employment in society subsequent to their exit from the drug trade? Some were able to reintegrate more readily than others, finding a steady line of work. Others floundered, moving from activity to activity, unsuccessful and unsatisfied. Their final exit from the drug trade also saw them move into a variety of different venues characterized by distinct patterns. Factors affecting dealers' reintegration were rooted in the periods prior to, during, and subsequent to their dealing careers.

Pre-Dealing Factors

One element influencing dealers' ability to ultimately reintegrate themselves into legitimate society was their *age at onset* in illicit activities. Individuals who become active in drug trafficking or other aspects of the underground economy at a young age remove themselves from pathways to options of legitimate success. Like Williams's (1989) cocaine kids, they drop out of school and fail to accumulate years of experience toward work in a lawful occupation. Their attitudes are also shaped by their early drug world experiences, so that they lose patience for legitimate work and seek the immediate reward of the scam and quick fix. When they become disenchanted with drug trafficking or are scared enough to think about quitting, they have no reasonable alternatives to consider. In contrast, individuals who enter the drug world after they have completed more schooling and/or have established themselves in lawful occupations have more options to pursue.

Very few of the dealers I studied entered the drug world at an early age. In fact, out of my original sample, only five people went directly from high school into supporting themselves through drug money. None of the members of my follow-up sample followed the early onset pattern. Those I recontacted had all been in their late twenties or early thirties prior to entering into the drug world. Nearly all of them had been to college, and over half had graduated. Ten had been married and four had borne children. This introduced an element of stability and responsibility into their lives, and gave them some years of investment in the legitimate world that they could draw on in their future.

Related to this were the *prior interests and skills* individuals developed in the legitimate economy before they began to earn most of their income from dealing drugs. Very often maturation and growth involves an identity-forming process where individuals gradually narrow the range of career or occupational options to those in which they are interested. During this time they may begin to pursue one or more of these avenues and gain knowledge or experience in these areas. Such occupational experience is later helpful in aiding dealers' reintegration because it can offer them an area to which they can return, an educational foundation, or a base of legitimate working experience that provides some transferrable knowledge of and confidence about the legitimate world.

From my follow-up sample, Dave had worked as a real estate agent for the four years immediately prior to entering the drug business. He had previously held jobs as an auto mechanic, an appliance salesman, and the editor/publisher of a surfing magazine. Jean had been a housewife and mother for many years, with only sales experience in retail stores. Jim had pursued a career as a photographer, holding a job on the staff of a major national news magazine for several years. Barney and Jeff had been involved in aviation. Lou had worked as an auto mechanic and auto body technician. Marty had been a teacher in the secondary school system and Bobby and Sandy had owned a fish store. Later, a couple of them returned to these early roots. For instance, Bobby and Marty resumed their original jobs as a retail fish store owner and a teacher, respectively, while Dave spent several years operating surf shops on both coasts. Jeff and Barney returned to the aviation business, and Lou not only returned to auto maintenance and repairing, but went back to live on his family's property.

A third factor affecting dealers' later reintegration was the *social class* in which they are born and raised. When people grow up and become accustomed to a certain standard of living, they are reluctant to engage in downward social mobility. One of the noteworthy aspects of the members of my sample is their middle-class background. They are likely representative of a more widespread, hidden, middle-class population that is involved in the illicit drug trade on either a full- or part-time basis (cf. Morley, 1989; Rice, 1989). Such people move into drug trafficking to enhance their middle-class, materialist lifestyle, and when they leave the fast money world their ties to the middle-class lifestyle force them to reintegrate into legitimate society more quickly. All of my subjects had grown up in upper-middle, middle, or lower-middle class backgrounds, with parents engaged in a variety of occupations from educators, to researchers, to career military, to manufacturers, and sales.

Concurrent Factors

The manner and style in which individuals comported their lives during the active phase of their trafficking careers also affected their later efforts at reintegrating. One of the most salient features toward this end was the dealers' degree of *outside involvement*. A large number of drug dealers were engaged in other ventures in addition to trafficking. At both the upper and lower levels of the drug trade, individuals can participate in trafficking on either a part- or full-time basis. For example, Reuter et al. (1990) found that the majority of the arrested lower-level crack dealers they surveyed in their Washington, D.C. sample were employed in full-time legitimate jobs but "moonlighted" as dealers to supplement their incomes. Similarly, at the upper levels, a whole coterie of accountants, bankers, lawyers, pilots, and other legitimate businesspeople are involved part-time in the drug economy, arranging smuggling runs or providing illicit services to full-time traffickers (Morley, 1989; Rice, 1989). These individuals, who deal only part-time, are likely to have more interpersonal, occupational, and economic factors tying them to society. When they renounce their dealing they have fewer reintegration obstacles to face because they are already more fully integrated into the legitimate economy.

In contrast, those who deal full-time, like Williams's (1989) youthful Dominican-American dealers, Hamid's (1990) Caribbean-American dealers, and my Caucasian upper-level dealers and smugglers, have more likely renounced their investment in socially sanctioned means of surviving financially. Of the 65 subjects in my original study, nearly one-third remained involved in their previous jobs for a significant period of time while they were dealing in large amounts. This was the case for all but one member of my follow-up sample as well. Eventually, they all renounced these jobs, however, and withdrew to dealing or smuggling as their primary activity and main source of economic support. Abandoning legitimate jobs or career tracks makes it significantly harder to reenter these lines after several years away, and only Marty, the teacher, who remained in the classroom well into his dealing career, was able to subsequently find another job in his profession.

Yet, even while engaged in full-time trafficking, individuals can become involved with legitimate front businesses on the side. Because they were making so much money, nearly two-thirds of my original sample had pretensions of being involved in a legitimate business (for the purpose of protecting themselves from the IRS) at one time or another. This figure roughly applies to the follow-up group as well. Jean, Jim, and Sandy worked in the catering business, Barney and Jeff worked with airplanes, Ben owned an automobile dealership, and Marsha ran an antique store. This kept these people partially tied to the legitimate economy and made it subsequently easier for them to reenter that economy on a serious basis once they left drug trafficking. Maintaining some connection to the lawful world of work, as Meisenhelder (1977) has noted, also implies a lifestyle commitment to keep some regular business hours. For these people, then, reintegration did not require as much of a lifestyle transformation as it did for those who had not worked at all. Thus, Jim eventually began his own successful catering business and Sandy worked in a restaurant, skills they had respectively acquired in their legitimate front businesses.

Knowledge and experience about legitimate work that was potentially useful to individuals' later reintegration could come not only from outside involvements, but from *trafficking-related skills* as well. For example, Dave used his connections in Mexico to find sources for buying Mexican ponchos and sweatshirts so he could sell them to surf stores all along the East Coast. He then parlayed this into a swap meet/flea market business, where he owned enough goods to travel around the country selling his products. His success in this venture enabled him to buy enough merchandise to open a surf store of his own. At the very least, the dealers and smugglers I studied became educated and trained in handling money, working on credit, calculating profits and expenses, and living with the uncertainty of entrepreneurship. Those with the discipline and business acumen to become successful in the drug world were often able to recreate some semblance of this outside that arena. Others with less reputable and reliable approaches, who had survived in the drug business primarily on the selling strength of the product, did not usually fare as well.

Instrumental aspects of these dealers' lives were not the only significant factors affecting their later reintegration. The strength of these traffickers' *outside associations* were important as well. This included interpersonal relationships with their children, parents, siblings, close friends, and other family members. Such associations were important because they kept these dealers integrated, to some degree, into mainstream society. These upper-level dealers and smugglers trod a delicate line, as they lived inside of conventional society, yet insulated themselves within it. That is, they ate at the same restaurants, sent their children to the same schools, and lived in the same housing developments as other people, yet they kept their social contacts with those outside the drug world to a minimum. For protection they removed themselves from the inquisitive prying of people who would not accept their occupation and lifestyle. Some Southwest County smugglers and dealers went for long periods, then, without seeing former friends and relatives. Others, though, kept in touch with their most important associates, whether they lived locally or at a distance. Through these ties they remained connected to individuals and social worlds outside of dealing. These associations would be crucial for them to draw upon in their reentry to the legitimate world.

Such outside associates are not likely to "steer individuals away" from their deviance, as Braithwaite (1989) has suggested, nor are they likely to provide a ratio of definitions favorable to the law and thereby reorient dealers' and smugglers' normative attitudes, as Sutherland's differential association theory holds. Rather, they hold traffickers, to greater or lesser degree, from totally removing themselves from society and provide a bridge back into it when these individuals feel an internal push to reenter society.

Both outside involvements and associations served as the type of "bonds to society" described by Hirschi's control theory. While people diminished these bonds during their careers in trafficking, they did not cut them entirely. They then reached out to strengthen them during their attempts to move out of dealing and reintegrate. Other *de-insulating factors* served as bonds to society as well, maintaining these dealers' connections to the mainstream and easing them back. This included ties like sports and hobbies (cf. Irwin, 1970), and could have included others such as religion. The dealers and smugglers in my sample all held onto some vestiges of their sport and hobby interests, rooting for their favorite teams, pursuing sports such as tennis or skiing, and indulging themselves in collecting things such as antiques or travel mementos. Religion, however, was not a significant part of their lives. Some individuals had come from religious backgrounds, attending parochial schools and church regularly, but this ended even before the onset of their dealing careers. While most of my follow-up subjects continued their sport and hobby interests after they quit dealing, none returned to religion.

A final factor characterizing dealers' active career behavior that affected their success and type of reintegration was the *degree of organizational sophistication* associated with their trafficking activity. Drug traffickers' involvement in deviant associations may follow a continuum of organizational sophistication, beginning with lone operators ensconced in a collegial subculture at the lowest end, and ascending to the loose associations of crack house crews, the more organized smuggling rings, the tighter and more serious delinquent gangs, and the deadly Colombian cartels or organized crime families at the highest end of the spectrum. We know from the broader study of deviance that individuals who are members of more organizationally sophisticated associations are more likely to be tied to those groups instead of integrated into society in a number of ways (see Best and Luckenbill, 1982).

The drug traffickers in my follow-up group, much like those from my original sample, represented a mixture of both dealers and smugglers. As such, their involvement in criminal organizations ranged from the lone operator to the member or leader of a smuggling ring. While they were clearly drawn into serious criminal activity and formed identities based on this occupation and lifestyle, they made no lifetime commitment to the pursuit. Detaching and reintegrating into society required a major change of master status (Hughes, 1945), but had fewer unbreakable side bets (Becker, 1960).

Post-Dealing Factors

Drug traffickers' success at reintegrating into society was also affected by several factors they encountered subsequent to their involvement in dealing. As they oscillated back and forth between their phases of dealing and quitting, the availability of *legitimate opportunities* seriously affected the permanence of their retirement. As Shover (1985) has noted in his study of thieves, finding a satisfying job could tie an individual to a line of activity. A positive experience at a legitimate job can draw an individual back into more conventional peer associations, reinforce a nondeviant identity, occupy significant amounts of time, and diminish the motivation to return to dealing. While "straight jobs" were often looked down upon with disdain by Southwest County dealers in their younger days, they were more likely to view them favorably at this later age. This was reflected in Jean's comments about her changed attitudes toward her current lifestyle and work. People who came out of drug trafficking with some money, usually those who consumed less drugs and who trafficked at the highest levels (smugglers), were often better able to create satisfying legitimate opportunities for themselves. As Barney commented:

> You spend the years from 25 to 35 in smuggling or dealing, you're too old to start a profession. But if you come out of it with some money you have a lot of options open to you. You can buy a job, buy a business, start your own business. You can lie on a resume. And you can do a lot of things when you're forced to that it would never occur to you that you can do. Like buy a passport, a birth certificate, a whole set of IDs. It's not as hard as you would think. And then you become someone else and you're free, the world opens up to you, once you have rid yourself of that financial restriction.

The importance of opportunity structures illustrates the value of Cloward and Ohlin's differential opportunity theory for reintegrating drug traffickers. Those who tried to oscillate out of dealing but could never find anything to support themselves in their hedonistic lifestyle returned to the drug world. Yet each time they attempted to quit it reflected a greater dissatisfaction with the dealing life. After a while, a less lucrative job opportunity, even Jean's bartending and waitressing job, appeared attractive.

Some drug traffickers were aided in their societal reintegration by *outside help.* As Braithwaite (1989:100–101) has noted, friends, associates, and acquaintances can aid former deviants' reintegration through "gestures of forgiveness" or "ceremonies to decertify offenders as deviant." Dealers may thus remove themselves from the scene, find a new life, make new friends, or meet a spouse (cf. Shover, 1985) who may help them start over. This begins the process of rebuilding the social bonds that tie individuals to legitimate society. For instance, Marty was strongly influenced in his move to reintegrate back into society by his new wife, who was opposed to his dealing activity, and Marsha was forcibly pulled from the dealing subculture by her boyfriend Vince, who had never liked her hanging around with the dealing crowd.

The extent and type of dealers' reintegration into society was ultimately affected by their *adaptability to the organizational world.* In my follow-up to Southwest County I observed a continuum between those whose experiences in the days of the wheeling and dealing and the big money had left them permanently unsuited for work as an employee in the organizational or bureaucratic world, and those who sought out and obtained jobs. Some of my subjects could never stoop to getting a job. They had entered the dealing world to secure freedom for their "brute being," and they would not endure the shackles of becoming an employee. Others were willing to get back into the working world, even if it meant taking a job at the bottom. Interestingly, finding oneself in "dire straits," as Dave and several others had, proved an insufficient inducement to an entrepreneurial, freedom-seeking person to get a job. They all had their limits, below which they would not stoop.

None of the wheeler-dealers, then, entered the confines of the straight "workaday" world they had either fled or disdained in the first place. Like many legitimate entrepreneurs, they could not imagine themselves punching a clock or working for someone else. Having tasted the excitement of the drug world, the straight world seemed boring. For them, staying within the world of independent business was associated with the potential for freedom and adventure. They could still dream of making the big killing and retiring. This also enabled them to avoid the awkwardness of trying to explain on a resume what they had been doing to earn a living during their dealing years. Like Dave and Barney, then, they became petty lawful entrepreneurs, leaving their glory days behind them.

In contrast, like Jean, some former dealers sought out a variety of jobs. Several of them had worked as employees prior to entering the drug world, while others tried to put together a legal front business that required them to work some regular hours during their dealing years. They did not feel uncomfortable, then, but rather enjoyed the assurance of a steady job and a predictable life. For them, quitting dealing and working legitimately became associated with security, domesticity, and freedom from paranoia. Their experiences with life as an employee, however, were never quite as predictable or as steady as the average worker.

Looking over the sum of their experiences, I found that my subjects were profoundly affected by their years spent in the illicit economy. Like other young people who failed, for various reasons, to enter career-tracking paths in the world of legitimate work, they found themselves having to make a mid-life career shift without any years of accumulation toward a secure future. Having earned significant sums of money early in their lives, they were also reluctant to later assume menial or entry-level jobs. Those who had earned credentials for legitimate careers often lost these, like Dave, due to arrest or imprisonment. They thus found themselves unemployable. Most reacted to this by eventually developing their own legitimate business ventures. Thus their years in trafficking were not wholly valueless, either financially or personally. The experience enabled them to see a side of life that might otherwise have remained blocked to them. They had lived with a passion and intensity known to few. They had traveled, met unusual people, and experimented with life in grand style. For those who survived, they were probably no worse off than many others who had lived for the present and let "mañana" take care of itself.

Discussion

While scholars have addressed the issue of exiting deviant careers (cf. Faupel, 1991; Frazier, 1976; Harris, 1974; Inciardi, 1975; Irwin, 1970; Meisenhelder, 1977; Petersilia, 1980; Ray, 1961; Shover, 1983; 1985), little has been written about the subsequent reintegration of former deviants into society. Brown (1991) has suggested that one way they do this is to capitalize on their former deviant status and become "professional ex-s," counseling and working to help others overcome their involvement in deviance. In Braithwaite's (1989) theory of crime, shame, and reintegration, he argues that individuals are steered away from their former deviant activities by caring others who accept them as essentially good, but reject their bad behavior. Rather than labeling and isolating them by casting the master status of deviant onto them, these friends, associates, and acquaintances aid former deviants' reintegration. Such reintegrative shaming, he argues, is only effective before individuals become ensconced in criminal subcultures, which support criminal behavior through their criminal opportunities, norms, values, and techniques of neutralization. At a more macro level, Braithwaite's theory suggests that "communitarian" cultures provide the most reintegrative form of shaming, by nurturing deviants within a network of attachments to conventional society.

While Braithwaite's theory of reintegration sheds light on the process by which individuals can be steered out of minor forms of deviance before they have significantly invested themselves in these behaviors and subcultures, it does not deal with the problem of reintegrating individuals who have already entered into criminal subcultures and seriously committed themselves to deviant or criminal activities, groups, and lifestyles.

Yet much crime is committed by individuals who begin criminal activities in their relative youth, much like drug traffickers, without intending to remain criminals all their lives. They go into these activities thinking they will make a lot of money and retire into some less dangerous line of work. Studies of deviant careers, in fact, show that large numbers of criminals and deviants (especially those who have never been incarcerated) naturally burn out, bottom out, grow out, and quit (Harris, 1974; Irwin, 1970; Waldorf, 1983; Waldorf, Reinarman, and Murphy, 1991). Once they have made the decision to exit deviance, their success depends largely on their ability to reintegrate into society. Braithwaite's theory, then, needs to be amended by a consideration of the reintegration of people who have passed the point at which he focuses.

My research suggests that shaming plays no role in these people's decisions to return to the more mainstream arena. Rather, they do it because they have evolved through the typical phases of their dealing careers and, like their peers, progress past the active into the inactive stage. With variations unique to each individual, dealers experience a progression through their early entry and involvement in the drug world, a middle period where they rise and experience shifts in their level and style of operation, an exit phase where they suddenly or gradually withdraw from the drug world, and the last phase, where they readapt themselves to the nondeviant world. Their eventual return to conventional society requires a process of reintegration, which is affected by the structural factors described here. They reintegrate, then, more because of "push" than "pull" factors, because the involvement in drug trafficking moves them past the point where they find it enjoyable, to the point where it is wearing and anxiety-provoking. Only once they have made the decision to leave the drug world, either temporarily or finally, do they reactivate their abandoned ties to the network of conventional society's attachments. This occurs, as Shover (1985) has noted, after they change their orientational (self-conceptions, goals, sense of time, tiredness) and interpersonal (ties to people or activities) foci, finding it preferable to detach from their deviant/criminal commitment and to reblend with the conventional society.

Their reintegration into this society is difficult, however. One of the hardest things is finding legitimate work. Years "derailed" from the mainstream in the career-building stage of their lives have blocked their entry into the professions and led to a failure to accrue connections and experience in legitimate occupational realms. They work, then, primarily in the entrepreneurial and secondarily in the employee (sales, unskilled, or semi-skilled labor) sector. Transferrable skills exist, but they are limited. Drug traffickers have gained experience working in an arena that functions more casually than most "straight" jobs. They could be irresponsible, be late, and be intoxicated for a drug deal, yet their connection would probably still wait for them because there was so much money to be made. Not many conventional jobs or deals are that profitable or forgiving. Former dealers then reenter the legitimate economy at an older age, where they are no longer the freshest and most attractive employees or trainees, bearing the stigma of unexplainable employment years. This limits their range of work opportunities. Yet compared to others who abandon youthful "compressed careers" (Gallmeier, 1987) in such fields as sport, art, drama, or music, drug traffickers have at least had the benefit of working in a business arena. This brings with it useful, and transferrable, skills. After ten years most had made the adjustment and were well ensconced within the legitimate business world; they were earning decent money and living fairly well.

The second hardest component of reintegrating is making the adjustment to the diminished lifestyle of the straight world. While their new jobs do not pay as well, traffickers' ties to the drug world were never significantly related to their work; relatively few individuals relished a deal well done or strove for intrinsic perfection in their operation. Rather, their satisfaction derived from the fast life and the easy money. They worked hard to play hard, not because they liked work. Many appreciate the mundane security of the everyday world, yet they never attain their former level of disposable income, excitement, flexibility, and the pleasure, spontaneity, and freedom they experienced during their halcyon days of drug trafficking. Some find a new identity and satisfaction in their post-dealing lifestyle, value system, and relationships, but this only occurs after a painful period of readjustment that includes feelings of relative deprivation and suffering.

Their post-dealing lives are thus profoundly affected by their years in the drug world. The attitudes, values, and lifestyle they adopted during the active phase of their dealing careers remain nascent within them. Most are straight for pragmatic rather than ideological or moral reasons. The quick buck and the "sweet" deal thus remain embedded within their vocabulary of motives. While they may be too old to keep up with their former drug-using pace or to return to the fast life, many still enjoy a touch of hedonism. In an era when the majority of middle-aged people are "former" marijuana smokers, party drinkers, and general revelers, these ex-drug traffickers still like to have adventures. It remains a part of their lifestyle and new identity, carried over from earlier times. Thus, while they have shed the dealing occupation, many retain some proclivity for deviant attitudes and lifestyles. They are post-dealers, but not completely reformed deviants. They live near the fringes of conventional society, trying to draw from both within and outside of it.

Author's Note

1. Previous studies of existing deviant careers have already identified age-related, structural, and social psychological variables as the prime factors driving most individuals to abandon their alternative lifestyles and careers (cf. Adler and Adler, 1983; Frazier, 1976; Inciardi, 1975; Irwin, 1970; Meisenhelder, 1977; Petersilia, 1980; Shover, 1983).

Discussion Questions

1. What factors preceding entry into the drug world influenced the ability of Adler's subjects later to become reintegrated into the straight world? Specifically, what role did age at onset into illicit activities, prior interests and skills, and social class background play in their ability to reintegrate?
2. What experiences in the drug world influenced the ability of Adler's subjects later to reintegrate into the straight world? What part did their involvement with activities, jobs, and individuals outside the drug world while they were dealing and smuggling play in their ability to reintegrate? What role did their trafficking-related skills play in their ability to reintegrate? Was the degree of organizational sophistication of their drug business important in the reintegration process? What part did "de-insulating factors" such as sports, hobbies, and religion play in reintegration?
3. How important were factors in the post-dealing careers of Adler's subjects in their reintegration? What role did legitimate opportunities, outsider help, and adaptability to legitimate organizations play in their reintegration?

Part *VII*

White-Collar Crime

Chapter *19*

White-Collar Crime and Criminal Careers*

David Weisburd, Ellen F. Chayet, and Elin J. Waring

In the previous selection, Adler uses the criminal careers perspective to look at the later stages of careers in drug dealing and smuggling. Here, Weisburd, Chayet, and Waring apply this perspective to a sample of convicted white-collar offenders by examining their age at onset of criminal activity, frequency of offending, prior arrest history, and specialization by type of crime. Their data provide some surprising conclusions that require revision of commonly held views of white-collar offenders.

The criminal career paradigm has begun to play a central role in the ways in which scholars and policymakers understand criminality. The paradigm directs attention to the factors that lead to participation in crime, the nature and extent of criminal activities of active offenders, and the duration of their involvement (e.g., see Blumstein and Cohen with Hseih, 1982; Blumstein et al., 1986). Scholars have increasingly focused upon the careers of "common criminals," but they have largely neglected the careers of white-collar offenders. Behind this neglect lies a common assumption about the nature of white-collar criminality. Although street criminals are assumed highly likely to recidivate, white-collar

* Research for this article was supported by the National Institute of Justice (Grant #88-IJ-CX-0046, entitled "White-Collar Criminal Careers: A Study of Sanctioning Effects"). The opinions expressed here are those of the authors and do not necessarily reflect the official policies or positions of the National Institute of Justice or the Department of Justice. We wish to express special appreciation to Robyn Lincoln, Paul Wilson, Martha J. Smith, and Neal Shover for their comments on earlier drafts of this article.

criminals are thought to be "one-shot" offenders unlikely to be processed in the justice system after their initial brush with the law. This assumption has little empirical support. But nonetheless, it is commonly stated by both researchers (see Edelhertz and Overcast, 1982) and criminal justice practitioners (e.g., see Benson, 1985; Wheeler, Mann, and Sarat, 1988).

This article examines the extent to which this image of white-collar criminals is reflected in the criminal records of defendants convicted under white-collar crime statutes in the federal court system. We find that a substantial proportion of such criminals are repeat offenders, and that a number have serious and lengthy criminal records. Following this, we explore parameters of criminality identified in the study of criminal careers in the context of this white-collar crime sample. We conclude with a discussion of the implications of these findings for white-collar crime research and policy.

The Sample

The sample was drawn from an earlier study of convicted white-collar criminals conducted by Wheeler, Weisburd, and Bode (1988; see also Wheeler, Weisburd, and Bode, 1982; Wheeler et al., 1988; Weisburd et al., 1991). They defined white-collar crime as "economic offenses committed through the use of some combination of fraud, deception, or collusion" (Wheeler, Weisburd, and Bode, 1982:642; see also Shapiro, 1980). Following this they examined eight such crimes in the federal system: antitrust offenses, securities and exchange fraud, postal and wire fraud, false claims and statements, credit and lending institution fraud, bank embezzlement, IRS fraud, and bribery. Wheeler and colleagues argued that their sample included those offenses "that would most frequently be identified by persons as 'presumptively' white-collar" (1982:643) and that most of the crimes identified in their sample fit one or another definition of white-collar crime (Wheeler et al., 1988:334). But they acknowledge that they cast a larger net for white-collar criminals than most other studies (see Weisburd et al., 1991).

The sample was drawn from seven federal judicial districts during fiscal years 1976–1978 with specific information about offenders coded from presentence investigation reports. The districts were chosen in part to provide geographic spread, in part because they were being examined in other studies, and in part because some of them were known to have a substantial amount of white-collar prosecution (see Wheeler et al., 1988). The districts (and their central cities) are: Central California (Los Angeles), Northern Georgia (Atlanta), Northern Illinois (Chicago), Maryland (Baltimore), Southern New York (Manhattan and the Bronx), Northern Texas (Dallas), and Western Washington (Seattle).

To allow a detailed reading of each presentence investigation, as well as to avoid having one or two offenses dominate, Wheeler, Weisburd, and Bode (1988; hereafter referred to as Wheeler et al.) chose to examine a random sample of 30 convicted defendants from each offense category in each of the seven districts.[1] The resulting sample therefore contained more antitrust and securities fraud offenders, and fewer postal fraud, IRS fraud and bank embezzlement offenders than a nonstratified random sample would. But it offered a broad and heterogeneous sample of those convicted under white-collar crime statutes in the federal courts.

TABLE 19-1   Social and Demographic Characteristics of Offenders in the Wheeler, et al. Sample, by Statutory Offense.

	Antitrust	Securities Fraud	Tax
Percentage White	100	100	87
Percentage unemployed	0	0	12
Percentage owners or officers	74	69	33
Percentage employed workers (nonmanagers)	0	17	27
Percentage in white-collar occupations*	100	97	74
Mean age	54	44	47
N†	27	65	210

* The definition of white-collar occupation is that used by the U.S. Census Bureau in their occupational classification system. See U.S. Bureau of the Census (1977, pp. 152-155)
† This is the maximum number of cases used. Specific statistics are calculated using at least 90% of the cases.

A brief review of background characteristics of the sample selected by Wheeler et al. illustrates the extent to which it reflects a white-collar population of criminal defendants (see Table 19-1). For example, only 8% of the sample as a whole were unemployed at the time they committed their crimes—a stark contrast to street criminals, most of whom are not employed in legitimate occupations (Sviridoff and McElroy, 1985). In the Wheeler et al. sample, most of those employed had "white-collar" jobs as defined by the federal government, and many were owners or officers of businesses. The sample also included a larger number of White offenders and a substantially older population of criminals than would be found in a sample of street criminals. Indeed, whereas bank embezzlers were on average 31 years old at the time of their conviction, the average tax offender was 47 years old, and the average securities offender was 44 years old.

TABLE 19-2   Prior Criminal Records of Offenders in the Wheeler et al. Sample, by Statutory Offense

	Antitrust	Securities Fraud	Tax
Percentage with any prior arrests	3	32	47
Percentage with any prior convictions	0	26	37
Percentage with 2 or more prior arrests	0	11	29
Percentage with 4 or more prior arrests	0	2	25
Percentage with prior felony convictions	0	15	23
Percentage previously incarcerated	0	4	14
Of those previously incarcerated			
Percentage serving more than 6 months	—	33	61
Percentage serving more than 1 year	—	33	57
N[a]	27	65	210

[a] This is the maximum number of cases used. Specific statistics are calculated on at least 90% of the cases.

Bribery	Credit Fraud	False Claims	Mail Fraud	Bank Embezzlement	Whole Sample
83	72	62	77	74	78
18	24	25	25	3	8
37	32	16	28	16	30
17	30	38	32	71	36
77	67	66	65	96	78
45	38	39	38	31	40
84	157	157	189	201	1,090

Prior Criminality of the Sample

Table 19-2 provides a general summary of the criminal histories of offenders within each of the statutory categories in the Wheeler et al. study. Of the eight white-collar crimes examined, only in the antitrust category did offenders fit traditional stereotypes of white-collar criminals. For every other offense, a substantial number of those examined had prior criminal records. Even in the case of embezzlement in banks where there are generally barriers to bank employment for those with criminal records, almost one-third of the offenders had prior arrests.

Many white-collar criminals evidenced multiple prior arrests. In the case of credit fraud, false claims and mail fraud violators, about 4 in 10 offenders had two or more prior arrests, and about 3 in 10 had four or more prior arrests. Although the extent of repeat

Bribery	Credit Fraud	False Claims	Mail Fraud	Bank Embezzlement	Whole Sample
23	55	56	54	29	43
19	46	45	41	22	34
13	42	40	37	13	28
8	29	28	27	6	12
9	29	31	29	11	21
6	25	22	23	7	15
60	63	63	63	33	60
60	47	50	61	25	52
84	157	157	189	201	1,090

offending was much lower in other crime categories, more than a quarter of tax offenders had two or more prior arrests, and more than 1 in 10 of bank embezzlers and bribery offenders had multiple prior arrests.

A substantial proportion of offenders in every crime category (with the exception of antitrust) also had prior convictions. The proportion ranged from a low of 19% for bribery offenders to a high of 46% for those convicted of a credit fraud.

The seriousness of the criminal records of these offenders may be gauged from the number with either prior felony convictions or previous incarcerations. More than 1 in 7 securities fraud violators in the sample had prior felony convictions, and this was the case for more than a quarter of those convicted of credit fraud, false claims, and mail fraud. Whereas only 1 in 25 securities violators had spent any time in jail or prison,[2] this was true for a fifth of credit fraud, false claims, and mail fraud offenders. And many of those in this latter group had served substantial periods of time behind bars.

Certainly, many of the white-collar criminals identified in the Wheeler et al. study were repeat offenders who evidenced criminality even before the felony convictions that brought them into the sample. Yet, the fact that antitrust offenders did not evidence substantial prior criminality raises an important question about the general validity of these findings. Is a high rate of recidivism common only among low-status criminals in the sample? Perhaps, more important, do those offenders who would fit the most restrictive definitions of white-collar crime also recidivate?

To address this question we restricted our criminal history analysis to a selected group of offenders who held elite positions or owned significant assets, and committed their crimes in the course of a legitimate occupation. Thus we selected (following Katz, 1979) only those sample members who worked within a bourgeois profession (such as doctors, lawyers or accountants), or who had positions as officers or managers, or who were owners of substantial capital (greater than $250,000)—and who used their occupation to commit their crimes. This procedure eliminated approximately two-thirds of the sample.[3] But even restricting the sample in this way we found that over a quarter had criminal records (see Table 19-3). Of this sample, 10% reported prior felony convictions, and 6% had prior records of incarceration. Accordingly, evidence of criminal careers can be found even within a highly restricted population of elite white-collar offenders.

TABLE 19-3   Prior Criminal Records of a Sample Restricted to High-Status White-Collar Offenders from the Wheeler et al. Sample*

	Percentage of Restricted Sample	N
Percentage with any prior arrests	28	319
Percentage with any prior convictions	22	316
Percentage with 2 or more prior arrests	13	317
Percentage with prior felony convictions	10	319
Percentage previously incarcerated	6	319

* See Author Note 3 for details about the definition of this sample.

White-Collar Criminals and Criminal Careers

Having established that many white-collar criminals do recidivate, we were led to ask how their criminal "careers"[4] are similar or different from those of street criminals. The Wheeler et al. data allowed us to focus upon three dimensions of offending identified in criminal career research (see Blumstein et al., 1986): frequency, or the intensity of offending; onset, or the age of the entrance of offenders into criminality; and specialization, or the extent to which criminals repeat crimes of a similar type. We were not able to speculate on other related dimensions of criminal careers, such as duration or desistance, because the sample was drawn at time of conviction and the study included no criminal history information subsequent to that conviction.

The Wheeler et al. data showed that there is a much higher frequency of offending for white-collar criminals than has commonly been thought. But the frequency of their offending is still much lower than that of other types of criminals. In a comparison sample of common crime offenders convicted under federal forgery and postal theft statutes, for example, Weisburd et al. (1991) found that 80% had prior arrests, and 74% had more than two prior arrests.[5] Similarly, studies of convicted street crime offenders have reported much higher rates of prior offending than found in this white-collar crime sample.[6]

These comparisons are, of course, complicated by the fact that the meaning of arrest for a white-collar crime is often different than that for a street crime. Prosecutors, not the police, are usually the primary investigators of white-collar crime (Katz, 1979). And white-collar offenders are often "arrested" much later in the investigative process than are street criminals, because their crimes are usually difficult to unravel and seldom have the advantage of identifiable victims (Braithwaite and Geis, 1982). Such offenders may not be arrested at all if prosecutors decide to use civil actions instead of a criminal prosecution (Mann, 1989). Accordingly, at least in regard to white-collar crimes,[7] we might expect official records to underestimate the frequency of offending for those in a white-collar crime sample.

This underreporting bias is exacerbated by the fact that white-collar crimes generally are of longer duration than are street crimes (see Wheeler et al., 1988). A land scheme that continues over several years may, for example, produce only one arrest. But it is certainly not comparable to a single theft or mugging. Even accounting for the fact that white-collar crimes prosecuted in the federal courts seldom approximate the spectacular offenses reported in the popular press, they generally represent more complicated and longer-lived crimes than the average street offense (Wheeler et al., 1988). In this sense, we might speculate that large gaps between officially reported crimes in a white-collar criminal "career" do not necessarily mean that such offenders are inactive in those periods.

The onset of offending in the Wheeler et al. sample also points to important differences between these offenders and street criminals. Whereas street offenders are usually arrested for the first time while teenagers, in every crime category we examined, white-collar offenders were, on average, adults before they committed their first offense (see Table 19-4). Indeed, for bribery, tax, and securities offenders the mean age of first arrest was over 40.

Of course it is problematic to speak of onset in a criminal career if there is no evidence that an offender will continue criminality after a first offense. And in fact, when we

TABLE 19.4   Age of Onset of Criminal Offending, From the Wheeler et al. Sample, by Statutory Offense

	Antitrust	Securities Fraud	Tax
Mean age at onset of offending for the whole sample	54	42	40
$N^\dagger$	27	65	210
Mean age at onset of offending for chronic offenders	—	29 (28)*	26
$N^\dagger$	0	6 (29)	56

* The figures in the parentheses represent the total national sample for securities offenders (see note 1)
† This is the maximum number of cases used. Specific statistics are calculated on at least 90% of the cases.

TABLE 19-5   Percent of Chronic Offenders With at Least 1 Prior White-Collar Crime, From Wheeler et al. Sample, by Statutory Offense

	Antitrust	Securities Fraud	Tax
Percentage with any known prior arrest for a white-collar crime	—	57 (45)*	25
N	0	7 (31)	59

* The numbers in parentheses represent the figures for the national sample of securities offenders (see note 1 for details).

examined only "chronic" offenders (See Table 19-4)—those with three or more arrests (see Tillman, 1987)[8]—we gained a substantially different portrait of the onset of offending in a white-collar crime sample. Although older, on average, than street criminals when they committed their first crimes, among chronic white-collar offenders the mean age of first arrest for each of the offense categories was between 20 and 30.

This discussion of white-collar criminal careers has so far not addressed the problem of specialization. The fact that white-collar crimes often demand special skills and particular organizational positions might lead to the assumption that white-collar criminals will specialize in white-collar type crimes. Although the Wheeler et al. data do not allow a precise tracking of the form of a criminal career, they do identify offenders who have some white-collar criminality in their pasts.[9] Table 19-5 shows the proportion of "chronic" offenders with at least one white-collar crime arrest prior to the conviction that brought them into the Wheeler et al. sample.

Only about a third of the chronic offenders have prior white-collar crime arrests. Least likely to evidence this type of specialization are bribery offenders and bank embezzlers; most likely are mail fraud and securities violators. In the latter case almost half of the chronic offenders, as we defined them, had at least one prior white-collar crime arrest. Although these data do not allow us to disentangle the complicated issues surrounding specialization, they do challenge the idea that there is much greater specialization in white-collar crime than in other types of offending.

Bribery	Credit Fraud	False Claims	Mail Fraud	Bank Embezzlement	Whole Sample
43	32	32	32	29	35
84	157	157	189	201	1,090
21	23	23	25	22	24
10	34	59	68	26	289

Bribery	Credit Fraud	False Claims	Mail Fraud	Bank Embezzlement	Whole Sample
20	39	28	46	23	34
10	64	61	68	26	295

We suspect that there are various types of criminal careers for those involved in white-collar crime. For some, like many of the securities violators in the Wheeler et al. sample, the skills needed to carry out an offense and the complexity of the crime scenarios involved may lead to a relatively late onset of criminality, a low frequency of offending, and a relatively high degree of specialization. For others, white-collar crime, often of a relatively trivial type,[10] represents only one part of a mixed bag of criminal activities. Such offenders are likely to begin offending much earlier in life and commit crimes (often not white-collar in nature) with much greater frequency. These scenarios represent perhaps the extremes of criminal "careers" in a white-collar crime sample and illustrate the diversity of offenders who are prosecuted under white-collar crime statutes.

Conclusions

Contrary to common assumptions, we found in a sample of offenders convicted of federal white-collar crimes that white-collar criminals are often repeat offenders. This fact led us to begin analyzing the criminal careers of such offenders, an effort that we are now continuing in the context of a National Institute of Justice-supported follow-up study of the Wheeler et al. sample.[11] Our initial findings suggest that white-collar criminals' "careers" begin later and evidence lower frequency of offending than do those of street criminals. They also challenge the assumption that such careers will be highly specialized.

The fact that white-collar criminals are often repeat offenders raises the question of whether it is useful to develop criminal justice policies for white-collar crime, like those for common crime (e.g., see Greenwood, 1985), that focus upon high-rate criminals. That many white-collar offenders commit crimes of a non-white-collar type appears to support those who argue that there is little use in making research or policy distinctions between white-collar criminals and other offenders (e.g., see Hirschi and Gottfredson, 1987).

The social backgrounds of offenders that fall within a white-collar crime sample appear to make them particularly susceptible to criminal justice intervention. As Zimring and Hawkins (1973:128) note, those with the most to lose in a society are also those who place the most at risk when they commit crimes (see also Benson and Cullen, 1988; Geis, 1977). Given the fact that white-collar crimes are assumed to be instrumental, rather than expressive (see Chambliss, 1984), we might expect that the threat of sanctions would be particularly salient for white-collar criminals. Accordingly, we believe there is good reason to focus research and policy on the problem of reducing individual recidivism among such offenders. What is less clear, however, is how different sanctions will affect higher status criminals. In fact, there is reason to suspect that simple assumptions linking harsher sanctions to greater deterrence will not apply for white-collar crime (e.g., see Benson and Cullen, 1988).[12]

Turning to the more general problem of whether it is useful to develop special policies for those who commit white-collar crimes, we think it is important to place our findings in the context of a more general understanding of the nature of white-collar criminality prosecuted in the federal courts. Weisburd et al. (1991) suggest that such crimes are most often committed by those who fall in the middle classes of our society. These are not those upper-class or elite criminals ordinarily associated with white-collar crime. But neither are they similar to the street criminals who have received the bulk of criminological attention. Clearly, we must reevaluate criminal justice policy with these offenders in mind.

Authors' Notes

1. Although this forms the primary sample in the Wheeler et al. study, they also collected information on all SEC and antitrust offenders convicted in the three-year period they examined.
2. Prior to the offense which led to their inclusion in the Wheeler et al. study.
3. We operationalized this by identifying those people who had at least one of the following characteristics: an occupational title of doctor, judge, lawyer, accountant, or clergyman; a social class of manager, owner, or officer; and assets of at least $500,000. The management class included government managers and inspectors. Of the sample, 370 individuals fit this definition of white-collar social class. Again, following Katz, those who did not use their occupations to commit their offenses were then eliminated, leaving 319 offenders in the sample.
4. We use the term "career" in reference to the crime patterns evidenced by offenders in the sample. We find it useful to use dimensions of offending identified with criminal career research, but we recognize that the criminal career paradigm may be especially problematic in the case of white-collar crime (see Gottfredson and Hirschi, 1988, for a more general critique of criminal career research).
5. This sample was made up of 210 individuals convicted of postal theft or postal fraud in the same districts and time period from which the Wheeler et al. white-collar sample was drawn. Postal theft cases generally involve thefts of government-issued checks for welfare or social security benefits, often from mail boxes on the day they arrive. The primary distinction between postal theft and postal forgery is simply whether the defendant is

caught at the time of the theft or when he or she tries to cash the check by forging the endorsement of the recipient.

6. For example, in a probability sample of defendants arrested for various felony crimes in New York City in 1971, almost two thirds of the defendants had prior arrest records, and one third had prior felony convictions (Vera Institute of Justice, 1977:21).

7. As we will discuss later, those convicted of white-collar crimes often have non-white-collar offenses in their criminal histories.

8. We included here the arrest that led to their inclusion in the Wheeler et al. sample, and thus for practical purposes a chronic offender was defined as any member of the sample with two or more prior arrests for any type of crime. As Tillman notes there is no agreement on what constitutes a chronic offender (1987:574). His definition is based on a comparison of arrest and police contact statistics, and attempts to find an arrest criterion equivalent to the five or more police contacts

threshold used by Wolfgang, Figlio, and Sellin (1972:219).

9. For this variable, all tax, business or personal frauds, other business violations (e.g., criminal violations of fair labor laws, health and safety laws of antitrust regulations), embezzlements, briberies and mail frauds, whether under state or federal statutes, were considered white-collar crimes.

10. Such as lying on credit card applications.

11. This study uses various criminal justice system data bases to track the post-sanctioning criminal careers of these defendants.

12. It is often suggested that more punitive sanctions will result in a greater deterrent influence on the offender (e.g., see Cook, 1980b). But in the case of white-collar crime there is strong reason to suspect that sanctions may also "backfire." In particular, we suspect that dramatic losses of prestige or status may reduce the cost of future criminality for white-collar offenders, thus increasing rather than decreasing recidivism.

Discussion Questions

1. Why have so few criminologists applied the criminal careers paradigm to white-collar offenders? What concepts from this paradigm do Weisburd, Chayet, and Waring use to examine the careers of white-collar criminals?

2. Who were the white-collar offenders studied by Weisburd, Chayet, and Waring? How did they select their sample? What other kinds of samples of white-collar offenders might criminologists study? Do you think that other kinds of samples might produce conclusions different from those reached by Weisburd, Chayet, and Waring? Why?

3. How are the white-collar offenders in Weisburd, Chayet, and Waring's study similar to or different from street criminals in terms of age at onset of offending, frequency of offending, prior arrest history, and specialization by type of crime? Do these white-collar offenders seem more like street criminals than popular beliefs suggest, or are they more like the elite white-collar offenders often portrayed in the mass media?

4. What implications does Weisburd, Chayet, and Waring's study have for law-enforcement policy?

Savings and Loan Fraud as Organized Crime*

Kitty Calavita and Henry N. Pontell

Gottfredson and Hirschi (1990) contend that white-collar criminals are similar to conventional offenders, and Weisburd, Chayet, and Waring (in selection #19) found that many white-collar offenders are not members of the business elite and have prior arrest records. Here, Calavita and Pontell use evidence from the recent savings and loan crisis to support their argument that some white-collar crime is analytically indistinct from what is commonly called organized crime. They distinguish corporate crime, which is committed by corporate officers for the benefit of the organization, from organized crime, which is carried out by organizations primarily designed to engage in criminal activity for personal profit, and conclude that some of the systematic looting of savings and loan institutions better fits their definition of organized crime. Rather than focus on the social status of the perpetrators of a crime, they argue, criminologists should study the methods and motives of the offenders.

* This research was supported by a grant from the Academic Senate, University of California, Irvine, and under award 90-IJ-CX-0059 from the National Institute of Justice, Office of Justice Programs, U.S. Department of Justice. Points of view in this document are those of the authors and do not necessarily represent the official position of the U.S. Department of Justice.

Source: Kitty Calavita and Henry N. Pontell, "Savings and Loan Fraud as Organized Crime: Toward a Conceptual Typology of Corporate Illegality," *Criminology* 31 (November 1993), pp. 519–48. Reprinted by permission of the American Society of Criminology.

Introduction

In 1970, Congress passed the Organized Crime Control Act, Title IX of which is known as the Racketeering Influenced Corrupt Organizations statute—or RICO (18 U.S.C. §§ 1961–1965). The chief counsel of the Senate subcommittee that drafted RICO explained that the law was enacted to facilitate certain types of prosecution and was not meant to apply only to the Mafia or organized crime narrowly construed. Defending the use of RICO in cases involving banks, securities brokers, and accounting firms, the counsel (Blakey, 1983:7) wrote, "the defense bar is claiming that it is unfair to bring 'racketeering' charges against 'legitimate' business people. In essence, these lawyers are suggesting that if certain ethnic groups wear black shirts and white ties and engage in criminal conduct it is all right to call them 'racketeers,' but individuals who wear Brooks Brothers suits and white collars and engage in similar conduct ought to be called by a less pejorative name."

There is an irony in Sutherland's (1940, 1941, 1949) contribution to criminology. On one hand, he advanced the understanding of the scope and nature of criminal behavior by calling attention to the previously neglected phenomenon of what he called "white collar crime." On the other hand, the very concept of white-collar crime suggests that criminal behavior on the part of white-collar offenders is qualitatively distinct from other types of crime, or at least distinct enough to merit a qualifying label. The concept itself implies that racketeers in "black shirts and white ties" are one thing and businessmen with white collars are quite another.

This paper reexamines the distinction between underworld racketeers and apparently legitimate entrepreneurs. Specifically, we argue that in some important instances, white-collar offenders for all intents and purposes engage in "organized crime." We begin by exploring a typology for distinguishing one form of white-collar crime—"corporate crime"—from "organized crime," based not on the social or occupational status of the offenders but on their differential purposes and methods. We then apply this typology to savings and loan fraud, arguably the largest set of white-collar heists in history, and demonstrate that the *modus operandi* of much executive misconduct approximates the organized crime model.

The typology and its application to the savings and loan case are important from both theoretical and policy perspectives. Theoretically, the typology contributes to the extrication of the concept of white-collar crime from the *ad hominem* limitations that from the beginning have crippled its conceptual potential. As Shapiro (1990:363) pointed out "it is time to integrate the 'white-collar' offenders into mainstream scholarship by looking beyond the perpetrators' wardrobe and social characteristics and exploring the modus operandi of their misdeeds. . . ." For too long the distinction between black shirts and white collars has fueled stereotypes about the relative villainy and moral culpability of mafiosi on one hand and high-status corporate offenders on the other.

More important, once the applicability of the organized crime model to some corporate offenders is understood, dynamics, patterns, and motivations can be exposed that are likely to have been concealed by preconceived notions about the nature of white-collar crime. For example, if savings and loan executives, by virtue of their white-collar status and executive positions, are assumed to be incapable of the kind of premeditated looting for personal gain more often associated with their lower-status counterparts in the underworld, a key ingredient in the etiology of the thrift crisis will be missed. A number of economists and financial experts (e.g., Ely, 1990; White, 1991) have depicted the savings and loan debacle as largely a case of mismanagement or excessive risk-taking, but rarely premeditated fraud. This view of the limited role of deliberate fraud is more consistent with stereotypical assumptions about the motivations of corporate actors than it is with the reality of extensive and organized insider abuse that will be portrayed here.

The conceptual clarification provided by the proposed typology and its application to the savings and loan case are thus important in understanding the causal dynamics of these white-collar crimes. At least as important, they may contribute to more effective policy-making. As we have explained in more detail elsewhere (Calavita and Pontell, 1990, 1991), the deregulation of the savings and loan industry in the early 1980s set the stage for insider abuse by providing extensive opportunities for fraud at little risk. In this analysis, we document the predictable response of thrift owners and directors to this "criminogenic environment" (Needleman and Needleman, 1979) as they looted their institutions into insolvency. In so doing, this analysis undermines the *ad hominem* moral distinctions between corporate actors and their organized crime counterparts, and it highlights the importance of rigorous control mechanisms and structural disincentives to fraud if comparable disasters are to be prevented in the future.

The data for this analysis were drawn from government reports, congressional hearings and debates, and open-ended interviews with Federal Bureau of Investigation (FBI) investigators, regulators in the Office of Thrift Supervision (the federal thrift regulator since 1989), and officials in the Federal Deposit Insurance Corporation (since 1989, the thrift insurance agency), and the Resolution Trust Corporation (the federal agency charged with the management and sale of insolvent thrifts' assets). These interviews took place in Washington, D.C., and in field offices in California, Texas, and Florida; they generally lasted between one and two hours, and some key respondents were interviewed several times over the course of two and a half years. Secondary sources and journalistic accounts of specific cases are used to supplement the congressional record, government reports, and interview material.

The paper is organized as follows. First, we discuss the general theoretical issues that are central to our argument, briefly reviewing traditional definitions of white-collar crime and organized crime, as well as pertinent criticisms of those definitions. The point here is not to present a general review of white-collar crime research, nor even to summarize all prevailing criticisms of the concept, a feat that is beyond the scope of this paper. Rather, our presentation focuses on those critiques of Sutherland's conceptualization that are relevant to the task at hand. Next, we propose a typology for the classification of corporate and organized crime that is based on their distinctive motives and methods, regardless of the occupational position, social prestige, or wardrobe of their participants. Third, we provide an overview of the thrift regulatory system and the savings and loan crisis. We then describe some typical patterns of fraud in the thrift industry and demonstrate that a significant portion of these crimes fit the organized crime model developed here. We conclude with a discussion of the theoretical and policy implications of the proposed typology and its application to a variety of white-collar offenses.

Theoretical Background

As introduced by Edwin Sutherland in his 1939 presidential address to the American Sociological Society, the term white collar crime referred to "crime committed by a person of respectability and high social status in the course of his occupation" (1949:9). The concept's broad theoretical and historical value can hardly be overstated; it swept aside the conceptual blinders that had led to defining crime as an exclusively lower-class activity. In this sense, it represented a substantial conceptual breakthrough and revealed the power of social science to reshape the thinking not only of academicians, but of policymakers and law enforcement officials as well (see Braithwaite, 1985b; Katz, 1980).

Recent efforts to understand more fully the dynamics and etiology of white-collar crime, however, have produced a substantial body of literature that is critical of the concept (Braithwaite, 1985b; Levi, 1987; Shapiro, 1980, 1990; Smith, 1980; Wheeler and Rothman, 1982; Vaughan, 1992). It has been pointed out that the generic term "white-collar crime" encompasses activities involving very different incentives, opportunity structures, and operating procedures.[1] Following this line of reasoning, Clinard and Yeager (1980), Coleman (1987), Wheeler and Rothman (1982), and others have recommended that a distinction be made between crimes committed by white-collar individuals on *behalf* of their organization or corporation and with the organization's support, and crimes engaged in by white-collar employees *against* an organization for personal gain. These scholars argue that in order for criminological theory to advance, further conceptual specificity is required—a notion that has given rise to more precise categories such as "corporate deviance" (Ermann and Lundman, 1982), "occupational crime" (Clinard and Quinney, 1973; Coleman, 1985), and "corporate crime" (Clinard and Quinney, 1973). Other classifications have focused on the various types of victims of white-collar crime (Snider, 1990) or whether the offense is a property crime or violent crime causing injury or death (Coleman, 1985:8).

More fundamental, however, is the criticism that the concept of white-collar crime is intrinsically flawed in that it constitutes a classification of crime according to the social status of the offender, rather than according to the nature of the criminal activity itself (Braithwaite, 1985b; Shapiro, 1980, 1990). For example, Shapiro (1990:346) noted the irony that although "the concept of white-collar crime was . . . born of Sutherland's efforts to liberate traditional criminology from the 'cognitive misbehavior' reflected in the spurious correlation between poverty and crime," his concept reproduces the correlation between social status and crime and in so doing "has become an imprisoning framework." Thus, while Sutherland contributed to dismantling the long-held assumption that upper-class individuals rarely commit crime, he nonetheless continued to define categories of crime in terms of social status.

Just as a growing body of literature criticizes the definition of white-collar crime handed down by Sutherland, criminologists have increasingly drawn attention to the inadequacies of the traditional depiction of organized crime—a depiction that was fashioned originally by policymakers and law enforcers. In 1951, Senator Estes Kefauver's Special Committee to Investigate Organized Crime in Interstate Commerce held a series of alarming hearings and launched over 30 years of research by academics and law enforcement agencies into organized crime. Kefauver's committee concluded that organized crime in the United States was committed by a syndicate known as the "Mafia," which was a transplant of the Italian operation (Kefauver, 1968). The President's Commission on Law Enforcement and Administration of Justice (1967:1–6, emphasis added) reiterated this definition of organized crime as an Italian-American phenomenon: "The core of organized crime activity is the supplying of illegal goods and services. . . . And to carry on its many activities secure from government interference, organized crime corrupts public officials. . . . *Their membership is exclusively men of Italian descent.* . . ." Other authorities agreed: "The fact is that the Italian gangs—Cosa Nostra—do make up the center of organized crime" (Salerno and Tompkins, 1969:89).

Donald Cressey, who had been a consultant to the President's Commission in 1967, laid out the scholarly basis for much subsequent organized crime research in *Theft of a Nation* (1969). Highlighting the Italian composition of organized crime in the United States, Cressey wrote that "the Cosa Nostra organization is so extensive, so powerful, and so central that precise description and control of it would be description of all but a tiny part of all organized crime" (p. 109). A number of major criminological texts and case studies have perpetuated this view of organized crime as synonymous with "the syndicate" or the "Mafia" and thus largely based on ethnicity and kinship (Abadinsky, 1981; Anderson, 1979; Clinard and Quinney, 1973).

Criticisms of this description of organized crime have focused on a variety of issues. The notion that the Mafia is a well-orchestrated transplant from the Italian syndicate has been questioned by those who maintain that there is no historical evidence for such a claim, or even that the historical evidence suggests otherwise (Block, 1978; Morash, 1984; Nelli, 1976; Smith, 1975:27–44). More widespread is the criticism that this depiction of the Mafia overstates the degree of structural rigidity and militaristic hierarchies of command that characterize organized crime. As early as 1953, Bell (1961:139) contested the Kefauver committee's portrayal of organized crime as a paramilitary organization with affiliated units across the United States. More recently, Hawkins (1969), Smith (1975), Block (1978), Albanese (1982), and others have challenged the traditional conspiratorial view of organized crime and pointed to evidence of a far less organized and monopolistic structure than suggested by the Mafia stereotype. Thus, Block (1980:10) defined organized crime simply as crime that depends on a "relationship binding members of the underworld to upperworld institutions and individuals," and he contended that these relationships are by no means confined to a Mafia syndicate with far-ranging influence and a fixed hierarchy. While these critics advance beyond a single-syndicate definition of organized crime, they continue implicitly or explicitly to define organized crime according to the participation of "members of the underworld" (Block, 1980:10).

A number of attempts have been made to demonstrate the parallels between and interactions among organized criminals and "legitimate" entrepreneurs. Albanese (1982) compared the Lockheed scandal and La Cosa Nostra, stressing the role of entrepreneurs and the facilitating function of political corruption in each. Others have pointed out that the line between organized crime and legitimate business is increasingly blurred as organized crime groups "diversify" by entering legitimate businesses and joining the ranks of white-collar executives (Meeker and Dombrink, 1984; Meeker et al., 1987). Those studies, however, generally do not replace the traditional definitions of organized and white-collar crime, and they continue to assume largely *ad hominem* distinctions between the two.

More relevant for our analysis are those works that extend and reconstitute the definition of organized crime by focusing on the nature of the activity, rather than the ethnicity or social respectability of its perpetrators. Smith (1980), for example, suggested eliminating altogether the notion of organized crime as a distinct phenomenon and replacing it with a "spectrum" of entrepreneurial activities ranging from criminal enterprises to legitimate businesses. Maltz (1976) treated white-collar crime as a subset of the broader category of organized crime, which he defined as "crime committed by two or more offenders who are or intend to remain associated for the purpose of committing crimes" (p. 342). This definition, which includes the dimensions of premeditation, organization, and continuity, avoids the traditional focus on offender characteristics, but it may be overly broad. Indeed, it does not distinguish organized crime from *any* ongoing criminal conspiracy. Maltz omitted an important component of the *modus operandi* of organized crime, that is, that it is facilitated by direct or indirect links to politicians or law enforcement agents. The "organization," in other words, is not just among the offenders themselves, but involves a network among offenders and local police, city hall, state officials, or anyone else in a position to minimize the risk of detection and prosecution. It is precisely this quality of organized crime that historically has hindered its prosecution and that led to the enactment of RICO in 1970.

A Reconceptualization of Organized and Corporate Crime

Sutherland's formal definition of white-collar crime included crimes committed by anyone of social respectability in the course of his or her white-collar employment. In fact, however, the bulk of Sutherland's research dealt with *corporate* crime, or crime committed by corporate executives on behalf of their companies. In a recent essay on white-collar crime, Geis (1992:35) noted that Sutherland's conceptualization was vague and shifted from one context to another. Geis concluded, however, that in addition to crimes by politicians and professionals, "Sutherland was most concerned with the illegal abuse of power by upper-echelon businessmen in the service of their corporations. . . ." (p. 35). Thus, in his landmark book *White Collar Crime,* Sutherland (1949) focused on price fixing, false advertising, and other statutory and regulatory violations aimed at enhancing corporate profits by curtailing competition, cutting costs, or expanding the market.

Subsequent research on corporate crime has generally followed Sutherland's example by examining the myriad ways that corporate managers violate and otherwise circumvent laws that stand in the way of larger profits. In his overview of corporate crime research, Coleman (1987:427) concluded that the "demand for profit is one of the most important economic influences on the opportunity structure for organizational crime." Geis's (1973) study of the electrical company price-fixing conspiracy revealed the central role played by the emphasis on profit maximization and the related corporate subculture that is conducive to, or at least tolerant of, illegal behavior in the interest of profits. Farberman (1975) argued that the necessity to maximize profits despite intense competition has produced a "criminogenic market structure" in the automobile industry. Cullen et al. (1987) and Dowie (1979) linked the corporate mandate to reduce costs and increase profits to the decision of Ford Motor Company managers in the 1970s to build the Pinto with a defective rear assembly despite their knowledge that it would lead to serious injury and death.

Much of the corporate crime literature examines the characteristics of firms and market structures that trigger differing amounts and types of crime in the search for reduced costs and increased profits. Wheeler and Rothman (1982:1425), summarizing Shapiro (1980), Staw and Szwajkowski (1975), and Kriesberg (1956), noted that "illegal behavior is found more often in newer, smaller, and less profitable organizations on the margins of more central business networks." Others have documented the ways in which a high degree of concentration facilitates price-fixing and other illegal conspiracies to maximize and stabilize profits (Asch and Seneca, 1969; Clinard et al., 1979; Hay and Kelly, 1974; Posner, 1970; Riedel, 1968).

While a heuristically useful definition of white-collar crime remains elusive, and debates continue to rage regarding its causal structure, there is at least an implicit consensus about this more narrow category of "corporate crime." The vast literature on corporate crime, a small portion of which was cited above, focuses on crimes committed by corporate owners and managers on behalf of their corporations or companies. While top managers may themselves stand to benefit financially from such crimes, the driving force and principal goal is to advance corporate profits (and indeed, it is generally only through increasing corporate profits that individual employees may indirectly accrue benefits from the illegal activity). Thus, Clinard and Quinney (1973:188) distinguished between "occupational crimes," in which employees violate the law on their own behalf, and "corporate crimes," in which executives violate the law on behalf of their corporations. Wheeler and Rothman (1982:1405) similarly drew a distinction between individual crimes against corporations and corporate crime: "Either the individual gains at the organization's expense, as in embezzlement [a crime against the corporation], or the organization profits . . . as in price-fixing [a corporate crime, committed on behalf of the corporation]." As Coleman (1987:407) argued, "The distinction between organizational crimes committed with support from an organization that is . . . furthering its own ends, and occupational crimes committed for the benefit of individual criminals . . . provides an especially powerful way of classifying different kinds of white-collar crime." This dichotomy is also apparent in Wheeler and Rothman's (1982) classification of the organization as either "weapon" or "victim." In contrast to the victimization of organizations by outsiders or individual insiders, in corporate crime the organization is used as a weapon to advance organizational goals.

Whether explicit or not, "corporate crime" is consistently treated in the literature as *an illegal act perpetrated by corporate employees on behalf of the corporation.* It is "corporate" not simply because corporate actors are involved but, more important, because the driving force and primary goal are to advance *corporate* interests. This definition makes intuitive and logical sense and is contrasted below to "organized crime," which is distinct in purpose and method, although as we discuss in regard to the savings and loan case, it too may involve corporate actors. Just as burglary, larceny, shoplifting, and other economic crimes are defined on the basis of their motives and methods rather than the nature of the offenders, it is useful to classify corporate crime and organized crime according to their distinctive intents and *modus operandi.*

In contrast to corporate crime, in which the primary goal is the pursuit of corporate interests, *in organized crime the purpose of the organization itself is illegal activity for personal gain.* Whether or not the organization appears to be a legitimate business, if a primary goal of the organization is to facilitate illegal transactions for personal profit, it qualifies here as organized crime. The *modus operandi* of organized crime is largely related to this goal. As discussed in the previous section, organized crime is premeditated, organized, continuous, and facilitated by relationships between its perpetrators and public officials.

At first glance, it may seem that there is overlap between the methods of organized crime and traditional corporate crime. For example, Sutherland (1940) and others (Coleman, 1985, 1987; Farberman, 1975; Geis, 1973) have discussed the organized nature of much corporate crime. No doubt most corporate crime is also premeditated in that it is based on a rational calculation of costs and benefits, a notable illustration of which is the Ford Motor Company decision to build the Pinto despite its defects (Cullen et al., 1987). Finally, some corporate crime is facilitated by captured regulatory agencies, campaign contributions to influential policymakers, or other forms of direct or indirect collusion with public officials (Calavita, 1983; Lowi, 1969; Snider, 1990; Yeager, 1991).

These operative qualities, however, take on a distinctive meaning within the context of organized crime's overriding purpose. Organized crime is premeditated not only in that the illegal activity is rationally calculated in advance, but in that the purpose of the organization itself is to provide a vehicle for committing illegal transactions for personal gain. Similarly, it is organized in the sense that networks inside and outside the organization are the conduit for illegal activity and are put in place for that purpose. Illegal activity by these networks is continuous rather than sporadic, because that is their primary function. Finally, while corporate criminals may develop connections to public officials in order to facilitate a "favorable business climate," which periodically includes illegal activity, in organized crime the *raison d'etre* of such relationships is to protect offenders from prosecution, just as illegal activity itself is the *raison d'etre* of their organizations.

The definitions proposed here implicitly locate "organized" and "corporate" crime within a larger typology of illegal activity based on their distinctive motives and methods. Thus, the analysis that follows is meant not only to provide a classificatory framework for understanding the etiology and dynamics of some savings and loan crimes, but also to begin to explore this broader typology with which to distinguish the various illegal activities of corporate actors. The white-collar crime literature, as well as the mass media, include empirical accounts of a wide variety of offenses by those in corporate management positions (e.g., Abolafia, 1984; Levi, 1981; Schlegel, 1993; Szockyj, 1993; Tomasic and Pentony, 1989). But, despite reference to such crimes in the literature, there have been few attempts to provide an analytic framework with which to distinguish these very different types of crimes. Indeed, there is a conspicuous gap between empirical accounts of the remarkably varied instances of fraud in the upper ranks of business organizations and the continued theoretical reliance on the concept of "corporate crime" as a relatively uniform activity engaged in by corporate actors on behalf of their organizations.

This analysis is an effort to fill that gap. While it is clearly beyond the scope of this paper to classify and discuss all the possible permutations of illegal activity by corporate actors, a few examples may underscore the broader utility of the typology that we begin to outline here. We have proposed that the motive for illegal activity (personal gain or corporate interests) is one central distinguishing feature of organized versus corporate crime. For the purpose of illustration, we turn our attention for the moment to those illegal acts that, like organized crime, are perpetrated for personal gain. This category of offenders might be called generically "self-dealers," their primary distinguishing mark being that, unlike corporate criminals, their illegal activity is oriented not toward corporate goals, but self-interest. Organized crime may then be thought of as a subset of self-dealers, whose criminal activity is premeditated, continuous, organized, and facilitated by links to public officials. It is possible to locate other types of "self-dealing" within this classifactory scheme. For example, self-dealers who trade on inside information acquired through their corporate positions may, like the "organized criminals" described here, be motivated by personal gain, but to the extent that they act on their own, outside of an organized network of co-conspirators, the *modus operandi* and etiology of these "unorganized" crimes are likely to be quite different.

Alternatively, there are self-dealers whose activity varies from the organized crime model primarily because it is not "premeditated" in the same way. Rather than getting into an organization with the intention of looting it, these offenders *fall into* illegal activity, seduced by the extensive opportunities or incentives in their work environment. Much savings and loan fraud was of this "opportunistic" nature. Indeed, government documents and reports are replete with illustrations of thrift owners and operators who, within the seductive environment of deregulation and the opportunities it presented, found themselves on the slippery slope of fraud. While it is possible for such offenders to form full-fledged "organized crime" networks over time, to the extent that they remain opportunists their criminal activity is likely to be less continuous in nature.

There undoubtedly exist in reality criminal conspiracies that defy easy classification, for example, that combine some qualities of organized and corporate crime. While a given criminal conspiracy may serve the primary purpose of enhancing corporate profits, it may be that some participants reap substantial personal profits and construct the offense accordingly. No doubt there are some corporate crimes in which not just the purpose, but the *modus operandi,* approaches that of organized crime. For example, there may be corporate crime schemes in which the sole function of networks with public officials is to shield the corporation from prosecution for illegal activity. The classification proposed here sets forth what should be considered "ideal types." Concrete instances of illegal activity can then be classified according to their proximity to these types.

We cannot overemphasize at this point that the classification of crime as organized or corporate is not to be based on the status of the offenders, but on the motives and methods of the offense. Thus, according to our definition, corporate offenders engage in organized crime if (1) the purpose of the corporation or company is primarily to provide a vehicle for the perpetration of illegal activity for personal gain and (2) the crimes are premeditated, organized, continuous, and facilitated by the participation of public officials. The remainder of this paper applies this typology to crime in the savings and loan industry, much of which fits the organized crime model. Before turning to the details of these savings and loan crimes, we provide a brief overview of the thrift industry and its regulatory structure.

Descriptive Background

In the 1970s, economic conditions began to undermine the financial health of the savings and loan industry. Committed to low-interest mortgages from previous eras, prohibited by regulation from paying more than 5.5% interest on deposits, and with inflation at more than 13% by 1979, the thrift industry suffered steep losses. Although policymakers had been considering loosening the restrictions on thrifts since the early 1970s, it was not until the deregulatory fervor of the early Reagan administration that this approach gained widespread acceptance as the solution to the escalating thrift crisis. Deregulators were convinced that the free enterprise system works best if left alone, unhampered by government regulation. Thus, in a few bold strokes, policymakers undid most of the thrift regulatory infrastructure. In 1980, the Depository Institutions Deregulation and Monetary Control Act (DIDMA; P.L. 96–221) phased out restrictions on interest rates paid by thrifts. However, the move to the free market was incomplete and accompanied by a decisive move in the opposite direction—the Federal Savings and Loan Insurance Corporation (FSLIC) increased deposit insurance from $40,000 to $100,000 per deposit.

In 1982, the Garn–St Germain Depository Institutions Act (P.L. 97–320) accelerated the phase-out on the interest rate ceiling initiated in 1980. Probably more important, it expanded thrifts' investment powers, authorizing them to make consumer loans up to 30% of their total assets; make commercial, corporate, or business loans; and invest in nonresidential real estate worth up to 40% of their assets. In addition, the new law allowed for 100% financing, which permitted thrifts to make loans with no down payment. The same year, federal regulators eliminated the requirement that thrifts have at least 400 stockholders with no one owning more than 25% of the stock, which opened the door for a single entrepreneur to own and operate a federally insured savings and loan.

Following these deregulatory reforms, thrift losses continued to mount. In 1982, FSLIC spent over $2.4 billion to close or merge insolvent thrifts, and by 1986, the federal insurance agency itself was insolvent (U.S. Congress, 1989a:286). With the number of insolvent thrifts climbing steadily, FSLIC, knowing it had insufficient funds to cope with the disaster, slowed the pace of closures, thereby allowing technically insolvent "zombie" thrifts to stay open, and continue to hemorrhage losses. In the first half of 1988, the thrift industry lost an unprecedented $7.5 billion (Eichler, 1989:119), and within weeks after the 1988 presidential election, a government bailout of the savings and loan industry was announced. In 1990, the General Accounting Office (GAO) estimated that the bailout of insolvent thrifts would cost at least $325 billion over the next several decades (General Accounting Office, 1990:1). Ed Gray, former chair of the Federal Home Loan Bank Board (FHLBB), has put the figure at over $1 trillion (personal interview). A *Stanford Law and Policy Review* article estimated the cost at $1.4 trillion (Hill, 1990:24).

There is abundant evidence that fraud was involved in a significant number of thrift insolvencies. Government reports suggest that criminal activity was a factor in 70% to 80% of thrift failures (General Accounting Office, 1989a; Federal Home Loan Bank Board, cited in U.S. Congress, 1988:51). In 1987, the FHLBB referred 6,205 savings and loan cases to the Justice Department for possible criminal prosecution, and an additional 5,114 cases were referred in 1988 (testimony before the Senate Committee on Banking, Housing and Urban Affairs, quoted in General Accounting Office, 1989a:11). A GAO study of 26 of the nation's most costly thrift failures found evidence of "numerous and sometimes blatant violations of laws and regulations" in every one of the thrifts in its sample (General Accounting Office, 1989b:51–52). The GAO concluded that criminal activity was the central ingredient in the collapse of all 26 institutions it examined.

The varieties and possible permutations of criminal activity perpetrated by thrift operators are extensive. By and large, however, the fraud falls into three general categories, described at length in our earlier work (Calavita and Pontell, 1990) as unlawful risk-taking, looting, and covering up. Deregulation allowed thrift operators to make risky investments in junk bonds, stocks, commercial real estate, land speculation, or virtually anything else they chose to speculate on. However, *unlawful risk-taking* involved investment activity that went beyond permissible levels of risk or compounded the risk by inadequate or nonexistent marketability studies or poor supervision of loan disbursements. Every deposit up to $100,000 was federally insured, which made these high-risk investments essentially risk free. Some of the high-risk transactions represented a last-ditch effort to save ailing institutions, in which case they more closely resemble traditional corporate crime than the organized crime described here.

In contrast, *looting* involved the siphoning off of thrift funds by its owners, operators, and affiliated outsiders, for personal gain.[2] It is this looting, or "collective embezzlement," as we have called it elsewhere (Calavita and Pontell, 1991), that is the primary focus of this analysis. It is not our position that all forms of thrift fraud were in effect organized crime. Rather, it is the looting, or collective embezzlement, which constituted a significant component of the thrift crisis, that fits the organized crime model outlined here.

Patterns of Fraud and Networks of Conspirators

A Senate Banking Committee memo (Alt and Siglin, 1990) delineates the four most common forms of transactions found at the center of the thrift crisis: land flips, nominee loans, reciprocal lending arrangements, and linked financing. In a *land flip,* a piece of property, usually commercial real estate, is sold back and forth between two or more partners, inflating the sale price each time and refinancing the property with each sale. It was not unusual in the mid-1980s for partners to sit down and in one afternoon "flip" a property until its value had increased several times over. The final loan was then defaulted on, leaving the partners with hefty profits and the lending institution with short-term points and fees but grossly inflated real estate. The playful jargon for this scheme was "cash-for-trash," and the loans were referred to as "drag-away loans," as the intention from the beginning was to default, dragging away the proceeds. By definition, this fraud requires an organized network of participants—at a minimum, two corrupt borrowers (who are often affiliated with the lending thrift) and a corrupt appraiser.

Nominee loans involve loans to a "straw borrower" outside the thrift who is indirectly connected to the institution. Nominee loans are used to circumvent the regulation limiting the permissible level of unsecured commercial loans made to thrift insiders. Don Dixon, owner and operator of Vernon Savings and Loan in northcentral Texas—one of the most expensive thrift insolvencies to date, costing taxpayers an estimated $1.3 billion (Pizzo et al., 1989:193)—was particularly adept at setting up nominee loans, which allowed him to raid his own bank. The schemes spun by Dixon were carried out within a network of over 30 subsidiary companies established for the purpose of making loans to himself and other insiders.

Reciprocal lending arrangements are similarly designed to evade restrictions on insider loans. These arrangements were used extensively in the mid-1980s by thrift officers and directors, who instead of making loans directly to themselves—which would have sounded the alarm among regulators—agreed to make loans to each other, with each loan contingent on receiving a comparable loan in return. One investigation in Wyoming in 1987 revealed a single "daisy chain" of reciprocal loans among four thrifts that by itself resulted in a $26 million loss to taxpayers (U.S. Congress, 1987:79–80, 129–30). A macabre variation on reciprocal lending involves the trading not of loans, but of bad assets. In this arrangement—the evocative jargon for which is "trading dead cows for dead horses"—networks of savings and loan executives traded their nonperforming loans back and forth to each other, temporarily getting them off the books and artificially enhancing their picture of financial health. These transactions were central to keeping zombie institutions open well after their insolvency so they could be further looted, which increased substantially the final cost of the bailout.[3] In one case, 19 of the largest thrifts in Texas sent representatives to a secret meeting in Houston in 1985 to exchange "dead cows and horses" for the explicit purpose of keeping regulators at bay (personal interviews; Pizzo et al., 1989:209–10).

Finally, *linked financing* is "the practice of depositing money into a financial institution with the understanding that the financial institution will make a loan conditioned upon receipt of the deposits" (U.S. Congress, 1988:42). These transactions usually involved brokered deposits in packages of $100,000, the limit on FSLIC insurance. In return for the deposits, brokers received a generous loan, which was not infrequently defaulted on; middlemen received a "finder's fee"; and thrift operators recorded hefty deposits, which spelled extra bonuses and dividends for insiders.

Investigators and regulators report finding variations of these four basic frauds over and over in their autopsies of insolvent savings and loans. As one regulator put it, the pattern was repeated so often, "it was as if someone had found a cookie cutter" (personal interview). What is important here is that these four fundamental types of illegal transactions found repeatedly in the thrift debacle, and labeled here "collective embezzlement," jeopardize the financial health of institutions while enriching the individual perpetrators. Unlike "corporate crimes," which are driven by the desire to maximize corporate profits, these illegal transactions are perpetrated by insiders and affiliated outsiders for the purpose of personal gain without regard for the impact on the institution. Indeed, thrift institutions were usually bankrupt as a result of such looting. These frauds resemble the Mafia "bustouts" described in the traditional organized crime literature and fit precisely our working definition of organized crime. Further, unlike illegal risk-takers, who were on a slippery slope of insolvency and tried to save their institutions through ever more risky activity, collective embezzlers often got into the business precisely to loot their institutions (Calavita and Pontell, 1990). Many of the biggest failures and the costliest insolvencies seem to have stemmed from such premeditated looting.[4]

As an indication not only of the premeditated nature of these crimes, but also the fraudulent purpose of the organization itself, regulators report that among the principal "red flags" apparent in the worst failures was a change of ownership in the early 1980s after deregulation opened the doors to control by one individual (personal interviews). Of the 26 failed thrifts studied by the GAO, 16 (62%) had undergone a change of control in the period preceding the insolvency (General Accounting Office, 1989b:15). The new owners were typically people who had never been in banking, and who were attracted to the opportunities of the newly deregulated "money machines." Don Dixon provides another good example. In 1981, Dixon, the owner of a multimillion dollar construction company in Texas, purchased Vernon Savings and Loan and quickly proceeded to use all four of the transaction scams described above. One observer noted that Dixon "flipped land deals [like] pancakes" (O'Shea, 1991:76). By 1990, eight Vernon officers and directors, including Dixon and four affiliated outsiders, had been convicted of bank fraud and related offenses (O'Shea, 1991; U.S. Department of Justice, 1990).

As one thrift regulator pointed out, the gleeful jargon used by the participants in these schemes provides "pretty clear indications that they knew there was fraud going on as opposed to simply risks" (personal interview). "Dead cows for dead horses," "kissing the paper," "cash for trash," "white knights"—the cynical terminology leaves little doubt about the fraudulent intent. In one infamous case, regulators seizing an insolvent thrift discovered a jingle scrawled on a notepad that mimicked the "Twelve Days of Christmas," in which the refrains were "banks a-failing," "checks a-bouncing," and "cops arresting." Another, to be sung to the tune of "Strangers in the Night," was entitled "Bilkers in the Night" (Pizzo et al., 1989).

This collective embezzlement was clearly premeditated, and the purpose of the organization itself was to serve as a vehicle for illegal transactions. In addition, these crimes were continuous and organized in the sense that they were carried out over the course of several months or years through a network of conspirators. A recurring theme emerging from the record on the thrift crisis is the degree to which insiders (savings and loan owners and operators) and outsiders (executives at other thrifts and banks, accountants, lawyers, appraisers, brokers, real estate agents, and developers) conspired to perpetrate fraud. Regarding the collapse of thrifts in Texas, a staff member of the Senate Banking Committee told us, "What you are going to find in these thrifts is sort of a mafia behind them. I don't mean Italians, but I'm using it in a generic sense: a fraudulent mutual support" (personal interview).

The nature of the four types of transactions described above requires this "mutual support." Indeed, in each of these schemes a network of participants is absolutely essential. Arthur Leiser, for 35 years an examiner with the Texas Savings and Loan Department, kept a diary and noted the relationships among savings and loan operators, developers, brokers, and a variety of borrowers. One network he recorded included 74 participants. According to Leiser's calculations, practically all the insolvent thrifts in Texas were involved in such networks (U.S. Congress, 1990a:804–72; see Adams, 1990:270–71, for a diagram of the network of thrift fraud "high-flyers"). One Texas thrift, Sunbelt Savings (nicknamed "Gunbelt" by regulators), was so permeated with fraud that 72 criminal referrals (involving 155 individuals) were ultimately filed, constituting perhaps the largest network of fraud involving a single institution yet uncovered (U.S. Congress, 1990b:20).

The conspiratorial quality of thrift fraud was by no means confined to Texas or the Southwest. In a speech to the American Bar Association in 1987, William Weld, assistant attorney general and chief of the criminal division at the Justice Department, told his audience, "We now have evidence to suggest a nationwide scheme linking numerous failures of banks and savings and loan institutions throughout the country" (quoted in Pizzo et al., 1989:279). The GAO reported that 85 criminal referrals had been made to the Department of Justice relating to the 26 insolvent thrifts in its study and they involved 182 suspects and 179 violations of criminal law (General Accounting Office, 1989a:51–53).

Finally, this collective embezzlement was facilitated by connections between its perpetrators and those in a position to shield them from prosecution. At the lowest level of field inspectors and examiners, that is, those with frontline responsibility for detecting and reporting fraud, evidence has surfaced of collusion with fraudulent thrift operators. One strategy of thrift executives was to woo examiners and regulators with job offers at salaries several times higher than their modest government wages. When "Erv" Hansen, owner of Centennial Savings and Loan in Santa Rosa, California, was questioned by examiners about his extravagant parties, excessive compensation schemes, and frequent land flips, he hired the deputy commissioner of the California Department of Savings and Loans as an executive vice-president and doubled his $40,000 a year state salary. According to an interview with Hansen's partner Beverly Haines, the new employee's chief assignment was to "calm the regulators down" (quoted in Pizzo et al., 1989:47). Similarly, Don Dixon at Vernon hired two senior officials from the Texas Savings and Loan Department and, according to one California regulator, "provided prostitutes along the way" (personal interview).[5]

More important than these relatively infrequent forms of outright collusion are connections between thrift industry executives and elected officials. Not only was the powerful U.S. League of Savings and Loans, with its generous campaign contributions and lobbying efforts, a significant force behind the deregulation that provided the opportunities for fraud,[6] but financial pressure was brought to bear by the operators of fraudulent institutions in order to avoid regulatory scrutiny. The "Keating Five" case is by far the most well-publicized instance of political influence peddling to stave off scrutiny of thrift fraud, but it is only part of a larger pattern, the repercussions of which go far beyond one or two institutions. The connections between former House Speaker Jim Wright, Rep. Tony Coelho, and thrift executives are illustrative of this pattern. Rep. Coelho of California was the chair of the Democratic Congressional Campaign Committee (DCCC) in the mid-1980s, whose task it was to solicit funds to be distributed to congressional Democrats' campaign chests. Coelho regularly went to the savings and loan industry as a major source of funds. Brooks Jackson (1988), an investigative reporter for the *Wall Street Journal* who gained access to the DCCC in the months preceding the 1986 elections, described Coelho's "code of ethics" in soliciting this critical "soft money"; "Doing official favors for donors was permitted. The unforgivable sin was to make the connection explicit" (p. 104). Coelho once explained to Jackson, "I don't mind donors bringing up that they have a problem with the government. But don't ever try to create the impression with me, or ever say it, if you say it's over, that your money has bought you something. That's a real delicate line there" (quoted in Jackson, 1988:105).

Coelho's relationship with Tom Gaubert, owner of Independent American Savings Association in Texas, is a good illustration of these networks of influence. Gaubert became a member of Coelho's "Speakers' Club," which for $5,000 assured members that they could "obtain personal assistance in Washington" (Jackson, 1988:98). Gaubert wrote checks for over $15,000 in his first six months as a club member and was invited on the annual backpacking trip for the elite of the Democratic Party. When Texas Rep. Jim Wright was up for reelection, Gaubert established a political action committee (PAC) called "East Texas First," the offices of which were located in a branch of Sunbelt Savings and Loan. The PAC raised money through contributions from 66 Texas thrift owners and borrowers, principally Dallas developers who had received hundreds of millions of dollars in thrift loans (Pizzo et al., 1989:216–17). The *Wall Street Journal* reported that the directors of Sunbelt were given "subsidies" by its owner to make $1,000 contributions to the PAC (cited in Jackson, 1988:266). In 1986, Gaubert became treasurer of the DCCC, and raised $9 million in that capacity (*Newsweek,* cited in Pizzo et al., 1989:217). The following year, he chaired a fundraiser that brought in $1 million for Jim Wright.

At the same time that Gaubert served as treasurer of the DCCC and was coordinating the thrift industry contribution to Democrats, he was under investigation by the FHLBB. In December 1984, thrift regulators forced Gaubert to resign from Independent American, which by then had a number of criminal referrals against it for serious regulatory violations. Two years later, he was prohibited from ever operating a federally insured thrift. Jim Wright intervened on Gaubert's behalf, threatening FHLBB chair Ed Gray that if he did not call off the investigation of Independent American, he (Wright) would hold up the urgently needed FSLIC recapitalization bill before Congress, which was to refurbish the depleted FSLIC coffers and allow for the closing down of insolvent savings and loans (personal interview). Gray refused and the recapitalization bill was tabled (U.S. Congress, 1989b; hereafter referred to as the Phelan report).

Wright was more successful in his efforts on behalf of Craig Hall, Dallas-based real estate syndicator and chair of Resource Savings Association of Dallas. In 1986, Hall was unable to service the many loans he had from thrifts in California and Texas, and he launched an effort at "global restructuring" of those loans under more favorable terms. Westwood Savings and Loan in Los Angeles was reluctant to restructure the loans on Hall's terms, which FHLB representative Scott Schultz had advised them was not in their best interests. Instead, Westwood announced that it would foreclose on Hall's properties, which would force him into bankruptcy. Wright once again called in Ed Gray and asked him to intervene on Hall's behalf. Gray soon learned that Wright had put a hold on the FSLIC recapitalization bill until something was done to accommodate Hall. As described in the Phelan report, "Gray and Fairbanks [FHLBB chief of staff] thus determined that if they were to obtain a recapitalization bill, they would have to facilitate a restructuring of Hall's loans" (U.S. Congress, 1989b:21). Gray removed Schultz from the Westwood case and replaced him with a representative who agreed to the restructuring. Commenting on the concessions made by the FHLBB and the special treatment that Texas thrifts received at Wright's request in the 1980s, one senior regulator remembered telling Gray, "He [Wright] just increases the demands, and the extortion just gets worse and worse. . . . The guy won't stay bought" (personal interview).

The Coelho, Wright, Texas thrift network offers a dramatic example of the political participation that greased the thrift money machines. Such ties were replicated throughout the country, most notably in California, Texas, Arkansas, and Florida, where thrift failures proliferated and losses soared.[7] One senior official in Florida reported that to his knowledge, *all* the Florida thrifts that managed to stay open after insolvency did so with the help of their owners' and operators' well-placed political connections (personal interview).

The political patrons of thrift offenders were regularly confronted with evidence of their clients' misdeeds. In the most notable case, in a two-hour meeting between San Francisco regulators and the "Keating Five," regulators explained to Senators DeConcini, McCain, Riegle, and Glenn (Senator Cranston stopped by to put on record that he "share[d] the concerns of the other senators on this subject") the irregularities at Lincoln. Michael Patriarca, senior regulator with the San Francisco FHLB, finally told the group of resistant senators, "I've never seen any bank or S&L that's anything like this. . . . They violate the law and regulations and common sense" (field notes of meeting, reproduced in Pizzo et al., 1989:418). Several months later, the San Francisco office was barred from any further inspections of Lincoln, and the case was eventually removed altogether from the jurisdiction of the San Francisco office.

In other instances, members of Congress actively chose not to be confronted with evidence of wrongdoing. One regulator recounted a meeting with House Speaker Jim Wright regarding Vernon Savings and Loan (owned by Don Dixon). As he remembers the meeting, "I got involved in attempting to defend the agency [the FHLB, in its actions against Vernon], and the Speaker went ballistic and started yelling. Thereafter . . . the Speaker's aides sought to get me fired" (personal interview). The same regulator was, without explanation, "disinvited" to testify before St Germain's House Banking Committee in 1987 on the subject of crime in the savings and loan industry. Having submitted his formal testimony 24 hours in advance as required, the regulator was met by House aides as he attempted to enter the Hearing room and was bluntly told that his testimony was no longer needed (personal interviews).

The degree to which public officials deliberately and explicitly conspired with thrift offenders is a difficult issue to resolve. In some instances (such as in the Keating Five meeting), there is evidence that the implicated officials were made aware of the transgressions that their intervention facilitated. In other cases, key policymakers clearly chose not to "know" of the crimes of their most generous clients. What is important for this analysis is that the intervention of influential politicians who were financially linked to the thrift industry provided a shield behind which thrift operators continued to loot and otherwise abuse their institutions.

It might be argued that this "networks of influence" quality of organized thrift crime is not substantially different from the connections that often link corporate criminals to politicians and captured regulatory agencies. However, there are at least two significant differences related to the underlying motives of organized, as opposed to corporate, crime. First, while the symbiotic links between corporate actors and state officials may occasionally facilitate the commission of crime as one element of a "favorable business climate," in organized crime such shielding from prosecution of illegal activity is the *raison d'etre* of these relationships. Second, and more important, unlike in the case of corporate crime, these thrift crimes enriched individual offenders at the expense of their corporations, hundreds of which collapsed as they were looted empty while politicians and regulators watched from the sidelines or turned a blind eye.

Discussion

Schlegel and Weisburd (1992:4) recently noted that "attention to white-collar crime will best be served in the future by studying the similarities and differences between white-collar crimes and those referred to as 'common crimes.'" We have examined the similarities between one form of white-collar crime by corporate executives and organized crime. We have argued that if *ad hominem* definitions of white-collar crime and organized crime are replaced with definitions that focus on the nature of the offenses themselves, it becomes apparent that certain forms of fraud by corporate offenders are for all intents and purposes "organized crime."

Whether or not a given corporate offense is "organized crime" is largely a matter of definition. Thus, we began by proposing a classification scheme for distinguishing corporate and organized crimes based on their respective motives and methods. Consistent with much of the corporate crime literature, we defined "corporate crime" as crime committed by corporate managers on behalf of their organizations. In contrast, "organized crime" involves criminal conspiracies for personal gain, regardless of the occupational status of the offender. Further, these criminal conspiracies are premeditated, continuous, organized in networks, and shielded by connections to public officials. While corporate crime too may be "premeditated" and facilitated by ties to regulators or other public officials, these operative qualities take on a distinctive meaning within the context of an organization whose primary function is illegal transactions for personal gain.

It might be argued that some other working definition of organized crime is more useful than the one proposed here. For example, some might suggest including in the definition the use of physical violence as a way to ensure compliance with group goals or to maintain control of markets. And indeed this would bring the definition closer to the traditional depiction of underworld syndicates. There is little evidence that violence or the threat of violence was used in the commission and cover-up of thrift crimes.[8] For one thing, these offenders were not involved in the sale of illegal goods or services, but in investment and development activity. While in the former a strictly controlled monopoly is critical to the maximization of profits, in the latter the "market" (or opportunity for investment) is effectively infinite, limited only by the entrepreneurial imagination and the flow of deposits attracted by pumped-up interest rates. Indeed, a key factor in explaining the enormous sums lost in the thrift debacle is that thrift management had the ability to expand continually the pool of money from which to embezzle. It was, in other words, not a zero-sum game.

Thrift executives not only had access to other people's money as a consequence of their occupation, but by using such strategies as land flips and nominee loans, they could inflate the size of their enterprise and, hence, their take. In part, this ability derived from their policymaking positions in the organization, but more fundamentally, it derived from the nature of the financial sector in which they operated. Unlike the legitimate manufacturing sector or the underground economy, in which consumers receive products or services for their money, in the case of some financial services, the consumer receives only a promise that some relatively ephemeral or distant service will be rendered. Since thrift managers need not actually produce anything in exchange for the cash flow of their customers (and because deposits are federally insured), opportunities for embezzlement can be expanded almost indefinitely (e.g., by raising the interest paid for deposits). They are unencumbered by the confines of the production process, which limit the expansion possibilities of legitimate manufacturing establishments and most underground enterprises. In this context of free-flowing cash, the preferred method of encouraging cooperation was the carrot, not the stick. Thus, the presence or absence of violence may simply be a correlate of the types of goods and services supplied and, related to this, whether or not the entrepreneurs are operating in a zero-sum context.

Although a primary purpose of this paper is to demonstrate the applicability of the organized crime model to fraud in the savings and loan industry, we do not mean to imply that *all* thrift frauds fit this model. Indeed, a significant component of illegal behavior by thrift executives may have involved efforts—albeit ill-conceived ones—to rescue their institutions through excessive risk. Nor do we mean to imply that all thrift executives engaged in misconduct. Despite the overwhelmingly criminogenic environment and structural incentives to commit fraud, a significant portion of thrift executives refrained from the kinds of fraudulent transactions described here. Future research might investigate the social-psychological or other micro factors that correlate with this restraint (see, e.g., Vaughan, 1992). The point we want to make here is that much of the extensive fraud that *was* committed more closely resembles organized crime than corporate crime, despite the corporate status of its perpetrators.

The typology we propose is meant to provide a heuristically useful classification of organized and corporate crime and to begin to unpack the *ad hominem* distinction between the two. It thus challenges the prevalent view of crime by corporate offenders as, by definition, distinct from other types of crime. Criminologists have spent much of the past 25 years attempting to debunk myths about what the "real" criminal looks like, but without much success. As Levi (1987:209) put it, white-collar offenders are still perceived as "essentially decent people" while organized criminals are "essentially nasty people." Recognizing certain types of fraud by corporate executives as organized crime will allow criminologists to advance beyond the *ad hominem* definitions that have constrained theoretical vision and contributed to perpetuation of the very stereotypes to be debunked. More important, it contributes to a better understanding of the etiology and dynamics of these crimes. Corporate crime has traditionally been defined as crime perpetrated by corporate managers on behalf of their corporations. Consistent with the emphasis on the perpetrator's status rather than on the dynamics of the crime, however, it has generally been assumed that *all* crime by corporate managers is "corporate crime" in this sense, perpetrated in the interests of the corporation. While a wide variety of crimes by corporate actors are included in mass media accounts and some academic literature, criminologists have been slow to integrate this empirical reality into their theoretical understanding and definitions of corporate illegality. Specifically, the corporate crime literature has generally failed to recognize the reality that corporate managers—acting as corporate managers—may conspire to commit crimes for personal gain, regardless of the negative impact on the institution.

This failure, and the stereotypes that underlie it, helps explain the otherwise perplexing inability on the part of some observers to recognize the important role of self-serving and deliberate fraud in the savings and loan crisis. These observers assume that corporate managers, while not always competent or effective, at least attempt to operate in the best interests of their corporations. This assumption precludes serious consideration of the possibility that intentional insider abuse played a significant role in the savings and loan crisis (see, e.g., Ely, 1990; White, 1991). As we have described, collective embezzlement by top management was extensive and drove the four major types of fraudulent transactions at the heart of the crisis. Once criminologists have drawn the distinction between corporate crime and organized crime *not* on the basis of corporate status but on the basis of motives and methods, it is more likely that they will be able to specify accurately the different types of thrift fraud and assess their roles in the financial debacle.

While thrift fraud is unusual in its scope and its impact on an entire financial sector, it is by no means unique with regard to the issues raised here. In fact, the proposed typology makes a contribution to the extent that it can be applied to a variety of sectors and types of crime. Most similar to thrift fraud are other instances of fraud in financial institutions, such as credit unions, the insurance industry, and pension funds. What these financial institutions have in common is that they manage other people's money and exchange cash for some ephemeral service rendered in the future. As we have shown elsewhere (Calavita and Pontell, 1991), some insurance fraud has much in common with collective embezzlement in the savings and loan industry. As a congressional subcommittee put it, "Pirates and dolts

... will plague an attractive industry such as insurance, where customers hand over large sums of cash in return for a promise of future benefits" (U.S. Congress, 1990c:iii). Not only did insurance executives loot their institutions, but as the same subcommittee showed, in some cases the primary function of their companies was to provide a vehicle for such embezzlement. Despite the corporate status of these offenders, their misconduct—like that of their thrift counterparts—more closely approximates organized crime than corporate crime, as we have defined it here.

As the primary locus of profit-making activity in the United States increasingly shifts from manufacturing enterprises to financial services, it is likely that the nature of much corporate illegal activity will shift as well. There is already some indication that "financial institution fraud" (FIF, as the Department of Justice now calls it) is beginning to outpace traditional corporate crimes in the manufacturing sector. It is in the nature of the financial services "production" process that financial institutions provide ideal vehicles for their own victimization. The typology explored here may be useful in distinguishing not just organized and corporate crime, but a wide variety of other permutations—such as the self-dealing described at the beginning of this paper—and may thus contribute to a better understanding of financial crimes, as well as their counterparts in the manufacturing sector. If future research is to provide accurate criminological analyses and build the groundwork for effective policy, criminologists must continue to refine the distinctions among different types of white-collar crime, based not on preconceived notions about corporate actors but on a careful examination of their motives and methods.

Authors' Notes

1. Other critics of Sutherland's concept and its subsequent application have pointed out that white-collar crime is in fact "democratic," involving lower-status individuals, as well as corporate executives (Edelhertz, 1970:3–4; Hagan et al., 1980; Shapiro, 1990; Weisburd et al., 1991; Vaughan, 1992); that the organizational component of white-collar crime has upstaged the equally important "micro" question of "why some do and why some don't" (Vaughan, 1992:127); and that the focus on corporate criminality obscures the potential for corporate self-regulation (Braithwaite, 1985a; Kagan and Scholz, 1984; Scholz, 1984).

2. *Covering up* (in slang, "cooking the books") was probably the most common form of thrift fraud. It involved the manipulation of thrift records in order to conceal the unlawful risk-taking and looting or to inflate the picture of financial health, thereby keeping regulators at bay.

3. A study by James Barth, former chief economist for the Office of Thrift Supervision (the thrift reg-

ulatory agency that replaced the FHLBB in 1989), reported that from 1980 to 1988, 489 savings and loans that stayed open after they were insolvent lost over $40 billion while operating in the red (cited in Brenner, 1990:H1).

4. As Michael Levi (1984:322) pointed out, "Since the aim of the more sophisticated fraudster is to manufacture the appearance of an ordinary business loss or at worst, of the 'slippery slope' rather than deliberate fraud ... the actual allocation of any given business 'failure' to any of these categories is highly problematic." What is problematic, of course, is that one is likely to underestimate the extent of deliberate fraud given the proclivity for fraudsters to disguise their intent.

5. According to one account, when a senior regulator was appointed director of the FHLB office in San Francisco, Charles Keating unsuccessfully attempted to "neutralize" him by offering his wife a position as an attorney (Pizzo et al., 1989:419).

6. Congressman Fernand St Germain (D-RI), chair of the House Banking Committee at the time, ini-

tiator of the 1980 increase in deposit insurance, and sponsor of the 1982 Garn–St Germain Act deregulating the thrift industry, was a major recipient of U.S. League of Savings and Loan largesse. Having been observed regularly dining out in Washington on the U.S. League expense account in 1981 and 1982 as the deregulation bill was being considered, St Germain was investigated by the Department of Justice. The Justice Department concluded that there was "substantial evidence of serious and sustained misconduct" by St Germain in his relationship to the thrift industry. A House Ethics Committee reported essentially the same findings. No prosecution was ever initiated, but in 1988 St Germain was voted out of office. Currently, St Germain is a lobbyist for the thrift industry (Jackson, 1988; Pizzo et al., 1989).

7. Sen. David Pryor of Arkansas, a state with a per capita thrift failure rate among the highest in the country, put a hold on the FSLIC recapitalization bill in the Senate, informing Ed Gray that unless he "correct[ed] the abuses which have been taking place in Arkansas" (meaning regulatory activity, not savings and loan abuses), the bill would remain on hold (letter quoted in Mayer, 1990:232).

8. Charles Keating, frustrated by the persistence of William Black, an aggressive San Francisco regulator, reportedly wrote a memo to a member of his staff in 1987: "Highest priority—GET BLACK—GOOD GRIEF—if you can't get Wright and Congress to get Black—kill him dead—you ought to retire" (Pizzo et al., 1989:420). Despite the violent metaphor, there is little indication that violence was part of the *modus operandi* of thrift crime.

Discussion Questions

1. What is the RICO law? Was it designed to punish only Mafia-style organized crime, or did the government intend it to be used to prosecute white-collar offenders?

2. What is organized crime? What is corporate crime? What characteristics do Calavita and Pontell use to distinguish between the two? How do the methods and motives of the two differ, and how do they differ in terms of links between offenders and public officials? Does the looting of savings and loan institutions have more in common with Calavita and Pontell's definition of organized crime, or more in common with their definition of corporate crime?

3. Were all savings and loan failures due to looting or collective embezzlement? If not, what distinguishes the failures due to organized criminal activity from those due to other causes?

4. What are the implications for law-enforcement policy of treating those who owned savings and loan institutions as organized criminals, racketeers, and gangsters? Will this redefinition of these "white-collar criminals" be accepted by lawmakers, judges, and the offenders themselves?

Part VIII

Deterrence, Treatment, and Punishment

$$Chapter \quad 21$$

Let's Do It: Deciding to Commit a Crime

Kenneth D. Tunnell

This selection examines the commonsense assumption that the threat of punishment deters criminals from breaking the law. The sixty property offenders interviewed by Kenneth Tunnell were men twenty-five or more years old who were serving at least their second prison term for a serious property crime and had served at least one term for burglary or armed robbery. To understand how these offenders decided to commit crime, Tunnell examined official state records, interviewed the men personally, and took field notes interpreting the information he gathered. Here he looks at the way that perceptions of formal and informal punishment influence, or fail to influence, the decision to commit a crime.

Previous researchers, when addressing the issue of crime specificity in decision-making research, suggest that the mode of resolving criminal decision problems may be related to the type of crime under consideration (e.g., Cornish and Clarke, 1987). Specificity may then be important when seeking individuals' explanations for their choosing to commit a particular crime over no crime at all (i.e., no action), a particular crime over another crime (i.e., displacement), or a particular crime over a legal alternative action. Researchers recently suggested that to differentiate between the resolutions of a variety of criminal decision problems, researchers should obtain a description of a *specific* crime rather than crime generally. This would allow reconstructions of specific events, whereas a discussion of their commission of crime in general would not. For example, to determine the factors

Source: Kenneth D. Tunnell, *Choosing Crime: The Criminal Calculus of Property Offenders.* (Chicago: Nelson-Hall, 1992), pp. 85–102. Reprinted by permission of the publisher and the author.

that comprise the decision to shoplift, a specific incident of shoplifting would need to be examined. Likewise, to determine the factors that comprise the decision to burgle, a specific incident of burglary would also need to be examined.

Thus, much of each interview with the sixty participants focused on one specific crime, the events leading up to that crime, and most important, the individual's thoughts and conversations during the actual decision to commit the crime. The crime itself and the target they selected were only of peripheral interest. Rather, the respondents were asked to recall the most recent crime they had committed and could remember clearly.[1] At that point in the interview, we then temporally reconstructed as many events as we could that both preceded the crime and that occurred during the crime itself. The emphasis, however, was on the decision to commit the crime. Focused attention was given to those variables of central importance within theoretical decision-making processes, namely, the individual's knowledge and perceptions of the likely positive and negative consequences of his actions.

Perceptions of Formal Punishment

Law-abiding citizens find it unfathomable that individuals have the ability to do something wrong and illegal without considering the risks that could occur. We assume that individual criminals think about the risks they take when choosing to commit a crime. Our public policies are designed to send threatening signals that deviance will not be tolerated and lawbreakers will be punished for their crimes. We create law, we install police forces, we establish courts, and we build increasing numbers of prisons for lawbreakers, and hence find it inconceivable that risk is not considered by such criminals. But, for this sample of criminals who we certainly would like to see deterred from committing crimes, risk represented little threat and, as a result, they went undeterred.

What is it about the nature of their decision making and their perceptions of legal punishment that explains this lack of deterrent effect? Three themes emerged from this study that explain an absence of deterrent effects on their decisions and actions and how they incorporated the threat of punishment into their decision making. First, they believed and hence operated under the assumption that they would not get caught for their crimes. The most active criminals, persistent offenders, knew from personal experience that the probability was low. In fact, recent research shows that the probability of arrest and imprisonment is less than the general public may like to believe. For example, one out of every three crimes is reported; one out of five reported offenses results in arrest; one out of two people arrested are formally charged; nine out of ten people charged are convicted; and one out of every two persons convicted receive prison sentences. Thus, the chances of being arrested are one in fifteen (Wright, 1985) or about as likely as being struck by lightning (Becker, 1970).

Second, they made decisions based on their belief that if they were caught they would be imprisoned for a relatively short period of time. Third, they made decisions to commit crimes based on their belief that prison was a nonthreatening environment. Each of these themes is explicated below and suggests that when the most active property offenders made their habitual decision to commit a crime, they operated beyond the long arm of the law and those policies designed to deter criminal behavior.

Beliefs About Arrest

All sixty respondents in this study reported that they and nearly every thief they had ever known simply did not think about possible legal consequences of their actions. This is especially true for very high-rate criminals who are of grave concern to deterrence-minded policymakers. Rather than thinking of the negative consequences of their actions, those offenders reported thinking primarily of the benefits that they anticipated from their actions.

Deterrence and decision-making theories inform us that risk theoretically is conceptualized and evaluated prior to acting. Again, contrary to decision-making theories, those few participants who conceptualized the possible negative consequences of committing a crime reported that they did not evaluate the consequences. They managed to put those thoughts of negative consequence out of their minds so they would be able to participate in the risky act. Their fear was neutralized as they turned away from signs of danger. Hence, this research suggests that the policy of influencing behavior through punitive policies for repeat property criminals may be ineffective, and has little empirical support.

Even more important, the respondents reported they rarely thought of being captured or being incarcerated in prison. Fifty-two of the sixty reported they simply believed they would not get caught and refused to think beyond that. One twenty-nine-year-old rural burglar and I had the following conversation:

Q: Come on now. You're not saying you didn't think about getting caught, are you?

A: I never really thought about getting caught until, pow, you're in jail, you're in juvenile or something. That's when you go to think about it.

And an inner-city hustler reported he had similar thoughts.

Q: So how much do you think you feared getting caught?

A: I didn't. I never did think about it really. Not to a point that it would make me undecided or anything like that. I knowed I wasn't supposed to get caught. I just figured every time I wouldn't get caught. I never thought that I would get caught for nothing that I did.

During the crime, thinking of risks was distracting and interfered with performing well in the task they had chosen. I asked a thirty-three-year-old burglar who specialized in stealing kitchen appliances from newly-built apartment complexes about his thoughts of risks prior to committing a crime.

Q: As you did burglaries, what came first—the crime or thinking about getting caught for the crime?

A: The crime comes first because it's enough to worry about doing the actual crime itself without worrying about what's going to happen if you get caught.

Even those who knew full well the possible consequences of their actions functioned with the belief that they would not be apprehended or suffer negatively. A twenty-nine-year-old armed robber described how the decision to do a crime was made even though he was aware of potentially negative consequences.

Q: So, it sounds like as you were approaching an armed robbery you thought about going to prison. And you said you also knew that your mama knew what you were into, and you said that bothered you. And you also just now said you were worried about getting killed or killing somebody. So knowing all those things . . . how did you manage to go ahead and do the armed robbery?

A: I was doing it just to get money. I didn't really think about all the trouble I'd end up in or anything.

Nearly all claimed to have rarely thought of the potential legal consequences of criminality. The following statement was volunteered by the second oldest sample member—a sixty-year-old armed robber.

A: I never cared about the risks. I don't think any man can care about the risk or he wouldn't do it. I would never let anything stop me from doing something because of the danger or the risk.

And the following conversation about risk took place with a thirty-three-year-old burglar serving his third prison sentence:

Q: These burglaries you committed, did you worry much about getting caught while you were doing them?

A: No.

Q: What about afterwards?

A: No-o-o. I didn't give a damn. And the police couldn't catch a damn cold if it wasn't for the snitches.

Like this individual, nearly all claimed to have rarely thought about the potential legal consequences of criminality.

The decision-making process does not appear to have been one of rational evaluation or calculation between perceived benefits and risks. Rather, the decision was one where the benefits only were considered and risks were (1) rarely thought about or (2) minimally considered but put out of their minds. Risk was a distraction to some individuals, who eventually were able to rid themselves of it. The decision was one of how to do the crime, predicated on the anticipated benefits alone and not the calculated results of the benefits versus the risks. The decision was one of coping with the action by putting the possible negative consequences out of mind—perceptions of consequences that distracted them from the act itself. A few reported that they could not commit a crime if the negative thoughts lingered in their minds. If they were unable to rid themselves of the perceptions of possible negative consequences, they would not go through with the act that they had previously decided to do. Among this sample, risk was not a variable that appeared in the calculus of typical crimes. When risk surfaced, it was evaluated (e.g., the individual asked if it was empirical or instinctive) and acted upon. It was typically cast aside and considered a hindrance to the task at hand.

Beliefs About Lengthy Prison Sentences

Many of the offenders had unrealistic or erroneous perceptions of the punishment severity for the crime they committed. Each participant reported that they knew their actions were illegal and therefore did their best to avoid capture. But, thirty-two of the participants did not know the severity of the punishment for that particular act until after their arrest. Most learned the "going rate" for certain crimes after their arrest rather than before (Walker, 1985). Their perceptions of the severity of legal sanction were unrealistic. Therefore, risk was weighted less than it ideally should have been. One armed robber, for example, thought that his first armed robbery conviction would result in a probationary sentence rather than a lengthy prison sentence. He never considered his chances of going to prison for a lengthy sentence.

Q: So, before you learned the penalty for armed robbery, did you know that you could go to the penitentiary for it?

A: I hadn't never got caught for robbery or nothing. I thought I'd go to jail and they'd put me on probation or something the first two times. So I really didn't pay too much attention to the penalty because I knew if I got caught that first time I might spend a few days in jail and I knew that my first time . . . I could get probation since it was my first offense. After my first conviction, five years for robbery, I really found out the penalty.

These men typically underestimated the prescriptive punishment for their crimes by believing that prison sentences would be considerably shorter than they actually were. I posed the following question to an inner-city offender who typically committed both armed robbery and strong-armed robbery.

Q: Did you have knowledge of the potential penalty for doing [strong-armed robbery]?

A: In the state of Tennessee, absolutely not. This class X crime penalty that's supposed to be a deterrent . . . I wasn't aware of any class X, I wasn't aware of any penalties whatsoever.[2]

The rationality of their decisions is questionable since they could not have realistically considered the possible outcomes of their actions. They were predisposed to calculate erroneously because they assessed the degree of punishment unrealistically. I asked a participant who specialized in burglary about his worries of incarceration as a juvenile.

Q: Did you know you could get some time as a juvenile for burglary?

A: Everybody told me, said "Hey, all they're going to do is give you probation."

They, therefore, resolved criminal decision problems without full knowledge about the real possible outcomes of various decisions and actions.

Beliefs About the Prison Environment

Prior to their first incarceration, when thinking about being sentenced to prison, these men had typical thoughts about the types of threats in such an environment (e.g., physical and verbal abuse, threats of sexual assault, restricted contact with the outside world). Such thoughts of prison, obviously, were not threatening enough to deter them. During their first incarceration, they concluded that the state's punishment for committing property crimes was not that severe. In other words, the worst punishment that the state could impose on them as property offenders, they discovered, could be endured relatively easily and was viewed from that time on as no great threat. The following dialogue with a twenty-eight-year-old burglar with a tenth grade education illustrates how he came to define prison as a fairly insignificant threat and how he also came to believe it contributed to his manhood.

Q: Prison must not be much of a threat to you.

A: It's not. Prison wasn't what I thought it was.

Q: What do you mean by that?

A: When I went in it . . . at that point in time it was kind of an awful thing to go to prison. That's what I had always heard. But, when I got there and then found out, "Well, hell, look who is here. I didn't know he was here or they was here." And then I seen that I'm a man just like they are and I can make it. And I went and come back so quick.

These individuals also learned the "ins and outs" of the correctional system (e.g., sentence reduction for "good and honor time"). They were then able to rationalize their sentences more easily by knowing that they actually would not serve their full sentence. After learning the ropes of the system, they calculated a second prison sentence as a fairly insignificant threat. Even so, there is no evidence from this study to substantiate the commonly held belief that a longer prison sentence or a harder time in prison would have sent a more threatening signal to these men as they decided to do crime. The conversation below is with a forty-eight-year-old who had committed hundreds of residential burglaries and who was serving his sixth prison sentence.

Q: When I asked you how much time you did, you said, "Nothing, eighteen months." Did that not seem like much time to you?

A: I always thought it wasn't nothing because I went and did it and come on back here. But it really wasn't eighteen months, it was thirteen months and something. See they give me eighteen months, see they give me so much off for good behavior. Just like this time I'm doing now. To you fifteen years would be a lot of time because you don't quite understand it. But, after you get into the system here then they give you so many points for this and so many points for that, and when you get through looking at that you really don't have to stay as long as you might think.

Thirty-six of these respondents reported that the possibility of incarceration was no threat to them and, as a result, was not calculated as a serious negative consequence. They typically did not think about formal, legal sanctions when deciding to commit crimes. Even those few who did consider the potential for legal punishment and those who had previously encountered legal punishment did not perceive it as a great threat.[3]

Although risk was relatively unimportant to them in their youth, there is evidence that they worried more about the risk of arrest and incarceration as they grew older. They also believed that, as they aged, their chances of arrest and incarceration increased. From their self-reporting, thoughts of formal punishment were rarely considered, but such thoughts do change with age (see also Shover, 1985). Table 21-1 illustrates the dynamics of their formal risk perceptions across three age periods.

While serving their first prison sentence, these offenders experienced a typical education about prison lifestyles and learned for the first time about prison sentences and the going rate for various crimes (Walker, 1985). For most of them, this represented new knowledge. Afterwards, some offenders desisted from crime for a time. Those who desisted attribute their decision to (1) their new knowledge of legal punishment and the threat it imposed and (2) interpersonal changes in their lives (e.g., newfound family commitments, abstinence from drugs and alcohol, legitimate employment). During this period, some claimed to have considered and pursued legitimate alternatives to crime for the first time since they began committing crimes frequently. Many also reported going through

TABLE 21-1   Self-Reported Worries About Arrest and Incarceration (by Percent and Age Category)

Response	Juvenile*	Young Adult[†]	Adult[§]
Never or occasionally worried about arrest	60%	56.7%	21.7%
Never or occasionally worried about going to jail	66.7	60	28.3
Believed their chances of arrest were low (1-4 on an 8-point scale)**	61.7	51.7	21.7
Believed their chances of incarceration were low (1-4 on an 8-point scale)**	60	50	18.3

* Juvenile period refers to younger than age 18
† Young adult period refers to the ages 18 through 26
§ Adult period refers to age 27 and older
** Responses are based on an 8-point Likert scale where 1 is representative of their belief that they had no chance of being arrested or incarcerated and 8 representing a certain chance. The respondents were asked to indicate their perceptions of their chances for the three age periods. These figures represent cumulative percentages for numbers 1 through 4 on the 8-point scale (i.e., their beliefs that their chances of arrest and incarceration were low).

phases of desistance which were not related to the threat of legal sanction. Rather, the phases were related to periods in their lives when conditions were positive and rewarding.

There is some mild support from these findings for temporary deterrence, since a few did desist for a time reportedly because of the threat of legal punishment. Recent research suggests that desistance "is not necessarily permanent and may simply be part of a continuing process of lulls in the offending of persistent criminals" (Clarke and Cornish, 1985:173). Thus, these respondents are among those who cyclically or temporarily desist from crime (Petersilia et al., 1977; Rowe et al., 1990). From the findings among this sample, the most significant indictment of deterrence theory and deterrence-guided policy is that the majority who temporarily desisted reportedly did so for reasons other than the threat of legal sanction.

Those who did not desist for a time and continued committing crimes after their first incarceration changed their decision making in one of two ways. Some thought about the possibility of legal sanction much more than they ever had before. This often led to, at best, improvements in planning crimes. Others claimed that they continued to simply not think about the legal consequences of their actions, a neutralization technique used among this sample to enable them to decide to commit crimes.

While committing crimes, nearly all sixty respondents (*N* - 51) considered themselves immune from arrest and incarceration, although they believed that every habitual criminal will eventually be arrested. They internalized and exhibited in their profession what Tom Wolfe (1979) referred to among test pilots as "the right stuff." Their belief in their own immunity disallowed adequate consideration of the likelihood of legal consequences.

Still, two participants in particular described being "torn" during their decision making—torn between whether or not to commit the crime. Their indecisiveness was exasperating to them and when describing their decisions to me, they were not all that clear as to why and how they finally chose the particular course of action they did choose. It is not that they were all that committed to their decision to commit a crime but rather they were committed to making some decision. They did consider the risks but they also considered the benefits from the crime. They did not make the decision based on some rational calculation but rather out of their desire to get beyond their indecisiveness. From the following dialogue with a thirty-seven-year-old burglar, we see how he made the decision to commit a crime in a frustrated manner and by "throwing up his hands."

Q: I've heard some of the other fellows I've talked to mention an expression similar to what you used then when you said, "Fuck it, I'll just go ahead and do it." Can you explain that to me? What did it mean to you when you said that to yourself, at that time?

A: When you say, "Fuck it" you don't want to deal with it, you just, whatever is up you're going for it. When you say "Fuck it," you're saying "Fuck it, I ain't going to worry about this no more." You ain't going to worry about nothing, you're fixing to go out there and just do whatever it is to do to get it. It's a problem that's up now that you don't want to deal with. So, you're running from the problem.

The second individual who made decisions in this manner was a thirty-eight-year-old armed robber serving his second prison sentence for the armed robbery that he described to me. He, like the burglar just quoted, described struggling with himself and his indecisiveness as he eventually made the decision to commit the crime, all the while waiting for his would-be victims. He described being undecided but then making a frustration-laden decision.

Q: So you stood around for about forty-five minutes waiting on them?

A: Right.

Q: What kinds of things did you think about?

A: I'm thinking, "Must I do this here or must I not?" I said, "I don't need to do this here." And I just said, "I'm going to do it, I'm going to just do it, I'm going to do it."

Although the decisions described here are in relation to crime and criminal decision making, such actions stemming from indecisiveness are not unique to criminal decision problems. Law-abiding individuals daily resolve legitimate non-criminal problems in much the same way. They decide by "throwing up their hands," so to speak, in exasperation. Thus, criminal decisions apparently are made not that differently from non-criminal decisions.

The great majority of these sixty criminals never thought of punishment or capture and did not feel guilty about what they had done. This is not to imply that they are amoral misfits, for my findings and earlier studies suggest that offenders are moral individuals who experience guilt feelings at some point in their criminal careers (e.g., Frazier and Meisenhelder, 1985). Even while frequently engaging in criminal actions, these offenders knew their actions were wrong. But, they were able to rationalize their feelings due to desire or necessity, or they were able to put the wrongfulness of their actions out of their minds and not dwell on them. Likewise, the offenders did not desire punishment.

Perceptions of Informal Punishment

Informal punishments are those beyond the parameters of the legal system. Informal punishment risks typically include sanction or punishment by one's parents, spouse, employer, peers, or significant others. Informal sanctions, however, represent much more far-reaching controls than simply the fear of sanction. They also include thoughts of disappointing significant others, such as family members or employers, the fear of losing a job or having difficulty securing employment in the future. The potential for informal sanctions theoretically acts as a control mechanism and hence serves as a deterrent to deviant behavior and to crime. The effects of these individuals' perceptions of informal sanctions were pursued during the interviews with each of the sixty criminals during their descriptions of a specific crime that they had committed. The findings indicate, not surprisingly, that deterrent effects from the potential for informal sanctions appear to have been nearly nonexistent.

These participants reported that they rarely worried about their family discovering they were committing crimes. The participants were asked if, while deciding to commit a crime, they thought of their parents and the effects on their parents. Almost all reported they did not think of them or worry that they would disappoint them or negatively affect their lives. This is odd since nearly all sixty reported that their parents represented the most significant others in their lives. They simply did not think about the possible hardships that would be imposed on their family as a result of their arrest or incarceration. When they finally witnessed firsthand the difficulties their family endured, they saw the results of their criminal actions, often for the first time in their lives.[4] One individual offered a sobering example of the effects that his crimes had on his family as he described how he, accompanied by his mother and girlfriend, had to face a shopkeeper to whom he had passed a forged check.

A: Well, when we got over there, the dude looked at me, and said, "Is this your son?" And she said "Yeah, do you have the picture? Would you let me see the picture?" He showed her the picture and sure enough it was a picture of me standing up there signing the check to get it cashed. So no way out. And my mom looked at me, man, and I seen that hurt in her eyes, and I just didn't know what to say. But then it hurt me just that much more because my girlfriend was standing behind me and she saw it too and it just, it was like I just shattered two lives right there, man. At that very moment I felt remorse. I felt bad about it.

During these conversations about the hardships their families had endured because of these men's crimes, the participants would often volunteer information about prison life as it related to negative effects on their family. One particular prisoner, who had committed burglaries and auto thefts at a high rate after becoming addicted to drugs, indicated once again that it typically was not until after arrest or imprisonment that the criminals considered the negative effects of their criminality on their families.

Q: What are the worst things about doing time?

A: Well, one of the worst is like when your family comes to visit you. You see them leave and see a lot of pain and a lot of hurt in their eyes. You know yourself that you're doing alright, but it hurts them a lot worse than it does you. You can see that. It's plain.

The fear of informal sanctions in one form or another from their friends was completely nonexistent. For example, according to reports of these participants, the potential for disappointing their friends who discovered they were committing crimes, or any thoughts about the effects of their incarcerations on these friendships, had no effect whatsoever on them, their criminal activity, or their criminal decision making. Because the friends of most of these individuals were also thieves, their behavior was not viewed by their associates and friends as deviant, but rather as normal, acceptable behavior. The following dialogue illustrates how most of their friends also committed crimes, as one thirty-six-year-old high-rate shoplifter and armed robber turned the tables on the researcher and did the questioning. The following questions are his and the answers mine.

Q: Okay, let me ask this here. Didn't the people that you grew up with always do crimes and stuff?

A: There were some people that I knew that were always into crimes, you know, like shoplifting. But as far as people I hung around with into more serious things—

Q: Such as?

A: Burglary or armed robbery . . . breaking and entering.

Q: Would you believe that, I don't have nothing personal against your crowd, but I never remember going to school with them. It seemed like everybody that I knew was damn near into the same things that I was, or they was wanting to be, or claiming to be, or something.

A: That's surprising.

Q: Well, your story is also surprising.

Thus, informal sanction risks were almost nonexistent in these men's lives and as a result, their perceptions of informal sanctions were calculated as insignificant. Their decision making about crime typically did not take into account the possibility of informal sanctions or the likelihood of negatively affecting their life or anyone else's. It was not until after they had been arrested, jailed, or imprisoned that they appreciated the gravity of their actions and the effects on family members and interpersonal relationships.

Conclusion

This chapter provides data on the way that decisions to commit crimes were made by this sample of repeat offenders. Nearly all sixty reported they rarely considered the threat of capture, arrest, and imprisonment and that risk was considered a nuisance rather than a real, tangible threat. Risk-related thoughts were considered distracting from their prime objective—committing the crime. Thus, many were simply able to not think about risks and to put them out of their minds.

These findings are incongruous with rational decision-making theories. Decisions, theoretically, are made by calculating the potential benefits and risks. Among this sample, such calculations remain theoretical, for there is little empirical support here for calculated action. Even risky legitimate decisions seemingly are calculated with more care and finesse than decisions found among these men.

For the behavior of this sample of very active repeat offenders, deterrence theory and policy lack an adequate explanation. This sample represents a criminal population that has committed a disproportionate number of street crimes and has done so with little concern for the law, arrest, or imprisonment. A crime control policy that uses harsher penalties may deter those individuals who either do not commit crimes or commit crimes infrequently, but appears dubiously successful when applied to those individuals who frequently commit crimes. Although these offenders represent a population that we as a society would most like to deter from committing property crimes, they view themselves as immune from criminal sanction and hence go undeterred. They tend to believe that they simply will not be apprehended for their criminal actions and if they are, they will be imprisoned for a very short time. Those who actually consider the possibilities of imprisonment view prison as a non-threatening environment and believe their stay will be short.

Although much has been written on the risk–benefit calculus, it is somewhat misleading for understanding criminal decision making. The decision-making process among this sample of chronic offenders appears to not be one of rational evaluation or calculation between potential benefits and risks. Rather, the decision was one where only the benefits were considered and risks were (1) rarely thought about or (2) minimally considered but were put out of mind.

Author's Notes

1. The individuals had earlier been asked to disclose the numbers and types of crimes they had committed, including both crimes for which they had been arrested and crimes that escaped official detection, that is, crimes that they had committed that they had not been arrested or punished for. But for a description of their decision making, I had each focus on only one typical crime that he had committed.

2. Class X legislation was passed in the state of Tennessee in the early 1980s. As a component of "sentencing reform," it mandates that individuals convicted of committing certain crimes (e.g., armed robbery and burglary) be sentenced to a determinant, fixed period of "flat time" in prison.

3. I provide descriptive statistics on two components of their decision making that demand further explanation. True, thirty-two of the sixty did not know the punishment severity for the crime they committed and thirty-six did not find imprisonment a threat. However, twenty-eight did know the punishment severity and twenty-four did find prison threatening. These latter individuals managed to make the decision to commit crimes any-

way. They managed to do so with the aid of neutralization techniques. They used these techniques to complete the risky action and then thought about the risk they had run afterwards. For example, forty-one of the sixty typically relied on alcohol or drugs to deaden their thoughts of negative consequences; sixteen of the sixty relied on the calming effect of conversation with their cohorts prior to committing a typical crime; fifty-four of the sixty (at some point in their lives) relied on the expertise of their older and hence wiser cohorts; and thirty-eight of the sixty managed to block out negative thoughts of capture and imprisonment until after the crime. These neutralization techniques represent tactics that allowed these individuals to avoid the fear of formal punishment.

4. Many now claim they do not want to cause their family similar hardships in the future. Those thirty-three participants who reported during the second interview that they had successfully desisted claimed that if they considered committing a crime, they would consider the effects of their criminal actions on their parents.

Discussion Questions

1. What role does the threat of imprisonment play for property offenders who are considering the commission of a crime? Is there any deterrent effect of the threat of punishment? If not, does this mean that we could eliminate the entire criminal justice system and experience no increase in crime? Or does it mean that those who are deterred by the threat of punishment are not included in Tunnell's sample? Who might these "deterrable" individuals be?

2. Do you think that a doubling in the chance of arrest would deter some of the property offenders studied by Tunnell? Why or why not? Would a doubling in the actual

length of time served in prison have a deterrent effect for these offenders? What would be the impact of a "three strikes and you're out" policy that provides a mandatory life sentence to anyone convicted of a third felony?

3.   What impact does the threat of informal punishment—that is, sanctions by family members, employers, and peers—have on the decision by property offenders to commit crime? Why do you think such consequences are unimportant for offenders? Would the strengthening of social bonds to family members, employers, and peers help to deter property criminals from crime?

The Effectiveness of Intervention: Recent Trends and Current Issues*

Ted Palmer

In 1974, Robert Martinson published an influential paper based on a systematic review of 231 evaluations of correctional programs and concluded that nothing that had yet been evaluated consistently rehabilitated offenders. The rehabilitative ideal then declined in credibility, but some scholars reacted by trying to reaffirm rehabilitation. Here Ted Palmer looks at recent trends in attitudes toward the effectiveness of correctional programs and cites evidence that some methods can rehabilitate certain kinds of offenders. Much of the evidence cited by Palmer is the result of studies that used a research technique known as meta-analysis, which uses the results of other studies as data for its own analysis. The meta-analyses discussed by Palmer and by Logan and Gaes in selection #23 examined the results of research projects that had tested the effectiveness of treatment programs.

The effectiveness of rehabilitation first became a major issue in the mid-1970s when Martinson and others seriously challenged it. This challenge lessened somewhat in the early 1980s as evidence of positive outcomes in the form of public protection as measured by

* Opinions expressed in this article are my own and do not necessarily reflect the California Youth Authority's official position. I wish to thank Don Gibbons for his many valuable suggestions regarding the article.

Source: Ted Palmer, *Crime & Delinquency* (Vol. 37, No. 3), pp. 330–46, copyright © 1991 by Sage Publications, Inc. Reprinted by permission of Sage Publications, Inc.

recidivism was slowly but increasingly recognized. Yet, even as of 1983–84, an unsettled atmosphere existed regarding effectiveness. Neither the global optimism of the 1960s nor the extreme pessimism of the middle and later 1970s seemed justified, and more moderate camps—the "skeptic" and "sanguine"—replaced them (Gendreau and Ross, 1979; Greenberg, 1977; Lipton, Martinson, and Wilks, 1975; Martinson, 1974; Palmer, 1975, 1978, 1983; Romig, 1978; van den Haag, 1975; von Hirsch, 1976; Wilson, 1975).

Within the skeptical camp, some individuals believed it was clear that few rehabilitation programs worked. They reached this conclusion on the basis of what they considered a sufficient body of adequately conducted research. Moreover, these skeptics held that those programs that did work probably reduced recidivism only by small amounts. These individuals felt that rehabilitation, while not a total failure, therefore held little promise and merited only a minor role in correctional programs.

Other individuals believed that very little could be asserted with confidence about the success of rehabilitation. They suggested that because of minor or major flaws in almost all studies, poor implementation of programs, or both, we do not know if any particular approaches work. These skeptics concluded that rehabilitation had not received a "fair trial." They suggested that although some approaches may perhaps work for some offenders, we are in the dark about them because research findings are neither ironclad for any one study nor entirely consistent across studies. As a result, these latter skeptics believed that although rehabilitation might well have promise, no specific approaches could yet be recommended, at least widely (Conrad, 1982; Empey, 1978; Martin, Sechrest, and Redner, 1981; Sechrest, White, and Brown, 1979).

Members of the more sanguine camp believed that many programs and approaches have been shown, with reasonable scientific assurance, to work for specific subgroups of offenders. Some persons, who might be called the Basic Treatment Amenability Group, claimed that "amenable" offenders respond positively to many approaches under a wide range of conditions; thus they are generally treatable. On the other hand, most "nonamenables" were thought to be largely unresponsive to any rehabilitation efforts.

Other proponents, who might be called the Differential Intervention Group (or, more colloquially, the "different strokes for different folks" camp), offered the somewhat different view that treatment affects offenders in a positive, neutral, or negative way, depending on the specific approach and external conditions to which they are exposed (Adams, 1974; Barkwell, 1980; Glaser, 1975; Hunt, 1971; Jesness and Wedge, 1983; Megargee and Bohn, 1979; Palmer, 1974, 1978; Quay, Gerard, and Levinson, 1970; Romig, 1978; Ross and Gendreau, 1980; Warren et al., 1966; Warren, 1971; Wilson, 1980).

Common Ground

Despite their differences, sanguines and skeptics shared some common ground. In particular, many of them largely agreed on at least three points regarding serious or repeat offenders. These were youths and adults who had received increasing attention since 1975; they were not uncommon among correctional—especially incarcerated—populations; some had committed violent offenses, and many were open to change and only moderately committed to illegal behavior:

1. To be effective with these individuals, intervention should be broadly based. More specifically, it should involve a multiple modality approach, for example, simultaneous or successive combinations of such program components as vocational or academic training, individual or group counseling, recreation, cultural enrichment, or other services or activities.

     2. Intervention should often be more intensive, for instance, contacts should be frequent.

     3. Differential intervention should be used, involving program and offender matching. A program's full range of resources should not automatically be applied to every type of offender subgroup. Instead, only some components or combinations should be used, at least at any one time, with any particular offender type. Intervention strategies should be adapted to the main needs and interests of each subgroup comprising the overall sample (Palmer, 1983).[1]

Together, these core elements of general agreement suggested that, for programs to substantially influence other-than-minor offenders or relatively "good risks," they should be better adapted to the life circumstances and personal as well as interpersonal features of those individuals.

Developments Since 1984–85

This core of similar views became apparent to many correctional practitioners and researchers by 1984–85. It helped initiate a quiet, osmoticlike process that, by the late 1980s, resulted in a tacit, de facto consensus regarding certain aspects of correctional intervention, one that was also accepted by various policymakers and academicians. This broadly held but still unsteady consensus was basically quite simple: First, in contrast to the clearly pessimistic outlook and the actively rejecting attitudes of the 1975–81 period, some forms of intervention *could* probably reduce recidivism and could promote public safety; thus rehabilitation/habilitation might be possible after all. Second, most standard forms and typical variants of intervention, such as types of individual or group counseling, were no longer thought to be intrinsically demeaning or necessarily onerous. Finally, when included in an intervention package that contained clear external controls and accountability, and that involved unpleasant consequences for infractions and illegal behavior, some forms of intervention, such as community-based approaches, were now considered less risky to the public, when used with selected offenders. This consensus received support from a collection of meta-analyses and literature reviews that began about 1984 (Davidson et al., 1984, 1987; Garrett, 1985; Geismar and Wood, 1985; Gendreau and Ross, 1979, 1987; Gensheimer, Mayer, Gottschalk, and Davidson, 1986; Graziano and Mooney, 1984; Lipsey, 1989; Mayer, Gensheimer, Davidson, and Gottschalk, 1986; Palmer, 1984). However, rather than being quiet and osmotic, their contributions were more active and visible. Selected meta-analyses are reviewed below.[2]

     This consensus was significant. For instance, by the late 1980s programs and research that involved rehabilitation or treatment were less often considered either anachronisms or exercises in naïveté and futility. In addition, correctional programs were less often described as repressive tools of a ruling-class conspiracy, made up of members of an upper-class "establishment"—which allegedly used various interventions, and incarceration per se, to curb crime in general and to control socially disadvantaged groups in order to maintain its social advantages. Nor was intervention as often considered brainwashing and intrinsically antithetical to various justice system reforms. Individuals who had earlier supported one or more such views were the American Friends Service Committee (1971), Lerman (1975), Mitford (1971, 1973), Platt (1969), Quinney (1974), Rothman (1971), and Schur (1973), among others.

In short, the sharp edges of the 1970s and 1980s had softened, and the tacit or implied consensus had helped reduce various scientific, philosophical, and political objections to program development and research. When combined with the core elements that helped produce it, the consensus had another outcome as well. (The core elements were multiple modality programming, increased intensity of contact, and greater attention to offender needs and characteristics.) For instance, those elements, supported by the growing consensus, gave new impetus to many research and development efforts directed at intervention. (To be sure, institutional crowding and societywide fiscal constraints had been more influential in reducing political impediments.)

More specifically, increased intensity of contact and multiple modality programming became central features of various intensive supervision and treatment efforts, particularly intensive or enhanced probation programs for juvenile recidivists and similar parole programs for relatively serious adults. Of course, other factors also contributed to the support for such programs, particularly those emphasizing external controls. Increased intensity of supervision was also related to the demands of some authorities and citizens for "stronger," more punitive approaches.

As impediments to intervention decreased during the mid-1980s, momentum for program development and research increased, at first slowly and then more rapidly. By 1987 multiple modality programming and offender-needs perspectives became incorporated in needs-assessment endeavors, in which attempts were made to identify offender needs and to determine appropriate strategies for meeting those needs. Needs-assessment efforts were also related to risk-assessment activities (Benoit and Clear, 1981; Clear, 1988; Gottfredson and Tonry, 1987; O'Leary and Clear, 1984). (Needs-assessments are usually designed to determine if areas such as employment, education, substance abuse assistance, and personal conflicts resolution require attention. In contrast, risk-assessment centers on an individual's likelihood of recidivating, as indicated by such factors as age at first offense, number of offenses, and type of offense.)

All in all, by the late 1980s the program-development efforts that existed during 1965–75 but which had then declined for several years had, to a large extent, returned. Many practitioners and researchers were again proceeding with the practical task of discovering useful intervention methods and strategies and of developing and evaluating possibly improved approaches. Despite their continued differences, many skeptics, sanguines, and others were moving in similar directions and were supporting similar goals (Altschuler and Armstrong, 1990; Andrews et al., 1990; Barton and Butts, 1990; Byrne, 1990; Cullen and Gendreau, 1989; Fagan, Forst, and Vivona, 1988; Gendreau and Andrews, 1989; Krisberg, Rodriquez, Baake, Neuenfeldt and Steele, 1989; Palmer and Wedge, 1989; Petersilia and Turner, 1990; van Voorhis, 1987). In short, the search for effective intervention had been relegitimized.

Nevertheless, uncertainty still exists regarding the effectiveness and utility of intervention. For instance, despite the changes described above and despite increased efforts, the consensus is far from universal, is only tacit, and covers only some offenders. In addition, important issues and differences remain. These issues are scientific, philosophical, and practical. Some of them are quite basic, focusing on such questions as what constitutes acceptable evidence of program effectiveness as well as on who should receive certain interventions.

Review of Meta-Analyses

Before we further examine the current status of intervention, two major meta-analyses of the 1980s should be reviewed. (Space limitations preclude examination of the results from several others, for example, Davidson et al. [1984, 1987]; Garrett [1985]; Gensheimer, Mayer, Gottschalk, and Davidson [1986]. However, a later section of this article contains an overview of findings from the combination of all major meta-analyses plus literature reviews such as those by Gendreau and Ross [1987]; Panizzon, Olson-Raymer, and Guerra [1991]; van Voorhis [1987]; Whitehead and Lab [1989].)

In meta-analyses, any collection of individual programs is said to comprise a "type-of-treatment" if they resemble each other on specified, salient, or dominant features—for example, family counseling or group counseling. In most meta-analyses and literature reviews, multicomponent programs such as those involving vocational training as well as recreation are routinely analyzed and reported in terms of their seemingly dominant component.

Lipsey recently described his meta-analysis of about 400 published and unpublished experimental studies of juvenile delinquents (mostly through age 18) in institutional and noninstitutional programs. Of these many studies, 86% were conducted during 1970–88. Based on a range of behavioral outcome measures (one per study), but most often arrests or police contacts and other justice system contacts, 64% of the results favored the treatment group. In 30% of the cases the control group received the greater benefits, and in 6% of the cases the results favored neither group. (*Favored* was defined as "in the direction of"—whether statistically significant or not.) Type of treatment was the factor most strongly related to program impact. Within the type-of-treatment factor, multimodal and behavioral approaches were most often effective, probation and parole enhancements had no positive impact, nor did broadly labeled approaches such as counseling and skill-oriented programs; and deterrence or shock approaches were associated with poorer outcomes for experimental than control cases. (From this point on, experimental cases will be designated as Es and control cases as Cs.)

Offender characteristics, such as first-timers versus repeaters, amenability, and interpersonal maturity level, were also important. Moreover, the results suggested the strong possibility that the most fully implemented programs outperformed the rest. Lipsey's analysis is the broadest and most systematic to date (Lipsey, 1989, 1991).

Whitehead and Lab analyzed 50 juvenile offender studies conducted in institutional and community settings from 1975 to 1984. Using fairly stringent success criteria, they found that 24% to 32% of the studies evidenced what they called "program effectiveness" (success). More specifically, to be considered effective, they required ø coefficients* (.20+ or .30+) that reflected large or major recidivism reductions—not just statistically significant E versus C differences or even any reduction, however small.

Of the five groups analyzed, those most often successful (40%) were system-diversion and community-corrections-oriented approaches (35%) such as probation or parole. Least successful were non-system-diversion (17%), that is, diversion outside the justice system (sometimes involving programming or contact), and institutional or residential programs

---

* [A ø coefficient is a statistical measure of association, or a measure of the strength of the relationship between two variables.]

(14%). Using a more common but less stringent criterion—a x^2 level of $p < .05$*—44% of the 50 programs had positive outcomes; that is, Es outperformed Cs (70% of the 50 programs showed outcomes in a positive direction—$p < .05$ or not). However, by using only the stricter criteria, Whitehead and Lab concluded that the results, collectively, "provide[d] little encouragement for advocates of correctional intervention. No single *type* [i.e., category] of intervention displays overwhelmingly positive results on recidivism" (emphasis added). Yet, since several individual programs within given types evidenced substantial gains for Es versus Cs, they acknowledged that some (individual) programs, for instance, system-diversion programs, "are able to reduce the recidivism among experimental clients significantly" (Whitehead and Lab, 1989:285, 289).

Whitehead and Lab's study is often cited by those who believe intervention does not work. However, this interpretation of the results rests on the following: First, focus exclusively on types or categories of intervention, viewed as undifferentiated entities, and ignore results from the individual studies that comprise those approaches. Second, require "overwhelmingly positive results," in terms of the success standard used. Third, generalize from a set of studies that represent the main range of intervention approaches. The third point applies to any meta-analysis, but regarding the Whitehead and Lab study the following should be noted: Of the 50 studies in their meta-analysis, 30 involved juvenile diversion alone; thus they largely generalized from this one approach to intervention as a whole. Moreover, earlier reviews and a 44-study meta-analysis had mostly shown that juvenile diversion was among the approaches least often successful when Es and Cs were compared on various measures of success (Davidson et al., 1984, 1987; Gensheimer et al., 1986; Whitehead and Lab, 1989).

Overview of Findings from Meta-Analyses and Literature Reviews

Taken together, the meta-analyses and literature reviews of the 1980s indicated the following:

1. When individual programs have been grouped together and analyzed as a single, undifferentiated type (e.g., "counseling"), many of them seemed unsuccessful in terms of recidivism reduction. Specifically, when judged by standard to fairly strict criteria (immediately below), these approaches showed neither statistically superior performance ($p < .05$) for Es versus Cs nor Es fairly consistently outperforming Cs (either by any amount or using $p < .05$), for instance, in at least two thirds of the programs that comprised any given grouping, such as counseling.

Lack of success in terms of those criteria was found for each of the following approaches: *confrontation* (deterrence or shock); *diversion* (at least "non-system" and perhaps other-than-behavior-based); *group therapy or counseling; individual therapy or counseling; physical challenge; probation or parole enhancements.*

* [x^2 (chi-square) is a statistical measure of the association between two variables. If the value of x^2 is statistically significant at less than the .05 level ($p < .05$), the chance that there is actually no "real" relationship between the two variables is less than five in one hundred. In other words, the data then strongly suggest that there is a "real" relationship between the two variables and that the association between the two is not just due to chance factors in the selection of samples.]

2. Despite the results described above for programs grouped together, Es outperformed Cs in many or most individual programs. Specifically, using any recidivism reduction ($p < .05$ or not), Es led Cs in about 65% of all programs while Cs were ahead in about 30%; and, using a $p < .05$ criterion they outperformed Cs in at least 25%–35% of all programs, while Cs led Es in about 10%.

Thus, if an investigator had categorized all programs but nevertheless reviewed them individually, he or she would have found statistically successful ($p < .05$) individual programs in almost every category, whether diversion, group therapy or counseling, or individual therapy or counseling. That is, successful individual programs would have been found that would not have emerged as "successful" if they had originally been merged into an overall category, such as diversion, and then had been considered only as part of that category.

3. Although many broad approaches (as vs. individual programs) seemed unsuccessful from an "E-*better-than*-C" perspective, some broad strategies and interventions were probably associated with *equal* outcomes. For instance, community-based and institutional programs seemed to yield comparable recidivism rates; and, under various conditions, even diversion's outcomes probably equalled those of further justice system processing.

4. Again at a broad level, the following interventions were usually regarded, on balance, as the most successful approaches: (a) behavioral, (b) cognitive–behavioral (also called social–cognitive), (c) family intervention, and (d) vocational training. Nevertheless, a minority of the meta-analyses and literature reviews did not find some of these approaches—chiefly behavioral and family intervention—successful. This inconsistency probably resulted from a combination of differing success criteria and the following factors:

First, the various individual programs that comprised those approaches were not entirely identical from one analysis or review to the next; for example, the overlap of programs across several analyses or reviews was about 60%–70%, mainly because of the partly different time periods or program settings that were involved in the respective analyses/reviews. Also reflected were the varied inclusion criteria that were used, that is, the differing bases for selecting programs in the first place, regardless of time and setting.

Second, the approaches, particularly behavioral and cognitive–behavioral, were defined somewhat differently in several meta-analyses and literature reviews, thus complicating the assessment of given approaches. Specifically, some of the inconsistent results from one study to the next were due to differing definitions. For example, in some analyses/reviews, behavioral intervention was defined in ways that substantively overlapped with cognitive–behavioral or vocational training in some other analyses/reviews. Similarly, vocational training, as defined in one or more analyses/reviews, included aspects of social skills, as defined in others. Finally, in some analyses/reviews, family intervention included programs that, in other analyses/reviews, appeared under behavioral or cognitive–behavioral. This apparently occurred because some behavioral or cognitive–behavioral principles and techniques were considered integral to the family interventions in question.

Thus varying and nonexclusive definitions complicated and rendered somewhat ambiguous the conceptualization and assessment even of various approaches that several meta-analysts and reviewers considered generally successful or at least among the most promising. Such definitional problems highlight the limitations of existing meta-analyses and reviews with respect to understanding the specific nature and impact of given approaches.

5. For positive-outcome studies, recidivism rates of Es averaged 17%–22% lower than those of Cs. About one of every four such studies had rather sizable recidivism reductions, for instance, 25% or more, and roughly one in five was under 10%. Positive-outcome studies were those in which Es outperformed Cs by any amount, whether or not the difference between Es and Cs was statistically significant. When those positive-outcome studies were averaged together with the negative-outcome studies, Es' recidivism rates were still lower than Cs'—10%–12% on average. Since these reductions applied to the overall target sample, they were undoubtedly larger for some offender subgroups than others, at least in many individual studies. Future research should give high priority to determining which subgroups are most and least responsive to the various methods and techniques.

Current Status of Effectiveness

Together, the several meta-analyses and literature reviews conducted since the mid-1980s helped change or modify many individuals' views about the effectiveness of correctional intervention. More specifically, they left a fairly strong, cumulative impression that several programs or approaches can very likely reduce recidivism under certain conditions, and not just for "treatment amenables" or low-risks. Currently, this impression is more widely and perhaps strongly held than in the early and mid-1980s. Moreover, largely because most meta-analyses indicate that many positive outcomes exist, this impression, or in some cases definite view, is seldom strongly challenged on empirical grounds.

This relative absence of challenge is nevertheless slightly surprising, since it exists despite the fact that the research designs of many individual studies that comprised the meta-analyses and literature reviews were much less than excellent and were in that respect open to valid question. On balance, it appears that many individuals' general impressions about effectiveness were probably shaped by the following combination of factors: First, many positive-outcome studies appeared to have scientifically adequate designs. Second, there was the sheer number of positive-outcome studies (especially across differing meta-analyses and literature reviews), together with the apparent convergence of evidence from various studies, several of which were good to excellent.[3] These factors may have tacitly reassured individuals that most studies do not have to be excellent in order to help one decide if intervention in general "works," or, at least, often works.

At any rate, based largely on the program developments and research efforts that occurred since 1984–85 in connection with core elements such as multiple modality programming and increased intensity of contact, and even apart from the meta-analyses and literature reviews mentioned above, the following seems clear: Intervention has a widely recognized and generally accepted role with at least serious and repeat offenders. This role involves not just control- or surveillance-centered approaches, but complex psychological and skill-development methods as well (Cullen and Gilbert, 1982; Fagan and Hartstone, 1986; Gendreau and Ross, 1987; Greenwood and Zimring, 1985; O'Leary and Clear, 1984). In the 1990s, particular focus should be placed upon the third core element: greater attention to offender needs and characteristics.

Equally important, however, is the following point. Neither meta-analyses nor recent literature reviews indicate that generic *types* of programs have been found that consistently produce *major* recidivism reductions. This absence of even a few clearly powerful yet widely applicable types of programs contributes to intervention's unsettled atmosphere. It may reflect any of several factors, the following being among the obvious, likely, and important ones. First, many positive-outcome programs may not be powerful or flexible enough to produce major reductions for all offenders combined. Some of them may have large effects on one or more types of offenders in the overall sample but may have limited relevance to the remaining types—those which might comprise much of the sample. Second, many programs that are grouped together and considered a "type" may not be very similar once they are closely examined. In addition, inadequate implementation often occurs, even in programs that *are* perhaps potentially powerful and widely applicable. If implementation were better, major reductions could occur more often. Finally, although many nontraditional, positive-outcome studies may be quite good themselves, various standard or traditional programs with which they were scientifically compared may have been quite good as well. This is a reasonable possibility, given the assumption that some standard programs, like some nontraditionals themselves, doubtlessly had a number of particularly competent or unusually talented line or supervisory staff and that such individuals had some effect on implementation and outcome.[4]

All in all, then, by 1989–90 the emerging picture or perhaps new implicit consensus among many skeptics, sanguines, and others was that "something" apparently works, although no generic method or approach (as vs. individual programs) especially shines. Stated differently, several methods seem promising, but none have been shown to usually produce major reductions when applied broadly to typical composite samples of offenders.

Greater acceptance of positive outcomes has not just resulted from meta-analyses, increased practical experience, and so on. It implicitly reflects the fact that relatively few researchers and academicians require that only excellent or near-perfect designs and analyses be considered when evaluating intervention. In this connection there now seems to be a combination of increased acquiescence and acceptance regarding studies that, on the surface at least, seem to meet long-established standards of scientific adequacy; and it is these studies that comprised a sizable portion of most meta-analyses and literature reviews. To be sure, there were many mediocre, that is, somewhat less than adequate, studies as well. This mixture of some excellent, many adequate, and many borderline and even poor studies leaves various assertions about correctional effectiveness open to valid question. Nevertheless, the large number and percentage of positive outcomes associated with studies that are at least adequate leaves little doubt that many programs work, and not just with one or two subgroups.

Closing Remarks

Knowledge Building

Intervention's continued progress into the mid-1990s and later, at least at other than a snail's pace, is far from assured. This applies, not just to knowledge building, but to the avoidance of a situation in which growth-centered intervention becomes little more than an appendage to either a management-and-control-centered strategy or a punishment- or just-desert-centered strategy, or little more than a vehicle for providing—at most—modest services to perhaps the majority of offenders, and somewhat more to those actively seeking them or in obvious need.

Regarding increased discovery of and knowledge about effective programs, and of how to establish and operate them, achievement of the following goals, at least 1, 4, and 5, would clearly promote progress:

1. Studies should be well designed. For instance, random assignment should be used wherever possible.

2. More studies should be designed as replications or partial replications. Replicated results could give practitioners and policymakers more confidence in particular programs or given approaches.

3. Purposive variations of earlier studies should be conducted. For example, a "variation" could test—with setting or population Y (say, urban males age 17–20)—results from a previously promising program that dealt with X (rural males age 13–16).

4. Wherever possible, each study should describe the offender subgroups that comprise the overall target sample, and separate outcome analyses should be conducted for each subgroup. These "differentiated analyses" would be especially valuable if differing interventions were used with those subgroups.

5. Intervention processes, for instance, specific techniques, strategies, and program features, should be examined closely and described more fully, so that researchers may obtain clues or strong evidence as to which of those factors substantially contribute to growth-centered intervention. If researchers could identify such "key elements," correctional knowledge and practice would be on firmer grounds and might advance more rapidly than by any other means.

Process or "black-box" descriptions should obviously include much more than names of particular approaches, for example, behavioral or group counseling, and more than brief or perhaps standard accounts of their main features or variants, for instance, contingency contracting or guided group interaction. Although detailed descriptions could be especially useful if provided separately by offender subgroups, they could also contribute without them. In addition, whether or not subgroups are delineated, key elements may be identified without meta-analysis.[5]

Whether or not goals 1 through 5 are achieved, sizable recidivism reductions should become increasingly possible or common insofar as such core elements as multiple modality programming and greater attention to offender needs and characteristics are increasingly used.

Legitimacy

A key issue that carried over from the 1970s to the 1980s involved intervention's legitimacy. Throughout 1975–81, numerous individuals virtually declared intervention illegitimate, that is, not just ineffective but inappropriate or at least of little use. However, in the 1980s, intervention in general and rehabilitation in particular more or less fought their way back from this alleged near-illegitimacy. They did so mainly via studies, meta-analyses, and literature reviews that, collectively, demonstrated frequent effectiveness,[6] and partly because personal as well as practical assistance was often provided and recognized as such, for instance, in areas of vocational and academic achievement. These findings and contributions increased or reestablished intervention's pragmatic legitimacy.

In addition, by the mid-1980s it was generally apparent that the *Clockwork Orange* stereotype of treatment as inhumane and dehumanizing—therefore morally illegitimate—seldom applied and was not intrinsic to intervention. (Abuses often existed before 1980, as did several questionable approaches [Mitford, 1971, 1973]. Moreover, these had been caused by neither institutional crowding nor fiscal constraints. Although not entirely absent, they are now much reduced.) Meanwhile, by the late 1980s, it was apparent that neither justice model proponents nor others had provided convincing arguments to the effect that rehabilitation, first, should be considered intrinsically inappropriate as a major correctional goal; second, was in fact unimportant or perhaps even harmful as a correctional activity; and, finally, should be secondary to punishment in any event, whether for short- or long-term goals. These developments helped maintain and, compared to the decade beginning in 1975, increase intervention's moral and philosophical legitimacy.

The Significance of Research

Finally, it should be mentioned that without scientifically sound research to determine independently if, and with whom, programs have worked, interventions that receive even strong testimonials and high acclaim—and that seem morally and philosophically legitimate—will probably fade after several years. This has occurred repeatedly in recent decades, even with programs deemed exemplary but whose research, when present and adequately reported, proved mediocre. In the long run, sound evaluation may be among the surest bases for a program's deserved confidence and survival, not just an appropriate basis for its legitimacy from the standpoint of increased public protection.

Over the decades, and despite its shortcomings, research has greatly contributed to intervention's progress. It should be challenged to continue contributing in the 1990s—in fact, to provide higher-quality information. Given the opportunity and resources, correctional researchers can meet this challenge. They already have the tools, and enough motivation exists.

Author's Notes

1. Thus differing subgroups would receive different combinations or amounts of those components. If only one component existed, differing amounts might be given to the different subgroups. Differential intervention proponents believed most samples contained at least two or three sizable subgroups, even if most individuals within those samples had a rather similar committing offense or offense history—for example, burglary or theft, sexual acting-out, or hard drug usage. Agreement between skeptics and sanguines about matching was only implicit, whereas it was explicit with regard to multiple modality programming and more intensive intervention.

2. Together, the literature reviews suggested that some methods or types of approach sometimes have a sizable impact, at least on particular offender groups. This suggestion, however, is not part of today's tacit consensus.

3. Regarding convergence of evidence, which occurred in positive-outcome studies within and across various approaches (e.g., behavioral and cognitive–behavioral) and which was found across as well as within given analyses or reviews, the following should be noted: Such evidence occurred in studies that resembled each other not just in name alone (e.g., behavioral programs), but on various offender, setting, structural, and program dimensions. As such, they in effect comprised—collectively—unplanned, partial replications of each other, and their resulting mutual reinforcement increased the contributions of all (Palmer, 1983).

4. Standard programs (controls, or Cs) doubtlessly vary among themselves in power and relevance—adequacy of implementation aside. The stronger ones, or those rather effective with certain types of offenders, may vigorously challenge many nontraditionals (experimentals, or Es)—particularly, but not only, since differences also exist among Es. Given the above, it would be surprising if C programs did not occasionally outperform Es, including those that were relevant and generally adequate with regard to staff and implementation. At any rate, nontraditional or experimental programs have no monopoly on talent, quality leadership, and even charisma, and Cs should not be stereotyped as almost always mediocre.

   Researchers might wish to pay increased attention to standard programs in the 1990s. Here a major goal might be to discover whether, why, and for whom selected C programs outperform other Cs, not just given Es. C versus C comparisons, that is, research on standard programs per se, could have practical benefits independent of those resulting from E/C studies themselves.

5. Meta-analyses conducted through 1989 did not focus on the techniques, strategies, and various related conditions, for instance, across-approach factors, underlying successful programs. This was partly because the necessary data seldom existed.

6. Detailed or "differentiated" analyses were not required in order to address overall effectiveness, for example, to determine if programs worked for their samples as a whole. Nevertheless, many 1960s-through-1980s studies did involve this kind of analysis. Differentiated research usually focuses on types of offenders, programs, or settings. For instance, in any given differentiated research study or set of studies, one might separately analyze the impact of two or more distinct offender characteristics, two or more program features, and so forth, on one or more outcome measures in turn, thus yielding estimates of differential impact. One might also analyze the impact of various offender/program combinations on those outcomes. Differentiated designs can be implemented identically in justice model and rehabilitation approaches. In this sense they can be philosophically neutral and scientifically independent of the content and underpinnings of given approaches.

Discussion Questions

1. What does a "skeptic" believe about the effectiveness of rehabilitation? What does a "sanguine" believe? How does each present his or her case, and how does the other respond? According to Palmer, what common ground do skeptics and sanguines now

share regarding treatment programs for serious offenders? Do you agree that skeptics now accept those assumptions about treatment for serious offenders?

2.   What conclusions does Palmer reach about the effectiveness of treatment programs from his study of meta-analyses and literature reviews? What goals does he propose for promoting progress in discovering and implementing effective treatment programs?

3.   If the relegitimation of rehabilitation that Palmer describes continues, how will it affect the policies of the criminal justice system? Look at the likely impact of such a trend on prison and community treatment programs, the "three strikes and you're out" policy, mandatory prison sentences, and the elimination of parole.

C h a p t e r *23*

Meta-Analysis and the Rehabilitation of Punishment*

Charles H. Logan and Gerald G. Gaes

Here Logan and Gaes take issue with the conclusions reached by Palmer in the selection #22. They argue that the meta-analyses cited to support the idea that some forms of treatment work are flawed. They then assert that even if effective correctional methods were found, rehabilitation should not be the goal of prisons; instead, prisons are designed to mete out justice through the confinement of offenders. Treatment programs can exist within prison walls, they say, but the correction of wrongdoers is not the mission of the prison.

The correctional rehabilitation ethic is a child of this century, born with the rise of Progressive ideology and reform in the early decades, growing strong with the development of social science in the thirties and forties, reaching maturity in the fifties when the medical model was at its peak, suffering a mid-life crisis and a loss of faith in the sixties and seventies, and essentially gone and forgotten by the eighties. As we enter the nineties, the rehabilitative ideal is showing signs of revival as some researchers, employing a new technology called "meta-analysis," believe they have detected life in the old body still. Were the rumors of the death of rehabilitation premature? Or is it time to give rehabilitation a decent burial and to consider a redefinition of penology without reference to "corrections?"

* This paper was written while the first author was a Visiting Fellow at the Federal Bureau of Prisons, Office of Research and Evaluation. That support is gratefully acknowledged, but the opinions expressed here are those of the authors and do not represent policies of the Bureau of Prisons or the Department of Justice.

Source: Charles H. Logan and Gerald G. Gaes, "Meta-Analysis and the Rehabilitation of Punishment," *Justice Quarterly* 10 (2): pp. 245–63. Copyright © by Academy of Criminal Justice Sciences. Reprinted with Permission of the Academy of Criminal Justice Sciences.

The debate over "treatment versus punishment" is rooted both in empirical research and in ideology; a candid discussion must address both of these aspects. Failure to do so has displaced onto seemingly objective questions (such as "Which is more effective: rehabilitation or punishment?") the kind of passion normally associated with ideological questions (such as "Which is a morally superior goal for criminal justice: rehabilitation or punishment?"). In this paper we intend, first, to challenge some of the recent empirical research being used to support claims for the effectiveness of rehabilitation. Second, we intend to argue that regardless of what such research shows, punishment is preferable to rehabilitation as an aim of criminal justice and, in particular, that punishment through confinement is the most appropriate mission for a prison. Meta-analysis of research on rehabilitation has not yet established that any particular method of treatment is significantly and reliably effective. We still do not know what "works" in correctional treatment, but it really wouldn't matter even if we knew, because the fundamental purpose of imprisonment is not the correction but the punishment of criminal behavior.

The Decline and Revival of Rehabilitation

Empirical research often has been used to support positions that are held primarily for ideological reasons. For many decades, a belief in the applicability of scientific method to the solution of social problems supported a system of indeterminate sentences based supposedly on objective expertise and knowledge and designed to allow for individualized treatment of offenders. The same belief led to a profusion of research aimed at discovering the most effective methods of providing this corrective treatment. Critical reviews of this research during the 1960s and 1970s, however, supported the conclusion that we do not know how to rehabilitate criminals (Bailey, 1966; Greenberg, 1977; Logan, 1972; Martinson, 1974; Robison and Smith, 1971; Sechrest, White, and Brown, 1979); other critics objected that discretionary treatment, however well motivated it might be, tends to be highly arbitrary and unjust (Allen, 1981; American Friends Service Committee, 1971; Szasz, 1965; von Hirsch, 1976).

Partly in response to this critical literature, indeterminate sentences and discretionary release largely have been replaced by sentences fixed according to statutes and guidelines. This reform was supported both by civil libertarians, who wanted to protect offenders from "benevolent" violation of their rights, and by conservatives, who believed that parole-adjusted sentences were too lenient. Individualized treatment has been pushed aside by the "justice model," in which offenders are to be treated impersonally and equally, according to the gravity of their crimes, and to receive the amount of punishment their acts deserve.

These reforms have been widely perceived as "getting tough on crime," and are believed by many to have led to overimprisonment and increased suffering by prisoners. In response to this perception, some people are attempting to revive the rehabilitative ethic in the belief that a treatment orientation will soften the alleged overemphasis on punishment (Cullen, 1986; Cullen and Gendreau, 1989; Cullen and Gilbert, 1982). In support of their position, the promoters of rehabilitation have been reviewing the research literature once again in an attempt to show that treatment does work after all, at least sometimes (Andrews et al., 1990a; Basta and Davidson, 1988; Cullen and Gendreau, 1989; Garrett, 1985; Gendreau, 1981; Gendreau and Andrews, 1990; Gendreau and Ross, 1979; 1987; Izzo and Ross, 1990; Lipsey, 1988, 1989, 1990; Palmer, 1983; Ross and Gendreau, 1980; van Voorhis, 1987).

Meta-Analysis: Discovery or Alchemy?

Advocates of rehabilitation believe that a powerful new tool known as "meta-analysis" can be used to mine the deposits of previous research, to uncover hidden veins of effective treatment not necessarily revealed by individual studies, and to refine the ore of prior findings to extract and combine the valuable elements. Critics of this approach believe that meta-analysis is being misused, like some kind of alchemy, in an attempt to turn the lead of inadequate experiments into the gold of established knowledge.

In less metaphorical terms, what meta-analysis does is to study other studies—in this case, studies that test the effectiveness of various programs of correctional treatment. Each study is coded on a number of variables such as characteristics of the research design, characteristics of the subjects studied, and characteristics of the treatment applied. In theory, by combining and reanalyzing studies, meta-analysis may be able to separate treatment effects from differences due to uncontrolled characteristics of the subjects, or other deficiencies of research design, even if those sources of error were not controlled adequately by any of the primary studies taken separately.

Meta-analysis is a legitimate research tool, but is easy to misuse. To be sure, meta-analysts are not deconstructionists who merely read into the literature whatever they please, but their technique imposes such demanding methodological requirements (Hedges and Olkin, 1985) that it is difficult to conduct a meta-analysis which controls and adjusts for errors in the primary studies without introducing new errors and biases of its own. It is not surprising, then, that separate reviews and meta-analyses of research on the effectiveness of correctional rehabilitation programs reach differing conclusions and criticize each other's validity (Andrews et al., 1990a, 1990b; Lab and Whitehead, 1990).

One recent meta-analysis can be used to illustrate the technique's ability to create spurious findings. This study has been hailed by influential scholars as proving that "something works"; it is part of a continuing body of research produced by a network composed mostly of Canadian researchers who appear to be having a considerable impact on that country's corrections system (Andrews et al., 1990a). This meta-analysis examined a sample of previous studies designed to test the effectiveness of various forms of treatment applied to juveniles and adults under correctional supervision. The researchers coded each of the original studies according to the quality of its research design, the type(s) of treatment it tested, and the size of the "treatment effect" found in the study. They found that the size of the treatment effect had only a minor relationship to the quality of the research design. In contrast, they found that both the size of the effect and whether it was positive or negative were related significantly to the type of treatment. More specifically, they found that treatment effects were strongest and most positive for what they called "appropriate treatment."

Treatment was labeled as "appropriate" under any of four conditions:

Any treatment, when applied to "high-risk" cases;

"Behavioral" treatment, except with "low-risk" cases;

Treatment matched to a client's "responsivity"; or

Treatment structured toward changing a "criminogenic need."

The keys to "appropriate treatment" in this scheme are the elements of "risk" and "receptivity." "Criminogenic needs" refer to "a subset of risk factors . . . that, when changed, are associated with changes in the chances of recidivism" (Andrews, Bonta, and Hoge, 1990:31).

This meta-analysis contains many problems (Lab and Whitehead, 1990; Logan et al., 1991), but the most serious is the apparently tautological character of the "appropriate treatment" label. Is treatment effective *because* it is appropriate, or is it *called* "appropriate" when it is seen to be effective? To avoid circular reasoning, one must be able to identify a particular treatment or form of treatment as "appropriate" or "inappropriate" without any prior knowledge of its effects. If a treatment were labeled "appropriate" or "inappropriate" according to theoretically based predictions of effectiveness *before* the point at which a research study measured the effect of applying that treatment to one group (a treatment group) and withholding it from another (a control group), there would be no problem in conducting a meta-analysis of many such studies to compare the effects of "appropriate" and "inappropriate" treatments. A problem *does* exist, however, when the original research studies seek and discover positive effects by reanalyzing their data to test the effectiveness of treatment under different conditions or on different subgroups, and *then* declare the treatment to be appropriate or inappropriate according to its differential effectiveness. This is the result in this meta-analysis when treatment is labeled "appropriate" or "inappropriate" according to its relation to the factors of "risk," "responsivity," and "need."

Did the meta-analysts know in advance what factors would indicate risk or responsivity, and why? They did not. They identified those factors through the meta-analysis itself. They identified both risk and responsivity by their relation to outcome, but distinguished them from each other by their *differential* relation to outcome. Age, for example, was determined to be a "risk" factor in a particular study if it proved in that study to be predictive of recidivism independently of treatment. If it *interacted* with treatment, however, so that treatment effects varied by age, then age was determined to be a "responsivity" factor. Thus three of the meta-analysts, writing elsewhere but describing one of the studies reviewed in the meta-analysis, found that offenders with certain traits were more "amenable" to treatment; in other words, treatment had a greater effect on them. In the absence of treatment, "amenables" and "nonamenables" did not differ in their recidivism. "That is, amenability was not a risk factor but a responsivity factor" (Andrews, Bonta, and Hoge, 1990:38).

Consider the history of a typical evaluation research project. An experimental group and a control group are compared, and no significant difference in outcome is found. The researcher, not satisfied with such an uninteresting and seemingly uninformative finding, asks "Aren't there are any conditions under which the effect I am looking for occurs?" In fact, even if an effect is found, most researchers will want to know what happens to that effect under different conditions. Thus the researcher starts to introduce third variables into the analysis, and tries holding them constant at different cutting points, until something interesting (or more interesting) results. At that point the researcher must give a name and an interpretation to the variable that has been discovered to condition the existence, strength, sign, or form of the treatment effect. Because the variables included in the original analysis, and thus available for the reanalysis, were chosen because they were thought to be predictors of outcome, the odds are good that some of the variables tested (age, race, sex, class, prior record, attitudes, personality traits, whatever) can be labeled elements of "risk" (i.e., predictors of outcome). Then the researcher's conclusion will be "Treatment has an effect, but only on offenders of a certain type (high- or low-risk)." If the control variable by itself does not predict outcome but does condition the effect of treatment, the researcher can label this interactive effect "responsivity." In such a case the conclusion will be "Treatment has an effect, but only on offenders who are responsive to this type of treatment."

Separately, studies like these are perfectly legitimate, but they do not prove anything. They are tautological; they explain their results with after-the-fact hypotheses but do not test those explanations. What, then, if a meta-analysis of 100 studies finds a significant relation between "risk" or "responsivity" or "needs," on the one hand, and treatment effect, on the other? Could this meta-analysis be regarded as confirmatory—a summary of replications? Not necessarily. If the operational definitions of "risk" and "responsivity" and "needs" (the predictor variables) differ from study to study, we will learn nothing from a meta-analysis showing that treatment effect depends on these factors. Even if "risk" always were based, say, on prior record, at least two problems still could exist. First, the criterion of how long or how serious a record had to be in order to be "risky" still could be defined differently, and ex post facto, for each study; thus "risk" still would be tautological. Second, researchers typically do not report all the interactions they test; they tend to report only those that make a difference. Thus most of the negative evidence showing that treatment effects do not vary by level of risk goes unreported. A bias is thereby created in favor of the conclusion that treatment works, if only for cases in which risk makes a difference and therefore is reported.

Andrews, Bonta, and Hoge (1990:31) define "criminogenic needs" as "a subset of risk factors" consisting of "dynamic attributes of offenders and their circumstances that, when changed, are associated with changes in the chances of recidivism." Thus all three concepts—risk, responsivity, and needs—lend themselves to circular reasoning. These concepts can be used as explanations whenever a researcher testing the effectiveness of treatment discovers some condition under which the treatment group has significantly lower recidivism than the control group. If treatment is more effective under Condition X, that fact alone is sufficient to support the interpretation that "Type X clients" or "clients under Condition X" are "more responsive" or that X indicates that the treatment must be targeting some "criminogenic need."

First, let's summarize in the language of statistics. If a variable has *main effects* on recidivism, it is a "risk" factor (unless it is something that is targeted for change by the treatment, in which case it is a "needs" factor). If the variable *interacts* with treatment in its effects on recidivism, it is a "responsivity" factor.[1] Treatment is declared to be "appropriate" and therefore effective only when it is tied to variables that are known to have either main or interactive effects on outcome.

Now let's put that in simple language. It is often said of psychotherapy that it "can be effective, but only if the patient *wants* to change." Likewise, treatment of criminals can be effective, but only if they need to change, want to change, are amenable to change, and receive treatment that is matched to their need, desire, and amenability to change. If this is what meta-analysts mean when they say that we are now beginning to know that "some things work sometimes," then in fact we are not far removed from the stage of "nothing works" or "we don't know what works."

The technique of meta-analysis has proved useful in medical research, albeit potentially harmful if applied poorly (Sacks et al., 1987). Likewise it may have a role in determining the effectiveness of certain forms of correctional treatment. Some meta-analytic research on the treatment of juvenile delinquents (Lipsey, 1990) has been more sophisticated statistically, more rigorous methodologically, and without the evangelical zeal of other meta-analytic research. Research on juveniles, however, much of it examining minor forms of delinquency, may have little bearing on the rehabilitation of adult offenders. In any case, the claim that meta-analysis now demonstrates that rehabilitative treatment "works" (in the sense of being significantly and reliably effective) as long as it is of the "appropriate" type and is applied "appropriately," is seriously flawed, unsubstantiated, and largely circular.

It may not be worthwhile to debate whether meta-analysis or other research has identified "what works" by way of prisoner rehabilitation. Engaging in such debate presupposes that effectiveness, or utility, is the crucial issue in discussing the value of rehabilitation in the criminal justice system generally and inside prisons in particular. Underlying the zeal with which meta-analysts claim to have proved scientifically that "something works after all" is the implicit argument that because rehabilitation can be made more scientific it is therefore both a viable and a desirable alternative to punishment. The meta-analysts believe that we turned away from treatment and toward punishment because Martinson and others convinced everyone that nothing works; therefore, convincing people of the opposite should help to turn them back in the "proper" policy direction. If only it could be shown that rehabilitation is technically feasible, then it could be taken for granted that it also is morally superior to punishment as a goal for the criminal justice system.

This presumption against punishment as a moral value is a subtext running through much of the new literature on "reviving" or "reaffirming" rehabilitation (Cullen, 1986; Cullen and Gendreau, 1989; Cullen and Gilbert, 1982). Many of these advocates argue that treatment ought to be the main goal of corrections for reasons that are more political or ideological than pragmatic. Even if the last vestiges of the instrumental purpose of treatment were discarded, such proponents still would argue that rehabilitation has an ideological, moral, and political basis. Yet although their support for rehabilitation is thus ultimately independent of the evidence, they still find it important to be able to back their claims, as far as possible, with research. As progressives, they believe that society can and should be reformed through "scientifically" directed government intervention, and they see in rehabilitation a potentially powerful vehicle with which to roll back the conservative political agenda and advance their own. They also see it as a politically suitable vehicle. Thus Cullen (1986:9) urges progressives to "think seriously about what ideology or correctional philosophy can gain sufficient support to permit the opportunity for reform to emerge and be realized." Toward that end, he argues "that rehabilitation is the most feasible ideology available and, thus, that it should be reaffirmed rather than be rejected."[2]

Because the case for rehabilitation is made on both utilitarian and nonutilitarian grounds, it is not enough merely to review and critique the empirical evidence offered by meta-analysts and others in favor of rehabilitation. We also must present an affirmative case, on moral and philosophical grounds, for punishment as opposed to rehabilitation. Assuming for the sake of argument that meta-analysis *could* tell us something significant about the effectiveness of different types of correctional treatment, would we be justified in giving rehabilitation a place of emphasis, or any place at all, in the mission of a prison system? Not if we understand that the essential purpose of imprisonment is punishment and that punishment is best defended on moral rather than instrumental grounds, by appeal to cultural values rather than to social utility.

The Value of Punishment

The biggest mistake in referring to the penal system as a "corrections" system is that it reinforces a false hierarchy of values in which "helping" is seen as superior to sanctioning. "Corrections" has adopted the language of treatment, which is the language of medicine, psychology, and education, largely as an attempt to acquire for itself some of the perceived legitimacy and prestige of those other professions. That has been a mistake. You can never feel good about yourself, or impress others, by pretending to be something you are not; the pretense is particularly pointless when what you are is already admirable. If the situation is not widely seen in that way, then some consciousness raising is needed.

If some people think that punishment is evil (perhaps a necessary evil but an evil nonetheless); that mercy is a higher value than justice; that compassion is more praiseworthy than fairness; that permissiveness and lenience are the marks of a kind and loving society, while accountability implies callousness; that forgiveness is divine, while judgment and enforcement are unpleasant human necessities; that the discretionary exercise of power and authority is trustworthy when the intent is benevolent and paternalistic but suspect when the purpose is disciplinary; or that teaching, helping, and treating offenders are laudable and prestigious activities while confining and managing them is a dirty job (though someone has to do it)—in short, that only a spirit of benevolence can give the criminal sanction any redeeming value—then perhaps those people have false values and need to be enlightened.

One source of enlightenment can be found in a recent book by David Garland (1990). In *Punishment and Modern Society,* Garland suggests that we need to concentrate less on the social, political, and instrumental purposes of imprisonment and more on its cultural, moral, and expressive values. In modern times, punishment has been overestimated as a social tool and underappreciated as a cultural value. As a social tool, punishment has been expected to accomplish all kinds of utilitarian objectives where other social institutions already have failed. It is expected to correct the incorrigible, to rehabilitate the wretched, to restrain the dangerous, to deter the determined, and in general to reinforce the social order. Punishment has at best only a limited capacity to achieve these ends, but in any case it should not be regarded as a form of social engineering, having worth only because it is useful. Rather, punishment is a significant aspect of culture, with meaning and merit in itself. It is a symbol and an expression of cultural and moral values. Punishment constructs and communicates some of the most important shared meanings, values, and beliefs that define the character of a culture. It "communicates meaning not just about crime and punishment but also about power, authority, legitimacy, normality, morality, personhood, social relations, and a host of other tangential matters" (Garland, 1990:252).

Those who exercise authority and impose sanctions are important cultural agents. They include not only the legislators and judges who define the purpose, nature, and targets of punishment, but also the agents who administer it, from the executive level to the line staff. The meaning and significance of the work they do should be viewed as a moral enterprise, an exercise in the philosophy of punishment.

One of the duties of prison officials is to help offenders understand the wrongfulness of their criminal conduct and accept responsibility and accountability for that conduct. This duty requires the imposition of punishment because the very concepts of wrongfulness, responsibility, and accountability must be socially defined and constructed through the use of sanctions. Thus punishment is a constructive, not a destructive, enterprise. When done right, it is a positive good rather than a necessary evil, but to do it right one needs the right people with the right attitudes. Hostility, contempt, and cruelty are inappropriate sentiments toward prisoners, but so too are pity, indulgence, or excessive sympathy and compassion. "Professionalism" is the most appropriate word to describe the proper attitude of impersonal authority, objectivity, and firm but respectful fairness that good officers have toward prisoners.

As agents of governmental authority, prison officers must understand that they are obliged to operate within rigid constraints. They ensure that justice is done, first and foremost, by following the rules that define the parameters of justice, the rules that determine what is too permissive and what is too harsh. If inmates are treated unfairly inside prison, they will find it hard to appreciate that it is fair for them to be in prison in the first place. To accept the justice of their punishment, inmates must understand that it is principled, not malicious. Prison officers, as representatives of society, must convey that message to them through their demeanor. First, however, prison officials and officers must accept without apology the fact that they are among society's "ministers of justice." Think about it: isn't that a more admirable mission than being a "correctional officer?"

Prison officers deserve a more favorable image as agents of punishment. The most negative result of emphasizing rehabilitation is that almost inevitably it demoralizes security and custody staff members who are portrayed (if only by implication) as less professional and less humane than the treatment and program staff. It also impugns the most important purposes of imprisonment—justice, punishment, and security—by portraying them as uninspiring, if not morally inferior. Prison professionals need to understand, to be reminded often, and to help the public appreciate that the job of confining and controlling an unwilling population without violating rights, the job of treating inmates "firmly but fairly," is every bit as praiseworthy as the pursuit of rehabilitation, if not more so.

Legal punishment is a legitimate and (if properly defined and administered) even a noble aspect of our culture. Imprisonment, in order to be respectable, need not be defined as "corrections," as "treatment," as "education," as "protection of society," or as any other instrumental activity that an army of critics will forever claim to be a failure. Instead, as Garland puts it, "the pursuit of values such as justice, tolerance, decency, humanity, and civility should be part of any penal institution's self-consciousness—an intrinsic and constitutive aspect of its role—rather than a diversion from its 'real' goals or an inhibition on its capacity to be 'effective'" (1990:292).

Punishment, Treatment, and Humanitarianism

To understand the expressive, or symbolic, importance of punishment is to achieve new insight into the question of treatment versus punishment as purposes of imprisonment and the question of treatment versus custody as functions within a prison. Treatment and confinement are not merely different means; they are also different ends in themselves. When they are debated as ends, the proponents of treatment often tend to assume the moral high ground and the proponents of confinement and punishment often tend to assume a defensive posture. The latter, however, have nothing to apologize for and should not allow others to disparage punitive confinement as "warehousing" or "caging." The stereotype of punishment as inherently cruel and inhumane is false and misleading, as is the stereotype of treatment as benevolent and humane.

Those who suppose that rehabilitative treatment is intrinsically more humane than punishment have bought into a false dichotomy between punishment and "humanitarianism." It is precisely within the context of punishment, as opposed to treatment, that humanistic concepts are most relevant. Principled and fair punishment for wrongdoing treats individuals as persons and as human beings rather than as objects. Punishment is an affirmation of the autonomy, responsibility, and dignity of the individual; paternalistic rehabilitative treatment is a denial of all three.

Proponents believe that rehabilitation programs reduce the harshness of imprisonment by softening and humanizing the prison environment. But what if this effect is more apparent than real? What if prisons merely pay lip service to the ideal of rehabilitation and create what amounts to a facade of fine-sounding programs that masks the harsh reality of doing time? Might this approach not reduce pressure from the public for real reform? A veneer of good intentions could undermine the vigilance and the restraint of power that we need to maintain a system of just punishment. Rather than softening the pains of imprisonment, the rehabilitative goal may even add injustice to injury because it encourages individualized treatment, which undermines consistency and fairness. Individualized treatment requires discretion, which lends itself to abuse in the form of arbitrary and capricious distinctions. In pursuit of rehabilitation, offenders who have committed similar wrongs often are treated differently because of differences in personality, background, and social skills. Furthermore, when rehabilitative treatment is defined as an official goal of the agents and institutions of authority, then treatment, too, becomes paternalistic and authoritarian. The result is cynicism and resistance on the part of the intended beneficiaries. If our goal is to reform the conditions of life inside prisons, it is better to do so directly than under the rubric of rehabilitation. The direct approach has less chance of backfiring.

But (as one of our reviewers suggested to us) wouldn't minimization of the treatment ideal and a formal acceptance of punishment as the primary goal of prisons tend to minimize programming and remove any possible incentive on the part of administrators to help inmates? As Cullen and Gilbert (1982:247) argue, "Rehabilitation is the only justification of criminal sanctioning that obligates the state to care for an offender's needs or welfare." We disagree. Rehabilitation raises the question of whether it is society's obligation to transform the inmate into a law-abiding citizen, not whether it is society's duty to treat the inmate humanely. None of the purposes of punishment directly defines a state's obligation to care for inmates. In fact, almost any justification of punishment might be interpreted to imply conditions that range from the brutal to the benign. Rehabilitation in some of its paternalistic forms is just as coercive as other justifications. Inmates may well be "encouraged," or "persuaded" into treatment against their wishes. Retribution, often associated with harsh treatment, also can imply that a prolonged separation from society, proportional to the crime, is sufficient punishment, but that the prison climate must be safe and must offer enough amenities so that prison life is not inhumane.

A state's obligation to its inmates is based on statutory, regulatory, and supervisory requirements. In practice, however, the quality of confinement is based on the funding levels, management capabilities, and external supervision of a prison or jail. The supervision can come from the legislature, the courts, or even the community. Because corrections is carried out behind walls, gates, and fences, both internal and external supervision are particularly important. We should not confuse supervision, however, with a model of treatment that calls for the transformation of individuals.

One also might argue that "treatment versus punishment" is a false dichotomy; that it is not necessary to abandon the goal of rehabilitation in order to pursue, or even to emphasize, the goal of punishment. That argument is certainly reasonable but we are more prepared to accept it in practice than in principle. In practice, the difference between punishment and treatment is often unclear, particularly to those on the receiving end; a prison that is literally all of one and none of the other is probably impossible as well as undesirable. Even so, an analytic distinction still is necessary. We believe that when the concepts are understood properly, it can be shown that a philosophy emphasizing punishment is more logically consistent, and even more true to the same general underlying values (such as humanitarianism, respect for the individual, human dignity, justice, fairness, decency, mercy, and compassion), than a philosophy emphasizing rehabilitation.

Later we will suggest that many of the activities which now occur under the heading of "programming" might still occur in a punishment-oriented prison. We do not object to treatment that is voluntary, is separated from punishment, and is not a privilege unavailable to those who are not in prison. We believe that even in a punishment model, inmates have as much (or as little) right as anyone else to a helping hand from government. The license to punish is not a license to deny to convicts any benefits to which they would be entitled if they were not in prison (with the exception of denials that are absolutely necessary for reasons of security). We also believe, however, that prison programs can be justified on grounds other (and better) than rehabilitation, and that for both conceptual and practical reasons, as discussed in the next two sections, the *idea* of inmate programs ought to be separated from the *ideal,* and the ideology, of rehabilitation.

The Conflicting Messages of Punishment and Treatment

As punishment, imprisonment conveys an important cultural message, but if the official mission of a prison is defined simultaneously as both punishment and rehabilitation conflicting and confusing messages are transmitted both inside and outside the prison walls. Inside the walls, such a definition conveys a message of rights without responsibility. When a prison system is mandated in its mission statement to attempt rehabilitation, or even merely to provide opportunities and resources for self-improvement, that mandate creates for inmates a legitimate claim (a right) to personally beneficial services. At the same time, it undermines inmates' accountability by defining them, like children, as insufficiently developed and disadvantaged persons for whose future behavior society must take some responsibility. Whereas imprisonment as punishment defines inmates as responsible for their *past* behavior, and whereas discipline within prison defines inmates as accountable for their *current* behavior, rehabilitation as a goal of the system defines inmates as not fully responsible for their *future* behavior.

Outside the walls, linking imprisonment with rehabilitation conveys a confusing message to the general public. As punishment, the message of imprisonment is "Felonies are very wrong acts, and those who commit them will be held to account." But the message of the rehabilitation ethic is "Felonies are the result of personal deficiencies (of knowledge, skills, habits, values, temperament, motivation, personality, and so on) on the part of the individual; society must attempt to correct those personal deficiencies." That is not an appropriate message for society to construct through its institutions of punishment. Such a message depicts criminal behavior in deterministic terms and portrays offenders as objects in need of adjustment, rather than as responsible human beings who must accept the consequences of their actions. It may not actually excuse their crimes, but it conflicts with and weakens the punishment message.

Separating Treatment from Punishment

Prison rehabilitation programs, especially if they are successful, confer valuable but unearned benefits on the undeserving at the expense of law-abiding taxpayers. To benefit convicts thus on the grounds that they have violated the law and may do so again is, in effect, to reward extortion. As an alternative, one legitimately might argue that prisoners deserve certain kinds of help merely because they are human beings, or because they are citizens toward whom, merely as citizens, society has some obligations and in whom it has some investment. That rationale would be legitimate, but only to the same extent as it would apply to all other citizens. Thus rehabilitation programs are more justifiable outside than inside the criminal justice system.

Treatment is more likely to be effective if it is voluntary. More important, the voluntary quality also makes it ethically more defensible. It is very difficult, however, to make treatment truly voluntary in the context of punishment. If judges, prison officials, probation officers, or parole boards place any great emphasis on rehabilitative programs and urge offenders to get involved in them, offenders would be foolish not to understand that some kind of consequences, however subtle, will follow from their agreement or refusal to do as they are urged. Also, within a system of coercion, all consequences, whether positive or negative, must be viewed as part of the coercion. To ensure voluntary involvement and to avoid the appearance of providing special benefits that are not available free to others who might be more deserving, it is necessary to disconnect treatment from imprisonment. The best way to do this would be to remove rehabilitative treatment entirely from the authority of the criminal justice system.

One way to achieve this separation would be to postpone treatment activities until after release from prison, or to send prisoners temporarily into the community to participate in such activities. Another way would be to make it clear that treatment is not the official business of the penal system, even while allowing it to be provided by other agencies either inside or outside the prison and to the same degree as it is available to nonprisoners.

Yet regardless of where these elective activities take place, their separation from the confinement mission should be emphasized by requiring that they be conducted and paid for by civilian (i.e., nonpenal) agencies, organizations, or individuals. That requirement could include activities conducted and paid for by prisoners themselves; what counts is that they are not sponsored by the penal system. Many such activities are permissible and desirable within a prison as long as they are compatible—and are not confused—with the prison's essential mission of confinement as punishment.

Prison Programs Under the Confinement Model

Another way to preserve treatment programs for prisoners would be to justify them on grounds that would be relevant even if rehabilitation were not an official goal of the system. Many programs currently offered in prisons could be separated from the context and vocabulary of "rehabilitation," and could be justified instead in the context and with the vocabulary of "confinement." Despite a decline in official endorsement of the rehabilitative ideal, many corrections officials continue to endorse programs because of their normalizing effect on the prison environment, not because they believe in effecting a change in the inmates. In addition, many corrections officials endorse the view that some programs work for some inmates in the sense that those who want to change should receive the opportunity to change. Both of these goals—time spent constructively and the opportunity to acquire skills—still can be pursued without the baggage of the rehabilitative ideal.

John DiIulio (1991:114) notes that most prison and jail administrators view correctional programs from what he calls an "institutional perspective." That is, they "evaluate programs not mainly in terms of what they do to reduce the likelihood of recidivism or otherwise affect inmates' post-release behavior but as institutional management tools." DiIulio also suggests that programs can be defended in less utilitarian terms simply as part of what we mean by humane conditions of confinement.

A "confinement model" of imprisonment (Logan 1991: ch. 1) would be a follow-up to the "justice model" of sentencing. The confinement model, like the justice model, is based on a purely retributive philosophy of punishment. In this philosophy, the essential purpose of imprisonment is to punish offenders—fairly and justly—through lengths of confinement proportionate to the seriousness of their crimes. Although confinement may serve other purposes in addition to justice and punishment, those are the necessary and sufficient conditions for justifying it. Thus the term *confinement model* may be regarded as a shorthand for a clumsier but more explicit label: the *doing-justice-through-confinement-as-a-form-of-punishment model.*

Under the confinement model, offenders are sent to prison *as* punishment, not *for* punishment. Thus, prisons operated on this model need not be harsh or internally punitive, nor would they be insensitive to the welfare of prisoners. Coercive confinement carries an obligation to meet prisoners' basic needs at a reasonable standard of decency, so measures of health care, safety, sanitation, nutrition, and other aspects of basic living conditions are relevant. Furthermore, confinement must meet constitutional standards of fairness and due process, so not only effectiveness and efficiency, but also the procedural justice with which confinement is imposed, are important. In addition—and most relevant to this discussion—programmatic activities such as education, recreation, and work can be viewed as part of the conditions of confinement, regardless of their alleged effects on rehabilitation. In short, confinement is much more than merely warehousing.

Here is a mission statement for a prison under the confinement model:

> The mission of a prison is to keep prisoners—to keep them in, keep them safe, keep them in line, keep them healthy, and keep them busy—and to do it with fairness, without undue suffering, and as efficiently as possible.

Many inmate programs currently offered in prisons—such as work, training, education, and recreation—can be justified under the heading of constructive activity ("keep them busy"). "Constructive" activity is not defined here as "contributing to the betterment of inmates" but as activity that is, on its face, consistent with the orderly, safe, secure, and humane operation of a prison. Idleness and boredom can be viewed as wrong from a work ethic standpoint, or as unnatural because human beings are not meant to be idle, or as so fundamentally related to mischief as to be undesirable for that reason. In any case, prison programs can be defended as forms of constructive and meaningful activity and as antidotes to idleness, without invoking claims of rehabilitative effectiveness. This is not to say that it does not matter whether the programs have any rehabilitative effects; it would be fine if they did so. But when we say that the primary purpose of prison is to punish through confinement, we become more interested in the operation of these programs inside the prison gates and less concerned about their effects beyond.

It is the duty of prisons to govern fairly and well within their own walls. It is not their duty to reform, rehabilitate, or reintegrate offenders into society. Though they *may* attempt these things, it is not their *duty* even to attempt these goals, let alone their obligation to achieve them. Prisons ought not to impose upon themselves, by inclusion in a mission statement, any responsibility for inmates' future conduct, welfare, or social adjustment. These are primarily the responsibility of the offenders themselves, and perhaps secondarily a concern of some others outside the justice system. They should not be declared the official business of prisons.

Authors' Notes

1. If the factor has both main and interaction effects, it is either a "risk/responsivity" or a "needs/responsivity" factor, in the terminology of Andrews et al.
2. The progressive ideology of Cullen and his colleagues extends well beyond the role of rehabilitation in prisons. It seeks also to "bring about a more equitable distribution of resources through a broad structural transformation of the social order" (Cullen and Gilbert, 1982:256). Whether these are noble goals or sheer folly depends on one's political perspective.

Discussion Questions

1.   How do Logan and Gaes differ from Palmer (selection #22) in their interpretation of the findings of meta-analyses? According to Logan and Gaes, is meta-analysis basically a flawed method, or has it simply been used inappropriately by researchers

seeking to reaffirm rehabilitation? Why do Logan and Gaes suggest that these researchers might have misused the technique of meta-analysis?

2.   What should be the mission of the prison, according to Logan and Gaes? How does the rehabilitative approach interfere with the achievement of that mission? How could treatment programs exist in prisons dedicated to the mission Logan and Gaes claim they should have?

3.   Is confinement for the purpose of meting out justice inhumane? Is rehabilitation a more humane approach? What evidence is there that the treatment philosophy is a more humane approach than an approach that emphasizes confinement as punishment?

References

Abadinsky, Howard. *Organized Crime.* Boston: Allyn & Bacon, 1981.

Abolafia, Mitchel Y. "Structured Anarchy: Formal Organization in the Commodities Futures Markets," in Patricia Adler and Peter Adler, eds., *The Social Dynamics of Financial Markets.* Greenwich, CT: JAI Press, 1984.

Adams, James Ring. *The Big Fix: Inside the S & L Scandal.* New York: Wiley, 1990.

Adams, Stuart. "Evaluative Research in Corrections: Status and Prospects," *Federal Probation* 38 (1974), 14–21.

Adler, Patricia A. *Wheeling and Dealing: An Ethnography of Upper-Level Drug Dealing and Smuggling Communities.* New York: Columbia University Press, 1985.

Adler, Patricia A., and Peter Adler. "Shifts and Oscillations in Deviant Careers: The Case of Upper-Level Drug Dealers and Smugglers," *Social Problems* 31 (1983), 195–207.

Agnew, Robert. "A Revised Strain Theory of Delinquency," *Social Forces* 64 (1985), 151–67.

Agopian, M. W. "Parental Child Stealing: Participants and the Victimization Process," *Victimology: An International Journal* 5 (1980), 263–73.

Agopian, M. W. *Parental Child Stealing.* Lexington, MA: Lexington Books, 1981.

Akers, Ronald L. "Delinquent Behavior, Drugs, and Alcohol: What Is the Relationship?" *Today's Delinquent* 3 (1984), 19–47.

Albanese, Jay S. "What Lockheed and La Cosa Nostra Have in Common: The Effect of Ideology on Criminal Justice Policy," *Crime & Delinquency* 28 (1982), 211–32.

Alfaro, Jose. "Studying Child Maltreatment Fatalities: A Synthesis of Nine Projects," in D. Besharov, ed., *Protecting Children from Abuse and Neglect: Policy and Practice.* Springfield, IL: Charles C. Thomas, 1988.

Alix, Ernest K. *Ransom Kidnapping in America 1874–1974: The Creation of a Capital Crime.* Carbondale: Southern Illinois University Press, 1978.

Allen, F. A. *The Decline of the Rehabilitative Ideal: Penal Policy and Social Purpose.* New Haven, CT: Yale University Press, 1981.

Allen, John [pseudonym]. *Assault with a Deadly Weapon: The Autobiography of a Street Criminal,* ed. by Dianne Hall Kelly and Philip Heymann. New York: McGraw-Hill, 1978.

Allen, R. E., and J. M. Oliver, "The Effects of Child Maltreatment on Language Development," *Child Abuse and Neglect* 6 (1982), 299–305.

Alt, Konrad, and Kristen Siglin. "Memorandum on Bank and Thrift Fraud to Senate Banking Committee Members and Staff." Unpublished paper, Senate Office Banking Committee, 1990.

Altschuler, David M., and Troy L. Armstrong. *Intensive Community-Based Aftercare Programs: Assessment Report.* Baltimore, MD: Johns Hopkins University Institute for Policy Studies, 1990.

American Friends Service Committee. *Struggle for Justice: A Report on Crime and Punishment in America.* New York: Hill and Wang, 1971.

Anderson, Annelise Graebner. *The Business of Organized Crime: A Cosa Nostra Family.* Stanford, CA: Hoover Institution Press, 1979.

Anderson, Elijah. *A Place on the Corner.* Chicago: University of Chicago Press, 1978.

Anderson, Elijah. *Streetwise: Race, Class, and Change in an Urban Community.* Chicago: University of Chicago Press, 1990.

Andrews, D. A., J. Bonta, and R. D. Hoge. "Classification for Effective Rehabilitation: Rediscovering Psychology," *Criminal Justice and Behavior* 17 (1990), 19–52.

Andrews, D. A., et al. "Does Correctional Treatment Work? A Clinically Relevant and Psychologically Informed Meta-Analysis," *Criminology* 28 (1990a), 369–404.

Andrews, D. A., et al. "A Human Science Approach or More Punishment and Pessimism: A Rejoinder to Lab and Whitehead," *Criminology* 28 (1990b), 419–29.

Anglin, M. Douglas, and Yih-Ing Hser. "Treatment of Drug Abuse," in M. Tonry and J. Q. Wilson, eds., *Drugs and Crime.* Chicago: University of Chicago Press, 1990.

Anglin, M. Douglas, Elizabeth S. Piper, and George Speckart. "The Effect of Legal Supervision on Addiction and Criminal Behavior." Paper presented at the 39th annual meeting of the American Society of Criminology, Montreal, Nov. 1987.

Anglin, M. Douglas, and George Speckart. "Narcotics Use, Property Crime, and Dealing: Structural Dynamics Across the Addiction Career," *Journal of Quantitative Criminology* 2 (1986), 355–75.

Archer, D., and R. Gartner. *Violence and Crime in Cross-National Perspective.* New Haven: Yale University Press, 1984.

Archer, John. "Childhood Gender Roles: Social Context and Organization," in J. McGurk, ed., *Childhood Social Development: Contemporary Perspectives.* Hillsdale, NJ: Lawrence Erlbaum, 1992.

Archer, John. "Violence Between Men," in John Archer, ed., *Male Violence.* London: Routledge, 1994, pp. 121–40.

Archer, John. "Testosterone and Aggression," in M. Hillbrand and N. Pallone, eds., *The Psychobiology of Aggression: Engines, Measurement, and Control.* Binghamton, NY: Haworth, 1995, pp. 3–26.

Archer, John, and N. Ray. "Dating Violence in the United Kingdom: A Preliminary Study," *Aggressive Behaviour* 15 (1989), 337–43.

Arendt, H. *On Violence.* New York: Harcourt Brace & World, 1970.

Ariz. Rev. Stat. Ann. 13-703(F)(4) (Supp. 1989).

Aronow, R., et al. "A Therapeutic Approach to the Acutely Overdosed Patient," *Journal of Psychedelic Drugs* 12 (1980), 259–68.

Asch, Peter, and J. J. Seneca. "Is Collusion Profitable?" *Review of Economics and Statistics* 58 (1969), 1–12.

Athens, L. H. *Violent Criminal Acts and Actors: A Symbolic Interactionist Study.* Boston: Routlege & Kegan Paul, 1977.

Auletta, Ken. *The Underclass.* New York: Random House, 1982.

Austin, James, and Aaron David McVey. *The Impact of the War on Drugs.* San Francisco: National Council on Crime and Delinquency, 1989.

Averill, J. *Anger and Aggression: An Essay on Emotion.* New York: Springer-Verlag, 1982.

Bachman, Jerald, Patrick O'Malley, and Jerome Johnston. *Youth in Transition,* Vol. VI, *Adolescence to Adulthood—Change and Stability in the Lives of Young Men.* Ann Arbor: Institute for Social Research, University of Michigan, 1978.

Bach-y-Rita, G., et al. "Episodic Dyscontrol: A Study of 130 Violent Patients," *American Journal of Psychiatry* 127 (1971), 1473–78.

Bach-y-Rita, G., et al. "Pathological Intoxication. Clinical and Electroencephalographic Studies," *American Journal of Psychiatry* 127 (1970), 698–703.

Bailey, W. C. "Correctional Outcome: An Evaluation of 100 Reports," *Journal of Criminal Law, Criminology and Police Science* 57 (1966), 153–60.

Bakan, D. *The Duality of Human Existence.* Boston: Beacon Press, 1966.

Baldus, David, Charles A. Pulaski, and George Woodworth. "Arbitrariness and Discrimination in the

Administration of the Death Penalty: A Challenge to State Supreme Courts," *Stetson Law Review* 15 (1986), 133.

Baldus, David, George Woodworth, and Charles Pulaski, Jr. "Monitoring and Evaluating Contemporary Death Sentencing Systems: Lessons from Georgia," *University of California Davis Law Review* 18 (1985), 1375.

Baldus, David, George Woodworth, and Charles Pulaski, Jr. *Equal Justice and the Death Penalty.* Boston: Northeastern University Press, 1990.

Ball, John C. "The Hyper-Criminal Opiate Addict," in Bruce D. Johnson and Eric Wish, eds., *Crime Rates Among Drug Abusing Offenders.* Final report to the National Institute of Justice. New York: Narcotic and Drug Research, Inc., 1986.

Ball, John C., John W. Shaffer, and David N. Nurco. "The Day-to-Day Criminality of Heroin Addicts in Baltimore: A Study in the Continuity of Offense Rates," *Drug and Alcohol Dependence* 12 (no. 1, 1983), 119–42.

Bandura, A. *Aggression: A Social Learning Analysis.* Englewood Cliffs, NJ: Prentice-Hall, 1973.

Barkwell, Lawrence J. "Differential Probation Treatment of Delinquency," in R. Ross and P. Gendreau, eds., *Effective Correctional Treatment.* Toronto: Butterworths, 1980, pp. 281–97.

Barnard, George, et al. "Till Death Do Us Part: A Study of Spouse Murder," *Bulletin of the American Academy of Psychiatry and Law* 10 (1982), 271.

Barr, William P. "The Case for More Incarceration." Washington, DC: U. S. Department of Justice, Office of Policy Development, 1992.

Barrett, Michael J. "The Case for More School Days," *Atlantic* 266 (1990), 78–106.

Barton, William H., and Jeffrey A. Butts. "Viable Options: Intensive Supervision Programs for Juvenile Delinquents," *Crime & Delinquency* 36 (1990), 238–56.

Basta, J. M., and W. S. Davidson. "Treatment of Juvenile Offenders: Study Outcomes Since 1980," *Behavioral Sciences and the Law* 6 (1988), 355–84.

Beck, Allen, et al. *Survey of State Prison Inmates, 1991.* Washington, DC: Bureau of Justice Statistics, 1993.

Becker, Howard S. "Notes on the Concept of Commitment," *American Journal of Sociology* 66 (1960), 32–42.

Becker, Howard S. "Conventional Crime: Rationalizations and Punishments," in Howard S. Becker, *Sociological Work: Method and Substance.* Chicago: Aldine, 1970, 329–39.

Bedau, Hugo Adam. *The Death Penalty in America,* 3rd ed. New York: Oxford University Press, 1982.

Bell, Daniel. "Crime as an American Way of Life," in Daniel Bell, ed., *The End of Ideology,* rev. ed. New York: Collier, 1961.

Benignus, V. A., et al. "Effects of Age and Body Lead Burden on CNS Function in Young Children. II: EEG Spectra," *Electroencephalography and Clinical Neurophysiology* 52 (1981), 240–48.

Benoit, Kevin, and Todd R. Clear. *Case Management Systems in Probation.* Washington, DC: U.S. Department of Justice, 1981.

Benson, M. L. "White-Collar Offenders Under Community Supervision," *Justice Quarterly* 2 (1985), 429–38.

Benson, M. L., and F. T. Cullen. "The Special Sensitivity of White-Collar Offenders to Prison: A Critique and Research Agenda," *Journal of Criminal Justice* 16 (1988), 207–15.

Berk, R., et al. "Mutual Combat and Other Family Violence Myths," in D. Finkelhor et al., eds., *The Dark Side of Families: Current Family Violence Research.* Beverly Hills, CA: Sage, 1981.

Berkowitz, L. "The Concept of Aggressive Drive: Some Additional Considerations," in L. Berkowitz, ed., *Advances in Experimental Social Psychology,* Vol. 2. New York: Academic Press, 1965.

Bernstein, Ilene Nagel, William R. Kelly, and Patricia A. Doyle. "Societal Reaction to Deviants: The Case of Criminal Defendants," *American Sociological Review* 42 (1977), 743–55.

Berry-Dee, Christopher, and Robin Odell. *A Question of Evidence.* London: Virgin True Crime, 1992.

Berry-Dee, Christopher, and Robin Odell. *Lady Killer.* London: Virgin True Crime, 1993.

Besag, V. E. *Bullies and Victims.* Milton Keynes, UK: Open University Press, 1980.

Best, Joel. "Rhetoric in Claims-Making: Constructing the Missing Children Problem," *Social Problems* 34 (1987), 101–21.

Best, Joel, ed. *Images of Issues.* Hawthorne, NY: Aldine de Gruyter, 1989.

Best, Joel, and David F. Luckenbill. *Organizing Deviance.* Englewood Cliffs, NJ: Prentice-Hall, 1982.

Bézard, Isabelle. "Images of the Serial Killer 1980–1982," *Memoire de Maitrise.* Paris: University of Paris, Institut d'Anglais Charles V, 1992.

Biederman, J., et al. "A Family Study of Patients with Attention Deficit Disorder and Normal Controls," *Journal of Psychiatric Research* 20 (1986), 263–74.

Biernacki, Patrick. *Pathways from Addiction: Recovery Without Treatment.* Philadelphia: Temple University Press, 1986.

Black, D. "Crime as Social Control," *American Sociological Review* 48 (no. 1, 1983), 34–45.

Blackburn, R. "Psychopathy, Arousal and the Need for Stimulation," in R. D. Hare and D. Schalling, eds., *Psychopathic Behaviour: Approaches to Research.* Chichester, England: Wiley, 1978.

Blakey, G. Robert. "White Collars vs. Organized Crime Act," *Los Angeles Times,* July 22, 1983, part 2, p. 7.

Block, Alan A. "History and the Study of Organized Crime," *Urban Life* 6 (1978), 455–74.

Block, Alan A. *East Side, West Side: Organizing Crime in New York, 1930–1950.* Cardiff, Wales: University College Cardiff Press, 1980.

Block, Carolyn. "Lethal Violence in Chicago over Seventeen Years: Homicides Known to the Police 1965–1981." Chicago: Illinois Criminal Justice Information Authority, 1985.

Block, Richard. *Violent Crime.* Lexington, MA: Lexington, 1977.

Blumstein, Alfred. "On the Racial Disproportionality of United States' Prison Populations" *Journal of Criminal Law and Criminology* 73 (1982), 1259–81.

Blumstein, Alfred. "Making Rationality Relevant— The American Society of Criminology 1992 Presidential Address," *Criminology* 31 (1993a), 1–16.

Blumstein, Alfred. "Racial Disproportionality of U.S. Prison Populations Revisited," *University of Colorado Law Review* 64 (1993b), 743–60.

Blumstein, Alfred, and J. Cohen, with P. Hseih. *The Duration of Adult Criminal Careers.* Washington, DC: National Institute of Justice, 1982.

Blumstein, Alfred, Jacqueline Cohen, and Daniel Nagin. *Deterrence and Incapacitation.* Report of the National Academy of Sciences Panel on Research on Deterrent and Incapacitative Effects. Washington, DC: National Academy Press, 1978.

Blumstein, Alfred, David P. Farrington, and Soumyo Moitra. "Delinquency Careers: Innocents, Desisters, and Persisters," in Michael Tonry and Norval Morris, eds., *Crime and Justice: An Annual Review of Research,* Vol. 6. Chicago: University of Chicago Press, 1985.

Blumstein, Alfred, et al., eds., *Criminal Careers and "Career Criminals".* Washington. DC: National Academy Press, 1986.

Blumstein, Alfred, et al. "Determinants of Sentences," in Alfred Blumstein et al., *Research on Sentencing: The Search for Reform,* Vol. 1. Washington, DC: National Academy Press, 1983.

Bohman, M., et al. "Predisposition to Petty Criminality in Swedish Adoptees: I. Genetic and Environmental Heterogeneity," *Archives of General Psychiatry* 41 (1982), 872–78.

Boritch, Helen, and John Hagan. "Crime and the Changing Forms of Class Control: Policing Public Order in 'Toronto the Good,' 1859–1955," *Social Forces* 66 (1987), 307–35.

Botvin, Gilbert J. "Substance Abuse Prevention: Theory, Practice, and Effectiveness," in M. Tonry and J. Q. Wilson, eds., *Drugs and Crime.* Chicago: University of Chicago Press, 1990.

Bouchard, T. J., Jr., and M. McGue. "Familial Studies of Intelligence: A Review," *Science* 212 (1981), 1055–59.

Bourgois, Phillippe. "In Search of Horatio Alger: Culture and Ideology in the Crack Economy," *Contemporary Drug Problems* 16 (1990), 619–49.

Bowker, L. *Beating Wife Beating.* Lexington, MA: Heath, 1983.

Brace, Charles Loring. *The Dangerous Classes of New York, and Twenty Years' Work Among Them.* New York: Wynkoop, 1872.

Braithwaite, John. *To Persuade or Punish: The Enforcement of Coal Mine Legislation.* Albany: State University of New York Press, 1985a.

Braithwaite, John. "White Collar Crime," *Annual Review of Sociology* 11 (1985b), 1–25.

Braithwaite, John. *Crime, Shame and Reintegration.* Cambridge, England: Cambridge University Press, 1989.

Braithwaite, John, and G. Geis. "On Theory and Action for Corporate Crime Control," in G. Geis, ed., *On White Collar Crime.* Lexington, MA: Heath, 1982, pp. 189–210.

Brenner, Joel Glenn. "S&L Bailout: How Delays Drove Up Cost," *Washington Post,* March 11, 1990, pp. H1, H4–5.

Brook, J. S., et al. "Stability of Personality During Adolescence and Its Relationship to Stage of Drug Use," *Genetic, Social and General Psychology Monographs* 111 (1985), 317–30.

Brown, G. L., et al. "Aggression in Humans Correlates with Cerebrospinal Fluid Amine Metabolites," *Psychiatry Research* 1 (1979), 131–39.

Brown, J. David. "The Professional Ex-: An Alternative for Exiting the Deviant Career," *Sociological Quarterly* 32 (1991), 219–30.

Browne, A. *When Battered Women Kill.* New York: Macmillan/Free Press, 1987.

Brownfield, David. "Social Class and Violent Behavior," *Criminology* 24 (1986), 421–71.

Bryce-Smith, D., and H. A. Waldron, "Lead, Behavior, and Criminality," *The Ecologist* 4 (1974), 367–77.

Bureau of Justice Statistics. *Correctional Populations in the United States, 1985.* Washington, DC: U.S. Department of Justice, Bureau of Justice Statistics, 1987.

Bureau of Justice Statistics. *Correctional Populations in the United States, 1986.* Washington, DC: U.S. Department of Justice, U.S. Department of Justice, 1989a.

Bureau of Justice Statistics. *Correctional Populations in the United States, 1987.* Washington, DC: U.S. Department of Justice, U.S. Department of Justice, 1989b.

Bureau of Justice Statistics. *Criminal Victimization in the United States, 1987.* Washington, DC: U.S. Department of Justice, Bureau of Justice Statistics, 1989c.

Bureau of Justice Statistics. *Correctional Populations in the United States, 1988.* Washington, DC: U.S. Department of Justice, U.S. Department of Justice, 1991a.

Bureau of Statistics. *Correctional Populations in the United States, 1989.* Washington, DC: U.S. Department of Justice, U.S. Department of Justice, 1991b.

Bureau of Justice Statistics. *Correctional Populations in the United States, 1991.* Washington, DC: U.S. Department of Justice, U.S. Department of Justice, 1993.

Bureau of Justice Statistics. *Child Rape Victims, 1992.* Washington, DC: U.S. Department of Justice, 1994a.

Bureau of Justice Statistics. *Murder in Families.* Washington, DC: U.S. Department of Justice, 1994b.

Burgess, Robert L. "Family Violence: Implications from Evolutionary Biology," in T. Hirschi and M. Gottfredson, eds., *Understanding Crime.* Beverly Hills, CA: Sage, 1980, pp. 91–101.

Byrne, James M. "The Future of Intensive Probation Supervision and the New Intermediate Sanctions," *Crime & Delinquency* 36 (1990), 6–41.

Cadoret, R. J., et al. "Adoption Study Demonstrates Two Genetic Pathways to Drug Abuse," *Archives of General Psychiatry* 52 (Jan. 1995), 42–52.

Cadoret, R. J., et al., "Alcoholism and Antisocial Personality: Interrelationships, Genetic and Environmental Factors," *Archives of General Psychiatry* 42 (1985), 161–67.

Cadoret, R. J., et al. "Studies of Adoptees from Psychiatrically Disturbed Biologic Parents. II. Temperament, Hyperactive, Antisocial and Developmental Variables," *Journal of Pediatrics* 87 (1975), 301–306.

Caesar, P. L. "Exposure to Violence in Families of Origin Among Wife Abusers and Maritally Nonviolent Men," *Violence and Victims* 3 (no. 1, 1988), 49–64.

Cahalan, Margaret Werner. *Historical Corrections Statistics in the United States, 1850–1984.* Washington, DC: U.S. Department of Justice, Bureau of Justice Statistics, 1986.

Cal. Penal Code §190.2(a)(11)-(13) (West Supp. 1990).

Calavita, Kitty. "The Demise of the Occupational Safety and Health Administration: A Case Study in Symbolic Action," *Social Problems* 30 (1983), 437–48.

Calavita, Kitty, and Henry N. Pontell. "'Heads I Win, Tails You Lose': Deregulation, Crime and Crisis in the Savings and Loan Industry," *Crime & Delinquency* 36 (1990), 309–41.

Calavita, Kitty, and Henry N. Pontell. "'Other People's Money' Revisited: Collective Embezzlement in the Savings and Loan and Insurance Industries," *Social Problems* 38 (1991), 94–112.

Campbell, Anne. "The Streets and Violence," in A. Campbell and J. Gibbs, eds., *Violent Transactions: The Limits of Personality.* Oxford and Boston: Basil Blackwell, 1986.

Campbell, Anne. *Girls in the Gang.* New York: Basil Blackwell, 1987.

Campbell, Anne. *Men, Women and Aggression.* New York: Basic Books, 1993.

Campbell, Anne, and S. Muncer. "Models of Anger and Aggression in the Social Talk of Women and Men," *Journal for the Theory of Social Behaviour* 17 (1987), 489–512.

Campbell, A., and S. Muncer. "Sex Differences in Aggression: Social Representations and Social

Roles," *British Journal of Social Psychology,* forthcoming.

Campbell, A., S. Muncer, and E. Coyle, "Social Representations of Aggression as an Explanation of Gender Differences: A Preliminary Study," *Aggressive Behaviour* 18 (no. 1, 1992), 95–108.

Campbell, A., S. Muncer, and B. Gorman. "Sex and Social Representations of Aggression: A Communal-Agentic Analysis," *Aggressive Behaviour* 19 (1993), 125–36.

Canadian Sentencing Commission. *Sentencing Reform: A Canadian Approach.* Ottawa: Canadian Government Publishing Centre, 1987.

Cantwell, D. P. "Minimal Brain Dysfunction in Adults: Evidence from Studies of Psychiatric Illness in the Families of Hyperactive Children," in L. Bellak, ed., *Psychiatric Aspects of Minimal Brain Dysfunction in Adults.* New York: Grune and Stratton, 1979, pp. 37–44.

Carlson, N. R., *Physiology of Behavior.* Boston: Allyn & Bacon, 1977.

Carpenter, Cheryl, et al. *Kids, Drugs, Alcohol, and Crime.* Lexington, MA: Lexington Books, 1988.

Carr, James. *Bad.* New York: Herman Graf, 1975.

Carroll, B. J., and M. Steiner. "The Psychobiology of Premenstrual Dysphoria: The Role of Prolactin," *Psychoneuroendocrinology* 3 (1987), 171–80.

Cate, R. M., et al. "Premarital Abuse: A Social Psychological Perspective," *Journal of Family Issues* 3 (1982), 79–90.

Cattell, R. B. *The Inheritance of Personality and Ability: Research Methods and Findings.* New York: Academic Press, 1982.

Chafe, William H. *The Unfinished Journey,* 2nd ed. New York: Oxford University Press, 1991.

Chaiken, Jan M., and Marcia R. Chaiken. *Varieties of Criminal Behavior.* Santa Monica, CA: Rand, 1982.

Chaiken, Marcia, "Crime Rates and Substance Abuse Among Types of Offenders," in Bruce D. Johnson and Eric Wish, eds., *Crime Rates Among Drug-Abusing Offenders.* Final report to the National Institute of Justice. New York: Narcotic and Drug Research, Inc., 1986.

Chaiken, Marcia, ed. *Street Level Enforcement: Examining the Issues.* Washington, DC: U.S. Government Printing Office, 1988.

Chaiken, Marcia R., and Jan M. Chaiken. "Who Gets Caught Doing Crime?" Discussion paper. Washington, DC: Bureau of Justice Statistics, 1985.

Chaiken, Marcia, and Jan M. Chaiken. *Redefining the Career Criminal: Priority Prosecution of High-Rate Dangerous Offenders.* Washington, DC: National Institute of Justice, 1989.

Chaiken, Marcia R., and Bruce D. Johnson. *Characteristics of Different Types of Drug-Involved Offenders.* Washington, DC: National Institute of Justice, 1988.

Chambliss, W. J. "Types of Deviance and the Effectiveness of Legal Sanctions," in W. J. Chambliss, ed., *Criminal Law in Action,* 2nd ed. New York: Wiley, 1984, pp. 398–407.

Chilton, Roland. "Continuity in Delinquency Area Research: A Comparison of Studies for Baltimore, Detroit and Indianapolis," *American Sociological Review* 29 (1964), 71–83.

Chiricos, Theodore G. "Rates of Crime and Unemployment: An Analysis of Aggregate Research Evidence," *Social Problems* 34 (1987), 187–212.

Christiansen, K. O. "A Review of Studies of Criminality Among Twins," in S. A. Mednick and K. O. Christiansen, eds., *Biosocial Bases of Criminal Behavior.* New York: Gardner Press, 1977, pp. 45–88.

Clare, A. W. "Hormones, Behaviour and the Menstrual Cycle," *Journal of Psychosomatic Research* 29 (no. 3, 1985), 225–33.

Clark, John P., and Richard E. Sykes. "Some Determinants of Police Organization and Practice in a Modern Industrial Democracy," in Daniel Glaser, ed., *Handbook of Criminology.* Chicago: Rand McNally, 1974.

Clark, Steve, and Mike Morley. *Murder in Mind: Mindhunting the Serial Killers.* London: Boxtree, 1993.

Clark, Stover. "Pennsylvania Corrections in Context," *Overcrowded Times* 3 (1992), 4–5.

Clarke, Ronald V., and Derek B. Cornish. "Modeling Offenders' Decisions: A Framework for Research and Policy," in Michael Tonry and Norval Morris, eds., *Crime and Justice: An Annual Review of Research,* Vol. 6. Chicago: University of Chicago Press, 1985, pp. 147–85.

Clarke, Stevens H. "North Carolina Prisons Growing," *Overcrowded Times* 3 (1992), 1, 11–13.

Clear, Todd R. "Statistical Prediction in Corrections," *Research in Corrections* 1 (1988), 1–52.

Cleckley, H. *The Mask of Sanity,* 4th ed. St. Louis, MO: Mosby, 1964.

Clinard, Marshall B., and Richard Quinney, eds. *Criminal Behavior Systems: A Typology,* 2nd ed. New York: Holt, Rinehart & Winston, 1973.

Clinard, Marshall B., and Peter Yeager. *Corporate Crime.* New York: Free Press, 1980.

Clinard, Marshall B., et al. *Illegal Corporate Behavior.* Washington, DC: Government Printing Office, 1979.

Cline, V. Privately published monograph. Salt Lake City: Department of Psychology, University of Utah, 1990.

Cloninger, C. R., T. Reich, and S. B. Guze, "The Multifactorial Model of Disease Transmission: II. Sex Differences in the Familial Transmission of Sociopathy (Antisocial Personality)," *British Journal of Psychiatry* 127 (1975), 11–22.

Cloninger, C. R., et al. "Implications of Sex Differences in the Prevalence of Antisocial Personality, Alcoholism, and Criminality for Familial Transmission," *Archives of General Psychiatry* 35 (1978), 941–51.

Cloward, Richard A., and Lloyd E. Ohlin. *Delinquency and Opportunity: A Theory of Delinquent Gangs.* New York: Free Press, 1960.

Coccaro, E. F. "Central Serotonin and Impulsive Aggression," *British Journal of Psychiatry* 115 (Suppl. 8, 1989), 52–62.

Coccaro, E. F., and J. L. Astill. "Central Serotonergic Function in Parasuicide," *Progress in Neuropsychopharmacology and Biological Psychiatry* 14 (1990), 663–74.

Coccaro, E. F., C. S. Bergeman, and G. E. McClearn. "Heritability of Irritable Impulsiveness: A Study of Twins Reared Together and Apart," *Psychiatry Research* 48 (1993), 229–42.

Coe, C. L., and S. Levine. "Biology of Aggression," *Bulletin of the American Academy of Psychiatry Law* 11 (1983), 131–48.

Cohen, Albert. *Delinquent Boys: The Culture of the Gang.* Glencoe, IL: Free Press, 1955.

Cohen, S. "Angel Dust," *Journal of the American Medical Association* 238 (1977), 515–16.

Cohen, S. "Alcoholic Hypoglycemia," *Drug Abuse and Alcoholism Newsletter* 9 (no. 2, 1980), 1–4.

Coid, J. "Mania a Potu: A Critical Review of Pathological Intoxication," *Psychological Medicine* 9 (1979), 709–19.

Coleman, D. H., and M. A. Straus. "Marital Power, Conflict and Violence in a Nationally Representative Sample of American Couples," *Violence and Victims* 1 (no. 2, 1986), 141–57.

Coleman, James S. "Social Capital in the Creation of Human Capital," *American Journal of Sociology* 94 (1988), S94–120.

Coleman, James William. *The Criminal Elite: The Sociology of White Collar Crime.* New York: St. Martin's Press, 1985.

Coleman, James William. "Toward an Integrated Theory of White-Collar Crime," *American Journal of Sociology* 93 (1987), 406–39.

Collins, James J., and Susan L. Bailey. *Early Drug Use and Criminal Careers.* Research Triangle Park, NC: Research Triangle Institute. Mimeographed, 1987.

Collins, James J., et al. *Criminality in a Drug Treatment Sample: Measurement Issues and Initial Findings.* Research Triangle Park, NC: Research Triangle Institute, 1982.

Colo. Rev. Stat. §16-11-103(6)(a) (Supp. 1986).

Colvin, Mark, and John Pauly. "A Critique of Criminology: Toward an Integrated Structural-Marxist Theory of Delinquency Production," *American Journal of Sociology* 89 (1983), 513–51.

Comings, D. E., et al. "The Dopamine D2 Receptor Gene: A Genetic Risk Factor in Substance Abuse," *Drug and Alcohol Dependence* 34 (1994), 175–80.

Congressional Record—Senate. *Statements on Introduced Bills and Joint Resolutions.* Oct. 27, 1983: S14787.

Conklin, John E. *Robbery and the Criminal Justice System.* Philadelphia: Lippincott, 1972.

Conrad, John P. "Research and Development in Corrections: A Thought Experiment," *Federal Probation* 46 (1982), 66–69.

Cook, Philip J. "Reducing Injury and Death Rates in Robbery," *Policy Analysis* 6 (1980a), 21–45.

Cook, Philip J. "Research in Criminal Deterrence: Laying the Groundwork for the Second Decade," in N. Morris and M. Tonry, eds., *Crime and Justice: An Annual Review of Research.* Chicago: University of Chicago Press, 1980b, pp. 211–68.

Cook, Philip J. "The Role of Firearms in Violent Crime: An Interpretive Review of the Literature," in M. E. Wolfgang and N. A. Weiner, eds., *Criminal Violence.* Beverly Hills, CA: Sage, 1982.

Cook, Philip J. "The Relationship Between Victim Resistance and Injury in Noncommercial Robbery," *Journal of Legal Studies* 15 (1986), 405–16.

Cook, Philip J., and D. Nagin. *Does the Weapon Matter?* Washington, DC: Institute for Law and Social Research, 1979.

Cornell Law Review. "Capital Punishment in 1984: Abandoning the Pursuit of Fairness and Consistency," *Cornell Law Review* 69 (1984), 1129.

Cornish, Derek B., and Ronald V. Clarke. "Understanding Crime Displacement: An Application of Rational Choice Theory," *Criminology* 25 (1987), 933–47.

Cressey, Donald. *Theft of the Nation: The Structure and Operations of Organized Crime in America.* New York: Harper & Row, 1969.

Crime Control Digest. "Massachusetts' New Missing Children Law Requires Immediate Reports, Investigations," *Crime Control Digest,* Jan. 14, 1985, p. 10.

Cullen, Francis T. "The Privatization of Treatment: Prison Reform in the 1980s," *Federal Probation* 50 (1986), 8–16.

Cullen, Francis T., and Paul Gendreau. "The Effectiveness of Correctional Rehabilitation: Reconsidering the 'Nothing Works' Debate," in L. Goodstein and D. L. MacKenzie, eds., *The American Prison: Issues in Research and Policy.* New York: Plenum, 1989, pp. 23–44.

Cullen, Francis T., and Karen E. Gilbert. *Reaffirming Rehabilitation.* Cincinnati, OH: Anderson, 1982.

Cullen, Francis T., Martha Todd Larson, and Richard A. Mathers. "Having Money and Delinquency Involvement: The Neglect of Power in Delinquency Theory," *Criminal Justice and Behavior* 12 (1985), 171–92.

Cullen, Francis T., William J. Maakestad, and Gray Cavender. *Corporate Crime Under Attack: The Ford Pinto Case and Beyond.* Cincinnati, OH: Anderson, 1987.

Cummings, Scott, and Daniel J. Monte. *Gangs.* Albany: State University of New York Press, 1993.

Currie, Elliott. *Confronting Crime: An American Challenge.* New York: Pantheon Books, 1985.

Curtis, Lynn A. "Race and Violent Crime: Toward a New Policy," in N. A. Weiner and M. E. Wolfgang, eds., *Violent Crime, Violent Criminals.* Newbury Park, CA: Sage, 1989, pp. 139–70.

Danto, B. "A Psychiatric View of Those Who Kill," in J. Bruhns, K. Bruhns, and H. Austin, eds., *The Human Side of Homicide.* New York: Columbia University Press, 1982, pp. 3–20.

Daro, Deborah, and Leslie Mitchel. "Child Abuse Fatalities Continue to Rise: The Results of the 1988 Annual Fifty State Survey." Report prepared for the National Center of Child Abuse Prevention Research. Washington, DC, 1989.

David, D., and R. Brannon. "The Male Sex-Role: Our Culture's Blueprint of Masculinity and What It's Done for Us Lately," in D. David and R. Brannon, eds., *The Forty-Nine Percent Majority: The Male Sex-Role.* Reading, MA: Addison-Wesley, 1976.

Davidson, J. *Conjugal Crime.* New York: Hawthorne Books, 1978.

Davidson, William S., II, et al. *Interventions with Juvenile Delinquents: A Meta-Analysis of Treatment Efficacy.* Washington, DC: National Institute of Juvenile Justice and Delinquency Prevention, 1984.

Davidson, William S., II., et al. "Diversion of Juvenile Offenders: An Experimental Comparison," *Journal of Consulting and Clinical Psychology* 55 (1987), 68–75.

Davis, B. A., et al. "Correlative Relationship Between Biochemical Activity and Aggressive Behavior," *Progress in Neuro-Psychopharmacology and Biological Psychiatry* 7 (1983), 529–35.

Dee Scofield Awareness Program. *Estimated Annual Missing Children.* Educational Report. Tampa, FL, Nov. 1983a.

Dee Scofield Awareness Program. *Federal Legislation: The First Steps.* Educational Report No. 5. Tampa, FL, 1983b.

Deer, Brian. "Maniacs Who Kill for Pleasure," *Sunday Times* (London), July 27, 1986.

DeFoe, Daniel. *An Effectual Scheme for the Immediate Prevention of Street Robberies and Suppressing of All Other Disorders of the Night.* London, 1730.

DeFries, J. C., and R. Plomin. "Behavioral Genetics," *Annual Reviews in Psychology* 29 (1978), 473–515.

Dembo, Richard, et al. "Heavy Marijuana Use and Crime Among Youths Entering a Juvenile Detention Center," *Journal of Psychoactive Drugs* 19 (1987), 47–56.

Denno, D. W. "Human Biology and Criminal Responsibility: Free Will or Free Ride?" *University of Pennsylvania Law Review* 137 (no. 2, 1988), 615–71.

Deykin, E. Y., J. C. Levy, and V. Wells, "Adolescent Depression, Alcohol and Drug Abuse," *American Journal of Public Health* 76 (1986), 178–82.

Dietz, Mary Lorenz. *Killing for Profit.* Chicago: Nelson-Hall, 1983.

DiIulio, J. J., Jr. *No Escape: The Future of American Corrections.* New York: Basic Books, 1991.

Dobash, R. E., and R. P. Dobash. *Violence Against Wives: A Case Against Patriarchy.* New York: Free Press, 1979.

Dohrenwend, B. P., and B. S. Dohrenwend. "Sex Differences in Psychiatric Disorders," *American Journal of Sociology* 81 (1976), 1447–71.

Dollard, J., et al. *Frustration and Aggression.* New Haven, CT: Yale University Press, 1939.

Domino, E. F. "Neurobiology of Phencyclidine—An Update," in R. C. Peterson and R. C. Stillman, eds., *Phencyclidine (PCP) Abuse: An Appraisal.* NIDA Research Monograph 21. Rockville, MD: National Institute on Drug Abuse, 1978.

Domino, E. F. "History and Pharmacology of PCP and PCP-Related Analogs," *Journal of Psychedelic Drugs* 12 (1980), 223–27.

Dowie, Mark. "Pinto Madness," in Jerome Skolnick and Elliott Currie, eds., *Crisis in American Institutions,* 4th ed. Boston: Little, Brown, 1979.

Downs, Donald A. *The New Politics of Pornography.* Chicago: University of Chicago Press, 1989.

Durkheim, E. "Individual and Collective Representations," in E. Durkheim, ed., *Sociology and Philosophy.* London: Cohen & West, 1953.

Dutton, D. G., and C. E. Strachen. "Motivational Needs for Power and Dominance as Differentiating Variables of Assaultive and Non-assaultive Male Populations," *Violence and Victims* 2 (1987), 145–56.

Eagly, A. *Sex Differences in Social Behavior: A Social Role Analysis.* Hillsdale, NJ: Lawrence Erlbaum, 1987.

Eagly, A., and V. J. Steffen. "Gender and Aggressive Behaviour: A Meta-Analytic Review of the Social Psychological Literature," *Psychological Bulletin* 100 (1986), 309–30.

Edelhertz, Herbert. *The Nature, Impact and Prosecution of White-Collar Crime.* Washington, DC: U.S. Department of Justice, 1970.

Edelhertz, Herbert, and T. D. Overcast, eds. *White Collar Crime: An Agenda for Research.* Lexington, MA: Heath, 1982.

Edsall, Thomas, and Mary Edsall. *Chain Reaction: The Impact of Race, Rights, and Taxes on American Politics.* New York: Norton, 1991.

Egeland, B., A. Stroufe, and M. Erickson. "The Developmental Consequences of Different Patterns of Maltreatment," *Child Abuse and Neglect* 7 (1983), 459–69.

Eichelman, B. S., and N. B. Thoa. "The Aggressive Monoamines," *Biological Psychiatry* 6 (no. 2, 1972), 143–63.

Eichler, Ned. *The Thrift Debacle.* Berkeley: University of California Press, 1989.

Eisenhower Foundation. *Youth Investment and Community Reconstruction.* Washington, DC: Milton S. Eisenhower Foundation, 1990.

Ekland-Olson, Sheldon. "Structured Discretion, Racial Bias and the Death Penalty," *Social Science Quarterly* 69 (1988), 853.

Elbow, M. "Theoretical Considerations of Violent Marriages," *Social Casework* 58 (1977), 515–26.

Ellickson, Phyllis L., and Robert M. Bell. *Prospects for Preventing Drug Abuse Among Young Adolescents.* Santa Monica, CA: Rand, 1990.

Elliott, Delbert S., and David Huizinga. "The Relationship Between Delinquent Behavior and ADM Problems." Proceedings of the Alcohol, Drug Abuse, and Mental Health Administration/Office of Juvenile Justice and Delinquency Prevention Research Conference on Juvenile Offenders with Serious Drug, Alcohol, and Mental Health Problems. Washington, DC, 1985.

Elliott, Delbert S., David Huizinga, and Scott Menard. *Multiple Problem Youth: Delinquency, Drugs, and Mental Health Problems.* New York: Springer-Verlag, 1989.

Ellis, L., and M. A. Ames. "Neurohormonal Functioning and Sexual Orientation: A Theory of Homosexuality–Heterosexuality," *Psychological Bulletin* 101 (1987), 233–58.

Ely, Bert. "Crime Accounts for Only 3% of the Cost of the S&L Mess." Unpublished report, 1990.

Emler, N. "Socio-Moral Development from the Perspective of Social Representations," *Journal for the Theory of Social Behaviour* 17 (1987), 371–88.

Empey, LaMar T. *American Delinquency: Its Meaning and Construction.* Homewood, IL: Dorsey, 1978.

Ermann, M. David, and Richard J. Lundman. *Corporate Deviance.* New York: Holt, Rinehart & Winston, 1982.

Eth, S., and R. S. Pynoos. "Developmental Perspective on Psychic Trauma in Childhood," in C. R. Figley, ed., *Trauma and Its Wake: The Study and Treatment of Post-Traumatic Stress Disorder.* New York: Brunner & Mazel, 1985, pp. 36–52.

Eysenck, Hans. *Crime and Personality.* London: Routledge & Kegan Paul, 1964.

Eysenck, Hans. *Crime and Personality,* rev. ed. London: Paladin, 1977.

Fagan, Jeffrey. "The Social Organization of Drug Use and Drug Dealing Among Urban Gangs," *Criminology* 27 (Nov. 1989), 633–70.

Fagan, Jeffrey. "Social Processes of Delinquency and Drug Use Among Urban Gangs," in C. Ronald Huff, ed., *Gangs in America.* Newbury Park, CA: Sage, 1990.

Fagan, Jeffrey. "Drug Selling and Licit Income in Distressed Neighborhoods: The Economic Lives of Street-Level Drug Users and Dealers," in Adele V. Harrell and George E. Peterson, eds., *Drugs, Crime, and Social Isolation.* Washington, DC: Urban Institute Press, 1991.

Fagan, Jeffrey. "The Political Economy of Drug Dealing Among Urban Gangs," in R. C. Davis, A. J. Lurigio, and D. P. Rosenbaum, eds., *Drugs and the Community.* Springfield, IL: Charles C. Thomas, 1993.

Fagan, Jeffrey, and A. Browne. "Marital Violence: Physical Aggression Between Women and Men in Intimate Relationships." Report to the Panel on Understanding and Control of Violent Behavior, National Academy of Sciences, Washington, DC, 1990.

Fagan, Jeffrey, Martin Forst, and T. Scott Vivona. *Treatment and Reintegration of Violent Juvenile Offenders: Experimental Results.* San Francisco: URSA Institute, 1988.

Fagan, Jeffrey, and Eliot Hartstone. *Innovation and Experimentation in Juvenile Corrections: Implementing a Community Reintegration Model for Violent Juvenile Offenders.* San Francisco: URSA Institute, 1986.

Fagan, Jeffrey, D. Stewart, and K. Hansen. "Violent Men or Violent Husbands? Background Factors and Situational Correlates of Domestic and Extra-Domestic Violence," in D. Finkelhor et al., eds., *The Dark Side of Families.* Beverly Hills, CA: Sage, 1983.

Fagan, Jeffrey, and Joseph G. Weis. *Drug Use and Delinquency Among Inner City Youth.* New York: Springer-Verlag, 1990.

Fagot, B. I., and R. Hagan. "Aggression in Toddlers: Responses to the Assertive Acts of Boys and Girls," *Sex Roles* 12 (no. 314, 1985), 341–51.

Fagot, B. I., et al. "Differential Reactions to the Assertive and Communicative Acts of Toddler Boys and Girls," *Child Development* 56 (1985), 1499–1505.

Farberman, Harvey A. "A Criminogenic Market Structure: The Automobile Industry," *Sociological Quarterly* 16 (1975), 438–57.

Farr, R. "Social Representations: A French Tradition of Research," *Journal for the Theory of Social Behaviour* 17 (1987), 343–70.

Farrington, David P. "Age and Crime," in Michael Tonry and Norval Morris, eds., *Crime and Justice: A Review of Research,* Vol. 7. Chicago: University of Chicago Press, 1986.

Farrington, David P., et al. "Unemployment, School Leaving and Crime," *British Journal of Criminology* 26 (1986), 335–56.

Fauman, M. A., and B. J. Fauman. "Chronic Phencyclidine (PCP) Abuse: A Psychiatric Perspective," *Journal of Psychedelic Drugs* 12 (1980), 307–14.

Faupel, Charles E. *Shooting Dope: Career Patterns of Hard-Core Heroin Users.* Gainesville: University of Florida Press, 1991.

Federal Bureau of Investigation. *Uniform Crime Reports—1985.* Washington, DC: U.S. Government Printing Office, 1986.

Federal Bureau of Investigation. *Uniform Crime Reports—1986.* Washington, DC: U.S. Government Printing Office, 1987.

Federal Bureau of Investigation. *Uniform Crime Reports—1987.* Washington, DC: U.S. Government Printing Office, 1988.

Federal Bureau of Investigation. *Uniform Crime Reports—1988.* Washington, DC: U.S. Government Printing Office, 1989.

Federal Bureau of Investigation. *Uniform Crime Reports—1992.* Washington, DC: U.S. Government Printing Office, 1993.

Feeley, Malcolm. *The Process Is the Punishment.* New York: Russell Sage, 1979.

Feeney, Floyd. "Robbers as Decision-Makers," in Derek B. Cornish and Ronald V. Clarke, eds., *The Reasoning Criminal.* New York: Springer-Verlag, 1986.

Felson, R. B. "Impression Management and the Escalation of Aggression and Violence," *Social Psychology Quarterly* 45 (1982), 245–54.

Felson, R. B. "Patterns of Aggressive Social Interaction," in A. Mummendey, ed., *Social Psychology of Aggression: From Individual Behavior to Social Interaction.* Berlin: Springer-Verlag, 1984.

Felson, R. B. "Sexual Coercion: An Interactionist Approach," in R. Felson and J. Tedeschi, eds., *Aggression and Violence: Social Interactionist Perspectives.* Washington, DC: American Psychological Association, 1993.

Felson, R. B., W. Baccaglini, and G. Gmelch. "Bar Room Brawls: Aggression and Violence in Irish and American Bars," in A. Campbell and J. Gibbs, eds., *Violent Transactions: The Limits of Personality.* Oxford and Boston: Basil Blackwell, 1986, pp. 153–66.

Finkelhor, David, Gerald Hotaling, and Andrea Sedlak. "The Abduction of Children by Strangers and Non-Family Members: Estimating the Incidence Using Multiple Methods," *Journal of Interpersonal Violence* 7 (June 1992), 226–43.

Fishbein, D. H. "Biological Perspectives in Criminology," *Criminology* 28 (1990), 27–72.

Fishbein, D. H. "Medicalizing the Drug War," *Behavioral Sciences and the Law* 9 (1991), 323–44.

Fishbein, D. H. "The Psychobiology of Female Aggression," *Criminal Justice and Behavior* 19 (no. 2, 1992), 99–126.

Fishbein, D. H., D. Lozovsky, and J. H. Jaffe. "Impulsivity, Aggression and Neuroendocrine Responses to Serotonergic Stimulation in Substance Abusers," *Biological Psychiatry* 25 (1989a), 1049–66.

Fishbein, D. H., and S. Pease. *The Dynamics of Drug Abuse.* Boston: Allyn & Bacon, in press.

Fishbein, D. H., et al. "Spontaneous EEG and Brainstem Evoked Response Potentials in Drug Abusers with Histories of Aggressive Behavior," *Biological Psychiatry* 26 (1989b), 595–611.

Fla. Stat. Ann. 921.141(5)(b)-(d) (West. Supp. 1989).

Foreman, J. "Kidnapped! Parental Child-Snatching, A World Problem," *Boston Globe,* March 16, 1980, p. B1.

Fortune, E. P., M. Vega, and I. J. Silverman. "A Study of Female Robbers in a Southern Correctional Institution," *Journal of Criminal Justice* 8 (1980), 317–25.

Frazier, Charles. *Theoretical Approaches to Deviance.* Columbus, OH: Charles Merrill, 1976.

Frazier, Charles, and Thomas Meisenhelder. "Criminality and Emotional Ambivalence: Exploratory Notes on an Overlooked Dimension," *Qualitative Sociology* 8 (1985), 266–84.

Freeman, Richard. "The Relation of Criminal Activity to Black Youth Employment," *The Review of Black Political Economy* 16 (1987), 99–107.

Freeman, Richard. "Crime and the Economic Status of Disadvantaged Young Men." Paper presented to Conference on Urban Labor Markets and Labor Mobility, Airlie House, Warrenton, VA, 1991.

Freeman, Richard, and Harry Holzer. "The Deterioration of Employment and Earnings Opportunities for Less Educated Young Americans: A Review of Evidence." Paper prepared for National Academy of Sciences Panel on High Risk Youth, Washington, DC, 1991.

Freud, S. "Triebe und Triebschicksale," in *Gesammelte Werke,* Vol. 10. London: Imago, 1915, 1946.

Frieze, I. H. "Investigating the Causes and Consequences of Marital Rape," *Signs* 8 (no. 3, 1983), 532–53.

Frieze, I. H., and A. Browne. "Violence in Marriage," in L. Ohlin and M. Tonry, eds., *Family Violence,* Vol. 11, *Crime and Justice: An Annual Review of Research.* Chicago: University of Chicago Press, 1989.

Frieze, I. H., and McHugh, M. C. "Violence in Relation to Power in Marriage." Paper presented to the Association for Women in Psychology. Santa Monica, CA, 1981.

Frodi, A., and J. Smetana. "Abused, Neglected, and Nonmaltreated Preschoolers' Ability to Discriminate Emotions in Others: The Effects of IQ," *Child Abuse and Neglect* 8 (1984), 459–65.

Frost, W. D., and J. R. Averill. "Differences Between Men and Women in the Everyday Experience of Anger," in J. R. Averill, *Anger and Aggression: An Essay on Emotion.* New York: Springer-Verlag, 1982, pp. 281–316.

Fujita, F., E. Diener, and E. Dandvik. "Gender Differences in Negative Affect and Well-Being: The Case for Emotional Intensity," *Journal of Personality and Social Psychology* 61 (1991), 427–34.

Furman v. *Georgia,* 408 U.S. 238 (1972).

Ga. Code Ann. §17-10-30(b)(1), (3), (8) (1982).

Gabor, Thomas, et al. *Armed Robbery: Cops, Robbers, and Victims.* Springfield, IL: Charles C. Thomas, 1987.

Galler, J. R., et al. "The Influence of Early Malnutrition on Subsequent Behavioral Development: II. Classroom Behavior," *Journal of the American Academy of Child Psychiatry* 24 (1983), 16–24.

Gallmeier, Charles P. "Dinosaurs and Prospects: Toward a Sociology of the Compressed Career," in K. M. Mahmoudi, B. W. Parlin, and M. E. Zusman, eds., *Sociological Inquiry: A Humanistic Perspective,* 4th ed. Dubuque, IA: Kendall-Hunt, 1987, pp. 95–103.

Gandossy, Robert P., et al. *Drugs and Crime: A Survey and Analysis of the Literature.* Washington, DC: U.S. Department of Justice, National Institute of Justice, 1980.

Ganley, A. L., and L. Harris, "Domestic Violence: Issues in Designing and Implementing Programs for Male Batterers." Paper presented to the American Psychological Association, Toronto, 1978.

Gans, Herbert. "Deconstructing the Under-Class: The Term's Danger as a Planning Concept," *Journal of the American Planning Association* 56 (1990), 271–77.

Garland, D. *Punishment and Modern Society: A Study in Social Theory.* Chicago: University of Chicago Press, 1990.

Garrett, Carol J. "Effects of Residential Treatment of Adjudicated Delinquents: A Meta-Analysis," *Journal of Research in Crime and Delinquency* 22 (1985), 287–308.

Gaylord, Mark, and John Galliher. *The Criminology of Edwin Sutherland.* New Brunswick, NJ: Transaction Books, 1988.

Geis, Gilbert A., "The Heavy Electrical Equipment Antitrust Case of 1961," in Marshall B. Clinard and Richard Quinney, eds., *Criminal Behavior Systems: A Typology.* New York: Holt, Rinehart & Winston, 1973.

Geis, Gilbert A., "The Heavy Electrical Equipment Antitrust Case of 1961," in G. Geis and R. F. Meier, eds., *White Collar Crime: Offenses in Business, Politics, and the Professions.* New York: Free Press, 1977, pp. 117–32.

Geis, Gilbert. "White-Collar Crime: *What Is It?,* in Kip Schlegel and David Weisburd, eds., *White-Collar Crime Reconsidered.* Boston: Northeastern University Press, 1992.

Geismar, Ludwig L., and Katherine M. Wood. *Family and Delinquency: Resocializing the Young Offender.* New York: Human Sciences, 1985.

Gelles, R. J. *The Violent Home: A Study of Physical Aggression Between Husbands and Wives.* Newbury Park, CA: Sage, 1974.

Gendreau, Paul. "Treatment in Corrections: Martinson Was Wrong!" *Canadian Psychology* 22 (1981), 332–38.

Gendreau, Paul, and D. A. Andrews. *What the Meta-Analysis of the Offender Treatment Literature Tells Us About "What Works."* Ottawa: University of Ottawa, Laboratory for Research on Assessment and Evaluation in Human Services, 1989.

Gendreau, Paul, and D. A. Andrews. "Tertiary Prevention: What the Meta-Analyses of the Offender Treatment Literature Tell Us About 'What Works,'" *Canadian Journal of Criminology* 32 (1990), 173–84.

Gendreau, Paul, and Robert R. Ross. "Effective Correctional Treatment: Bibliotherapy for Cynics," *Crime and Delinquency* 25 (1979), 463–89.

Gendreau, Paul, and Robert R. Ross. "Revivification of Rehabilitation: Evidence from the 1980s," *Justice Quarterly* 4 (1987), 349–407.

General Accounting Office. "Failed Thrifts. Internal Control Weaknesses Create an Environment Conducive to Fraud, Insider Abuse and Related Unsafe Practices." Statement of Frederick D. Wolf, assistant comptroller general, before the Subcommittee on Criminal Justice of the Committee on the Judiciary, U.S. House of Representatives, 1989a.

General Accounting Office. *Thrift Failures. Costly Failures Resulted from Regulatory Violations and Unsafe Practices. Report to the Congress.* GAO/AFMD-89-62. Washington, DC: U.S. General Accounting Office, 1989b.

General Accounting Office. "Resolving the Savings and Loan Crisis: Billions More and Additional Reforms Needed." Testimony of Charles A. Bowsher, comptroller general, before the Committee on Banking, Housing and Urban Affairs, U.S. Senate. GAO/T-AFMD-90-15. Washington, DC: U.S. General Accounting Office, 1990.

Gensheimer, Leah K., et al. "A Meta-Analysis of Intervention Efficacy," in S. Apter and A. Goldstein, eds., *Youth Violence: Programs and Prospects.* New York: Pergamon, 1986, pp. 39–57.

Gerstein, Dean R., and Henrik J. Jarwood. *Treating Drug Problems.* Report of the Committee for Substance Abuse Coverage Study, Division of Health Care Services, National Institute of Medicine. Washington, DC: National Academy Press, 1990.

Ghodsian-Carpey, J., and L. A. Baker. "Genetic and Environmental Influences on Aggression in 4- to 7-Year-Old Twins," *Aggressive Behavior* 13 (1987), 173–86.

Gibbons, Don C. "From the Editor's Desk: A Call for Some 'Outrageous Proposals' for Crime Control in the 1990s," *Crime & Delinquency* 36 (1990), 195–203.

Gillespie, Cynthia. *Justifiable Homicide*. Columbus: Ohio State University Press, 1989.

Gilliard, Darrell K. *National Corrections Reporting Program, 1987*. Washington, DC: U.S. Department of Justice, Bureau of Justice Statistics, 1992.

Gilligan, C. *In a Different Voice: Psychological Theory and Women's Development*. Cambridge, MA: Harvard University Press, 1982.

Gillis, A. R. "Crime and State Surveillance in Nineteenth-Century France," *American Journal of Sociology* 95 (1989), 307–41.

Ginsburg, B. E., and B. F. Carter. *Premenstrual Syndrome: Ethical and Legal Implications in a Biomedical Perspective*. New York: Bantam, 1987.

Girouard, D. "Les Femmes Incarcerées pour Vol Qualifié, en Quebec, en 1985: Importance de Leur Rôle," *Canadian Journal of Criminology,* April 1988.

Glaser, Daniel. "Achieving Better Questions: A Half Century's Progress in Correctional Research," *Federal Probation* 39 (1975), 3–9.

Glueck, Sheldon, and Eleanor Glueck. *Unraveling Juvenile Delinquency*. Cambridge, MA: Harvard University Press, 1950.

Glueck, Sheldon, and Eleanor Glueck. *Delinquents and Nondelinquents in Perspective*. Cambridge, MA: Harvard University Press, 1968.

Goldstein, Paul J. "The Drugs/Violence Nexus: A Tripartite Conceptual Framework," *Journal of Drug Issues* 15 (1985), 493–506.

Goodenough, F. *Anger in Young Children*. Minneapolis: University of Minnesota Press, 1931.

Gottfredson, Donald M., and Michael H. Tonry, eds. *Prediction and Classification*. Chicago: University of Chicago Press, 1987.

Gottfredson, Michael. *Victims of Crime: The Dimensions of Risk*. London: HMSO, 1984.

Gottfredson, Michael R., and Travis Hirschi. "Science, Public Policy, and the Career Paradigm," *Criminology* 26 (1988), 37–55.

Gottfredson, Michael R., and Travis Hirschi. *A General Theory of Crime*. Stanford, CA: Stanford University Press, 1990.

Gough, Harrison G. "A Sociological Theory of Psychopathy," *American Journal of Sociology* 53 (1948), 359–66.

Gove, W., and J. Tudor, "Adult Sex Roles and Mental Illness," *American Journal of Sociology* 78 (1973), 812–35.

Gove, W. R., and C. Wilmoth. "Risk, Crime and Physiological Highs: A Consideration of Neurological Processes Which May Act as Positive Reinforcers," in L. Ellis and H. Hoffman, eds., *Evolution, The Brain and Criminal Behavior: A Reader in Biosocial Criminology*. New York: Praeger, 1990.

Graziano, Anthony M., and Kevin C. Mooney. *Children and Behavior Therapy*. Chicago: Aldine, 1984.

Greenberg, D. F. "The Correctional Effects of Corrections: A Survey of Evaluations," in D. F. Greenberg, ed., *Corrections and Punishment*. Newbury Park, CA: Sage, 1977, pp. 111–48.

Greenwood, Peter. "The Incapacitative/Deterrent Role of Increased Criminal Penalties," *Proceedings of the Attorney-General's Crime Conference 85*. Sacramento: California Department of Justice, 1985.

Greenwood, Peter, and Franklin E. Zimring. *One More Chance: The Pursuit of Promising Intervention Strategies for Chronic Juvenile Offenders*. Santa Monica, CA: Rand, 1985.

Grogger, Jeff. "The Effect of Arrest on the Employment Outcomes of Young Men." Unpublished manuscript, University of California at Santa Barbara, 1991.

Gross, Samuel, and Robert Mauro. *Death and Discrimination*. Boston: Northeastern University Press, 1989.

Gurin, G., J. Veroff, and S. Feld. *Americans View Their Mental Health: A Nationwide Interview Survey*. New York: Basic Books, 1960.

Guze, S. B., et al. "Psychiatric Illness in the Families of Convicted Criminals: A Study of 519 First-Degree Relatives," *Diseases of the Nervous System* 28 (1967), 651–59.

Hagan, John. *Structural Criminology*. New Brunswick, NJ: Rutgers University Press, 1989.

Hagan, John. "Destiny and Drift: Subcultural Preferences, Status Attainments, and the Risks and

Rewards of Youth," *American Sociological Review* 56 (1991), 567–82.

Hagan, John, and Celesta Albonetti. "Race, Class and the Perception of Criminal Injustice in America," *American Journal of Sociology* 88 (1982), 329–55.

Hagan, John, and Kristin Bumiller. "Making Sense of Sentencing: A Review and Critique of Sentencing Research," in Alfred Blumstein et al., eds., *Research on Sentencing: The Search for Reform,* Vol. II. Washington, DC: National Academy Press, 1983.

Hagan, John, A. R. Gillis, and John Simpson. "The Class Structure of Gender and Delinquency: Toward a Power-Control Theory of Common Delinquent Behavior," *American Journal of Sociology* 90 (1985), 1151–78.

Hagan, John, and Fiona Kay. "Gender and Delinquency in White-Collar Families: A Power-Control Perspective," *Crime & Delinquency* 36 (1990) 391–407.

Hagan, John, Ilene H. Nagel (Bernstein), and Celesta Albonetti. "The Differential Sentencing of White-Collar Offenders in Ten Federal District Courts," *American Sociological Review* 45 (1980), 802–20.

Hagan, John, and Alberto Palloni. "The Social Reproduction of a Criminal Class in Working Class London, Circa 1950–1980," *American Journal of Sociology* 96 (1990), 265–99.

Hagan, John, and Patricia Parker. "White Collar Crime and Punishment: The Class Structure and Legal Sanctioning of Securities Violations," *American Sociological Review* 50 (1985), 302–16.

Hagedorn, John M.. *People and Folks: Gangs, Crime and the Underclass in a Rustbelt City.* Chicago: Lakeview Press, 1988.

Hagedorn, John M. "Gangs, Neighborhoods, and Public Policy," *Social Problems* 38 (1991), 529–42.

Hamid, Ansley. "The Political Economy of Crack-Related Violence," *Contemporary Drug Problems* 17 (no. 1, 1990), 31–78.

Hamid, Ansley. "The Development Cycle of a Drug Epidemic: The Cocaine Smoking Epidemic of 1981–1991," *Journal of Psychoactive Drugs* 24 (1992), 337–48.

Hamilton, Stephen F. *Apprenticeship for Adulthood: Preparing Youth for the Future.* New York: Free Press, 1990.

Hamparian, D. M., et al. *The Violent Few: A Study of Dangerous Juvenile Offenders.* Lexington, MA: Lexington/Heath, 1978.

Hannerz, Ulf. *Soulside: Inquiries into Ghetto Culture and Community.* New York: Columbia University Press, 1969.

Hanson, Bill, et al. *Life with Heroin: Voices from the Inner City.* Lexington, MA: Lexington Books, 1985.

Haran, James F. *The Loser's Game: A Sociological Profile of 500 Armed Bank Robbers.* Ph.D. dissertation, Department of Sociology, Fordham University, 1982.

Hare, R. D. *Psychopathy: Theory and Research.* New York: Wiley, 1970.

Hare, R. D., and D. Schalling. *Psychopathic Behavior.* New York: Wiley, 1978.

Harlow, C. W. *Special Report: Robbery Victims.* Washington, DC: Bureau of Justice Statistics, 1987.

Harris, Mervyn. *The Dilly Boys.* Rockville, MD: New Perspectives, 1974.

Harrison, Bennett, and Barry Bluestone. *The Great U-Turn.* New York: Basic Books, 1988.

Harrison, Shirley. *The Diary of Jack the Ripper.* New York: Hyperion, 1993.

Harry, B., and C. Balcer. "Menstruation and Crime: A Critical Review of the Literature from the Clinical Criminology Perspective," *Behavioral Sciences and the Law* 5 (no. 3, 1987), 307–22.

Haskett, R. F. "Premenstrual Dysphoric Disorder: Evaluation, Pathophysiology and Treatment," *Progress in Neuro-Psychopharmacology and Biological Psychiatry* 11 (1987), 129–35.

Hawkins, Gordon. "Organized Crime and God," in Norval Morris and Gordon Hawkins, eds., *The Honest Politician's Guide to Crime Control.* Chicago: University of Chicago Press, 1969.

Hay, George, and Daniel Kelly. "An Empirical Survey of Price-Fixing Conspiracies," *Journal of Law and Economics* 17 (1974), 13–39.

Hazelwood, R. R., and J. Warren. "The Serial Rapist: His Characteristics and Victims," *FBI Law Enforcement Bulletin,* Jan. 1989, pp. 10–17.

Hedges, L. V., and I. Olkin. *Statistical Methods for Meta-Analysis.* San Diego: Academic Press, 1985.

Herzberger, S. "Social Cognition and the Transmission of Abuse," in D. Finkelhor et al., eds., *The Dark Side of Families.* Beverly Hills, CA: Sage, 1983.

Herzlich, C. *Health and Illness: A Social Psychological Analysis.* London: Academic Press, 1973.

Hill, G. Christian. "A Never Ending Story: An Introduction to the S&L Symposium," *Stanford Law and Policy Review* 2 (1990), 21–24.

Hindelang, Michael J. "Age, Sex, and the Versatility of Delinquent Involvements," *Social Problems* 18 (1971), 522–35.

Hindelang, Michael J. *Criminal Victimization in Eight American Cities: A Descriptive Analysis of Common Theft and Assault.* Washington, DC: Law Enforcement Assistance Administration, 1976.

Hindelang, Michael J. "Race and Involvement in Common Law Personal Crimes," *American Sociological Review* 43 (1978), 93–108.

Hindelang, Michael J. "Variations in Sex-Race-Age-Specific Incidence Rates of Offending," *American Sociological Review* 46 (1981), 461–74.

Hindelang, Michael J., Michael R. Gottfredson, and James Garofalo. *Victims of Personal Crime.* Cambridge, MA: Ballinger, 1978.

Hindelang, Michael J., Travis Hirschi, and Joseph G. Weis, "Correlates of Delinquency," *American Sociological Review* 44 (1979), 995–1014.

Hindelang, Michael J., Travis Hirschi, and Joseph G. Weis. *Measuring Delinquency.* Beverly Hills, CA: Sage, 1981.

Hirschi, Travis. *Causes of Delinquency.* Berkeley: University of California Press, 1969.

Hirschi, Travis. "Social Class and Crime," in Gerald W. Thielbar and Saul D. Feldman, eds., *Issues in Social Inequality.* Boston: Little, Brown, 1972.

Hirschi, Travis, and M. Gottfredson. "Causes of White Collar Crime," *Criminology* 25 (1987), 949–74.

Home Office. *Protecting the Public.* London: H. M. Stationery Office, 1990.

Horowitz, Ruth. *Honor and the American Dream: Culture and Identity in a Chicano Community.* New Brunswick, NJ: Rutgers University Press, 1983.

Hotaling, G. T., and D. B. Sugarman. "An Analysis of Risk Markers in Husband to Wife Violence: The Current State of Knowledge," *Violence and Victims* 1 (no. 2, 1986), 101–24.

House, T. H., and W. L. Milligan, "Autonomic Responses to Modeled Distress in Prison Psychopaths," *Journal of Personality and Social Psychology* 34 (1976), 556–60.

Howard, R. C. "The Clinical EEG and Personality in Mentally Abnormal Offenders," *Psychological Medicine* 14 (1984), 569–80.

Howell, Joseph T. *Hard Living on Clay Street: Portraits of Blue Collar Families.* New York: Anchor Press, 1973.

Huff, C. Ronald. *Gangs in America.* Newbury Park, CA: Sage, 1990.

Hughes, Everett C. "Dilemmas and Contradictions in Status," *American Journal of Sociology* 50 (1945), 353–59.

Hunt, Dana. "Drugs and Consensual Crimes: Drug Dealing and Prostitution," in Michael Tonry and James Q. Wilson, eds., *Drugs and Crime,* Vol. 13 of *Crime and Justice: A Review of Research.* Chicago: University of Chicago Press, 1990.

Hunt, David. *Matching Models in Education.* Toronto: Ontario Institute for Studies in Education, 1971.

Ignatieff, Michael. *A Just Measure of Pain: The Penitentiary in the Industrial Revolution, 1750–1850.* New York: Pantheon Books, 1978.

In re Nehra v. Uhlar, 43 N.Y. 2d 242, 1977.

Inciardi, James A. *Careers in Crime.* Chicago: Rand McNally, 1975.

Inciardi, James A. "Beyond Cocaine: Basuco, Crack, and Other Coca Products." Paper presented at the annual meeting of the Criminal Justice Sciences Association. St. Louis, MO, March 1987.

Inciardi, James A. "The Crack–Violence Connection Within a Population of Hardcore Adolescent Offenders," in M. De La Rosa, E. Y. Lambert, and B. Gropper, eds., *Drugs and Violence: Causes, Correlates, and Consequences.* Rockville, MD: National Institute on Drug Abuse, 1990, pp. 92–111.

Innes, Christopher A. *Profile of State Prison Inmates, 1986.* Special report. Washington, DC: Bureau of Justice Statistics, 1988.

Irwin, John. *The Felon.* Englewood Cliffs, NJ: Prentice-Hall, 1970.

Izzo, R. L., and R. R. Ross. "Meta-Analysis of Rehabilitation Programs for Juvenile Delinquents," *Criminal Justice and Behavior* 17 (1990), 134–42.

Jackson, Brooks. *Honest Graft: Big Money and the American Political Process.* New York: Alfred A. Knopf, 1988.

Jankowski, Martín Sánchez. *Islands in the Street: Gangs and American Urban Society.* Berkeley: University of California Press, 1991.

Jaspars, J. M. F., and C. Fraser. "Attitudes and Social Representations," in R. M. Farr and S. Moscovici, eds., *Social Representations.* New York: Cambridge University Press, 1984.

Jencks, Christopher, and Susan E. Mayer. "The Social Consequences of Growing Up in a Poor Neighborhood," in Lawrence Lynn and Michael

McGeary, eds., *Inner-City Poverty in the United States.* Washington, DC: National Academy Press, 1990.

Jencks, Christopher, et al. *Inequality: A Reassessment of the Effect of Family and Schooling in America.* New York: Basic Books, 1972.

Jenkins, Philip. "Myth and Murder: The Serial Murder Panic of 1983–1985," *Criminal Justice Research Bulletin* 3 (1988, no. 11), 1–7.

Jenkins, Philip. "Changing Perceptions of Serial Murder in Contemporary England," *Journal of Contemporary Criminal Justice* 7 (no. 4, 1991), 210–31.

Jenkins, Philip. *Intimate Enemies: Moral Panics in Contemporary Great Britain.* Hawthorne, NY: Aldine de Gruyter, 1992.

Jensen, Gary F., and Kevin Thompson. "What's Class Got to Do With It? A Further Examination of Power-Control Theory," *American Journal of Sociology* 95 (1990), 1009–23.

Jesness, Carl F., and Robert F. Wedge. *Manual for Youth Counselors.* Sacramento: California Youth Authority, 1983.

Jessor, Richard, John Donovan, and Frances Costa. *Beyond Adolescence: Problem Behavior and Young Adult Development.* New York: Cambridge University Press, 1991.

Joe, George W., and D. Dwayne Simpson. "Mortality Rates Among Opioid Addicts in a Longitudinal Study," *American Journal of Public Health* 77 (1987), 347–48.

Johnson, Bruce D., et al. *Taking Care of Business: The Economics of Crime by Heroin Abusers.* Lexington, MA: Lexington Books, 1985.

Johnson, Richard E. "Social Class and Delinquent Behavior: A New Test," *Criminology* 18 (1980), 86–93.

Johnston, D. A. "Psychological Observations of Bank Robbery," *American Journal of Psychiatry* 135 (1978), 1377–79.

Johnston, Lloyd D., Patrick M. O'Malley, and Jerald G. Bachman. *Use of Licit and Illicit Drugs by America's High School Students, 1975–84.* Rockville, MD: National Institute on Drug Abuse, 1985.

Johnston, Lloyd D., Patrick M. O'Malley, and Jerald G. Bachman. *Drug Use Among American High School Students, College Students, and Other Young Adults, National Trends Through 1985.* Rockville, MD: National Institute on Drug Abuse, 1986.

Joyce, I. *Never Talk to Strangers: A Book About Personal Safety.* Racine, WI: Western Publishing Company, 1967.

Juvenile Justice Digest. "Kidnapping and Abuse: Rep. Hyde Seeks Life in Prison or Mandatory Death Sentence for Crimes Against Children," *Juvenile Justice Digest,* July 1, 1985a, p. 4.

Juvenile Justice Digest. "National Campaign to Locate Abducted Children Enters Phase II," *Juvenile Justice Digest,* Feb. 25, 1985b, p. 2.

Kagan, Robert, and John Scholz. "The Criminology of the Corporation and Regulatory Enforcement Strategies," in K. Hawkins and J. Thomas, eds., *Enforcing Regulation.* Boston: Kluwer-Nijhoff Publishing, 1984.

Kandel, Denise B., Ora Simcha-Fagan, and Mark Davies. "Risk Factors for Delinquency and Illicit Drug Use from Adolescence to Young Adulthood," *Journal of Drug Issues* 16 (1986), 67–90.

Kantor, G. K., and M. A. Straus. "The 'Drunken Bum' Theory of Wife Beating," *Social Problems* 34 (1987), 213–31.

Kappeler, V. E., and J. B. Vaughn. "The Myth and Fear of Child Abduction: Defining the Problem and Solutions," *The Justice Professional* 3 (no. 1, 1988), 56–69.

Katz, Jack. "Legality and Equality: Plea-Bargaining in the Prosecution of White-Collar and Common Crime," *Law and Society Review* 13 (1979), 431–59.

Katz, Jack. "The Social Movement Against White-Collar Crime," *Criminology Review Yearbook* 2 (1980), 161–84.

Katz, Jack. *Seductions of Crime: Moral and Sensual Attractions in Doing Evil.* New York: Basic Books, 1988.

Kefauver, Estes. *Crime in America.* New York: Greenwood Press, 1968.

Keiser, R. Lincoln. *The Vice Lords.* New York: Holt, Rinehart & Winston, 1979.

Kellam, S. G., M. E. Ensminger, and M. B. Simon. "Mental Health in First Grade and Teenage Drug, Alcohol, and Cigarette Use," *Drug and Alcohol Dependence* 5 (1980), 273–304.

Kessler, Ronald. *The FBI.* New York: Pocket Books, 1993.

Kiloh, L. G., A. J. McComas, and J. W. Osselton. *Clinical Electroencephalography,* 3rd ed. London: Butterworths, 1972.

Kitsuse, John I., and Joseph W. Schneider, "Preface," in Joel Best, ed., *Images of Issues.* Hawthorne, NY: Aldine de Gruyter, 1989, pp. xi–xiii.

Kleiman, Mark A. R., and Kerry D. Smith, "State and Local Drug Enforcement: In Search of a Strategy," in Michael Tonry and James Q. Wilson, eds., *Drugs and Crime,* Vol. 13 of *Crime and Justice: A Review of Research.* Chicago: University of Chicago Press, 1990.

Klein, Malcolm W. *Street Gangs and Street Workers.* Englewood Cliffs, NJ: Prentice-Hall, 1971.

Klein, Malcolm W. "Offense Specialization and Versatility Among Juveniles," *British Journal of Criminology* 24 (1984), 185–94.

Klein, Malcolm W. "The New Street Gang . . . Or Is It?" *Contemporary Sociology* 21 (1992), 80–82.

Klein, Malcolm W., and Cheryl L. Maxson. "Gangs and Cocaine Trafficking," in Craig Uchida and Doris Mackenzie, eds., *Drugs and the Criminal Justice System.* Newbury Park, CA: Sage, 1993.

Klein, Malcolm W., Cheryl L. Maxson, and Lea C. Cunningham. "Crack, Street Gangs, and Violence," *Criminology* 29 (1991), 623–50.

Klein, Stephen, Joan Petersilia, and Susan Turner. "Race and Imprisonment Decisions in California," *Science* 247 (1990), 812–16.

Kohn, Melvin. *Class and Conformity.* Chicago: University of Chicago Press, 1977.

Kreuz, L. E., and R. M. Rose. "Assessment of Aggressive Behavior and Plasma Testosterone in a Young Criminal Population," *Psychomatic Medicine* 34 (1971), 321–32.

Kriesberg, Louis. "National Security and Conduct in the Steel Industry," *Social Forces* 34 (1956), 268–77.

Krisberg, Barry A., et al. *Demonstration of Post-Adjudication Non-residential Intensive Supervision Programs: Assessment Report.* San Francisco: National Council on Crime and Delinquency, 1989.

Kruttschnitt, C. "Gender and Interpersonal Violence." Report to the Panel on the Understanding and Control of Violent Behavior, National Academy of Sciences, Washington, DC, 1990.

Ky. Rev. Stat. Ann. §532.025(2)(a)(6) (Baldwin 1989).

La. Code Crim. Proc. Ann. art. 905.4(A)(7) (West Supp. 1989).

Lab, S. P., and J. T. Whitehead. "From 'Nothing Works' to 'The Appropriate Works': The Latest Stop on the Search for the Secular Grail," *Criminology* 28 (1990), 405–17.

Langan, Patrick A. "Racism on Trial: New Evidence to Explain the Racial Composition of Prisons in the United States," *Journal of Criminal Law and Criminology* 76 (1985), 666–83.

Langan, Patrick A. *Race of Persons Admitted to State and Federal Institutions, 1926–86.* Washington, DC: U.S. Department of Justice, Bureau of Justice Statistics, 1991.

Larson, C. J. *Crime, Justice and Society.* New York: General Hall, 1984.

Larzelere, Robert E., and Gerald R. Patterson. "Parental Management: Mediator of the Effect of Socioeconomic Status on Early Delinquency," *Criminology* 28 (1990), 301–24.

Laub, John, and M. Joan McDermott. "An Analysis of Crime by Young Black Women," *Criminology* 23 (1985), 81–98.

Lejeune, R. "The Management of a Mugging," *Urban Life* 6 (no. 2, 1977), 123–48.

Lemann, Nicholas. "The Origins of the Underclass," *The Atlantic,* Part I, June 1986, 31–55; Part II, July 1986, 54–68.

Lerman, Paul. *Community Treatment and Social Control: A Critical Analysis of Juvenile Correctional Policy.* Chicago: University of Chicago Press, 1975.

Lester, M. L., and D. H. Fishbein. "Nutrition and Neuropsychological Development in Children," in R. Tarter, D. H. Van Thiel, and K. Edwards, eds., *Medical Neuropsychology: The Impact of Disease on Behavior.* New York: Plenum, 1987.

Levi, Michael. *Phantom Capitalists: The Organisation and Control of Long-Firm Fraud.* London: Heinemann, 1981.

Levi, Michael. "Giving Creditors the Business: The Criminal Law in Inaction," *International Journal of the Sociology of Law* 12 (1984), 321–33.

Levi, Michael. "Crisis? What Crisis? Reactions to Commercial Fraud in the United Kingdom," *Contemporary Crises* 11 (1987), 207–21.

Liebow, Elliot. *Tally's Corner: A Study of Negro Streetcorner Men.* Boston: Little, Brown, 1967.

Lincoln, Yvonna S., and Egon G. Guba. *Naturalistic Inquiry.* Beverly Hills, CA: Sage, 1985.

Linder, R. L., S. E. Lerner, and R. S. Burns. "The Experience and Effects of PCP Abuse," in R. L. Linder, S. E. Lerner, and R. S. Burns, *The Devil's Dust: Recognition, Management, and Prevention of Phencyclidine Abuse.* Belmont, CA: Wadsworth, 1981.

Linnoila, M., et al. "Low Cerebrospinal Fluid 5-Hydroxyindoleacetic Acid Concentration Differentiates Impulsive from Nonimpulsive Violent Behavior," *Life Sciences* 33 (1983), 2609–14.

Lipsey, Mark W. "Juvenile Delinquency Intervention," in H. S. Bloom, D. S. Cordray, and R. J. Light, eds., *Lessons from Selected Program and Policy Areas*. San Francisco: Jossey-Bass, 1988.

Lipsey, Mark W. "The Efficacy of Intervention for Juvenile Delinquency." Paper presented at the annual meeting of the American Society of Criminology, Reno, NV, Nov. 1989.

Lipsey, Mark W. "Juvenile Delinquency Treatment: A Meta-Analytic Inquiry into the Variability of Effects." Paper presented for the Research Synthesis Committee of the Russell Sage Foundation, 1990.

Lipsey, Mark W. *Juvenile Delinquency Treatment: A Meta-Analytic Inquiry into the Viability of Effects*. New York: Russell Sage, 1991.

Lipton, Douglas R., Robert Martinson, and Judith Wilks. *The Effectiveness of Correctional Treatment: A Survey of Treatment Evaluation Studies*. New York: Praeger, 1975.

Littleton, Christine A. "Restructuring Sexual Equality," *California Law Review* 75 (1987), 1279.

Lloyd, B., and C. Smith. "The Effects of Age and Gender on Social Behaviour in Very Young Children," *British Journal of Social Psychology* 25 (1986), 219–30.

Loeber, R., and T. Dishion. "Early Predictors of Male Delinquency: A Review," *Psychological Bulletin* 94 (1983), 68–99.

Loeber, R., T. Dishion, and Magda Stouthamer-Loeber. "Family Factors as Correlates and Predictors of Juvenile Conduct Problems and Delinquency," in M. Tonry and N. Morris, eds., *Crime and Justice: An Annual Review of Research*, Vol. 7. Chicago: University of Chicago Press, 1986, pp. 29–149.

Logan, C. H. "Evaluation Research in Crime and Delinquency: A Reappraisal," *Journal of Criminal Law, Criminology and Police Science* 63 (1972), 378–87.

Logan, C. H. *Well Kept: Comparing Quality of Confinement in a Public and a Private Prison*. Washington, DC: National Institute of Justice, 1991.

Logan, C. H., et al. *Can Meta-Analysis Save Correctional Rehabilitation?* Washington, DC: Federal Bureau of Prisons, 1991.

Lorenz, K. *On Aggression*. London: Methuen, 1966.

Los Angeles Times. "Jones Day's Chief to Step Down; Successor Named," Nov. 10, 1992, p. D7.

Lowi, Theodore. *The End of Liberalism*. New York: Norton, 1969.

Luckenbill, D. F. "Criminal Homicide as a Situated Transaction," *Social Problems* 25 (1977), 176–86.

Luckenbill, D. F. "Patterns of Force in Robbery," *Deviant Behavior* 1 (1980), 361–78.

Luckenbill, D. F. "Generating Compliance: The Case of Robbery," *Urban Life* 10 (1981), 25–46.

Maccoby, E. *Social Development: Psychological Growth and the Parent-Child Relationship*. New York: Harcourt Brace Jovanovich, 1980.

Maccoby, E. "Gender as a Social Category," *Developmental Psychology* 24 (1988), 755–65.

MacCoun, Robert, and Peter Reuter. "Are the Wages of Sin $30 an Hour? Economic Aspects of Street-Level Drug Dealing," *Crime & Delinquency* 38 (1992), 477–491.

MacLeod, Jay. *Ain't No Makin' It: Leveled Aspirations in a Low-Income Neighborhood*. Boulder: Westview, 1987.

Maletsky, B. M. "The Diagnosis of Pathological Intoxication," *Journal of Studies on Alcohol* 37 (1976), 1215–28.

Maltz, D., and R. Borker. "A Cultural Approach to Male–Female Miscommunication," in J. Gumperz, ed., *Language and Social Identity*. New York: Cambridge University Press, 1982.

Maltz, Michael D. "On Defining 'Organized Crime': The Development of a Definition and a Typology," *Crime & Delinquency* 22 (1976), 338–46.

Mande, Mary J., and Kim English. *Individual Crime Rates of Colorado Prisoners*. Denver: Colorado Department of Public Safety, Division of Criminal Justice, 1988.

Mann, K. "Sanctioning White Collar Offenders." Paper presented to the School of Criminal Justice, Rutgers, the State University of New Jersey, Feb. 1989.

Mann, Paul. "The Net Tightens on 'Family' Killers," *New Idea*, Sept. 23, 1989.

Marinacci, A. A. "Special Types of Temporal Lobe Seizures Following Ingestion of Alcohol," *Bulletin of the Los Angeles Neurological Society* 28 (1963), 241–50.

Marks, Carole. "The Urban Underclass," *Annual Review of Sociology* 17 (1991), 445–66.

Marrs-Simon, P. A., et al. "Analysis of Sexual Disparity of Violent Behavior in PCP Intoxication,"

Veterinary and Human Toxicology 30 (no. 1, 1988), 53–55.

Marsh, P., and A. Campbell. *Final Report to Whitbread Ltd.* Oxford, England: Contemporary Violence Research Centre, 1979.

Marsh, P., E. Rosser, and R. Harre. *The Rules of Disorder.* London: Routledge & Kegan Paul, 1978.

Marshall, L. L., and P. Rose. "Gender, Stress and Violence in the Adult Relationships of a Sample of College Students," *Journal of Personal and Social Relationships* 4 (1987), 299–316.

Martin, Susan E., Lee B. Sechrest, and Robin Redner. *New Directions in the Rehabilitation of Criminal Offenders.* Washington, DC: National Academy Press, 1981.

Martinson, R. "What Works? Questions and Answers About Prison Reform." *The Public Interest* 35 (1974), 22–54.

Matsueda, Ross. "Testing Control Theory and Differential Association: A Causal Modeling Approach," *American Sociological Review* 47 (1982), 489–504.

Matsueda, Ross, and Karen Heimer. "Race, Family Structure and Delinquency: A Test of Differential Association and Social Control Theories," *American Sociological Review* 52 (1987), 826–40.

Mattes, J. A., and M. Fink. "A Family Study of Patients with Temper Outbursts," *Journal of Psychiatric Research* 21 (1987), 249–55.

Matza, David. *Delinquency and Drift.* New York: Wiley, 1964.

Matza, David. "The Disreputable Poor," in Reinhard Bendix and Seymour M. Lipset, eds., *Class, Status and Power.* New York: Free Press, 1966.

Mayer, Jeffrey P., et al. "Social Learning Treatment Within Juvenile Justice," in S. Apter and A. Goldstein, eds., *Youth Violence: Problems and Prospects.* New York: Pergamon, 1986, pp. 24–38.

Mayer, Martin. *The Greatest Ever Bank Robbery: The Collapse of the Savings and Loan Industry.* New York: Charles Scribner's Sons, 1990.

McCardle, L., and D. H. Fishbein. "The Self-Reported Effects of PCP on Human Aggression," *Addictive Behaviors* 4 (no. 4, 1989), 465–72.

McCarthy, Bill, and John Hagan. "Homelessness: A Criminogenic Situation?" *British Journal of Criminology* 31 (Autumn 1991), 393–410.

McClelland, D. C. *The Achieving Society.* New York: Free Press, 1961.

McClelland, D. C. *Power: The Inner Experience.* New York: Irvington Publishers, 1975.

McClintock, F. H., and T. B. Haden. "Law and Social Control Systems: A Functional Analysis," in J. A. Jolowicz, ed., *The Division and Classification of the Law.* London: Butterworth, 1970.

McCord, Joan. "Some Child-Rearing Antecedents of Criminal Behavior in Adult Men," *Journal of Personality and Social Psychology* 37 (1979), 1477–86.

McCord, William, and Joan McCord. *Origins of Crime: A New Evaluation of the Cambridge–Somerville Study.* New York: Columbia University Press, 1959.

McCoy, M. *Parental Kidnapping: Issues Brief No. ID 77117.* Washington, DC: Congressional Research Service, 1978.

McDonald, Douglas, and Ken Carlson. *Sentencing in the Federal Courts: Does Race Matter?* Washington, DC: Department of Justice, Bureau of Justice Statistics, 1993.

Mealey, L. "The Sociobiology of Sociopathy: An Integrated Evolutionary Model," *Behavioral and Brain Sciences,* forthcoming.

Mednick, S. A., W. F. Gabrielli, Jr., and B. Hutchings. "Genetic Influences in Criminal Convictions: Evidence from an Adoption Cohort," *Science* 224 (1984), 891–94.

Mednick, S. A., T. E. Moffitt, and S. A. Stack. *The Causes of Crime: New Biological Approaches.* New York: Cambridge University Press, 1987.

Meeker, James W., and John Dombrink. "Criminal RICO and Organized Crime: An Analysis of Appellate Litigation," *Criminal Law Bulletin* 20 (1984), 309–20.

Meeker, James W., John Dombrink, and Henry N. Pontell. "White-Collar and Organized Crime: Questions of Seriousness and Policy," *Justice Quarterly* 4 (1987), 73–98.

Megargee, Edwin I., and Martin J. Bohn, Jr. *Classifying Criminal Offenders: A New System Based on the MMPI.* Beverly Hills, CA: Sage, 1979.

Meisenhelder, Thomas. "An Exploratory Study of Exiting from Criminal Careers," *Criminology* 15 (1977), 319–34.

Menninger, Karl, *The Crime of Punishment.* New York: Viking, 1957, 1968.

Merton, Robert K. "Social Structure and Anomie," *American Sociological Review* 3 (1938), 672–82.

Merton, Robert K. *Social Theory and Social Structure.* New York: Free Press, 1957, 1968.

Michaud, Stephen G., and Hugh Aynesworth. *The Only Living Witness.* New York: Simon & Schuster, 1983.

Michaud, Stephen G., and Hugh Aynesworth. *Ted Bundy: Conversations with a Killer.* New York: New American Library, 1989.

Mieczkowski, Thomas. "Geeking Up and Throwing Down: Heroin Street Life in Detroit," *Criminology* 24 (Nov. 1986), 645–66.

Miller, Judith D., et al. *National Survey on Drug Abuse: Main Findings 1982.* Report no. (ADM)83-1263. Rockville, MD: National Institute on Drug Abuse, 1983.

Miller, Stuart J., Simon Dinitz, and John P. Conrad. *Careers of the Violent.* Lexington, MA: Heath, 1982.

Miller, Walter B. "Lower Class Culture as a Generating Milieu of Gang Delinquency," *Journal of Social Issues* 14 (1958), 5–19.

Minow, Martha. "Foreword: Justice Engendered," *Harvard Law Review* 101 (1987), 10.

Missing Children's Assistance Act of 1983, 28 U.S.C. 534.

Missing Children's Assistance Act of 1984, 42 U.S.C. 5772.

Mitford, Jessica. "Kind and Usual Punishment in California," *Atlantic Monthly* 227 (March 1971), 45–52.

Mitford, Jessica. "The Torture Cure," *Harpers* 247 (Aug. 1973), 16–30.

Moffitt, T. E. "The Learning Theory Model of Punishment: Implications for Delinquency Deterrence," *Criminal Justice and Behavior* 10 (1983), 131–58.

Moffitt, T. E., S. A. Mednick, and W. F. Gabrielli, "Predicting Careers of Criminal Violence: Descriptive Data and Predispositional Factors," in D. A. Brizer and M. Crowner, eds., *Current Approaches to the Prediction of Violence.* Washington, DC: American Psychiatric Press, 1989.

Monkkonen, Eric H. *Police in Urban America, 1860–1920.* New York: Cambridge University Press, 1981.

Monroe, Sylvester, and Peter Goldman. *Brothers: Black and Poor—A True Story of Courage and Survival.* New York: William Morrow, 1988.

Moore, Joan W. *Homeboys: Gangs, Drugs, and Prison in the Barrios of Los Angeles.* Philadelphia: Temple University Press, 1978.

Moore, Joan W. *Going Down to the Barrio: Homeboys and Homegirls in Change.* Philadelphia: Temple University Press, 1991.

Moore, L. S., and A. I. Fleischman. "Subclinical Lead Toxicity," *Orthomolecular Psychiatry* 4 (1975), 61–70.

Moore, Mark H. "Supply Reduction and Drug Law Enforcement," in Michael Tonry and James Q. Wilson, eds., *Drugs and Crime,* Vol. 13 of *Crime and Justice: A Review of Research.* Chicago: University of Chicago Press, 1990.

Morash, Merry. "Organized Crime," in Robert F. Meier, ed., *Major Forms of Crime.* Beverly Hills, CA: Sage, 1984.

Morley, Jefferson. "Contradictions of Cocaine Capitalism," *The Nation,* Oct. 2, 1989, pp. 341–47.

Moscovici, S. *La Psychanalyse: Son Image et Son Public.* Paris: Presses Universitaires de France, 1976.

Moscovici, S. "On Social Representations," in J. Forgas, ed., *Social Cognition: Perspectives on Everyday Understanding.* London: Academic Press, 1981.

Moynihan, Daniel Patrick. "Iatrogenic Government— Social Policy and Drug Research," *American Scholar* 62 (1993), 351–62.

Muhlbauer, H. D. "Human Aggression and the Role of Central Serotonin," *Pharmacopsychiatry* 18 (1985), 218–21.

Myrdal, Gunnar. *Challenge to Affluence.* New York: Pantheon Books, 1963.

NAACP Legal Defense and Educational Fund. *Death Row U.S.A.,* Jan. 1991.

Nakell, Barry, and Kenneth Hardy. *The Arbitrariness of the Death Penalty.* Philadelphia: Temple University Press, 1987.

National Governors' Association. *Policy on Missing and Exploited Children,* 1985.

National Institute on Drug Abuse. *National Household Survey on Drug Abuse: Population Estimates 1990.* Washington, DC: U.S. Government Printing Office, 1991.

Needleman, H. L., et al. "Deficits in Psychologic and Classroom Performance of Children with Elevated Dentine Lead Levels," *New England Journal of Medicine* 300 (1979), 689–85.

Needleman, Martin, and Carolyn Needleman. "Organizational Crime: Two Models of Criminogenesis," *The Sociological Quarterly* 20 (1979), 517–39.

Nelli, Humbert S. *The Business of Organized Crime.* New York: Oxford University Press, 1976.

Nettler, G. *Killing One Another.* Cincinnati, OH: Anderson, 1982.

New York Times. Nov. 4, 1990, VII, 8:1.

New York Times. "4 Convicted of Defrauding Texas Savings and Loans," Nov. 7, 1991, p. C16.

Newcomb, Michael D., and Peter M. Bentler. *Consequences of Adolescent Drug Use Impact on the Lives of Young Adults.* Beverly Hills, CA: Sage, 1988.

Newson, J., and E. Newson. *Four-Year-Olds in an Urban Community.* London: Allen & Unwin, 1968.

Noble, E. P., et al. "Allelic Association of the D2 Dopamine Receptor Gene with Cocaine Dependence," *Drug and Alcohol Dependence* 33 (1993), 271–85.

Novaco, R. "The Functions and Regulation of the Arousal of Anger," *American Journal of Psychiatry* 133 (no. 1, 1976), 1124–28.

Nugent, S., et al. *Risks and Rewards in Robbery.* Sydney: Australian Institute of Criminology, 1989.

Nurco, David N., et al. "Differential Criminal Patterns of Narcotic Addicts over an Addiction Career," *Criminology* 26 (1988), 407–23.

Nye, F. Ivan, and James F. Short, Jr. "Scaling Delinquent Behavior," *American Sociological Review* 22 (1957), 326–31.

Oakes, Jeannie. *Keeping Track: How Schools Structure Inequality.* New Haven, CT: Yale University Press, 1985.

Office of National Drug Control Policy. *National Drug Control Strategy—January 1990.* Washington, DC: Office of National Drug Control Policy, 1990.

O'Leary, Vincent, and Todd R. Clear. *Directions for Community Corrections in the 1990s.* Washington, DC: National Institute of Corrections, 1984.

Oliver, William. *The Violent Social World of Black Men.* New York: Lexington, 1994.

Olweus, D. A., et al. "Circulating Testosterone Levels and Aggression in Adolescent Males: A Causal Analysis," *Psychosomatic Medicine* 50 (no. 3, 1988), 261–72.

O'Shea, James. *The Daisy Chain: How Borrowed Billions Sank a Texas S & L.* New York: Pocket Books, 1991.

Owen, D., and J. O. Sines. "Heritability of Personality in Children," *Behavior Genetics* 1 (1970), 235–48.

Padilla, Felix. *The Gang as an American Enterprise.* New Brunswick, NJ: Rutgers University Press, 1992.

Pagelow, M. D. *Family Violence.* New York: Praeger, 1984.

Palmer, Ted. "The Youth Authority's Community Treatment Project," *Federal Probation* 38 (1974), 3–14.

Palmer, Ted. "Martinson Revisited," *Journal of Research in Crime and Delinquency* 12 (1975), 133–52.

Palmer, Ted. *Correctional Intervention and Research: Current Issues and Future Prospects.* Lexington, MA: Lexington, 1978.

Palmer, Ted. "The 'Effectiveness' Issue Today: An Overview," *Federal Probation* 47 (1983), 3–10.

Palmer, Ted. "Treatment and the Role of Classification: A Review of Basics," *Crime & Delinquency* 30 (1984), 245–67.

Palmer, Ted, and Robert F. Wedge. "California's Juvenile Probation Camps: Findings and Implications," *Crime & Delinquency* 35 (1989), 234–53.

Panizzon, Ann, Gayle Olson-Raymer, and Nancy Guerra. *Delinquency Prevention: What Works/What Doesn't.* Sacramento, CA: State Office of Criminal Justice Planning, 1991.

Parsons, T., and R. F. Bales. *Family Socialization and Interaction Process.* New York: Free Press, 1955.

Patterson, Gerald R. "Children Who Steal," in T. Hirschi and M. Gottfredson, eds., *Understanding Crime.* Beverly Hills, CA: Sage, 1980, pp. 73–90.

Patterson, Gerald R., Patricia Chamberlain, and John B. Reid. "A Comparative Evaluation of a Parent-Training Program," *Behavior Therapy* 13 (1982), 636–50.

Patterson, G. R., B. D. Debaryshe, and E. Ramsey. "A Developmental Perspective on Antisocial Behavior," *American Psychologist* 44 (1989), 329–35.

Perkins, Craig. *National Corrections Reporting Program, 1989.* Washington, DC: U.S. Department of Justice, Bureau of Justice Statistics, 1992.

Perkins, Craig. *National Corrections Reporting Program, 1990.* Washington, DC: U.S. Department of Justice, Bureau of Justice Statistics, 1993.

Perkins, Craig, and Darrell K. Gilliard. *National Corrections Reporting Program, 1988.* Washington, DC: U.S. Department of Justice, Bureau of Justice Statistics, 1992.

Perls, F. *In and Out of the Garbage Pail.* Lafayette, CA: Real People's Press, 1969.

Petersilia, Joan. "Criminal Career Research: A Review of Recent Evidence," in M. Tonry and N. Morris, eds., *Crime and Justice: An Annual Review of Research,* Vol. 2. Chicago: University of Chicago Press, 1980, pp. 321–79.

Petersilia, Joan, Peter Greenwood, and Marvin Lavin. *Criminal Careers of Habitual Felons.* Washington, DC: U. S. Department of Justice, 1977.

Petersilia, Joan, and Susan Turner. "Comparing Intensive and Regular Supervision for High-Risk Probationers: Early Results from an Experiment in California," *Crime & Delinquency* 36 (1990), 87–111.

Phillips, Kevin. *The Politics of Rich and Poor.* New York: Random House, 1990.

Pihl, R. O., and M. Parkes. "Hair Element Content in Learning Disabled Children," *Science* 198 (1977), 204.

Pihl, R. O., and D. Ross. "Research on Alcohol Related Aggression: A Review and Implications for Understanding Aggression," in S. W. Sadava, ed., *Drug Use and Psychological Theory.* New York: Haworth Press, 1987.

Pihl, R. O., et al. "Hair Element Content of Violent Criminals," *Canadian Journal of Psychiatry* 27 (1982), 533.

Piliavin, Irving, and Scott Briar. "Police Encounters with Juveniles," *American Journal of Sociology* 70 (1964), 206–14.

Pincus, J., and G. Tucker. *Behavioral Neurology.* New York: Oxford University Press, 1974.

Piore, Michael J. *Notes for a Theory of Labor Market Stratification.* Working Paper no. 95. Cambridge, MA: Massachusetts Institute of Technology, 1972.

Pizzo, Stephen, Mary Fricker, and Paul Muolo. *Inside Job: The Looting of America's Savings and Loans.* New York: McGraw-Hill, 1989.

Platt, Anthony M. *The Child Savers: The Invention of Delinquency.* Chicago: University of Chicago Press, 1969.

Pleck, E., et al. "The Battered Data Syndrome: A Reply to Steinmetz' Article," *Victimology* 2 (1977–1978), 680–84.

Plomin, R., and D. Daniels. "Genetics and Shyness," in W. H. Jones, J. M. Cheek, and S. R. Briggs, eds., *Shyness: Perspectives on Research and Treatment.* New York: Plenum, 1986.

Plomin, R., J. C. DeFries, and G. E. McClearn. *Behavioral Genetics: A Primer.* San Francisco: W. H. Freeman, 1980.

Plomin, R., T. T. Foch, and D. C. Rowe. "Bobo Clown Aggression in Childhood: Environment, Not Genes," *Journal of Research in Personality* 15 (1981), 331–42.

Plomin, R., K. Nitz, and D. C. Rowe, "Behavioral Genetics and Aggressive Behavior in Childhood," in M. Lewis and S. M. Miller, eds., *Handbook of Developmental Psychopathology.* New York: Plenum, 1990, pp. 119–33.

Plomin, R., et al. "EAS Temperaments During the Last Half of the Life Span: Twins Reared Apart and Twins Reared Together," *Psychology and Aging* 3 (1988), 43–50.

Pollak, Otto. *The Criminality of Women.* Philadelphia: University of Pennsylvania Press, 1950.

Pontius, A. A., and K. F. Ruttiger. "Frontal Lobe System Maturational Lag in Juvenile Delinquents Shown in Narratives Test," *Adolescence* 11 (no. 44, 1976), 509–18.

Posner, Richard. "A Statistical Study of Antitrust Enforcement," *Journal of Law and Economics* 13 (1970), 365–420.

Powers, Richard Gid. *G-Men: Hoover's FBI in American Popular Culture.* Carbondale: Southern Illinois University Press, 1983.

Powers, Richard Gid. *Secrecy and Power: The Secret Life of J. Edgar Hoover.* New York: Free Press, 1987.

Preble, Edward, and John J. Casey, Jr. "Taking Care of Business: The Heroin User's Life on the Street," *International Journal of the Addictions* 4 (1969), 1–24.

Prentky, R., A. W. Burgess, and D. L. Carter. "Victim Responses by Rapist Type: An Empirical and Clinical Analysis," *Journal of Interpersonal Violence* 1 (1986), 73–98.

President's Commission on Law Enforcement and Administration of Justice. *The Challenge of Crime in a Free Society.* Washington, DC: U.S. Government Printing Office, 1967a.

President's Commission on Law Enforcement and Administration of Justice. *Task Force Report: Organized Crime.* Washington, DC: U.S. Government Printing Office, 1967b.

President's Commission on Model State Drug Laws. *Final Report.* Washington, DC: U.S. Government Printing Office, 1993.

Quay, H. C. "Psychopathic Personality as Pathological Stimulation Seeking," *American Journal of Psychiatry* 122 (1965), 180–83.

Quay, H. C., Roy Gerard, and Robert B. Levinson. *Differential Treatment . . . A Way to Begin.* Washington, DC: U.S. Department of Justice, 1970.

Quinney, Richard, ed. *Criminal Justice in America.* Boston: Little, Brown, 1974.

Rachall, J. V., et al. *A National Study of Adolescent Behavior, Attitudes and Correlates.* Final Report to the National Institute on Alcohol Abuse and Alcoholism, Rockville, MD, 1975.

Rada, R. T., et al. "Plasma Androgens in Violent and Nonviolent Sex Offenders," *Bulletin of the American Academy of Psychiatry Law* 11 (1983), 149–58.

Raine, A. *The Psychopathology of Crime: Criminal Behavior as a Clinical Disorder.* New York: Academic Press, 1993.

Rapaport, Elizabeth. "Some Questions About Gender and the Death Penalty," *Golden State University Law Review* 20 (1990), 501.

Ray, Marsh. "The Cycle of Abstinence and Relapse Among Heroin Addicts," *Social Problems* 9 (1961), 132–40.

Redl, F., and H. Toch. "The Psychoanalytic Perspective," in H. Toch, ed., *Psychology of Crime and Criminal Justice.* Prospect Heights, IL: Waveland Press, 1986.

Regnery, A. A. "A Federal Perspective on Juvenile Justice Reform," *Crime & Delinquency* 32 (1986), 39–51.

Reich, Robert B. "The Real Economy," *The Atlantic* 267 (1991), 35–52.

Reinarman, Craig, and Harry G. Levine. "Crack in Context: Politics and Media in the Making of a Drug Scare," *Contemporary Drug Problems* 16 (1990), 535–77.

Reiss, Albert J., Jr., and Jeffrey Roth. *Understanding and Controlling Violence. Report of the National Academy of Sciences Panel on the Understanding and Control of Violence.* Washington, DC: National Academy Press, 1993.

Repella, J. "Prosecution of Child Abuse Deaths—Statutory Framework." Alexandria, VA: National Center for the Prosecution of Child Abuse, 1989.

Ressler, R. K., A. W. Burgess, and J. E. Douglas. *Sexual Homicide.* Lexington, MA: Lexington Books, 1988.

Ressler, R. K., and T. Schachtman. *Whoever Fights Monsters.* New York: St. Martin's, 1992.

Reuter, Peter. "Can the Borders Be Sealed?" *The Public Interest* 92 (1988), 51–65.

Reuter, Peter, Robert MacCoun, and Patrick Murphy. *Money from Crime.* Santa Monica, CA: Rand Corporation, 1990.

Rice, Berkeley. *Trafficking.* New York: St. Martin's, 1989.

Riedel, Marc. "Corporate and Interfirm Organization: A Study of Penalized Sherman Act Violations," *Graduate Sociology Club Journal* 8 (1968), 74–97.

Riedel, Marc, and Margaret Zahn. *The Nature and Patterns of American Homicide.* Washington, DC: U.S. Department of Justice, 1985.

Riesman, David. *Abundance for What.* Garden City, NY: Doubleday, 1964.

Riley, David, and Margaret Shaw. *Parental Supervision and Juvenile Delinquency.* Home Office Research Study no. 83. London: HMSO, 1985.

Rimland, B., and G. E. Larson. "Hair Mineral Analysis and Behavior: An Analysis of 51 Studies," *Journal of Learning Disabilities* 16 (1983), 279–85.

Riordan, William L. *Plunkitt of Tammany Hall.* New York: Dutton, 1963.

Roberts, Julian V. "Public Opinion, Crime, and Criminal Justice," in M. Tonry, ed., *Crime and Justice: A Review of Research,* Vol. 16. Chicago: University of Chicago Press, 1992.

Robins, Lee. *Deviant Children Grown Up.* Baltimore: Williams & Wilkins, 1966.

Robins, Lee. "Aetiological Implications in Studies of Childhood Histories Relating to Antisocial Personality," in R. Hare and D. Schalling, eds., *Psychopathic Behavior.* New York: Wiley, 1978, pp. 255–71.

Robins, Lee, Darlene H. Davis, and Eric Wish. "Vietnam Veterans Three Years After Vietnam: How Our Study Changed Our View of Heroin," in L. Brill and C. Winick, eds., *Yearbook of Substance Abuse.* New York: Human Sciences Press, 1980.

Robins, Lee, P. A. West, and B. L. Herjanic. "Arrests and Delinquency in Two Generations: A Study of Black Urban Families and Their Children," *Journal of Child Psychology and Psychiatry* 16 (1975), 125–40.

Robinson, Jane, "On the Trail of the Serial Killers," *Queensland Northern Star,* Dec. 13, 1989.

Robison, J., and G. Smith. "The Effectiveness of Correctional Programs," *Crime and Delinquency* 17 (1971), 67–80.

Rogeness, G. A., et al. "Plasma Dopamine-B-Hydroxylase, HVA, MHPG, and Conduct Disorder in

Emotionally Disturbed Boys," *Biological Psychiatry* 22 (1987), 1155–58.

Rojek, Dean, and Maynard Erickson. "Delinquent Careers," *Criminology* 20 (1982), 5–28.

Romig, Dennis A. *Justice for Our Children.* Lexington, MA: Lexington Books, 1978.

Rose, Dan. *Black American Street Life: South Philadelphia, 1969–1971.* Philadelphia: University of Pennsylvania Press, 1987.

Rose, Harold M., et al. *The Labor Market Experience of Young African American Men from Low-Income Families in Wisconsin.* Milwaukee: University of Wisconsin-Milwaukee Employment and Training Institute, 1992.

Rosenbaum, A., and R. D. O'Leary. "Marital Violence: Characteristics of Abusive Couples," *Journal of Consulting and Clinical Psychology* 49 (1981) 63–76.

Ross, Robert R., and Paul Gendreau. *Effective Correctional Treatment.* Toronto: Butterworths, 1980.

Rothman, David. *The Discovery of the Asylum: Social Order and Disorder in the New Republic.* Boston: Little, Brown, 1971.

Rowe, D. C. "Biometrical Genetic Models of Self-Reported Delinquent Behavior: A Twin Study," *Behavior Genetics* 13 (1983), 473–89.

Rowe, D. C. "Genetic and Environmental Components of Antisocial Behavior: A Study of 265 Twin Pairs," *Criminology* 24 (no. 3, 1986), 513–32.

Rowe, D. C., M. Clapp, and J. Wallis. "Physical Attractiveness and the Personality Resemblance of Identical Twins," *Behavior Genetics* 17 (1987), 191–201.

Rowe, D. C., and D. W. Osgood. "Heredity and Sociological Theories of Delinquency: A Reconsideration," *American Sociological Review* 49 (1984), 526–40.

Rowe, D. C., D. Wayne Osgood, and W. Alan Nicewander. "A Latent Trait Approach to Unifying Criminal Careers," *Criminology* 28 (1990), 237–70.

Roy, A., et al. "Monoamines, Glucose Metabolism, Suicidal and Aggressive Behaviors," *Psychopharmacology Bulletin* 22 (no. 3, 1986), 661–65.

Rule, Andrew. *Cuckoo.* Melbourne, Australia: Floradale Press, 1988.

Rushton, J. P., et al. "Altruism and Aggression: The Heritability of Individual Differences," *Journal of Personality and Social Psychology* 50 (no. 6, 1986), 1192–98.

Russell, William Felton, as told to William McSweeny. *Go Up to Glory.* New York: Coward-McCann, 1966.

Rutter, Michael, and Henri Giller. *Juvenile Delinquency: Trends and Perspectives.* New York: Guilford, 1984.

Sacks, H. S., et al. "Meta-Analyses of Randomized Controlled Trials," *New England Journal of Medicine* 316 (1987), 450–55.

Salerno, Ralph, and John S. Tompkins. *The Crime Confederation: Cosa Nostra and Allied Operations in Organized Crime.* Garden City, NY: Doubleday, 1969.

Sampson, Robert J. "Urban Black Violence: The Effect of Male Joblessness and Family Disruption," *American Journal of Sociology* 93 (1987), 348–82.

Sampson, Robert J., and W. Byron Groves. "Community Structure and Crime: Testing Social-Disorganization Theory," *American Journal of Sociology* 94 (1989), 774–802.

Sampson, Robert J., and John H. Laub. "Stability and Change in Crime and Deviance over the Life Course: The Salience of Adult Social Bonds," *American Sociological Review* 55 (1990), 609–27.

Sampson, Robert J., and John H. Laub. *Crime in the Making: Pathways and Turning Points Through Life.* Cambridge, MA: Harvard University Press, 1993.

Sanchez, Jose E., and Bruce D. Johnson. "Women and the Drugs–Crime Connection: Crime Rates Among Drug-Abusing Women at Rikers Island," *Journal of Psychoactive Drugs* 19 (no. 2, 1987), 205–16.

Saunders, D. "When Battered Women Use Violence: Husband-Abuse or Self-Defense?" *Victims and Violence* 1 (1986), 47–60.

Schechter, Harold. *Deranged.* New York: Pocket, 1990.

Schiavi, R. C., et al. "Sex Chromosome Anomalies, Hormones, and Aggressivity," *Archives of General Psychiatry* 41 (1984), 93–99.

Schlegel, Kip. "Crime in the Pits: The Regulation of Futures Trading," *The Annals of the American Academy of Political and Social Science* 525 (1993), 59–70.

Schlegel, Kip, and David Weisburd, eds. *White-Collar Crime Reconsidered.* Boston: Northeastern University Press, 1992.

Schoenberger, R. W., and W. A. Thomas. "Missing Children in Michigan: Facts, Problems, Recommendations," *Juvenile Justice Digest* 31 (1985), 7–8.

Scholz, John. "Deterrence, Cooperation and the Ecology of Regulatory Enforcement," *Law and Society Review* 18 (1984), 179–224.

Schuckit, M. A., and M. A. Morrissey. "Propoxyphene and Phencyclidine (PCP) Use in Adolescents," *Journal of Clinical Psychiatry* 39 (1978), 7–13.

Schur, Edwin M. *Radical Non-intervention: Rethinking the Delinquency Problem*. Englewood Cliffs, NJ: Prentice-Hall, 1973.

Schwartz, Richard, and Jerome Skolnick. "Two Studies of Legal Stigma," in Howard Becker, ed., *The Other Side: Perspectives on Deviance*. New York: Free Press, 1964.

Sechrest, Lee B., Susan O. White, and Elizabeth D. Brown. *The Rehabilitation of Criminal Offenders: Problems and Prospects*. Washington, DC: National Academy Press, 1979.

Seigal, R. K. "Phencyclidine, Criminal Behavior, and the Defense of Diminished Capacity," in R. C. Peterson and R. C. Stillman, eds., *Phencyclidine (PCP) Abuse: An Appraisal*. NIDA Research Monograph 21. Rockville, MD: National Institute on Drug Abuse, 1978.

Sellin, Thorsten. *The Penalty of Death*. Beverly Hills, CA: Sage, 1980.

Shapiro, Susan P. *Thinking About White Collar Crime: Matters of Conceptualization and Research*. Washington, DC: National Institute of Justice, 1980.

Shapiro, Susan P. "Collaring the Crime, Not the Criminal: Reconsidering the Concept of White-Collar Crime," *American Sociological Review* 55 (1990), 346–65.

Shaw, Clifford R., and Henry D. McKay. *Juvenile Delinquency and Urban Areas*. Chicago: University of Chicago Press, 1942.

Shields, N., C. R. Hanneke, and G. J. McCall. "Patterns of Family and Non-Family Violence: Violent Husbands and Violent Men," *Violence and Victims* 3 (1988), 83–98.

Short, James F., and Fred L. Strodtbeck. *Group Process and Gang Delinquency*. Chicago: University of Chicago Press, 1965.

Shover, Neal. "The Later Stages of Ordinary Property Offender Careers," *Social Problems* 31 (1983), 208–18.

Shover, Neal. *Aging Criminals*. Beverly Hills, CA: Sage, 1985.

Sigvardsson, D., et al. "Predisposition to Petty Criminality in Swedish Adoptees. III. Sex Differences and Validation of the Male Typology," *Archives of General Psychiatry* 39 (1982), 1248–53.

Silver, Allan. "The Demand for Order in Civil Society: A Review of Some Themes in the History of Urban Crime, Police and Riot," in David J. Bordua, ed., *The Police: Six Sociological Essays*. New York: Wiley, 1967.

Silverman, B. S. "The Search for a Solution to Child Snatching," *Hofstra Law Review* 11 (1983), 1073–1117.

Simcha-Fagan, Ora, and Joseph E. Schwartz. "Neighborhood and Delinquency: An Assessment of Contextual Effects," *Criminology* 24 (1986), 667–95.

Skogan, Wesley G. "Weapon Use in Robbery," in James A. Inciardi and Anne E. Pottieger, eds., *Violent Crime: Historical and Contemporary Issues*. Beverly Hills, CA: Sage, 1978.

Skolnick, Jerome H. "The Social Structure of Street Drug Dealing," *American Journal of Police* 9 (1990), 1–41.

Smith, D. E., and D. R. Wesson. "PCP Abuse: Diagnostic and Pharmacological Treatment Approaches," *Journal of Psychedelic Drugs* 12 (1980), 293–99.

Smith, Douglas, and Christy Visher. "Street Level Justice: Situational Determinants of Police Arrest Decisions," *Social Problems* 29 (1981), 167–77.

Smith, Dwight C., Jr. *The Mafia Mystique*. New York: Basic Books, 1975.

Smith, Dwight C., Jr. "Paragons, Pariahs, and Pirates: A Spectrum-Based Theory of Enterprise," *Crime & Delinquency* 26 (1980), 358–86.

Snider, Laureen. "Cooperative Models and Corporate Crimes: Panacea or Copout?" *Crime & Delinquency* 36 (1990), 373–90.

Sonkin, D. J., and M. Durphy. *Learning to Live Without Violence: A Handbook for Men*, 2nd ed. San Francisco: Volcano Press, 1985.

Soubrie, P. "Reconciling the Role of Central Serotonin Neurons in Human and Animal Behavior," *The Behavioral and Brain Sciences* 9 (1986), 319–64.

Sourcebook of Criminal Justice Statistics. Washington, DC: Department of Justice, Bureau of Justice Statistics, 1978–1992.

Spergel, Irving A., and G. David Curry. "Strategies and Perceived Agency Effectiveness in Dealing with the Youth Gang Problem," in C. Ronald Huff, ed., *Gangs in America.* Beverly Hills, CA: Sage, 1990.

Standing Committee on Justice and the Solicitor General. *Crime Prevention in Canada: Toward a National Strategy.* Ottawa: Canada Communication Group, 1993.

Stark, E., A. Flitcraft, and W. Frazier. "Medicine and Patriarchical Violence: The Social Construction of a Private Event," *International Journal of Health Services* 9 (1979), 461–93.

Staw, Barry M., and Eugene Szwajkowski. "The Scarcity–Munificence Component of Organizational Environments and the Commission of Illegal Acts," *Administrative Science Quarterly* 20 (1975), 345–54.

Steffensmeier, Darrell J., and M. Cobb. "Sex Differences in Urban Arrest Patterns 1934–1979," *Social Problems* 29 (1981), 37–50.

Steffensmeier, Darrell J., et al. "Age and the Distribution of Crime," *American Journal of Sociology* 94 (1989), 803–31.

Stewart, M. A., and C. S. de Blois. "Father–Son Resemblances in Aggressive and Antisocial Behavior," *British Journal of Psychiatry* 142 (1983), 78–84.

Stewart, M. A., C. S. de Blois, and C. Cummings. "Psychiatric Disorder in the Parents of Hyperactive Boys and Those with Conduct Disorder," *Journal of Child Psychology and Psychiatry* 21 (1980), 283–92.

Stewart, M. A., and L. Leone. "A Family Study of Unsocialized Aggressive Boys," *Biological Psychiatry* 13 (1978), 107–17.

Storr, A. *Human Aggression.* New York: Atheneum, 1968.

Straus, M. A. "Victims and Aggressors in Marital Violence," *American Behavioral Scientist* 23 (no. 5, 1980), 681–704.

Straus, M. A. "Assaults by Wives on Husbands: Implications for Primary Prevention of Marital Violence." Paper presented to the American Society of Criminology, Reno, NV, 1989.

Straus, M. A., and L. Baron. *Sexual Stratification, Pornography, and Rape.* Durham: Family Research Laboratory, University of New Hampshire, 1983.

Straus, M. A., and R. J. Gelles. *Physical Violence in American Families: Risk Factors and Adaptations to Violence in 8,145 Families.* New Brunswick, NJ: Transaction, 1990.

Straus, M. A., R. J. Gelles, and S. Steinmetz. *Behind Closed Doors: Violence in the American Family.* New York: Anchor Press, 1980.

Strauss, Anselm L. *Qualitative Analysis for Social Scientists.* Cambridge, England: Cambridge University Press, 1987.

Streib, Victor. "The Death Penalty for Female Offenders," *Cincinnati Law Review* 58 (1990), 845.

Streib, Victor. "Capital Punishment for Female Offenders: Present Female Death Row Inmates and Death Sentences and Executions of Female Offenders, January 1, 1973, to March 1, 1991." Unpublished manuscript. Cleveland, OH: Cleveland-Marshall College of Law, 1991.

Sullivan, Mercer L. "Youth Crime: New York's Two Varieties," *New York Affairs* 8 (1983), 31–48.

Sullivan, Mercer L. *Getting Paid: Youth Crime and Work in the Inner City.* Ithaca, NY: Cornell University Press, 1989.

Summers, Anthony. *Official and Confidential: The Secret Life of J. Edgar Hoover.* New York: Putnam, 1993.

Sunday Times (London), July 27, 1986.

Sutherland, Edwin H. "White-Collar Criminality," *American Sociological Review* 5 (1940), 1–12.

Sutherland, Edwin H. "Crime and Business," *The Annals of the American Academy of Political and Social Science* 217 (1941), 112–18.

Sutherland, Edwin H. *White Collar Crime.* New York: Dryden, 1949.

Sutherland, Edwin H., and Donald R. Cressey, *Criminology.* Philadelphia: Lippincott, 1970.

Sutter, Alan G. "Worlds of Drug Use on the Street Scene," in D. R. Cressey and D. A. Ward, eds., *Delinquency, Crime, and Social Process.* New York: Harper & Row, 1969, pp. 802–29.

Sviridoff, Michele, and J. E. McElroy. *Employment and Crime: A Summary Report.* New York: Vera Institute of Justice, 1985.

Sviridoff, Michele, et al. *The Neighborhood Effects of Street-Level Drug Enforcement.* New York: Vera Institute of Justice, 1992.

Syndulko, K. "Electrocortical Investigations of Sociopathy," in R. D. Hare and D. Schalling, eds., *Psychopathic Behavior: Approaches to Research.* Chichester, England: Wiley, 1978.

Syndulko, K., et al. "Psychophysiology of Sociopathy: Electrocortical Measures," *Biological Psychology* 3 (1975), 185–200.

Szasz, T. *Psychiatric Justice.* New York: Macmillan, 1965.

Szockyj, Elizabeth. "Insider Trading: The SEC Meets Carl Karcher," *The Annals of the American Academy of Political and Social Science* 525 (1993), 46–58.

Tanay, E. *The Murderers.* Indianapolis: Bobbs-Merrill, 1976.

Tanner, Julian, and Harvey Krahn. "Part-Time Work and Deviance Among High School Seniors," *Canadian Journal of Sociology* 16 (1991), 281–302.

Tarter, R. E., A. I. Alterman, and K. L. Edwards. "Vulnerability to Alcoholism in Men: A Behavior-Genetic Perspective," *Journal of Studies on Alcoholism* 46 (no. 4, 1985), 329–56.

Tarter, R. E., and K. Edwards. "Vulnerability to Alcohol and Drug Abuse: A Behavior-Genetic View," *Psychological Bulletin* 102 (1987), 204–18.

Tavris, C. *Anger: The Misunderstood Emotion,* 2nd ed. New York: Touchstone Books, 1989.

Taylor, Carl. *Dangerous Society.* East Lansing: Michigan State University Press, 1990.

Taylor, Laurie. *In the Underworld.* London: Unwin, 1985.

Tedeschi, J. T., R. B. Smith, and R. C. Brown. "A Reinterpretation of Research on Aggression," *Psychological Bulletin* 81 (1974), 540–62.

Tellegen, A., et al. "Personality Similarity in Twins Reared Apart and Together," *Journal of Personality and Social Psychology* 54 (no. 6, 1988), 1031–39.

Thiessen, D. D. *The Evolution and Chemistry of Aggression.* Springfield, IL: Charles C. Thomas, 1976.

Thornberry, Terence P., and R. L. Christenson, "Unemployment and Criminal Involvement: An Investigation of Reciprocal Causal Structures," *American Sociological Review* 49 (1984), 398–411.

Thornton, J. "The Tragedy of America's Missing Children," *U.S. News and World Report,* Oct. 24, 1983, pp. 63–64.

Thrasher, Frederic. *The Gang: A Study of 1,313 Gangs in Chicago.* Chicago: University of Chicago Press, 1927, 1963.

Tillman, R. "The Size of the 'Criminal Population': The Prevalence and Incidence of Adult Arrest," *Criminology* 25 (1987), 561–80.

Tittle, Charles R., and Robert F. Meier. "Specifying the SES/Delinquency Relationship," *Criminology* 28 (1990), 271–99.

Tittle, Charles R., Wayne J. Villemez, and Douglas A. Smith. "The Myth of Social Class and Criminality: An Empirical Assessment of the Empirical Evidence," *American Sociological Review* 43 (1978), 643–56.

Toch, H. *Violent Men: An Inquiry into the Psychology of Violence.* Chicago: Aldine, 1969.

Tomasic, Roman, and Brendan Pentony. "Insider Trading and Business Ethics," *Legal Studies Forum* 13 (1989), 151–69.

Tombs, Robert. "Crime and the Security of the State: The 'Dangerous Classes' and the Insurrection in Nineteenth-Century Paris," in V. A. C. Gartrell, Bruce Lenman, and Geoffrey Noel Parker, eds., *Crime and the Law: The Social History of Crime in Western Europe Since 1500.* London: Europa Publications, 1980.

Tonry, Michael. *Malign Neglect: Race, Crime, and Punishment in America.* New York: Oxford University Press, 1994.

Treanor, B. "Picture Our Missing Children: The Problem Is Blown Far Out of Proportion," *The Houston Chronicle,* Feb. 1, 1986.

Trunnell, E. P., and C. W. Turner. "A Comparison of the Psychological and Hormonal Factors in Women with and Without Premenstrual Syndrome," *Journal of Abnormal Psychology* 97 (1988), 429–36.

TV Guide, Nov. 14–20, 1992.

Twito, T. J., and M. A. Stewart. "A Half-Sibling Study of Aggressive Conduct Disorder," *Neuropsychobiology* 8 (1982), 144–50.

Ungar, Sanford J. *FBI.* Boston: Little, Brown, 1976.

United States Attorneys Bulletin, April 29, 1983, p. 31.

U.S. Bureau of the Census. *Public Use of Basic Records from the 1970 Census: Description and Technical Documentation.* Washington, DC: Government Printing Office, 1972.

U.S. Bureau of Justice Statistics. *Report for the Nation on Crime and Justice,* 2nd ed. Washington, DC: Government Printing Office, 1988.

U.S. Bureau of Justice Statistics. *Capital Punishment 1988.* Washington, DC: Government Printing Office, 1989.

U.S. Bureau of Justice Statistics. *Profile of Felons Convicted in State Courts, 1986.* Washington, DC: Government Printing Office, 1990.

U.S. Congress. *Adequacy of Federal Efforts to Combat Fraud, Abuse, and Misconduct in Federally Insured Financial Institutions.* Hearings before the Committee on Government Operations, Subcommittee on Commerce, Consumer, and Monetary Affairs. 100th Cong., 1st Sess. Washington, DC: Government Printing Office, 1987.

U.S. Congress. *Combating Fraud, Abuse, and Misconduct in the Nation's Financial Institutions: Current Federal Efforts Are Inadequate.* Committee on Government Operations. Committee Report No. 100-1088. Washington, DC: Government Printing Office, 1988.

U.S. Congress. *Financial Institutions Reform, Recovery, and Enforcement Act of 1989 (H.R. 1278).* Hearings before the Committee on Banking, Finance and Urban Affairs, Subcommittee on Financial Institutions Supervision, Regulation and Insurance. 101st Cong., 1st Sess. Washington, DC: Government Printing Office, 1989a.

U.S. Congress. *Report of the Special Outside Counsel in the Matter of Speaker James C. Wright, Jr. (Richard J. Phelan, Special Outside Counsel).* Committee on Standards of Official Conduct. Washington, DC: Government Printing Office, 1989b.

U.S. Congress. *Effectiveness of Law Enforcement Against Financial Crime.* Hearings before the Committee on Banking, Finance and Urban Affairs. Part 1. 101st Cong., 2nd Sess. Washington, DC: Government Printing Office, 1990a.

U.S. Congress. *Effectiveness of Law Enforcement Against Financial Crime.* Hearings before the Committee on Banking, Finance and Urban Affairs. Part 2. 101st Cong., 2nd Sess. Washington, DC: Government Printing Office, 1990b.

U.S. Congress. *Failed Promises: Insurance Company Insolvencies.* A Report by the Committee on Energy and Commerce, Subcommittee on Oversight and Investigations. Washington, DC: Government Printing Office, 1990c.

U.S. Department of Justice. *Sixth Report to Congress on Implementation of the Parental Kidnapping Prevention Act of 1980.* Washington, DC: U.S. Department of Justice, 1983.

U.S. Department of Justice. *Attacking Savings and Loan Institution Fraud.* Department of Justice Report to the President. Washington, DC: U.S. Department of Justice, 1990.

U.S. General Accounting Office. *Drug Abuse: Research on Treatment May Not Address Current Needs.* Washington, DC: U.S. General Accounting Office, 1990.

USA Today, Sept. 30, 1992.

USA Today, Jan. 14, 1993, p. 6A.

USA Today, May 18, 1993, p. 3A.

Valzelli, L. *Psychobiology of Aggression and Violence.* New York: Raven Press, 1981.

van den Haag, Ernest. *Punishing Criminals.* New York: Basic Books, 1975.

van Praag, H. M., et al. "Denosologization of Biological Psychiatry or the Specificity of 5-HT Disturbances in Psychiatric Disorders," *Journal of Affective Disorders* 13 (1987), 1–8.

van Voorhis, Patricia. "Correctional Effectiveness: The High Cost of Ignoring Success," *Federal Probation* 51 (1987), 56–62.

Vaughan, Diane. "The Macro–Micro Connection in White-Collar Crime Theory," in Kip Schlegel and David Weisburd, eds., *White-Collar Crime Reconsidered.* Boston: Northeastern University Press, 1992.

Venables, P. H. "Autonomic Nervous System Factors in Criminal Behavior," in S. A. Mednick, T. E. Moffitt, and S. Stack, eds., *The Causes of Crime: New Biological Approaches.* New York: Cambridge University Press, 1987.

Vera Institute of Justice. *Felony Arrests: Their Prosecution and Disposition in New York City Courts.* New York: Vera Institute of Justice, 1977.

Virgil, James Diego. *Barrio Gangs: Street Life and Identity in Southern California.* Austin: University of Texas Press, 1988.

Virkkunen, M., and S. Narvanen. "Plasma Insulin, Tryptophan and Serotonin Levels During the Glucose Tolerance Test Among Habitually Violent and Impulsive Offenders," *Neuropsychobiology* 17 (1987), 19–23.

Virkkunen, M., et al. "Cerebrospinal Fluid Monoamine Metabolite Levels in Male Arsonists," *Archives of General Psychiatry* 44 (1987), 241–47.

Virkkunen, M., et al. "Relationship of Psychobiological Variables to Recidivism in Violent Offenders and Impulsive Fire Setters," *Archives of General Psychiatry* 46 (1989), 600–03.

Viscusi, Kip. "Market Incentives for Criminal Behavior," in Richard Freeman and Harry Holzer, eds., *The Black Youth Employment Crisis.* Chicago: University of Chicago Press, 1986.

Visher, Christy. "The Rand Second Inmate Survey: A Reanalysis," in Alfred Blumstein et al., eds., *Criminal Careers and "Career Criminals,"* Vol. 2. Washington, DC: National Academy Press, 1986.

von Hirsch, Andrew. *Doing Justice: The Choice of Punishments.* New York: Hill and Wang, 1976.

Waldorf, Dan. "Natural Recovery from Opiate Addiction: Some Social-Psychological Processes of Untreated Recovery," *Journal of Drug Issues* 13 (no. 2, 1983), 237–80.

Waldorf, Dan. *Final Report of the Crack Sales, Gangs, and Violence Study: NIDA Grant 5#R01DA06486.* Alameda, CA: Institute for Scientific Analysis, 1993.

Waldorf, Dan, Craig Reinarman, and Sheigla Murphy. *Cocaine Changes: The Experience of Using and Quitting.* Philadelphia: Temple University Press, 1991.

Walker, L. E. *The Battered Woman Syndrome.* New York: Springer, 1984.

Walker, Samuel. *Sense and Nonsense About Crime.* Monterey, CA: Brooks/Cole, 1985.

Walker, Samuel. *Sense and Nonsense About Crime,* 2nd ed.. Pacific Grove, CA: Brooks/Cole, 1989.

Wallgren, H., and H. Barry. *Action of Alcohol.* Vols. 1 and 2. New York: Elsevier, 1970.

Walsh, D. *Heavy Business: Commercial Burglary and Robbery.* London and Boston: Routledge & Kegan Paul, 1986.

Walters, G. D., and T. W. White. "Heredity and Crime: Bad Genes or Bad Research?" *Criminology* 27 (1989), 455–86.

Ward, Benjamin, Commissioner, New York City Police Department, press release No. 17, May 22, 1989.

Warren, Marguerite Q. "Classification of Offenders as an Aid to Efficient Management and Effective Treatment," *Journal of Criminal Law, Criminology, and Police Science* 62 (1971), 239–58.

Warren, Marguerite Q., et al "Interpersonal Maturity Level Classification: Juvenile. Diagnosis and Treatment of Low, Middle, and High Maturity Delinquents." Sacramento: California Youth Authority, 1966.

Weingartner, H., et al. "Effects of Serotonin on Memory Impairments Produced by Ethanol," *Science* 221 (1983), 472–74.

Weis, Joseph G. "Social Class and Crime," in Michael Gottfredson and Travis Hirschi, eds., *Positive Criminology.* Beverly Hills, CA: Sage, 1987.

Weisburd, D., et al. *Crimes of the Middle Classes: White-Collar Offenders in the Federal Courts.* New Haven, CT: Yale University Press, 1991.

West, Donald, and David Farrington. *The Delinquent Way of Life.* London: Heinemann, 1977.

West, W. Gordon. "The Short-Term Careers of Serious Thieves," *Canadian Journal of Criminology* 20 (1978), 169–90.

Westat, Inc. *Study Findings: Study of National Incidence and Prevalence of Child Abuse and Neglect: 1988.* Washington, DC: U.S. Department of Health and Human Services, 1988.

Wheeler, Stanton, K. Mann, and A. Sarat. *Sitting in Judgment: The Sentencing of White Collar Offenders.* New Haven, CT: Yale University Press, 1988.

Wheeler, Stanton, and Mitchell Lewis Rothman. "The Organization as Weapon in White-Collar Crime," *Michigan Law Review* 80 (1982), 1403–26.

Wheeler, Stanton, D. Weisburd, and N. Bode. "Sentencing the White Collar Offender: Rhetoric and Reality," *American Sociological Review* 47 (1982), 641–59.

Wheeler, Stanton, D. Weisburd, and N. Bode. *Study of Convicted Federal White-Collar Crime Defendants.* National Archives of Criminal Justice Data. The Inter-University Consortium for Political and Social Research. Ann Arbor: University of Michigan, 1988.

Wheeler, Stanton, et al. "White Collar Crimes and Criminals," *American Criminal Law Review* 25 (1988), 331–57.

White, Helene Raskin, Robert J. Pandina, and Randy LaGrange. "Longitudinal Predictors of Serious Substance Use and Delinquency," *Criminology* 25 (1987), 715–40.

White, Lawrence J. *The S&L Debacle: Public Policy Lessons for Bank and Theft Regulation.* New York: Oxford University Press, 1991.

Whitehead, John T., and Steven P. Lab. "A Meta-Analysis of Juvenile Correctional Treatment," *Journal of Research in Crime and Delinquency* 26 (1989), 276–95.

Whyte, William Foote. *Street Corner Society.* Chicago: University of Chicago Press, 1943.

Widom, C. S. "Toward an Understanding of Female Criminality," *Progress in Experimental Personality Research* 8 (1978), 245–308.

Widom, C. S. "Child Abuse, Neglect, and Adult Behavior: Research Design and Findings on Criminality, Violence, and Child Abuse," *American Journal of Orthopsychiatry* 59 (1989), 355–67.

Wilbanks, W. "The Female Homicide Offender in Dade County, Florida," *Criminal Justice Review* 8 (1983), 9–14.

Williams, Terry. *The Cocaine Kids.* Reading, MA: Addison-Wesley, 1989.

Williams, Terry, and William Kornblum. *Growing Up Poor.* Lexington, MA: Lexington Books, 1985.

Williams, Wendy. "The Equality Crisis: Some Reflections on Culture, Courts, and Feminism," *Women's Rights Law Reporter* 7 (1982), 175.

Williamson, H. *Hustler! The Autobiography of a Thief.* New York: Doubleday, 1965.

Willis, P. *Learning to Labour.* London: Saxon House, 1977.

Willis, P. *Profane Culture.* London: Routledge & Kegan Paul, 1978.

Willwerth, James. *Jones.* New York: M. Evans, 1974.

Wilson, Colin, and Donald Seaman. *The Serial Killers.* London: Virgin True Crime, 1992.

Wilson, James Q. *Thinking About Crime.* New York: Basic Books, 1975.

Wilson, James Q. "'What Works?' Revisited: New Findings on Criminal Rehabilitation," *The Public Interest* 61 (1980), 3–17.

Wilson, James Q. "Drugs and Crime," in M. Tonry and J. Q. Wilson, eds., *Drugs and Crime.* Chicago: University of Chicago Press, 1990.

Wilson, James Q., and R. J. Herrnstein. *Crime and Human Nature.* New York: Simon & Schuster, 1985.

Wilson, William Julius. *The Truly Disadvantaged: The Inner City, the Underclass, and Public Policy.* Chicago: University of Chicago Press, 1987.

Wilson, William Julius. "Studying Inner-City Social Dislocations: The Challenge of Public Agenda Research," *American Sociological Review* 56 (1991), 1–14.

Wish, Eric D., and Bruce D. Johnson. "The Impact of Substance Abuse on Criminal Careers," in Alfred Blumstein, et al., eds., *Criminal Careers and "Career Criminals,"* Vol. 2. Washington, DC: National Academy Press, 1986.

Wolfe, Tom. *The Right Stuff.* New York: Farrar, Straus, and Giroux, 1979.

Wolfgang, Marvin E. *Patterns in Criminal Homicide.* Philadelphia: University of Pennsylvania Press, 1958.

Wolfgang, Marvin E. "A Sociological Analysis of Criminal Homicide," in M. E. Wolfgang, ed., *Studies in Homicide.* New York: Harper & Row, 1967.

Wolfgang, Marvin E., and F. Ferracuti, *The Subculture of Violence.* New York: Barnes & Noble, 1967.

Wolfgang, Marvin E., Robert M. Figlio, and Thorsten Sellin. *Delinquency in a Birth Cohort.* Chicago: University of Chicago Press, 1972.

Wood, Floris W. *An American Profile: Opinions and Behavior, 1972–1989.* New York: Gale Research, 1990.

Wright, Erik Olin. *Classes.* London: Verso, 1985.

Wright, James D., and Peter H. Rossi. *Armed and Considered Dangerous.* New York: Aldine de Gruyter, 1986.

Wright, Kevin N. *The Great American Crime Myth.* New York: Praeger, 1985.

Yeager, Peter. *The Limits of Law: The Public Regulation of Private Pollution.* Cambridge, England: Cambridge University Press, 1991.

Yeudall, L. T., O. Fedora, and D. Fromm. *A Neuropsychosocial Theory of Persistent Criminality: Implications for Assessment and Treatment.* Alberta Hospital, Edmonton, Research Bulletin #97, 1985.

Zahn, M. A. "Homicide in the Twentieth Century: Trends, Types and Causes," in T. R. Gurr, ed., *Violence in America,* Vol. 1, *The History of Violence.* Beverly Hills, CA: Sage, 1989.

Zillmann, D. *Hostility and Aggression.* Hillsdale, NJ: Lawrence Erlbaum, 1979.

Zimring, Franklin E. "Kids, Groups and Crime: Some Implications of a Well-Known Secret," *Journal of Criminal Law and Criminology* 72 (1981), 867–85.

Zimring, Franklin E., and G. J. Hawkins. *Deterrence: The Legal Threat in Crime Control.* Chicago: University of Chicago Press, 1973.

Zimring, Franklin E., and Gordon Hawkins. "The Growth of Imprisonment in California," *British Journal of Criminology* 34 (1994), 83–95.

Zimring, Franklin E., and James Zuehl. "Victim Injury and Death in Urban Robbery: A Chicago Study," *Journal of Legal Studies* 15 (1986), 1–40.

Zuckerman, M. "A Biological Theory of Sensation Seeking," in M. Zuckerman, ed., *Biological Basis of Sensation Seeking, Impulsivity and Anxiety.* Hillsdale, NJ: Lawrence Erlbaum Associates, 1983.

Easy
Weeknight
Dinners

Easy
Weeknight
Dinners

100 fast, flavor-packed meals
for busy people who still
want something good to eat

The New York Times
Cooking

Emily Weinstein

TEN SPEED PRESS
California | New York

Contents

Introduction

It's 4 p.m., and I'm thinking about dinner.

Will it be chicken? Tofu? Pasta? Should I defrost the salmon? What about those black beans in the fridge? Are there vegetables to use up? What do I have? What do I want? How much energy am I willing to spend on this tonight? Should we just get takeout?

You can be as passionate about food as I am—food and the act of cooking it are central to my daily life—and still find yourself spinning out over dinner and the immediate yet eternal question of what to cook. Dinner, again, and again, and again, and it has to be something you can get on the table quickly and that everyone will eat. And in a perfect world, it also tastes great. Even if you love to cook, which not everyone does, this dinner situation gets to be a lot.

That's why we've created this cookbook. It's for busy people—like you—who still want something good to eat but don't know where to start or what to make. This collection of 100 recipes will not only solve the dinner problem, but will inspire you with ideas and lead you somewhere delicious—even when you don't have much time.

I love recipes, and I put a lot of faith in them. I love the possibility of them, imagining the flavors, textures and varying bites. I also love the fact that a good recipe is a map to deliciousness: follow it, step-by-step, and you'll arrive at your destination.

Because of my job—I'm the editor in chief of Cooking and Food at *The New York Times*—people sometimes assume I'm a chef or went to culinary school. Nope! I don't have any formal culinary training, and while I grew up well fed with endless helpings of chicken cutlets, spaghetti and boxed macaroni and cheese, I didn't learn to cook at home as a kid. I learned to cook as an adult, from excellent recipes and early failures.

Oh, the failures. I had no sense of how to chop or season ingredients. I was sloppy. I burned things. I'd invite friends over to keep me company and share the food, but I couldn't time anything right and often served dinner way after 10 p.m., even though I'd told them 8. My small apartment kitchen was a mess; once in such a state of chaos that when a stove burner flared up, it set fire to a stack of oil-spattered recipes on the counter, and then a vase of dried hydrangeas nearby. I had to run to the bathroom, throw the flowers in the tub and yank on the cold water to put out the fire.

But I also remember some amazing moments in those early days, meals I was shocked that I actually made myself. There was a roast chicken dinner where I sat down at the table and felt things had started to click: the chicken was bronzed and juicy, the carrots sweet and tender. I cooked and cooked, leisurely picking up ingredients on the way home from work based on what I was in the mood to make. On weekends, I'd often disappear into the kitchen for entire days to make huge dinners for parties.

At the same time, cooking had become more central to my work life. By then, I'd worked at *The New York Times* for a few years, and I'd started editing recipes, which taught me about how the best ones are written (clear and to the point, not too long, with enough visual cues to help cooks know when the food is done). I also learned what good ideas look and taste like.

I got married. I had a baby, and then another. I kept cooking, though now, of course, it was different because I—a person with a full-time job, a partner and two kids—needed those recipes to be as fast and simple as possible. Gone were the evenings when I stopped at the market to buy mussels to cook on a whim; now I planned, plotting out meals and getting groceries on Sunday for the week ahead.

Personally and professionally, this was the moment I started to zero in on quick, easy dishes, recipes that were delicious but also doable. This is the food I needed, and I knew others needed, too, no matter where they were in life, whether younger or older; single or partnered; living with children at home, or past that stage, or never planning to enter it at all. It doesn't matter how much you love to cook. Sometimes you just don't want to spend hours in the kitchen prepping, cooking and cleaning. (My husband did and still does all the cleaning up, an arrangement I highly recommend if you have a partner, love to cook and hate to clean.)

I began writing a newsletter with dinner recipes, Five Weeknight Dishes and, with my coworkers, publishing the recipes that fill the book that you're holding in your hands.

Every one of these recipes can be made in under an hour, and many of them in less than 30 minutes. They're genuinely quick, and if they take a bit longer, the work is hands-off: you slide a pan into the oven, set a timer and walk away. They don't require more than two pots or pans, and they don't call for special equipment beyond a blender, just to make cleanup a little easier.

Sometimes simple recipes can be dull or dutiful, and they can be boring to eat day after day. Not these recipes. These recipes are inspired. They pop. They use electrifying ingredients (gochujang, chile crisp, Tajín!), clever techniques and brilliant shortcuts.

They're rooted in cultures around the world, but they've been remixed into something wholly new. They make it easy to cook and exciting to eat, and that's true whether it's a Tuesday or a Saturday (because really, weeknight recipes taste just as good on the weekends).

Many of the recipes in this book are the ones I have on repeat in my own kitchen. The revelation that feta is delicious baked in a hot oven has changed my weeknights, with recipes like Ali Slagle's sheet-pan feta with chickpeas and tomatoes (page 247) in heavy rotation. Kay Chun's pork meatballs with ginger and fish sauce (page 170) are as genius as she is; I eat them over rice, piled with fresh herbs. Melissa Clark's fast garlicky chicken with lemon-anchovy sauce (page 33) was the recipe that awakened me to the necessity of anchovies. Tejal Rao's eggs Kejriwal (page 229) are a favorite, especially because I almost always have the ingredients on hand (eggs, Dijon mustard, jalapeños, toast), and they add up to something much bolder than the sum of their parts. Eric Kim's gyeran bap (page 230)—rice with a buttery soy sauce–fried egg on top—has revolutionized both lunch and dinner in my kitchen. And throughout this book, you'll see comments from real cooks in the NYT Cooking community, endorsing their favorite recipes. (I've created a recipe index for you on pages 12 to 15 to help you find your way to the recipes you want as quickly as possible.)

> It doesn't matter how much you love to cook. Sometimes you just don't want to spend hours in the kitchen.

I've always described my newsletter as being for busy people who still want something good to eat. That's me, and my friends and family, and I'm guessing you, too. It's hard to throw cooking into the whirring cycles of daily life. I hope these recipes make it a little easier, and life more delicious. After all these years of cooking and building confidence in the kitchen, I still love recipes, and I keep coming back to them. I hope you do, too.

How to Use This Book

We want to solve the dinner problem for you. The recipes in this book, all originally published on NYT Cooking, are easy to make, with ingredients that you should be able to find at large supermarkets around the country. None of the recipes call for more than two pots or pans—because cleanup should be easy, too.

What to Know Before You Get Cooking

- The chapters in this book are organized by ingredient, with recipes appearing in order of shortest cook time to longest.

- The ingredients in our recipes are listed in the order you use them (and water doesn't usually appear in the ingredients list, even if it's called for in a step).

- On page 12, you'll find a special index we created to help you decide what you want to cook tonight.

A Note About Salt

The majority of recipes in this book call for "kosher salt" for seasoning. We tested all of these recipes with Diamond Crystal salt. Some recipes call for "coarse kosher salt." We tested those recipes with Morton's salt.

It's important to use the type of salt called for in each recipe, as the weight (and therefore levels of saltiness) is different between types of salt (and from brand to brand!). For example, 1 tablespoon of Diamond Crystal salt is equal to 10 grams, while 1 tablespoon of table salt comes in at almost double the weight: 19 grams.

Our Beloved Recipe Developers

The recipes in this book, a curated collection of some of my NYT Cooking favorites, were developed by a number of different recipe writers. There may be some variation in style or technique from recipe to recipe, but all of the recipes have been thoroughly tested and edited, and they'll work. You can find bios of all of the recipe contributors on page 16.

Our Valued Home Cooks

Alongside some of the recipes, you'll see comments from home cooks like you, just a handful of the millions of NYT Cooking readers who have made and loved these recipes. These commenters keep us honest, too. They've cooked every single one of these recipes—and they let us know when something doesn't work!

Pots, Pans and Other Tools

You don't need any fancy equipment to make good food, and in these recipes, you don't need much equipment at all. (A few recipes also give instructions for grilling; if you don't have a grill, use your broiler, which you can basically treat as an upside-down grill inside your oven.) A skillet, a saucepan and a large pot will be fine for nearly all of them, as well as a baking dish and a sheet pan (also known as a baking sheet or a rimmed baking sheet).

About that sheet pan: If you don't have one, it's worth getting one right now. In fact, it's one of the only pieces of cookware I'll ever recommend that you buy. Sheet pans are simple and affordable, and if you buy a sturdy one (a good idea!), it'll last forever. They make it simple to cook a full meal in one pan, and they're versatile. Technically, what you want is a half sheet pan: about 18 x 13 inches. (Full sheet pans are giant, and they're used in commercial kitchens.) Do not buy nonstick, and do not get rimless cookie sheets. Those are different.

Need Help Deciding?

Looking for a meal easy to freeze ahead of time, or scale down for a solo portion? Looking for something even your picky kids will (maybe) enjoy? Are you obsessed with sheet pans? Here are some suggestions to make your dinner decision making process easier.

Truly Fifteen-Minute Recipes (We Promise)

Tastes Like Pizza

I Only Cook on a Sheet Pan

Good for Freezing

Vegan (or Easy to Veganize) Dinners

Hand-Held Dinners

Dinner Party Vibes, But on a Tuesday

One Pot, Minimal Dishes

Make It Spicy

If You're Really Feeling Lazy

Emily's Most Repeated Weeknight Dinners at Home

Five-Star Recipes with 5,000+ Comments

Honestly, Just Go Make This Right Now

Picky Kids Might Actually Eat This

Easy Recipes to Adapt for One Person

Minimum Effort For Maximum Magic

Need Help Deciding?

Need Help Deciding?   15

Meet the Contributors

Yossy Arefi is a Brooklyn-based recipe developer, photographer and food stylist. She is the author of *Snacking Bakes: Simple Recipes for Cookies, Bars, Brownies, Cakes, and More* and *Snacking Cakes: Simple Treats for Anytime Cravings*.

Mark Bittman is the author of the How to Cook Everything series and *Animal, Vegetable, Junk*. After three decades at *The New York Times,* he is now editor in chief of *The Bittman Project,* a professor at Columbia's Mailman School of Public Health and the founder of Community Kitchen.

Kay Chun is a recipe developer and regular contributor to NYT Cooking. She has been a writer and editor at several food publications, including *Food & Wine, Bon Appétit, Gourmet* and *Real Simple*.

Melissa Clark is a food reporter and columnist for *The New York Times* and NYT Cooking, for which she creates recipes, hosts videos and is one of the writers of the Cooking newsletter. She's also written dozens of cookbooks. A native of Brooklyn, she knows where to find the best bagel.

Sarah DiGregorio is a critically acclaimed journalist. Her work has appeared in major national publications, and she is the author of two reported nonfiction books and one cookbook.

Yasmin Fahr is a regular contributor to NYT Cooking. She is the author of three books, including *Cook Simply, Live Fully,* and was nominated for a Webby Award for her work with *The Kitchn*.

Colu Henry is a writer, cook and contributor to *The New York Times* and *Food & Wine*. She is the author of two books, including *Colu Cooks: Easy Fancy Food,* and a weekly newsletter, Colu Cooks.

Lidey Heuck is a cook, writer, contributor to NYT Cooking and the author of *Cooking in Real Life*.

Eric Kim is a food columnist for *The New York Times Magazine* and a recipe developer and video host for NYT Cooking. A native of Atlanta, he is also the author of the cookbook *Korean American*.

Genevieve Ko is a deputy editor of NYT Cooking and Food at *The New York Times,* where she also writes a column, develops recipes and appears in videos. In addition to writing her own cookbook, *Better Baking,* she has contributed to more than twenty cookbooks.

Yewande Komolafe is a cooking writer and columnist for *The New York Times* and a recipe developer and video host for NYT Cooking. She is also the author of the cookbook *My Everyday Lagos.*

Priya Krishna is a food reporter for *The New York Times* and a recipe developer and video host for NYT Cooking. She is the author of multiple cookbooks, and her stories have been included in *The Best American Food Writing*.

Francis Lam is the host of *The Splendid Table* and vice president and editor in chief at Clarkson Potter. He has written for numerous publications, including *The New York Times Magazine*.

Sue Li is a food stylist and recipe developer and is a frequent contributor to NYT Cooking. She previously worked at *Bon Appétit.*

Vallery Lomas is the author of *Life Is What You Bake It.* She's a contributor to *The New York Times* and columnist of "The Bakeaway" with the *Wall Street Journal*. She was the winner of the fourth season of ABC's *The Great American Baking Show*.

J. Kenji López-Alt writes a column for *The New York Times* on food and science. He is also the author of *The Food Lab* and *The Wok,* the creator and host of *Kenji's Cooking Show* on YouTube and co-creator of the podcast *The Recipe with Kenji and Deb*.

Rick A. Martínez is a regular contributor to *The New York Times* and the author of *Mi Cocina.* He co-hosts the podcast *Borderline Salty* and hosts the video series *Mi Cocina, Sweet Heat* and *Pruébalo*.

Hetty Lui McKinnon is a cook, food writer and regular contributor to *The New York Times*. She is the author of *Tenderheart* and four other cookbooks.

Dawn Perry is a writer and cookbook author, who served as the food director for *Real Simple*. She is a contributor to *The New York Times* and the author of *Ready, Set, Cook*.

Tejal Rao is a critic for *The New York Times* covering restaurants and food culture. She has won two James Beard Foundation awards for restaurant criticism and contributed to several anthologies. She lives in Los Angeles.

Zainab Shah is a regular contributor to NYT Cooking and the vice president of audience strategy at the American Journalism Project.

Sam Sifton is the founding editor of NYT Cooking and an assistant managing editor leading culture and lifestyle coverage for *The New York Times*. He is also a cookbook author and one of the writers of the Cooking newsletter.

Ali Slagle is a recipe developer and regular contributor to NYT Cooking who specializes in low-effort, high-reward recipes. She is also the author of the cookbook *I Dream of Dinner (so You Don't Have To)*.

Alexa Weibel is a senior staff editor and recipe developer at NYT Cooking. She was previously an editor at *Rachael Ray Magazine,* a cookbook editor and a restaurant line cook.

Korsha Wilson is a food writer for publications like *The New York Times, Eater, Saveur,* and *The New Yorker*. She is the founder and host of the podcast *A Hungry Society*.

Sheet-Pan Gochujang Chicken
and Roasted Vegetables, page 48

Chicken

Chicken

Crispy, juicy, easy to cook and easy to love—chicken dinners are among the most popular recipes on NYT Cooking, and I understand why. You can cook chicken every which way, and it takes well to pretty much any flavor you throw at it. It's affordable and universally liked, and it can be quite healthy, depending on the cut and how you prepare it. And, of course, a great chicken dish is truly delicious.

But chicken, made the same way week after week, can also get dull. This chapter is devoted to what I think of as chicken inspiration, ideas for different tastes and cuts, techniques and shortcuts.

Looking for big flavors? Turn to the recipe for Sheet-Pan Gochujang Chicken and Roasted Vegetables on page 48, which practically vibrates with ginger, scallions and a few generous tablespoons of gochujang, Korean red pepper paste. (Swap some or all of the vegetables in that recipe with precut veggies from the store, to save some prep time.) Or there's the Tajín

Grilled Chicken on page 43, seasoned with the beloved chile-lime spice mix from Mexico, which you normally see sprinkled on fruit or coating the rim of a margarita. This is chicken gone electric.

A few recipes in this chapter are from my favorite genre of cooking: something simple plus an amazing sauce. Think Garlic Chicken with Guasacaca Sauce, a version of a dish from Venezuela (page 44), or Mayo-Marinated Chicken with Chimichurri (page 23), a recipe that not only includes one of the best sauces on Earth, but also gives you a brilliant trick for cooking the chicken. (The beauty of these two recipes—aside from how good they are—is that you can double the sauce and keep it in the fridge for a few weeks for next time.)

If you're looking to start somewhere simple, try the Baked Mustard-Herb Chicken Legs on page 55—a true crowd-pleaser, perfect for any age or taste.

Most of the recipes in this chapter are made with boneless chicken thighs, because boneless cuts cook faster than bone-in, and thighs won't dry out as easily as breasts when you cook them. The few bone-in recipes in this chapter will take closer to an hour to cook, but they've got fairly minimal prep and most of the cooking time is unattended. Trust me: they're here because they're worth it.

Mayo-Marinated Chicken with Chimichurri

time   about 10 minutes

yield   2 to 4 servings

The magic of mayo is that it helps your other marinade ingredients spread evenly across the surface of the meat, delivering more consistent flavor, while improving browning. (Don't worry, the cooked meat doesn't taste like mayo.) In this recipe, that means chicken cutlets that cook through and brown in about four minutes, with deep chimichurri flavor enhanced by a post-grill drizzle of fresh sauce. This recipe will work with nearly any marinade, exactly as written: you could use pesto, salsa verde, bottled barbecue sauce, jarred Thai curry paste, teriyaki sauce or mole, all with equal success.

—J. Kenji López-Alt

4 chicken breast cutlets (4 to 5 ounces each), pounded about ¼-inch thick

Kosher salt and black pepper

⅓ cup store-bought or homemade mayonnaise

1 cup chimichurri (recipe follows)

1. Season the chicken cutlets on both sides with salt and pepper and set aside.

2. Whisk together the mayonnaise and ¼ cup chimichurri in a large bowl. Reserve remaining chimichurri. Add the chicken cutlets to the mixture and turn to coat. Cook immediately, or for better flavor, transfer to a sealed container and refrigerate for 4 to 24 hours.

3. To cook on the grill: Heat a gas or charcoal grill over high heat for 10 minutes. Cook the chicken cutlets directly over high heat, turning and flipping occasionally, until just cooked through and lightly charred all over, 4 to 5 minutes. Transfer the chicken to a serving platter. Spoon some of the remaining chimichurri over the chicken and serve the rest in a small bowl on the side.

   To cook in a skillet: Heat a large (12-inch) cast-iron or nonstick skillet over medium-high heat until a drop of water immediately balls up and dances across the surface. Add the chicken cutlets in a single layer and cook, swirling them and flipping them occasionally until browned all over and just cooked through, about 4 minutes. Transfer the chicken to a serving platter. Spoon some of the remaining chimichurri over the chicken and serve the rest in a small bowl on the side.

Chimichurri

time   35 minutes

yield   about 1 cup

Chimichurri is a herbaceous and vinegary sauce from Argentina that's classically paired with grilled meats, especially beef, but its uses don't end there. Combine chimichurri with equal parts olive oil to use as a marinade and dressing for grilled vegetables. Add a few crushed cloves of garlic to that same mixture, brush it on a split ciabatta or baguette, and grill or broil it for an oregano-packed take on garlic bread. Chimichurri can be stored in the refrigerator for several weeks; it will lose its bright green color, but it will improve in flavor with time.

¼ cup dried oregano

1 teaspoon sweet paprika

½ teaspoon red pepper flakes (more or less to taste)

½ teaspoon ground cumin (optional)

½ cup hot water

Kosher salt

¼ cup red wine vinegar

8 medium garlic cloves

2 tablespoons olive oil (it need not be extra-virgin, but it can be), plus more as needed

¼ cup fresh oregano leaves, finely minced

1 tightly packed cup fresh parsley leaves, finely minced

Black pepper

1. Combine the dried oregano, paprika, red pepper flakes and cumin (if using) in a large bowl. Add the water and a big pinch of salt and stir with a fork. Add the vinegar and stir to combine.

2. Smash the garlic with a pinch of salt in a mortar and pestle to form a rough paste, then drizzle in about 2 tablespoons olive oil and work the garlic and oil around the mortar until it emulsifies and no loose oil remains. Scrape the garlic mixture into the bowl with the oregano mixture and stir to combine. (Alternatively, smash the garlic cloves on a cutting board with the flat side of a chef's knife. Sprinkle with a pinch of kosher salt, then use the side of your knife to scrape the mixture back and forth until a paste forms. Drizzle a little olive oil over the paste and work it in with the side of the knife. Repeat until you've added about a tablespoon of olive oil, then scrape the mixture up and transfer it to the bowl with the oregano mixture, add the remaining olive oil, and stir to combine.)

3. Add the fresh oregano and parsley and stir to combine. Set aside at room temperature for at least 30 minutes, or in the refrigerator overnight, to allow the dried oregano to rehydrate and the flavors and texture to develop. Stir vigorously before tasting, then adjust the seasoning with salt and black pepper.

Ginger-Scallion Chicken

time   15 minutes

yield   4 servings

In this easy stir-fry, adapted from Lan Hing Riggin, a home cook from Virginia who grew up cooking with her family in Hong Kong, slivers of ginger and scallion turn golden, adding their sweetness and pungency to the oil. Soy sauce provides saltiness and depth, while a cupful of cilantro leaves, used as garnish, makes the dish a bit lighter and fresher. Fire seekers can add a sliced chile or two along with the ginger.

—Melissa Clark

2 large scallions

¼ cup peanut oil or neutral oil (such as grapeseed or sunflower), plus more if needed

1¾ pounds boneless, skinless chicken thighs or breasts, cut into 1-inch chunks

½ teaspoon kosher salt

1 cup roughly chopped fresh cilantro leaves and tender stems

1 (2½-inch) piece fresh ginger, peeled and cut into thin matchsticks (3 tablespoons)

3 tablespoons soy sauce

Large pinch of granulated sugar

1. Trim the scallions, cut lengthwise into quarters, then cut crosswise into 1½-inch-long pieces. You should end up with thin blades of scallion. Separate out the dark green tops from the pale green and white parts. (You don't have to be very thorough; some mixing of colors is fine.)

2. Heat the oil in a wok or large skillet over very high heat. When it's shimmering but not smoking, stir in the chicken and salt. Cook, stirring almost constantly, until the chicken is just cooked through and no longer pink, 3 to 5 minutes. Use a slotted spoon to transfer the chicken to a serving plate, leaving the oil in the pan. Immediately scatter the cilantro and scallion greens (not the pale green and white parts) over the hot chicken.

3. Return the wok to medium-high heat. Make sure there are at least 2 tablespoons oil in the wok. If not, add more oil. Stir in the ginger and cook until lightly browned, about 1 minute. Stir in the scallion whites and pale green parts, soy sauce and sugar and cook for another 30 seconds (if using a skillet, remove from the heat). Immediately spoon the contents of the pan evenly over the chicken and herbs. Serve right away.

"Recommend chopping the cilantro in a mini processor. Once all the ingredients were prepared, this was a quick breeze to put together. Quite simple to make and a joy to consume."

—Kathy A

Easy Kung Pao Chicken

time   15 minutes

yield   4 servings

Sweet, sour and a little spicy, this meal tastes like home—specifically the home of Pearl Han, a talented cook originally from Taiwan who naturally streamlined dishes while raising three kids and managing a busy career in California. Her younger daughter, Grace Han, shared this recipe: "quick, easy and my mom's favorite." First, dried chiles sizzle in oil to impart heat to the whole dish, then chicken browns in a single layer—no high-heat stir-frying necessary—to create a tasty caramelized crust before the pieces are flipped together. Coated in a dead-simple kung pao sauce that delivers the dish's signature salty tang, the chicken begs to be spooned over steamed rice. Serve with stir-fried vegetables as well for a complete meal.

—Genevieve Ko

1 pound boneless, skinless chicken breasts, cut into ½-inch chunks

3 tablespoons soy sauce

2 teaspoons cornstarch

Kosher salt and black or Sichuan pepper

1½ tablespoons Chinkiang (black) vinegar or balsamic vinegar

2 teaspoons granulated sugar

¼ cup neutral oil, such as grapeseed

½ cup small dried red chiles (½ ounce; see Tip)

1. In a medium bowl, mix together the chicken, 1 tablespoon of the soy sauce, 1 teaspoon of the cornstarch, and a big pinch each of salt and pepper until the chicken is evenly coated. Let sit while you prepare the sauce.

2. In a small bowl, stir together the vinegar, sugar and the remaining 2 tablespoons soy sauce and 1 teaspoon cornstarch.

3. Combine the oil and chiles in a wok or large nonstick skillet and set over medium heat. When the chiles start to sizzle and brown, after about 15 seconds, push them to one side of the pan. Add the chicken to the other side and spread in a single layer. Cook the pieces, without moving them, until the bottoms are dark golden brown, 3 to 5 minutes. If the chiles start to blacken, put them on top of the chicken so they don't burn.

4. Using a large spatula, flip the chicken in portions. Cook just until the meat almost loses all of its pinkness, 1 to 2 minutes more. Stir the sauce and pour it into the pan. Stir until the sauce thickens and slicks the chicken evenly. Immediately transfer to a plate and serve hot.

Tip

The small dried red chiles typically used in kung pao dishes are available in Chinese markets. Any small dried red chiles work, though they do range in heat. For a similar spice level, use chiles de árbol.

Sheet-Pan Miso-Honey Chicken and Asparagus

time 20 minutes, plus
up to 30 minutes
for marinating

yield 4 servings

This easy meal is broiled instead of baked, which chars the marinade slightly on the chicken, browns the asparagus for maximum flavor and cuts the cooking time to around 10 minutes. The miso-honey mixture packs a punch, with lots of garlic, ginger and as much hot sauce as you like. Make sure to arrange the chicken thighs in a single layer so they cook and char evenly, and keep an eye on the pan, as some broilers have hot spots.

—Yossy Arefi

3 tablespoons white miso

3 tablespoons mild honey

3 tablespoons soy sauce or tamari

1 tablespoon rice vinegar

2 teaspoons peeled, grated fresh ginger

2 teaspoons grated garlic

2 teaspoons chile-garlic sauce or other hot sauce

1 tablespoon plus 2 teaspoons neutral oil, such as grapeseed or canola

1½ to 2 pounds boneless, skinless chicken thighs

1 large bunch asparagus (about 1 pound), trimmed

Kosher salt and black pepper

2 scallions, thinly sliced

Hot steamed rice, for serving (optional)

1. In a small bowl, whisk together the miso, honey, soy sauce, vinegar, ginger, garlic, chile-garlic sauce, 1 tablespoon of the oil and 1 tablespoon water. Refrigerate half of the mixture to use as a sauce for serving.

2. Place the chicken in a large, shallow dish or resealable plastic bag and pour the remaining miso-honey mixture over the top. Toss the chicken until coated and cover the dish, or seal the bag and turn a few times to coat. Marinate the chicken in the refrigerator for up to 30 minutes. (Marinating longer may dry out the chicken.)

3. When you're ready to cook, heat the broiler with a rack about 6 inches from the heat source. Line a large sheet pan with foil.

4. Remove the chicken from the marinade, scraping off and discarding any excess. Place the chicken, flatter side up, in a single layer on one side of the pan. Place the asparagus on the other side. Drizzle the asparagus with the remaining 2 teaspoons oil, then season with salt and pepper, toss to coat and spread in a single layer.

5. Broil until the chicken is cooked through with some charred spots and the asparagus is browned, about 10 minutes.

6. To serve, drizzle the chicken with the reserved miso-honey and sprinkle with the scallions. Serve with rice, if desired.

"This was so easy. Next time I will double the sauce, then freeze half. The kids who never agree on anything had seconds."

—Nisey

Garlicky Chicken with Lemon-Anchovy Sauce

time   25 minutes

yield   4 servings

There's nothing wrong with a dinner of pan-seared chicken seasoned with salt and pepper. But there's everything right about the same chicken when you add anchovies, capers, garlic and plenty of lemon to the pan. What was once timid and a little dull turns vibrant and tangy. Most people would probably want to use the workhorse of all poultry dinners to make this dish: the boneless, skinless breast. But thighs are easier to cook, in that they're more difficult to overcook. However, if your family insists on white meat, you can substitute breasts and subtract about 3 minutes from the cooking time. There's no need to mention the anchovies until after people have complimented you on the meal.

—Melissa Clark

1¼ pounds boneless, skinless chicken thighs (4 to 5 thighs)

1 teaspoon coarse kosher salt

Black pepper

6 garlic cloves, smashed, then peeled

¼ cup extra-virgin olive oil

5 anchovy fillets

2 tablespoons drained capers, patted dry

Large pinch of red pepper flakes

1 lemon, halved

Chopped fresh parsley, for serving

1. Heat the oven to 350 degrees. Season the chicken thighs all over with the salt and some pepper and let rest while you prepare the anchovy-garlic oil. Mince one of the garlic cloves and set it aside for later. Heat the oil in a large, ovenproof skillet over medium-high heat. When the oil is hot, add the remaining 5 smashed garlic cloves, the anchovies, capers and pepper flakes. Let cook, stirring with a wooden spoon to break up the anchovies, until the garlic browns around the edges and the anchovies dissolve, 3 to 5 minutes.

2. Add the chicken thighs and cook until nicely browned on the underside, 5 to 7 minutes. Flip the thighs, place the pan in the oven and bake the chicken until it's cooked through, another 5 to 10 minutes.

3. When the chicken is done, transfer the thighs to a plate (be careful, as the pan handle will be hot). Place the skillet back on the stovetop over medium-high heat, add the minced garlic and squeeze in the juice from a lemon half. Cook for about 30 seconds, scraping up the browned bits on the bottom of the pan. Return the chicken to the pan and cook it in the sauce for another 15 to 30 seconds.

4. Transfer everything to a serving platter. Squeeze the juice from the remaining lemon half over the chicken, sprinkle with parsley and serve.

Green Chile Chicken Tacos

time   30 minutes

yield   4 servings

This weeknight chicken dinner takes advantage of canned green chiles, a flavorful and time-saving pantry staple. The green chiles have already been roasted, peeled and chopped for ease; simply combine them with spices and broth for a quick sauce with nice mild heat and smoky notes. Chicken thighs are an affordable cut that's juicy, tender and rich with flavor, but chicken breast could also be used here for leaner (but just as tasty) tacos. Leftovers can be turned into a zesty pasta salad or used as a hearty omelet or frittata filling.

—Kay Chun

¼ cup safflower or canola oil

½ teaspoon dried oregano

½ teaspoon ground cumin

1½ pounds boneless skinless chicken thighs, chopped into ½-inch pieces

Kosher salt and black pepper

½ cup finely chopped yellow onion (from ½ medium onion)

½ cup finely chopped green bell pepper (from ½ bell pepper)

3 garlic cloves, minced

2 (4-ounce) cans chopped green chiles, drained

1 cup low-sodium chicken broth

8 (6-inch) corn tortillas, warmed or toasted

Shredded cabbage, store-bought pico de gallo or salsa, sliced avocado, sour cream, and cilantro leaves and tender stems, for serving

Lime wedges, for serving

1. In a small bowl, mix the oil with the oregano and cumin. Heat a large nonstick skillet over medium-high heat. To the skillet add 2 tablespoons of the seasoned oil and half of the chicken and season with salt and pepper. Cook, stirring occasionally, until the chicken is no longer pink and is lightly golden, about 5 minutes. Using a slotted spoon or spatula, transfer the chicken to a plate. Add 1 tablespoon of the oil and remaining chicken to the skillet and repeat.

2. Add the remaining 1 tablespoon oil, onion and bell pepper to the empty skillet and season with salt and pepper. Cook, stirring occasionally, until softened, about 3 minutes. Stir in the garlic until fragrant, 30 seconds to 1 minute. Add the green chiles, broth and chicken (along with any accumulated juices) and bring to a simmer. Cook, stirring occasionally, until all of the liquid is absorbed, the mixture is thick and the chicken is cooked through, about 8 minutes.

3. Divide the chicken mixture among the tortillas. Top with the shredded cabbage, pico de gallo, avocado, sour cream and cilantro. Serve with lime wedges.

"Beautiful marriage of flavors that taste a little like posole, a little like chile rellenos. The sauce is silky when reduced down, and there is hardly any need for condiments other than good tomatoes and crisp iceberg lettuce. Great weeknight dish!"

—Jennie VT

"One of the best chicken dishes I have ever made. The yogurt marinade made the chicken so tender and I grilled it inside on a grill pan and it was DELICIOUS!"

—Rena T.

Grilled Za'atar Chicken with Garlic Yogurt and Cilantro

time 30 minutes, plus
at least 2 hours
for marinating

yield 4 to 6 servings

This garlicky, herby chicken is full-flavored and very tender, thanks to its piquant yogurt marinade. It's flexible, too. You can marinate the meat for as little as a couple of hours or as long as overnight. You can substitute chicken breasts for the thighs; just watch them closely as they cook. And the chicken is just as good cooked under the broiler as it is on the grill. This dish goes with almost anything, but it's especially nice with pita or other flatbread and a big cucumber and tomato salad.

—Melissa Clark

6 garlic cloves, grated, pressed or minced

2 lemons, zested

1 cup whole-milk plain yogurt

¼ cup chopped fresh cilantro, plus sprigs for serving

3 tablespoons extra-virgin olive oil, plus more for serving

1½ tablespoons za'atar

1 tablespoon chopped fresh oregano or marjoram, plus sprigs for serving

1¾ teaspoons kosher salt, plus more for the yogurt sauce

¼ teaspoon black pepper, plus more for the yogurt sauce

2¼ pounds boneless, skinless chicken thighs

1. In a large bowl or other food-safe container, stir together 5 of the garlic cloves, half of the lemon zest, ⅓ cup of the yogurt, the cilantro, oil, za'atar, oregano, salt and black pepper. Add the chicken and toss until well coated. Cover and refrigerate for at least 2 hours or up to overnight.

2. When ready to cook, prepare a grill for direct cooking over medium heat or heat the broiler with the rack 3 inches from the heat source. Remove the chicken from the bowl, shaking off any excess marinade and grill or broil on one side until charred in spots, 5 to 8 minutes. Flip the chicken and grill or broil until just cooked through, another 5 to 8 minutes.

3. While the chicken is cooking, put the remaining ⅔ cup yogurt into a small bowl. Stir in the remaining garlic and lemon zest and season with salt and pepper. Cut 1 zested lemon in half and set aside for serving (save the other zested lemon for another use).

4. Place the chicken on a serving platter and drizzle with oil and a large squeeze of juice from the zested lemon. Top with cilantro and oregano sprigs and serve with the yogurt sauce.

Tip

If you're broiling instead of grilling, you can line your sheet pan with foil for easier cleanup. Don't use parchment paper, as it may burn.

Chicken Katsu

time 30 minutes

yield 4 servings

In this version of katsu, the popular Japanese comfort food, boneless chicken breasts are pounded thin, dredged in flour, egg and panko, and then fried until golden brown for an irresistible crispy crust that yields to—and protects—juicy meat inside. The traditional accompaniments are a mound of crunchy shredded cabbage, steamed rice and a generous drizzle of sweet-savory katsu sauce (also called tonkatsu sauce), a Japanese-style barbecue sauce made with soy sauce, Worcestershire sauce, tomatoes, ginger and clove. Although you can purchase bottles of the sauce in Asian markets or online, it's easy to make, lasts indefinitely in the fridge and serves as a great all-purpose dip.

—Kay Chun

For the tonkatsu sauce

6 tablespoons ketchup

6 tablespoons Worcestershire sauce

4 teaspoons unsulfured molasses

2 teaspoons low-sodium soy sauce

2 teaspoons granulated sugar

¼ teaspoon peeled, grated fresh ginger

⅛ teaspoon ground cloves

For the chicken katsu

Vegetable oil, for frying

½ cup all-purpose flour

2 large eggs, beaten

1½ cups panko bread crumbs (about 3½ ounces)

2 (½-pound) boneless, skinless chicken breasts, halved crosswise, then pounded ¼ inch thick

Kosher salt and black pepper

4 tightly packed cups finely shredded green cabbage (about 12 ounces)

Hot steamed rice and lemon wedges, for serving

1. Prepare the tonkatsu sauce: In a small bowl, combine all the ingredients and stir well.

2. Prepare the chicken: Pour oil to a depth of ⅓ inch into a large cast-iron or other heavy skillet. Heat over medium heat until an instant-read thermometer registers 350 degrees.

3. Place the flour, eggs and bread crumbs in three separate wide, shallow bowls or large plates.

4. Season the chicken cutlets on both sides with salt and pepper. Working with 1 cutlet at a time, dredge in flour until fully coated, then shake off the excess. Dip into the egg, coating both sides and letting the excess drip off, then press

"Great as leftovers too. A cutlet on a good toasted bun with shredded cabbage and tonkatsu sauce on top. We always make more than one meal out of this."

—Charlie

into the bread crumbs until well coated. Transfer to a clean plate and repeat with the remaining 3 cutlets.

5. Gently lower 2 cutlets into the oil and fry until golden on the underside, about 2 minutes. Adjust the heat to keep it as close to 350 degrees as possible. Turn the chicken over and fry until golden on the second side and cooked through, 1½ to 2 minutes longer. Transfer to a paper towel–lined plate to drain and season with salt. Repeat with remaining 2 cutlets.

6. Cut the cutlets into thick slices and transfer to four plates. Divide the cabbage evenly and arrange in a mound next to the katsu. Drizzle the katsu with some of the tonkatsu sauce. Serve with small bowls of rice and with lemon wedges and the remaining tonkatsu sauce on the side.

Pan-Seared Ranch Chicken

time   35 minutes
        plus at least
        15 minutes
        for marinating

yield   4 servings

In this recipe, America's favorite salad dressing serves double duty as a creamy, herbaceous sauce and as a marinade. But don't reach for bottled ranch. Instead, quickly make your own brighter, tangier version using Greek yogurt. Unlike lemon- or vinegar-based marinades, which can toughen meat, yogurt tenderizes even the leanest of chicken breasts. When the chicken is seared in a hot pan, the yogurt-mayo coating forms a flavorful, caramelized crust. (It also makes an excellent marinade for fish, pork, shrimp or sturdy vegetables.)

—Ali Slagle

¾ cup Greek yogurt

¼ cup mayonnaise

3 tablespoons finely chopped fresh chives, or ½ teaspoon dried, plus more for serving

3 tablespoons finely chopped fresh dill or parsley, or ½ teaspoon dried, plus more for serving

¾ teaspoon garlic powder

Kosher salt and black pepper

1½ to 2 pounds boneless, skinless chicken breasts or thighs

2 tablespoons extra-virgin olive oil

1. Make the ranch: In a measuring cup or small bowl, stir together the yogurt, mayonnaise, chives, dill and garlic powder; season with 1½ teaspoons salt and a few grinds of pepper. Transfer half of the ranch to a medium bowl.

2. Pat the chicken dry. If thickness varies greatly, pound to an even thickness of about ½ inch. Season both sides with salt and pepper, then transfer the chicken to the medium bowl with the ranch and toss to coat. Let sit for at least 15 minutes or cover and refrigerate for up to overnight. (Let the chicken come to room temperature before cooking.)

3. Heat the oil in a large nonstick skillet over medium-high heat. Working in batches if necessary, cook the chicken (with the marinade still on it), turning once, until deeply caramelized on the outside, it releases from the pan and its juices run clear, 4 to 6 minutes per side. Turn down the heat if the chicken is browning too quickly.

4. If the ranch in the measuring cup is too thick, add a little bit of water to loosen it. (You should be able to drizzle it easily.) Serve the chicken with the ranch passed at the table and more herbs if you like.

"So surprisingly tasty! Loved how the chicken got crispy on the outside. For the reserved dressing, I thinned it with lemon juice and used it to dress leafy greens to serve alongside."

—Jennifer

"We ate it with lime cilantro rice, vaquero beans with some of the sauce added, and mango salsa with avocado. I love a dish that can please people with different eating preferences without sacrificing flavor."

—Maura

Easy Weeknight Dinners

Tajín Grilled Chicken

time   35 minutes

yield   4 servings

Tajín—the Mexican seasoning made from ground dried red chiles, salt and lime—is great sprinkled over cut fresh fruit like mango and pineapple, or coating the rim of an ice cold margarita. But it's also an easy way to add chile and lime to your favorite grilled meats, rubs or sauces. In this dish, the lime in the Tajín cuts the sweetness from the agave syrup, while the red chiles complement the smoky flavor of the chipotles. Serve the chicken as is or on toasted hamburger buns with mayonnaise, chopped grilled scallions, cilantro leaves and sliced pickled jalapeños. This Tajín sauce would also pair well with cod or salmon, grilled bass or with shrimp skewers.

—Rick A. Martínez

Vegetable oil, for the grill

8 boneless, skinless chicken thighs (about 2 pounds)

Sea salt or kosher salt

½ cup light agave syrup or honey

1 teaspoon grated orange zest

½ cup fresh orange juice

3 chipotle chiles in adobo, finely chopped, plus ¼ cup adobo sauce

6 garlic cloves, grated

2 tablespoons extra-virgin olive oil

1 tablespoon Tajín Clásico

8 scallions, trimmed

½ cup fresh cilantro leaves and tender stems, for serving

1. Prepare a grill for direct cooking over medium-high heat. Clean the grates well, then brush them with vegetable oil. Alternatively, heat a grill pan over medium-high heat and brush the pan with vegetable oil.

2. Arrange the chicken on a sheet pan and generously season on both sides with salt. In a medium bowl, whisk together the agave syrup, orange juice, orange zest, chipotle chiles, adobo sauce, garlic, olive oil and Tajín.

3. Brush the chicken on both sides with the Tajín sauce. Grill the chicken, turning and basting often with the Tajín sauce, until cooked through, charred but brick red and glazed, 7 to 9 minutes. Grill the scallions, turning occasionally, until lightly charred on all sides, about 5 minutes.

4. Serve the chicken with the grilled scallions, topped with the cilantro.

Garlic Chicken with Guasacaca Sauce

time   45 minutes

yield   4 servings

Simple to make, versatile in use and complex in flavor, guasacaca sauce is one of the wonderful condiments of Venezuelan cuisine. Creamy from the addition of avocado with a bright and tangy herb and lime base, it makes an evocative pairing for any vegetarian, seafood or meat dish. Here it accompanies a sheet-pan dinner of roasted chicken and carrots, but will do just as well with anything from the grill.

—Yewande Komolafe

½ cup olive oil

3 large garlic cloves

1½ pounds carrots, scrubbed, trimmed and cut into 2-inch lengths (½-inch wide)

Kosher salt and black pepper

2½ to 3 pounds bone-in, skin-on chicken thighs, drumsticks, breasts or a combination, patted dry

1 avocado, pitted and chopped

1 jalapeño, stemmed and chopped

2 tablespoons rice vinegar

Zest and juice of 1 lime

1 cup chopped fresh parsley leaves with tender stems

1 cup chopped fresh cilantro leaves with tender stems

1. Heat the oven to 425 degrees. In a medium bowl, combine ¼ cup of the oil and grate in 2 of the garlic cloves using a zester. Add the carrots and toss to coat. Lightly season with salt and black pepper and transfer to a sheet pan, reserving the garlic oil in the bowl. Add the chicken to the bowl and coat with the remaining garlic oil. Arrange in a single layer on the sheet pan skin-side up between the carrots.

2. Roast until the carrots are tender and the chicken is cooked through with crispy skin that's browned in spots, 35 to 40 minutes.

3. While the chicken cooks, in a food processor or blender or using a mortar and pestle, combine the avocado, jalapeño, vinegar, lime zest and juice, remaining garlic clove, half the chopped parsley and cilantro, ½ teaspoon salt and ¼ teaspoon black pepper. Purée or pound into a coarse mixture. With the machine running or while mixing with a pestle in a mortar, slowly drizzle in the remaining ¼ cup oil and 1 tablespoon room-temperature water. Purée or stir until the sauce is smooth and creamy. Taste and adjust the seasoning with additional salt if necessary. The sauce can be made a few hours in advance and refrigerated in an airtight container.

4. Scatter the remaining ½ cup each parsley and cilantro over the chicken and carrots. Transfer to individual plates along with any pan juices. Spoon a few tablespoons of the guasacaca sauce on the side for dipping. Serve warm with additional sauce on the side.

"Incredible! Never had guasacaca sauce before but I'm amazed. I'm a sauce lover so doubled the sauce, honestly didn't need to, a little goes a long way."

—Jade

"This recipe doesn't just go into the standard repertoire, it goes into the secret-weapon-for-dinner-parties repertoire."

—VSB

Skillet Chicken with Tomatoes, Pancetta and Mozzarella

time   45 minutes

yield   4 servings

With a topping of tomato sauce and mozzarella, it's no wonder that this easy skillet dish has been dubbed "pizza chicken." It's a tangy, milky, gooey, lovable meal that's somewhat reminiscent of chicken Parmesan, but with succulent bone-in chicken pieces instead of breaded and fried cutlets. Even better, it has pancetta and anchovies for complexity of flavor, and the whole thing comes together in under an hour.

—Melissa Clark

3½ pounds bone-in, skin-on chicken pieces, or 1 (3½-pound) chicken cut into 8 pieces

2 teaspoons kosher salt

1 teaspoon black pepper

1 tablespoon extra-virgin olive oil

4 to 5 ounces pancetta, diced

3 garlic cloves, thinly sliced

2 anchovy fillets

¼ teaspoon red pepper flakes

1 (28-ounce) can whole plum tomatoes

1 large basil sprig, plus chopped fresh basil for serving

8 ounces bocconcini, halved, or fresh mozzarella, cut into ¾-inch pieces

1. Heat the oven to 400 degrees. Pat the chicken dry and season on both sides with the salt and black pepper.

2. Heat the oil in a large ovenproof skillet over medium-high heat. When the oil is hot, add the pancetta and cook, stirring frequently, until browned. Use a slotted spoon to transfer the pancetta to a paper towel–lined plate.

3. Add the chicken to the skillet and sear, turning only occasionally, until well browned on all sides, about 10 minutes. Transfer to a large plate. Pour off all but 1 tablespoon oil.

4. Add the garlic, anchovies and red pepper flakes to the skillet and fry, stirring, for 1 minute. Stir in the tomatoes and basil sprig and cook, breaking up the tomatoes with a spatula, until the sauce thickens somewhat, about 10 minutes.

5. Return the chicken to the skillet. Transfer the skillet to the oven and cook, uncovered, until chicken is no longer pink, about 30 minutes.

6. Remove the skillet from the oven and scatter the bocconcini evenly over the top. Adjust the oven temperature to broil. Return the skillet to the oven and broil until the cheese is melted and bubbling, 2 to 3 minutes (watch closely to make sure the top does not burn).

7. Top with the reserved pancetta and chopped basil and serve.

Sheet-Pan Gochujang Chicken and Roasted Vegetables

time   45 minutes

yield   4 to 6 servings

Gochujang, the Korean fermented chile paste, can enliven a straightforward dinner of roast chicken and vegetables with a salty, spicy and umami-rich layer of flavor. Freshly grated ginger, sliced scallions and quick-pickled radishes elevate the flavor even further. This recipe calls for a wintry mix of squash and turnips, but equal amounts of root vegetables, like carrots, potatoes and beets, or lighter vegetables, such as cauliflower, brussels sprouts and broccoli, will work well, too.

—Yewande Komolafe

3 tablespoons gochujang

2 tablespoons soy sauce

1 (1-inch) piece fresh ginger, peeled and grated (1 tablespoon)

3 tablespoons neutral oil, such as grapeseed or canola, plus more for drizzling

2 pounds winter squash, such as butternut, acorn or delicata, unpeeled, seeded and cut into 2-inch pieces (about 5 loose cups)

1 pound turnips, trimmed and cut into 2-inch pieces (about 3½ loose cups)

10 scallions, trimmed, green and white parts separated

Kosher salt

2½ to 3 pounds bone-in, skin-on chicken thighs, drumsticks or breasts

1 bunch radishes (about 10 ounces), trimmed

2 tablespoons rice vinegar

1 tablespoon sesame oil (optional)

Hot steamed rice, for serving (optional)

1. Heat the oven to 425 degrees. Combine the gochujang, soy sauce, ginger and neutral oil in a medium bowl or resealable plastic bag. Add the squash, turnips and scallion whites and toss to coat with the glaze or seal the bag and shake to coat. Lightly season with salt and transfer to a sheet pan. Pat the chicken dry, season on both sides with salt and then toss to coat in whatever is left of the glaze in the bowl or bag. Arrange the chicken, skin side up, among the vegetables on the sheet pan.

2. Roast until the vegetables are tender and the chicken is cooked through and its skin is crispy and browned in spots, about 40 minutes.

3. While the chicken cooks, thinly slice the scallion greens. Using a sharp knife or a mandoline, cut the radishes into thin rounds. In a small bowl, toss the sliced scallion greens and radishes with the vinegar and sesame oil (if using). Season with salt and set aside to pickle lightly.

4. Top the roast chicken and vegetables with the scallion-radish mix and transfer to serving plates. Serve with rice, if desired.

"The squash was tasty, the chicken was very, very, very good, but the turnips were unparalleled. I got up (twice) in the evening to reheat a few more veggies."

—Kate

Lemony White Bean Soup with Turkey and Greens

time   45 minutes

yield   4 servings

Bright with lemon and herbs and packed with hearty greens, this highly adaptable soup—the only turkey recipe to sneak into the chicken chapter—can be either light and brothy or thick and stew-like, depending on your preference. Smashing some of the beans to release their starch will give you a thicker soup that's almost worthy of a fork. To keep it on the brothy side, add a little more liquid and leave the beans intact. Either way, it's a warming, piquant one-pot meal that's perfect for winter.

—Melissa Clark

3 tablespoons olive oil

1 large onion, diced

1 large carrot, diced

1 bunch sturdy greens, such as kale, broccoli rabe, mustard greens or collard greens

1 tablespoon tomato paste

¾ teaspoon ground cumin, plus more to taste

⅛ teaspoon red pepper flakes, plus more for serving (optional)

½ pound ground turkey

3 garlic cloves, minced

1 tablespoon peeled, grated fresh ginger

Kosher salt

4 cups chicken stock

2 (15-ounce) cans white beans, drained and rinsed

1 cup chopped fresh soft herbs, such as parsley, mint, dill, basil, tarragon or chives or a combination

Fresh lemon juice, to taste

1. Heat a large pot over medium-high heat for 1 minute or so to warm it up. Add the oil and heat until it shimmers, about 30 seconds. Add the onion and carrot and cook, stirring occasionally, until very soft and brown at the edges, 7 to 10 minutes.

2. Meanwhile, rinse the greens and pull the leaves off the stems. Tear or chop the leaves into bite-size pieces and set aside.

3. When the onion is golden, add the tomato paste, cumin and red pepper flakes and cook, stirring frequently, until the tomato paste darkens, about 1 minute. Add the turkey, garlic, ginger and 1 teaspoon salt and cook, stirring often and breaking up the turkey with your spoon until it is browned in spots, 4 to 7 minutes.

4. Add the stock and beans, stir well and bring to a simmer. Simmer until the soup is thick and flavorful, tasting and adding more salt if needed, 15 to 25 minutes. If you prefer a thicker broth, smash some of the beans with the back of the spoon to release their starch.

> "My 11-year-old son just made this yesterday at his cooking class with his grandma. It is so, so good. They skipped the fresh herbs and lemon (none on hand) and upped both the chile flakes and ginger. It was divine. My son was so proud to serve it to us for lunch."
>
> —Compostista

5. Add the greens and simmer until very soft. This will take 5 to 10 minutes for most greens, but tough collard greens might take 15 minutes. (Add a little water if the broth reduces too much.)

6. Stir the herbs and lemon juice into the pot, then taste and add more salt, cumin and lemon juice until the broth is lively and bright tasting. Serve topped with a drizzle of oil and a sprinkle of red pepper flakes, if you like.

Sticky Coconut Chicken and Rice

time   45 minutes

yield   4 servings

This comforting one-pot chicken dish features fragrant coconut rice infused with aromatic ginger, garlic and scallion and studded with toasty cashews. The cashews soften as the rice steams, adding subtle nuttiness to the dish. Chicken thighs absorb the coconut milk as they cook, which keeps the meat tender and juicy. Chopped fresh cilantro brightens the dish, while hot sauce adds nice heat and tang to balance the creamy, rich and slightly sweet rice.

—Kay Chun

1½ pounds boneless, skinless chicken thighs, each cut in half

4 tablespoons neutral oil, such as safflower or canola

2 teaspoons kosher salt

½ teaspoon black pepper

2 tablespoons peeled, minced fresh ginger

1 tablespoon minced garlic

1½ cups short-grain white rice, rinsed until water runs clear

1¾ cups low-sodium chicken stock

1 (13-ounce) can full-fat coconut milk

1 yellow bell pepper, cut into ½-inch pieces

½ cup roasted cashews, coarsely chopped

3 scallions, thinly sliced (½ packed cup)

2 tablespoons coarsely chopped fresh cilantro

Hot sauce, for serving

1. Heat the oven to 375 degrees. Rub the chicken on both sides with 1 tablespoon of the oil and season with 1 teaspoon of the salt and ¼ teaspoon of the pepper.

2. Heat 2 tablespoons of the oil in a large Dutch oven over medium heat. Working in two batches, brown the chicken, turning once at the halfway point, until no longer pink, about 5 minutes per batch. As each batch is ready, transfer to a plate.

3. Add the remaining 1 tablespoon oil, the ginger and the garlic to the empty pot and stir until fragrant, about 30 seconds. Add the rice and stir until evenly coated in the oil. Add the stock, coconut milk, bell pepper, cashews, scallions and the remaining 1 teaspoon salt and ¼ teaspoon pepper and stir to dislodge any browned bits on the bottom of the pot. Arrange the chicken on top of the rice mixture, add any accumulated juices from the plate, increase the heat to high and bring to a boil.

4. Cover, transfer to the oven and bake until all the liquid is absorbed, the rice is tender and chicken is cooked through, about 25 minutes. Remove from the oven, scatter the cilantro over the chicken and rice and then divide among bowls. Serve with hot sauce.

"Made with basmati rice. Loved it with green Tabasco. Extremely easy."

—Janet

"This recipe is so simple and the result is luscious and delicious. The quality of the Dijon mustard is key."

—Karen M.

Baked Mustard-Herb Chicken Legs

time 45 minutes

yield 4 servings

This recipe for baked chicken is adapted from chef Gary Danko, whose whole "deviled" legs, coated with Dijon mustard and tossed in bread crumbs, are a model of simplicity. It's dinner party–worthy fare, made just as easily on a weeknight.

—Mark Bittman

4 bone-in, skin-on whole chicken legs, each cut into drumstick and thigh pieces, or 8 bone-in, skin-on chicken thighs

1½ cups coarse fresh bread crumbs

2 teaspoons minced garlic

2 tablespoons chopped fresh parsley

1 teaspoon chopped fresh tarragon or the herb of your choice

Kosher salt and black pepper

6 tablespoons Dijon mustard

1. Heat the oven to 400 degrees. Trim the excess skin and fat from the chicken. Mix together the bread crumbs, garlic, parsley and tarragon on a plate and season with salt and pepper. Spread the mustard lightly on the chicken, covering completely. Carefully coat the chicken with the bread crumb mixture.

2. Gently place the chicken in a roasting pan. Bake until cooked through, 30 to 40 minutes. Serve hot or cold.

Sheet-Pan Chicken Thighs with Spicy Corn

time   55 minutes,
       plus at least
       30 minutes
       for marinating

yield 4 to 6 servings

The spicy, salty jalapeño brine balances sweet corn kernels, which roast on a sheet pan alongside chicken thighs in this simple, summery weeknight meal. The chicken, marinated with basil, garlic and a little mayonnaise, stays juicy even after a brief stint under the broiler. You can serve this hot from the oven or at room temperature—it's equally good each way—and cold leftovers are excellent piled onto lettuce or avocado for a salad the next day.

—Melissa Clark

2 pounds boneless, skinless chicken thighs

1¾ teaspoons fine sea or table salt

2 tablespoons mayonnaise

¼ cup finely chopped basil, plus more for garnish

2 garlic cloves, finely grated or minced

⅓ cup chopped pickled jalapeños, plus brine from the jar

4 cups fresh or frozen corn kernels (from about 4 ears)

3 tablespoons olive oil, plus more for drizzling

5 scallions, thinly sliced

1 jalapeño, sliced into rings

1 lime, halved

1. Season the chicken all over with ¾ teaspoon of the salt. In a large bowl, stir together the mayonnaise, basil, garlic and 2 tablespoons jalapeño brine. Add the chicken to the marinade. Cover and refrigerate for 30 minutes and up to 6 hours.

2. Heat the oven to 425 degrees. In a medium bowl, toss together the corn, pickled jalapeños, oil, remaining 1 teaspoon salt and half of the scallions (save remaining scallions for serving).

3. Arrange the chicken on a baking sheet, spacing it out. Roast for 12 minutes. Spoon the corn mixture onto the empty parts of the baking sheet. Drizzle the chicken and corn with oil. Continue to roast until the chicken is cooked through, 10 to 15 minutes longer, stirring the corn once while roasting.

4. Turn the broiler on high and broil the chicken and corn until golden brown in spots, 2 to 4 minutes (watch carefully so it doesn't burn, though a little blistering is nice).

5. Scatter the basil, remaining scallions and fresh jalapeño slices over the chicken and corn. Sprinkle with more pickled jalapeño brine and squeezes of lime juice. Serve hot or at room temperature.

"This was eyes-rolled-
  back-in-your-head
  good. The fat from the
  chicken and the olive
  oil, the acid and spice
  from the jalapeños,
  sweetness from the
  corn, and generous
  salt, this was perfect.
  So, so, so good. My
  husband is still talking
  about it."

  —Audrey

Blistered Broccoli Pasta
with Walnuts, Pecorino
and Mint, page 79

Pasta and Noodles

Pasta and Noodles

The fork swirled with spaghetti, the thick slurp of udon—few foods are as fun and pleasing as pasta and noodles. Affordable, customizable, easy to make and extremely tasty, they're staples of my weeknight cooking repertoire.

That's in part because of how pantry-friendly they are. No matter how bare the fridge is, I always have what I need to make a dish like the San Francisco–Style Vietnamese American Garlic Noodles on page 63, or a version of the Blond Puttanesca (Linguine with Tuna, Arugula and Capers) on page 83. Arugula, by the way, is a permanent item on my grocery list. The leaves mix in brilliantly with all kinds of pasta and grain dishes, or they can make the simplest side salad with lemon and olive oil if you're looking to get a fast vegetable in.

But it's not just arugula. Pasta and noodles are dream vehicles for all kinds of vegetables, which become far more delicious when they're tumbled with sauce and other elements. Take the Blistered

Broccoli Pasta on page 79: the broccoli is seared, which deepens its flavor while keeping its snap. It's then tossed with tender fusilli, crunchy walnuts and leafy herbs, topped with a flurry of cheese and spritzed with lemon juice. If you're trying to persuade someone to love vegetables, start with recipes like this one.

Noodles and pasta also play well with enormous and sometimes unexpected flavors. Those buttery garlic noodles teem with them—soy sauce, fish sauce, oyster sauce and twenty cloves of garlic. The Chile Crisp Fettuccine Alfredo on page 75 is another strong example: a tablespoon of the fiery, onion-flecked Chinese condiment turns classic fettuccine Alfredo into something far more exciting. (A full package of baby spinach stirred into the pan makes that dish greener than your typical Alfredo, too.)

But the star of one of my favorite recipes here isn't exactly a noodle. It's potato gnocchi, a pantry staple that feels like a luxury but is priced like a basic. Until recently, I didn't know I needed gnocchi, and now I don't go without it. (You can find it prepackaged in the pasta aisle.) Gnocchi is especially good if you let the dumplings toast in the pan, so they're crisp on the outside and irresistibly chewy within.

"Unusual for me, completely followed the recipe, no changes. I'll never cook pasta in a pot again. Added a fair amount of the pasta water to the end product, and it tasted like a cream sauce. This is amazing, no leftovers!"

—Michelle

San Francisco–Style Vietnamese American Garlic Noodles

time   15 minutes

yield   4 servings

These noodles, based on a dish originally created and served by Helene An at San Francisco's Thanh Long restaurant, are extraordinarily simple and delicious on their own, but that doesn't mean you can't fancy them up a bit. They go very well with seafood, and some raw, shell-on shrimp stir-fried along with the garlic right from the start would be an excellent addition.

—J. Kenji López-Alt

4 tablespoons unsalted butter

20 medium garlic cloves, minced or smashed with a mortar and pestle

4 teaspoons oyster sauce

2 teaspoons light soy sauce or shoyu (Japanese-style soy sauce)

2 teaspoons fish sauce

1 pound spaghetti

Heaping ¼ cup grated Parmesan or Pecorino Romano (1 ounce)

Small handful of thinly sliced scallions (optional)

1. Melt the butter in a wok or large saucepan over medium heat. Add the garlic and cook, stirring, until fragrant but not browned, about 2 minutes. Add the oyster sauce, soy sauce and fish sauce and stir to combine. Remove from the heat.

2. Meanwhile, add water to a depth of 1½ inches to a large skillet or sauté pan and bring to a boil over high heat. (Alternatively, heat up just enough water to cover the spaghetti in a large Dutch oven or saucepan.) Add the pasta, stir a few times to make sure it's not clumping, and cook, stirring occasionally, until just shy of al dente, about 2 minutes short of the recommended cook time on the package.

3. Using tongs, transfer the cooked pasta to the garlic sauce along with whatever water clings to it. (Reserve the remaining cooking water.)

4. Return the wok or large saucepan to high heat, add the cheese and stir and toss vigorously with a wooden spatula or spoon until the sauce is creamy and comes together, about 30 seconds. If the sauce looks too watery, continue to reduce it over high heat. If it looks greasy, splash some cooking water into it and let it come together again. Stir in the scallions (if using) and serve immediately.

One-Pot Pasta with Ricotta and Lemon

time   15 minutes

yield   4 servings

This elegant, bright pasta comes together in about the same amount of time it takes to boil noodles and heat up a jar of store-bought marinara. The no-cook sauce is a fifty-fifty mix of ricotta and Parmesan, with the zest and juice of a lemon thrown in. That's it. You could toss a handful of peas, cut-up asparagus or spinach leaves into the boiling water with the pasta during the last few minutes of cooking, or add arugula or watercress with the sauce in Step 3. It's a weeknight and for-company keeper any way you stir it.

—Ali Slagle

Kosher salt and black pepper

1 pound short, ribbed pasta, such as gemelli or penne

1 cup whole-milk ricotta (8 ounces)

1 cup grated Parmesan or pecorino (4 ounces), plus more for garnish

1 tablespoon grated lemon zest

¼ cup fresh lemon juice (from 1 to 2 lemons)

Red pepper flakes, for serving

¼ cup thinly sliced or torn fresh basil leaves, for serving (optional)

1. Bring a large pot of salted water to a boil. Add the pasta and cook until al dente, according to package instructions. Reserve 1 cup of the cooking water, then drain the pasta.

2. In the same pot, make the sauce: Add the ricotta, Parmesan, lemon zest and juice and ½ teaspoon each salt and black pepper and stir until well combined.

3. Add ½ cup of the cooking water to the sauce and stir until smooth. Add the pasta and continue to stir vigorously until the noodles are well coated. Add more cooking water as needed for a smooth sauce.

4. Divide the pasta among bowls and top each serving with some of the sauce that has pooled at the bottom of the pot. Garnish with Parmesan, black pepper, red pepper flakes and basil (if using) and serve immediately.

"I made this with the addition of arugula. So good! Just tossed in the arugula at the end for some green, peppery flavor."

—Vanessa

Somen Noodles with Poached Egg, Bok Choy and Mushrooms

time   20 minutes

yield   2 servings

The perfect meal for cold winter days, this vegetarian noodle soup can be cobbled together in an instant. Its quick, flavorful broth is made with just four ingredients: soy sauce, toasted sesame oil, scallions and shiitake mushrooms. Poached eggs add richness to the finished soup. The main keys to getting that teardrop shape during poaching are to use eggs that are as fresh as possible, and to let them simmer without disturbing them until they're cooked.

—Sue Li

2 tablespoons vegetable oil

3 scallions, trimmed, whites and greens separated and thinly sliced

8 ounces fresh shiitake mushrooms, stemmed and caps thinly sliced (about 3 cups)

Kosher salt

1 medium bok choy (about 4 ounces), cut into bite-size pieces

3 tablespoons soy sauce

2 teaspoons toasted sesame oil, plus more for drizzling

2 bundles (about 7 ounces total) somen noodles or any thin wheat or rice noodle

2 large eggs

1. Bring a large saucepan of water to a simmer.

2. Heat the vegetable oil in a medium pot over medium heat. Add the scallion whites and mushrooms, season with salt and cook, stirring occasionally, until browned, 5 to 6 minutes.

3. Add 3 cups water to the pot with the mushrooms, increase the heat to medium-high and bring to a simmer. Add the bok choy and cook until crisp-tender, about 1 minute. Stir in the soy sauce and sesame oil and season to taste with salt. Turn off the heat and cover to keep warm.

4. Meanwhile, cook the somen in the large saucepan of simmering water according to the package instructions. Using a slotted spoon or spider, divide the noodles among bowls, leaving the simmering water in the saucepan. Crack each egg into its own small bowl, discarding the shells. Swirl the simmering water in the saucepan, creating a vortex by stirring with a wooden spoon. Add the eggs, one right after another, and cook over medium-low until the whites are set, about 3 minutes. Use a slotted spoon to transfer the eggs to the bowls of noodles.

5. Ladle the hot shiitake broth into the bowls. Top with the scallion greens, drizzle with sesame oil and serve.

Honey-Glazed Mushrooms with Udon

time 20 minutes

yield 4 servings

In this fast dish, caramelized mushrooms are bathed in a satiny glaze of honey and butter, delivering the winning combination of sweet, savory and earthy flavors. Creminis are the hardest workers of the mushroom world; they are inexpensive and accessible, and while they may not feel as fancy as some wild varieties, they burst with complex flavor once they've spent some time in the pan. (Button mushrooms also do the job well.) Chubby udon noodles are the ideal carriers for the luscious sauce. For the most satisfying results, use fresh or frozen noodles rather than the thinner dried strands (though in a pinch, they work too).

—Hetty Lui McKinnon

Kosher salt and black pepper

1½ pounds fresh or frozen udon noodles

2 tablespoons neutral oil, such as vegetable or grapeseed

1 pound cremini mushrooms, stemmed and caps cut into ¼-inch-thick slices

4 garlic cloves, finely chopped

3 tablespoons honey

4 tablespoons butter, preferably salted; if not, add an additional ¼ teaspoon salt in step 2

½ small head napa cabbage, thinly sliced (about 1 pound)

3 tablespoons soy sauce

2 scallions, thinly sliced

1 tablespoon toasted sesame seeds

1. Bring a large pot of salted water to a boil. Add the noodles and cook, using chopsticks or tongs to gently loosen the noodles from their tight bundle, for about 2 minutes. Drain, rinse with cold water and leave to continue draining while you prepare the remaining ingredients.

2. Heat a wok or large skillet over medium-high heat until very hot. Add the oil and mushrooms and stir-fry, leaving undisturbed for 30 seconds to 1 minute at a time to allow them to caramelize, for 7 to 8 minutes. (Be patient: The mushrooms will release a lot of liquid, then start to brown.) Add the garlic, ½ teaspoon salt and a few turns of pepper. Drizzle the mushrooms with 2 tablespoons of the honey, then add 3 tablespoons of the butter and toss to coat evenly.

3. Add the noodles, cabbage and soy sauce to the pan, then toss until the cabbage is wilted and everything is well combined, about 2 minutes. Remove from the heat, add the remaining 1 tablespoon each honey and butter and toss. Taste and season with more salt and pepper if needed. To serve, scatter with the scallions and sesame seeds.

"Just before eating, a spritz of lime on the noodles brings the dish alive! Dish now on family meal rotation."

—LB

Cold Noodle Salad with Spicy Peanut Sauce

time   20 minutes

yield   4 servings

Soba, Japanese buckwheat noodles, are ideal for salads because they taste particularly great when they're served cold. But it's the crunchy vegetables that are the highlight here, adding crisp, fresh texture in every bite. Substitute any raw vegetables you have on hand, such as cabbage, carrot, fennel, asparagus, broccoli or cauliflower. The spicy peanut sauce is very adaptable: If you don't want to use peanut butter, you can use any nut or seed butter, like cashew, almond or sunflower butter, or even tahini.

Both the soba and the peanut sauce can be prepared ahead of time and stored in the fridge overnight, but wait to combine them until you are ready to eat for the best texture and consistency. The peanut sauce thickens as it sits, so add a tablespoon or two of water to loosen it up if necessary.

—Hetty Lui McKinnon

For the salad

Kosher salt

10 ounces soba noodles

1 medium zucchini or cucumber (about 6 ounces)

5 radishes (about 4 ounces), trimmed

1 bell pepper (any color)

1 tablespoon toasted sesame oil

½ cup salted roasted peanuts (about 2 ounces), roughly chopped

2 scallions, finely chopped

Handful of fresh cilantro leaves

1 lime, cut into wedges, for serving

For the spicy peanut sauce

½ cup smooth peanut butter (not natural peanut butter)

¼ cup soy sauce

2 tablespoons maple syrup

2 tablespoons fresh lime juice (from 1 lime)

1 tablespoon toasted sesame oil

2 teaspoons chile oil or hot sauce, plus more to taste

1 garlic clove, grated

1. Cook the noodles: Bring a large pot of salted water to the boil. Add the soba, stir to prevent sticking, and cook until just tender, according to package instructions. Drain and rinse under cold water until completely cold.

2. Meanwhile, make the sauce: In a medium bowl, combine the peanut butter, soy sauce, maple syrup, lime juice, sesame oil, chile oil and garlic. Add ¼ to ½ cup water, 1 tablespoon at a time, and whisk until the sauce is a pourable consistency. Taste and add more chile oil as desired. Set aside.

"This was so easy and so good and so versatile. Everyone loved it. The sauce is just perfect. We added extra hot sauce and extra lime juice, just because that's what we love."

—Lenna

3. To finish the salad, cut the zucchini and radishes into ⅛-inch-thick slices, then cut into thin matchsticks. Cut the bell pepper into ⅛-inch pieces. Put them all into a large bowl.

4. Loosen the soba noodles by briefly holding them under running cold water, then drain again. Add the noodles and the remaining 1 tablespoon sesame oil to the vegetables and toss to combine.

5. When you're ready to serve, drizzle the salad with the peanut sauce and top with the peanuts, scallions and cilantro. Serve immediately, with the lime wedges alongside.

Dumpling Noodle Soup

time   25 minutes

yield 4 servings

Keep a package or two of frozen dumplings in your freezer for this warming weeknight meal. This recipe is loosely inspired by wonton noodle soup but replaces homemade wontons with store-bought frozen dumplings for a quick alternative. The soup base, which comes together in just 10 minutes, is surprisingly rich and full-bodied, thanks to the trio of ginger, garlic and turmeric. Miso paste brings extra savoriness, but you could substitute soy sauce or tamari. Scale up on veggies if you like; carrots, peas, snow peas or mushrooms would be excellent additions. Any type of frozen dumpling works in this dish, making it easy to adapt for vegan, vegetarian or meat-loving diners.

—Hetty Lui McKinnon

Kosher salt

6 ounces thin, dried wheat, egg or rice noodles

1 tablespoon toasted sesame oil

1 (2-inch) piece fresh ginger, peeled and grated (about 2 tablespoons)

2 garlic cloves, grated

1 teaspoon ground turmeric

6 cups vegetable stock

2 tablespoon white miso paste

16 ounces frozen dumplings (not thawed)

4 baby bok choy (about 12 ounces), trimmed and each cut into 4 pieces through the stem

1 small head broccoli (about 9 ounces), cut into bite-size florets

Handful of fresh cilantro or chopped scallions, for serving

1. Bring a large pot of salted water to a boil. Add the noodles and cook according to package instructions, until the noodles are just tender. Drain, rinse with cold water and drain well again. Divide them among four serving bowls.

2. Place the same large pot over medium heat and add the sesame oil, ginger and garlic. Stir and cook until aromatic, about 30 seconds. Add the turmeric and stir until fragrant, about 15 seconds.

3. Pour the vegetable stock into the pot, then season with 1 teaspoon salt. Cover and cook for 8 to 10 minutes on medium heat, to allow flavors to meld.

4. Remove the lid and add the miso paste, stirring constantly until it is dissolved. Taste and season with more salt, if needed.

5. Increase the heat to medium-high and carefully drop the dumplings into the broth. When they float to the top, add the baby bok choy and broccoli, and cook just until the broccoli is crisp-tender, about 2 minutes.

6. Ladle the broth, dumplings, baby bok choy and broccoli into the four bowls over the noodles. To serve, top with cilantro or chopped scallions.

"Made this last night with only a few veg substitutions (what was in the fridge) and it was so very delicious, we just 'mmmmm'd our way through dinner."

—Jean

"This tastes like a decadent dish you'd pay a lot for in a restaurant. Definitely add chile crisp on top when plating the dish—SO good!"

—ReadyAbout

Chile Crisp Fettuccine Alfredo with Spinach

time   25 minutes

yield   6 servings

Swirling spinach and chile crisp, the popular Chinese condiment, into fettuccine Alfredo gives you an immensely satisfying meatless one-dish dinner. The firecracker crunch of chile crisp intensifies when it's sizzled in butter, before cream tempers its heat, while Parmesan heightens the savory umami of the sauce. This astoundingly simple meal—it doesn't even require any chopping—comes together in under 30 minutes but tastes as complex as anything you'd get at a restaurant.

—Genevieve Ko

Kosher salt

4 tablespoons butter

1 to 2 tablespoons chile crisp (see Tip), plus more for serving if you'd like

1 cup heavy cream

1 pound fettuccine

1 (5-ounce) package baby spinach

¾ cup grated Parmesan (3 ounces), plus more for serving

1. Bring a large pot of salted water to a boil.

2. While the water heats, melt the butter with the chile crisp in a very large skillet or a large Dutch oven over low heat. Whisk in the cream and keep warm over low heat. (It should steam, not bubble.)

3. Add the fettuccine to the boiling water and cook until al dente, according to the package instructions. Use tongs to transfer the noodles to the cream mixture, reserving the cooking water. Add the spinach to the noodles and turn with tongs until the noodles are well coated.

4. Add the Parmesan and toss, still over low heat, until the noodles are slicked with a creamy sauce, adding a spoonful or two of the cooking water if needed to loosen the sauce. Divide among plates or bowls and top with Parmesan and with chile crisp, if you'd like. Serve immediately.

Tip

You can easily find chile crisp in supermarkets or online. It varies in spiciness, so adjust the amount to your taste. For this dish, try to add more of the solids than the oil to the sauce for the most flavorful dish.

Crispy Gnocchi with Burst Tomatoes and Mozzarella

time   25 minutes

yield   4 servings

Store-bought gnocchi can be quickly pan-fried for an exciting mix of crispy outsides and chewy middles, no boiling required. Here the gnocchi are studded with juicy tomatoes and melty pockets of mozzarella. Use cherry tomatoes, which are reliably flavorful year-round—unlike larger varieties, like beefsteak tomatoes, which can be watery. (That said, taste your tomatoes, and if they're more tart than sweet, add ½ teaspoon sugar in step 3.) You'll toss the tomatoes with browned butter, red pepper flakes and garlic, then hit them with a little heat so they'll burst into a bright sauce.

—Ali Slagle

2 tablespoons extra-virgin olive oil, plus more for drizzling

2 (12- to 18-ounce) packages shelf-stable or refrigerated potato gnocchi

4 tablespoons unsalted butter

4 garlic cloves, thinly sliced

¼ teaspoon red pepper flakes, plus more for garnish

Kosher salt and black pepper

2 pints cherry or grape tomatoes, such as Sungold (about 4 cups)

¼ cup thinly sliced or torn fresh basil leaves, plus more for garnish (optional)

8 ounces fresh mozzarella, cut or torn into ½-inch pieces

1. Heat the broiler with a rack about 6 inches from the heat source.

2. Heat 1 tablespoon of the oil in a large skillet or well-seasoned cast-iron skillet over medium-high heat. Add half of the gnocchi to the pan in a single layer, breaking apart any that are stuck together. Cover and cook, undisturbed, until the gnocchi are golden brown on the underside, 2 to 4 minutes. Transfer to a medium bowl. Repeat with the remaining 1 tablespoon oil and gnocchi.

3. Add the butter to the skillet and cook over medium-high heat, stirring often, until golden brown and toasty, 1 to 2 minutes. Add the garlic, red pepper flakes, 1½ teaspoons salt and a few grinds of pepper, reducing the heat slightly if necessary to avoid scorching. Add the tomatoes and 3 tablespoons water and cook, shaking the pan occasionally, until the tomatoes have softened and the liquid has slightly thickened, 4 to 6 minutes. Smash the tomatoes as they burst to help them along.

4. Return the seared gnocchi to the pan, add the basil (if using) and stir to coat, then shake into an even layer. Top evenly with the mozzarella and drizzle lightly with oil. Broil until the cheese is melted and browned in spots, 2 to 4 minutes. Top with basil, red pepper flakes and black pepper if you'd like and serve immediately.

"Seared gnocchi draped in broiled cheese? Stay out of my daydreams."

—plumping iron

"Absolute slam dunk. I prepped the lemon zest, grated cheese, measured walnuts, etc., and the whole thing came together between boiling the water and sprinkling the parsley. Delicious!!"

—Izzy

Blistered Broccoli Pasta with Walnuts, Pecorino and Mint

time   25 minutes

yield   4 servings

There are two tricks to creating deeply browned, pan-seared broccoli: high heat and no touching. Allowing your florets and stems to sear over high heat in an even layer, undisturbed, gives them time to blister without cooking all the way through, so they retain some crunch. While many pasta sauces are finished with starchy pasta water, this one isn't, because the hot water would strip the broccoli of that color and crunch you worked so hard to achieve. Instead, toss the cooked pasta in the skillet with the broccoli, walnuts and cheese. A drizzle of olive oil and a squeeze of lemon will provide any additional moisture you need.

—Dawn Perry

Kosher salt and black pepper

12 ounces fusilli or other short pasta

½ cup olive oil, plus more for drizzling

½ cup walnuts or pecans, chopped

¼ to ½ teaspoon red pepper flakes (optional)

1 bunch broccoli or cauliflower (about 1½ pounds untrimmed), florets roughly chopped and stalks peeled and sliced ¼ inch thick

1 lemon, zested (about 1 teaspoon), then quartered, for serving

½ cup grated Pecorino Romano or Parmesan (2 ounces), plus more for serving

1 packed cup fresh mint or parsley leaves

1. Bring a large pot of salted water to a boil. Add the pasta and cook until al dente, according to the package instructions.

2. Meanwhile, heat the oil in a large skillet over medium-high heat. Add the walnuts and red pepper flakes (if using) and cook, stirring, until golden and fragrant, about 1 minute. Use a slotted spoon to transfer the walnuts and red pepper flakes to a small bowl. Season the nuts with a little salt and black pepper.

3. Return the skillet to medium-high heat, add the broccoli and toss to coat in the oil. Shake the skillet so the broccoli settles in an even layer. Cook, undisturbed, for 2 minutes. Toss and shake to arrange in an even layer again and cook, undisturbed, for another 2 to 3 minutes. Season with salt and pepper and remove from the heat.

4. Drain the pasta and add to the skillet along with the lemon zest, cheese, toasted walnuts and half of the mint. Toss to combine. Divide among plates or bowls and top with the remaining mint, more cheese and a drizzle of oil. Serve with the lemon wedges for squeezing juice on top.

Easy Spaghetti with Meat Sauce

time   30 minutes

yield   4 servings

The secret ingredient in this ultrafast sauce based on long-cooking Bolognese is Worcestershire sauce. The vinegar, molasses and anchovies in the condiment season the ground beef mixture with salt, acid, sweetness and funk in one shot. Once the sauce has simmered, use tongs to transfer the pasta directly from the pot to the skillet, then toss in some of the starchy pasta cooking liquid for a glossy, saucy finish.

—Dawn Perry

Kosher salt and black pepper

2 tablespoons olive oil

1 medium yellow onion, finely chopped

2 garlic cloves, finely chopped

½ pound ground beef (preferably 20% fat), pork or dark meat turkey

12 ounces spaghetti, pappardelle or other long pasta

¼ cup tomato paste

2 teaspoons Worcestershire sauce

Grated Parmesan, for serving

1. Bring a large pot of salted water to a boil. Heat oil in a large skillet over medium-high heat. Add the onion, garlic and ½ teaspoon salt and cook, stirring often, until the onions begin to soften, 3 minutes. Add the beef and cook, breaking it up with a wooden spoon, until no longer pink, about 3 minutes.

2. Add the pasta to the pot and cook according to package instructions until al dente.

3. Meanwhile, add the tomato paste to the skillet and cook, stirring, until darkened, about 1 minute. Add 1 cup water, the Worcestershire, ½ teaspoon pepper and ½ teaspoon salt and simmer until slightly reduced, about 5 minutes.

4. Using tongs, transfer the pasta directly from the pot to the skillet along with 1 cup pasta cooking water. Increase the heat to high and simmer vigorously, tossing, until the sauce reduces and coats the pasta, about 2 minutes. Season to taste with salt and pepper. Serve with Parmesan.

"Cooked this a few times, a cup of white wine makes it sweeter and enhances the aroma! So many other options too; this is a great base recipe since it's simpler and quicker than the other tomato meat sauces."

—Rodrigo

"This is so easy and delicious. I add lots of extra greens to not feel guilty about how often I make this. I use whatever fish I have—it's just as good with leftover salmon as the tuna."

—A New Week Night Staple

Easy Weeknight Dinners

Blond Puttanesca
(Linguine with Tuna, Arugula and Capers)

time   30 minutes

yield   4 servings

Garlic, anchovies, capers and tuna come together in this briny, tomato-less take on the classic pasta puttanesca. The sauce is prepared while the pasta cooks, so you can get dinner on the table in no time. If you want to go the extra mile, roughly chopped green pitted olives would be a nice addition, as would topping the dish with toasted panko bread crumbs tossed with lemon zest.

—Colu Henry

Kosher salt and black pepper

12 ounces linguine

3 tablespoons olive oil

3 garlic cloves, thinly sliced

½ teaspoon red pepper flakes, plus more for serving if desired

10 anchovies, roughly chopped

3 tablespoons capers, rinsed well if salt-packed

5 ounces baby arugula or other young greens, such as pea shoots or kale

1 (6-ounce) jar oil-packed Italian tuna, drained and flaked

¼ cup chopped Italian parsley, plus more for serving, if desired

Flaky salt, for serving (optional)

Lemon wedges, for serving (optional)

1. Bring a large pot of well-salted water to a boil. Add the pasta and cook until it is just under al dente, about 7 minutes. Drain, reserving 1½ cups of the pasta cooking water.

2. While the pasta cooks, heat the olive oil in a large skillet over medium-low heat. Add the garlic and red pepper flakes and cook until the garlic is pale golden, about 1 minute. Add the anchovies and capers and cook until the anchovies have melted and the capers begin to brown slightly, 1 to 2 minutes.

3. Increase the heat to medium. Ladle ½ cup of the reserved cooking water into the skillet and bring the mixture to a simmer. Cook until the mixture is reduced by about half, 2 to 3 minutes. Add the arugula and ladle in an additional ½ cup of pasta cooking water, tossing together until wilted.

4. Increase the heat to medium-high and scoop the pasta directly into the skillet, tossing with sauce until well coated. Add the tuna to the pasta and toss again until it is just warmed through, about 1 minute. Ladle in an additional ¼ cup pasta cooking water or more to loosen the sauce and toss again. Sprinkle the parsley over top and toss again. Season with salt and pepper.

5. Serve in bowls, with flaky salt, a squeeze of lemon and additional parsley and red pepper flakes, if desired.

Pasta with Andouille Sausage, Beans and Greens

time   30 minutes

yield   4 to 6 servings

This one-dish dinner is perfect for cold, cozy nights when you want something hearty, but it will satisfy any time. It features ingredients that aren't typically seen in pasta recipes: highly seasoned andouille sausage, which makes the dish extra zippy, and the combination of white beans and collard greens, which gives it rustic flair. Swirling in lemon juice and olive oil just before serving adds freshness and ties all the flavors together.

—Vallery Lomas

Kosher salt and black pepper

1 pound rigatoni or any pasta with ridges

2 tablespoons extra-virgin olive oil, plus more for drizzling

¾ pound andouille sausages, diced

1 shallot, minced

2 garlic cloves, minced

1 bunch collard greens, stems discarded and leaves coarsely chopped (4½ cups)

1 tablespoon fresh thyme leaves

1 (15-ounce) can cannellini beans, drained and rinsed

1 cup diced tomato (about 1 large)

¼ cup chopped fresh flat-leaf parsley

¼ cup thinly sliced fresh chives

¼ cup grated Parmesan (1 ounce)

1 lemon, zested, then cut into wedges, for serving

1. Bring a large pot of salted water to a boil. Add the pasta and cook until al dente, according to the package instructions.

2. Meanwhile, heat the oil in a large, heavy-bottomed skillet over medium-high heat. Add the sausage and cook, stirring occasionally, until browned, 5 to 7 minutes. Add the shallot and garlic and cook, stirring often, until translucent, about 2 minutes.

3. Add the collard greens and toss to wilt, 2 to 3 minutes. Season with salt and pepper. Add the thyme, beans and tomato and toss until warmed through. Season again with salt and pepper to taste.

4. Reserve ½ cup of the cooking water, then drain the pasta, return it to the pot and set over medium-low heat. Add the sausage mixture and toss to combine, gradually adding the reserved cooking water as needed to create a sauce.

5. Remove from the heat and sprinkle with the parsley, chives, lemon zest and Parmesan. Season with salt and pepper to taste. Divide among bowls, drizzle with oil and serve with the lemon wedges for squeezing on top.

"This was a big hit with my family! I used spinach instead of collard greens. Will definitely add this to our rotation. Perfect winter dish!"

—Eileen O.

"Loved this dish so much. It was easy to make, tasty and nutritious to boot. I can't stop raving about it to my friends."

—Cheah

Easy Weeknight Dinners

Pasta e Ceci (Italian Pasta and Chickpea Stew)

time   30 minutes

yield   4 servings

There are countless recipes for this classic Roman dish, and everyone has an opinion on how it should be prepared. This version is more stew than soup, but it can be loosened up with a bit more water for a brothier dish. It begins with cooking onion, tomatoes, garlic and rosemary in olive oil, then tossing in the chickpeas and smashing some of them to give the stew a creamy texture. Water is added and then uncooked pasta, which cooks as the stew simmers (and results in one less dish to wash). Escarole is stirred in right before serving. This flexible stew can go in a number of directions, so tweak it as you see fit, but don't forget to finish each bowl with grated cheese and a drizzle of olive oil.

—Colu Henry

3 tablespoons olive oil, plus more for drizzling

1 medium yellow onion, finely chopped

3 garlic cloves, finely chopped

2 teaspoons chopped fresh rosemary

½ teaspoon red pepper flakes

Kosher salt and black pepper

1 packed cup drained canned whole tomatoes

1 (15-ounce) can chickpeas, drained and rinsed

1 cup ditalini

4 cups roughly chopped escarole, Tuscan kale or radicchio

Grated pecorino or Parmesan cheese, for serving

1. Heat the oil in a large stockpot or Dutch oven over medium heat. Add the onion and cook, stirring occasionally, until softened but not taking on any color, 4 to 5 minutes. Add the garlic, rosemary and red pepper flakes and cook, stirring occasionally, for 1 minute more. Season well with salt and black pepper.

2. Stir in the tomatoes and chickpeas, breaking up the tomatoes with the back of a spoon or spatula and smashing about ½ cup of the beans.

3. Add 3 cups water, increase the heat to high, and bring to a boil. Add the pasta and simmer, stirring often to make sure nothing sticks to the bottom of the pot, until the pasta is al dente, about 10 minutes. The water will mostly be absorbed by the pasta, but if you prefer a brothier dish, you can add ½ to 1 cup water and simmer until warmed through, about 1 minute more. Season with salt and black pepper.

4. Add the escarole and stir until wilted. Taste and adjust the seasonings if needed. Ladle into bowls and top with pecorino and a drizzle of oil.

Taiwanese Meefun

time 35 minutes

yield 4 to 6 servings

Meefun is a stir-fried rice noodle dish very common in Taiwan, and many cooks claim that their version is the best. Traditionally, meefun has dried shrimp, but this vegetarian version gets its umami from dried shiitake mushrooms and gains a little heft from eggs. It's delicious when it's first made, but it can also be served at room temperature, so it will travel well to a picnic or other gatherings.

—Sue Li

5 ounces rice vermicelli

4 dried shiitake mushrooms

5 tablespoons vegetable oil

2 large eggs, lightly beaten

2 large shallots, thinly sliced

Kosher salt

1 large carrot, cut into thin matchsticks (about 2½ cups)

¼ small green cabbage, shredded (about 2½ cups)

8 ounces baked or smoked tofu, cut into thin matchsticks (about 2 cups)

3 tablespoons soy sauce

1 teaspoon ground white pepper

¼ cup fresh cilantro, roughly chopped

Chile oil, for serving

1. In a medium bowl, soak the rice vermicelli in cold water to cover until softened, 5 to 10 minutes. Drain and set aside. In a small bowl, soak the mushrooms in warm water to cover until hydrated and softened, about 10 minutes. Drain, remove and discard the stems, slice the caps ¼ inch thick and set aside.

2. Heat 2 tablespoons of the vegetable oil in a large, deep skillet over medium heat. When the oil is hot, add the eggs, swirl the pan to create an even layer and cook until set and cooked through, about 1 minute. Transfer the cooked eggs to a cutting board and let cool slightly. Cut into matchsticks and set aside.

3. Return the skillet to the stove over medium-high heat. Add the remaining 3 tablespoons vegetable oil, the shallots and mushrooms and season with salt. Cook, stirring frequently, until the edges of the shallots begin to brown, 3 to 4 minutes.

4. Add the carrot, season with salt and cook, stirring frequently, until softened but still crisp, 1 to 2 minutes. Add the cabbage, season with salt and cook, stirring frequently, until slightly wilted, 1 to 2 minutes.

5. Add the tofu, soy sauce, drained rice vermicelli and 1 cup water and cook, stirring frequently, until the noodles absorb the water, 5 to 6 minutes. Season with salt and white pepper, add the reserved eggs and stir to mix well. Serve topped with the cilantro and a drizzle of chile oil.

"We loved this. I used fresh shiitakes, a bag of shredded coleslaw mix, sesame flavored baked tofu. It was delicious! Would definitely make again."

—Molly

"I followed recipe as is and took on the tips from others to include dill (it's a stand-out flavor in this dish) along with the zest of 1 lemon, which lifted from the creamy tones."

—Joelene

Easy Weeknight Dinners

Baked Spanakopita Pasta with Greens and Feta

time   40 minutes

yield   4 servings

This baked pasta is inspired by spanakopita, the classic Greek spinach and feta pie. This loose interpretation combines pasta with gooey mozzarella, briny feta, plenty of greens and a rich cream sauce, which is then piled into a dish and baked until golden. The key to this dish is in the greens: Use at least three kinds—a mellow one, a peppery one and a fresh herb or two—to create an exciting mix of flavors. No need to sauté them; just salt and massage them until they wilt slightly. This cozy dish might be the best way to eat your greens all year long.

—Ali Slagle

Kosher salt and black pepper

4 cups chopped spinach, Swiss chard or other mild greens (tough stems removed)

4 cups chopped arugula, watercress or other peppery greens

1 cup chopped fresh dill or parsley leaves and tender stems, or a combination

6 scallions, trimmed and thinly sliced, whites and dark green parts separated

1 pound tubular or curvy pasta, like rigatoni or fusilli

2 tablespoons unsalted butter

4 garlic cloves, thinly sliced

8 ounces cream cheese (1 cup), cut into ½-inch cubes

4 ounces mozzarella, grated (1 cup)

4 ounces crumbled feta (1 cup)

1. Bring a large pot of salted water to a boil. Heat the oven to 450 degrees.

2. In a 3-quart/9 x 13-inch baking dish, toss the chopped spinach, arugula, herbs and scallion greens with 2 teaspoons salt and a few grinds of pepper. Squeeze the mixture with your hands to wilt, then set aside.

3. Cook the pasta until 2 minutes shy of al dente; reserve 1 cup pasta cooking water, then drain pasta and set aside. Return the pot to the stove.

4. Melt the butter in the pot over medium heat. Add the scallion whites, garlic and a pinch of salt and sauté until softened, 4 to 5 minutes. Add the cream cheese and cooking water and stir until smooth. Stir in the wilted greens, half the mozzarella and half the feta until combined. Stir in the pasta until combined. Taste and adjust the seasonings as needed.

5. Transfer the pasta to the baking dish, then top with remaining mozzarella and feta. Bake until the sauce is thick and bubbly and the top has browned in spots, 10 to 15 minutes. If you like a crispier top, broil for a few minutes.

Pasta with Sausage, Squash and Sage Brown Butter

time   40 minutes

yield   4 servings

Whether you're after a night in with your special someone or your sweatpants, this is your pasta: a cozy combination of spicy sausage and squash that's glossed with nutty, sage-spiked butter and Parmesan. It's inspired by the cavatelli with sausage and browned sage butter at the beloved Brooklyn restaurant Frankies Spuntino—the most ordered dish on dates, according to the owners, but appealing no matter the occasion, according to us. The key to making the dish sing is its unsexy color (brown). You'll want to get a hard sear on the sausage and the squash, and let the butter bubble until brown and toasty. If you're looking for a vegetarian option, omit the sausage. The meat will be gone, but the comfort won't be.

—Ali Slagle

Kosher salt and black pepper

1 pound hot Italian sausages

2 tablespoons extra-virgin olive oil, plus more for the pasta

12 ounces butternut squash, peeled, seeded and cut into ½-inch cubes (about 2 cups)

1 pound cup-shaped or short tube pasta, such as orecchiette or penne

6 tablespoons unsalted butter

8 fresh sage leaves

½ cup grated Parmesan (2 ounces), plus more for serving

1. Bring a large pot of heavily salted water to a boil.

2. Meanwhile, cook the sausages: In a sauté pan or skillet large enough to hold all the pasta, add the sausages and enough cold water to cover. Set over medium-high heat, then remove from the heat when the water hits a boil, 8 to 10 minutes.

3. Transfer the sausages to a cutting board and cut into ½-inch-thick coins. Discard the water in the pan and dry the pan.

4. Return the pan to the stovetop over high heat, add the oil and heat until nearly smoking. Add the sausage slices and cook, flipping once, until dark brown on both sides, 5 to 7 minutes. Transfer to a paper towel–lined plate to drain. Turn down the heat to medium, add the squash and a pinch of salt to the pan and cook, stirring briefly and scraping up any browned bits on the bottom of the pan, until browned, 5 to 7 minutes.

5. While the squash is browning, add the pasta to the boiling water and cook until al dente, according to the package instructions. Reserve 1 cup of the cooking water, then drain the pasta.

"This has become a weeknight staple in our house. It's delicious, easy and inexpensive. I just crumble and sauté the sausage instead of boiling and slicing it— gets rid of a couple of steps, and it tastes great."

—Emma

6. When the squash is nicely browned, add the butter and sage and cook until the butter is golden, nutty smelling and foaming, just a minute or two, then immediately remove the pan from the heat and add back the sausages.

7. Add the pasta to the pan and mix with the brown-butter sauce (if the pasta has cooled off quite a bit, return the pan to low heat while you combine everything). Stir in the cheese, then add the cooking water as needed to smooth the sauce. Taste and add salt and pepper if needed. Serve with extra Parmesan.

Rice and
Other Grains

Shrimp Fried Rice, page 106

Rice and Other Grains

Fried rice had a renaissance in my home after the twin arrivals of my younger child and the pandemic. I'd always liked fried rice, but at that moment I embraced it. There's its unparalleled convenience; the satisfying way it absorbs other leftovers (cooked vegetables, roast chicken); its all-ages appeal; the fact that it can be made with ingredients I keep in the fridge (eggs), pantry (rice) and freezer (peas, shrimp); and the savory satisfaction it delivers. The Shrimp Fried Rice on page 106 is entirely within reach anytime, and I especially love the Kimchi Fried Rice on page 103.

Rice, more than any other ingredient featured in this book, is ideal for cooking ahead and keeping on hand, not just for fried rice but for other fast meal prep. I always have a large container of cooked rice in the fridge for quick reheating to serve with beans, tofu or any number of other recipes in this book. Rice also freezes like a dream. Sprinkle it with water and reheat it, covered, in the microwave at medium-low power and it springs back to life. But nothing compares to a freshly steamed pot of rice, especially when you top it with a fried egg, as in the recipe for Gyeran Bap (Egg Rice) on page 230. The aroma alone will bring you joy.

But we're not only about rice over here. We've got Warm Roasted Carrot and Barley Salad (found on page 110 and drizzled with a warmly spiced tahini dressing) and a Quinoa Salad with Chicken, Almonds and Avocado (page 100). Yet nubby, chewy farro is my favorite. I like how its nutty flavor plays against sweeter elements, like the juicy tomatoes in the Farro with Blistered Tomatoes, Pesto and Spinach on page 115. Farro is simple to cook: just boil it in salted water, the same way you'd cook pasta. Easy!

"Thayir saadham is classic comfort food! Had a bowl almost every single day of my childhood. At its simplest it's just plain cooked rice mixed with plain yogurt with some salt, and this is it at perhaps its fanciest."

—Nilla S.

Cumin and Cashew Yogurt Rice

time   10 minutes

yield   4 servings

Yogurt rice is a nostalgic dish for many South Asians, and especially South Indians. It's the ultimate comfort food, and a no-fuss dinner that's easy to put together. Cool, creamy yogurt and crunchy, warm spices create a dreamy contrast that makes this dish feel more whole meal–worthy than snack-friendly (though it'll serve you well for both). Traditional versions include mustard seeds, curry leaves and urad dal, but this variation includes a different set of pantry staples: cumin seeds, cashews and red chile powder. The trio, plus fresh green chiles, gets sizzled in ghee, enhancing all the rich, smoky, spicy flavors, then gets poured directly over the yogurt rice. Add grated carrots and zucchini to give the rice more heft, or try it with a different combination of spices.

—Priya Krishna

3 cups cooked long-grain basmati rice, at room temperature

1 (1-inch) piece fresh ginger, peeled and minced (1 tablespoon)

1 teaspoon coarse kosher salt

2½ cups full-fat plain yogurt

2 tablespoons ghee (or unsalted butter)

¼ cup raw, unsalted cashews

1 Indian green chile or serrano chile, minced

1 tablespoon cumin seeds

¼ teaspoon red chile powder (such as Kashmiri chile powder or ground cayenne)

¼ teaspoon asafetida (optional)

2 tablespoons roughly chopped fresh cilantro

1. In a bowl, combine the cooked rice, ginger and salt. Fold in the yogurt. The yogurt should evenly coat the rice, so that it resembles a thick rice pudding.

2. In a small saucepan, melt the ghee over medium heat. Add the cashews and chile and cook, stirring occasionally, until the cashews are lightly browned, 2 to 3 minutes. Shift the cashews and chile to the side of the pan and add the cumin seeds, toasting until they are slightly browned, 30 seconds to 1 minute. Stir in red chile powder and asafetida (if using), then turn off the heat.

3. Pour the spice mixture over the rice and serve with cilantro.

Quinoa Salad with Chicken, Almonds and Avocado

time   20 minutes

yield   4 to 6 servings

Tricolor quinoa combines the tenderness of white quinoa with the pop of the red and black grains. All soak up a Dijon-sherry vinaigrette in this blend of chewy, tangy cranberries, crunchy salty almonds, creamy avocado and refreshing parsley. This salad—tasty warm, at room temperature or cold—is a great way to use up leftover or rotisserie chicken. It's perfectly satisfying without the chicken, too, if you're vegetarian.

—Genevieve Ko

2 cups tricolor quinoa (12 ounces), rinsed well and drained

¼ cup finely diced shallot or onion

3 tablespoons sherry vinegar

1 tablespoon Dijon mustard

⅓ cup extra-virgin olive oil

Kosher salt and black pepper

2 cups leftover chicken meat, torn from a rotisserie bird

¾ cup dried cranberries

2 cups fresh flat-leaf parsley, chopped

½ cup roasted salted almonds, chopped

1 avocado, pitted and thinly sliced

1. Bring a large saucepan of generously salted water to a boil. Add the quinoa and cook, stirring occasionally, until tender, 10 to 15 minutes.

2. Meanwhile, in a very large bowl, whisk the shallot, vinegar, mustard, oil and a generous pinch of salt. When the quinoa is done, drain very well, then add it to the dressing, along with the chicken, cranberries and parsley. Fold until evenly mixed and cooled, then season to taste with salt and pepper.

3. Divide the salad among dishes and top with the chopped almonds and avocado.

Tip

It's fastest and easiest to rinse grains in a sieve. Simply run cold water over them while gently shaking the sieve, then gently shake dry. It's important to rinse grains to clean them and in the case of quinoa, to remove saponins, which can leave a bitter or soapy aftertaste. Since it's also tough to get flavors into grains once they're cooked, it's a good idea to season them with salt at this point.

"This is completely addictive. Make as written. Do not substitute. You won't be sorry. You will only contemplate how empty your life was before this recipe."

—Matt

Kimchi Fried Rice

time   30 minutes

yield   2 servings

Not the high-heat stir-fry you might expect, this home-style fried-rice recipe, adapted from a home cook named Grace Lee, uses a simple technique: make an easy, flavorful kimchi sauce mellowed out with butter and cook leftover rice in it. It's perfect for a snack or a quick, no-fuss meal. The Spam, though optional, reflects many Koreans' love of foods introduced by the American military.

—Francis Lam

3 tablespoons unsalted butter

½ small onion, diced

1 cup roughly chopped kimchi (6 ounces)

2 tablespoons kimchi juice, plus more to taste if needed

½ cup small-dice Spam, ham or leftover cooked meat (optional)

2 cups cooked white rice (preferably short grain)

2 teaspoons soy sauce, plus more to taste

1 teaspoon toasted sesame oil, plus more to taste

2 teaspoons vegetable oil

2 eggs

Kosher salt

Crumbled or slivered nori (roasted seaweed), for garnish

Sesame seeds, for garnish

1. Melt the butter in a nonstick sauté pan or well-seasoned cast-iron skillet over medium-low heat. Add the onion and cook, stirring, until the onion starts to sizzle, about 2 minutes. Add the kimchi and kimchi juice and stir until the mixture comes to a boil, about 3 minutes. Add the Spam (if using) and cook until the sauce has nearly evaporated, about 5 minutes.

2. Break up the rice in the pan with a spatula and stir it to incorporate. Increase the heat to medium and cook, stirring, until the rice has absorbed the sauce and is very hot, about 5 minutes. Stir in the soy sauce and sesame oil. Taste and adjust with more soy sauce, sesame oil and kimchi juice to your taste. Turn down the heat slightly, but let the rice continue to cook, undisturbed, to lightly brown while you cook the eggs.

3. Heat the vegetable oil in a small nonstick sauté pan over medium heat. When the oil is hot, crack the eggs into the pan, season with salt and fry to your desired doneness.

4. To serve, divide the rice between plates and top with the fried eggs, the nori and a sprinkle of sesame seeds.

Baked Risotto with Greens and Peas

time   30 minutes

yield   4 servings

This easy baked risotto eliminates the constant stirring required in traditional risotto recipes. It's laden with vegetables, namely kale and spinach, but other leafy greens like Swiss chard or collard greens would work equally well. If you happen to have some extra asparagus, you can use it instead of the peas. You can make it into a more filling vegetarian main course by topping it with sautéed mushrooms, a fried egg or crispy tofu slices. Leftovers can be refrigerated for two days and reheated with more stock, or repurposed into crunchy rice cakes or arancini. Simply shape the risotto into patties or balls, coat them in bread crumbs and shallow-fry until golden and crunchy.

—Kay Chun

4 ounces curly or Tuscan kale (about ⅓ bunch)

2 tablespoons extra-virgin olive oil

½ cup finely chopped yellow onion

1 small garlic clove, minced

1 cup arborio rice (about 7 ounces)

Kosher salt and black pepper

3½ cups low-sodium chicken stock (or use vegetable or mushroom stock)

4 ounces baby spinach (about 4 packed cups)

1 cup frozen peas (5 ounces), thawed

¾ cup grated Parmesan (3 ounces), plus more for garnish

3 tablespoons unsalted butter

1 tablespoon fresh lemon juice

1. Heat the oven to 375 degrees. Separate the stems from the kale leaves and thinly slice the stems. Stack the leaves and cut crosswise into ¼-inch-wide ribbons. You should have about 4 packed cups leaves and stems.

2. Heat the oil in a large Dutch oven over medium heat. Add the onion and cook, stirring occasionally, until softened, about 3 minutes. Add the garlic and stir until fragrant, about 1 minute. Add the rice, season with salt and pepper and stir until coated in oil and lightly toasted, about 2 minutes.

3. Add the kale, season with salt and pepper and stir until wilted, about 30 seconds. Add the stock, increase the heat to high and bring to a boil.

4. Cover, transfer to the oven and bake until almost all the liquid is absorbed and the rice is tender, about 20 minutes.

5. Stir in the spinach and peas until the spinach is wilted. Add the Parmesan, butter and lemon juice and stir until well blended and saucy. (Liquid will continue to be absorbed as the risotto sits.) Season with salt and pepper. Divide among bowls, garnish with Parmesan and serve.

"Always a big hit with my family and guests. Easy too! I add spinach right before serving so it is not too wilted."

—Shrudds

Shrimp Fried Rice

time   30 minutes

yield   4 to 6 servings

Inspired by the fire-kissed flavor of Japanese steakhouse and hibachi fare, especially at the Kani House restaurants in Georgia, this quick fried-rice dish is a true comfort. Frying the shrimp first in oil, just until they're cooked, and then reserving them to add back at the end of cooking helps them stay tender. Plus, you're left with the most aromatic shrimp oil in which to fry the rice and vegetables. The shortcut of bagged frozen mixed vegetables comes in handy here, not least because they don't need to be defrosted first. And the Yum Yum Sauce, a mayo-ketchup dipping sauce that is ordinarily reserved for grilled hibachi meats, tastes fabulous splattered over the finished rice.

—Eric Kim

¼ cup olive oil, plus more as needed

1 pound peeled and deveined medium shrimp, thawed if frozen

Kosher salt

½ teaspoon garlic powder

1 medium onion, diced

1½ cups frozen mixed vegetables (any mix of carrots, peas, corn and green beans)

6 cups cooked jasmine or other long-grain white rice, preferably cold and day old

¼ cup soy sauce, plus more to taste

2 tablespoons unsalted butter

4 large eggs

Yum Yum Sauce (recipe follows), for serving

1. Heat a very large nonstick or cast-iron skillet over high heat. Add the oil and shrimp and sprinkle with salt and the garlic powder. Cook, stirring occasionally, until the shrimp is no longer translucent and begins to turn golden at the edges, 2 to 4 minutes. Use a slotted spoon to transfer the shrimp to a plate and set aside.

2. Add the onion and mixed vegetables to the shrimpy oil and cook, stirring occasionally, just until the onion loses its raw edge but is still crunchy and the vegetables are mostly thawed, 1 to 2 minutes. Add the rice and soy sauce and cook, stirring occasionally, until well combined and the rice begins to crisp underneath where it meets the pan, 5 to 7 minutes. Taste and adjust the seasoning with more soy sauce as needed.

3. Scooch the rice to one side of the pan, lower the heat to medium and melt the butter on the empty side of the pan. Crack the eggs into the melted butter, break the yolks and stir vigorously to scramble the eggs, cooking just until they have set but are still tender, about 1 minute. Stir the soft scrambled eggs into the rice, add the reserved shrimp and any accumulated juices and remove the pan from the heat.

"Delicious and easy to make. It's become one of my 13-year-old's favorite dishes and she's even learning to make it herself."

—Kate

4. Let the fried rice sit for a few minutes so it can continue to crisp in the pan's residual heat. (If you haven't already made the Yum Yum Sauce, this is the perfect time to do it.)

5. Drizzle most of the Yum Yum Sauce over the fried rice in the skillet, holding back some, if desired, to serve in a small dish on the side for dipping the shrimp.

Yum Yum Sauce

time   5 minutes

yield   about ¾ cup

This mayonnaise-based Japanese steakhouse sauce tastes glorious with grilled shrimp, chicken and vegetables, or drizzled over a plate of fried rice. Slather it on a burger, serve it as a dipping sauce for fried tofu, French fries and pizza crusts, or even use it as a salad dressing for crunchy iceberg, romaine or Little Gem lettuce. An all-purpose sauce for everyday pleasure, yum yum sauce should taste both savory and sweet and have a touch of acid and gosoham, the Korean word often used to describe the nuttiness of sesame oil. Remember to salt generously so all the flavors can shine.

—Eric Kim

1 teaspoon garlic powder

½ teaspoon sweet paprika

1 tablespoon warm water

½ cup mayonnaise

¼ cup ketchup

2 teaspoons rice vinegar

1 teaspoon toasted sesame oil

Kosher salt

In a medium bowl, stir together the garlic powder, paprika and warm water. Add the mayonnaise, ketchup, vinegar and oil, season generously with salt and stir until smooth. The sauce will keep in an airtight container in the refrigerator for up to 5 days.

"This is so good, it ruined me. I will never be able to enjoy the sub-par, far too sweet yum yum sauce at my go-to hibachi joint. I will be the person who brings their own sauce."

—Anna

Warm Roasted Carrot and Barley Salad

time   35 minutes

yield   6 servings

There's something exciting about transforming a bunch of carrots into a deeply flavorful and satisfying weeknight meal. Carrots are given a lot of love here: Leaving the skin on adds texture, slicing them into thin batons ensures that they cook quickly and evenly and drizzling them with honey right out of the oven amplifies their natural sweetness. A sprinkle of lemon zest adds brightness. Fragrant ras el hanout, a North African spice blend of coriander, cumin, ginger, clove and turmeric, brings warmth and richness to the tahini.

—Hetty Lui McKinnon

1 cup pearled barley

Kosher salt and black pepper

2 pounds carrots, washed, trimmed and cut into 3-inch-long, scant ½-inch-wide batons

2 tablespoons extra-virgin olive oil

2 teaspoons runny honey, such as clover honey

½ teaspoon fresh lemon zest (from ½ lemon)

2 cups arugula

A handful of fresh parsley

¼ cup toasted sliced almonds

For the spiced tahini

¼ cup tahini

1 tablespoon fresh lemon juice (from ½ lemon)

1 teaspoon ras el hanout, store-bought or homemade (see Tip)

1 small garlic clove, grated

1. Place a rack on the lowest level and heat the oven to 425 degrees. In a medium saucepan, combine the barley with 4 cups water and season with ½ teaspoon salt. Bring to a boil over medium-high heat. Reduce the heat to low and simmer until tender, 20 to 25 minutes. If the barley hasn't absorbed all of the water, drain off the excess.

2. Meanwhile, place the carrots on a sheet pan, drizzle with the olive oil and toss to coat, spreading into an even layer. Season with salt and pepper. Roast until tender and starting to turn golden, about 15 minutes. Remove from the oven, toss and continue roasting until completely tender, 5 to 7 minutes more.

3. While the carrots are roasting, make the dressing: In a medium bowl, whisk together the tahini, lemon juice, ras el hanout, garlic and ½ teaspoon salt. Add 3 to 4 tablespoons water, 1 tablespoon at a time, until it is smooth and has a pourable consistency.

Ras el Hanout

Using ground spices, combine 1 teaspoon each turmeric, coriander, ginger, cumin, cardamom and nutmeg, plus ½ teaspoon each aniseed, caraway seeds, fennel seeds, cloves and black pepper. Store leftover ras el hanout in a sealed container, away from light and heat.

"YUM. A great recipe base that you can make your own with whatever spice or flavor/ingredient tweaks that you like."

—SG

4. When the carrots are ready, remove them from the oven, drizzle with honey and sprinkle with lemon zest. Season with a pinch of salt and toss to coat.

5. In a serving bowl, combine the carrots with the barley, arugula and parsley. Drizzle with the spiced tahini and sprinkle with almonds.

Quick Jambalaya

time   35 minutes

yield   2 to 4 servings

This recipe makes quick work of jambalaya by using leftover rice, and it tastes great with freshly cooked grains too. To make this meal meatless, use vegan andouille sausage, or stick with pork sausage, if you prefer. Either option, along with Creole seasoning and the classic trinity of Creole cooking—onion, celery and green bell pepper—results in a dish that is unmistakably Louisianan. Although many jambalaya recipes skip tomatoes, this version uses a blend of tomato paste and diced tomatoes to add bulk and an acidity that helps lighten up the otherwise hearty one-pot meal.

—Vallery Lomas

2 tablespoons extra-virgin olive oil

1 medium yellow onion, diced

2 pork or vegan andouille or chorizo sausage (6 ounces), cut into ½-inch pieces

2 celery stalks, thinly sliced

1 green bell pepper, diced

4 garlic cloves, minced

1 tablespoon tomato paste

2 cups cooked long-grain white rice (see Tip)

1 tablespoon Creole seasoning

Kosher salt and black pepper

1 (15-ounce) can diced tomatoes

1 tablespoon hot sauce, plus more for serving

2 tablespoons sliced scallions

1. Heat 1 tablespoon oil in a large skillet over medium heat. Add the onion and cook, stirring often, until softened, 5 to 7 minutes. Add the sausage and cook until starting to brown, about 5 minutes.

2. Add the remaining 1 tablespoon oil, then add the celery and bell pepper and cook, stirring occasionally, until softened, 5 to 7 minutes. Stir in the garlic and cook until fragrant, about 1 minute. Stir in the tomato paste and cook until very fragrant, about 1 minute.

3. Reduce the heat to low and add the cooked rice. Sprinkle with the Creole seasoning and ½ teaspoon each salt and pepper. Stir in the tomatoes and hot sauce and cook until warmed through. Season with additional salt and pepper as needed. Garnish with the scallions and serve with more hot sauce.

Tip

This recipe is a great use of leftover cooked rice, but if you are making the rice from scratch, cook it in vegetable stock with 2 teaspoons Creole or Cajun seasoning for an extra kick of flavor.

"I love recipes like this: a great basis for endless adaptations with mostly pantry staples. This was simple, comforting and delicious."

—Chef Agostino

"Followed the recipe with the exception of making an arugula pesto, since I had some on hand. Delicious. Will make again. Leftovers destined for breakfast topped with a fried egg."

—Donna

Farro with Blistered Tomatoes, Pesto and Spinach

time   40 minutes

yield   4 servings

This is an Italian-inspired recipe that uses store-bought or homemade pesto to season farro, which is then tossed with fresh spinach, roasted tomatoes, red onions and mozzarella for a complete vegetarian meal. Make it with fresh-from-the-market cherry tomatoes when they're in season, but during the rest of the year, use grape tomatoes, as they tend to be more flavorful than cherry during the colder months. If you'd like, substitute arugula, or cooked broccoli rabe or kale, for the spinach. It tastes delicious warm or cold the next day—and topping it with shrimp, chicken or scallops can make it feel new again. Before reheating, add a bit more spinach, drizzle it with a little olive oil and give it a good stir.

—Yasmin Fahr

Kosher salt and black pepper

1 cup farro, rinsed

2 pints cherry or grape tomatoes

1 small red onion, peeled, quartered and cut into 1-inch wedges

2 tablespoons olive oil, plus more for the farro

½ teaspoon red pepper flakes

¼ cup store-bought or homemade pesto, plus more to taste

1 lemon, zested (about 1 tablespoon) and juiced (about 2 tablespoons)

2 packed cups baby spinach

1 (4-ounce) ball fresh mozzarella, torn into chunks, or ½ cup ricotta salata, crumbled (optional)

¼ cup fresh flat-leaf parsley or basil leaves and tender stems, roughly chopped

1. Heat the oven to 400 degrees. Bring a large pot of well-salted water to a boil. Add the farro and adjust the heat to maintain a medium boil. Cook, uncovered, stirring occasionally to make sure nothing is sticking to the bottom, until tender and not too chewy, about 30 minutes.

2. Meanwhile, on a sheet pan, combine the tomatoes and onion wedges with the oil, making sure everything is well coated and glistening, then season with salt, pepper and the red pepper flakes. Roast until the tomatoes blister and slightly deflate, 25 to 30 minutes.

3. When the farro is done, drain, then pour into a serving bowl or back into the pot. Toss with some olive oil, then mix in the pesto. Add the lemon zest and juice, then stir in the spinach. Set aside to cool slightly.

4. Scrape the onions, tomatoes and their juices into the farro and season with salt and pepper as needed. Add the cheese (if using), then serve with the herbs.

Farro with Roasted Squash, Feta and Mint

time   45 minutes

yield   4 to 6 servings

Falling somewhere between a grain bowl and a warm grain salad, this colorful dish is substantial enough to be a meatless main course, or it makes a hearty side dish to simple roasted meat or fish. You can use whatever kind of squash you like here, either peeled or unpeeled. Squash skin is perfectly edible; let anyone who objects cut theirs away at the table (though see if you can get them to try it first). Cooking the farro in apple cider makes this dish extra special, but you can use water instead if you'd like. If you don't have farro, you can substitute brown rice. Just increase the cooking time by about 20 minutes.

—Melissa Clark

For the squash

3 tablespoons extra-virgin olive oil

2 teaspoons granulated sugar

¾ teaspoon ground cinnamon

¾ teaspoon fine sea salt

¼ teaspoon black pepper

⅛ teaspoon ground cayenne, or to taste

3 pounds winter squash, such as kabocha, Carnival or butternut, seeded and cut into ½-inch-thick slices (unpeeled or peeled)

For the farro

1½ cups apple cider (optional)

2½ teaspoons kosher salt, plus more if needed

1½ cups farro

2 tablespoons apple cider vinegar, plus more if needed

2 garlic cloves, grated or minced

½ teaspoon black pepper

7 tablespoons extra-virgin olive oil, plus more as needed

3 ounces feta, crumbled (about ¾ cup)

Fresh mint and/or arugula leaves, for serving

1. Heat the oven to 450 degrees. Prepare the squash: In a large bowl, mix together the oil, sugar, cinnamon, salt, black pepper and cayenne. Add the squash and toss to coat well with the spiced oil. Lay the squash pieces in a single layer on one or two sheet pans.

2. Roast the squash pieces until the undersides are golden, 10 to 15 minutes. Carefully turn the pieces over and continue to roast until tender, 10 to 20 minutes longer.

3. Meanwhile, make the farro: In a medium pot, bring the apple cider (if using), 2 cups water and the kosher salt to a simmer. (If you're not using cider, add 1½ cups more water to the pot.) Add the farro and simmer, uncovered, until the water is absorbed and the farro is tender, 20 to 30 minutes. If the liquid evaporates before the farro is done, add a little more water. Or if the farro is done and liquid remains, drain the farro.

"Really enjoyed this dish! The squash is phenomenal cooked this way. My only complaint is that there was not enough."

—JCW in PDX

4. In a large bowl, whisk together the vinegar, garlic and pepper, then whisk in the oil. Add the farro and toss well. Taste and add more vinegar, oil and salt if needed.

5. To serve, spoon the farro onto a platter and top with the squash, feta, mint and a drizzle of olive oil.

"My son declared this 'amazing.' So fast, easy, adaptable. I followed the recipe precisely but will add more squash next time. So happy to have such a hit to use up all that CSA squash!!!"

—Jenn L.

Butternut Squash Congee with Chile Oil

time   45 minutes

yield   4 to 6 servings

Congee comes in many textures and flavors, under a number of different names, and is eaten widely across East, Southeast and South Asia. This particular version, which is not traditional to any region or cuisine, is an interpretation that incorporates butternut squash for a warming, naturally sweet, earthy glow. The chile oil delivers a lively counter to the mellow nature of this congee, delivering both heat and savoriness. Using leftover rice gives you a hearty congee in just about 30 minutes, but make sure you give it a good stir at the end to further break up the rice and create a creamy finish. Butternut can be awkward to handle, so try cutting it into smaller pieces before slicing the skin off with a sharp knife or peeler. Quicker still, opt for precut cubes of butternut, which can be found in many supermarkets.

—Hetty Lui McKinnon

2 tightly packed cups leftover medium- or long-grain rice, preferably refrigerated

1 tablespoon neutral oil, such as canola

1 teaspoon kosher salt, plus more if needed

6 cups vegetable stock

4 garlic cloves, crushed

1 pound butternut squash (about ½ small), peeled, seeded and cut into 1-inch dice

1 small piece kombu (optional)

2 scallions, thinly sliced, for serving

Chile oil or chile crisp, for serving

1. Place the rice, oil and salt in a large pot and stir to combine, breaking up any clumps of rice. Add the stock, garlic, squash and kombu (if using) and bring to a boil over medium-high heat. Reduce the heat to low, cover and simmer for 30 minutes.

2. Uncover, stir and increase the heat to medium. Simmer until the rice has broken down, 5 to 10 minutes.

3. Turn off the heat and, if you like, discard any larger pieces of kombu, though it is fine to leave it in. Using a wooden spoon, stir vigorously to break up the rice, squash and garlic. Some of the squash pieces will stay intact, while others will break apart and impart a beautiful golden hue to the dish. Taste and adjust with salt if needed.

4. To serve, divide among bowls and top with the scallions and a few drops of chile oil.

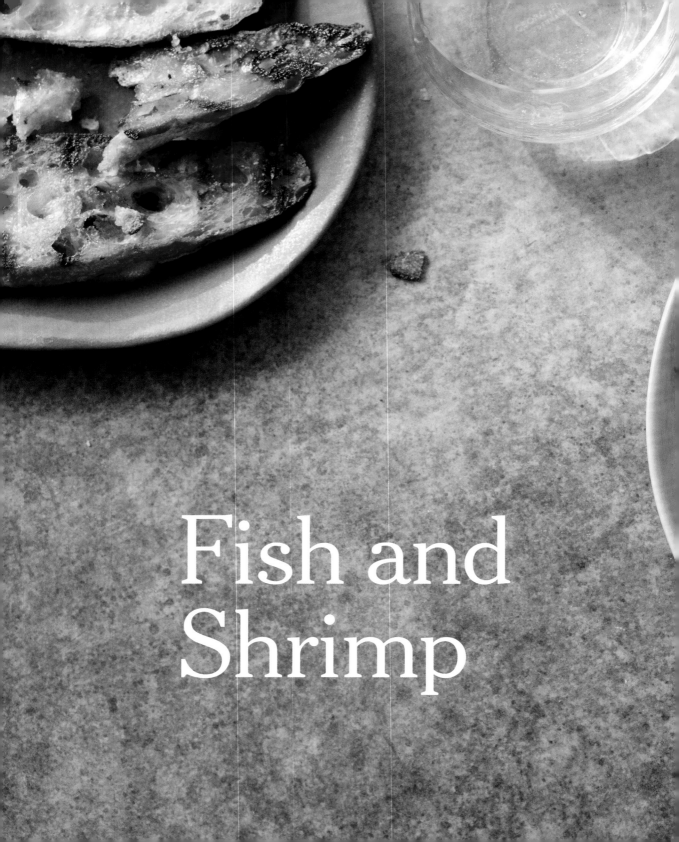

Fish and Shrimp

Coconut Fish and
Tomato Bake, page 134

Fish and Shrimp

Imagine a beachy, breezy platter of shrimp, tortillas and all the fixings for tacos landing on your dinner table at the end of a very long day. All you'd need is a cold beer, maybe a margarita. The recipe for the Shrimp Tacos of your dreams is on page 154 and I think you should bookmark it.

Another dreamy keeper: our Coconut Fish and Tomato Bake, in which fillets are cloaked in a ginger-lime coconut sauce (page 134). And the Sheet-Pan Shrimp with Tomatoes, Feta and Oregano on page 127 is a very relaxed ten-minute dinner that's reminiscent of Greece.

For food that's so transporting, seafood is easy to find and maybe even easier to prepare. It also cooks quickly, which makes it ideal for weeknights.

Fish doesn't need to be expensive, either. (No one's expecting you to cook bluefin tuna for dinner, and if they are, just tell them no.)

I cook seafood weekly, and pretty much always keep shrimp and salmon in my freezer, both great staples to have on hand; my kids like the plush texture and flavor of salmon, and often ask for seconds. (I have yet to convince them to eat shrimp, but I'm trying.) I'm also very attached to canned tuna, which never gets any love but deserves it all. The recipe for Tuna Crunch Sandwiches on page 124 is the only one you need for either a simple version or an upgrade. I also keep tuna on hand for emergency pastas, like a pared-down version of the Blond Puttanesca, back on page 83.

A few tips: Buy fish at a store you trust and use it within a few days if it's fresh (there's a myth that you have to use it immediately, but you don't), or buy frozen and defrost it right before you plan to use it. Follow the recipe in front of you and keep a close eye on it to avoid overcooking; setting a timer is smart, too. By cooking the fish relatively quickly, you reduce the risk of lingering scents in your home.

And however you cook it, I recommend giving it a last generous spray of lemon or lime juice before eating. Seafood loves a citrus spritz.

Tuna Crunch Sandwiches

time   5 minutes

yield   2 sandwiches

A tuna salad and potato chip sandwich may not be quite as classic a pairing as peanut butter and jelly, but it is no less delicious. Beyond crunch, chips also add stability to the sandwich, holding the tuna salad in place as you eat. There's no wrong way to make the sandwich, but seasoning tuna salad with red onion and celery, plenty of olive oil and a little lemon juice, and using kettle-style salt and vinegar potato chips makes it especially alluring. There's the word "optional" next to some ingredients below, but consider everything other than the tuna, bread and chips to be adaptable according to your own taste (or how your mom made it).

—J. Kenji López-Alt

1 (5-ounce) can solid white albacore or skipjack tuna (see Tip)

1 hard-boiled egg, peeled

1 celery stalk, finely minced

3 tablespoons extra-virgin olive oil (see Tip)

2 tablespoons finely minced red onion, shallot or scallions

2 tablespoons finely minced fresh parsley, chives, tarragon or a mix (optional)

2 tablespoons mayonnaise, plus more for spreading (see Tip)

1 tablespoon sweet pickle relish or chopped dill pickles (optional)

2 teaspoons freshly squeezed lemon juice

A few large handfuls of hearty potato chips or corn chips (see Tip)

Kosher salt and black pepper

4 slices thick, soft sandwich bread, such as Texas toast, toasted, if desired

2 lettuce leaves, such as iceberg, romaine, green leaf or Bibb

Tip

You can use oil- or water-packed tuna here; make sure the tuna is well drained. Save the expensive stuff for other recipes. This recipe calls for olive oil, but for a more classic flavor, omit the olive oil and use up to 4 tablespoons of mayonnaise instead. For the chips, Ruffles, Fritos or kettle-style chips work best (especially salt and vinegar flavor).

1. Open the can of tuna, leaving the lid in place after opening it. Invert the whole can over the sink and press the lid into the tuna firmly to squeeze out as much excess water or oil as you can. (Be careful not to cut your fingers on any sharp edges.) Transfer the tuna to a medium bowl.

2. Wash your hands well, then grab the boiled egg and squeeze it through your fingers into the bowl with the tuna. Add the celery, olive oil, onion, herbs (if using), mayonnaise, relish (if using) and lemon juice. Using a fork, gently fold together all the ingredients, trying to leave the tuna in relatively large chunks. Grab a few chips and, using your hands, crumble them into the bowl. Season lightly with salt and pepper, and fold again to combine. Taste and adjust seasoning—more salt, pepper and lemon juice if it tastes bland, and more olive oil or mayonnaise if it tastes dry.

3. Spread each slice of bread generously with mayonnaise. Place lettuce on each bottom slice of bread, then top each with half of the tuna salad mixture. Add a generous handful of potato chips on top of each (more than seems reasonable), then close the sandwiches. Press down firmly so the chips break and embed themselves into the tuna salad and the bread. Cut into triangles and serve with extra chips on the side.

"Served hot with crusty bread and salad for dinner this evening and will throw the chilled leftovers over a Greek salad for tomorrow's lunch."

—Elyse

Easy Weeknight Dinners

Sheet-Pan Shrimp with Tomatoes, Feta and Oregano

time 10 minutes

yield 4 servings

Shrimp is among the most popular seafood in America, and it's certainly the most versatile. In this one-pan recipe, the shrimp is coated with garlic, oregano and black pepper and broiled for just a few minutes. For the most part, the shrimp will tell you when they're done. Certainly they're ready once they're pink, though very large shrimp may need an extra minute to cook through. To check, slice one in half; if it's opaque, or even nearly so, season to taste and start eating. Serve with a hearty salad, bread or both.

—Mark Bittman

1 garlic clove

1 teaspoon kosher salt

1 tablespoon chopped fresh oregano

1 tablespoon fresh lemon juice

2 tablespoons olive oil

Black pepper

1½ pounds peeled shrimp, preferably wild

Chopped tomatoes, for serving

Crumbled feta, for serving

1. Heat the broiler with a rack close to the heat source.

2. In a small bowl, mash the garlic with the salt until a paste forms. Add the oregano, lemon juice, oil and lots of black pepper and mix well. Rub the paste all over the shrimp.

3. Spread the shrimp out on a sheet pan and broil, 2 to 3 minutes per side. Served topped with the tomatoes and feta.

Sheet-Pan Salmon and Broccoli with Sesame and Ginger

time   20 minutes

yield   4 servings

This healthy sheet-pan dinner comes together in just 20 minutes. Brushing a simple sesame-ginger glaze onto the salmon before it roasts promotes caramelization on the fish, a feat not easily accomplished when roasting salmon fillets. The garnishes give this dinner a lovely finish: A squeeze of lime juice, a sprinkle of sesame seeds and a handful of thinly sliced scallions make for a beautiful plate.

—Lidey Heuck

4 tablespoons toasted sesame oil

2 tablespoons soy sauce or tamari

1 tablespoon rice vinegar

1 tablespoon honey

1 (2-inch) piece fresh ginger, peeled and grated (about 2 tablespoons)

1 garlic clove, grated

1 pound broccoli, trimmed and cut into florets, thick stems discarded

2 scallions, trimmed and cut on the diagonal into 1½-inch segments, plus thinly sliced scallions for garnish

1 tablespoon olive oil, plus more for brushing

Kosher salt and black pepper

4 (6-ounce) skin-on salmon fillets

½ lime, for serving

Sesame seeds, for serving

1. Heat the oven to 425 degrees. In a small bowl, whisk 3 tablespoons of the sesame oil with the soy sauce, vinegar, honey, ginger and garlic until smooth. Set the glaze aside.

2. Place the broccoli florets and 1½-inch scallion segments on a sheet pan. Drizzle with the olive oil and the remaining 1 tablespoon sesame oil, sprinkle with ½ teaspoon salt and ¼ teaspoon black pepper and toss well. Roast for 5 minutes.

3. While the broccoli and scallions roast, place the salmon fillets on a plate and pat dry with paper towels. Brush all over with olive oil and sprinkle with salt and pepper.

4. Toss the broccoli and scallions and move to the edges of the pan, clearing space in the center for the salmon fillets. Place the salmon fillets, evenly spaced, on the center of the pan. Brush the fillets generously with the glaze.

5. Return the pan to the oven and roast until the salmon is cooked through but still slightly rare in the center, about 12 minutes.

6. Squeeze the lime half over the broccoli and sprinkle with salt. Scatter the sliced scallions and sesame seeds over the salmon. Serve hot.

Salmon with Garlic Butter and Tomato Pasta

time   20 minutes

yield   4 servings

In less than a half-hour of swift multitasking, you'll be feasting on crisp-skinned salmon and delicate noodles dotted with caramelized tomatoes and fresh basil. Start by broiling salmon, skin side up, alongside little tomatoes. Without flipping or stinking up the house, the salmon skin sears and protects the tender flesh from overcooking, while the tomatoes grow juicier and char in spots. Meanwhile, cook angel hair pasta on the stovetop with garlic and butter. When everything is done cooking, stir the tomatoes into the pasta: They're like water balloons of sweetness and tang among the glossy, unapologetically garlicky noodles.

—Ali Slagle

4 (4- to 6-ounce) skin-on salmon fillets, patted dry

1 pint cherry or other small tomatoes (about 2 cups)

1½ tablespoons extra-virgin olive oil

Kosher salt and black pepper

3 tablespoons unsalted butter

5 garlic cloves, finely chopped or grated

3 basil sprigs, plus ½ cup torn fresh leaves

8 ounces angel hair pasta

1. Heat the broiler with a rack about 6 inches from the heat source. Line a sheet pan with foil. Place the salmon and tomatoes on the prepared pan, coat them all over with the oil and season all over with salt and pepper. Arrange the salmon skin side up. Broil until the tomatoes are blistered, the salmon skin is crisp and the salmon flesh flakes easily with a fork, 6 to 10 minutes. Halfway through broiling, check on the sheet pan: If the tomatoes are burning, give them a stir. If the salmon skin is burning, move the rack to the center of the oven and keep cooking.

2. Meanwhile, melt 2 tablespoons of the butter in a large skillet over medium-high heat. Add the garlic and stir until fragrant, 1 to 2 minutes. Add 3 cups water, 1½ teaspoons salt, the basil sprigs and a generous sprinkling of black pepper and bring to a boil. Add the pasta, breaking the noodles in half if they don't fit in the skillet. Cook the pasta, tossing often with tongs or a fork, until al dente, 5 to 8 minutes. It's okay if the pasta is ready and the water isn't completely absorbed. But if the skillet looks dry (no liquid is visible on the bottom) and the pasta is not yet ready, add a few tablespoons of water. If the pasta is done before the salmon, remove from the heat and cover to keep warm.

> "Cooked this with a toddler hanging on me. This will now become a go-to for busy weeknights. One sheet pan and a sauté pan and dinner is on the table with almost no chopping other than garlic."
>
> **—Tomaha**

3. When the salmon and tomatoes are out of the oven, transfer the salmon, skin side up, to plates to rest. Remove and discard the basil sprigs from the pasta, then add the remaining 1 tablespoon butter to the pasta and toss until melted and glossing the noodles. Add the tomatoes, any juices from the sheet pan and the basil leaves to the pasta and stir just once to combine. Season to taste with salt and pepper. Serve the noodles alongside the salmon.

"Just made this according to the recipe (but with skin-on salmon), and it was divine. The deliciousness: effort ratio on this one is quite high. Will make this again and again."

—David

Sheet-Pan Chile Crisp Salmon and Asparagus

time   20 minutes

yield   4 servings

A mixture of chile crisp, soy sauce and honey coats salmon bites that roast alongside scallions and asparagus for a quick and colorful weeknight dinner. While the salmon doesn't need to be cubed, it's an easy and enjoyable way to eat it; the bite-size pieces can be served over rice, other cooked grains in a bowl or big salads. Finish it as you'd like: Try some gently torn fresh cilantro, toasted sesame seeds, flaky sea salt, lime slices or an extra drizzle of chile crisp.

—Yasmin Fahr

1 tablespoon chile crisp, plus more for serving

1 tablespoon soy sauce

1 teaspoon honey

2 pounds skinless, center-cut salmon (1 to 1½ inches thick), cut into 1- to 1½-inch cubes

1 bunch scallions, light green and white parts thinly sliced (reserve dark greens for another use)

1 bunch asparagus, trimmed

Kosher salt

2 tablespoons olive oil

Cooked grains or salad greens, for serving (optional)

1. Heat the oven to 400 degrees. In a large bowl, stir together the chile crisp, soy sauce and honey. Add the salmon and scallions and toss to coat.

2. Place the asparagus on a sheet pan. Season with salt, drizzle with the oil and toss until the asparagus is shiny. Add the salmon mixture to the pan, nestling the salmon between the asparagus spears or on top if needed to fit. Place any larger cubes near the edges of the pan so they'll cook evenly.

3. Roast until the salmon is just cooked through and the asparagus is crisp-tender, about 12 minutes. Season with salt. Serve over cooked grains, if you'd like.

Coconut Fish and Tomato Bake

time   20 minutes, plus
        15 to 30 minutes
        for marinating

yield   4 servings

A coconut-milk dressing infused with garlic, ginger, turmeric and lime coats fish fillets in this sheet-pan dinner. Accompanying the fish are bright-tasting cherry tomatoes, which turn jammy under the broiler and relinquish some of their juices to the pan sauce. This sauce is silky enough to coat a spoon and packed with flavor. It pairs well with anything from snapper to flounder and even salmon, so choose the fillets that look best at the market. You'll want to sop up the sauce with thick grilled or toasted baguette slices or spoon it over steamed rice.

—Yewande Komolafe

¾ cup unsweetened coconut milk

1 tablespoon honey

1 (1-inch) piece fresh ginger, scrubbed (unpeeled) and grated

1 garlic clove, grated

½ teaspoon ground turmeric

½ teaspoon red pepper flakes

Kosher salt

2 limes

½ cup chopped fresh cilantro

4 (6-ounce) skin-on or skinless fish fillets, such as snapper, haddock, striped bass, fluke, sablefish or salmon

2 pints cherry or grape tomatoes (about 4 cups)

3 tablespoons olive oil

1. In a large bowl, whisk together the coconut milk, honey, ginger, garlic, turmeric, red pepper flakes and 1 teaspoon salt.

2. Zest and juice 1 lime directly into the coconut milk mixture. Stir in ¼ cup of the cilantro. Add the fish fillets and turn to coat. Cover and marinate in the refrigerator for 15 to 30 minutes.

3. Meanwhile, position an oven rack in the lower-middle of the oven. Position a second rack as close as possible to the broiler heat source. Heat the oven to 425 degrees.

4. Place the tomatoes on a large sheet pan. Drizzle with 2 tablespoons of the oil, season with salt and toss to coat. Place the marinated fish between the tomatoes and spoon all the marinade from the bowl over the fish. Drizzle the remaining 1 tablespoon oil over the fish. Transfer the pan to the lower-middle oven rack and roast until the surface of the fish is opaque but the center is not cooked through, 8 to 10 minutes. The timing depends on thickness of the fish. The fish should not flake easily with a fork. Remove the pan from the oven and heat the broiler.

"This was sooooo good, even my picky 3-year-old was sopping up the sauce. I used frozen cod and it was perfect."

—Nikki B.

5. When the broiler is ready, place the pan on the rack closest to the heat source and finish cooking, rotating the pan once 180 degrees halfway through cooking, until the fish is tender and the tomatoes are just beginning to brown in spots, 5 to 6 minutes. Again, the timing depends on the thickness of the fish. While the fish cooks, cut the remaining lime into wedges.

6. Divide the tomatoes and fish among plates and tip the pan juices over the fish. Garnish with the remaining ¼ cup cilantro and serve with the lime wedges.

"Delicious for a cold January night. Citrus salad made me feel like we weren't experiencing -7 degrees in Chicago. The citrus dressing flaky salt also cut the sharp flavors of radish and grapefruit. Will make again!"

—MaliaZ

Ginger-Dill Salmon

time 25 minutes

yield 4 servings

Salmon, gently roasted to a buttery medium-rare, stars in this make-ahead-friendly dish. Fruity citrus and dill join spicy radishes and ginger, and the result is a refreshing, jostling mix of juicy, crunchy, creamy, spicy and sweet. Both the salad and the salmon can be made two days ahead, and everything is good at room temperature or cold. To embellish further, consider baby greens, thinly sliced cucumbers or fennel, roasted beets, soba noodles, tostadas, furikake or chile oil.

—Ali Slagle

1 (1½-pound) salmon fillet, skin-on or skinless

Kosher salt and black pepper

6 tablespoons finely chopped dill

1 (2-inch) piece ginger, scrubbed (unpeeled) and finely grated

2 tablespoons extra-virgin olive oil, plus more for serving

1 grapefruit

2 oranges

6 small radishes, trimmed and cut into thin wedges

1 avocado

Flaky sea salt, for finishing (optional)

1. Heat the oven to 325 degrees. Line a sheet pan with parchment paper. Pat the salmon dry, then place on the tray skin-side down (if there is skin) and season with salt and pepper.

2. In a medium bowl, stir together the dill, ginger and olive oil until combined. Season with salt and pepper. Spread half of the dill-ginger mixture over the top of the salmon. (Reserve the remaining dill-ginger mixture.) Bake until cooked through, 15 to 20 minutes. (You'll know the salmon is done when the fish flakes or an instant-read thermometer inserted into the thickest part is 120 degrees.)

3. As the salmon cooks, cut off the top and bottom of the grapefruit and set the grapefruit down on one of the cut sides. Follow the curve of the fruit to cut away the peel and pith. Squeeze the peels into the remaining dill-ginger mixture to get out any juice. Cut the fruit in half from top to bottom, then slice into ¼-inch-thick half-moons and remove the seeds. If your pieces are especially large, halve them again. Transfer the fruit and any juice on the cutting board to the bowl. Repeat with the oranges. Add the radishes, season generously with salt and stir gently to combine.

4. Break the salmon into large pieces and divide across plates with the citrus salad. Peel and pit the avocado, then quarter lengthwise and add to the plates. Season with salt. Spoon the juices from the bowl over the top and season with pepper, another drizzle of olive oil and flaky sea salt (if using).

Blackened Fish with Quick Grits

time   25 minutes

yield   4 servings

Blackening is a cooking technique that uses high heat and lots of seasoning to develop distinctive flavor by nearly charring the food in a cast-iron skillet. It's particularly good for lean white fish, such as catfish, snapper, trout and redfish. The fish is traditionally dipped in melted butter, then cooked in a dry skillet, but that can create billows of smoke. This smokeless method cooks seasoned fillets in oil to create a lovely texture. The cheese grits cook in just under 5 minutes, but they are extra flavorful from cooking in chicken stock and still creamy as a result of added milk and butter.

—Vallery Lomas

For the fish

1 tablespoon plus 1½ teaspoons sweet paprika

1 tablespoon black pepper

2¼ teaspoons dried thyme

2¼ teaspoons dried oregano

1½ teaspoons garlic powder

1½ teaspoons kosher salt

½ to 1 teaspoon ground cayenne, depending on heat preference

4 (5- to 6-ounce) skinless white fish fillets, such as snapper, catfish, trout or tilapia

1 tablespoon extra-virgin olive oil

1 tablespoon unsalted butter

For the cheese grits

3½ cups low-sodium chicken stock or water

1 teaspoon kosher salt, plus more to taste

1 cup quick-cooking grits

½ cup whole milk

2 tablespoons unsalted butter

1 cup grated sharp Cheddar (4 ounces), plus more for garnish

½ teaspoon black pepper

1. Prepare the fish: In a small bowl, whisk the sweet paprika, black pepper, thyme, oregano, garlic powder, salt and cayenne. Pat the fish fillets dry, then sprinkle enough seasoning over both sides of the fillets to completely coat. Reserve remaining seasoning for another use. Allow the fish to sit for 15 minutes at room temperature.

2. While the fish sits, make the cheese grits: In a large saucepan, bring the chicken stock and salt to a boil. Add the grits while whisking and lower the heat to maintain a simmer. Allow the grits to thicken, about 5 minutes or so, then stir in the milk, butter and cheese. Season with pepper and more salt to taste. Keep over the lowest heat possible until ready to serve.

"Southerner here: Tennessean by birth, Mississippian by trade. I've grown up with grits and would like to add that quick/instant grits can actually be quite tasty (provided you add enough cream and *butter*)."

—William

3. Meanwhile, cook the fish: In a large cast-iron skillet heat the olive oil and butter over medium-high heat. Add the fish fillets, and cook until the spices are darkened and aromatic and the fish flakes easily with a fork, 2 to 4 minutes per side.

4. Divide the grits among serving dishes and nestle the fish on top. Garnish the grits with more shredded cheese and the whole dish with the scallions. Serve immediately with lemon wedges for squeezing over the fish.

"This is the best, most adjustable, best scented recipe we make on repeat. Recently cooked for company and the only request from someone at the table was for a twist of ground pepper. Okay—you do you."

—Anita A

Coconut-Miso Salmon Curry

time 25 minutes

yield 4 servings

This light, delicate weeknight curry comes together in less than 30 minutes and is defined by its deep miso flavor. Miso is typically whisked into soups toward the end of the recipe, but sweating it directly in the pot with ginger, garlic and a little oil early on helps the paste caramelize, intensifying its earthy sweetness. Adding coconut milk creates a rich broth that works with a wide range of seafood. Salmon is used here, but flaky white fish, shrimp or scallops would all benefit from this quick poaching method. A squeeze of lime and a flurry of fresh herbs keep this curry bright and citrusy. For a hit of heat, garnish with slices of jalapeño or serrano chile.

—Kay Chun

2 tablespoons safflower or canola oil

1 medium red onion, halved and sliced ½ inch thick (about 2 cups)

1 (1-inch) piece fresh ginger, peeled and minced (1 tablespoon)

3 garlic cloves, thinly sliced

Kosher salt and black pepper

¼ cup white miso

½ cup unsweetened full-fat coconut milk

1 (1½-pound) salmon fillet, cut into 2-inch pieces

5 ounces baby spinach (about 5 packed cups)

1 tablespoon fresh lime juice, plus lime wedges for serving

Hot steamed rice, such as jasmine or basmati, for serving

¼ cup chopped fresh basil

¼ cup chopped fresh cilantro

1. Heat the oil in a large pot over medium heat. Add the onion, ginger and garlic, season with salt and pepper, and cook, stirring occasionally, until softened, about 3 minutes. Add the miso and cook, stirring frequently, until miso is lightly caramelized, about 2 minutes.

2. Add the coconut milk and 3 cups water, increase the heat to high and bring to a boil. Cook until liquid is slightly reduced, about 5 minutes. Stir in the salmon, reduce the heat to medium-low and simmer gently until just cooked through, about 5 minutes. Turn off the heat and stir in the spinach and lime juice.

3. Divide the rice among bowls. Top with the salmon curry, basil and cilantro. Serve with lime wedges for squeezing on top.

Baked Cod with Buttery Cracker Topping

time   25 minutes

yield   4 servings

Baked stuffed fish is an old-school restaurant staple in New England. Covering the fish in lemony, butter-soaked cracker crumbs is a wonderful way to eat mild white fish like cod or haddock. The dish has a long history and relies on two ingredients New Englanders have in abundance: fresh seafood and crackers, which are descended from sailors' hardtack. Some modern versions use saltines, others use butter crackers like Ritz and many enrich the crackers with crabmeat. This recipe is an easy weeknight variation: Instead of rolling the fish up around the stuffing, which requires long, thin fillets, it is generously covered in the stuffing and roasted until the cracker topping is toasted and the fish flakes.

—Sarah DiGregorio

4 ounces butter-flavored crackers, such as Ritz (about 1½ sleeves; 1½ cups crushed)

5 tablespoons unsalted butter, melted

¼ cup minced fresh chives

¼ cup minced fresh flat-leaf parsley

½ lemon, zest and juice, plus lemon wedges for serving

1 teaspoon onion powder

1 teaspoon garlic powder

4 (6- to 8-ounce) white fish fillets, such as cod, haddock or halibut

Coarse kosher salt and black pepper

Sweet paprika, for garnish

1. Heat the oven to 425 degrees. Put the crackers into a medium bowl and crush them with your hand until finely crushed. (Some coarser bits are okay.) Add 4 tablespoons of the butter, the chives, parsley, lemon zest and onion and garlic powders and stir to mix evenly, making sure all the crumbs are moistened.

2. Put the fish fillets into a large, ovenproof skillet. Drizzle the remaining 1 tablespoon butter over the fish and turn to coat. Season the fish on all sides with salt and pepper. Mound the cracker mixture on top of the fish, covering it. (Some cracker crumbs will fall off the fish.)

3. Roast for 10 to 16 minutes, depending on the thickness of the fillets. Plan for about 10 minutes per inch; the fish should flake easily, and the juices should be bubbly around the edges. Squeeze the lemon juice over the top. Sprinkle with paprika and serve with lemon wedges on the side.

"I prepared per the recipe with no changes and served with baked butternut squash and lemony rice. Simple, fast, and elegant."

—Polly

"I toasted the orzo to a deep brown and used lots of parsley at the end, and ended up with something slightly nutty and herbal. Will cook again regularly."

—Jessica

Shrimp Scampi with Orzo

time   25 minutes

yield   4 servings

The universal appeal of shrimp scampi isn't the shrimp but the pan sauce: garlicky butter lightened with white wine and bursts of lemon, parsley and red pepper flakes. Scampi is often tossed with pasta or served with crusty bread, but this version uses orzo, which simmers directly in the pan sauce, imparting a starchy gloss and soaking up the garlicky flavors. Toss the shrimp with some garlic, lemon zest and red pepper flakes and let them marinate while the orzo gets a head start on the stove, then simply lay the shrimp on top of the orzo to steam. It all comes together in a flash and feels effortless. Pair this dish with Caesar salad, arugula or steamed broccoli, or bask in its simple comfort, straight from a spoon.

—Ali Slagle

1 pound large shrimp, peeled and deveined

3 tablespoons extra-virgin olive oil

1 tablespoon grated lemon zest

½ teaspoon red pepper flakes

Kosher salt and black pepper

4 garlic cloves, minced

2 tablespoons unsalted butter

1 cup orzo

⅓ cup dry white wine

2 cups boiling water, seafood stock or chicken stock

3 tablespoons finely chopped fresh parsley

1 tablespoon fresh lemon juice

1. In a medium bowl, stir together the shrimp, 1 tablespoon of the oil, the lemon zest, red pepper flakes, ½ teaspoon salt, ¼ teaspoon black pepper and half of the garlic. Set aside to marinate. (This step can be done up to 1 hour in advance and refrigerated.)

2. In a medium skillet, combine the butter, the remaining 2 tablespoons oil and the remaining garlic over medium heat. When the butter starts to bubble, add the orzo and ½ teaspoon salt and cook, stirring often, until the orzo is toasted, about 2 minutes, adjusting the heat as necessary to prevent the garlic from burning. Carefully add the wine—it will bubble—and stir until absorbed, about 1 minute. Stir in the water, reduce the heat to low, cover and cook until the orzo is al dente, about 12 minutes.

3. Add the shrimp in a snug, even layer on top of the orzo, cover and cook until all the shrimp are pink and cooked through, 2 to 4 minutes. Remove the pan from the heat and let sit, covered, for 2 minutes.

4. Sprinkle with the parsley and lemon juice, season with salt and pepper and serve immediately.

Sheet-Pan Cod and Scallions
with Cucumber Yogurt

time   25 minutes

yield   4 servings

You can use any mild, flaky fish for this quick recipe. The scallions add sweetness and crunch to the delicate fish, which is flavored with soy sauce and fish sauce for an extra-salty depth. Then it's all dolloped with a tart, creamy yogurt sauce that's both pungent from the garlic and cool and crisp from the chopped cucumber. Serve this dish with more sliced cucumber on the side and some pita bread or a baguette to soak up any remaining sauce. You won't want to waste even a drop.

—Melissa Clark

1 bunch scallions

3 tablespoons extra-virgin olive oil, plus more for drizzling

Fine sea salt and black pepper

4 (6- to 8-ounce) skinless cod fillets

1½ teaspoons soy sauce

1 teaspoon fish sauce

⅔ cup plain Greek yogurt

⅔ cup finely chopped Persian or English (hothouse) cucumber

1 tablespoon minced fresh dill or mint

2 teaspoons fresh lemon juice, plus more for serving

1 garlic clove, grated or mashed to a paste

Red pepper flakes (Urfa or Espelette are nice if you have them)

Flaky sea salt, for serving (optional)

1. Heat the oven to 450 degrees. Finely chop 1 to 2 scallions (you want to end up with about 2 tablespoons of chopped scallions); set aside. Halve the remaining scallions lengthwise. Place the halved scallions in a bowl and toss with 1 tablespoon oil and a pinch of salt; set aside.

2. Season the cod with salt and pepper, and place on a rimmed baking sheet. Drizzle the cod with a little oil, soy sauce and fish sauce. Add the halved scallions to the baking sheet, spreading them out in one layer around the fish. Transfer to the oven and roast until the fish is opaque in the center and golden at the edges, and the scallions are browned in spots, 8 to 12 minutes.

3. While the fish roasts, make the sauce: In a small bowl, mix together the remaining 2 tablespoons olive oil with 1 tablespoon chopped scallions, the yogurt, cucumber, dill, lemon juice, garlic and salt and pepper to taste.

4. To serve, put the cod and scallions on plates and squeeze lemon over the top. Dollop yogurt sauce over the cod and garnish with the remaining chopped scallions, red pepper flakes, more black pepper and sea salt, if you like.

"Excellent. I offered roasted sweet potatoes with the dish. It was a feast."

—Claire

Fried Snapper with Creole Sauce

time   30 minutes

yield   4 servings

Best enjoyed using local snapper, this bright dish represents the protein part of fish and fungi, a classic duo on dinner tables in the Virgin Islands. The fish is topped with plenty of thyme-laced, tomato-based Creole sauce and is typically served over a bed of fungi, the classic Virgin Islands side dish of buttery cooked cornmeal with sliced, boiled okra. This recipe was adapted from Michael Anthony Watson and Judy Watson, husband-and-wife owners of Petite Pump Room in St. Thomas, who traditionally use whole fried snapper, but you can use fish fillets. For authenticity, serve the snapper with plenty of hot sauce on the side for extra heat.

—Korsha Wilson

For the Creole sauce

3 tablespoons olive oil

3 medium yellow onions, halved and cut into ¼-inch-thick slices

1 red bell pepper, cored and cut into ¼-inch-thick slices

1 green bell pepper, cored and cut into ¼-inch-thick slices

4 garlic cloves, sliced

1 (14-ounce) can tomato sauce

4 fresh thyme sprigs

4 teaspoons distilled white vinegar

4 teaspoons seasoning salt, such as Creole seasoning or Lawry's

Kosher salt and black pepper

For the pan-fried snapper

⅓ cup vegetable oil

½ cup all-purpose flour

1½ teaspoons seasoning salt, such as Creole seasoning or Lawry's

4 skin-on red snapper fillets (about 6 ounces each)

Hot sauce (optional)

1. Prepare the sauce: In a large skillet, heat the olive oil over medium until shimmering. Add the onions, red and green bell peppers and garlic and cook, stirring occasionally, until fragrant and just starting to brown, about 7 minutes.

2. Stir in the tomato sauce, thyme and 1¾ cups water and bring to a boil over high.

3. Stir in the vinegar and seasoning salt, reduce the temperature to medium-low and simmer for 10 minutes. Season to taste with salt and pepper. Cover and keep warm.

4. Meanwhile, prepare the fish: Heat the vegetable oil in a large frying pan over medium. On a large plate, mix the flour and seasoning salt with a fork.

5. Pat the snapper fillets dry using paper towels, and season 2 fillets with salt and pepper before dipping them into the flour mixture until coated on both sides.

"Delicious. Reminded us of the snapper you can find in the lolos in St. Martin. The recipe makes a ton of sauce. Luckily it freezes well and is equally good on eggs."

—Raehay

6. Once the oil is shimmering, gently lay the floured fillets in the hot oil, skin-side down, and cook until skin is crispy, 3 to 4 minutes. Using a fish spatula, carefully flip fillets and cook for an additional 2 to 3 minutes, until cooked through.

7. Transfer the fish to a large paper towel–lined plate. Cover loosely with foil and repeat with the remaining fillets.

8. Divide fish among plates, skin side up, and top with the Creole sauce. Serve immediately, passing hot sauce at the table.

"This was quick and easy and SO COZY! I doubled it for four and it was the perfect amount with plenty of crusty garlic bread to sop it all up. I will make this again and again."

—Barrett

Easy Weeknight Dinners

Lemony Shrimp and Bean Stew

time   30 minutes

yield   4 servings

With minimal prep and a quick cook time, this shrimp stew feels elegant for such an easy weeknight meal. You can also take the dish in a number of directions: Substitute the shrimp with an equal amount of flaky white fish or even seared scallops, or stretch the dish into a meal for six by stirring in some butter and serving over cooked spaghetti or rigatoni.

—Sue Li

1 teaspoon grated lemon zest

1 teaspoon sweet or smoked paprika

2 garlic cloves, grated

Kosher salt and black pepper

1 pound peeled and deveined large shrimp, tails removed

2 large leeks, or 1 large onion

4 tablespoons unsalted butter

1 (15-ounce) can cannellini beans, drained and rinsed

2 cups chicken stock or vegetable stock

2 tablespoons finely chopped fresh parsley

2 tablespoons fresh lemon juice

Toasted bread, for serving

1. Mix together the lemon zest, paprika, garlic and ¾ teaspoon each salt and pepper in a medium bowl. Add the shrimp, toss to coat and set aside. If using leeks, trim the ends, halve lengthwise and cut the white and light green parts crosswise into ½-inch-thick slices. If using the onion, mince it.

2. In a large pot, melt the butter over medium-high heat. When butter is foaming, add the shrimp and cook, stirring occasionally, until pink and starting to curl, 2 to 3 minutes. Use a slotted spoon to transfer shrimp to a plate; set aside.

3. Reduce the heat to medium, add the leeks or onion, season with salt and pepper and cook, stirring occasionally, until soft and starting to brown on the edges, 4 to 5 minutes. Add the beans and stock, increase the heat to high and bring to a boil. Lower the heat to a simmer and cook, 8 to 10 minutes.

4. Stir in the reserved shrimp and any juices from the plate, parsley and lemon juice and season with salt and pepper. Serve with toasted bread.

Roasted Fish and Broccolini
with Tamarind and Black Pepper

time 35 minutes,
      plus at least
      15 minutes
      for marinating

yield 4 servings

A single skillet is all you need for this delicious, convenient and comforting weeknight meal of simple baked fish fillets. Rich with coconut milk enlivened by tangy tamarind, and infused with garlic, ginger and freshly ground black pepper, the quick marinade glazes the fish and bathes the vegetables. Broccolini is used here, but cauliflower, brussels sprouts or hearty leafy greens such as chard, turnip or beet greens can be substituted. This sauce is versatile and pairs well with most fish, so go with the fillets that look freshest at the market.

—Yewande Komolafe

4 fish fillets (6 ounces each), such as snapper, haddock, cod, striped bass, fluke, sablefish or salmon, skin on or off

Kosher salt and black pepper

¼ cup store-bought tamarind purée or 1 tablespoon tamarind paste (see Tip)

1 tablespoon molasses

1 (1-inch) piece fresh ginger, scrubbed (unpeeled) and grated (1 tablespoon)

2 garlic cloves, finely grated

½ cup unsweetened coconut cream or coconut milk

3 tablespoons olive oil, plus more for drizzling

1 bunch scallions, trimmed

1 pound broccolini (2 to 3 bunches), cut into 3-inch pieces

¼ cup chopped cilantro

Steamed grains, such as rice or fonio, for serving

1 lime, sliced into wedges, for serving

1. Season both sides of the fish lightly with salt and black pepper. In a large bowl, combine the tamarind purée, molasses, ginger, garlic, coconut cream, 1 tablespoon olive oil, ½ teaspoon salt and ½ teaspoon black pepper. Thinly slice 2 scallions and add to the marinade. Cut the remaining scallions into 1-inch pieces and set aside. Add the fish to the marinade and turn to coat. Refrigerate for at least 15 minutes and up to 12 hours.

2. Heat the oven to 450 degrees. In a large (12-inch) oven-safe skillet, combine the broccolini and chopped scallions. Toss with 1 tablespoon oil and season lightly with salt and pepper. Spread in an even layer, then place the fish right on top of the vegetables and pour any leftover marinade over the fish.

Tip

Tamarind can be purchased as a purée or paste and varies in degrees of concentration. Taste it first to determine how acidic it is and how much to use in the marinade. Find it online or at African, Caribbean or Asian grocery stores.

"SO GOOD! I used the rest of the coconut milk to make the rice."

—Greta

3. Roast until the fish is opaque but the center is not cooked through, 8 to 10 minutes, depending on the thickness of the fish. The fish should not flake easily with a fork. Remove the pan from the oven and heat the broiler to high. Drizzle the remaining tablespoon of oil over the fish.

4. Move the pan to the broiler and finish cooking, rotating the pan once, until the fish is tender and flakes easily and the broccolini is just tender and beginning to brown in spots, 6 to 7 minutes. Remove the pan from the broiler and sprinkle the fish with chopped cilantro.

5. Serve the fish and broccolini over steamed grains, such as rice or fonio. Tip the pan juices over the fish and serve with lime wedges for squeezing.

Shrimp Tacos

time   35 minutes

yield   4 servings

Spiced shrimp and quick-pickled red cabbage fill corn tortillas for dressed-up tacos that are easy to put together and sure to be a favorite. The seasoned shrimp is cooked in a hot skillet for a slight char. Be sure to resist the temptation to move the pieces before the contact side is properly browned. You can keep the add-ons simple with slices of creamy avocado, bits of fresh cilantro and acidic bursts from lime slices. Or you can bulk up with dollops of guacamole, chunky pico de gallo (see page 174) and sour cream.

—Yewande Komolafe

1 pound peeled and deveined shrimp, tails removed

½ teaspoon ground cumin

¼ teaspoon ground cayenne

½ teaspoon onion powder

½ teaspoon garlic powder

¼ teaspoon black pepper

3 tablespoons neutral oil, such as grapeseed or canola

Kosher salt

2 limes

1½ cups thinly sliced red cabbage (¼ small cabbage)

12 corn tortillas

Guacamole (see Tip), sour cream or crema, pico de gallo (see page 174) and fresh cilantro leaves, for serving

Guacamole

In a medium bowl, combine ½ cup finely chopped white onion with 2 tablespoons lime juice, and season with salt and pepper. Finely chop 1 jalapeño, and then add it to the bowl. Scoop out the flesh from 2 ripe avocados, add to the bowl and then mix and mash to your desired consistency. Add more salt and some chopped cilantro, if you'd like.

1. In a medium bowl, toss the shrimp with the cumin, cayenne, onion powder, garlic powder, black pepper and 1 tablespoon of the oil. Season the shrimp lightly with salt. If you have time, you can refrigerate the shrimp to marinate for at least 30 minutes or up to 12 hours.

2. Squeeze 1 tablespoon juice from 1 lime. Cut the remaining lime into wedges for serving. To quick pickle the cabbage, in a small bowl, toss together the cabbage, lime juice and a pinch of salt. Set aside.

3. Heat a large skillet over medium heat. Warm a tortilla in the dry skillet, flipping once, until soft and pliable, about 30 seconds. Place in a dish towel to keep warm. Repeat until all the tortillas are warmed, stacking and wrapping them in the dish towel until ready to use.

4. Heat 1 tablespoon of the oil in the skillet over medium-high heat. Add half of the shrimp and cook, without stirring. until the contact side is browned around the edges, about 3 minutes. Flip the shrimp over and cook on the other side until fully cooked, 1 to 2 minutes. Transfer the shrimp to a plate. Cook the remaining shrimp the same way, heating up the remaining 1 tablespoon oil before adding the shrimp to get a nice sear.

"Quick recipe with tons of flavor payoff—the best kind. The shrimp were restaurant quality. I'm already dreaming up different ways to incorporate them into other dishes. Maybe over crunchy greens with a mango vinaigrette next!"

—Stephanie

5. To assemble, spread some guacamole down the middle of each warm tortilla. Divide the shrimp among the tortillas and top with sour cream, pico de gallo, quick-pickled cabbage and cilantro. Serve immediately, with the lime wedges for squeezing.

"This is such a wonderful recipe. I added cubed mango, edamame and avocado. Can't go wrong with whatever goodies you add. Will add pickled shallots next time."

—Julie

Sesame Salmon Bowls

time 40 minutes

yield 4 servings

This one-pot meal, which is inspired by chirashi, or Japanese rice and raw fish bowls, features a savory vinegared rice that's typically served with sushi. Traditionally, the rice is cooked first, then mixed with vinegar, but here, the rice is cooked in vinegar-seasoned water to eliminate a step. The result is sticky rice that's tangy and sweet, and a perfect bed for fatty salmon. The salmon is added toward the end to steam directly on top of the rice for an easy one-pan meal. Packaged coleslaw is a time saver, eliminating extra knife work. Make a double batch of the zesty dressing for drizzling over roasted vegetables or green leafy salads the next day.

—Kay Chun

¼ cup unseasoned rice vinegar

3 tablespoons granulated sugar

1 teaspoon kosher salt, plus more for seasoning

1½ cups sushi rice (short-grain white rice), rinsed until water runs clear

1½ pounds skinless salmon fillet, cut into 1-inch cubes

½ teaspoon toasted sesame oil

¼ cup low-sodium soy sauce

3 tablespoons distilled white vinegar

2 tablespoons safflower or canola oil

2 tablespoons coarsely chopped scallions

1 (2-inch) piece fresh ginger, peeled and minced (about 2 tablespoons)

3 Persian cucumbers, thinly sliced

8 ounces green coleslaw mix (about 3 packed cups)

1 avocado, halved, pitted and thinly sliced

Torn toasted nori sheets, for garnish (optional)

1. In a large saucepan, combine the rice vinegar, sugar and salt; stir to dissolve the sugar. Add the rice and 1¾ cups water and mix well. Bring to a boil, then cover and reduce the heat to low. Cook until the rice is tender and most of the liquid is absorbed, about 20 minutes.

2. In a small bowl, toss the salmon with ¼ teaspoon sesame oil and season with salt. Once the rice is tender, arrange the salmon in an even layer on top of the rice. Cover and steam over low heat until fish is cooked to medium, about 12 minutes.

3. Meanwhile, in a small bowl, combine the soy sauce, white vinegar, safflower oil, scallions, ginger and the remaining ¼ teaspoon sesame oil. Mix well and season with salt.

4. Scoop the salmon and rice into bowls. Top each with some cucumbers, coleslaw mix and avocado. Drizzle with the vinaigrette. Top with nori (if using).

Beef and Pork

Black Pepper Beef and
Cabbage Stir-Fry, page 166

Beef and Pork

A truth of home cooking is that it's often easier to cook meat than it is to cook vegetables—and by that I mean easier to cook them deliciously. Meat, after all, is laced with fat and full of flavor. All you need to make beef taste good is salt, pepper and the wherewithal to not overcook it. (Not that cooking vegetables is hard, but let's agree they typically need a little help in the form of oil or butter.)

Assuming you're not making a roast or stew—please, don't do that to yourself on a Wednesday!—then beef cooks quickly, too, and rarely faster than in the Black Pepper Beef and Cabbage Stir-Fry on page 166, which is an excellent dinner.

Pork sausage is another heroic weeknight ingredient because it arrives preseasoned and ready to roast, broil, grill or pan-fry. If you're cooking sausage in a pan, its fat flavors everything around it, as in the Sheet-Pan Sausage with Peppers and Tomatoes on page 165.

I love meatballs, a crowd-pleaser that never goes out of style. Never, ever make a single batch of meatballs, and especially not the Pork Meatballs with Ginger and Fish Sauce (page 170), one of my favorite NYT Cooking recipes. Double, triple or even quadruple the recipe so you have extra to freeze in meal-size portions, a weeknight gift to your future self.

And I've come to realize that there's nothing that tastes better than a grilled steak and a cold drink on a summer night. It's just another truth of home cooking, and a delectable one at that. Good steak doesn't need any help, but the bright green sauce in the recipe for Grilled Steak with Sauce Rof on page 182 would make even an oven mitt taste good.

Beef Short Rib Rice Bowls

time   15 minutes, plus
at least 5 minutes
for marinating

yield   4 servings

Inspired by galbi, or Korean barbecued short ribs, this recipe takes a sharp turn away from the traditional sweet, fruity treatment and instead skews savory, with warm spices like cumin, coriander and turmeric. Meaty short ribs generally require a lengthy cook time, but slice them thinly off the bone and they'll tenderize quickly when seared on the stovetop—or you could use slivers of skirt steak or hanger steak instead. The skinny strips also have a higher surface area, which means they'll quickly soak up the flavors of the marinade. Rice is the perfect canvas for the meat, and celery and lettuce balance out the bold flavors with lightness and crunch.

—Sue Li

1 pound boneless beef short ribs, sliced ¼ inch thick

2 tablespoons soy sauce

1 tablespoon peeled, grated fresh ginger

1 tablespoon light brown sugar

2 garlic cloves, grated

1 teaspoon ground coriander

1 teaspoon ground cumin

1 teaspoon ground turmeric

½ teaspoon red pepper flakes

Kosher salt

2 tablespoons vegetable oil

4 cups hot cooked short-grain rice

1 small head green-leaf lettuce, shredded

2 celery stalks, thinly sliced crosswise

Fresh cilantro, for serving

Lime wedges, for serving

1. Combine the short ribs, soy sauce, ginger, sugar, garlic, coriander, cumin, turmeric, red pepper flakes and 1 teaspoon salt in a medium bowl and toss to coat. Cover, transfer to the fridge and let marinate for at least 5 minutes or up to 8 hours.

2. Heat the oil in a large skillet over medium heat. Working in batches, cook the meat until browned all over, about 3 minutes per side.

3. Divide the rice and short ribs among bowls. Top with the lettuce, celery and cilantro. Serve with lime wedges for squeezing on top.

"This is a perfect, bright, light and flavorful weeknight meal. I pulse the garlic and ginger together quickly in a food processor to speed up prep, as opposed to using a grater. Also, it's worth noting you can ask your butcher to debone the short ribs."

—PJ

"Excellent! Hit the mark for an easy family dinner. Lined sheet pan with foil to reduce cleanup."

—Elizabeth

Easy Weeknight Dinners

Sheet-Pan Sausage with Peppers and Tomatoes

time   20 minutes

yield   4 servings

Good, flexible and fast, this recipe is a surefire standby: all you have to do is toss the ingredients together on a sheet pan, then slide the entire thing under the broiler. In just 15 minutes, you'll have nicely seared sausages, tomatoes and peppers, all of which have released juices that you should dunk bread into or spoon over pasta or rice. Experiment with adding cumin, paprika, oregano or red pepper flakes in Step 1, or swap the garlic for scallions or red onion. You could also scatter crumbled feta, lemon slices, olives, pickled hot peppers or green beans across the top in the last few minutes of broiling.

—Ali Slagle

1 pound fresh sausages, such as sweet or hot Italian

1 pound sweet or mild peppers, such as mini sweet peppers, bell or Cubanelle, cut into 2-inch-wide strips if large

1 pound cherry or grape tomatoes

4 garlic cloves, thinly sliced

2 shallots, cut into ½-inch wedges

3 tablespoons extra-virgin olive oil

Kosher salt and black pepper

1. Heat the broiler with a rack about 6 inches from the heat source. Score each sausage in a few places on both sides, making sure not to cut all the way through. In a shallow baking dish or sheet pan, toss the sausages with the peppers, tomatoes, garlic, shallots and oil. Season with salt and pepper and spread in a single layer.

2. Broil until the sausages are cooked through and the peppers and tomatoes are nicely charred, 10 to 15 minutes. Rotate the pan and the ingredients as needed so everything gets under the broiler. If everything is charring too quickly, cover the pan with foil. Serve immediately.

Black Pepper Beef and Cabbage Stir-Fry

time   20 minutes

yield   2 to 4 servings

Coarsely crushed black peppercorns star in this quick dish, which is built primarily from pantry staples. Don't be shy about adding the entire tablespoon of pepper, as it balances out the richness of the beef and adds a lightly spicy bite to the dish. A quick rub of garlic, brown sugar, salt, pepper and cornstarch seasons the beef; the cornstarch helps tenderize the beef and later imparts a silky texture to the sauce. Feel free to marinate the beef up to 8 hours ahead and cook when you're ready. If leftovers remain, tuck them into a crunchy baguette or roll them into a wrap.

—Sue Li

1 tablespoon black peppercorns, coarsely crushed with the bottom of a cup or pan

3 garlic cloves, grated

2 teaspoons light brown sugar

1 teaspoon cornstarch

Kosher salt

¾ pound sirloin steak, thinly sliced crosswise

3 tablespoons sunflower or other neutral oil

2 tablespoons soy sauce

½ head small green cabbage (about 8 ounces), thinly sliced

1 tablespoon sherry vinegar

1 tablespoon toasted sesame seeds, crushed with your fingertips

2 scallions, thinly sliced

Hot cooked rice, for serving

1. Add the peppercorns, garlic, sugar, cornstarch and 1 teaspoon salt to a medium bowl and stir to mix. Add the steak slices and toss to coat.

2. Heat the oil in a large cast-iron skillet over medium-high heat. Add the steak and cook, stirring frequently, until some of the edges are lightly browned, 3 to 4 minutes. Add the soy sauce and toss the beef to coat, about 1 minute. Use a slotted spoon to transfer beef to a bowl or plate.

3. With the skillet still over medium-high heat, add the cabbage and spread in an even layer. Let cook, undisturbed, for 1 minute so some pieces caramelize in the pan. Toss and cook the cabbage, stirring occasionally, until crisp-tender, 4 to 6 minutes. Stir in the vinegar and season with salt.

4. Return the steak and any juices to the skillet and stir until well combined with the cabbage and warmed through, about 1 minute. Top with the sesame seeds and scallions and serve with rice.

"I made this recipe exactly as is, and it is SPECTACULAR! I suppose I may have to make one change next time since my husband and I devoured it all at once: I'll double the entire recipe so I end up with leftovers to look forward to!"

—Alexa

"Super easy and delicious every time. I have been making this for years and love it with blackberry preserves, Dijon, and I don't add the water."

—Julia

Pork Chops with Jammy-Mustard Glaze

time   20 minutes

yield   4 servings

Fruit and mustard are two classic accompaniments to pork, and a juicy chop doesn't need much more than that for a sweet and tangy sauce. First, mix together water, grainy mustard and any fruit preserve that's good with pork, such as cherry, fig, peach or apricot. Next, sear bone-in pork chops mostly on one side to prevent overcooking, then pour the fruit-mustard mixture into the skillet while they rest. The pork will stay moist, and its juices will have time to mingle with the sauce. Then just slice the pork and drape it in the velvety two-ingredient sauce. Eat with mashed or roasted potatoes and a green salad.

—Ali Slagle

2 tablespoons cherry, fig, peach or apricot preserves, plus more if needed

2 tablespoons whole-grain mustard, plus more if needed

4 (6- to 8-ounce) pork rib chops (½ to ¾ inch thick)

Kosher salt and black pepper

2 tablespoons neutral oil, such as canola or grapeseed

1. In a small bowl, stir together ¼ cup water, the preserves and mustard. Set near the stove. Pat the pork chops dry and season all over with salt and pepper.

2. In a large cast-iron skillet, heat the oil over medium-high heat. Add the pork chops and cook, occasionally pressing down to make good contact with the skillet, until browned on the underside, 4 to 5 minutes. Reduce the heat to low, flip the chops over and cook until opaque on the other side, 1 to 2 minutes. Pour in the jam-mustard mixture, turn off the heat and let rest for 5 minutes.

3. Transfer the chops to plates, then return the skillet to medium-low heat and simmer the sauce, scraping up browned bits on the pan bottom, until slightly thickened, 1 to 3 minutes. Taste and adjust the seasonings if needed. Every jam is different, so if the sauce is too sweet, add more mustard, salt or pepper; if it's too salty, add a little more jam; if it's too intense or thick, add a little more water; and if it's flat, add salt. Spoon the sauce over the pork chops and serve.

Pork Meatballs with Ginger and Fish Sauce

time   20 minutes

yield   4 servings

These nuoc cham–inspired meatballs are perfect to fill lettuce cups topped with fresh basil or cilantro. (Add steamed rice for a more substantial meal.) The Ritz crackers here make for a juicier meatball, but feel free to substitute plain dried bread crumbs. To make the Ritz crumbs, place the crackers in a resealable plastic bag and lightly crush them with the back of a wooden spoon or the bottom of a measuring cup. For an easy dipping sauce, spike ¼ cup mayonnaise with 2 teaspoons toasted sesame oil or soy sauce. And save any leftover meatballs: They're great simmered in chicken stock the next day. The ginger and garlic in them release their aromatics into the stock for a deeply flavorful soup base.

—Kay Chun

2 tablespoons peeled, minced fresh ginger

1 tablespoon minced garlic (from about 3 large cloves)

1 tablespoon fish sauce

1 teaspoon black pepper

½ teaspoon kosher salt

½ cup finely crushed Ritz crackers (12 crackers)

1 pound ground pork

1. Heat the oven to 425 degrees.

2. In a large bowl, combine the ginger, garlic, fish sauce, pepper, salt, crackers and pork and use your hands to mix gently.

3. Shape the meat into 12 golf-ball-size spheres (about 2 inches in diameter) and arrange on a greased rimmed baking sheet.

4. Bake until golden and cooked through, about 15 minutes. Serve warm.

Tip

Leftover meatballs freeze well and can be reheated in the oven at 375 degrees until warmed through (about 20 minutes).

"These were great! While they baked, I stir-fried some snow peas and made a quick mint salad to accompany with rice. Delicious, easy dinner!"

—Joe

"This was an absolute-hands-down-midweek-let's-have-friends-over crowd pleaser. Very simple—easy to scale when appetites outrun initial supply."

—Rich

BLT Tacos

time 25 minutes

yield 4 servings

Without the bread muffling the crunch of bacon and crisp lettuce, BLT tacos are a lot more texturally exciting than the usual sandwich, and perfect for brunch, lunch or a light, fast dinner. Here, hot sauce-spiked mayonnaise adds spice; avocado adds creaminess; and chopping the tomatoes into a salsa with jalapeño, lime juice and cilantro makes everything juicy and bright. Choose a tangy, vinegar-based hot sauce here, such as Cholula or Tabasco; just avoid Sriracha, which will be too sweet.

—Melissa Clark

1 pound thick-cut bacon

1 pint cherry tomatoes, quartered (mixed colors are pretty here)

1 small jalapeño, seeded or not, finely chopped

2 tablespoons cilantro, chopped

1½ teaspoons fresh lime juice, plus more to taste

Kosher salt

½ cup mayonnaise

1½ teaspoons Cholula or other hot sauce, or to taste, plus more for serving

8 (6-inch) corn or flour tortillas

Romaine lettuce leaves, torn into bite-size pieces

1 avocado, sliced (optional)

1. Heat the oven to 400 degrees. Lay the bacon in an even layer on a rimmed baking sheet and bake until browned and crisp, 15 to 20 minutes. Transfer to a paper towel–lined plate and let cool.

2. While bacon is cooking, in a medium bowl, toss together tomatoes, jalapeño, cilantro, lime juice and a large pinch of salt. Taste and add more lime juice and salt, if needed.

3. In a small bowl, whisk together the mayonnaise and hot sauce.

4. Lay a clean kitchen towel in a medium bowl. Using the open flame from a stovetop gas burner (or in a skillet placed on an electric burner), warm and lightly char the tortillas, 30 seconds to 1 minute per side. Transfer warmed tortillas to the towel-lined bowl and cover with the towel to keep warm while you finish the remaining tortillas.

5. Serve, letting each person make their own tacos by layering bacon, salsa, lettuce, spicy mayonnaise and avocado (if using) on tortillas. Top with more hot sauce, if desired.

Hot Dogs with Pico de Gallo

time   30 minutes

yield   4 servings

Tanya Sichynsky, a New York Times Cooking editor, tops salty, snappy grilled hot dogs with bright pico de gallo. Combining those two elements of fully loaded Mexican hot dogs makes these easy to cook for a crowd and tote to a cookout. You can prepare the pico de gallo early in the day and keep it in an airtight container until ready to pile onto the hot dogs, split to cradle the fresh filling. Be sure to keep the grill heat moderate. Too hot, and the hot dogs—and buns—will burn and dry out. Too cool, and they won't take on a smoky char.

—Genevieve Ko

4 hot dogs and buns

2 tablespoons mayonnaise (optional)

For the pico de gallo

2 ripe but firm tomatoes (1 pound), cored, seeded and diced (2 cups)

½ small white onion, finely diced (1 cup)

2 jalapeños, stemmed, seeded (if desired) and finely chopped (⅓ cup)

½ cup cilantro leaves and tender stems, finely chopped

1 teaspoon fresh lime juice, plus more to taste

Kosher salt

1. Prepare an outdoor charcoal grill or a gas grill to medium heat. You should be able to hold your hand 5 inches above the coals for 7 to 9 seconds before it becomes too hot. Or heat a grill pan on the stovetop over medium heat.

2. Make the pico de gallo by combining the tomatoes, onion, jalapeños, cilantro and lime juice in a medium bowl. Season with salt and mix well. Taste and add more lime juice and salt, if desired.

3. Butterfly the hot dogs: Slice them in half lengthwise without cutting all the way through the skin, then open them so they sit flat. Place them on the grill, cut side down, and cook until grill marks appear, 3 to 5 minutes. Flip the hot dogs and cook skin side down until the skin deepens in color, 2 to 4 minutes.

4. Meanwhile, open the hot dog buns and spread the mayonnaise on the cut sides, if you like. Grill, cut side down, until toasted, 1 to 2 minutes, then flip and grill until lightly toasted, about 1 minute.

5. Place the grilled hot dogs in the toasted buns, cut side up, then pile the pico de gallo into the butterflied opening. Serve immediately, with any remaining pico de gallo on the side.

"If you want to elevate your picnic game, this is the hot dog recipe that will do it! And don't skip the recommendation to use mayonnaise on the hot dog buns as you grill them—it adds more depth to the overall taste."

—Dick T.

"Oh my gosh. Husband
is not a fan of
sausages (I know!)
or mustard but loves
brussels sprouts . . .
yet I forged ahead.
This was his response:
'I think this is one of
the best things you've
ever made. Mic drop.'"

—Michelle

Easy Weeknight Dinners

Sheet-Pan Sausage and Brussels Sprouts with Honey Mustard

time   30 minutes

yield   4 servings

This hearty pan of sticky, honey mustard-glazed sausages, brussels sprouts and potatoes only adds to the argument that sheet-pan dinners make the best weeknight meals. As the sausages roast, they yield a delicious fat that coats and seasons the caramelized vegetables. Use any fresh sausage you like as long as it pairs well with the honey mustard. Feel free to substitute or add other vegetables, such as squash, cherry tomatoes, broccoli, carrots or cabbage. The mustard seeds and nuts provide texture and crunch, but leave them out if you prefer.

—Ali Slagle

1 pound fresh sausages, such as sweet or hot Italian or bratwurst

1 pound brussels sprouts, trimmed and halved lengthwise

1 pound small potatoes, such as baby Yukon Gold or red potatoes, halved

2 tablespoons extra-virgin olive oil, plus more as needed

Kosher salt and black pepper

4 teaspoons honey

1 tablespoon Dijon mustard

1 tablespoon yellow mustard seeds (optional)

¼ cup almonds or walnuts, chopped (optional)

1. Place a sheet pan in the oven and heat the oven to 450 degrees. Score each sausage in a few places on both sides, making sure not to cut all the way through. Transfer to a large bowl, add the brussels sprouts, potatoes and oil and stir until coated. If the mixture seems dry, add a little more oil. Season with salt and pepper.

2. Remove the sheet pan from the oven and spread the mixture in a single layer on the hot pan, arranging the vegetables cut side down. Roast until the brussels sprouts and potatoes start to soften, about 15 minutes. (The sausages will not be cooked through yet.)

3. Meanwhile, in a small bowl, stir together the honey, mustard and mustard seeds (if using).

4. Drizzle the honey mustard over the sausages and vegetables and toss to coat or shake the pan to coat. Flip the sausages. Sprinkle with the almonds (if using). Roast until the sausages are cooked through and the vegetables are golden and tender, another 10 minutes or so. Season to taste with salt and pepper and serve.

Pork Chops in Lemon-Caper Sauce

time   35 minutes

yield   4 servings

Here's my favorite recipe in Toni Tipton-Martin's excellent and invaluable cookbook *Jubilee: Recipes from Two Centuries of African American Cooking*. A dish of smothered pork chops, essentially, it's a glorious remix of a recipe that the chef Nathaniel Burton collected into his 1978 opus, *Creole Feast: Fifteen Master Chefs of New Orleans Reveal Their Secrets*, glossed-up here with lemon zest, juice and extra butter. It's African American French food that is also Italian, totally elegant and thus absolutely from New Orleans, and every time I make it, there is absolute joy at the table.

—Sam Sifton

4 bone-in pork chops
(about 8 ounces each)

Kosher salt and freshly cracked black pepper

½ teaspoon dried thyme leaves

2 tablespoons olive oil

4 tablespoons unsalted butter

1 very small shallot, minced
(about 1 tablespoon)

2 garlic cloves, minced (about 1 teaspoon)

2 teaspoons all-purpose flour

1 cup dry white wine

1½ cups chicken stock, homemade, or low-sodium, if store-bought

2 tablespoons drained capers

2 tablespoons minced fresh parsley, plus more for garnish

1 teaspoon grated lemon zest

2 tablespoons fresh lemon juice

Hot sauce, for seasoning (optional)

1. Pat the chops dry with paper towels and season aggressively with salt, pepper and the thyme. Swirl the olive oil into a large skillet and heat over medium heat until the oil begins to shimmer. Add the chops and cook until well browned on each side and cooked through, about 5 minutes per side. Transfer the chops to a plate and cover to keep warm.

2. Drain the fat from the skillet, then return the skillet to medium heat, add 2 tablespoons of the butter and melt until sizzling. Add the shallot and garlic and cook, until softened, reducing the heat if necessary to prevent scorching, about 1 minute. Sprinkle in the flour and cook, stirring, for 2 minutes. Whisk in the wine and stock, increase the heat to high and bring to a boil, scraping up the browned bits on the bottom of the pan. Reduce the heat to medium-high and cook, uncovered, until the liquid is reduced by half, 7 to 10 minutes.

"Amazing, I let my husband make this for me (I usually do the cooking but a girl needs a day off). Spent the tail end of my night eating the sauce out of the pan. Pairs amazingly with a crisp Sauvignon Blanc."

—Kami M.

3. Stir in the capers, parsley, lemon zest and juice and hot sauce to taste (if using) and simmer for 1 to 2 minutes. Stir in the remaining 2 tablespoons butter until melted and the sauce looks smooth. Nestle the pork chops into the sauce and allow them to warm up for a couple of minutes. Transfer the chops to plates, pouring the pan sauce over each chop to taste. Serve with more fresh parsley.

Loaded Baked Frittata

time   45 minutes

yield   4 to 6 servings

Sautéed onion, pepper and spinach lace this sturdy frittata that's as good warm out of the pan as it is cold. Bacon and goat cheese enrich the mix, which can be eaten alone or put in a sandwich (see Tip). This recipe is, of course, delicious as is, but you can also take a cue from one of our commenters, Joan, who made this with leftover peppers and onions, adding sliced roasted baby potatoes. Ready in 45 minutes, it lasts for up to three days in the refrigerator, so you can enjoy it as long as it lasts—which may not be very long.

—Genevieve Ko

8 large eggs

½ cup whole milk

Kosher salt and black pepper

½ cup finely diced uncooked bacon

1 cup diced onion (from 1 small onion)

2 cups diced red or orange bell pepper (from 2 peppers)

1 (5-ounce) package baby spinach

4 ounces fresh goat cheese

1. Heat the oven to 375 degrees. In a medium bowl, beat the eggs, milk, 1 teaspoon salt and ½ teaspoon pepper until smooth. Set aside.

2. In a 10- to 12-inch cast-iron or oven-safe nonstick skillet, cook the bacon over medium heat, stirring occasionally, until browned, 4 to 5 minutes.

3. Add the onion, peppers and ½ teaspoon each salt and pepper and cook, stirring often, until the onions are translucent, 6 to 7 minutes. Add the spinach a handful at a time, stirring after each addition, to wilt.

4. Reduce the heat to low and pour in the egg mixture. Stir well to evenly distribute the vegetables, then smooth the top. Drop small nuggets of goat cheese evenly on top. Transfer to the oven.

5. Bake until the top is golden brown and the eggs are set, 20 to 25 minutes. When you shake the pan, the eggs shouldn't jiggle. Cool on a rack for about 10 minutes.

6. Cut into wedges to serve warm or at room temperature.

Tip

To make into sandwiches, slide the frittata onto a cutting board. Cut to match the dimensions of your bread, trimming the rounded edges if needed. Sandwich between the bread and serve immediately or wrap tightly in foil, plastic wrap or wax paper for later.

Grilled Steak with Sauce Rof

time   45 minutes,
        plus at least
        15 minutes
        for marinating

yield   4 servings

A combination of onion, parsley, scallions and chile, classic Senegalese rof adds complexity to dishes. Typically used to stuff fish as a marinade and top it as a bold relish, it is also great for tempering the smoky char of grilled chicken or steak. In this recipe, sauce rof is used as a marinade and served as a topping for steak. The relish is thinned with a dash of olive oil and gets a splash of lemon juice, which adds a lovely sparkle. Go for a nice marbled cut of meat—the fat intensifies the flavor of the grilled meat, and the sauce rof cuts through the richness. The condiment can be made up to 24 hours in advance and refrigerated in an airtight jar.

—Yewande Komolafe

1½ pounds skirt steak or boneless short ribs (see Tip)

Coarse kosher salt and black pepper

1 medium white or yellow onion

2 garlic cloves, peeled

1 serrano chile or jalapeño, stemmed

4 scallions, trimmed and thinly sliced

1 small bunch parsley, leaves and tender stems only (about 2 ounces)

1 lemon

4 tablespoons extra-virgin olive oil

1. Pat the steak dry and season lightly with salt.

2. In a food processor, pulse the onion until roughly chopped. Add the garlic and chile and pulse to combine. Add the scallions and parsley and pulse until all the ingredients are reduced to a coarse paste. Transfer the paste to a large bowl and zest the lemon directly into it. Stir in 2 tablespoons of the oil, 1 teaspoon salt and ½ teaspoon pepper. (Alternatively, finely chop the onion, chile, garlic, scallions and parsley to a coarse paste by hand. Transfer to a large bowl, zest the lemon into the bowl, add the oil, salt and pepper and stir to mix well.)

3. Transfer about ¾ cup of the paste to a small bowl. Add the meat to the large bowl and turn to coat. Marinate at room temperature for at least 15 minutes or cover and marinate in the refrigerator for up to 12 hours.

4. Combine the reserved marinade with the remaining 2 tablespoons oil and squeeze in about 2 tablespoons lemon juice. Season with ¼ teaspoon salt and a pinch of black pepper, stir to combine and set aside.

5. Heat a charcoal or gas grill to medium-high.

Tip

If your boneless short ribs are already in slices ½ inch thick or thinner, you can use them as they are. If they're thicker, lay several strips on a piece of plastic wrap, spacing them about ½ inch apart, and top with another piece of plastic wrap. Pound the meat with a rolling pin or the bottom of a heavy bottle until the strips are flattened to about ½ inch thick.

"I left out the chile and my 3- and 1-year-olds loved it. I served with rice, asparagus and corn, and the sauce went well on everything."

—Christina

6. Scrape any excess marinade off the steak and discard the marinade. Grill the steak until the contact side is seared, 4 to 5 minutes. Flip and cook for an additional 3 minutes for medium-rare. Cook for an additional minute on each side for medium.

7. Transfer the steak to a cutting board to rest for at least 5 minutes. Slice and transfer to a serving platter. Spoon the marinade dressing over the steak and serve immediately.

"I liked this technique for deeply browning the ground meat with the onions and spices sprinkled on top. It really did something special to the flavor and texture of the beef. A keeper."

—Stephanie

Easy Weeknight Dinners

Easy Burritos

time   50 minutes

yield   6 burritos

Saucy and savory with just ground beef, beans and cheese, this easy recipe is inspired by Los Angeles–style burritos. The filling eschews guacamole, sour cream, rice and raw vegetables, which means it freezes well for up to three months. The seared ground beef is simply spiced, but feel free to swap in a stewed meat like birria or tinga de pollo, or make it vegetarian with just beans and cheese.

—Ali Slagle

1 pound ground beef

1 medium yellow or white onion, finely chopped

1½ teaspoons ground cumin

½ teaspoon smoked paprika, or chipotle or ancho chile powder

½ teaspoon dried oregano

Kosher salt and black pepper

1 (15-ounce) can black or pinto beans

1 large tomato, coarsely chopped

2 teaspoons lime juice or apple cider vinegar

6 burrito-size (about 10-inch) flour tortillas

2 cups (8 ounces) shredded Monterey Jack or Mexican blend cheese

Hot sauce, for drizzling (optional)

1. In a large skillet, press the beef into an even layer to fill the skillet. Sprinkle with the onion. Cook over medium-high heat, undisturbed, until the meat is deeply browned underneath, 6 to 8 minutes. Sprinkle with the cumin, smoked paprika and oregano and season with salt and pepper. Break up the beef into small pieces, then cook, stirring occasionally, until the onion is softened and the spices are fragrant, 2 to 4 minutes.

2. Add the beans, including the liquid, and the tomato and simmer, stirring and scraping up browned bits, until the liquid has evaporated and the mixture starts to sizzle, 8 to 10 minutes. Turn off the heat, stir in the lime juice and season with salt and pepper.

3. Arrange the tortillas on a clean work surface. Sprinkle half the cheese across the center of the tortillas, left to right, leaving a 1-inch border. Top each with ⅔ cup of the beef-bean mixture, followed by the remaining cheese. Drizzle on hot sauce (if using). Fold the tortilla's short sides over the filling, then fold the bottom of the tortilla snugly over the filling. Tightly roll away from you until the burrito is sealed. Repeat with the other tortillas.

4. When ready to eat, in a nonstick skillet over medium, place the burritos seam side down. Cook, turning occasionally, until golden all over, 3 to 5 minutes. Serve with desired toppings.

Tip

To make ahead, prepare through step 3. Let cool slightly, then wrap in aluminum foil. Refrigerate for up to 24 hours or freeze for up to 3 months. To reheat, remove the foil and wrap the burrito in a damp paper towel. Microwave, seam side down, until warm, 1 to 4 minutes. Remove the towel and continue to step 4.

Red Curry Lentils with
Sweet Potatoes and
Spinach, page 222

Vegetables, Beans and Tofu

Vegetables, Beans and Tofu

The single biggest shift in my diet in the past few years has been toward cooking meatless meals. The game changer has been beans, which are big in my home. Cooking them from scratch will always taste best, and you can do it last minute if you invest in an electric pressure cooker (like an Instant Pot). But you're busy! Take the shortcut and use canned beans, which are a convenience food like none other. I keep them stocked in my pantry to use in recipes like the Braised White Beans and Greens with Parmesan on page 211.

It's especially easy to make black beans kid-friendly, if that's who you're feeding. My children love black beans, and even demand them; they've become a sort of gateway bean for us, leading my kids to try other kinds. If you look at your kids and think, "That's impossible!"—I swear, put the beans in front of them a few times and see what happens. I particularly love the Coconut-Ginger Black Beans on page 215.

If you never cook tofu, what's holding you back? It's versatile and easy. Find a brand you like and stick with it—the taste and texture of tofu can vary widely. The cool Silken Tofu with Spicy Soy Dressing on page 191 is a NYT Cooking staff favorite and an unparalleled meal for a hot day when you can't bear to turn on the stove.

And, of course, you can just focus on vegetables, no beans, tofu, eggs or any other staples of vegetarian cooking. I find that if they're seasoned boldly enough, they can be the star of a meal, especially when they're paired with rice or other grains. (I'm looking at you, Sweet-and-Sour Eggplant with Garlic Chips, page 200.) If you're concerned about a vegetable dish not being filling, add nuts, cheese or a dollop of Greek yogurt for extra oomph.

"This is a nice variation on something I regularly ate in my childhood. So yummy and refreshing, especially in the hot Florida summers!"

—TamagoGohan

Easy Weeknight Dinners

Silken Tofu with Spicy Soy Dressing

time   5 minutes

yield   4 servings

This recipe is inspired by the many cold silken tofu dishes from East Asia, like Japanese hiyayakko and Chinese liangban tofu. It's a no-cook dish that's handy to have up your sleeve, especially for warm evenings when the desire to cook is nonexistent. Silky soft tofu is draped in a punchy soy dressing, creating a lively dish with little effort. The tofu is ideally served cold, but 10 minutes at room temperature can take the edge off. Make it your own with other fresh herbs, such as Thai basil, mint or shiso leaves, or add crunch with fried shallots or roasted peanuts. A salty, fermented element like kimchi, pickled radish or ja choi, also known as zha cai, a Sichuan pickled mustard root, would work well, too. One block of silken tofu is usually enough to feed two people, but for a more substantial meal, serve it with hot rice or noodles to create a pleasing contrast of temperatures.

—Hetty Lui McKinnon

For the spicy soy dressing

¼ cup soy sauce

1 tablespoon rice vinegar

1 tablespoon sesame oil

1 tablespoon chile oil

1 tablespoon toasted sesame seeds

2 teaspoons granulated sugar

1 scallion, green and white parts, thinly sliced

For the tofu

2 (14-ounce) blocks silken tofu (2 packages), cold

1 scallion, green and white parts, thinly sliced

Handful of fresh cilantro leaves

1. Make the dressing: Combine the soy sauce, vinegar, sesame oil, chile oil, sesame seeds, sugar and scallion in a small bowl. Whisk until the sugar dissolves.

2. Open a tofu package, carefully drain off the liquid and gently tip the block onto a kitchen towel. (Try to keep the block in one piece, if possible, but don't worry if it falls apart; it will still taste great.) Pat with another clean kitchen towel, removing as much liquid as possible. Repeat with the second package and a second towel. Transfer the blocks to one large plate or two smaller plates. Leave whole or cut into 1-inch cubes. Spoon the soy dressing over the top until the tofu is completely covered. Top with the scallion and cilantro and serve.

Cheesy, Spicy Black Bean Bake

time   15 minutes

yield   4 servings

Black beans shine in a deep-red mixture of fried garlic, caramelized tomato paste, smoked paprika and cumin. The whole skillet gets coated in a generous sprinkling of sharp Cheddar or Manchego cheese, then baked until melted. The result is what you hope for from a really good chili or stew, but in a lot less time. For a spicier rendition, add a pinch of cayenne with the paprika, or douse the final skillet with hot sauce. Serve with tortillas, tortilla chips, rice, a baked potato or fried eggs.

—Ali Slagle

3 tablespoons extra-virgin olive oil

5 garlic cloves, sliced

¼ cup tomato paste

1½ teaspoons smoked paprika

1 teaspoon ground cumin

¼ teaspoon red pepper flakes

2 (14-ounce) cans black beans, drained and rinsed

½ cup boiling water

Kosher salt and black pepper

1½ cups grated Cheddar or Manchego cheese (6 ounces)

1. Heat the oven to 475 degrees. In a 10-inch oven-safe skillet, heat the olive oil over medium-high heat. Fry the garlic until lightly golden, about 1 minute. Stir in the tomato paste, paprika, cumin and red pepper flakes (be careful of splattering), and fry for 30 seconds, lowering the heat as needed to prevent the garlic from burning.

2. Add the beans, water and generous pinches of salt and pepper and stir to combine. Sprinkle the cheese evenly over the top, then bake until the cheese has melted, 5 to 10 minutes. If the top is not as browned as you'd like, run the skillet under the broiler for 1 or 2 minutes. Serve immediately.

"I absolutely loved this. It's the perfect pantry dish—I ate it with tortilla chips, like a spoiled child."

—mrb

"Fantastic with last of the summer homegrown tomatoes! Added shredded chicken to make it more substantial."

—cgrant38

Tortizzas

time   15 minutes

yield   4 servings

Inspired by California Pizza Kitchen's now-discontinued Greek pizza, as well as the Manhattan bar Our/New York's also-discontinued tortilla pizzas (affectionately called "tortizzas" by the patrons who remember them), this quick lunch or light dinner builds on a sturdy base of crispy, cheesy flour tortillas. A fresh mix of cucumbers, tomatoes and avocado mounded atop the tortillas makes you feel like you're eating a salad with your hands. Feta delivers sharpness and creaminess, as does the simple garlicky yogurt sauce that drapes each tortizza. A drizzle of honey at the end might sound out of place here, but it really brings together all the flavors, and is a popular dipping sauce for pizza in South Korea.

—Eric Kim

3 to 4 Persian or mini seedless cucumbers, cut into ½-inch dice (about 2 cups)

2 ripe medium tomatoes, cut into ½-inch dice (about 2 cups)

1½ teaspoons kosher salt

8 (6-inch) soft flour tortillas

2 cups shredded low-moisture mozzarella

2 teaspoons dried oregano, za'atar or Italian seasoning

1 cup plain yogurt

1 large garlic clove, grated

1 tablespoon fresh lemon juice

2 teaspoons honey, plus more for drizzling

1 cup crumbled feta

1 ripe avocado, thinly sliced

½ packed cup fresh flat-leaf parsley leaves and tender stems

1. Position oven racks in the upper third and lower third of the oven and heat the oven to 400 degrees. Line two large sheet pans with parchment paper.

2. Combine the cucumbers, tomatoes and ½ teaspoon of the salt in a colander set in the sink and toss to mix. Let sit to drain the excess liquid, about 10 minutes.

3. Meanwhile, arrange the tortillas on the sheet pans, dividing them evenly between the pans, and sprinkle each tortilla evenly with the mozzarella and oregano. Bake until the cheese is melted and lightly browned and the edges of the tortillas are crispy but still pale, 8 to 10 minutes.

4. While the tortillas are baking, make the yogurt sauce: In a small bowl or measuring cup, whisk together the yogurt, garlic, lemon juice, honey and the remaining 1 teaspoon salt.

5. To serve, evenly divide the drained cucumbers and tomatoes among the tortillas. Top evenly with the feta, avocado and parsley and spoon the yogurt sauce over everything, leaving some back to serve on the side. As a final flourish, lightly drizzle the tortizzas with honey. You can eat the tortizzas flat like mini pizzas or folded like tacos.

Beans and Greens Alla Vodka

time 20 minutes

yield 4 servings

Pasta alla vodka is a classic because all of the ingredients work together beautifully: the heat of the red pepper flakes and vodka, the sweetness of the tomato and the richness of the cream. And that combination works equally well with beans and greens. Use chickpeas or white beans and kale or any other dark leafy green, like Swiss chard or broccoli rabe. The finished dish keeps for up to three days in the fridge. Eat it on its own, with crusty bread for dunking, or over pasta.

—Ali Slagle

3 tablespoons olive oil

1 yellow onion, chopped

4 garlic cloves, chopped

Kosher salt

1 (6-ounce) can tomato paste

¼ cup vodka

½ teaspoon red pepper flakes

2 (15-ounce) cans white beans (such as cannellini or Great Northern) or chickpeas, drained but not rinsed

1 bunch kale, ribs removed, leaves torn or coarsely chopped

¼ cup heavy cream

Grated Parmesan, as needed

1. In a large pot or Dutch oven, heat the olive oil over medium-high heat. Add the onion and garlic, season with salt and cook, stirring occasionally, until softened, 3 to 5 minutes. Add the tomato paste, vodka and red pepper flakes. Cook, stirring, until the tomato paste is a shade darker and starts to stick to the bottom of the pot, 2 to 3 minutes.

2. Add 2 cups water, the beans and the kale, season with salt and bring to a simmer. Lower the heat to maintain a simmer, cover, and cook until the liquid is flavorful and the kale is tender, 7 to 10 minutes.

3. Remove from the heat and stir in the heavy cream. Taste and if it needs more salt, stir in some grated Parmesan. Serve with more Parmesan on top.

"Great one to riff on, and I love a recipe that uses a whole can of tomato paste! Swapped the kale for spinach and used bone broth in place of water. The whole thing was super rich and very comforting."

—Lindsay A.

Soy-Braised Tofu with Bok Choy

time   20 minutes

yield   4 servings

This Chinese-style braised tofu is an ideal midweek dinner over rice or noodles. Shallow frying the tofu first makes it sturdier and prevents it from breaking apart in the sauce. (You could also deep-fry it or use an air fryer.) Cutting the tofu into thicker pieces means that each mouthful is crisp yet plump with a soft interior. This is an adaptable dish; when adding the bell peppers, you could add more vegetables, such as broccoli, cauliflower, carrots, snow peas or whatever you have on hand. Those familiar with restaurant-style braised tofu may expect more sauce, but in this homestyle version, the seasoning sauce delicately coats the tofu and vegetables without drowning them. That said, double the sauce if you prefer.

—Hetty Lui McKinnon

For the tofu

1 (14-ounce) package extra-firm tofu, drained and patted dry

Neutral oil, such as grapeseed or vegetable, for cooking

Kosher salt and black pepper

1 tablespoon doubanjiang (chile bean paste) or chile oil

2 garlic cloves, finely chopped

1 (1-inch) piece fresh ginger, peeled and finely chopped (1 tablespoon)

4 scallions, trimmed, white and green parts separated and cut into 1-inch pieces

1 bell pepper (any color), cut into 1-inch pieces

2 teaspoons Shaoxing wine (optional)

4 baby bok choy, trimmed and halved lengthwise

Hot cooked rice or noodles, for serving

For the seasoning sauce

2 tablespoons soy sauce

1 tablespoon vegetarian stir-fry sauce or oyster sauce

1 teaspoon cornstarch

½ teaspoon granulated sugar

1. Prepare the tofu: Cut the tofu crosswise into ¾-inch-thick slices, then cut each slice in half. You should have roughly 12 squares.

2. Heat a large, deep nonstick or well-seasoned cast-iron skillet over medium-high heat. When hot, add 1 tablespoon neutral oil and swirl to coat the bottom. Place the tofu in a single layer in the pan, season each piece with a little salt and black pepper, and fry until golden and crispy, 3 to 4 minutes. Flip and cook on the other side until golden and crispy, 3 to 4 minutes more, adding more oil if needed to prevent sticking. Transfer the tofu to a plate and set aside.

3. Make the seasoning sauce: In a small bowl, whisk together the soy sauce, stir-fry sauce, cornstarch, sugar and ⅓ cup water until smooth.

"Baked the tofu, doubled the sauce, added shiitake mushrooms. Delicious! Great weeknight meatless meal!"

—Elizabeth Ball

4. Return the skillet to medium heat. Add the doubanjiang and about 1 teaspoon vegetable oil, or add the chile oil without additional oil, and stir for 15 seconds. Add the garlic, ginger and white scallion parts and toss until the scallions are softened and everything is fragrant, 1 to 2 minutes. If the pan starts to look dry, add a drop of vegetable oil.

5. Add the bell pepper and wine (if using) and stir-fry until slightly softened, 2 to 3 minutes. Pour in the seasoning sauce and let it sizzle for 30 seconds, stirring once or twice.

6. Add the bok choy, tofu and green scallion parts and toss gently to coat the tofu. Reduce the heat to low and simmer the mixture simmer until the sauce thickens, the baby bok choy is wilted but still green and crisp-tender and the tofu has absorbed some of the sauce, 1 to 2 minutes. Serve immediately with rice or noodles.

Vegetables, Beans and Tofu

Sweet-and-Sour Eggplant with Garlic Chips

time   20 minutes

yield   2 to 4 servings

This vibrant eggplant dish relies heavily on simple pantry staples but gets its complex flavor from the clever use of garlic. First, you make garlic chips, then you fry eggplant in the remaining garlic-infused oil. Since garlic chips can burn easily, the key here is to combine the garlic and oil in an unheated pan for even cooking. As the oil heats up, the garlic will sizzle rapidly as the moisture cooks off. When it slows down, the garlic slices should be crisp. Be sure to remove the chips just as they begin to turn golden, as they will continue to cook after they are out of the oil. The rest is easy: Cook the eggplant, create a quick soy sauce glaze, sprinkle with herbs and garlic chips and serve.

—Sue Li

4 garlic cloves, very thinly sliced

¼ cup sunflower or other neutral oil

Kosher salt

3 medium Japanese eggplants (about 1 pound total), quartered lengthwise, then cut crosswise into 2-inch pieces

3 tablespoons low-sodium soy sauce

2 tablespoons light brown sugar

1 tablespoon rice vinegar

½ to 1 teaspoon red pepper flakes

½ cup fresh cilantro leaves, roughly chopped

¼ cup fresh basil leaves, roughly chopped

1. Set a small sieve over a small heatproof bowl. Line a small plate with a paper towel. Combine the garlic and oil in a medium skillet and heat over medium-low heat. Cook the garlic until light golden brown and crisp and the bubbles have subsided, 3 to 4 minutes, then quickly drain the garlic chips into the sieve. Transfer the garlic chips to the paper towel–lined plate, season with salt and set aside. Return the garlic oil to the skillet.

2. Heat the garlic oil over medium-high heat. Add the eggplant pieces in batches, adding more as they shrink in size and space permits, and cook, stirring occasionally, until the cut sides of the eggplant are golden brown and the skins are slightly wrinkled, 6 to 8 minutes.

3. Add the soy sauce, sugar, vinegar and red pepper flakes and reduce the heat to medium-low. Simmer, tossing the eggplant to coat, until the sauce thickens, 1 to 2 minutes. Serve topped with the cilantro, basil and garlic chips.

"I am addicted to this dish. As always, ignore the recommended garlic quantity and measure the slices out with your biting, burning, garlic-soaked, vampire-protected soul."

—ejb

Kaddu (Sweet-and-Sour Butternut Squash)

time   about 25 minutes

yield   4 servings

This cozy vegetable main is an ode to earthy, maple-y fenugreek, a staple spice of Indian cooking that is a perfect match for the mild sweetness of butternut squash. Normally roasted, butternut squash is gently stewed here with ginger, onion, turmeric, tomatoes and brown sugar, bringing out a unique and addictive sweet-and-sour flavor. Kaddu is traditionally paired with puri, a type of fried bread, but roti, tortillas or even toast works well with this bright and hearty one-pot dish.

—Priya Krishna

2 tablespoons olive oil

1 teaspoon fenugreek seeds

½ teaspoon ground turmeric

1 small yellow onion, finely diced

2 tablespoons peeled, minced fresh ginger

½ teaspoon red chile powder, such as cayenne

¼ teaspoon asafetida (optional)

1 medium butternut squash (about 2 pounds), peeled, seeded and cut into ½-inch cubes

1 teaspoon kosher salt, plus more as needed

4 medium plum tomatoes, cut into ½-inch cubes

2 tablespoons fresh lime juice (from about 1 lime), plus more as needed

2 tablespoons light brown sugar

2 tablespoons chopped fresh cilantro (stems and leaves), for garnish

1. In a large, deep sauté pan, warm the oil over medium heat. Once the oil begins to shimmer, add the fenugreek seeds and cook until they start to sputter, which should be within seconds. Reduce the heat to medium-low and swirl in the turmeric. Add the onion and cook, stirring often, just until it starts to soften, 3 to 4 minutes. Add the ginger, chile powder and asafetida (if using) and cook, stirring, for 1 minute. Add the squash and salt, stir well, cover and cook until the squash is tender, 10 to 15 minutes.

2. Stir in the tomatoes, lime juice and brown sugar, reduce the heat to low, re-cover and cook until the tomatoes are soft but still retain their shape, about 5 minutes. Remove from the heat. Taste and adjust the seasoning with lime juice and salt as needed. Top with the cilantro and serve warm.

Green Curry–Glazed Tofu

time   25 minutes

yield   2 servings

To make crispy, flavorful tofu without having to press it first, use this smart method from Andrea Nguyen, the author of *Asian Tofu* and other cookbooks: Warm the tofu in a pan with a small amount of flavorful sauce. As it cooks, it will dry out and absorb the flavors of the sauce. Next, you add oil to the pan, which crisps the tofu. In Ms. Nguyen's recipe, soy sauce is used, but here, the aromatics in Thai green curry paste and the sugars in coconut milk toast and caramelize on the tofu. Once the tofu has a deep-brown crust, remove it, sear a quick-cooking vegetable in the same pan and then reduce the remaining curry-coconut mixture to a fragrant, sweet-and-spicy glaze.

—Ali Slagle

1 (14- to 16-ounce) package extra-firm tofu, drained

Kosher salt

1 (14-ounce) can unsweetened full-fat coconut milk

3 to 4 tablespoons Thai green curry paste

1 tablespoon neutral or coconut oil, plus more as needed

2 cups chopped vegetables, such as snap or snow peas, asparagus, broccoli, kale, fennel or corn kernels, or a combination (see Tip)

2 tablespoons fresh lime juice (from about 1 lime)

Hot cooked rice or other grain, for serving

1. Cut the tofu in half lengthwise, then slice crosswise into 6 sections. (You'll have a total of 12 squares.) Transfer to a paper towel–lined plate and pat dry, then sprinkle with salt.

2. Transfer the coconut milk to a liquid measuring cup or medium bowl, add the curry paste, stir with a fork until smooth and then season to taste with salt. (Be aware that some curry pastes are quite salty.)

3. Arrange the tofu in a single layer in a large nonstick or well-seasoned cast-iron skillet. Pour 2 tablespoons of the coconut-curry mixture over the tofu and flip the tofu to coat. Set the skillet over medium-high heat and cook the tofu without flipping until the skillet is dry and the underside of the tofu pieces is speckled golden, 3 to 5 minutes.

4. Add the oil, swirl to coat the bottom of the pan and then flip the tofu. Cook until browned and crisp on the underside, 3 to 5 minutes, then flip once more until the remaining side is browned and crisp, 1 to 2 minutes, adding additional oil as needed to prevent sticking. Transfer to a plate.

Tip

This recipe accommodates any vegetable that will cook in 6 to 8 minutes. If you'd like to use a vegetable that takes longer, like sliced carrots or winter squash, sear it for a few additional minutes, tossing occasionally, before pouring in the coconut-curry mixture.

"This was a huge hit, including with my son, who hates tofu. The texture of the tofu was perfect—crisp on the outside, tender on the inside—and the sauce was delicious, restaurant quality."

—Kathleen

5. If the skillet is dry, add more oil over medium-high heat, then add the vegetables, season with salt and cook, without stirring, until charred on the underside, 2 to 3 minutes. Pour in the remaining coconut-curry mixture, bring to a boil and boil, stirring occasionally, until the vegetables are crisp-tender and the liquid has thickened to a glaze, 4 to 5 minutes. (The sauce is ready when a spoon dragged across the bottom of the skillet leaves a trail.) Turn off the heat, stir in the lime juice and then add the tofu and stir gently to coat. Season to taste with salt. Eat on top of rice.

"I made this as a vegetarian dish for a family gathering. A delicious change from the ubiquitous eggplant parm. I added thinly sliced firm tofu underneath the cheeses and breadcrumbs to increase protein."

—Christine

Sheet-Pan Mushroom Parmigiana

time   30 minutes

yield   4 servings

This smart weeknight dinner offers all the comforting flavors of a classic Parmigiana, but with minimal work. Earthy portobello mushrooms are used here, offering a perfect cradle for the red sauce and creamy mozzarella. Use good-quality store-bought marinara sauce (vodka, arrabbiata or amatriciana), a much-underrated pantry item that can turn around a meal quickly. This flexible recipe can be scaled up or down without too much fuss. It accounts for two portobello mushrooms per person, but if you're serving them with pasta or a salad, you could reduce to one each. The basil-scented bread crumbs finish the mushrooms with a lovely, herbaceous crunch. Extra bread crumbs keep well in an airtight container and are wonderful for topping pasta, salads, soups and roasted vegetables.

—Hetty Lui McKinnon

10 ounces cherry or grape tomatoes, halved (1 pint)

2 garlic cloves, finely chopped

Extra-virgin olive oil

Kosher salt and black pepper

8 portobello mushrooms, stems removed

3 cups store-bought or homemade marinara sauce

3 cups shredded low-moisture mozzarella (12 ounces)

1 cup panko bread crumbs

½ cup basil leaves, finely chopped, plus more leaves for topping

1. Heat the oven to 425 degrees. Arrange the cherry tomatoes on a sheet pan, along with half the garlic and drizzle with 1 to 2 tablespoons of olive oil. Season with ½ teaspoon salt and ½ teaspoon pepper and toss to coat the tomatoes.

2. Add the mushroom caps in between the tomatoes, gill side up, and drizzle each generously with olive oil. (Don't skimp here, as the olive oil will add lots of rich flavor.) Scatter the mushrooms with the remaining garlic and season each mushroom with salt and pepper. Fill each mushroom with marinara sauce and top with cheese. Roast until the cheese is melted, bubbly and golden, 25 to 20 minutes.

3. Meanwhile, heat a medium skillet over medium-high heat. Add 1 tablespoon olive oil and add the bread crumbs, basil and ½ teaspoon salt. Stir constantly for 2 to 3 minutes, until golden. Remove from the heat and immediately transfer to a bowl or jar.

4. To serve, transfer the mushrooms to serving plates, along with a few of the roasted cherry tomatoes. Top each mushroom with the basil bread crumbs and scatter with a few basil leaves.

Crispy Tofu with Cashews and Blistered Snap Peas

time   30 minutes

yield   4 servings

A ginger and coconut milk reduction can coat pretty much anything that browns nicely on its own. Here, it's pieces of pan-seared tofu, but small morsels of chicken and pork will work just as well. The soy and the teaspoons of molasses give the sauce a little caramelization and a little shine and gloss. For a fresh side, toss blistered snap peas with sliced scallions, a little mint and a splash of rice vinegar. Snow peas, green beans, broccoli or asparagus? If it's fresh and green, it'll work just fine.

—Yewande Komolafe

1 (14-ounce) package firm or extra-firm tofu, drained

3 tablespoons neutral oil, such as grapeseed, vegetable or canola, plus more as needed

Kosher salt and black pepper

12 ounces snap peas, trimmed

1 (2-inch) piece fresh ginger, peeled and grated (about 2 tablespoons)

2 garlic cloves, grated

1 (13-ounce) can unsweetened coconut milk (light or full-fat)

1 tablespoon soy sauce

2 teaspoons molasses, dark brown sugar or honey

½ cup toasted cashews

1 tablespoon rice vinegar

4 scallions, trimmed and thinly sliced

¼ cup fresh mint leaves, torn if large

½ to 1 teaspoon red pepper flakes (optional)

Hot rice or other steamed grain, for serving

1. Slice the tofu in half horizontally. Transfer to a paper towel–lined plate to dry any excess liquid.

2. In a medium skillet or cast-iron pan, heat 1 tablespoon of the oil over medium-high heat until it shimmers. Season both sides of the tofu pieces with salt and pepper, place in the pan and sear without moving until the underside is golden brown, about 4 minutes. Flip the pieces and sear on the second side until golden brown, about 4 minutes more. Transfer the tofu to a plate.

3. Add 1 tablespoon of the oil to the pan over medium-high heat. Add the snap peas and cook, stirring occasionally, until blistered and just tender, about 3 minutes. Season with salt and move to a medium bowl.

4. Heat the remaining 1 tablespoon oil in the pan, add the ginger and garlic and cook, stirring, until fragrant, about 30 seconds. Pour in the coconut milk, soy sauce and molasses and simmer, stirring frequently, until the sauce is reduced

"This is how I got my kid to eat tofu. The sauce is simple and yummy, but it's the plentiful seasoning and crisp texture of the tofu that's the difference."

—JDubs

and its color deepens to a dark brown, 6 to 8 minutes. It should coat a spoon without running right off. Stir in the cashews, break the tofu into 1-inch pieces and toss in the pan to coat with the sauce. Remove from the heat and taste and adjust the seasoning if necessary.

5. Add the vinegar, scallions, mint and red pepper flakes (if using) to the snap peas and toss to mix well. Divide among plates along with the tofu and cashews. Serve with rice or any steamed grain.

Vegetables, Beans and Tofu

"Excellent dish! Perfect for a rainy evening with a nice crusty bread. Flavorful and complex. Agree with others that the lemon is key, and lemon rind is a nice addition."

—Yvette

Braised White Beans and Greens with Parmesan

time   30 minutes

yield   4 servings

Inspired by the Italian dish of sautéed puntarelle (an Italian variety of chicory) and white beans, this recipe makes a satisfying vegetarian main course or a hearty side dish for roast chicken or sausages. It opts for canned white beans, for the sake of weeknight convenience, and Swiss chard, which is much milder than puntarelle and easier to find in the United States. Kale or escarole would also work well, if that's what you've got. Serve in shallow bowls with toasted country bread to mop up the garlicky broth.

—Lidey Heuck

¼ cup olive oil

1 small fennel bulb, trimmed, cored and finely diced

1 small yellow onion, finely diced

2 teaspoons minced fresh rosemary or thyme leaves

5 garlic cloves, minced

¼ teaspoon red pepper flakes, plus more for serving

1 large or 2 small bunches Swiss chard, escarole or kale, stems removed (10 to 12 ounces)

2 (15-ounce) cans cannellini beans, drained and rinsed

2 cups low-sodium vegetable or chicken stock

Kosher salt and black pepper

1 tablespoon fresh lemon juice

½ cup shredded mozzarella (optional)

3 tablespoons grated Pecorino Romano or Parmesan, plus more for serving

Toasted country bread, for serving

1. In a large, deep skillet or a Dutch oven, heat the oil over medium heat. Add the fennel, onion and rosemary and cook, stirring occasionally, until tender, 4 to 6 minutes. Add the garlic and red pepper flakes and cook until fragrant, about 1 minute.

2. Begin adding handfuls of the greens, cooking and stirring until the leaves wilt.

3. Add the beans, stock and ¼ teaspoon black pepper and stir to combine. Bring to a boil, then turn down the heat to low and simmer, mashing some of the beans with a wooden spoon, until the liquid has reduced and thickened, 6 to 8 minutes.

4. Remove from the heat, stir in the lemon juice and then the mozzarella (if using) and Pecorino Romano. Taste and season with salt and pepper. Divide among shallow bowls and top with more Pecorino Romano. Serve with toasted bread and a small dish of red pepper flakes on the side.

Vegetable Pajeon
(Korean Scallion Pancakes with Vegetables)

time   30 minutes

yield   3 to 4 servings

Crisp at the edges, soft at the center and filled with scallions and other vegetables, these irresistible, comforting pancakes adapted from chef Sohui Kim make for a quick dinner that you can throw together on any given weeknight. The recipe is extremely forgiving, so feel free to use whatever vegetables you have on hand. Ms. Kim recommends finely shredded raw vegetables, or even leftover cooked vegetables. And if you don't have the bandwidth to make a dipping sauce, a drizzle of soy sauce and a squirt of Sriracha add verve without any work. Serve pajeon by itself or topped with a fried egg or two if you want to add protein.

—Melissa Clark

For the pancakes

½ cup all-purpose flour

½ cup potato starch, or ¼ cup each white rice flour and cornstarch

¾ teaspoon fine sea salt, plus more as needed

½ teaspoon baking powder

¾ cup ice water

1 large egg

¼ cup finely chopped kimchi

4 cups finely chopped or grated mixed vegetables, such as carrot, zucchini, bell pepper, kale or whatever you've got

4 scallions, trimmed, cut into 2-inch-long sections and thinly sliced lengthwise

2 tablespoons grapeseed or peanut oil, plus more as needed

For the dipping sauce

3 tablespoons soy sauce

2 teaspoons rice vinegar, plus more to taste

1 teaspoon peeled, grated fresh ginger or garlic (optional)

½ teaspoon sesame oil, plus more to taste

Pinch of granulated sugar

1. Prepare the pancakes: In a large bowl, whisk together the flour, potato starch, salt and baking powder.

2. In a medium bowl, whisk together the water, egg and kimchi until blended. Whisk the kimchi mixture into the flour mixture until smooth. Stir in the vegetables and about three-fourths of the scallions. Reserve the remaining scallions for serving.

3. In a large nonstick skillet, heat the grapeseed oil over medium heat. Scoop ¼-cup portions of the batter into the skillet, adding only as many as will fit

"I made these with my 3-year-old (I prepped the veggies and did the frying on my own, he did everything else). He loved helping and he LOVED eating these."

—Jane

without touching. Flatten each portion and fry until dark golden on the underside, 2 to 3 minutes. Flip and continue to fry until the other side is dark golden, 2 to 3 minutes longer. Transfer to a paper towel–lined plate, sprinkle with a little salt. Repeat with the remaining batter.

4. While the pancakes cook, make the dipping sauce: In a small bowl, stir together the soy sauce, vinegar, ginger (if using), sesame oil and sugar.

5. Sprinkle the reserved scallions over the pancakes and serve immediately with the dipping sauce on the side.

"Flavorful comfort food and a quick and easy lunch! A good shake-up from the usual Tex-Mex black bean flavorings. Used unsweetened coconut flakes toasted in a pan instead of the plantain chips."

—Hannah

Easy Weeknight Dinners

Coconut-Ginger Black Beans

time 30 minutes

yield 4 servings

The velvety combination of beans and coconut milk is found in a number of African and Caribbean dishes, like Nigerian frejon and Haitian sos pwa nwa. In this recipe, black beans are simmered in coconut milk with a healthy dose of fresh ginger, then finished with lime juice. The result is a light vegan main or side dish. Finish with crushed plantain chips seasoned with lime zest for sweetness and crunch, or top with coconut flakes or tortilla chips, which are also excellent.

—Ali Slagle

2 (15-ounce) cans black beans

2 tablespoons coconut oil or extra-virgin olive oil

1½ teaspoons ground cumin or coriander

1 (3-inch piece) fresh ginger, peeled and finely grated (about 3 tablespoons)

1 (13-ounce) can unsweetened full-fat coconut milk

Kosher salt and black pepper

½ cup plantain chips or toasted coconut flakes

1 teaspoon grated lime zest

About 2 tablespoons fresh lime juice

Hot sauce, for serving (optional)

1. Open, drain, and rinse 1 can of black beans and set aside. Open the second can and reserve. In a large saucepan, heat the coconut oil over medium heat. Add the cumin and half of the ginger and cook, stirring constantly, until fragrant, 1 to 2 minutes. Add the rinsed black beans, the second can of black beans with their liquid and the coconut milk and season generously with salt and pepper.

2. Increase the heat to medium-high and bring the beans to a boil. Then reduce the heat to a simmer and cook, stirring occasionally, until the beans are soft and the mixture is flavorful, 15 to 20 minutes. (If you want a thicker consistency, smash some of beans with the back of a spoon as the mixture cooks and simmer longer.)

3. Meanwhile, in a small bowl, crumble the plantain chips into bite-size pieces. (If using coconut flakes, leave as they are.) Add the lime zest and a few generous grinds of pepper and stir to combine.

4. Remove the beans from the heat. Stir in the remaining ginger and season with salt and pepper. Stir in the lime juice a little at a time until the beans taste bright but the coconut flavor is still rich. Top with the seasoned plantain chips and serve with hot sauce (if using) for more kick.

Cauliflower Adobo

time 45 minutes

yield 4 servings

Chicken adobo, the beloved Filipino dish, is made by braising chicken in a salty, sour and sweet mixture of mostly soy sauce and vinegar. In this vegetarian version, cauliflower, rather than chicken, is caramelized on one side, then simmered in the pungent but not prickly sauce until it's tender. The simmer mellows the vinegar and soy sauce into a sauce interlaced with pepper, garlic and something herbal but not immediately traceable—that's the bay leaves. Serve the cauliflower and sauce over rice or another grain with something green on the side.

—Ali Slagle

1 large cauliflower (2½ to 3 pounds)

Kosher salt

2 teaspoons black pepper, plus more as needed

3 tablespoons canola oil, plus more as needed

½ cup rice vinegar

5 tablespoons soy sauce

2 teaspoons raw or light brown sugar

6 garlic cloves, smashed and peeled

3 bay leaves

1 Thai chile, halved lengthwise, or ¼ teaspoon red pepper flakes

3 scallions, thinly sliced, for serving (optional)

Rice

If you plan to eat rice with the adobo, bring 1¾ cups water to a boil in a medium saucepan before you start the recipe. Stir in 1 teaspoon salt and 1 cup long-grain rice, cover, and let simmer on the lowest heat possible for 18 minutes. Proceed with the adobo. Let the rice sit, covered and off the heat, until the adobo is ready. Fluff rice with a fork before serving.

1. Trim the leaves and woody stalk from the cauliflower, then cut through the root into 8 wedges. Season both sides of each wedge with salt and pepper. Reserve any loose cauliflower pieces.

2. In a large skillet or Dutch oven, heat the oil over medium-high heat. Place one layer of the wedges in the skillet cut side down and cook without moving them until well browned on one side, 3 to 4 minutes. Transfer to a plate and continue until all the cauliflower is seared, adding more oil as needed. Return all the cauliflower to the pan with uncooked side facing down.

3. Add ¼ cup water, any loose cauliflower pieces, 2 teaspoons black pepper, rice vinegar, soy sauce, sugar, garlic, bay leaves and Thai chile. Cover and let simmer over medium heat until the cauliflower is crisp-tender, about 5 minutes.

4. Uncover, turn the heat to medium-high and cook, basting the cauliflower occasionally with the sauce, until the cauliflower is tender and the sauce has thickened and reduced to about ¾ cup, 8 to 10 minutes.

5. Serve the cauliflower with plenty of sauce and a sprinkle of scallions (if using).

"I make this often and I love it. I like adding a package of firm tofu, cut into squares and browned on both sides, then added in with the liquid."

—Sean C.

Mushroom and Eggplant Yassa

time   45 minutes

yield   4 servings

Sauce yassa is a richly flavored Senegalese stew typically made with poultry, meat or fish. It's the result of slowly caramelized onions, chile, garlic and ginger simmered in stock and finished with a splash of lime juice. This vegetable version, a vegan adaptation, uses mushrooms and eggplants, which both add layers of depth to the sauce. A shower of thinly sliced fresh scallions announces itself with its delicate yet crisp bite. Serve a generous helping of the sauce over steamed rice, millet or fonio.

—Yewande Komolafe

6 tablespoons neutral oil, such as grapeseed or canola, plus more as needed

1 pound cremini or button mushrooms, sliced

Kosher salt and black pepper

8 thyme sprigs

2 large yellow onions (about 1½ pounds), thinly sliced

1 Scotch bonnet chile

4 garlic cloves, thinly sliced

1 (2-inch) piece fresh ginger, scrubbed (unpeeled) and grated (2 tablespoons)

2 fresh or dried bay leaves

1 medium eggplant (about 1¼ pounds), cut into 1-inch cubes

2 cups vegetable stock

2 limes

1 tablespoon Dijon mustard

2 scallions, thinly sliced

Hot steamed rice, millet or fonio, for serving

1. Heat 1 tablespoon of the oil in a large skillet over medium-high heat. Add half of the mushrooms in an even layer to the hot oil. Season with salt and pepper and add half of the thyme sprigs. Sear, stirring, until lightly browned on both sides, about 4 minutes. Transfer the mushrooms to a plate and repeat with 1 tablespoon of the oil and all the remaining mushrooms and thyme sprigs.

2. Return the skillet to medium-high heat and add 2 tablespoons of the oil. Add the onions, season with salt and pepper and cook, stirring occasionally, until softened and browned along the edges, about 5 minutes. Reduce the heat to medium and continue to cook, stirring frequently, until caramelized, about 12 minutes.

3. Add the remaining 2 tablespoons oil to the skillet over medium-high heat. Poke holes in the Scotch bonnet with the tip of a sharp knife and drop it into the oil. Add the garlic, ginger and bay leaves and stir and cook until the chile starts to soften, about 1 minute. Add the eggplant, season lightly with salt and stir to coat with the onion mixture. Return the mushrooms to the pan along with any liquid that has collected on the plate. Add the stock and simmer, stirring frequently, until the liquid is saucy, about 8 minutes.

"This recipe has incredible depth of flavor. I cooked it longer—until almost all liquid was evaporated. The next day, I put the leftovers on toast for breakfast. YUM!"

—dlt

4. Juice 1 lime and cut the second lime into wedges. Add the lime juice and mustard to the sauce and cook, stirring, until the sauce thickens, about 4 minutes. Stir in the scallions and cook for an additional minute. Taste and adjust with more salt or lime juice if needed. Spoon the warm yassa over rice and serve with the lime wedges for squeezing.

Sabich Bowls

time   45 minutes

yield   4 servings

The Israeli sandwich known as sabich features fried eggplant that's tucked into pitas and topped with sliced hard-boiled eggs, chopped tomato-cucumber salad, pickles, tahini sauce and sometimes shredded cabbage. This weeknight recipe turns the popular sandwich into a one-bowl meal that is prepared on a sheet pan. Eggplant and chickpeas are roasted side by side; the eggplant becomes tender and creamy, while the chickpeas turn golden and crispy. Canned chickpeas do double duty: Some are a part of the roast, while the remaining beans transform into a luscious, garlicky tahini sauce. The eggplant mixture is served on top of rice here but all sorts of grains would work, including bulgur, farro and quinoa.

—Kay Chun

1½ pounds Italian eggplant (1 large), cut into 1-inch cubes (8 cups)

Kosher salt and black pepper

8 tablespoons extra-virgin olive oil

1 (15-ounce) can chickpeas, drained and rinsed

¼ cup tahini

3 tablespoons fresh lemon juice

1 teaspoon minced garlic

1 teaspoon low-sodium soy sauce

8 ounces grape or cherry tomatoes, chopped (1 heaping cup)

1 Persian cucumber, cut into ¼-inch cubes (½ cup)

2 tablespoons coarsely chopped fresh parsley, plus more for garnish

4 cups hot cooked rice or grains, for serving

Shredded cabbage, pickles (preferably Israeli), hot sauce and hard-boiled or fried eggs, for topping (optional)

1. Heat the oven to 425 degrees. On a large sheet pan, season the eggplant with salt and pepper, drizzle with 3 tablespoons of the oil and toss to coat evenly. Push the eggplant to one side. In the empty space, combine 1 cup of the chickpeas and 1 tablespoon of the oil and season with salt and pepper. Toss to coat evenly, then mix with the eggplant and spread the mixture in an even layer. Roast, stirring halfway, until the eggplant is tender and the chickpeas are golden and crispy, about 30 minutes.

2. Meanwhile, in a food processor, combine the remaining chickpeas with the tahini, 2 tablespoons of the lemon juice, the garlic, soy sauce and ¼ cup water and pulse to combine. With the machine running, drizzle in the remaining 4 tablespoons oil and purée until smooth. Season with salt and pepper.

"A real crowd pleaser and easy to prep ahead for a group. Roasted cauliflower, with a little smoked paprika, and flash-sautéed kale are my favorite additions."

—Jenn

3. In a small bowl, combine the tomatoes, cucumber, parsley and the remaining 1 tablespoon lemon juice. Season with salt and pepper and mix well.

4. Divide the rice among bowls. Top with separate piles of the eggplant mixture, tomato salad and other toppings of choice. Drizzle generously with some of the tahini sauce. Top with parsley and serve warm.

Red Curry Lentils with Sweet Potatoes and Spinach

time   1 hour

yield   4 to 6 servings

In this vegetarian main inspired by Indian dal, lentils are cooked with an aromatic blend of Thai spices—fresh ginger, turmeric, red curry paste and chile—then simmered in coconut milk until fall-apart tender. Browning the sweet potatoes before cooking them with the lentils brings out their sweetness, tempering the heat from the chile and curry paste, while baby spinach tossed in just before serving adds fresh flavor. Serve over steamed white or brown rice or with toasted flatbread on the side.

—Lidey Heuck

3 tablespoons olive oil

1 pound sweet potatoes (about 2 medium), peeled and cut into ¾-inch cubes

1 medium yellow onion, chopped

3 tablespoons Thai red curry paste

3 garlic cloves, minced (about 1 tablespoon)

1 (1-inch) piece fresh ginger, peeled and grated (1 tablespoon)

1 fresh red chile, such as Fresno or serrano, seeds and ribs removed, then minced

1 teaspoon ground turmeric

1 cup red lentils, rinsed

4 cups low-sodium vegetable stock

Kosher salt

1 (13-ounce) can unsweetened full-fat coconut milk

1 (4- to 5-ounce) bag baby spinach (4 to 5 packed cups)

½ lime, juiced

Fresh cilantro leaves, for serving

Toasted unsweetened coconut flakes, for serving (optional)

1. In a Dutch oven or other heavy pot, heat 2 tablespoons of the oil over medium-high heat. Add the sweet potatoes and cook, stirring occasionally, until browned all over, 5 to 7 minutes. Transfer to a plate and set aside.

2. Add the remaining 1 tablespoon oil to the pot and reduce the heat to medium-low. Add the onion and cook, stirring occasionally, until translucent, 4 to 6 minutes. Add the curry paste, garlic, ginger, chile and turmeric and cook until fragrant, about 1 minute.

3. Add the lentils, stock, 2 teaspoons salt and the browned sweet potatoes to the pot, increase the heat to high and bring to a boil. Lower the heat to a simmer and simmer uncovered, stirring occasionally, until the lentils are just tender, 20 to 25 minutes.

4. Add the coconut milk and continue to simmer, stirring occasionally, until the liquid has reduced and the lentils are creamy and falling apart, 15 to 20 minutes.

5. Add the spinach and stir just until wilted, 2 to 3 minutes. Remove from the heat, stir in the lime juice and season to taste with salt.

6. Divide among shallow bowls, top with cilantro and coconut flakes (if using) and serve.

Chilaquiles, page 248

Eggs and Cheese

Eggs and Cheese

Is there any food as exuberant as a burst egg
yolk, or as enticing as oozing cheese? I think most
omnivores lean too much on meat when they're
putting together meals, and so I'm here to remind
you that eggs and cheese can be just as satisfying.

Egg dishes exist in countless cuisines, whether
they turn up in cameos (accessorizing a bowl of
noodles) or serve as the star (whisked and folded
into a classic omelet). Topping a dish with an egg
instantly improves it. Handsomely salted eggs are
one of my favorite foods, whether they are poached,
scrambled, soft-boiled or fried. A carton of them
lasts weeks in your fridge and goes brilliantly with
just about everything. They are so good, so fast,
so versatile! I love them for it.

Eggs go particularly well with hot peppers and chile sauces of all kinds; their richness is a good counterpoint to blazing chile heat. Look at chilaquiles, on page 248, which uses fried eggs to top tortilla chips soaked in red chile sauce. (The most transcendent chilaquiles are made with tortillas that are cut up and freshly fried, but it's still delicious if you use store-bought tortilla chips.) In the Sheet-Pan Bibimbap on page 244, a clever spin on the classic Korean dish, an egg crowns a bowl of rice, roasted vegetables and spicy gochujang.

Greek feta cheese has been a weeknight revelation to me in the past few years, as I started using it more as a way to add bright, briny flavor and heft to vegetarian meals. It's especially good roasted in the oven, as it is in the technicolor Sheet-Pan Baked Feta with Broccolini, Tomatoes and Lemon on page 241. I love paneer, the fresh Indian cheese, and it turns up here in a shortcut version of Mattar Paneer (page 238) that tastes as if luxuriated at a simmer for hours, rather than coming together in mere minutes. Finally, it took having children for me to rediscover the rapture of a golden, crispy-edge quesadilla (page 233)—another dish that would only be made better if it were topped with a fried egg.

Eggs Kejriwal

time   10 minutes

yield   2 servings

This spicy egg and cheese on toast has its roots in the social club circuit of Mumbai, though chefs in London, New York and California have riffed on it, too. The dish is quick and simple, ideal for breakfast, a hearty snack between meals or a lightning-speed dinner, and it can be customized with a variety of cheeses and toppings. To make this updated version, toast good bread and smear it with mustard, then pile on some grated cheese mixed up with chopped green chiles, red onion and cilantro leaves. Once the cheese is bubbling under the broiler, pull it out and slide on a fried egg.

—Tejal Rao

1 tablespoon butter, softened

2 thick Pullman bread slices

2 teaspoons mustard

4 ounces Cheddar cheese, grated (1 cup)

1 serrano chile, thinly sliced

2 tablespoons fresh cilantro leaves, chopped

1 tablespoon minced red onion

2 eggs

Kosher salt and black pepper

Ketchup, for serving (optional)

1. Butter the bread slices on both sides and lightly brown in a frying pan (use the pan you like most for frying eggs). Smear one side of the toasts with mustard, and transfer to a sheet pan, mustard-side up. Heat the broiler with a rack about 6 inches from the heat source.

2. In a small bowl, mix together the cheese, chile, cilantro and onion. Divide the mixture evenly between the toasts. Place under the broiler just until the cheese is melted.

3. While the cheese is melting, place the same pan you used to make the toast. Crack the eggs into the pan and fry until the edges of the whites are crisp but the yolks are still soft. Gently loosen the eggs from the pan and slide one on top of each toast. Season with salt and pepper and serve with ketchup on the side, if you like.

Gyeran Bap (Egg Rice)

time 10 minutes

yield 1 serving

Gyeran bap is a lifesaving Korean pantry meal of fried eggs stirred into steamed white rice. In this version, the eggs fry and puff up slightly in a shallow bath of browned butter. Soy sauce, which reduces in the pan, seasons the rice, as does a final smattering of salty gim or nori (roasted seaweed). A dribble of sesame oil lends comforting nuttiness, and runny yolks act as a makeshift sauce for the rice, slicking each grain with eggy gold. (You can cook the eggs to your preferred doneness, of course.) This dinner-for-one can be scaled up to serve more: Just double, triple or quadruple all the ingredient amounts, using a larger skillet or repeating the steps in a small one.

—Eric Kim

½ tablespoon unsalted butter

2 large eggs

1 teaspoon soy sauce

1 teaspoon toasted sesame oil

1 cup hot steamed white rice, preferably short or medium grain

1 (5-gram) packet roasted, salted seaweed, such as gim (optional)

1. Melt the butter in a small nonstick skillet over medium heat. Continue cooking, stirring occasionally with a heat-resistant rubber spatula, until the melted butter starts to darken from yellow to light brown, 1 to 1½ minutes.

2. Crack in the eggs and drizzle the soy sauce and sesame oil on top. Cook until the whites puff up slightly around the edges of the pan and the translucent parts around the yolks start to turn opaque, 2 to 2½ minutes. Watch that the soy sauce doesn't burn, removing the pan from the heat if necessary.

3. Scoop the rice into a medium bowl and top with the fried eggs, including all the buttery soy sauce drippings from the pan. If using the seaweed, crush it directly over the eggs, piling it high. This will seem like a lot of seaweed, but it will wilt as you mix everything together with a spoon, which you should do to disperse the ingredients before eating.

"I make this for my kid often. It's his favorite snack/meal and mine, too, because it's simple, healthy, and no fuss. As a fellow Korean brother, my approach is almost as described with a couple of additional garnishes that are stock in any Korean kitchen/cupboard: a sprinkle of sesame seeds and green onions."

—Wilson

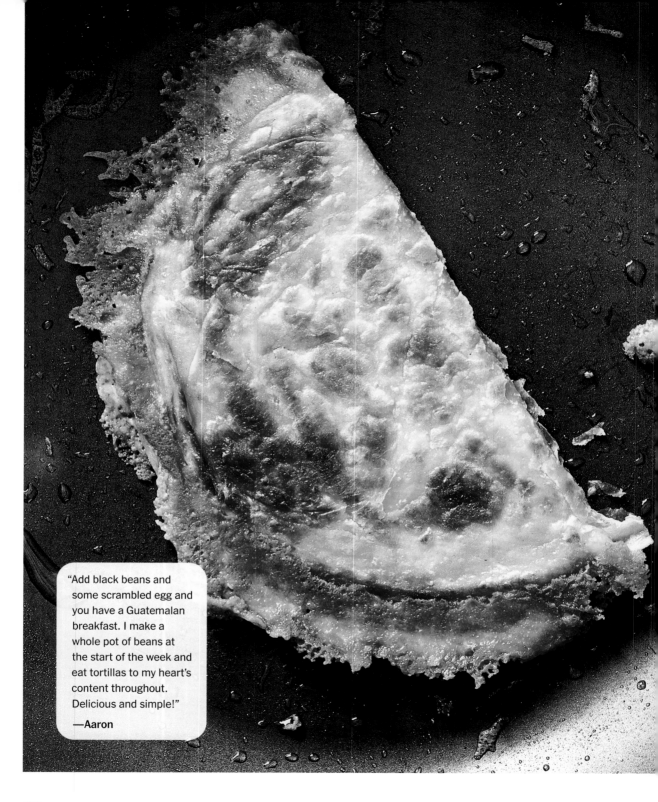

"Add black beans and
some scrambled egg and
you have a Guatemalan
breakfast. I make a
whole pot of beans at
the start of the week and
eat tortillas to my heart's
content throughout.
Delicious and simple!"

—Aaron

Crispy-Edged Quesadilla

time   10 minutes

yield   1 quesadilla

This straightforward quesadilla has an unexpected twist: a border of salty, crispy cheese surrounding the tortilla. Achieving it couldn't be easier: Just press down on the folded tortilla as it heats up in the pan so the cheese spills out and turns golden. A nonstick pan is key here. Otherwise, the melted cheese will glue itself onto the cooking surface. Medium heat is just the right temperature for a quesadilla: It's hot enough to crisp up the cheese but low enough to prevent the cheese from burning.

—Melissa Clark

2 teaspoons oil, such as olive, grapeseed or sunflower

1 (8-inch) flour tortilla

⅔ cup shredded cheese, such as Cheddar, Monterey Jack or Mexican cheese blend (about 2½ ounces)

1. Place a medium nonstick skillet over medium heat and add the oil. Let the oil heat for 20 seconds, swirling the pan so the oil coats the bottom.

2. Place the tortilla in the skillet and sprinkle the cheese evenly over the top. Once the cheese begins to melt, after 30 seconds to 1 minute, use a spatula to fold the tortilla in half. Using the spatula, press down firmly on the top of the tortilla until some of the cheese runs out into the pan. Let the quesadilla cook until the cheese that has leaked out solidifies and turns brown, 2 to 3 minutes.

3. Flip the quesadilla over and let cook on the other side until the cheese is crisp and golden, 1 to 2 minutes longer. Slide the quesadilla onto a plate and serve immediately.

Kimchi Grilled Cheese

time   15 minutes

yield   1 serving

Spicy heat plays well with melty cheese (think: queso dip, stuffed jalapeños, Buffalo wings and blue cheese). Here, kimchi and mozzarella cheese come together for a twist on the classic grilled cheese. Mildly flavored mozzarella is an especially good choice in this recipe because it lets the kimchi shine, but you could also add ¼ cup of grated Cheddar, Monterey Jack or even pepper Jack for more kick. If you have grilled steak, roasted vegetables or practically any other savory leftover in your fridge, chop it up and add about ¼ cup to your sandwich along with the kimchi. Smearing mayonnaise on the bread, instead of butter, might sound weird, but it won't burn as quickly as butter, allowing the cheese ample time to melt, and the bread to toast up to golden perfection.

—Ali Slagle

2 slices bread, either soft sandwich bread or large rustic slices, not more than ½ inch thick

1 tablespoon mayonnaise

½ cup grated mozzarella, Cheddar or other mild, semi-firm cheese

¼ cup drained and coarsely chopped kimchi

1. Heat a heavy skillet over medium-low. Thinly spread 1 side of each slice of bread with ½ tablespoon mayonnaise. Place the bread, mayonnaise side down, in the skillet and divide the mozzarella evenly over the slices.

2. When the cheese has just melted (no individual shreds of cheese remain), 6 to 10 minutes, add the kimchi to one side. Use a spatula to top with the other slice of bread, cheese side down. Press with the spatula to meld, then let cook, covered, flipping as needed to prevent burning, until the bread is crusty-brown and the sandwich is warmed through, 2 to 4 minutes.

"This is a wonderful sandwich—even better with homemade kimchi. A variation of this is to add an egg or two, serve on a Kaiser roll and make a kimchi egg and cheese."

—steve

"Nice recipe and so easy. I put the bread into the skillet of red pepper and butter to coat on both sides, then toasted it in the oven. Perfection."

—Dani

Çilbir (Turkish Eggs with Yogurt)

time 20 minutes

yield 2 servings

This traditional Turkish egg dish of garlicky yogurt with poached eggs and a drizzle of spicy butter is rich, luscious and faintly smoky. Typically served as a meze among a spread of other dishes, it makes a light lunch or dinner that comes together in the time it takes to poach eggs. For your base, opt for Greek yogurt to mimic the thicker yogurt common in Turkey. Next, bloom Aleppo pepper in butter or olive oil. Also known as pul biber, it delivers about as much heat as chipotle chile, with smoky notes and a fruity flavor. This version of çilbir is adapted from Özlem Warren, a cookbook author and blogger. Although the dish is traditionally served without herbs, she recommends dill or parsley for a modern flourish.

—Alexa Weibel

1 cup thick, strained plain yogurt, such as Greek yogurt, at room temperature

1 small garlic clove, grated

3 tablespoons unsalted butter or olive oil, or a combination

1 tablespoon Aleppo pepper, or 1 teaspoon red pepper flakes

4 large eggs

2 tablespoons white vinegar

Kosher salt and black pepper

Chopped fresh dill or parsley leaves, for serving (optional)

Toasted crusty bread or flatbread, for serving

1. Bring a medium saucepan of water to a simmer over medium heat.

2. Prepare the garlic yogurt: In a small bowl, stir together the yogurt and garlic. Divide between two shallow bowls, using the back of a spoon to spread it out.

3. In a small saucepan or skillet, melt the butter over medium heat. Add the Aleppo pepper and stir until fragrant, about 30 seconds. Remove from the heat.

4. Crack the eggs into four separate small bowls. Add the vinegar to the simmering water. (You want the water to be at a low simmer, with very small bubbles rising to the surface. Reduce the heat to medium-low if needed.) Using a slotted spoon, give the water a swirl, then gently add 1 egg at a time, trying to space them evenly apart. (Swirling the water helps the egg whites form tight, round nests as they cook.) Cook the eggs just until the whites are cooked through, 2 to 3 minutes.

5. Using the slotted spoon, transfer 2 eggs to each bowl of yogurt, lifting out one at a time and dabbing the bottom of the spoon with a folded paper towel to remove excess water.

6. Season the eggs with salt and black pepper, then drizzle with the spiced butter and sprinkle with herbs (if using). Serve immediately with bread.

Mattar Paneer (Peas and Paneer in Spiced Tomato Gravy)

time   25 minutes

yield   2 to 4 servings

Traditionally, roasted and crushed cashews are puréed with cooked onions and tomatoes to make the base for this comforting vegetarian dish. This version skips the hassle of puréeing and instead uses a hefty amount of cashew butter for the same nutty flavor and creamy texture. Red chile powder, ginger and garlic provide the perfect backbone for the sauce. Substitute tofu for the paneer if you like; the mildness of either lends itself well to this unexpectedly luxurious dish.

—Zainab Shah

¼ cup ghee or neutral oil (such as grapeseed or canola)

8 ounces paneer or extra-firm tofu, cut into 1-inch cubes and patted very dry

1 medium yellow onion, finely chopped

½ teaspoon ginger paste or peeled, grated fresh ginger

½ teaspoon garlic paste or grated garlic

1 teaspoon cumin seeds

¾ teaspoon Kashmiri or other red chile powder

¼ teaspoon turmeric powder

3 medium plum tomatoes, finely chopped

1 teaspoon fine sea salt

2 tablespoons cashew butter

1¾ cups fresh or frozen peas (about 8 ounces; no need to thaw)

3 tablespoons heavy cream or cashew cream (optional)

½ teaspoon garam masala

Hot cooked rice or roti, for serving

1. Heat the ghee in a large skillet or medium wok over high heat until it melts, about 30 seconds. Lower the heat to medium, add the paneer cubes and lightly fry, turning frequently, until golden on all sides, about 5 minutes. Remove and set aside on a plate lined with a paper towel.

2. With the pan still over medium heat, add the onion, ginger and garlic and cook, stirring occasionally, until the onion is translucent, 5 to 7 minutes.

3. Add the cumin, chile powder and turmeric and stir until fragrant, 30 seconds to 1 minute. Stir in the tomatoes and salt and add ¾ cup water. Bring to a simmer and simmer until the mixture thickens slightly, 3 to 5 minutes.

4. Lower the heat to medium-low and stir in the cashew butter. Add the peas and paneer, stir to combine and simmer until the mixture reaches your desired thickness, usually about 5 minutes.

5. Top with the cream in a swirl, if you like, then sprinkle with the garam masala. Serve with rice.

"This was so flavorful and delicious, made as written, that my partner asked if we could have it for dinner every day. My only disappointment was that I didn't double the recipe."

—Hally

Sheet-Pan Baked Feta with Broccolini, Tomatoes and Lemon

time   25 minutes

yield   4 servings

When it's baked, feta gains an almost creamy texture, similar to goat cheese but with its characteristic tang. In this easy vegetarian sheet-pan dinner, broccolini (or broccoli), grape tomatoes and lemon slices roast alongside the feta until the broccolini crisps, the tomatoes burst and the lemon rinds soften. (Remember, broccolini has a tender, delicious stalk so only the bottom ½-inch needs to be trimmed.) Serve this dish over a pile of orzo for a complete meal. If you like, cut the broccolini, feta and lemon into bite-size pieces and toss them with the orzo.

—Yasmin Fahr

1 bunch broccolini, ends trimmed, thick stalks split lengthwise, or 1 head of broccoli, stalks trimmed and cut into bite-size pieces

1 pint grape tomatoes, halved (about 2 cups)

1 small red onion, peeled, quartered and cut into 2-inch wedges

1 lemon, ½ cut into thin rounds and the remaining ½ left intact, for serving

3 tablespoons olive oil, plus more for serving

1 teaspoon ground cumin

½ teaspoon red pepper flakes

Kosher salt and black pepper

2 (6- to 8-ounce) blocks feta, cut into 1-inch slices

Cooked orzo or farro, for serving

½ cup fresh basil or cilantro leaves and fine stems, roughly chopped (optional)

1. Heat the oven to 400 degrees with a rack set in the lower third. On a sheet pan, combine the broccolini, tomatoes, onion and lemon slices with the olive oil and toss. Add the cumin and red pepper flakes, season with salt and pepper and toss again until evenly coated. Nestle the feta slices into the vegetables. (It's okay if they break apart a little.)

2. Roast 15 to 20 minutes, stirring halfway through but leaving the feta in place, until the broccolini is charred at the tips, the stems are easily pierced with a fork and the tomato skins start to blister and break down.

3. Serve over orzo or farro. Drizzle with olive oil and serve with the remaining lemon half for squeezing. Top with fresh herbs (if using).

Tip

Avoid feta made with cow's milk, which does not have enough fat to withstand roasting.

Plantains with Jammy Tomatoes and Eggs

time   30 minutes

yield   4 servings

Plantains are nutrient-rich starches that can sweeten as they cook, and in many parts of the world, they find their way into the best stews and porridges. This recipe is based on tomato eggs, a dish popular in Lagos, Nigeria, and beyond West Africa. Tomato eggs can be made with yams or plantains, and here, firm yellow plantains work best because they hold their shape and texture while absorbing the flavors of the surrounding stew. It's a perfect meal for days when you want something hot but not too heavy or filling. Any herbs you have on hand will work well, and the dish can be made vegan by substituting medium-firm or soft tofu for the eggs.

—Yewande Komolafe

2 firm yellow plantains (about 1 pound)

3 tablespoons neutral oil, such as grapeseed or canola

1 small yellow onion, chopped

2 garlic cloves, sliced

1 (12-ounce) jar roasted red peppers, drained and chopped

1 fresh or dried bay leaf

1 Scotch bonnet chile, or 1 teaspoon red pepper flakes

Kosher salt

1 (14-ounce) can whole tomatoes, with their juices

4 large eggs

½ cup fresh herb leaves, such as dill or flat-leaf parsley, chopped, for garnish

1. Cut off both ends of each plantain. Using a sharp knife, cut along the length of the peel of each plantain without cutting into the flesh. Remove the peels and discard. Cut the plantains into 2- to 3-inch-long pieces and then cut each piece in half lengthwise.

2. Heat 2 tablespoons of the oil in a large skillet over medium heat. When the oil shimmers, place the plantain pieces, long cut side down, in the skillet. Sear until the cut sides are deep golden brown, about 5 minutes. Transfer the plantains to a plate and set aside.

3. Pour in the remaining 1 tablespoon oil. Add the onion and garlic and cook, stirring often, until softened, about 2 minutes. Stir in the roasted peppers and bay leaf, drop in the chile and season with salt. Cook, stirring, until the liquid released by the peppers evaporates, about 2 minutes.

4. Add the tomatoes with their juices to the skillet and, using a spatula, carefully break the tomatoes into smaller pieces. Fill the tomato can with 1 cup water, swirl to rinse the sides and pour the liquid into the skillet. Increase the heat to high and bring the sauce to a simmer. Allow the sauce to simmer, stirring

"In the summer, I used fresh garden tomatoes and in the winter I used canned—it's great both ways."

—Amy K.

occasionally, until thickened and reduced by about one-fourth, about 5 minutes. Taste and season with additional salt if necessary.

5. Reduce the heat to medium and return the plantains to the skillet, nestling each piece, seared side up, in the sauce until almost submerged. Cook until the plantains are just soft and the tomatoes are jammy, 4 to 6 minutes. When you poke the plantains with a fork, there should be little resistance.

6. Remove and discard the bay leaf and chile. Make four wells in the sauce, spacing them out evenly, and gently crack an egg into each well. Cover with a lid or foil and cook until the whites of the eggs are set and the yolks are runny, 6 to 8 minutes. Remove the skillet from the heat. Garnish with the herbs and serve immediately.

Sheet-Pan Bibimbap

time   35 minutes

yield   4 servings

Bibimbap, the Korean mixed rice dish, is a kaleidoscope of flavors and textures. The popular dish has multiple origin stories and, like banchan and kimchi, many variations. Cooks who ordinarily keep namul (seasoned vegetable) banchan in the fridge may add them to a bowl with leftover rice and seasonings like spicy-sweet gochujang and nutty sesame oil, for example. Others, starting their bibimbap from scratch, will prep each component separately. But here's a fun way to accomplish everything at once: Roast a mélange of bits and bobs on one sheet pan as rice heats and eggs "oven-fry" on another. The caramelized sweet potato and salty kale in this formula come highly recommended, but you can use any vegetables on hand, reducing cook times for delicate options, such as spinach, scallions or asparagus.

—Eric Kim

6 ounces oyster mushrooms, torn into bite-size pieces

1 medium sweet potato (about 6 ounces), unpeeled, halved lengthwise and thinly sliced crosswise into half-moons

1 small red onion (about 6 ounces), thinly sliced crosswise into half-moons

3 packed cups coarsely chopped Tuscan or curly kale (from 1 small bunch)

6 tablespoons olive oil

Kosher salt and black pepper

4 cups cooked medium-grain white rice, preferably cold leftovers

4 large eggs

4 teaspoons toasted sesame oil, or more to taste, for serving

4 teaspoons gochujang, or more to taste, for serving

Kimchi, for serving (optional)

1. Position oven racks in the upper third and lower third of the oven and heat the oven to 450 degrees.

2. On a large sheet pan, arrange the mushrooms, sweet potato, red onion and kale into separate quadrants. Drizzle the vegetables with 3 tablespoons of the olive oil, season with salt and pepper and toss to coat, keeping the types of vegetables separate. Try to not crowd the vegetables; you want them to brown, not steam. Roast on the top rack until the sweet potato is fork-tender, the onion and mushrooms are slightly caramelized and the kale is crispy but not burnt, 20 to 25 minutes.

3. Meanwhile, place another large sheet pan on the bottom rack to heat. When the vegetables are almost done cooking, in the last 5 minutes or so, remove the heated pan from the oven and evenly drizzle the remaining 3 tablespoons olive oil on it. Spread the rice over half of the pan. Crack the eggs onto the other half and

"This is a go-to meal for us! So easy and delicious. I usually double the vegetables and do this on two sheets, great leftovers!"

—Emmy

carefully transfer to the oven. Bake until the whites of the eggs are just set and the yolks are still runny, 3 to 6 minutes (the time can vary depending on your oven, so watch closely).

4. To serve, divide the rice evenly among four bowls. Now, divide the vegetables evenly among the bowls, placing them in four neat piles over each portion of rice. Use a spatula to slide the eggs over the vegetables. Drizzle each bowl with 1 teaspoon of the sesame oil and dollop with 1 teaspoon of the gochujang, adding more of both if desired. Mix everything together with a spoon or chopsticks before diving in and serve kimchi alongside, if you prefer.

"So good as is! I've been making this a few evenings a week as a quick dinner. I do it in the air fryer and have been putting it on top of some penne for a delicious & easy pasta salad."

—Carrie

Easy Weeknight Dinners

Sheet-Pan Feta with Chickpeas and Tomatoes

time   40 minutes

yield   4 servings

In a spread of Greek appetizers, or meze, there's often a warm feta dish like bouyiourdi (baked feta with tomato and chiles) or a saganaki (fried cheese). This recipe combines elements of these two classic appetizers into a sheet-pan meal. Softened feta provides a salty, creamy counterpoint to sweet, juicy tomatoes and chickpeas that are sticky from honey and spicy from dried chile. Try this version, then riff wildly: Switch out the tomatoes for mini peppers, olives, dates or cauliflower. Swap the hot honey for anchovies, harissa, smoked paprika or turmeric. Eat with pita, grains, salad greens, hummus or yogurt.

—Ali Slagle

3 cups cooked chickpeas (homemade or two 15-ounce cans), drained, rinsed and shaken dry

2 pints cherry tomatoes, such as Sungold (about 4 cups)

1 shallot, thinly sliced

¼ cup extra-virgin olive oil

2 tablespoons hot honey

1 teaspoon mild chile flakes, such as gochugaru, or ½ teaspoon red pepper flakes

Kosher salt

2 (6- to 8-ounce) blocks feta (see Tip, page 241), sliced 1 inch thick

1. Heat the oven to 400 degrees. On a sheet pan, stir together the chickpeas, tomatoes, shallot, oil, honey and chile flakes. Season with salt, then spread in an even layer. Arrange the feta among the chickpeas.

2. Roast until the feta and tomatoes are soft and the chickpeas are golden brown, 30 to 35 minutes (no need to stir). Eat right away. (The feta will harden as it cools; reheat leftovers.)

Chilaquiles

time   45 minutes

yield   4 servings

Chilaquiles are an incredibly comforting, quick and easy Mexican dish whose origins and name are believed to go back to the Aztecs. (In Nahuatl, the Aztec language, the name means "submerged in chile sauce.") It was—and is—a great way to use up stale tortillas because they soften and absorb the flavor and color of the chiles. For chilaquiles rojos, guajillo chiles are used to add that familiar brick-red color as well as an earthiness that counters the sweetness and acidity of the tomatoes. Chiles de árbol add heat, but if you don't have them, you can use one or two chipotles in adobo for heat and a bit of smokiness. Top with shredded rotisserie chicken or roasted vegetables to make a hearty meal.

—Rick A. Martínez

Vegetable oil, about 4 cups for deep-frying, plus about 5 tablespoons for the salsa and eggs

7 medium guajillo chiles, stemmed and seeded

3 ripe medium tomatoes, cored

3 dried chiles de árbol, stemmed (and seeded if you like less heat), or 2 chipotle chiles in adobo

2 garlic cloves

½ teaspoon dried oregano, preferably Mexican

¼ teaspoon cumin, seeds or ground

Kosher salt

16 stale corn tortillas, cut into triangles if deep-frying, left whole if baking (see Tip)

4 large eggs

Sliced red onion, chopped fresh cilantro, sliced avocado, crumbled queso fresco and crema, for serving

1. Fit a medium, heavy pot with a deep-fry thermometer and pour in enough oil to come halfway up the sides of the pot. Heat over high heat until the thermometer registers 350 degrees.

2. Meanwhile, make the salsa guajillo: In a large saucepan, combine the guajillo chiles, tomatoes, chiles de árbol, garlic, oregano, cumin, 1½ teaspoons salt and 3 cups water and bring to a boil over high heat. Reduce the heat to a gentle boil (medium-low heat), cover and cook for 5 minutes. Remove from the heat and let sit, covered, until the tomatoes and chiles are tender, about 10 minutes. Transfer to a blender and purée until smooth.

3. In a medium saucepan, heat 2 tablespoons oil over medium-high heat. Carefully add the tomato-chile purée to the hot oil. The mixture will sputter but will rapidly settle down. Cook, stirring occasionally, until the mixture has thickened slightly and has become a darker brick red, about 5 minutes. Keep warm over low heat.

4. Make the totopos (chips): Line a large heatproof bowl with paper towels. Working in two batches, deep-fry the tortillas in the hot oil, stirring occasionally, until

Tip

You can skip deep-frying the tortillas and instead bake them whole on two sheet pans set on the upper and lower racks of a 350-degree oven until crisp, 35 to 45 minutes, then break them into pieces. Or you can use store-bought tortilla chips and skip Steps 1 and 4.

"This recipe is really good. Guajillo chiles add a complex, smoky flavor. Baking the tortillas is genius!"

—Camlam

lightly golden brown and crispy, 3 to 4 minutes. Transfer to the prepared bowl and season lightly with salt.

5. Heat 3 tablespoons oil in a large nonstick skillet over medium-high heat. Crack the eggs into the skillet, leaving space around each one, and cook until the whites are set and the edges are crisp, about 4 minutes. Season with salt and transfer to a plate.

6. For softer chilaquiles, toss the totopos in the warm salsa guajillo and cook over medium-high heat, tossing to coat completely, until very hot. For crispier chilaquiles, remove the paper towels from the bowl holding the totopos. Pour three-fourths of the warm salsa guajillo over the totopos and toss until completely coated.

7. To serve, divide the chilaquiles among four plates and top each serving with a fried egg, red onion, cilantro, avocado, queso fresco and crema. If serving crispier chilaquiles, top with the remaining salsa guajillo.

Acknowledgments

I'd like to thank the entire NYT Cooking team for their colossal creativity, talent, and dedication to making our work the best in the world. Thanks to Genevieve Ko, Emily Fleischaker and Krysten Chambrot, in particular, for their leadership of the Cooking editorial team and the sparkling intelligence they bring to all that they do. I'm extremely grateful for Camilla Velasquez, the general manager of Cooking and my partner in all things related to it, for her vision, her staggering smarts and her friendship. The gratitude I feel for Sam Sifton, the founding editor of Cooking and a mentor to me, could fill this entire page.

Caitlin Roper, Trish Daly, Erik Borenstein, Brian Rideout, Debbie Beshaw-Farrell, and Alena Cerro at The New York Times, Kari Stuart, Molly Birnbaum and the team at Ten Speed Press brought this book to life expertly. The photo team—Kim Gougenheim, David Malosh, Simon Andrews and Megan Hedgpeth—made it look delicious, and Deb Bishop designed a beautiful cover. Thank you all so much.

Special thanks to the extraordinary recipe developers whose work fills this book, and to the devoted community of readers whose comments bring Cooking to life. I appreciate you deeply. And thank you to my husband, Blake Wilson, and our two beloved daughters, for everything and then some.

Index

Text copyright © 2024 by The New York Times Company
Photographs copyright © 2024 by The New York Times Company

All rights reserved.
Published in the United States by Ten Speed Press, an imprint of the Crown Publishing Group, a division of Penguin Random House LLC, New York.
TenSpeed.com

Ten Speed Press and the Ten Speed Press colophon are registered trademarks of Penguin Random House LLC.

Page 203, adapted from: Krishna, Priya with Krishna, Ritu. *Indian-Ish: Recipes and Antics from a Modern American Family.* New York: Harvest, 2019.
Page 63, adapted from: López-Alt, J. Kenji. *The Wok: Recipes and Techniques.* New York: W. W. Norton and Company, 2022.
Page 178, adapted from: Tipton-Martin, Toni. *Jubilee: Recipes From Two Centuries of African American Cooking.* New York: Clarkson Potter, 2019.

Typefaces: New York Times' Cheltenham and Franklin

Library of Congress Cataloging-in-Publication Data is on file with the publisher.

Hardcover ISBN: 978-0-593-83632-3
Ebook ISBN: 978-0-593-83633-0

Printed in China

Acquiring editor: Molly Birnbaum
Production editor: Terry Deal
Editorial assistant: Gabby Ureña Matos
Designer and art director: Annie Marino
Production designer: Mari Gill
Cover designer: Deb Bishop
Production manager: Jane Chinn
Prepress color manager: Claudia Sanchez
Cover and chapter opener photography: David Malosh
Food stylist: Simon Andrews
Prop stylist: Megan Hedgpeth
Copyeditor: Sharon Silva
Proofreaders: Miriam Garron and Monika Dziamka
Indexer: Barbara Mortenson
Publicists: David Hawk and Jana Branson
Marketer: Stephanie Davis

10 9 8 7 6 5 4 3 2 1
First Edition

Photographers

Andrew Purcell 78, 81, 86, 167, 201
Andrew Scrivani 27, 117, 172
Armando Rafael 42, 183
Beatriz Da Costa 111
Bryan Gardner 240
Christopher Simpson 71, 136, 139, 175, 190
Christopher Testani 28, 46, 49, 118, 150, 184, 193, 236, 249
Con Poulos 51, 102
Dane Tashima 125, 221
David Malosh 22, 25, 31, 32, 35, 45, 57, 66, 89, 107, 126, 131, 163, 164, 168, 180, 194, 209, 214, 217
James Ransom 132
Jenny Huang 65
Johnny Miller 41, 69, 85, 206
Joseph De Leo 235
Julia Gartland 54, 114, 140, 171, 210, 232
Kate Sears 74
Kelly Marshall 113, 153, 155
Linda Pugliese 239
Linda Xiao 39, 73, 77, 82, 90, 93, 101, 129, 135, 144, 147, 149, 156, 176, 213, 219, 223, 243, 245
Nico Schinco 98
Ryan Liebe 36, 197, 199, 202, 205, 228, 231, 246
Sang An 53, 62, 143
Sarah Anne Ward 178
Yossy Arefi 105

Food stylists

Barrett Washburne 25, 54, 65, 86, 98, 118, 125, 132, 136, 167, 171, 180, 201, 205, 213, 228, 240
Brett Regot 219
Carrie Purcell 78, 81
Chris Lanier 49
Cyd Raftus McDowell 183
Erika Joyce 221
Hadas Smirnoff 73, 74, 243
Jerrie-Joy Redman-Lloyd 51, 102
Judy Kim 149, 245
Liza Jernow 140
Maggie Ruggiero 178, 231
Monica Pierini 39, 90, 77, 129, 135, 144, 147, 156, 176, 223, 232, 235, 239
Rebecca Jurkevich 69, 85, 111
Roscoe Betsill 113, 153
Simon Andrews 28, 31, 32, 35, 36, 42, 45, 46, 53, 57, 62, 66, 71, 89, 107, 126, 131, 139, 143, 150, 163, 168, 175, 184, 190, 193, 194, 197, 199, 202, 206, 209, 214, 217, 236, 246, 249
Susan Spungen 41
Vivian Lui 164

Prop Stylists

Carla Gonzalez-Hart 49
Maeve Sheridan 113
Megan Hedgpeth 73, 228
Paige Hicks 28, 153, 175
Paola Andrea 178
Sophia Pappas 231